ACTS OF THE MIND
IN
JEWISH RITUAL LAW

An Insight into Rabbinic Psychology

דעת יצחק

ACTS OF THE MIND
IN
JEWISH RITUAL LAW

An Insight into Rabbinic Psychology

Isaac Cohen

Acts of the Mind in Jewish Ritual Law: An Insight into Rabbinic Psychology
by Isaac Cohen

ISBN 13: 978-965-7108-83-3
ISBN 10: 965-7108-83-7

Urim Publications
P.O. Box 52287, Jerusalem 91521 Israel

Lambda Publishers Inc.
3709 13th Avenue Brooklyn, New York 11218 U.S.A.
Tel: 718-972-5449 Fax: 718-972-6307, mh@ejudaica.com

www.UrimPublications.com

This work is dedicated to the loving
memory of a perfect Soul Mate

Fanny Cohen, ז״ל

איטא פיגא

בת דוב ורודא למשפחת וייספוגל
אשה יראת ה׳ היא תתהלל

הרב זלמן יצחק כהן ז״ל
נפטר ביום ו׳, כ׳ בכסלו תשס״ח

RABBI DR. ISAAC COHEN, 1914–2007

Rabbinical minds are not merely the repositories of Jewish law. In every generation rabbis have learned, practised, codified, condensed and commented on the laws that Moses received on Mount Sinai. Their devotion to their Halakhic duties has preserved and kept the Jewish people.

Isaac Cohen's 93 years of life bridged three centuries. He was educated under the still powerful influence of the 19th century. As a rabbi, he ministered throughout the 20th century against the backdrop of the Holocaust and the founding of the New Zion. His life came to an end in the 21st century, while living and working in Jerusalem, where he brought forth his own special contribution to rabbinical continuity – *Acts of the Mind in Jewish Ritual Law: An Insight into Rabbinic Psychology.*

The first time I met Rabbi Cohen was during the *shivah* for Fanny, his dear wife of over 60 years. Already then, in February 2007, he was in poor health. Yet, when it came time for him to recite Kaddish for Fanny, he did so with surprising strength. He chanted the words to a slow, dignified rhythm no longer heard, a rhythm that stretched back to a time before he was born in 1914.

Two days before Yom Kippur of the same year, I brought Rabbi Cohen two bound sample copies of his book. Finally, after decades of work, he held his book in his hands. Because he had had a tracheotomy, speaking proved nearly impossible. We communicated in writing. But then, quite unexpectedly, he plugged the hole in his throat with his finger. Suddenly, he was speaking. His voice was thick and sounded far away. I bent down, with my ear close to his lips, to hear what he was saying. It was the Bracha for Thanksgiving: *"...Shehekhiyanu, veKiyemanu veHigiyanu laZman haZeh."*

At his funeral on the dark and misty Motzei Shabbat of December 1, 2007, Stuart Davies rose to eulogize his Uncle Isaac. As the nephew spoke his first words, it began to rain mightily, drumming on the roof with a terrible din; but as soon as he finished speaking, the downpour ended, as if turned off. On our way to the gravesite, Rabbi Cohen's advocate Shmuel Becker observed that because the Cohens had not been blessed with children to cry for their departed parents, the skies cried in their stead. No more rain fell after that, and not a drop struck the mourners by the graveside.

Despite his advanced age, in his last year of life Rabbi Cohen overcame several major abdominal operations and bouts of pneumonia. He survived, because he was determined to see his book published. He did not quite make it. Yet this book דעת יצחק, the wisdom of Rabbi Isaac Cohen, will live on and continue to teach as he taught during his life, according to Bet Hillel, a kind, compassionate and loving understanding of the Law of Moses.   (D.B.)

זכרונו לברכה לחיי העולם הבא

Office of the

CHIEF RABBI

London

Rabbi Dr. Isaac Cohen has produced a truly monumental work of Jewish scholarship, majestic in scope, riveting in detail, enthralling in its overarching theme. What he has provided us with is a systematic exploration of the role of mental acts, motives and intentions in virtually every aspect of Jewish law and life. Drawing on a range of disciplines, psychological, philosophical and jurisprudential, Dr. Cohen shows us how Jewish law is concerned not only with outward behaviour but also with inward acts of conscious thought, and that Judaism is not just about the soul but also and more precisely about the mind. A magnificent achievement, highly recommended.

Rabbi Sir Jonathan Sacks
Chief Rabbi of the United Hebrew Congregations of the Commonwealth

צבי א' טל שופט (בדימוס)

ב"ה ירושלים,

הרב יצחק כהן הי"ו, לפנים רבה הראשי של אירלנד, הניף ידו על ים הת־
למוד והפוסקים, ראשונים ואחרונים, כדי להוציא לאור את השקפת חכמינו
על יסוד הרצון הכוונה והדעת שבמעשי האדם.

חיבורו מקיף הלכות שבין אדם לקונו, בין אדם לחבירו ובין אדם לחברה.
ענייני מוסר ומצפון, כמו גם ענייני גטין וקדושין, קניין וחוזים, אמונה וקדו־
שה, תפילה וצדקה, שבת ומועד, נדרים ושבועות, ועוד.

החיבור אינו מתיימר להיות מדעי-ביקורתי, אבל יש בו עיון הלכתי למן
המשנה והגמרא, דרך פוסקי ההלכות לרבדיהם ולדורותיהם. בכולם מחפש
הרב כהן את היסוד הנפשי הנותן טעם והקובע את תוקף המעשה.

כל המבקש לדעת ולהבין את אורח החיים, ההלכה והמשפט היהודיים
מן הצד הפסיכולוגי והיסוד הנפשי שבהם, לרבות מי שלא למד דברים אלה
מעולם - ימצא בחיבורו של הרב כהן שפע ועושר רב.

צבי א' טל

שופט לשעבר של בית המשפט העליון בישראל

ירושלים, אייר תשס"ה (מאי 2005)

Zvi Tal
Former Justice of the Israel Supreme Court

Jerusalem
Iyyar 5765 – May 2005

Dr. Isaac Cohen, the former Chief Rabbi of Ireland, has performed a worthy task by exploring the ocean of Talmud and Jewish religious law, ancient and modern, with the aim of bringing to light the views of our Sages on the role of Will, Intention and Intellect in the actions of Man.

His new book discusses the Jewish legal view of Man's relationship with God, his fellow human beings and the society in which he lives. It also goes into questions of morality and conscience regarding marriage and divorce, property and contracts, faith and holiness, prayer and charity, Sabbaths and festivals, oaths and vows.

Although Dr. Cohen, an Orthodox rabbi, did not aim to write a critical, "scientific" treatise, his work amounts to a panoramic study of Jewish law from the Mishnah and Gemara onwards, ranging through the various strata and generations of halakhic decision makers (*posekim*). In each case treated, he pursues the spiritual factor that lends significance to, and determines the validity of, an action.

All who wish to gain a better knowledge of the spiritual and psychological aspects of Jewish law and the Jewish way of life, as well as those completely unfamiliar with these subjects, will discover a wealth of information in Dr. Isaac Cohen's book.

Zvi Tal

(This is a translation of the original Hebrew on the previous page.)

The Ludwig and Erica Jesselson
Institute of Advanced Torah
Studies
Bar-Ilan University
Ramat Gan 52900, Israel
Rabbi Prof. Daniel Sperber
President

המכון הגבוה לתורה
ע״ש לודביג ז״ל ואריקה יסלזון (ע״ר)
אוניברסיטת בר–אילן
רמת גן 52900
הרב פרופסור דניאל שפרבר
נשיא

I have read several chapters of Rabbi Isaac Cohen's manuscript on *Acts of the Mind in Jewish Ritual Law*, in which he identifies the components of knowledge and intent in the vast repository of Jewish law. This is a pioneer study not only in its compass but also in the clarity of analysis and formulation. Complex legal issues are explained in a manner understandable to all, and the reader gains a lucid overview both diachronic and dogmatic of extensive areas both of Jewish ritual law and of other juristic fields. Rabbi Cohen's work will be of interest and value to a broad readership, both those well acquainted with the Talmud and the Codes, and those less knowledgeable thereof. I certainly enjoyed reading the sample chapters I received and benefited for their perusal.

Daniel Sperber

July 5, 2005

Prof. Stefan C. Reif, Director,
Taylor-Schechter Genizah Research Unit,
Cambridge University Library

It has a wealth of interesting content with much good discussion, generally clear presentation and broad coverage of the topic in its various manifestations within the rabbinic tradition. The approach is a traditional one and the work sets out to describe, rather than to analyse in a critical fashion, the specific technical topics that exemplify the overall legal structure. The whole of the rabbinic tradition is seen to extend from the earliest biblical times until the modern period and is viewed as a unit and not within distinct historical frameworks. There is no comparison with other treatments of the subject or any survey of the current state of scholarship in the field.

Stefan Reif

Rabbi Emanuel Quint,
Dean, Jerusalem Institute of Law
Author of *A Restatement of Rabbinic Civil Law*

When I first picked up to read the manuscript of *Acts of the Mind* and saw the Contents, I thought to myself that Rabbi Dr. Isaac Cohen had undertaken a monumental task. Most authors who write a book dealing with so many profound, distinct subjects do justice to none of them. As I read chapter by chapter, it became apparent that Rav Cohen was able to handle in a very capable manner the variety and wide scope of topics about which he was writing. He writes in a very lucid manner and this makes the philosophical, legal and technical chapters readable and understandable.

He thus goes from *Emunah* to *Kedushah*, *Kavannah*, *Teshuvah*, *Middot*, *Korbanot*, Shabbath, Festivals, Marriage, Divorce, Oaths and Vows, *Ayin ha-Ra*, Contracts and The Rabbinic Concept of Mind and Will. As can be seen from the names of the chapters, they all entail Acts of the Mind. Many readers will have some knowledge of some of these topics, but here one can learn about topics that he is not all that familiar with. That makes this book so valuable on one's book shelf.

His opening chapter "*Emunah* – Faith, Belief, Trust", which is more theological, is written in the same precise, clear manner as his other chapters which are more instructional. This first chapter which describes the bedrock of our faith flows naturally into the next two chapters dealing with Holiness and Attentive Devotion. One who reads this book cannot but think the next time that he performs a mitzvah, does he have the proper *kavannah*? In his chapters dealing with Halachah, he describes the subject matter in an easygoing, interesting manner. His chapter dealing with Repentance reminds the reader of the classical *seforim* dealing with getting ready for Rosh Hashanah.

In his chapter on Contracts he covers all the aspects

of contracts so that the book could very well be used as a law school textbook for teaching contracts in Halachah. For example, in this chapter he has sections on Will and Consent; Intention; Conditions; Consideration; Fraud and Misrepresentation; Duress – *Oness;* Mistake; Gift; Inheritance – *Yerusha*; Warranty; and Suretyship – *Arevut.* Since his thesis is the Acts of the Mind, he approaches the laws of contracts in a very novel way and in the manner it would be seen in a halachic society.

I highly recommend this book as a welcome addition to all libraries, public and individual. I suggest that after reading the book that the reader then slowly read one chapter at a time and then put it aside as he absorbs and integrates into his mind and life the chapter he has read. When he feels comfortable with that chapter he should reread the next chapter.

The author, very erudite, has rendered us a service by writing this book that can have a positive impact on all of us.

Emanuel Quint

PREFACE

Preface

Every human being is endowed with a personality of his own, which is normally exhibited as a composite presentation of the individual as he would wish to be seen. The inner thoughts and intentions of each individual are, however, unseen and unknown to any observer and may be entirely undisclosed. These unspoken intentions will vary from one individual to the other. A person or government wishing to hide their real intention will speak in "double talk" which can then become their normal manner of "double think" (Orwell, *1984*).

An artistic portrayal of this concept may be found in Leonardo da Vinci's painting, *La Gioconda,* better known as the "Mona Lisa" (Louvre). One cannot help wondering about the mysterious look in her eyes. The portrait as a whole is striking, but it is impossible to discern the thoughts which that look conceals.

In rabbinical literature the term *Da'at* has a wide meaning signifying mind, thought, intellect, will, desire, intention, *kavvanah*, attention, emotion, and movement, etc. Modern science locates each action in a particular section of the brain which, overall, is controlled by the man himself. The old Kabbalistic system distinguished between a large number of different activities and attributed each activity to a different universal heavenly sphere, known as *sefirot* (Moses de Leon, *Sefer ha-Nefesh ha-Hakhamah*). This mystical system, however, bears no relationship with halakha, which is concerned with the acts a man performs and his responsibility for such actions.

The manner and extent of belief is inscrutable to the onlooker, just as every purpose and intention of any visible action cannot be known. In Jewish ritual law, much of the required actions must be accompanied by full integrity of intention of the purpose to fulfil in this manner the requirements of the Jewish law. To believe in a supernatural existence is quintessentially and purely an act of the mind.

The ramifications of Jewish ritual law, as found in the rabbinic teaching of the Talmud and codes, are the product of the social, theological and moral background of the ordinances specified in the Torah. When religious guidance was sought by the individual, all these conditions were included in the purview of the Sages, resulting in debated decisions of an individual's guilt or innocence. Sometimes the same action may be approved or forbidden according to the circumstances of that individual.

In the rubric of Jewish daily prayers, before addressing any glorification of the Almighty or prayer to Him, it is customary to declare: "I hereby commit myself to fulfil the law, 'And thou shalt love thy neighbour as thyself'"(Lev. 19:18) – הריני מקבל עלי מצות עשה של ואהבת לרעך כמוך. The Biblical verse concludes with the words, "I am the Lord" – אני ה'. It is possible for anyone to make a show of loving his neighbour while in his private thoughts deceiving him; but the Torah teaches us that man's secret thoughts are known to the Almighty, who judges him.

Rabbi Akiva declared that this law is the great principle governing all the laws of the Torah – אמר ר' עקיבא זה כלל גדול בתורה. The *tanna* Ben Azzai expounded Rabbi Akiva's principle, in the same Midrash, teaching that "thy neighbour" includes every human being – not just one's brother, friend and racial or religious colleague, but every fellow man. Such wider instruction was indicated in the Biblical verse, "This is the book of the generations of humanity" (Gen. 5:1) – זה ספר תולדות אדם כלל גדול מזה. The brotherhood of all mankind is enunciated in another Biblical verse, "In the image of God He created him" (Gen. 1:27) – בצלם אל-הים ברא אותו. The power of the occult personality that man possesses is itself an attribute of God, as the Bible tells us that the Almighty created man in His own image, endowing him with the power and propensity of free will in the use of his innate intelligence.

The conduct of man demonstrates the fact that, on his own, he would not always do what was right and just in the eyes of his Creator. The Almighty therefore wished to find a man who could understand the ways of God and spread the knowledge of Him throughout mankind. Choosing the one man who could perform such a mission, God called on Abram to shoulder this fateful task in his own way (cf. *Ned.* 32a). Yet Abram had been born and reared in Ur of the Chaldees, in a society abounding with idols and idolaters. It was therefore necessary to change his former outlook and character, to transform him into a new and elevated personality.

The Almighty proceeded to achieve this change in various stages, from which our Sages learned what would be needed to effect a change in a person's character. He called on Abram to take the first step by leaving the country of his birth and separating himself entirely from the influence of his family and of idolatrous Chaldea. He ordered him to set out for an unfamiliar, new land where he would experience the reality of God's presence. He then changed his name to Abraham, which embraced God's blessing and the creation of his new spiritual character (Gen. 17:5).

Abraham's son Ishmael did not give up his evil ways, although Abraham tried, unsuccessfully, to train him in the right way (Gen. R. 148:13; 53:11; *Tosefta Sota* 6:6). God did not change him into a better person; only Ishmael himself could have done so; and he did not. Ishmael became identified as the ancestor of the Ishmaelites, and neighbouring tribes, who often named their sons Ishmael (Ginzberg, *Legend*s, 5, 223, 234).

Abraham underwent ten tests of his faith, and even after ordeals of heart-rending tribulations, culminating in the command to sacrifice his son Isaac, he remained unshaken in his deep belief in God (Gen. 22:1, Ibn Ezra *ad loc.*; *Avot* 5:3, Maim., Rashi, *ad loc.*; *Avot de-R. Natan* 33:2).

Abraham now emerged as the first of the patriarchs of Israel. In the Hebrew form of his name, Avraham, the word *Av* means "father" and *raham* is an old Semitic term meaning "numerous". Abraham thus became an emissary of God endowed with the title, "father of a multitude of nations" (Gen. 17:5) – אב-המון גויים. From Abraham's experience our Sages deduced the factors required to transform an individual's personality, and they often used that pattern as a model for themselves.

Modern thought asserts that every human being's life is, to a great extent, predetermined by his genetic make-up. The ancients believed that the nature and government of an individual's life are controlled by the chance phenomena obtaining among the heavenly bodies at the time of his birth. The knowledge of astrology acquired by ancient priests was used to read the stars and foretell the future – a practice forbidden in Jewish law (Deut. 18:10).

Jewish teaching maintained that Israel need not be dominated by astrological conditions, since the power of man's life force is governed only by his Divine creation. The Sages expressed this teaching in the adage, "Israel has no permanent good or ill fortune" – אין מזל לישראל (Shab. 156a). His existing genetic destiny may be changed by the will of the Almighty.

An individual can inaugurate this process by altering his way of life and, according to the Sages, even a change of name could effect a change in his own biotic function. This teaching was expressed by the traditional adage: "A change of name brings a change in fortune" – שינוי שם שינוי מזל (Gen. R. 44:15).

The Sages declared that a person's evil fate can be averted if he changes his own nature to such an extent that he is no longer the individual whom the heavenly decree condemned. "R. Yitzhak said: 'Four things annul an evil decree: charity, prayer, change of name and change of conduct'. Some add: change of residence" – אמר ר' יצחק: ד' דברים מקרעין גזר דינו של אדם: צדקה, צעקה, שינוי השם ושינוי מעשה. ויש אומרים שינוי מקום. A well-known adage simply has it that "a change of residence and a change of name transform one's ordained fate" – שינוי מקום ושינוי שם משנה מזל (RH 16b; Rashi, Maharsha ad loc.).

On visiting a gravely ill person one is urged to pray for his recovery and to bestow on him a change of name (Gen. R. 44:15; *Zohar, Ra'aya Meheimna,* Pinhas, p. 217), so that the decreed sickness will not harm this new individual (*Sh. Ar. Yoreh De'ah* 335:10, REMA). The Torah also states that in order for Abraham to become a new personality, one fit to be the bearer of God's word, he renounced his idolatrous people, left his family home and was given a new name.

All the physical changes that Abraham experienced could not, however, guarantee the creation of a new person. One thing more was needed, and this additional quality is described in the Book of Nehemiah.

Nehemiah, who governed Judea in the time of Ezra, inspired the religious reformation of the people of Israel and laid the spiritual foundations of the new Judean Commonwealth (5th cent. BCE). He called on his people to confess their sins and pray for forgiveness. He also begged the Almighty to remember His call to Abraham: "Thou art the Lord the God, who didst choose Abram, and broughtest him forth out of Ur of the Chaldees and gavest him the name of Abraham; and foundest his heart faithful before Thee" (Neh. 9:7–8). In his concluding words Nehemiah emphasized that Abraham's change of name and abode were external matters; they did nothing to secure the elevation of his personality.

The one important change was that Abraham's new faith in the Almighty had become deeply rooted in his consciousness, which is why Nehemiah added: "and foundest his heart faithful before Thee" – ‏ומצאת את-לבבו נאמן לפניך‎. Abraham's change of personality was effected only when he himself maintained in his consciousness a powerful act of the mind. When his heart and mind remained steadfast in a perfect faith, God chose him as the new man fit to convey Divine instruction. A reminder of this essential act of the mind occurs in the daily Morning Service, where this passage from Nehemiah is quoted.

✡

The Torah's specific legislation for the People of Israel was described in this manner by Jethro to Moses: "And thou shalt teach them the statutes and the laws, and shalt show them the way wherein they must walk, and the work that they must do" והזהרתה אתהם את החקים ואת-התורות והודעת להם את-הדרך ילכו בה – ואת המעשה אשר יעשון (Ex. 18:20).

This teaching was repeated by the lawgiver: "And Moses called unto all Israel, and said unto them: 'Hear, O Israel, the statutes and the ordinances which I speak in your ears this day, that ye may learn them, and observe to do them'" – ויקרא משה אל כל ישראל ויאמר אליהם שמע ישראל את החקים ואת המשפטים אשר אנכי דובר באזניכם היום ולמדתם אותם ושמרתם לעשותם (Deut. 5:1). As stated in the first passage of the *Shema*, however, Moses added: "And thou shalt love the Lord thy God with all thy heart, and with all thy soul, and with all thy might" – ואהבת את ה' אל-היך בכל לבבך ובכל נפשך ובכל מאדך (Deut. 6:5).

The present work studies those aspects where the two are interrelated – the action and the heart. The combination of both constitutes the morality of the outer action.

Use has been made of a number of classical rabbinical interpreters of the Bible texts, a list of which has been added in the Appendix – such as Maimonides, Rashi, Nahmanides, Ibn Ezra, and Sforno. When considering various interpretations of Biblical passages, rabbinical scholars always relied first and foremost on the lucid expositions of Rashi (R. Shelomo Yitzhaki, 1040–1105, Troyes, north-west France). It was maintained by many that he was "Divinely inspired" in his work, like the saintly ARI (R. Yitzhak Luria). (HIDA, Hafetz Hayyim, Hazon Ish; R. Yitzhak Frankel: *Zekhor le-David*, Jerusalem 2000).

Many Scriptural passages may be appreciated simply as they appear in the text, but on deeper examination they raise considerable problems. Such difficulties of understanding are frequently explained by the Sages of the Talmud and Midrash. It is significant to note that Rashi himself in his commentary on the first verse of Genesis found difficulty in understanding the grammatical form used in the text. He wrote: "This verse presents considerable problems in describing the creation and

cannot be understood without some further clarification". He
taught, as a general rule, that when we are unable to offer
a satisfactory explanation of the text, only the traditional
interpretation of the Sages should be followed, for any other
interpretation was probably contrived and tentative. Thus, on
this verse describing the creation Rashi stated that the text
is beyond our understanding and we are obliged to follow
only the interpretation traditionally given by the Sages –
אין המקרא הזה אומר אלא דורשני כמו שדרשו חז"ל (Gen. 1:1,
Rashi).

Years of intensive research paved the way for this book,
which is specifically entitled *Acts of the Mind in Jewish Ritual
Law: An Insight into Rabbinic Psychology*. Its Hebrew title,
Da'at Yitzhak (דעת יצחק), is a traditional form of title, being
a combination of the subject of the book and the name of its
author. The work is not intended as a text book of Jewish
ritual, or a compendium of Jewish law, but is confined to
such aspects of Jewish ritual where, in the action performed,
the accompanying inner thought and intention of the mind
determine the rightfulness of the action or its culpability. I
have closely examined the entire Babylonian Talmud, and
its accompanying rabbinic literature, and I have analysed the
laws of every situation in which *Da'at* is involved.

The concluding chapter is an extract from my study,
The Notion of the Will in the Old Testament (Ph.D. thesis,
Edinburgh University, 1957), reprinted in *Essays Presented
to Chief Rabbi Israel Brodie* (Soncino, London, 1967). It
embraces the entire concept of Mind as a decisive factor in
the undertaking of actions in Jewish religious law.

Scriptural passages are quoted from the Hebrew Bible and
English translations from the Revised Version, unless otherwise
stated. Talmudic citations are normally from tractates of the
Babylonian Talmud (*Bavli*); those referring to the Jerusalem
Talmud (*Yerushalmi*) are indicated by the abbreviation T.J.
Other rabbinic sources (notably the Midrashim) are indicated
by their titles. Citations from Maimonides refer to his *Yad ha-
Hazakah* code, unless otherwise stated. References to the legal

code (*Shulḥan Arukh*) of Joseph Caro are entitled according to its four separate divisions. All translations of rabbinic literature are my own, following the explanations given by halakhic authorities.

The account of Sabbath and Holy Day observances conforms with the order of Festivals given in the *Shulḥan Arukh*. Some technical terms and the names of different Sages have been transliterated from the original Hebrew or Aramaic. A glossary of Hebrew and Aramaic terms and an index of the abbreviations used for books and authors that I have appended are based on the Soncino Press translation of the Babylonian Talmud edited by Isidore Epstein (London, 1952). A description of the classical Hebrew texts is included in an Appendix.

Readers will appreciate the fact that my use of the terms 'we' and 'our' in describing religious duties comes naturally to one whose viewpoint is that of a traditionally observant Jew, and the work is a committed portrayal of orthodox Jewish practice. The masculine form in all these laws is used for convenience, but generally they refer to both men and women.

Wherever necessary, I have provided a general introduction to each chapter, referring only to those situations in which the effect of an "act of the mind" is particularly involved. I have included a chapter on contract, although this topic is not strictly within the purview of ritual law but rather of civil law. It is, however, replete with acts of the mind and constitutes a vital aspect of daily life. Torts and criminal law are subjects that require separate treatment and they are not covered in this work.

When planning each exposition I have taken into account the fact that most readers will have a limited acquaintance with the subject discussed. However, even those completely unfamiliar with Jewish legal matters will find it possible to understand the various ritual procedures and to follow the logical sequence of the laws. In the course of explaining each regulation I have also endeavoured to supply all the relevant background in order to ensure that the place of every law discussed can be understood by the general reader.

The text presents different rulings by different Sages. These rulings enable us to judge how the one scholar's outlook differed from the other. Many of those differences were not rooted in the law *per se* but in the way Jewish scholars read the purpose and intention in the mind of an individual. It is from such discussions that one can gain a valuable insight into rabbinic psychology and the making of rabbinic law.

In some chapters certain subjects may be dealt with, which had already been studied in previous chapters. This is done in order to make each chapter, as much as possible, a complete study in itself. without having to refer back to previous pages.

The totality of this work may serve as an extensive sourcebook of the consequential effect of intention in Jewish ritual law.

My sincerest thanks are due to Dr. Gavriel Sivan who skillfully edited the entire book, and offered many valuable suggestions which I have incorporated.

My heartfelt thanks are given to Judge Zvi Tal for his continuing encouragement in my work, and his painstaking review particularly of many halakhic sections of this book. My grateful thanks are likewise due to Chief Rabbi Sir Jonathan Sacks of London, and to Prof. Daniel Sperber, and Rabbi Emanuel Quint, as well as to Prof. Stefan Reif of Cambridge, my former student and constant friend, for their kindness in reviewing my book and offering me their much appreciated commendations.

I wish to thank David Brauner for his efficient proofreading and for his devotion to the project. I also owe my many thanks to my good friend and neighbor Itzchak Teichtal, to Tali Ilan for the cover design, to Rachel Twito (Muvan Office Services) and to Eli Cohen (Graphics Centre) for their most helpful assistance in my printing requirements.

Finally, I wish to express my sincere appreciation to Mr. Zamir Bar-Lev, president of Printiv Press, for his helpful suggestions and guidance in seeing the book through the press.

Even though every effort has been made to avoid any error in the text, I am mindful of an early saying of scholars, "In the finest flour one can find some chaff".

In conclusion I offer thanksgiving to the Almighty who has sustained me and enabled me to present this work of Torah research.

ירושלים עיה"ק, ערב יום הכיפור, תשס"ח, שנת "עת לחננה כי בא מועד" לפ"ק (תהלים קב:יד).

Isaac Cohen

Jerusalem 2007

CONTENTS

Chapter 1

Faith, Belief, Trust – *Emunah*

1 Faith, Belief, Trust – Emunah

The word *emunah*, denoting "faith, belief, trust", has various meanings, all of which stem from the root a-m-n, "to be firm, strong, unchanging, constant, trustworthy, reliable". As an expression of religious belief, it means to have confidence in the truth and reliability of one's religion, i.e., complete acceptance of the truth of a religious doctrine.

A. Belief in God

Faith as the First Principle

In *Hovot ha-Levavot* (ch. 1, introd., *Yihud*), R. Bahya Ibn Pakuda (Spain, 11th cent.) states that the foundation of the Jewish religion is belief in the existence and unity of God. The acceptance of this belief is ordained in the First Commandment – "I am the Lord thy God, who brought thee out of the land of Egypt, out of the house of bondage. Thou shalt have no other gods before Me" (Ex. 20:2, 3).[1] It is the duty of every Jew to believe with perfect faith that the Almighty is the Creator of the universe, and that there is no sovereign creator other than He. Moses, the prophet of God, repeated this teaching in the words, "Hear, O Israel: the Lord our God, the Lord is one" (Deut. 6:4);[2] or, in Jewish tradition, "the Lord is our Almighty God; the Lord is one". By the expression, "Hear, O Israel" – *Shema Yisra'el* – Moses meant not just "hearing" but "understanding" and "being convinced of the truth of" this declaration and consequently obeying its injunctions. Hence

---

אנכי ה׳ אל-היך... לא יהיה לך אל-הים אחרים על פני   1

שמע ישראל ה׳ אל-הינו ה׳ אחד   2

Israel was commanded, "Hear therefore, O Israel, and observe to do it" (Deut. 6:3).[3]

The first paragraph of the *Shema* enunciates the components and subsequent unfolding of the duties resulting from the affirmation of this belief. After we express our belief in the unity of the omnipotent Divine Creator, it becomes our duty to love God with all our heart, as He commanded us: "And thou shalt love the Lord thy God with all thy heart, and with all thy soul, and with all thy might" (Deut. 6:5).[4] Secondly, we must engrave our duties to God firmly in our hearts and conscience, as the law continues: "And these words, which I command thee this day, shall be upon thy heart" (Deut. 6:6).[5] For this purpose we must study them and teach them continually to our children,[6] so that we will not be unmindful of our duty to God at any given moment.

David proclaimed: "I have set the Lord always before me". He said that at all times he conjured up in his mind that he was confronted by the presence of the Lord; and so long as he was aware that God was before him, and saw all his conduct, he would not sin (Ps. 16:8, *Metzudat David, ad loc.*).[7]

A similar thought is expressed in the Rabbinic interpretation of the temptation of Joseph by the wife of Potiphar. Throughout his exile in Egypt it was Joseph's practice to keep the figure of his father always before him. When he was about to yield to his mistress's lures, the vision of his father appeared before him and reminded him of the sanctity of his destiny. He was told that his name was destined to appear on the sacred *ephod* (the special jeweled vest) worn by the High Priest in the Temple. By that vision he was restrained submitting to a shameful act of immorality (Gen. 39:11, 12,[8] Rashi *ad loc.;* Sotah 36b.).[9]

---

3   ושמעת ישראל ושמרת לעשות

4   ואהבת את ה' אל-היך בכל לבבך ובכל נפשך ובכל מאדך

5   והיו הדברים האלה אשר אנכי מצוך היום על לבבך

6   ושננתם לבניך

7   שויתי ה' לנגדי תמיד

8   ויעזב בגדו בידה וינס ויצא החוצה

9   באותה שעה באתה דיוקנו של אביו ונראתה לו בחלון

We are thus required to have practical reminders of God's omnipresence – signs on our arm and head, and on the door-posts of our home: "And thou shalt bind them for a sign upon thy hand, and they shall be for frontlets between thine eyes. And thou shalt write them upon the door-posts of thy house, and upon thy gates" (Deut. 6:8-9).[10] The fulfillment of all these requirements is a declaration of our belief in God.[11] Only after this complete acceptance of God are we able to assume the consequent responsibility of observing His commandments, as Bahya states.[12] Just as it is our duty to affirm our belief in God, as a matter of faith, so is it our duty to understand the truth of this dogma by the effort of our intellect. Thus Moses declared: "Know this day, and lay it to thy heart, that the Lord, He is God in heaven above and upon the earth beneath; there is none else" (Deut. 4:39).[13]

Accordingly, in addition to affirming his belief in the Creator, each individual should endeavour to attain an understanding of the Sovereignty of God, in accordance with his intellectual ability. Solomon was instructed by his father, David, to understand God's sovereignty in order to serve Him "with a whole heart" (1 Chron. 28:9).[14] Jeremiah likewise declared that the highest achievement of man, of which one should be proud, was not the acquiring of philosophical wisdom or scientific knowledge, not power or wealth, but an understanding of the truth, justice and righteousness of God (Jer. 9:22–23).[15]

Like Bahya, Maimonides wrote that the first principle of Judaism is belief in the One omnipotent, incorporeal Creator and Controller of the universe. In his Thirteen Articles of Faith Maimonides listed, as his first principle, faith in the existence

---

10 וקשרתם לאות על ידך והיו לטוטפות בין עיניך
11 קבלת עול מלכות שמים
12 ואחר כך יקבל עליו עול מלכות שמים
13 וידעת היום והשבת על לבבך כי ה' הוא האל-הים בשמים ממעל ועל הארץ מתחת, אין עוד
14 ואתה שלמה בני דע את אלו-הי אביך ועבדהו בלב שלם ובנפש חפצה
15 ואל יתהלל חכם בחכמתו.... כי אם בזאת יתהלל המתהלל השכל וידוע אותי

of God as the cause of the existence of all other beings
(Maim., Commentary on the Mishnah, introd. to *Sanhedrin*
10). The duty to believe this is reflected in the first of the Ten
Commandments: "I am the Lord thy God" (Ex. 20:2).[16] Any
deviation from this belief constitutes a denial of the Almighty
Himself (Maim., Code, *Yesodei ha-Torah* 1.6).[17]

Godliness and the Divine

The first act in the Jewish concept of man's relationship with
his Creator is an act of the mind – an act of belief, not just
of the intellect but of a faith that is rooted in man's entire
personality. The three paragraphs of the *Shema* recited daily
express the totality of Jewish belief; they depart from their
strict order in the Torah, although the basic *Shema Yisra'el*
passage is said first. The Sages taught that our belief must start
with the full acceptance of God's sovereignty and, as a result,
the believer will fulfil all the laws ordained in the Torah (*Ber.*
13a).[18]

While plural in form, the Hebrew term for God (*elohim*) has
a grammatically singular sense. The Torah thus teaches us that
the universe was not created by two or more separate powers
– good and evil or mercy and judgment. The Sages laid down
as axiomatic that there are no universal powers other than the
One Creator (Midrash: Gen. R. 12:15; 1:1).[19]

The Sages also regarded judgment and mercy as attributes of
the Divine. They taught that the Almighty considered whether
He should create the world in the attribute of judgment or of
mercy. "Should I create it only in the practice of judgment and
retribution", He said, "the world could not manage to survive.

---

16 אנכי ה' אל-היך
17 כופר בעיקר
18 אמר ר' יהושע בן קרחה... כדי שיקבל עליו עול מלכות שמים תחלה ואחר כך
    מקבל עליו עול מצוות
19 אין שתי רשויות

Both judgment and mercy are therefore needed" (Gen. R. 1:1).[20]

Faced with the awesome powers of nature, notably fire, water, wind, heat and cold, men attributed a special potency to each. These mighty powers were represented in the form of idolatrous gods, whom worshippers called *elohim* or *elim*. Moses therefore warned the people of Israel not to follow the practice of heathen nations: "The Lord will bring thee, and thy king whom thou shalt set over thee, unto a nation that neither thou nor thy fathers have known; and there shalt thou serve other gods of wood and stone" (Deut. 28:36).[21]

The early Semitic term *El* denoted "a mighty power", or a "superpower" invested with superhuman authority and a godlike majesty. This term was retained in Hebrew when referring to Divine power in the highest degree, especially the plural form *Elohim*, which we translate as "All-Powerful God". In the Song ofMoses at the crossing of the Red Sea, after Israel's deliverance from enslavement in Egypt, Moses declared: "Who is like Thee, O Lord, among the gods *(elohim)*?" (Ex. 15:11).[22] In other words, what power is there that can be compared with that of the true God?Daniel also termed one of the heathen deities *elo'ah nekhar*, "a foreign god" (Dan. 11:39).[23] Torah teaching holds all these forces of nature to be Divine creations, their powers being harnessed in the service of God, the Supreme Creator. In our daily prayers, immediately after the *Shema*, we proclaim our faith in the Lord as "Rock of our salvation", adding that "there is no God beside You".[24]

Angels as Servants of God

In the vision of Isaiah, the Almighty is seated on his throne

---

20 אם אני בורא את העולם במדת הדין אינו יכול לעמוד, אני בורא את העולם במדת הרחמים

21 ועבדתם שם אלהים אחרים עץ ואבן

22 מי כמוך באלים

23 אלהי נכר

24 אין אל-הים זולתך

and surrounded by a heavenly court of ministering angels (Isa. 6:1–2). These angels are servants of God entrusted with various missions. They may be employed to deliver a message to man or they may serve as instruments of Divine judgment and providence (Gen. 18:1*ff*; 1 Kings 22:19).

The English word "angel" derives from the Greek term *angelos* ("messenger"). This is a translation of the Hebrew *mal'akh,* signifying a messenger of God who fulfils His commands, as in the verse: "God hath sent His angel, and hath shut the lions' mouths, that they have not hurt me" (Dan. 6:22). The Bible also refers to angels serving as instruments of Divine providence (Ps. 103:19-21).[25] Even the elements are referred to as *mal'akhim:* "Who maketh winds His messengers, flaming fire His ministers" (Ps. 104:4).

The function of angels is to execute God's decrees; they never serve as emissaries of mankind. It is therefore useless for man to call on an angel to help him in his hour of need or to intercede with God on his behalf. Help comes only from the Lord (Ps. 121:1–2), and it is to Him alone that prayers should be addressed. The Sages declared: "Should any trouble befall a man, let him not call upon [the angel] Michael or Gabriel but appeal directly to Me, and I the Lord will answer his prayer" (TJ *Ber.* 1:1; cf. Moshe ben Yosef di Trani [HA-MABBIT], *Bet Elohim*, Part 1, *Tefillah*, section 1).[26]

Jews who adopted the custom of praying at the graves of eminent holy men (e.g., R. Shim'on bar Yoḥai and R. Meir Ba'al ha-Nes) did not believe that their plea for a blessing or for the cure of an ailment would be answered by the dead. A deceased person's spirit was thought to continue hovering over the grave in some mysterious way, which endowed it with sanctity and made it a suitable place for individual prayers and petitions. When the Lord answered these pleas, He was simply acknowledging the merit of the righteous.

---

25 ברכו ה׳ כל צבאיו משרתיו עשי רצונו

26 אם באת על אדם צרה לא יצווח לא למיכאל ולא לגבריאל אלא לי לצווח ואני ענה לו מיד

According to the KOL BO, a mediaeval compendium of Jewish practice attributed to R. Aharon ha-Kohen of Lunel, it was customary in some communities to visit the graves of parents and holy men on the eve of Rosh ha-Shanah and on Fast days, when petitions to God were usually made.

The Sages enquired about the reason for paying these customary visits to the burial ground and praying there.[27] Some authorities held that it was meant to reinforce an awareness of our mortality. Others believed that the souls of the departed would implore God to have mercy on those visiting their graves (*Ta'an.* 16a, *Tos.* '*yotze'in*').[28] Just as all things in nature are drawn to their origin, so the body and soul of a righteous person maintain a certain attachment even after they are parted.

Although it is written that "the dust returneth to the earth as it was, and the spirit returneth unto God who gave it" (Eccles. 12:7),[29] the Sages taught that a man's body continues to exist for twelve months after death, during which time his soul moves up and down between heaven and earth. After twelve months the body ceases to exist; the soul rises to heaven and never returns to earth (*Shab.* 152b).

An early teaching of the Sages affirms, however, that the righteous soul has the power to return to its previous corporeal abode whenever it so desires (*Shab.* 153a, *Tos.* s.v. '*venishmato*'). They maintained that the soul, which is pure, can reconnect with the body of the righteous person, which is also pure (*Shab.* 152b; *BB* 58a).

This explains why the custom developed for Jews to visit the graves ofrighteous people, where they felt able to pour out their souls to God.

The presence of a special sanctity obtained particularly in a place where God had already revealed Himself in answer to man's prayer. That is why Jacob, on his flight from Esau, went especially to Beth-El because Abraham and Isaac had

---

למה יוצאין לבית הקברות   27

כדי שיבקשו עלינו מתים רחמים   28

וישב העפר על הארץ כשהיה והרוח תשוב אל האל-הים אשר נתנה   29

previously communed with God there. In Talmudic literature the Sages identified this Biblical Beth-El with the site of Jerusalem (Gen. 28:16, 17;[30] 35:1, Rashi *ad loc.*; *Hullin* 91b).

Abraham's Faith

The first man to recognize God was Abraham. From the moment of this recognition, every external prompting of his intellect was subordinated to his religious faith. The Sages concluded that Abraham came to know God as a boy, in the home of his idol-worshipping family. Through his contemplation of the meaning of existence, he decided that this could only be explained as the work of a supreme Creator. He smashed the powerless idols of his father and embraced the idea of spreading monotheism (Gen. R. 95.2, 64.4, 39.1). Abraham's belief in the Divine promise of the gift of an abundant progeny, even at his advanced age, was an act of faith. The Almighty showed him the countless stars in the heavens, saying "So shall thy seed be",[31] and Abraham firmly believed that God would fulfil His promise. That complete trust was expressed in the words, "And he believed in the Lord",[32] despite the fact that Abraham had obviously long believed in God. Such loyalty was reckoned to be an act of righteous faith on Abraham's part (Gen. 15:5–6; Rashi and Sforno, *ad loc.*).

Faith as Yir'at Elohim – Divine Awe

The duty to believe in God and worship Him was described by Moses as "fear of the Lord" *(yir'at Elohim)* and formulated by him in the words: "And now, Israel, what doth the Lord thy God require of thee, but to fear the Lord thy God, to walk in all His ways, and to love Him, and to serve the Lord thy God

---

30 ויאמר מה נורא המקום הזה אין זה כי אם בית אל-הים וזה שער השמים

31 כה יהיה זרעך

32 והאמין בה'

with all thy heart and with all thy soul; to keep the Lord's commandments and His statutes, which I command thee this day, for thine own good?" (Deut. 10:12-13, Rashi *ad loc.*; *Ber.* 33b).[33]

The Talmud relates that, on this basis, R. Haninah taught: "Everything is in the power of Heaven except the fear of Heaven".[34] *Yir'at Elohim* is determined by man. The elated condition of *yirat Elohim* is entirely dependent on man's own decision to embrace it. Yet "fear of God" does not mean that we are terrified to be in the Lord's presence and wish to hide from Him. It is rather a way of expressing the awe and reverence that we feel when drawing closer to the Divine.

The sense of *yir'at Elohim* flows from our consciousness of the Lord's all-powerful greatness, as seen in the universal acts of His creation, His supreme wisdom and His loving care for man.

Our response to the Almighty's proclamation in the Decalogue, "I am the Lord thy God" (Ex. 20:1), is "Thou art my God" (Isa. 44:17; Ps. 22:11, 118:28) or our daily conscious acknowledgment in the *Shema* prayer: "The Lord is our God" (Deut. 6:4). This acknowledgment is not something imposed on man but a spontaneous, reverent response flowing from his heart and mind, in recognition of the Creator's infinite majesty, love and providence. It causes us to distance ourselves from anything that might displease Him and make us unworthy of His love.

The feeling of reverence for the Almighty extends to everything related in our mind to the works of God. We have respect for all of His creations as well as for the teachings that bear His Name.

One's duty to "fear God" – *yir'at Elohim* – was further taught by David to Solomon in the following words: "And thou, Solomon my son, know thou the God of thy father, and serve Him with a perfect heart and with a willing mind… If thou seek Him, He will be found of thee" (1 Chron.

---

33   ועתה ישראל מה ה' אל-היך שואל מעמך כי אם ליראה את ה' אל-היך
34   הכל בידי שמים חוץ מיראת שמים

28:9).[35] In David's teaching the attainment of this "fear of God" – *yir'at Elohim* – would result from obeying the call to "seek to understand the God of thy father" and serve Him wholeheartedly.

King Solomon, in a summation of his philosophical enquiry, concluded that the only meaningful realization of man's life on earth was as follows: "The end of the matter, all having been heard: fear God, and keep His commandments; for this is the whole duty of man" (Eccles. 12:13).[36]

Conscious of His all-embracing power and wisdom, we safely entrust ourselves to His commands and exhortations as our surest guide in life. The Psalmist declared: "Trust in the Lord, and do good" (Ps. 37:2).[37] As a tender of sheep, accustomed to show loving care for his flock, David affirmed: "The Lord is my shepherd; I shall not want" (Ps. 23:1).[38]

A spontaneous feeling of reverence before God is insufficient, however, if it does not find expression in our acts and speech. A devout communion with God in our heart alone will not bring us the spiritual satisfaction that we seek, if we do not also give it outward expression through appropriate speech and the fulfilment of His laws in our relationship with Him and with our fellow human beings. David portrayed the completeness of his own devotion to God in the following words: "With my whole heart have I sought Thee; O let me not wander from Thy commandments" (Ps. 119:10).[39]

Displaying a respectful awareness, at all times, of our presence before God is held out by the Sages as the first rule of our daily life. The great principle of Torah teaching is a cognizance of the ideal: "I have set the Lord always before me" (Ps. 16:8).[40] As a result of such awareness of God's presence we will be able to fulfil the teaching of R. Yehudah

---

35   ואתה שלמה בני דע את אל-הי אביך ועבדהו בלב שלם ובנפש חפצה... אם
      תדרשנו ימצא לך

36   סוף דבר הכל נשמע את אל-הים ירא ואת מצוותיו שמור כי זה כל האדם

37   בטח בה' ועשה טוב

38   ה' רעי לא אחסר

39   בכל לבי דרשתיך אל תשגני ממצותיך

40   שויתי ה' לנגדי תמיד

ben Tema: "Be bold as a leopard, swift as an eagle, fleet as a deer and strong as a lion, to do the will of your Father who is in Heaven" (*Avot* 5.23; *Sh. Ar., Ora*ḥ *Hayyim* 1.1).[41]

Jeremiah proclaimed that trusting in the Lord is man's surest safeguard: "Blessed is the man that trusteth in the Lord, and whose trust the Lord is" (Jer. 17:7).[42] When man has faith, the Almighty will protect him and he need fear no evil, as this agricultural metaphor implies: "For he shall be as a tree planted by the waters, that spreadeth out its roots by the river, and shall not fear when heat cometh, but his leaf shall be green..." (Kimḥi, commenting on Jer. 17:7–8).

The Sages recognized that there are two approaches towards the fulfilment of *yir'at Elohim* – a superficial or external attitude and a deeper, internal one. The superficial approach results from one's fear of Divine punishment or anticipation of heavenly reward, as well as the need for protection from the ills of misfortune, adversity and suffering. The deeper, internal approach results from a knowledge of the overwhelming wonders of God's creation as revealed by natural science, together with the marvels of humankind. Although the *yir'at Elohim* resulting from an external approach was also commendable, it was to the other, deeper fear of God that David pointed his son: "And thou, Solomon my son, know thou the God of thy father", meaning that his successor should gain the same intimate knowledge of God that he had acquired.

The Sages realized, however, that such an achievement – on the strength of one's own intellectual effort – was only granted to a few exceptional individuals. Referring to Moses the lawgiver's injunction "to fear the Lord thy God", they stated that this was a small demand for Moses alone; but for people in general it was no light task.[43]

They nevertheless insisted that *yir'at shamayim* – "the fear of Heaven" – was within the power of man alone to achieve,

41   וגבור כארי לעשות רצון אביך שבשמים
42   ברוך הגבר אשר יבטח בה' והיה ה' מבטחו
43   אטו יראת שמים מילתא זוטרתא היא, אין לגבי משה מילתא זוטרתא היא

and not a gift bestowed by God, for "everything is in the power of God except the fear of God" (Deut. 10:12, Rashi *ad loc.*; *Ber.* 33b).[44]

Similarly, one's "love of God" – *ahavat Hashem* – could derive from external, ulterior motives, such as finding favor in God's sight, and reaping the rewards of success, honour, wealth or even eternal bliss in the World to Come. The truer level of *ahavat Hashem* results from our boundless admiration of the vast complex of Divine creation and our feeling that we are indeed privileged to be associated with the Creator's universal scheme. Hence this exhortation of Moses to his people, enjoining them to keep God's commandments: "Know therefore this day, and lay it to thy heart, that the Lord, He is God in Heaven above and upon the earth beneath; there is none else" (Deut. 4:39[45]; R. Yeshayahu Horowitz, *Kitzur Shenei Luḥot ha-Berit, Sha'ar ha-Yir'ah*).

B. Faith vs. Reason

Faith in God – *emunah ba-Shem* – consists of a wholehearted belief in the sovereignty of the all-powerful Creator and in the Torah's Divine authority. Only such *emunah* can help man to attain spiritual excellence and synergy with the Divine Spirit, thus giving rise to prophecy and even to the working of miracles. No amount of intellectual exploration in science and philosophy can elevate man to such spiritual heights. Only perfect *emunah* can raise a man above the confines of natural existence. As R. Yosef Albo phrased it, complete belief in the truth of God's doctrine – *emunah ba-Shem* – surpasses man's highest intellectual attainment (*Sefer ha-Ikkarim*, I, 21, section 9).[46]

---

44   הכל בידי שמים חוץ מיראת שמים

45   וידעת היום והשבות אל לבבך כי ה' הוא האל-הים בשמים ממעל ועל הארץ מתחת אין עוד

46   כי האמונה היא למעלה מן הידיעה המחקרית

Abraham, the progenitor of Israel, achieved *emunah ba-Shem* despite the conflicting demands of his intellect. Scripture records that when God assured the aged but childless patriarch that he would still be blessed with numerous offspring, Abraham had complete faith that this Divine promise would be fulfilled, as it is written: "And he believed in the Lord".[47] That faith and trust was acknowledged by God, who "counted it to him for righteousness" (Gen. 15:6).[48]

Emunah ba-Shem thus denotes complete faith and trust in the word of God, that it is true and will undoubtedly be fulfilled. A momentary lapse on the part of Moses, his failure to trust in God's promise to bring forth water from the rock only by speaking to it, woulddisqualify him from bringing Israel into the Promised Land. "Because ye believed not in Me...." [49,] Scripture explains; Moses obviously *believed* in God, yet disobeyed His clear instruction, since he evidently *did not believe* that water could be obtained without striking the rock. By contrast, when the Israelites experienced their miraculous escape through the parted waters of the Red Sea and then saw the pursuing Egyptians drown in those same waters, "the people feared the Lord", had complete faith in His sovereignty and "believed in His servant Moses" (Ex. 14:31).[50]

Likewise, at the Sinaitic Revelation, God tells Moses that when the Decalogue is proclaimed to Israel, the voice of God will be heard speaking to Moses. As a result, the people will believe with complete faith that these laws are Divinely commanded; they will thus trust Moses unreservedly when he conveys to them God's further teachings: "And they will also believe thee forever" (Ex. 19:9).[51] Albo states that this is not an irrational belief in something that does not exist. It accepts what truly exists as a fact; and even if the intellect fails to grasp it, one can be certain of its truth because it is the word of God (*Sefer ha-Ikkarim*, I, 21, section 1).

---

47   והאמין בה׳
48   ויחשבה לו צדקה
49   יען לא האמנתם בי
50   ויאמינו בה׳ ובמשה עבדו
51   וגם בך האמינו לעולם

R. Yehudah Halevi maintained that there is nothing in the Bible that contradicts reason. At the same time, however, the Bible is a source of higher and surer truth than men can attain rationally. Knowledge reached by philosophical methods is inherently faulty, since philosophers themselves often refute each other. The Jewish religion is not irrational, but suprarational. The God of Abraham is the God of living experience, known personally to Abraham and, through him, to Israel in a manifestation of Divine providence, whereas the God of Aristotle, a supreme achievement of the human intellect, is still no more than an abstract philosophical principle. Halevi concludes, as Albo did later, that faith is a higher source of truth than intellectual research (Yehudah Halevi, *Kuzari*, I, 4, 13; IV, 16–18).[52]

Maimonides interpreted the Torah in the light of Rabbinic teaching and endeavoured to reconcile philosophy with Jewish tradition. He describes intellectual inquiry as the stage following the primary one of accepting Torah by belief, since intellectual excellence is attained only by a few "not many are wise" (Job 32:9).[53] Every man is endowed with the Divine gift of intellect, but for one reason or another, physical, sensual, or mental slothfulness, man's intellect is far from perfect; and some mystical concepts of the Divine are entirely beyond the reach of his understanding (Maim. Code, *Yesodei ha-Torah* 2:10–12).

The Sages described the sequence to be followed in gaining a knowledge of Torah. Having first accepted the concept of its truth, one must learn what the Torah actually teaches. Then one must understand what actions are required in the light of Torah wisdom and elucidate the way it perfects man's conduct. Hence the Sages declared: "When man is brought to judgment in the World to Come, he is asked: Did you study Torah regularly; did you investigate the reasoning behind your knowledge; and, finally, did you learn how to control

---

52 האמונה היא למעלה מן הידיעה המחקרית

53 לא רבים יחכמו

your behaviour?"[54] Even so, the Sages concluded, everything depends on whether complete faith in the Almighty was one's most precious possession (*Shab.* 31a; Maim., *Guide*, III, 54).[55]

C. Other Meanings of *Emunah*

In the Rabbinic teaching mentioned above, another meaning of the word *emunah* is found. Among the questions put to man on the Day of Judgment is, firstly, "Did you conduct your daily business faithfully [i.e., honestly]?" Such conduct is described as *be-emunah*. Thus the Sages declared: "When a man is brought to Final Judgment, he is first asked, Did you deal honestly with your fellow man?" (*Shab.* 31a).[56]

This idea of faithfulness and steadfastness occurs frequently and in Biblical sources the term "faith" has many nuances. The following selection displays various aspects of the concept and its usage:"Trust in the Lord, and do good; dwell in the land, and cherish faithfulness" (Ps. 37:3).[57] "I have chosen the way of faithfulness" (Ps. 119:30).[58] "A God of faithfulness and without iniquity, just and right is He" (Deut. 32:4).[59] "A faithful witness will not lie; but a false witness uttereth lies" (Prov. 14:5).[60] "Most men will proclaim every one his own kindness; but a faithful man who can find?" (Prov. 20:6).[61] "Moreover they reckoned not with the men, into whose hand they delivered the money to give to them that did the work: for they dealt faithfully" (2 Kings 12:16).[62] "His compassions fail not. They are new every morning; great is Thy faithfulness"

קבעת עתים לתורה, פלפלת בחכמה, היבנת דבר מתוך דבר   54

יראת ה׳ היא אוצרו   55

בשעה שמכניסין אדם לדין אומרים לו נשאת ונתת באמונה   56

ורעה אמונה   57

דרך אמונה בחרתי   58

א-ל אמונה ואין עול, צדיק וישר הוא   59

עד אמונים לא יכזב   60

ואיש אמונים מי ימצא   61

כי באמונה הם עושים   62

(Lam. 3:22-23).[63] "How is the faithful city become a harlot!" [i.e., the city that was true and upright is now faithless] (Isa. 1:21).[64] "My servant Moses is not so; he is trusted in all My house" (Num. 12:7)[65] "I will betroth thee unto Me in faithfulness" (Hos. 2:22).[66] "But the righteous shall live by his faith" (Hab. 2:4).[67]

The Sages quoted this last verse when they summed up the whole of Torah teaching: "Habakkuk encapsulated all that God required of man in the words, 'The righteous shall live by his faith'" (commentary on Micah 6:8 – "He hath told thee, O man, what is good; and what the Lord doth require of thee: but to do justly, and to love mercy, and to walk humbly with thy God").[68] Thus the faith of the righteous encompasses belief in God and constant loyalty to that belief. His life will be complete because of his faith (*Mak.* 24a).

A further sense of *emunah* can be gauged from its use in the first verse quoted above (Ps. 37:3): "Trust in the Lord, and do good; dwell in the land, and cherish faithfulness". Here, "dwell in the land" could be understood to mean "engage in agriculture", "live humbly" or "dwell in the land of Israel". An even more appropriate meaning can be derived from an interpretation of Balaam's words blessing the people of Israel: "He couched, he lay down as a lion, and as a lioness; who shall rouse him up?" (Num. 24:9).[69] Now a moralistic teaching of the Sages compares Israel to a lion and quotes R. Yehuda ben Tema: "Be... strong as a lion to perform the will of your Father in heaven" (TUR, *Sh. Ar., Orah Hayyim* 1:1).[70]

However, in accordance with their plain meaning, Balaam's words are a reference to the strength of Israel as a people. It is instinctive for a lion, whenever and wherever he lies down, to

---

63   רבה אמונתך

64   איכה היתה לזונה קריה נאמנה

65   בכל ביתי נאמן הוא

66   וארשתיך לי באמונה

67   וצדיק באמונתו יחיה

68   עשות משפט ואהבת חסד והצנע לכת

69   כרע שכב כארי וכלביא מי יקימנו

70   הוי עז כנמר ..... וגבור כארי לעשות רצון אביך שבשמים

fiercely defend that spot. Nothing will make him quit his lair and he is the master of his terrain. This is how the people of Israel are called upon to settle their land (Num 24:9, *Targum,* Rashi and Ibn Ezra, *ad loc.*). The words of the Psalmist can therefore be taken to mean: "Put your trust in the Lord and act righteously; settle your land in a resolute manner and pasture your herds like afaithful shepherd".

Emunah, in this context, is also associated with the revival or resurrection of the dead. In his vision concerning the "Valley of Dry Bones", Ezekiel prophesied that the Almighty would raise His people from their graves, restore them to life and bring them back to their land (Ezek. 37:12-14).[71] Elsewhere in the Bible we are told: "Many of them that sleep in the dust of the earth shall awake, some to everlasting life..." (Dan. 12:2). Maimonides, who declared an unshaken belief resurrection (*tehiyyat ha-metim*)[72] one of the basic tenets of Judaism, listed it as the final article in his Thirteen Principles of Faith (Maim. Mishnah Commentary, intro. to *Sanhedrin* 10). This declaration, which was accepted by all later Jewish philosophers, is repeated in the daily *Amidah* prayer: "You are faithful to resurrect the dead".[73]

God promised Abram, "all the land which thou seest, to thee will I give it, and to thy seed forever" (Gen. 13:15).[74] A more explicit covenant was later made with the patriarch: "I will give unto thee and to thy seed after thee, the land of thy sojournings, all the land of Canaan, for an everlasting possession" (Gen. 17:8).[75] Later, at the time of the Exodus, God confirmed the promise made to Abraham, and renewed to Isaac and Jacob, that Israel would inherit Canaan, "a land flowing with milk and honey" (Ex. 13:5, 11). The Sages noted that the patriarchs themselves had never taken possession of the land, where they always remained sojourners. It was only in the days of Joshua that Israel conquered its inhabitants and

---

71   והעליתי אתכם מקברותיכם עמי
72   תחיית המתים
73   ונאמן אתה להחיות מתים
74   כי את כל הארץ אשר אתה רואה לך אתננה ולזרעך עד עולם
75   ונתתי לך ולזרעך אחריך את ארץ מגוריך את כל ארץ כנען לאחזת עולם

assumed possession. Was there a contradiction here? The Almighty had sworn that He would give the land of Canaan "to thee" (i.e. to each of the patriarchs), whereas the text should presumably read "to you" (i.e. their descendants).

According to the Sages, however, God meant that Israel's forefathers will possess the land of Canaan in time to come, when the resurrection of the dead takes place, thus substantiating the truth of expression "to you". The Talmud records a statement by R. Simlai, affirming that these words show that the principle of *tehiyyat ha-metim* was already embodied in the Torah (*Sanh.* 90b). According to Nehemia, when Israel's newly returned exiles held a joyous assembly in their homeland, they offered thanksgiving and proclaimed "Thou art the Lord the God, who didst choose Abram... and madest a covenant with him to give the land of the Canaanite, the Hittite, the Amorite and the Perizzite and the Jebusite, and the Girgashite, even to give it unto his seed, and hast preformed thy words; for Thou art righteous" (Neh. 9:7,8).

D. *Emunah* in Action

Habakkuk prophesied that when Nebuchadnezzar exiled the Jews to Babylon during the reign of King Jehoiachin, those who remained loyal to their faith and trusted in God would not disappear in exile but return to their land with their faith intact (Rashi, Kimhi *ad loc.*). Hence the Sages declared that everything the Lord asked of them could be condensed in one requirement – to be steadfast in their faith in God (Hab. 2:4).[76]

King Jehoshaphat thus instructed magistrates in Jerusalem to render judgment "in the fear of the Lord, faithfully, and with a perfect heart" (2 Chron. 19:9).[77]

"I will betroth thee unto Me in faithfulness", said the

---

76 צדיק באמונתו יחיה
77 ביראת ה' באמונה ובלבב שלם

prophet (Hos. 2:22).[78] This means that the relationship between God and Israel will be described as strong and enduring as a faithful marriage, but only on condition that Israel practises"righteousness and justice" – *tzedakah u-mishpat* (Gen. 18:19). In return, God will show Israel "kindness and mercy" – *hesed ve-rahamim*. This He will also do because of Israel's unwavering trust and confidence in the prophetic assurances of God's redemption, and so "thou shalt know [the love of] God" (*Idem* Rashi *ad loc.*).

The prophet castigated the speakers of falsehood who had "grown strong in the land but not for truth". People can kill, said the prophet, with their evil speech. "They bend their tongue as it were their bow for falsehood." In this way, as with an arrow, they kill a person from afar" (Jer. 9:2). [79]

After King Josiah cleansed Judea of idolatry and ordered that the Temple be repaired, the Levites gave the Temple money to reliable craftsmen, who did all their work faithfully (*be-emunah*; 2 Chron. 34:12).[80] As mentioned earlier, the Sages declared that when a man is brought to Heavenly judgment in the World to Come, he must answer questions about his religious conduct and devotion to Torah. One of those questions will be: "Did you deal truly and honestly with your neighbour?"[81] The outcome depends on whether he is judged to possess *yir'at Hashem* – "fear of God" (*Shab.* 31a).

---

78 וארשתיך לי באמונה וידעת את ה'
79 וידרכו את לשונם קשתם שקר ולא לאמונה גברו בארץ
80 והאנשים עושים באמונה במלאכה
81 נשאת ונתת באמונה

Chapter 2

Holiness – *Kedushah*

2 *Holiness* – Kedushah

A. The Concept of Holiness

The entire concept of holiness in Judaism is a religious one, founded on a belief in the existence of God as the sole Creator of the universe, in God's covenant with the patriarchs and His Sinaitic revelation as described in the Torah, as well as in Divine Providence as experienced by Israel's ancestors (Ex. 20:1; Deut. 5:4). This belief embraces the inviolable sanctity of God and the admiration and love of that unique sanctity which determines man's obligations and his longing to dedicate himself to the ethic in which that sanctity is expressed (Ex. 34:6, 7). The idea of God's holiness is based on belief in His supreme majesty and moral perfection, which demands the undivided worship and obedience of man (Ps. 99:3).

The Biblical command to attain holiness is expressed in the words: "Ye shall be holy; for I the Lord your God am holy" (Lev. 19:2).[1] The Sage Abba Shaul said of the Biblical expression, "This is my God, and I will glorify Him" (Ex. 15:2), that man is in duty bound to imitate the character of God: "As He is gracious and merciful, so shall you be gracious and merciful" (*Shab.* 133b). Divine holiness is seen as the ideal model for man to follow.

The Hebrew root *k-d-sh* expresses the notion of "separateness, dedication, sacredness", and describes the holiness of God as a sanctity separate from and above all defilement (Isa. 6:3).[2] Similarly, the term can refer to objects and places sanctified and set apart by God's Presence, notably the Tabernacle (Lev. 10:17) and Jerusalem (Isa. 11:9; Ps. 20:3). Holiness may also relate to elements of Divine worship, such as sacrificial offerings and the service of priests, as well as to the covenant that God made with Israel (Ex. 30:10; Lev. 2:3; Dan. 11:28, 30).

Israel is called upon to be holy by separating itself from impurity, sin and defilement (Lev. 19:2; Lev. 11:44). R. Pinhas ben Ya'ir taught that holiness appears in man after his purification from sin and defilement, making possible the attainment of the Holy Spirit (*AZ* 20b). The term "holiness" is also applied to the Sabbath and festivals as times consecrated to the worship of God (Gen 2:3, Ex. 20:8-11; Lev. 23:4*ff.*). Holiness entails a separation from everything opposed to God's will, and dedicates man to His service. Such holiness governs the domain of religion in an abhorrence of idolatry and its debasing practices and in following instead a form of worship that ennobles man's spirit. In the moral sphere, holiness demands resistance to the baser urges of nature which inhibit the ethical life prescribed by the Torah. Holiness likewise ensures the perfect mould of man's character. Torah instruction is the ideal way for man to attain the desired state of holiness.

David gave expression to Jewish thought when he said: "The law of the Lord is perfect, restoring the soul" (Ps. 19:8).[3] He affirmed that Torah law encompasses every aspect of man's existence, enabling one to realize all the physical and mental, earthly and heavenly aspects of life, which results in the spiritual invigoration of "restoring the soul".

Maimonides concluded his treatise on the laws of forbidden sexual relationships by repeating the teaching of the Sages that, human nature being what it is, one of the most difficult laws to observe is the prohibition against immorality. People have a deep-seated urge to engage in forbidden relationships, just as they have to commit petty theft or to indulge in gossip. Human nature has not changed throughout the generations (*Hag.* 11b; *Mak.* 23b; *BB* 164b–165a).[4]

---

3   תורת ה' תמימה משיבת נפש

4   אמר מר גזל ועריות נפשו מחמדת ומתאוה להם (חגיגה יא)

The Sages outlined their warning not to fall into moral transgression when they quoted the teaching of R. Hanania ben Akashyah: "It was because the Almighty wished to purify Israel in thought and action that He gave them numerous laws and commandments, ordering them to busy themselves with their thoughts and actions, as the prophet Isaiah declared: 'The Lord was pleased, for His righteousness' sake, to make the Torah great and glorious'" (*Avot* 1:18; Isa. 42:21; Maim. Code, *Issurei Bi'ah* 22.18–21).[5]

R. Avraham ben David of Posquières (RAVAD) expounded two avenues for pursuing holiness: in action, and in speech and thought. He derived his exposition from the Torah law ordaining the separation of man from impurity and ritual abomination, in which it is stated: "Sanctify yourselves therefore, and be holy; for I am holy" (Lev. 11:44).[6] RAVAD explained that in the first expression, *ve-hitkaddishtem* – "sanctify yourselves", man is required to avoid any contact with impurity. This is followed by the exhortation, "and be holy" – *vi-heyitem kedoshim*, requiring that he should keep his mind free from any thought that may involve impurity. It is also emphasized that just as the Almighty is free from all association with impurity and any thought of impurity, so does He require that man should keep himself holy, "for I am holy" – *ki kadosh Ani* (RAVAD, *Ba'alei ha-Nefesh,* ch. 7, *Sha'ar ha-Kedushah,* beginning, ed. Yosef Kappah, Mosad Ha-Rav Kook, Jerusalem, 1964, p. 112*ff.*).

The Almighty is described as holy – *kadosh* – since He is a unique external Being, set apart and different from any other type of existence – *ein od mi-levaddo* (Deut. 4:35; RAMBAN *ad loc*).[7] The root meaning of the word kadosh is "separation" or "consecration" (Maim. Code, *Yesodei ha-Torah* 1.1–4).

For his part, man is enjoined to imitate the holiness of God by attaining the highest degree of sanctification (Lev. 19:2).[8]

---

5   ה׳ חפץ למען צדקו יגדיל תורה ויאדיר
6   והתקדשתם והייתם קדשים כי קדוש אני
7   אין עוד מלבדו
8   קדשים תהיו כי קדוש אני ה׳ אל-היכם

This can be attained through virtuous restraint from physical
desire and through seeking devekut – nearness to God – by the
meticulous fulfillment of all the laws of the Torah, as well as
by maintaining ritual purity and separation from all sources of
abomination and ritual impurity (Maim. *Guide* III, 33, 47).

Since the people of Israel are ordered to keep themselves
holy in imitation of God, they are further commanded to sanctify
the Name of God and to refrain from any action that might
besmirch His Name (*hillul Hashem*). Beyond all thought of
self-preservation, they must abstain from anything associated
with idol worship and from immoral behaviour or the killing
of a fellow human being. One should be prepared to accept
martyrdom rather than defile God's Name by committing any
such cardinal transgression (*Sanh.* 74a; *AZ* 27b.; *Tos. ad loc.,*
"Yakhol"; Maim. Code, *Yesodei ha-Torah* 5.1, 2, 6, 7).[9]

Just as the law of God may not be broken or the world of
God defiled, so must the written Name of God be preserved
as holy and not obliterated, for which offence one would be
liable to the punishment of "lashes" (Maim. Code, *Yesodei
ha-Torah* 6:1).[10]

B. Purity of Mind and Speech

The thoughts in a person's mind reflect his inner character
while his speech represents his outer one. The Sages declared
that just as the Holy Ark in the Tabernacle was covered with
pure gold, within and without, so must a Torah scholar be pure
in both mind and outward appearance (*Tanhuma, Va-Yakhel*
7;[11] Ex. 37:2; *Ber.* 28b).[12]

One must not give a false impression of oneself, but should

בעל עבירות שבתורה אם אומרין לאדם עבור ואל תהרג יעבור ואל יהרג חוץ   9
מעבודת אלילים וגילוי עריות ושפיכות דמים

כל המאבד שם מן השמות הקדושים הטהורים שנקרא בהם הקב״ה לוקה מן   10
התורה

מכאן שיהא תלמיד חכם תוכו כברו שנאמר מבית ומחוץ תצפנו   11

ר׳ גמליאל מכריז ואמר כל תלמיד שאין תוכו כברו לא יכנס לבית המדרש   12

be identical in speech and inner thought (*Ber.* 28a). The mind should think only of truth; and verbal expression, prompted by the individual's heart or will, should reflect only that truth. According to the Sages, man's character has its seat in the heart. In this sense, R. Yohanan ben Zakkai praised the reply of his pupil, R. Eleazar ben Arakh, to his question: "Which is the proper quality in man that one should cultivate?" R. Elazar said that "the good way in life", one that includes all other good ways, is the cultivation of a "a good heart" – *lev tov*, which will spontaneously choose whatever is true and good. By keeping to this habit, one will grow into a virtuous individual (*Avot* 2.13).[13]

The Sages taught that when a man entertains impure thoughts during the day, he causes an impure emission during the night (*Hul.* 37b; Maim. Code, *Issurei Bi'ah* 21.21).[14]

They also recorded a saying of Rav's: "There are three transgressions which no one can ever avoid, namely, immoral thoughts, a disturbed attitude in prayer, and mischievous gossip about people".[15] They then modified this statement, declaring that most people fall victim to the sin of theft, some to that of immorality, and everyone to some form of evil gossip (*BB* 164b–165a; *Tos. ad loc., s. v. "Iyyun Tefillah"*).

The Sages taught that all conduct is prompted by thoughts that exist in the mind. Thus the exhortation to "keep yourselves holy" – *ve-hitkaddishtem* – refers especially to purity of the mind. Accordingly, Maimonides urged, a man should endeavour to cultivate pure thoughts and remain in a state of holiness, precisely to avoid these transgressions. He should therefore guard himself by abstaining from hard liquor, by having a wife and, especially, by concentrating his thoughts on Torah (Maim. Code, *Issurei Bi'ah* 22:18–21).

The Jewish Bible commentators explain that since man is composed of both body and spirit, of dust of the earth endowed

---

13 צאו וראו איזו היא דרך טובה שידבק בה האדם... ר' אליעזר אומר לב טוב
14 שלא הרהרתי ביום לבא לידי טומאה בלילה
15 שלש עבירות אין אדם ניצול מהן בכל יום הרהור עבירה ועיון תפילה ולשון הרע

with a heavenly soul, he naturally hovers between the spiritual and physical elements of his being. The man who lives his life in holiness and Torah wisdom can become entirely identified with the spiritual element, like one of the angels. Hence the prophet Malachi's description of the righteous priest: "The law of truth was in his mouth, and unrighteousness was not found on his lips; he walked with Me in peace and uprightness.... For the priest's lips should keep knowledge, and they should seek the law at his mouth; for he is the messenger of the Lord of Hosts" (Mal. 2:6–7; *BB* 164b, MAHARSHA *ad loc., s. v. "shalosh averot").[16]

It is related of the saintly R. Yehudah bar Ilai that he would dance before the bride at a wedding and not be affected by her beauty (*Ket.* 17a). The Sages affirmed that "whoever keeps his distance from immorality is called holy". Thus the Shunammite woman referred to Elisha as a "holy man" because of his unblemished conduct (2 Kings 4:9; Lev. R. 35:1).

According to Nahmanides (RAMBAN), the cultivation of holiness stems from a conscious attitude of self-restraint towards life in general. The Biblical precept, "Ye shall be holy" (Lev.19:2), was understood by the Sages to refer particularly to abstention from prohibited sexual relationships (Rashi *ad loc.*); but they also taught that the duty of separation (*perishut*) applies to all Torah laws. While certain things are completely forbidden by the Torah, even those which are not forbidden require the exercise of self-restraint (Lev. R. 24:5–6).[17]

Marital sex is permitted, but not in excess; drinking wine is permitted, but only in moderation. Food that is permitted should be eaten with discrimination; speech should be clean and without evil intent. General social relationships must be honest and without deceit, based on truth and magnanimity. Holiness does not require abstention from normal daily life but its sanctification. That is the sense of the general exhortation, "Ye shall be holy" – *kedoshim tiheyu* (Lev.19.2, RAMBAN *ad loc*).

---

16   כי שפתי כהן ישמרו דעת ותורה יבקשו מפיהו כי מלאך ה׳ צבאות הוא

17   כל מקום שאתה מוצא בו גדר ערוה אתה מוצא קדושה

Speech is considered an act of man's sacred life force, an expression of his spirit. In the creation of man Scripture affirms that he "became a living soul", an expression which the Targum Onkelos translates as "he had the power of speech" (Gen.2:7; *Targum ad loc.*).[18] Speech is the instrument of thought – *keli ha-mahshavah* (Bahya ben Asher, *Kad ha-Kemah*, *Reshut* 62.2). It must be used with great care and restraint, never wantonly, since tremendous power for good or evil lies in the tongue. The Psalmist observes: "Who is the man that desireth life, and loveth days, that he may see good therein? Keep thy tongue from evil, and thy lips from speaking guile" (Ps. 34:13-14).[19]

The Sages declared that life and death are "in the power of the tongue" (Prov. 18:21).[20] Shim'on the son of Rabban Gamaliel said: "All my life I have grown up among the Sages, and I have discovered that nothing is more suited to a man than silence" (*Avot* 1:17).[21] A popular adage had it that silence was twice as valuable as speech. One's speech should be kept to a minimum, for "a word may be worth a *sela*, but silence is worth two" (*Meg.* 18a; Maim. Code, *De'ot* 2:4).[22]

It is related in *Midrash Yelammedenu* that there was no greater holiness in people than that found in Aaron and Miriam. Thanks to the great merit of Miriam, the well of water miraculously supplied the needs of Israel in the wilderness; and thanks to that of Aaron, the heavenly clouds protected Israel. When they spoke evil against Moses, however, the Almighty did not overlook their sin (Num. 12:1, 20:1-2; *Yalkut Shim'oni, Beha'alotekha* 11, 12; *Ta'an.* 9a).[23]

Four types of people are excluded from the Divine Presence (*Shekhinah*): scoffers, flatterers, liars and slanderers (*Sot.* 42a).

---

18   ויהי האדם לנפש חיה – והות באדם לרוח ממללא
19   נצור לשונך מרע ושפתיך מדבר מרמה
20   מות וחיים ביד הלשון
21   לא מצאתי לגוף טוב משתיקה
22   מלה בסלע משתוקא בתרין
23   ג' מתנות טובות ניתנה על ידם ואלו הן באר בזכות מרים וכו'

General reference: R. Eliyyahu Vidas, *Reshit Hokhmah, Sha'ar Kedushah,* 2, 160b *ff.*

Kiddush Hashem and Hillul Hashem

The two opposing concepts of *Kiddush Hashem* (sanctification of the Divine Name) and *Hillul Hashem* (defamation of the Divine Name) have been described as an original contribution by the Jewish faith in the concept of monotheistic belief. They denote two aspects of the glorification of God, one in its positive service of God, of belief in God and the other denotes a person's failure to act in a manner that resulted in the glorification of God, but rather in a manner that brought shame and debased the name of God.

The principle of *Kiddush Hashem* and *Hillul Hashem* was ordained in a general form in the Biblical command: "And ye shall not profane My Holy Name but will be hallowed among the children of Israel" (Lev. 22:32). A basic rule in the observance of the laws of Judaism is enunciated in the exhortation of the Almighty to the people of Israel: "Ye shall therefore keep my statutes and my judgements; which if a man do, he shall live in them (Lev. 18:5). R. Levi taught (TJ *Taan.* 4:5, Lev. 22:32, Rashi; *Encyclopaedia Judaica, Kiddush Hashem,* Vol. 10, p. 979; TJ *Sanhedrin* 74a; TJ *Sanhedrin* 21a; *Yoma 8a*) whereas for the transgression of other offenses against the Almighty's prohibitions one may obtain remission of his sins by repentance – *teshuvah* on the Day of Atonement (Lev. 16:30), the sin of defiling the Name of God will not be atoned for except by the infliction of its due penalty, even the extreme penalty of death (*Yoma* 8b). The call to martyrdom is spoken of as an atonement for *Hillul Hashem* (Ezek. 36:23).

R. Papa asked Abaye (Babylon, 4th cent.), "Why is it that for the early Sages miracles took place, but for us, although we are devoted scholars at the Torah, no miracles are granted to us". The reply given to him was "The early Sages gave their lives for the sanctification of the Name, but we do not give our lives" (*Ber.* 20).

As an example of *Kiddush Hashem,* Yehuda Hanasi told of a Jewish woman who was taken into captivity with her seven sons. Each son was ordered by the Roman emperor on pain of death to prostrate himself before an idol. Each one refused to do so, proclaiming his belief in the one God and suffered painful martyrdom, sanctifying the Name of God – *al kiddush Hashem (Git.* 57b*).* A similar record is given in the Book of Maccabees of Hannah and her seven sons at the time of the Macabeean revolt. The greatest of the early Sages suffered the most cruel forms of martyrdom for their faith such as in the account of the ten martyrs during the Roman persecution under Hadrian (1st cent.) when Jews were taken out indiscriminately to the stake "as sheep to the slaughter".

The principle was laid down that it was one's duty to accept martyrdom rather than worship idolatry (*AZ* 27b) – one must refuse to sin in unchsastity, in forbidden sexual relationships, idolatry and murder (*Sanh.* 74a). The concept of *Kiddush Hashem* was always prominent in the Judaic faith. When Judaism was confronted with the violent and coercive missionary methods of the pagan cultures the Jew emboldened his faith in the face of cruel torture. The Book of Daniel (3:26, 6:23) tells of three Jews, Shadrakh, Meshakh and Abednego, who refused determinedly to obey the command of Nebukhadnezzar to worship an idol, and were miraculously saved from a fiery furnace. At the time of the overpowering policy of Hellenisation wrought by Antiochus Epiphanes death was usually chosen above apostasy. Men women and children died for their faith (Daniel 7:23; II Maccabees IV 6:18; *Pes.* 53b). During the Hadarian persecutions (1st cent.) Jews were taken out to the stake or thrown into arenas to fight with wild beasts, "as sheep taken to the slaughter". The Talmud tells of ten illustrious Rabbis, including R. Akiva, who nobly suffered martyrdom for their faith, thus sanctifying the name of God before the eyes of Jew and gentile alike – *al kiddush Hashem* (*Git.* 57b; Ezek. 36:23).

The accepted expression for dying a martyr's death is "to die for the sanctification of the Name – *al kiddush Hashem.* At the same time it was recognized that not everyone possessed the heroic strength to face martyrdom.

During the religious persecutions by the Romans the priestly Hasmoneans raised the standard of revolt. In the Middle Ages when the religiously fanatical Crusaders swept through the Rhine district towards the Holy Land Jews were forced to convert to Christianity but thousands bravely chose to suffer a painful death for the sake of the honour – *al Kiddush Hashem*. During the infamous Crusader persecutions of 1096 and 1146 (*gezerot tatnu* and *tatkav*) entire Jewish communities were massacred, and their brave martyrdom is recalled in a special dirge which is included in the Sabbath morning prayers (*Av ha-Rahamim*). Likewise in Spain persecution and martyrdom were the fate of the entire Jewish communities (14th cent.).

At the great rabbinical council in Lydda (2nd cent.) the laws of martyrdom were formulated. *Kiddush Hashem* was declared obligatory in the case of three commandments and a person had to suffer death rather than violate them: idolatry, unchastity – *gilui arayot* (including incest, adultery and, under certain circumstances, any infraction of the moral code) and murder (*Sanh.* 74a). But all other commandments should be violated rather than suffer death. Nevertheless if a Jew is coerced into transgressing any of these other laws in the presence of ten other Jews ("a community") in order to demonstrate his apostacy in public, he must sanctify God's Name and choose death. If ten Jews were not present he should transgress rather than be killed. Talmudists debated whether the duty to choose martyrdom overrode the duty to preserve life (Lev. 18:5). It was agreed that martyrdom was meritorious although not mandatory (*Tos. AZ* 27b). Maimonides, however, ruled that a person who chose *Kiddush Hashem* where the law decided in favour of life, was culpable (Maim. *Yad, Yesodei ha-Torah* 5:1, 3).

C. Aids to Holiness

Peace of Mind – Shalom

The various elements of which man is composed, like the four which were believed to constitute the universe (earth, air, fire and water), are such that they normally conflict with each other. This conflict is a perpetual one, so that nothing remains as it was before. Likewise, a person's condition is always changing, according to whichever element gains ascendancy over the others. The different physical conditions prevailing in the body result in different states of mind and behaviour patterns, an individual being strong or weak, hot-tempered or phlegmatic, proud or modest, greedy or content, ambitious or humble, smart or dull (Maim. *De'ot* 1.1). In the combination of opposing physical conditions within the human body a person is not exactly the same today as he was yesterday, or as he will be tomorrow.

A happy balance between these opposing forces, not the elimination of one or the other, results in peaceful coexistence – *shalom*. Thus, within the universe, God is described as follows: "I form the light and create darkness; I make peace and create evil; I am the Lord that doeth all these things" (Isa. 45:7).[24] According to the Sages, heaven is composed of water and the stars of fire, yet they exist side by side because the Almighty ensures a peaceful relationship between them (Job 25:2). Life's continuity is due to peaceful coexistence between all the different forces of nature (TJ *RH* 2.4, R. Shim'on bar Yohai; TB *RH* 23b).

The Torah relates that God created Adam in a perfect state, "in His own image" (Gen.1:27).[25] Hence every individual can declare in his morning prayers: "The soul which You have given me is pure" (*Ber.* 60b).[26] In discussing the condition

---

24 ארבע כיתות אין מקבלות פני שכינה
25 בצלם אל-הים ברא אותו
26 אל-הי נשמה שנתת בי טהורה היא

of the soul within the body, our Sages said: "Just as the Holy One blessed be He is pure, so the soul of man is pure" (*Ber.* 10a).[27]

After his creation, man is given the task of maintaining the purity of his soul and a peaceful balance in his own nature, harnessing all the opposing forces within him despite the efforts made by each element to gain ascendancy. It is by achieving this personal control that man attains his greatness. In that sense the Psalmist proclaimed: "Thou hast made him but little lower than God" (Ps. 8:6).[28]

Maintaining this peaceful balance requires a considerable effort on man's part. The Sages taught that the most important condition to be achieved by every person, in order to receive the Divine blessing, is an assured peaceful balance among the natural urges within himself, which may be called attaining peace of mind. In describing the abundant future rewards of the righteous, R. Shim'on ben Halafta said: "The Almighty finds no better receptacle for blessing in Israel than the condition of peace within oneself" (*Mishnah, Uktzin* 3:12).[29]

The Torah relates that, in his zeal for the honour of God, Pinhas the priest slew Zimri and Cozbi, killing those sinners in flagrante delicto instead of bringing them to trial. The Almighty acknowledged the righteousness of his zeal in the exceptional circumstances of the time, and assured Pinhas that he would be blessed forever with God's covenant of peace (Num. 25:12).[30]

By contrast, lack of internal peace leads an individual to sin. Accordingly, in the words of the prophet, a sinner knows no rest: "The wicked are like the troubled sea... There is no peace, saith my God, for the wicked" (Isa. 57:20–21).

In the Priestly Benediction (*Birkat Kohanim*), the prayer for physical blessing, *Yevarekhekha Hashem ve-yishmerekha* – "The Lord bless thee and keep thee", is followed by a plea

---

27   מה הקב"ה טהור אף נשמה טהורה
28   ותחסרהו מעט מאל-הים
29   לא מצא הקב"ה בלי מחזיק ברכה לישראל אלא השלום
30   הנני נותן לו את בריתי שלום

for the Almighty to favour us in His graciousness and answer our prayers, even though we are unworthy – *Ya'er Hashem panav elekha vi-huneka*. These two prayers require an extra one for harmony, allowing each to be present in due proportion and resulting in a symbiosis of peace – *ve-yasem lekha shalom* (Num. 6:24–26; Albo, *ha-Ikkarim,* IV, 51; Prayer Book, *Otzar ha-Tefillot, Etz Yosef, 'yevarekhekha'*).

The theological disquisition of R. Hayyim Berlin of Volozhin includes the following commentary on the Biblical verse relating the creation of man in the image of God (Gen. 1:27). Just as the Almighty is the reservoir of all powers that exist in the universe and controls them according to His will, so man in his intelligence and speech is endowed with the power to master countless forces in the world and, in conjunction with the Divine, to control them according to his will (R. Hayyim Berlin, *Nefesh Hayyim*, I, ch. 2).

This sheds light on King David's assertion: "Thou hast made him but little lower than God (R.V., but Jewish Version JPSA "than angels"), and crowned him with glory and honour. Thou hast made him to have dominion over the works of Thy hands; Thou hast put all things under his feet" (Ps. 8:6–7, Rashi, Ibn Ezra).[31] We therefore pray that just as the Almighty makes peace in all his heavenly constellations, so may He bring peace to us and help us to achieve peace of mind within ourselves (Daily Prayer Book, *Amidah* and *Kaddish*).[32]

Similarly, at the end of each *Amidah* prayer, when we recite "Grant peace" – *Sim shalom*, we pray for a number of blessings: for the Divine gifts of mercy, of spiritual inspiration through learning Torah, and of life itself, as well as for the all-important blessing of peace that frees us from war and aggression of any kind. Yet the first prayer is for peace within ourselves – *Sim shalom... aleinu* – and this is the foundation of all other blessings (*Otzar Tefillot* Prayer Book, note of *Dover Shalom* by R. Yitzhak Eliyyahu Landau of Vilna).

---

31   תמשילהו במעשי ידיך
32   עושה שלום במרומיו הוא יעשה שלום עלינו

Shalom generally describes a nation's desire for peace, i.e., for the absence of war and foreign aggression, as well as freedom from internal strife and dissension. This state of peace is a basic yearning of mankind, for without it we cannot survive. The Psalmist describes the blessing of this ideal condition: "Mercy and truth are met together; righteousness and peace have kissed each other" (Ps. 85:11).[33]

The Almighty assured the people of Israel that if they followed the laws of the Torah in everything they did, He would fill their land with bountiful produce and bestow peace on the land. They would live in safety, without fear of attack by wild beasts or of aggression by an enemy (Lev. 26:6).[34] Rabbinical commentators explained that "no sword shall pass" (*ve-herev lo ta'avor*) meant freedom from enemy attack, while "peace" (*shalom*) meant freedom from fraternal strife, since internal peace was the fount of all blessings (*ibid.*, RAMBAN, Rashi).

Trust in God – Bittaḥon ba-Shem

The meaning of *bittaḥon* (trust in God) is well indicated in the Scriptures, particularly in the psalms of David, whose own life was an outstanding example of faith in the Almighty.

David summed up the peace of mind enjoyed by the righteous in his first psalm: "He shall be like a tree planted by the streams of water... whose leaf also doth not wither" (Ps. 1:3).[35] This confidence is echoed by Jeremiah: "Blessed is the man that trusteth in the Lord, and whose hope the Lord is. For he shall be as a tree planted by the waters, and that spreadeth out his roots by the river, and shall not fear when heat cometh, but his leaf shall be green" (Jer. 17:7–8.).[36]

Moses declared: "The Rock, His work is perfect; for all

---

33   צדק ושלום נשקו
34   ונתתי שלום בארץ ושכבתם ואין מחריד
35   והיה כעץ שתול על פלגי מים
36   ברוך הגבר אשר יבטח בה

His ways are judgment; A God of faithfulness and without iniquity, just and right is He" (Deut. 32:4).[37]

Faith in God stems from complete trust in His dispensation, based on the assurance of His love. That faith is naturally accompanied by man's sense of gratitude for the gifts readily bestowed on him by the Almighty and his acknowledgment of the justice of God's judgment. David expressed such faith in these words: "Thou openest Thine hand, and satisfiest the desire of every living thing. The Lord is righteous in all His ways, and gracious in all His works" (Ps. 145:16–17).[38]

Since we believe that the Almighty is aware of man's needs and, in His love and compassion for him, wishes only to do him good, we have faith and confidence in God's Providence and we are happy to conduct ourselves faithfully according to His teachings. David offered these words of guidance: "Trust in the Lord, and do good; dwell in the land, and cherish faithfulness. Delight thyself in the Lord; and He shall give thee the desires of thy heart" (Ps.37:3–4).[39] Complete faith is shown in the next verse: "Commit thy way unto the Lord; trust also in Him, and He will bring it to pass" (Ps. 37:5, Rashi and Ibn Ezra *ad loc.*).[40] The Hebrew for "commit thy way unto the Lord", *gol al Hashem*, means "roll it on to Him", as expressed in the phrase "Cast thy burden upon the Lord, and He will sustain thee" (Ps. 55:23).[41]

The Sages urged: "Learn to say that whatever the Almighty does is done for our own good" (*Ber.* 60b).[42]

While maintaining faith in God's goodness and the belief that God will sustain him, man must labour for his daily needs, trusting that whatever God wishes him to have will be duly obtained. If man applies his own effort, the Almighty will help him to attain that goal; as Solomon, often repeating

---

37 א-ל אמונה ואין עול צדיק וישר הוא

38 צדיק ה׳ בכל דרכיו וחסיד בכל מעשיו

39 בטח בה׳ ועשה טוב

40 גול על ה׳ דרכך ובטח עליו

41 השלח על ה׳ יהבך והוא יכלכלך

42 כל דעביד רחמנא לטב עביד

his father's instruction, observed: "A man's heart deviseth his way; but the Lord directeth his steps" (Prov. 16:9).[43] David taught: "Blessed is every one that feareth the Lord, that walketh in His ways. When thou shalt eat the labour of thine hands, happy shalt thou be, and it shall be well with thee" (Ps. 128:1–2).[44]

Man must not presume that just because he put his trust in God, he can then just wait idly for his sustenance to come to him and that God will sustain him. Indolence will bring about his own death, and the Torah prohibition, "Thou shalt not murder" – *lo tirtzah* (Ex. 20:13), would apply to such behaviour.

The place of *bittahon* in the life of King David is illustrated throughout Psalm 27. Though surrounded by foes intent on destroying him, David has no fear because God will bring him the light of hope and salvation from his enemies (Ps 27:1).[45] Without faith in God's protection he could never have withstood enemy attacks: "If I had not believed to look upon the goodness of the Lord in the land of the living!" (Ps. 27:13).[46] Only a profound belief that his just efforts would be rewarded during his own lifetime (*be-eretz hayyim* – "in the land of the living") gave him the strength to vanquish his opponents. As a result of this firsthand experience, David urges everyone to preserve this staunch and constant faith in God: "Wait for the Lord [i.e., put your trust in Him]; be strong, and let thy heart take courage; yea, wait thou for the Lord" (Ps. 27:14).[47]

The grammatical imperative, *kavveh*, means "wait, look eagerly for, hope". An alternative meaning of the Hebrew expression that follows, *hazak ve-ya'ametz libbekha*, is supplied by Ibn Ezra: "Keep yourself strong, and the Lord will add strength to you heart"; the lesson is that whatever a man endures, he should hold on to his faith in God (Ibn Ezra

---

43   לב אדם יחשב דרכו וה׳ יכין צעדו

44   אשרי כל ירא ה׳ ההלך בדרכיו יגיע כפיך כי תאכל אשריך וטוב לך

45   ה׳ אורי וישעי ממי אירא

46   לולא האמנתי לראות בטוב ה׳ בארץ חיים

47   קוה אל ה׳ חזק ויאמץ לבך וקוה אל ה׳

ad loc.). David's song, calling on the faithful to keep their trust in God, declares: "Be strong, and let your heart take courage, all ye that hope in the Lord" (Ps. 31:25).[48] In his commentary, Kimhi (*ad loc.*) gives this translation of the verse: "Be strong, all you that hope for the Lord, and He will strengthen your heart" (*Bahya, Hovot ha-Levavot, Sha'ar ha-Bittahon*, ch. 4).

D. Outward Demonstrations of Faith

The Sabbath – Shabbat

Among the basic laws of the Decalogue is the commandment: "Remember the Sabbath day to keep it holy" (Ex. 20:8).[49] A prime example of all-embracing conduct that gives expression to holiness is found in Sabbath observance. The Sages declared that the merit earned by observing the Sabbath is as great as the merit of fulfilling all the precepts of the Torah (TJ *Ber.* 1.8;[50] TJ *Ned.* 3.14).

The Sabbath is the Almighty's precious gift to Israel (*Shab.* 10b;[51] *Betzah* 16a). Keeping the Sabbath is recognized by the Almighty as the special expression of Israel's faith in and devotion to God.

Emphasis on "remember" in this commandment indicates the need for an unwavering awareness of the Sabbath day's holiness. That awareness fills the mind of every observant Jew throughout the working week, as each new day leads him towards the Sabbath. The whole conduct of an individual on the Sabbath is marked by an ever-present feeling of special sanctity – in his thoughts, actions, speech, meals and dress, in his study of Torah and in a powerful communion with his

---

48 חזקו ויאמץ לבבכם כל המיחלים לה׳
49 זכור את יום השבת לקדשו
50 מצות שבת שהיא שקולה כנגד כל מצוותיה של תורה
51 מתנה טובה יש לי בבית גנזי ושבת שמה

Maker. It is known that those who observe the sanctity of the Sabbath experience their home throughout the Sabbath day filled with an unusual aura of sanctity (Maim. Code, *Shabbat* 30.1; *Shab.* 113b; *Mekhilta, Yitro*, on Ex. 20:8; *Torat Kohanim* on Lev. 23:35 and *Rashi ad loc.*).

The Sages declared that the Sabbath, in its observance, always increases the holiness of the individual (*Mekhilta, Naso*).[52]

The thoughts and outlook of a person observing the Sabbath are quite unlike those occupying his mind during the rest of the week. In addition to observing the laws that oblige one to refrain from all prohibited work, as God Himself ceased from all His creation on the seventh day, one is obliged to fulfil the positive commandment (*mitzvat aseh*) to sanctify all one's thoughts in devotion to God's own holiness, keeping the Sabbath as the day of the Lord – *Shabbat la-Shem*. In this sense the Torah orders man to create the Sabbath day's sanctity within himself through close communion with the Holy Spirit. We observe the Sabbath by sanctifying ourselves continuously throughout the day. Commenting on the Biblical verse, "Wherefore the children of Israel shall keep the Sabbath, to observe the Sabbath throughout their generations" (Ex.31:16), the Sages noted that the Hebrew expression *la'asot et ha-Shabbat* (translated as "to observe") actually reads in the text "to make the Sabbath".[53] Hence whoever abides by the spirit and laws of the Sabbath "makes" the Sabbath (*Mekhilta ad loc.*).

The Sabbath was a special work of the Creator, giving the finishing touch to all His creation. This special act is implied in the Biblical verse: "And on the seventh day God finished His work which He had made; and He rested on the seventh day from all His work which He had made".[54] Superficially, it would appear that everything was finished on the sixth day,

---

52   השבת מוספת קדושה על ישראל
53   לעשות את השבת לדרתם ברית עולם
54   ויכל אל-הים ביום השביעי מלאכתו אשר עשה

as indeed the seventy rabbis wrote in the Septuagint; but the Hebrew text states that "on the seventh day God finished His work", indicating that man still lacked the occasion to satisfy his need for rest, which the Almighty then supplied on the seventh day by creating the Sabbath (Gen.2:2, Rashi *ad loc.*; *Torah Temimah ad loc.*).

The Almighty endowed the Sabbath with its own special holiness, separate from other days of the week, just as His own holiness was different from that of any other existence. Hence it is stated that He bestowed His blessing on the seventh day and sanctified it: "God blessed the seventh day, and hallowed it; because on it He rested from all His work which God had created and made" (Gen. 2:3 RV; JPSA, Jewish Version "in creating had made").[55]

R. Shim'on ben Lakish declared that, from the time the Almighty created man, He endowed him with an additional soul on the eve of Sabbath, which departed from him at the Sabbath's termination.[56] This "additional soul" (*neshamah yeterah*) is alluded to in the statement: "And on the seventh day He rested and was refreshed" (Ex. 31:17).[57] The Hebrew phrase *shavat va-yinnafash* suggests that during His rest He made a new soul (*Betzah* 16a). This "additional soul" was given to man because the entire concept of holiness – *kedushah* – is rooted in a person's thought. Therefore, in order to preserve the holiness of the Sabbath, one must maintain one's thoughts in a special state of holiness throughout the day, keeping in mind only thoughts of a spiritual nature instead of one's ordinary material concerns. To achieve this, man is vested with additional spiritual power, the "additional soul" of the Sabbath. This should be treasured in a state of sanctity and nourished particularly by devotion in prayer and deep Torah study, to an even greater extent than on a weekday.

The holiness of the Sabbath differed from that of the festivals.

---

55 ויברך אל-הים את יום השביעי ויקדש אותו

56 נשמה יתירה נותן הקב"ה באדם ערב שבת

57 וביום השביעי שבת וינפש

The appointing of a given day as the festival depended on how the Sages determined the beginning of the month by the confirmed appearance of the New Moon, whereas the Sabbath day was established by God permanently in the nature of creation (TJ *Meg.* 1:4; Gen. 2:3, *Torah Temimah ad loc.*).[58] This difference is indicated in the festival *Amidah* prayer, which concludes its special blessing with the statement that God sanctifies Israel, who in turn hallow the festive seasons. In the Sabbath *Amidah* prayer, however, God sanctifies the Sabbath directly.[59]

The Sabbath day possesses its own holiness, and Israel is commanded to participate in that holiness by keeping the laws of the Sabbath and observing the holiness of the day. Thus the Torah prescribes: "Ye shall keep the Sabbath therefore, for it is holy unto you" (Ex. 31:14).[60] The opportunity to share in this Divine holiness was a special gift bestowed on Israel, and its observance was an outward sign of Israel's devotion to God and of God's devotion to Israel (Ex. 31:17; *Shab.* 10b).[61]

The feeling of sanctity should be so powerful that its impact will also be felt during the ensuing days of the week, when one allots some time each day to purely spiritual matters, trusting in Divine Providence to help secure one's daily needs. Shammai affirmed that Torah study should become a regular daily activity (*Avot* 1.15).[62] R. Meir said that, as a daily rule, one should reduce the amount of time spent pursuing one's normal daily work and devote more time to study, for the blessing of Torah will increase the success of one's work (*Avot* 4:12; *Reshit Hokhmah, Sha'ar ha-Kedushah,* 3, 165a).[63]

---

58   את ששמחתו תלויה בבית דין יצא זה ששמחתו תלויה בידי שמים

59   מקדש השבת וישראל והזמנים

60   כי קדש היא לכם

61   ביני ובין בני ישראל אות היא לעולם

62   עשה תורתך קבע

63   הוה ממעט בעסק ועסק בתורה

The Phylacteries – Tefillin

In order to help maintain man's constant devotion to God, the Torah prescribed certain outward signs as continual reminders of his duty to the Creator. According to the Sages, whoever wears *tefillin* on his head and arm and *tzitzit* on his garment and who also has a *mezuzah* on his door-post is unlikely to engage in sin (*Men.* 43b).[64] The observant Jew likewise bears the sign of circumcision – *ot milah* – and that of the holy Sabbath – *ot ha-Shabbat*. These signs, together with his devotion to Torah, help to ensure the purity of his soul – *tahorat ha-neshamah*.

When prescribing the laws relating to the Exodus from slavery in Egypt, the Torah exhorts Israel always to remember the mighty hand of God's deliverance and, to keep this remembrance fresh in mind, Israel is commanded to bind the *tefillin* on his arm. Referring to the *tefillin*, Scripture states: "And it shall be for a sign unto thee upon thy hand, and for a memorial between thine eyes, that the law of the Lord may be in thy mouth; for with a strong hand hath the Lord brought thee out of Egypt" (Ex. 13:9).[65] Similarly, another Bible verse ordains: "And these words, which I command thee this day, shall be upon thy heart... And thou shalt bind them for a sign upon thy hand, and they shall be for frontlets between thine eyes" (Deut. 6:6, 8).[66]

Torah law requires that the *tefillin* be composed of leather boxes containing the four related Scriptural passages pertaining to this law, and that they be bound with leather straps on the arm and on the head. These four passages, handwritten on parchment, are: Ex. 13:1–10, Ex. 13:11–16, Deut. 6:4-9 and Deut. 11:13–21 (*Sh. Ar., Orah Hayyim*, 32:1).

In fulfilling this commandment one is required to bear in mind the wonders of God's deliverance of Israel and the

---

64 כל שיש לו תפלין בראשו ותפילין בזרועו וציצית בבגדו ומזוזה בפיתחו הכל בחזיק שלא מטא

65 כי ביד חזקה הוציאך ה' ממצרים

66 וקשרתם לאות על ידך והיו לטטפות בין עיניך

obligation to serve God through the observance of His Torah (*Sh. Ar., Orah Hayyim*, 25.5).

The straps of the *tefillin* should be bound around the left arm nearest the heart and on the head, as the thoughts of the mind were considered to emanate from both the heart and the head. This action symbolized the individual's complete dedication to the service of God and taught the wearer that the thoughts of the mind should be governed by holiness, resulting in the practical effect of sanctified action (*Sefer ha-Hinnukh*, 421; *Men.* 37b).

Just as it is stated that earnest Torah study leads to the fulfilment of all the precepts (*Pe'ah* 1:1; *Shab.* 127a),[67] so the diligent observance of *tefillin* is regarded as equivalent to being engaged in the study of Torah and thus fulfilling all of the 613 Commandments (*Zohar: Tikkunim*).

Scripture required the study of Torah "day and night" (Josh. 1:8)[68] and the Sages regarded the wearing of *tefillin* as equivalent to reading the Torah (Minor Tractates: *Tefillin*, 17; *Midrash Pesikta Zutarti* on Ex.12; *Ber.* 9b).[69] Thus, the Pious Men of olden days (*Hasidim Rishonim*) wore their *tefillin* throughout the day (*Men.* 43b). It is related in the Midrash in the name of R. Eliezer: "Israel said to the Almighty, 'We would like to engage in Torah study day and night, but our work does not allow us to do so'. The Almighty replied: 'Observe the law of wearing *tefillin* and reciting the *Shema*, and I will consider it as equivalent to your studying Torah day and night'" (*Reshit Hokhmah, Sha'ar ha-Kedushah*, 128a).

The generally accepted practice since the era of the Sages, apart from a few exceptions such as Elijah Gaon of Vilna, is to wear *tefillin* only while reciting the Morning Prayers, because of the need to be punctilious in maintaining a state of purity out of respect for the holiness of the *tefillin* (Asher ben Yehiel, *Hilkhot Tefillin*, 26; *Men.* 99b).

---

67   ותלמוד תורה כנגד כולם
68   והגית בו יומם ולילה
69   הלכה בתפילין כאחרים בקריאת שמע כוותיקין

The Sages declared that the Almighty Himself "lays" *tefillin* (*Ber.* 6a). This is deduced from the Torah's account of the Revelation of God to Moses in response to the latter's request that the Almighty show him His glory. The Almighty replied that His face cannot be seen, but allowed Moses to see His back. The Sages interpreted this to mean that what Moses saw was a vision of the Holy One wearing *tefillin* on His head. Moses, of course, could not see the invisible Divine Spirit, but "the Almighty showed him the knot binding the *tefillin* at the back of His head" (*Ber.* 7a).[70] They thus understood that as God Himself wore *tefillin*, it was a tremendous privilege for man to perform this sanctified act and that the Almighty delights in this demonstration of Israel's loving devotion to Him (MAHARSHA, *Ber.* 6a).

The word "phylacteries" is derived from the Greek term for "protective amulet", whereas the word *tefillin* stems from the Hebrew root *p-l-l*, meaning "to judge" and "to pray". Thus the *tefillin* are intended to serve as a practical reminder that we acknowledge God's love for us, that all our actions should begin with a determination of the mind and its elevation to lead a righteous life in the service of God (*Sh. Ar., Orah Hayyim,* 25:5).

This action signifies a conscious commitment to our constant duty to God. The physical binding of His teachings in the *tefillin* on the arm and on the head expresses our humble submission to God's will and therefore, when a man dons his *tefillin*, the spirit of God rests within him (*Zohar, Toledot* 141a).

R. Zeira observed that, through the continuous presence of the *tefillin* on his body, he was able to maintain himself in a constant state of holiness. One should always "serve the Lord with gladness" (Ps. 100:2), but even in a moment of great joy that rejoicing can contain an awareness of solemnity (Ps. 2:11; *Ber.* 30b).[71]

---

70 הראה הקב״ה למשה קשר של תפילין
71 עבדו את ה׳ ביראה וגילו ברעדה

R. Yohanan, who made it his practice to wear tefillin throughout the day, keeping himself in a state of purity, affirmed: "Whoever cleanses his body, washes his hands, lays *tefillin*, and recites the *Shema* and the *Amidah* prayer achieves a state of holiness like one who built the Sanctuary altar and offered up a sacrifice to God" (*Ber.* 15a).[72]

Extensive descriptions of the spiritual insights and mystical symbolism of the *tefillin* are given in rabbinic sources and especially in the *Zohar*. The leather of the *tefillin* was, for example, described as a "sequel" to the garments of skin that God provided for Adam and Eve (Gen. 3:21; *Reshit Hokhmah, Sha'ar ha-Kedushah, 6, passim*).

In the blessing of Moses, the wearing of tefillin is the distinctive pride of the children of Israel, whereby all peoples recognize their unique spirituality (Deut. 28:10; *Ber.* 6a).[73]

The Fringes – Tzitzit

Among the religious aids for attaining holiness as a state of mind, great value is attached to observance of the law of "fringes" – *tzitzit*. The Torah required Israel to insert fringe threads, *tzitzit*, in the four corners of garments, entwining around these threads a thread of blue – *tekhelet* (Num. 15:38).[74]

The *tzitzit* are obviously an adjunct to the garment, placed there as a visible reminder to the wearer of the many commandments issued to him by God. The wearing of a garment was described at the time of Creation as clothing for the human body after Adam and Eve had followed the inclination of their "heart and eyes" that led them to sin (Gen.3:21). The *tzitzit* should therefore be seen as a reminder "that ye go not after your own heart and your own eyes" and

---

72 מעלה עליו הכתוב כאילו בנה מזבח והקריב עליו קרבן

73 מניין שהתפלין עוז הם לישראל דכתיב וראו כל עמי הארץ כי שם ה' נקרא עליך
ויראו ממך

74 ועשו להם ציצת על כנפי בגדיהם לדרתם ונתנו על ציצת הכנף פתיל תכלת

"that ye may remember to do all My commandments, and be holy unto your God" (Num. 15:37-41; Ibn Ezra *ad loc.*).[75]

The blue shade of the special fringe added to those in white suggests the colour of the heavens, making it a visible reminder of the invisible God above, whose Revelation taught man a higher obligation than mere striving for animal gratification (*Sot.* 17a; *Sifri*, Numbers, *Shelah*, 15:68).

The Sages pointed to a further significance in the fact that the number of thread windings and knots traditionally prescribed add up to 613, i.e., the total number of precepts revealed in the Torah (*Sefer ha-Hinnukh, Shelah*, 386, 387; Num. 15:39–40, *Rashi ad loc.*).

The religious insight derived from the precept to wear *tzitzit* is described as resembling the insight one derives from observing the Sabbath, which leads to fulfilment of all the commandments (Num. 15:39, Rashi *ad loc.*; *Shab.* 118b; Maim. *Shabbat* 30:15).

The Sages taught: "Whoever observes the law of fringes will be considered as one fulfilling all the commandments, since they lead to an acceptance of God's sovereignty and the binding force of all His laws, as the Rabbis said: 'Seeing leads to remembering and remembering to fulfilling'" (*Men.* 43a; *Sifri* Num. 15.69; *Ned.* 25a).[76]

Great emphasis is laid by the Sages on the need to wear a four-cornered garment, which obliges one to insert the required *tzitzit*. Immediately upon rising in the morning (even at first light), after his ablutions, a man should wrap himself in the four-cornered garment known as a *tallit* and recite the appropriate benediction. Wearing a *tallit* is particularly required during the morning recitation of the *Shema* (*Sh. Ar., Orah Hayyim* 8:1, 18:3; Maim. Code, *Tzitzit* 3:11, 12).

---

75   וראיתם אותו וזכרתם את כל מצות ה' ועשיתם אתם
76   שקולה מצות ציצית כנגד כל מצוות שבתורה

The Mezuzah

The state of holiness in man derives from the fulfillment of his duty to God, which the Sages designate "accepting the Sovereignty of heaven".[77] The most explicit statement recognizing the sovereignty of God is found in the scriptural passage known as the *Shema*: "Hear O Israel: the Lord is God, the Lord is One" (Deut. 6:4).[78] To this the following passage is added: "And thou shalt love the Lord thy God with all thy heart, and with all thy soul, and with all thy might" (Deut. 6:5).[79]

An awareness of our duty to obey the word of God should accompany us at all times and be the fount of all our thoughts and actions. Accordingly, this passage of Torah, in the form of the *tefillin* straps, should be bound each day "on thy hand" and "between thine eyes". These words should likewise be written, in the form of the *mezuzah*, "upon the door-posts of thy house" (Deut. 6:8–9).[80]

Just as wearing *tefillin* inspires us to be conscious each day of our love of God and our desire to fulfil all His commandments, so the presence of these words of Torah on the door-posts of our house is a continual reminder of our obligations towards Him.

The small parchment in the case housing the *mezuzah* contains the handwritten texts of two passages: Deut. 6:4–9 and Deut. 11:13–21. The first of these passages, the *Shema*, proclaims our love of God and includes the commandment pertaining to the *mezuzah*. The second passage assures us of the blessings that flow from obedience to the Torah and warns us to refrain from transgression.

The *mezuzah* is affixed to the right-hand door-post of the entrance to the house as well as to the entrance of each living room. It is customary to place one's hand on the *mezuzah* on

---

77   קבלת מלכות שמים
78   שמע ישראל ה׳ אל-הינו ה׳ אחד
79   ואהבת את ה׳ אל-היך בכל לבבך ובכל נפשך ובכל מאדך
80   וקשרתם לאות על ידך... וכתבתם על מזוזות ביתך ובשעריך

entering and leaving the house and then kiss the hand as a mark of love (*Sh. Ar., Yoreh Deah*, 285, 288; *Men.* 28a).

Man's conscious creation of a state of mind in which an awareness of God is always present – *yir'at Hashem* – leads him to a life of perfection and holiness. This is the basic requirement of the religious life, as Moses declared: "And now, Israel, what doth the Lord thy God require of thee, but to fear the Lord thy God..." (Deut. 10:12).[81] Thus Solomon, in his instructions with regard to the training of a wise son, urged that he should always revere God: "Be in the fear of the Lord all day long" (Prov. 23:17).[82] Rabbenu Yonah, the pious scholar and moralist (13th cent. Spain), wrote that this teaching is the pillar on which the whole Torah rests, as David affirmed: "I have set the Lord always before me; because He is at my right hand, I shall not be moved" (Ps. 16:8; Rabbenu Yonah, *Iggeret ha-Teshuvah; Sha'arei Teshuvah*, 3:7; *Reshit Hokhmah, Sha'ar ha-Yir'ah*, 15, 101b).[83]

In view of the paramount need for *yir'at Hashem* at all times, Israel was instructed to set the words of Torah, especially these basic passages, always before his eyes through studying Torah, wearing *tallit* and *tefillin,* and attaching them to the door-posts of his home. Just as David expressed his immense joy at being in God's house (Ps. 84:2),[84] so also can every individual sanctify his home and bring the Divine Presence into it, thus making it a house in which God dwells. His presence is indicated by the *mezuzah* on the front door-post, which serves as a constant reminder of the *yir'at Hashem* injunction.

The home of each individual therefore acquires the sanctity of the Temple, and of each individual living in that home it can be said: "Happy are they that dwell in Thy House; they will ever be praising thee" (Ps. 84:5).[85] On entering and leaving our home each day, we look at the *mezuzah* and thereby express

---

81 מה ה' אל-הך שאל מעמך כי אם ליראה את ה' אל-היך
82 כי אם ביראת ה' כל היום
83 שויתי ה' לנגדי תמיד
84 נכספה וגם בלתה נפשי לחצרות ה'
85 אשרי יושבי ביתך עוד יהללוך סלה

our love of God and our happiness that this home is sanctified by the Almighty (*Reshit Hokhmah, Sha'ar ha-Ahavah*, 1:63, 10:108).

The practice of affixing a *mezuzah* to the door-post of one's house is an ancient one, dating back to the time of Moses. Josephus, the first-century Jewish historian, relates that *mezuzot* were to be found in all Jewish homes (*Antiquities* IV, 6.13).

The presence of a *mezuzah* at the entrance or front door always distinguished a Jewish from a non-Jewish home. That, however, was not its religious significance. The basic purpose of the *mezuzah* was to emphasize, in the mind of the Jew, the supreme influence that God's word should constantly exert over all his actions.

Although a *mezuzah* gave those occupying the house an assurance of protection from harm (*Darkhei Mosheh* on *Yoreh Deah*, 237), it was never regarded as a magical charm or amulet. According to the Sages, it gave protection in a different sense. This they explained by elucidating a text from Proverbs on the supreme value of Torah: "For wisdom is better than rubies, and all things desirable are not to be compared unto her" (Prov. 8:11).[86] In the story they told, Artavan, king of Persia, sent the gift of a precious stone to R. Yehudah ha-Nasi, expecting the Sage to present him with a gift of equal value in return. However, R. Yehudah sent Artavan a *mezuzah*. The monarch complained that whereas the present he had sent was of great value, the one he had received was worth only a florin. R. Yehudah replied: "The precious gift that you sent me is one that I myself will have to guard; but the teachings contained in the gift that I sent you, should you make them your own, will always guard you" (Gen. R. 33:4; TJ *Pe'ah* 1:1, 15d).

Maimonides warned against regarding the *mezuzah* as some sort of amulet containing Divine Names that would serve to protect the owner. He was vehemently opposed to the insertion of kabbalistic formulas (such as the names of angels) in the text of the *mezuzah*. Those who did so, "with their foolish hearts", turned a sacred precept – aimed at emphasizing one's love of God and homage to His Sovereignty – into a mere amulet for their physical protection (Maim. *Yad, Tefillin* and *Mezuzah*, 5.4).

The religious significance of the *mezuzah* is illustrated in the following passage from the Talmud. Onkelos the Proselyte, reputedly a nephew of Emperor Titus, infuriated the latter by embracing Judaism. The Emperor dispatched soldiers to arrest him and, as they were leaving, Onkelos saw the *mezuzah* on his door-post and placed his hand upon it. He then told the soldiers that a mortal king usually dwells within his residence, while his servants keep guard on him from without. However, in the case of the Holy One, Blessed be He, His servants dwell within, while He keeps guard on them from without, as it is written: "The Lord shall guard thy going out and thy coming in, from this time forth and for ever" (Ps. 121:8; *AZ* 11a).[87]

Chapter 3

Intention – *Kavvanah*

3 *Intention* – Kavvanah

A. Introduction: The Psychological
Meaning of the *Mitzvot*

Every moral injunction is considered a religious requirement, so that one's devotion to God demands the claims of morality. The source of man's behaviour is always an act of his autonomous free will, but the moral quality of what he does depends on the extent to which it conforms with the ethical standards taught by God. The uniqueness of man lies in his faith that by his creation he knows the difference between good and bad, and that in his autonomous will he may choose what pleases him and reject the moral imperative of God's law: "Behold, the man is become as one of us, to know good and evil" (Gen. 3:22, Sforno).[1] Targum Onkelos expresses this view in his rendering, "to know the difference between good and bad".[2]

In certain actions the moral quality of what is done may not be recognizable by another person, so that an evil intention maybe disguised as genuinely moral behavior. The Torah urges man to control his inner thoughts, and the Sages, accordingly, transmitted this dictum: "In every matter known only in the heart of the performer, you shall fear your God" (*BM* 58b).[3]

Torah law gave examples of such conduct: "Thou shalt not curse the deaf, nor put a stumbling-block before the blind, but thou shalt fear thy God" (Lev.19:14). Likewise, "Thou shalt honour the face of the old man, and thou shalt fear thy God: I am the Lord" (Lev. 19:32); "Thou shalt love him [the stranger] as thyself... Just balances, just weights, shall ye have: I am the

---

1   הן אדם כאחד ממנו לדעת טוב ורע
2   למידע טב וביש
3   כל דבר המסור ללב נאמר בו ויראת מאלקים

Lord your God"(Lev. 19:34, 36); "Take no usury of him; but fear thy God" (Lev. 25:36); and "If thy brother sell himself unto thee... thou shalt not rule over him with rigour; but shalt fear thy God" (Lev. 25:39, 43).

Torah laws cover every aspect of man's life – personal, social, religious and intellectual. Through his obedience to them, every part of a Jew's life is spiritualized and brought into association with the Divine. These laws are called "the statutes of life" – *hukkot ha-hayyim* (Ezek. 33:15; cf. Lev. 26:15) – which God taught Israel out of love for His people. The aim of the Torah is the idealization of all our earthly actions, bringing every detail of life into touch with the Divine (I. Epstein: Judaism, chap. 3). The early Rabbis expressed this teaching in a simple phrase: "The mitzvot were given by the Creator with the special aim of purifying His creatures" (Gen. R. 44.1).[4] The more one grasps this association, the better one will succeed in adopting this programme of life and achieving its desired sanctification.

Kavvanah in the Performance of Mitzvot

It would appear self-evident that any religious duty (*mitzvah*) should be performed in a careful manner and in full awareness of one's action as a specific act of worship. One would not expect one's religious duty as having been fulfilled if the ceremonial act was performed in a thoughtless, careless manner. In fulfilling every *mitzvah* one must carry it through until it is completed. The Sages said that the *mitzvah* can not be considered performed unless it is completed. They added the exhortation, "When one begins to perform a *mitzvah* we say to him 'finish it'" (TJ *Pes.* 37:4)[5]. While doing so one is even exempted from the duty of carrying out a different *mitzvah* (*Ber.* 11a; *Suk.* 25a).[6]

לא נתנו המצות אלא לצרף בהן את הבריות   4
כל המתחיל במצוה אומרים לו גמור   5
העוסק במצוה פטור מן המצוה   6

The early codifiers took it for granted that the fulfilment of a religious commandment required a person's full attention and concentration. R. Yosef Caro, in his *Shulḥan Arukh*, followed the great early codifiers, the RIF, Rambam, Rashi and ROSH, in laying down the principle that every religious duty must be performed with full awareness of one's action and with the intention of performing the act in order to fulfil one's religious obligation (*mitzvot tzerikhot kavvanah*). While acknowledging that there were other opinions, R. Caro concluded that this was to be accepted as the general rule (*Oraḥ Hayyim* 60:4).

Likewise, in reciting a blessing over food it is required that the individual have in mind the full intention of making a blessing for that specific purpose. Thus, the case is discussed in the Talmud where someone holding a glass of beer mistakenly began to recite the blessing over wine (*borei peri ha-gefen*), but realized midway that it was beer and concluded with the appropriate benediction (*she-ha-kol*). Since in making a blessing no physical act was performed, and the entire action was really a mental act of intention (*kavvanah*), the *kavvanah* had to be complete (*Ber*. 12a; R. Yonah *ad loc*.).[7]

The Talmudic Sages also ruled that in the performance of every religious duty one must concentrate fully on the intention to fulfil that *mitzvah*. Thus, when reciting the *Shema*, a tannaitic Sage laid down in a *Baraita* that it is essential that one must concentrate one's mind entirely on the words of the *Shema* (*Ber*. 13a; *Ber*. 2a, *Tos*., s.v. *mei'eimatai; Oraḥ Hayyim* 60:4,5; 61:1).[8]

The Sages differed, however, as to whether the *mitzvah* had been fulfilled if the *kavvanah* was lacking. According to one tannaitic opinion, it was essential that there be due *kavvanah* in order to fulfil the *mitzvah* (*Er*. 95b). However, Rabban Gamliel, held that even though *kavvanah* had been lacking, the proper action in performing the *mitzvah* was sufficient to fulfil it (*Er*. 95b).

---

7   פתח ומברך אדעתה דשכרא

8   הקורא את שמע ולא כיון לבו בפסוק ראשון שהוא שמע ישראל לא יצא ידי
חובתו

Early codifiers likewise differed in their rulings. R. Hai Gaon accepted the *mitzvot* even without *kavvanah*, but the RIF declared that *kavvanah* was essential. Maimonides required full concentration particularly in fulfilling the duty to pray (*kavvanat ha-lev*). Thus, a sick person, or one who is so tired that he is unable to concentrate before eating some food, or one who is resting, must not pray until his mind is settled (Maim. *Tefillah* 4:1, 15).[9]

Some authorities required that in order to direct one's attention to the *mitzvah* being performed, one should first declare that it is undertaken in fulfilment of that particular *mitzvah*,[10] e.g., as in the prayer book text before the benedictions recited on counting the Omer (*sefirat ha-omer*) and prior to binding *tefillin* on the arm (Ari). Other authorities, however, objected that this was an unnecessary distraction, since one had already demonstrated one's intention by actually performing the *mitzvah* (Vilna Gaon).

It is generally accepted that *kavvanah* is particularly required when there is no outward sign that a *mitzvah* is being performed. Thus, when one reaps wheat before Passover especially for the baking of "guarded" unleavened bread (*matzah shemurah*), which might appear to be harvested for normal use, one should declare that one is doing so especially for this *mitzvah* (*Matteh Mosheh* 577).[11]

R. Hai Gaon and R. Yonah stated, as a general rule, that the performance of *mitzvot* was fulfilled even where full *kavvanah* was absent.[12] The RIF, however, determined that *kavvanah* was essential in the fulfillment of all *mitzvot* (*Gufei Halakhot* 98).

Those who maintained the rule that lack of *kavvanah* did not invalidate the fulfillment of the *mitzvah* referred only to such *mitzvot* as were performed by some physical action (e.g., *tefillin*, *sukkah* and *lulav*), since the very performance

---

9   כל תפלה שאינה בכונה אינה תפילה
10 הנני מוכן ומזומן לקיים מצות עשה של ספירת העומר
11 לשם מצות שמורה
12 מצוות אין צריכות כוונה

of the action indicated one's intention to fulfil the *mitzvah*. All the authorities nevertheless agreed that where the mitzvah involved no physical action but depended on mental attention alone, in thought or speech[13] as in prayer, complete mental attention was necessary to grasp the meaning of the words uttered, as though one were carefully reading a passage of the Torah.

Intentions and Actions

The Sages considered the question of when the mental act of intention (*mahashavah*) can be considered an act of performance (*ma'aseh*). The Sages stated as a general rule: "A good intention is reckoned with the action performed" (*Kid.* 40a).[14] R. Assi expounded the rule further, saying that even if one intended to perform the act of fulfilling the *mitzvah* but was unavoidably prevented from doing so, the Torah considers it as though one had actually performed the act. On the other hand, "an evil intention is not reckoned by the Almighty as the actual committing of a sin".[15] This rule is further defined thus: "If the intention produced an action, the Almighty reckons as sinful the intention as well as the resulting act and renders the act doubly sinful; but a sinful intention that does not result in an action is not considered the same as the performance of a sinful act".[16]

Thus, if one considered performing a *mitzvah* but did not, this is simply a case of not fulfilling a *mitzvah*. If a man had every intention of fulfilling the *mitzvah*, and the reason for not doing so was his subjection to *force majeure* (*ne'enas*), he was deemed no less meritorious than someone who had performed the *mitzvah*. Where someone intended to commit a transgression but never did so, he would not incur punishment

---

13 מצוות התלויות בלב ובאמירה
14 מחשבה טובה מצרפה למעשה
15 מחשבה רעה אין הקב״ה מצרפה למעשה
16 מחשבה שעושה פרי הקב״ה מצרפה למעשה

merely for a thought that did not lead to the action intended, i.e., one that had no actual result.

Clearly, if the intention resulted in a sinful act, one would be punished for having actually transgressed; but here the Sages enlarged on their interpretation of this case. If the evil thought continued to result in further transgressions, one would be additionally penalized for the evil thought that gave rise to the sins. This was the meaning of the idea of "a thought that produced further results".[17] The evil thought had proved to be of a graver nature. If, however, the evil thought resulted only in a particular transgression and was not followed by others, punishment would be restricted to that one action and not extend to any intention of performing others which, in fact, never occurred.

Another interpretation of this teaching of the Sages is that, for the first transgression, the evil thought is not additionally punished; but if there are any further thoughts of transgressing, even if they are not put into effect, the evil intention itself is punished by the Almighty, "for He knows the thoughts of man" (*Kid.* 40a, Rashi).[18]

It is further explained that it would not be just for a man to be punished on account of his thoughts; for the Sages taught that harbouring of evil thoughts in the mind is a common, inescapable experience. "There are", they said, "three everyday transgressions that no one can avoid: firstly, evil thoughts about committing a sinful act; failure to concentrate during one's prayer; and, finally, slander (*BB* 164b; Rashi, *Tos.*, Maharsha *ad loc.*).[19]

In the light of this teaching, it is maintained that punishment for evil intentions only relates to a case where one fully intended to do wrong, but was prevented from doing so by *force majeure*. Here, even one's intention is culpable, as if the transgression had actually been committed. The transgression referred to is, of course, one against religious law – an affront

---

17   מחשבה שעשה פרי

18   עבירה שעושה פירות כגון חילול ה'

19   שלש עבירות אין אדם ניצול מהן בכל יום

to God, who is the Judge of human intentions – but not a breach of civil law, where testimony would be required in a court of law (Maharsha on *Kid.* 40a).

Levirate Marriage – Yibbum ve-Halitzah

Special identification with a *mitzvah* is clearly demonstrated in the law of levirate marriage (*yibbum ve-halitzah*). In the procedure of levirate marriage, the brother of a man who died without offspring is required to marry that man's surviving widow, the purpose being to father a child who will perpetuate "the name of his brother" and "build up his brother's house" (Deut. 25:5–6, 9).[20] Thus, although Torah law normally forbids a man to marry a woman who is or was his brother's wife (Lev. 18:16; *Sh. Ar., Even ha-Ezer* 15.22), it is nevertheless laid down exceptionally that in the case of a levirate marriage the *yavam* is obligated to marry his brother's widow (TJ *Ned.* 3.2, 37d; *Sifrei*, Deut. 233).[21]

Since the purpose of such a marriage was nothing other than the fulfilment of this Torah obligation, the *tanna* Abba Shaul held that if personal attraction was also a motivating factor, the marriage would be forbidden as incestuous – *issur ervah* (*Yev.* 39b; Mish., *Bek.* 1.7, Rashi *ad loc.*). However, the early Sages maintained that *yibbum* was preferable even in these circumstances, as the Torah itself had commanded it and what mattered was not the brother's inclination but the law's implementation.[22]

Abba Shaul's opinion was, however, accepted by later authorities. They ruled that in view of prevailing moral standards, one could not assume that the intention of the *yavam* would be wholly religious (*le-shem mitzvah*) and he was even forbidden to contract such a levirate marriage.[23] Thus, in all

20   יבמה יבוא עליה ולקחה לו לאשה ויבמה
21   והיה הבכור אשר תוליד יקום על שם אחיו המת
22   וחכמים אומרים יבמה יבוא עליה — מכל מקום

circumstances, he had to release her from the marriage by performing the ceremony of *halitzah* (Deut. 25:7–10; *Yev.* 39b, *Tos. ad loc., s.v. "amar Rav"*; ROSH, *ibid.*, 17; *Even ha-Ezer* 165.1, REMA *ad loc.*).

The Shofar

The vital importance of *kavvanah* in fulfilling the *mitzvot* is discussed in the Talmud, with particular reference to one's obligation to hear the blowing of the *shofar* on Rosh ha-Shanah, the Jewish New Year.

Biblical law required the blowing of the *shofar*, a ram's horn, on Rosh ha-Shanah: "On the first day of the seventh month, ye shall have a solemn assembly... a day of sounding the *shofar*" (Num. 29:1; Lev. 23, 24; Maim. *Shofar* 1.1; *Hinnukh* 405). Since this is the Day of Judgment for all mankind, the sound of the *shofar* proclaims that the Divine court is in session, and it calls on everyone to subdue all evil desires and pray for forgiveness with awe and humility. The essential purpose of this religious act is that each individual should be fully conscious that, as he hears the call of the *shofar*, he is standing in judgment before the Almighty. In order to achieve this spiritual effect, he must listen to the *shofar* with a total awareness of its religious meaning.

However, since the idea of consciousness and kavvanah maybe open to different interpretations, the Sages of the Talmud endeavoured to establish guidelines defining the extent to which consciousness is essential in order to fulfil this Biblical law. Although the general rule states that everyone is obligated to fulfil the law of "sounding the shofar" (RH 29a),[24] it is the accepted practice, after the Torah reading in synagogue, for an officiant (*toke'a*) to recite the benediction,

23   אין מניחים ליבם

24   הכל חיבים בתקיעת שופר

"Who commanded us to hear the sound of the *shofar*",[25] and then to blow prescribed blasts on behalf of the entire congregation, which listens to them (RH 29b; Maim. *Shofar* 3.10). This practice is based on the fact that not everyone is capable of sounding the shofar correctly or even possesses one. Maimonides therefore states that "all are obligated to hear the sound of the shofar" (Maim. *Shofar* 2:1). Although Rabbenu Tam declared that the text of the blessing should read, "to sound the shofar", the codifiers followed the view of the Jerusalem Talmud and recorded it as "to hear the sound of the shofar",[26] since even one who blows the ram's horn must also listen to it with due kavvanah (RH 4.10).

The duty to "hear the *shofar*" requires that the entire "sounding" be performed with the specific aim of fulfilling one's religious duty. This law applies both to the officiant who sounds the *shofar* and to the one who hears it.[27] Rabban Gamliel determined that the blowing of the *shofar* by the *toke'a* would enable the congregation to fulfil its duty (*RH* 38b).[28] Thus, if a man walks by the synagogue, hears the *shofar* blown within and, on hearing it, directs his mind to fulfilling his religious duty (not just listening to a musical instrument), such "hearing" is recognized as a proper fulfilment of the *mitzvah*. In this case, it is also understood that the officiant's "blowing" of the *shofar* possesses the *kavvanah* necessary for those who listen as well, thus fulfilling the double requirement of "sounding" and "hearing" (*RH* 28b; *Sh. Ar., Orah Hayyim* 589.9).

Shehitah

In the prescribed ("kosher") slaughter of animals for food, it is an essential requirement that the due procedure of *shehitah* be

---

25 הכל חיבים לשמוע קול שופר
26 לשמוע קול שופר
27 שיתכון שומע ומשמיע
28 שליח ציבור מוציא את הרבים ידי חובתן

followed, whatever other intention one might have in mind. The only external restrictions are that the slaughter may not be carried out within the Temple precincts, and that there must be no thought in the mind of the slaughterer (*shohet*) that the slaughter was being done for an idolatrous purpose. It is as though such an abominable thought injected venom into the beast, rendering it forbidden (Maim. *Shehitah* 2.1, 12, 14–15). Therefore, apart from the exceptional case of an animal being slaughtered for the purpose of idol worship, the capability of an individual was not questioned but the method of slaughter (*Hul.* 2a; Maim. *Tanna* 12; Rashi; *Git.* 22; Maim. *Shehitah* 2.11–12, Radbaz).[29]

An instance occurred in Caesarea, where an Israelite duly slaughtered an animal and afterwards expressed his intention to sprinkle the blood in an idolatrous ritual (*Hul.* 39b).[30] The Sages considered whether, since he had shown himself to be an apostate, he also had that thought in mind at the time of the slaughter, in which case the animal would be forbidden. The view of R. Shim'on ben Gamliel was upheld, that "his last act proves what he had in mind at the beginning".[31] We must therefore assume that he was also intent on idolatry when he slaughtered the animal, which was accordingly forbidden (Maim. *Shehitah* 2:16).

Mitzvot as Spiritual Satisfaction

In the Talmudic discussion as to whether the performance of a religious duty in fulfilment of a *mitzvah* gives one "a pleasurable benefit" (*le-hana'ah*), the view of Rava is accepted – that the fulfilment of a *mitzvah* is a personal obligation, not a satisfaction.[32] Thus, where it is an individual's duty to sound the prescribed *shofar* blasts on Rosh ha-Shanah, blowing the

---

29   הכל שוחטין וכולן ששחטו אומרים רואין איתן שחיטתן כשרה
30   שוחטה ואחר כך כיתב עליה ליצרק דמה לעבודת אילים
31   הוכיח סופו על תכילתו
32   ומצוות לאו להנות נתנו

shofar is accepted as a fulfilment of his duty, even if the use of the *shofar* was ritually forbidden to him, when it came from an animal already sanctified as an offering, for example, or when he was already bound by a vow prohibiting use of the *shofar*. The reason given is that the performance of a *mitzvah* in fulfilment of God's law is not undertaken for any satisfaction that maybe derived from it, but essentially in obedience to a Divine command. This is expressed halakhically by the rule, *mitzvot lav le-hannot nittenu*. Rashi explains that the *mitzvah* of blowing the *shofar* is not performed to gratify one's pleasure in the sound of the music or any other urge, but to fulfil an obligation imposed by the Creator.[33] The satisfaction gained is entirely spiritual, for having righteously obeyed God's command (*RH* 28a, Rashi *ad loc.*; *Sh. Ar.*, *Yoreh De'ah* 121.11).

Maimonides accordingly rules that since blowing the *shofar* on Rosh ha-Shanah is a positive Torah injunction, even if using that *shofar* was prohibited because it derived from an animal already sanctified as an offering (in accordance with the law of *me'ilah*), the blowing of such a *shofar* is nevertheless accepted as the fulfilment of a *mitzvah*. Maimonides adds, with reference to the argument that one takes pleasure in hearing the sound of the *shofar*, that the fulfilment of a *mitzvah* should not be regarded as any type of physical gratification – according to the same principle of *mitzvot lav le-hannot nittenu* (Maim. Code, *Shofar* 1.3).

One might well assume that the fulfilment of a *mitzvah* gives one spiritual satisfaction or even the benefit of heavenly reward, which could certainly be regarded as *hana'ah*, but this is a metaphysical pleasure, not a physical one. If, however, the performance of the *mitzvah* was inevitably accompanied by physical pleasure (which would neither apply to blowing the *shofar* nor to taking an *etrog* on Sukkot), the presence of such a *hana'ah* would have to be reckoned with; hence, whatever is forbidden may not be used for a *mitzvah*, despite the *mitzvot lav le-hannot nittenu* ruling.

Rava, who enunciated this principle, made the distinction in his additional statement (*ad loc.*) that if someone vowed not to benefit from a certain spring by bathing in it, he could ritually immerse himself in it during the winter; but during the summer, when fulfilment of the *mitzvah* would also afford enjoyment of the cool water, such immersion would be forbidden (*RH* 28a).[34] Thus, although ritual immersion even in winter affords a personal benefit, removing impurity and enabling one to enjoy things forbidden in an impure state, the pleasure is spiritual and the benefit is not gained directly from the act of immersion but after immersion, thus excluding it from the prohibited *hana'ah* (RASHBA *ad loc.* and commentary on *Suk.* 31a).

Similarly, in the *halitzah* procedure (as above) that releases a widow from an obligatory levirate marriage (Deut. 25:5-10), if the sandal worn by her brother-in-law (*Yev.* 103b) has been put to idolatrous use, any benefit from it would normally be forbidden, but for the purpose of *halitzah* even an "idolatrous sandal" may lawfully be used.[35] Here, it is explained that although the widow enjoys the benefit of her freedom after the ceremony, the act of *halitzah* itself is not a source of enjoyment and is performed solely in obedience to the Divine command. This ruling accords with the principle of *mitzvot lav le-hannot nittenu* (*Yev.* 103b; *Sh. Ar., Even ha-Ezer* 169.23; see discussion in *Avnei Millu'im* on *Even ha-Ezer* 28.60).

According to the same interpretation, this would also apply in the case of *shehitah*. Even if the slaughtering knife (*hallaf*) has been defiled by idolatrous use,[36] *shehitah* performed with it is kasher, because the procedure is a religious duty and the benefit derived from the animal's having been made fit for consumption is secondary to the obligatory performance of *shehitah* (*Hul.* 8a; *Sh. Ar., Yoreh De'ah* 10.1).

---

34 במהודר הנאה ממיאן טובל בה טבילה של מצות בימות הגשמים אבל לא בימות
    החמה
35 סנדל של עבודה זרע
36 סכין של עבודה זרע

B. In Prayer

Kavvanah in Prayer

The duty to pray to God every day is an ordinance of the Torah as it is written "And thou shalt love the Lord thy God with all your heart". The Sages explained that service of God in the heart is by means of prayer (*Taan.* 2a). Although Moses excelled in the performance of righteous deeds his prayers were only answered after he prayed to God (*Ber.* 4b, 32a).

The three daily prayers (morning, afternoon and evening) correspond with the three daily sacrificial acts. Yehuda Halevi wrote: Each hour of prayer is the climax of that part of the day (*Kuzari,* III, V). "No other hours are better fitted to turn the souls and minds of men towards God than the hours of sunrise and sunset" (*Ya'avetz*, Daily Prayer Book). "At sunrise man is rejuvenated with new strength and vigour while at sundown in the veil of darkness he entrusts his fate in the hand of the Omnipotent creator". In the morning man's heart is filled with gratitude for God's mercy in restoring to him his vitality, recognizing God's *middat rahamim.* He begins his morning prayers by praising God for the wonders of man's creation – *asher yatzar et ha-adam behokhmah.* In the evening he stands before God to render an account of his day's activities at the time of God's judgement – *middat hadin*, and he prays that his judgement will be tempered with mercy, with forgiveness of iniquities – *vehu rahum yekhapper avon.* On both occasions he adds a hymn of trust in God and His exaltation *adon olam,* generally ascribed to the scholar-poet Solomon Ibn Gabirol, and by some to Rav Hai Gaon (*Tur, Orah Hayyim,* par. 235).

These were the times when prayers had been successfully addressed to God by Abraham, Isaac and Jacob *(Ber.* 26b; Gen. 19:27; 24; 63; 28:11). But R. Joshua ben Levi said the daily prayers of the Amida were introduced by the Men of the Great Synagogue to replace the daily sacrifices which had been offered in the Temple in the morning, afternoon and evening (*Ber.* 26b).

Awareness of the Almighty

Rabbi Akiva said: "Beloved is man in that he was created in the image of God. But it was with greater Divine love that it was made known to him that he was created in the image of God, as it is written in the Torah, "for in the image of God He made man" (*Avot* 3:14, Gen. 1:27).[37]

To the extent that man is bound to nature, so is he bound to religion. Within religion man and God meet, and in that sphere the conscience of man encounters the awareness of the Almighty, and it is there that the relationship of man to his God takes shape (Abraham Joshua Heschel, *Bitzaron,* Vol. 3, no. 346).

When praying man must disengage himself from mundane, everyday affairs and endeavour to reach that vital degree of awareness of the divine side of his existence.

The *mitzvah* of prayer is different from the fulfilment of other *mitzvot.* The performance of other *mitzvot* involve some action on the part of the worshipper such as *tefillin, sukkah, mikveh,* tithes, charity. By the very fact of doing these actions one has fulfilled the *mitzvah* whether there is *kavvanah* in fulfilling them or not; but prayer is entirely an act of thought. Therefore, it must only be done with due *kavvanah* (*RH* 28b; *Ber.* 30b).[38]

The duty of prayer which is not a physical action is fulfilled only when it is accompanied by full invidivual thought and attentiveness (Deut. 11:13).[39]

Man is different from the animal. Man is endowed with intelligence which is given to him by the Almighty as part of His own heavenly throne – *mi-kiseh hakavod.* Man stands upright turning his face heavenward, whereas the animal having no intellect is rooted on the earth and walks on four legs with its head turned downward. Man who is endowed

---

37   חביב אדם שנברא בצלם, חבה יתרה נודע לו שנברא בצלם, שנאמר בצלם אל-
        הים עשה את האדם

38   מצות אין צריכות כונה

39   ולעבדו בכל לבבכם

with intelligence uses that intelligence in worship and supplication to God. The Psalmist David described this as a manner of subservience: the standing of the righteous during their prayer demonstrates that they are the servants of God – *avdei Hashem* (Ps. 134:1).[40]

It was the practice to stand throughout the Temple worship and the sacrificial procedure. The person in prayer is in communion with God and therefore must stand as a mark of his subservience to God.

The central prayer of all our daily prayers is the Amida during which our thoughts are completely directed to God. Then like angels in Divine worship we stand with our feet together as the angels are described as standing before God as though standing on one leg: the Sages described this worship thus *"ve-ragleihem regel yeshara"* (*Ber.* 10b, 12b; 34a).[41]

In reciting the first and closing blessings of the *Amidah* we are bidden to bow before God. These two blessings are praises of God, while the other intervening blessings are prayers of personal requirements.

The ritual of the recital of one's daily prayers was required to be in the Hebrew language as it was specified in the Torah, and the worshipper was instructed to express every word and every letter punctiliously. Nevertheless, since the most important element in prayer is understanding the words recited, and doing so with full devotion, the Sages ruled that one may also say the prayers in any language with which he is most familiar (*Ber.* 13a; *Sotah* 32a; *Sh. Ar., Orah Hayyim* 62:2).[42]

The Sages praised the Jewish people for remaining true to their language. The Hebrew language, throughout Jewish history, has been one of the strongest links binding together Jews from all parts of the world into one national unit and implanting in the heart of every Jew the knowledge that he belonged to the Children of Israel. All authoritative scholars

---

40   ברכו את ה׳ כל עבדי ה׳ העומדים בבית ה׳ בלילות

41   ורגליהם רגל ישרה

42   וחכמים אומרים בכל לשון שאתה שומע

urged that people say their prayers in the original Hebrew and
to make every effort to learn the meaning of them.

When presenting our supplication before God one must not
think that because the worshipper is himself righteous it is due
to him that the Almighty fulfil his request. He should know
that any granting of his supplication is an act of mercy on the
part of God and not due to any obligation by the Almighty
to grant his request. Thus, the Sages declared, when you
pray to God do not think His response is due to you for it is
only by God's grace that his prayer will be answered. The
Sages said: "Do not consider the result of your prayer as the
automatic response to your worthiness, but only as a part of
the Almighty's grace to you" (*Avot* 2:18).[43]

Prayer at Fixed Times

The Sages instituted fixed times for the recital of the morning,
afternoon and evening prayer. By this means one's own prayer
is joined with the prayers of the large body of worshippers and
they said one should always endeavour to pray together with
a congregation, which is defined as a minimum of ten adult
males, known as a *minyan*.

R. Yohanan in the name of R. Shimon ben Yohai said that
praying together with a congregation renders one's prayer
acceptable before God as it is written: "And as for me, may
my prayer unto Thee, O Lord, be in an acceptable time (Ps.
69:14; *Ber.* 7b–8a).[44]

A Cry in Distress

The act of praying is frequently called *tze'akah,* meaning a
loud cry to God for his help in our distress. Man is required to

---

43   כשאתה מתפלל אל תעש תפלתך קבע, אלא רחמים ותחנונים
44   ואני תפילתי לך עת רצון

call on God for help and not take it for granted that He knows the prayer we have in our hearts. The expression of Psalm 20:2, 10 is expressed in our daily prayers: "May the Lord hear thee in the day of trouble... Save, Lord O King, who hears us on the day when we call" (Ps. 77:2).[45]

In the account of the suffering of their Egyptian bondage, it is written, "And the children of Israel sighed by reason of their bondage and they cried and their cry rose up to God by reason of the bondage".[46]

The Almighty said, "The sin of Sodom and Gomorrah is very grievous; I will go down, and see whether they have done altogether according to the cry of it, which is come to Me" (Gen. 18:20–21).[47]

In the words of the Psalmist, "To God I will cry aloud, to God I will cry aloud. In the day of my trouble I sought the Lord" (Ps. 77:2).[48]

But devotion in prayer need not necessarily be by loud supplication. Silent prayer, heard only by the supplicant is equally a proper way to pray. At the opening of the Book of Samuel I we are told that Hannah the wife of Elkana poured out her heart before God in the Temple in Shiloh because she had failed to give birth to a son. She wept bitterly but no words of prayer were heard from her. The High Priest Eli thought she was just mumbling in a state of drunkenness, but she explained that it was because of the deep grief in her heart that she was praying to God for His blessing. Her prayer was duly answered, and she bore a son whom she called Samuel (Sam. 1:1–20).[49]

Congregational Prayer

The prayers composed by the Sages were primarily composed

---

45   יענך ה׳ ביום צרה... ה׳ הושיעה המלך יעננו ביום קראנו
46   ויאנחו בני ישראל מן העבודה ויזעקו
47   הכצעקתה הבאה אלי עשו כלה
48   קולי אל אל-הים ואצעקה
49   רק שפתיה נעות וקולה לא ישמע

for recitation by a congregation – although the obligation to
utter these prayers rests on the individual even if no gathering
of a congregation is available. The Sages taught that by
reciting the prayers at the same time when they are said in
the synagogue it is considered as though the individual was
praying with the congregation (*Ber.* 29b; TJ *Ber.* 5:1).

Prayer to God is based on the belief that God is the all-
powerful Sovereign of the world and that He is gracious and
merciful.

The more concentration and devotion we put into our prayers
directing our thoughts only to God, where the more deeply
we become involved in our awareness of God, whereupon
we become closer to the Divine. We are told that pious men
of old would wait an hour before praying so that they may
concentrate their thoughts on their Maker (*Ber.* 32b).

Repentance before Prayer

Prayer to the Almighty should always be preceded by a solemn
act of repentance, *teshuvah,* for one's past sins. When Samuel
wanted to pray that Israel be delivered from the Philistines, he
called on Israel to gather in Mitzpeh where he would pray for
them, and the people fasted on that day and confessed: "We
have sinned to the Lord", and the Lord delivered them from
the Philistines (1 Sam. 7:6; cf. Dan. 10:12).

We find throughout the Scriptures that it was the practice in
time of trouble to go to the prophet or saintly person and ask
him to pray for them (Jer. 42:2; *Ber.* 42a) since the prayer of a
righteous man would be more effective than their own.

Customs When Praying

It is customary for the Reader of the prayers in the congregation,
the *ḥazan,* to stand in a low place among the congregants
instead of on an elevated platform. This practice is based on
the words of the Psalmist: "Out of the depths, I have cried

unto Thee, Lord" (Ps. 130:1; *Ber.* 10b; Rashi *ad loc.*; Maim. *Yad, Tefillah* 9:1).[50]

The scholars differed on whether it is good practice to sway the body to and fro or from side to side during prayer. The custom was based on the words, "All my bones shall say Lord who is like Thee" (Ps. 35:10).[51]

It is a custom to recite one's prayers and the study of the Scriptures and Talmud with a familiar melody, which action encouraged concentration. R. Akiva said, "Chant it every day" (*Sanh.* 99a). In Temple times the Levites accompanied all their Services with song and musical instruments (Ps. 27:6; stet Chron. 25:7).

General References:

Abudraham on the Prayer Book rubric (R. Dabid ben Yosef, Spain, 1341); *Siddur Ya'avetz* (Ya'akov ben Zvi Emden, Altona, Germany 18th cent.); Elie Munk, *The World of Prayer* (Feldheim, New York, 1954); Samson Raphael Hirsch, *Commentary on Prayer Book*; Elbogen, *Gottesdienst* (German and English translation); Idelsohn, *Liturgy*.

The Meaning of Prayer

The first thoughts in the mind of a person who wakes up in the morning from an apparent state of unconsciousness to a state of awareness bringing to mind the dogma of "the revival of the dead" (*mehayeh metim*), are those expressed in the words of the Psalmist: "How mighty are Thy works, O Lord!" (or "how manifold") – *Mah-rabbu ma'asekha Hashem* (Ps. 104:24, Kimhi *ad loc.*).[52] On retiring to sleep at night one utters the

---

50 ממעמקים קראתיך ה'
51 כל עצמותי תאמרנה ה' מי כמוך
52 מה רבו מעשך ה'

prayer, "Lighten mine eyes, lest I sleep the sleep of death" (Ps.13:3).[53] On our awakening our morning prayer expresses our thanks to God, "Who keepeth His faith with those that sleep in the earth",[54] refering both to "the rivival of the dead" and the restoration of consciousness after sleep, as Isaiah said, "Awake and sing, ye that dwell in the dust" (Isa. 26:19).[55]

In the Jewish morning service, the daily benedictions commence with thanksgiving for the blessing of consciousness and intelligence vouchsafed to us by the Almighty when we awake from sleep. This is followed by our recognition that it is by the grace of God that we are able to see, stand and clothe ourselves with dignity.

It may seem odd that all these blessings begin with an acknowledgment that God endowed the cockerel with the ability to recognize the passage from night to morning, when "the rising of the sun calls it to crow" (George Eliot). The clarion call of the cockcrow at dawn arouses man from his sleep. The cockerel possesses an understanding beyond mere instinct that enables it to distinguish day from night. The benedictions giving thanks for our sight, strength and freedom therefore commence: "Blessed art Thou, O, Lord our God, King of the universe, who hast given the cock intelligence to distinguish between day and night" – *Barukh attah Hashem ... asher natan la-sekhvi vinah le-havhin bein yom u-vein layelah*"[56] (*Ber.*60b).

The celebrated Gaon of Vilna, in his commentary on the prayer book, explained that through these blessings man is encouraged to recognize the wonders of God's creation, particularly those things which he normally takes for granted. Man prides himself on his intellect, but the dawn crowing of the cock should make us realize that it has also been endowed with an understanding that we can admire. This first morning benediction therefore expresses our thanks for God's gift of

---

53   האירה עיני פן אישן המות

54   המקים אמונתו לישיני עפר

55   הקיצו ורננו שכני עפר

56   ברוך אתה ה'...אשר נתן לשכוי בינה להבחין בין יום ובין לילה

intelligence, thought and understanding (Vilna Gaon, *Siddur Ma'aseh Rav*).[57]

True prayer was described by the late Chief Rabbi A. Y. Kook as the supreme spiritual joy that is experienced by reaching into the depths of natural sanctity within our hearts and drawing that sanctity into the consciousness of our daily existence. This discovery of one's own spiritual depths can only be achieved by assiduously clearing the mind of all thoughts of evil or self-indulgence and purifying one's thoughts by raising them nearer to the realm of Divine spirituality.

Man can experience no greater joy in life than achieving, through attentive devotion in prayer (*kavvanah*), the holiness of a closer identification with the holiness of God and in rediscovering the true path of human life by a personal awareness of the necessity and joy of living according to God's precepts (Rav A. Y. Kook, *Olat Re'ayah, Seder ha-Tefillah*, pp. 13, 19; quoted by R. Yissakhar Jakobson in *Netiv Binah*, vol. 1, p. 33).

The Torah requires one to "love the Lord your God, and serve Him with all your heart" (Deut. 11:13). This duty the Sages took to mean *avodah she-ba-lev* – "service in [or of] the heart", which is prayer (*Ta'an.* 2a). The further verse states, "Therefore ye shall lay up these my words in your heart and in your soul; and ye shall bind them for a sign upon your hand... and ye shall teach them your children..." (Deut. 11:18, 19). The Sages understood these words to mean the study and practice of the Torah (*Sifri*, Deut. *Ibid*; Maim. *Sefer ha-Mitzvot, mitzvot aseih*, sect. 5).[58]

Specific forms or times of prayer are not prescribed in the Torah, except for a few particular formulas, such as the Priestly Benediction (Num. 6:24–26),[59] the offering of first fruits (Deut. 26:2–10)[60] and the dedication of tithes (Deut.

---

57 מעשה רב
58 לשון ספרי, ולעבדו זו תפילה, ואמרו גם כן ולעבדו זו תלמוד
59 ברכת כהנים
60 מקרה בכורים

26:13–15).[61] Although detailed instructions are not set forth in the Torah, it was the practice of Jews from the time of Moses to worship daily in the threefold manner of praising God, asking for and turning to one's special needs, and then giving thanks for the blessings one had received (Maim. *Tefillah* 1:1). King David mentioned the custom of praying daily, in the evening, the morning and at noon[62] (*Arvit, Shaḥarit, Minḥa*).

The Sages commended the introduction of some innovation in prayer rather than the habitual repetition[63] which could lead to thoughtless gabbling by rote (*Ber.* 29b).[64] It was realized, however, that not everyone is able to formulate his own mode of expression when praying for himself or for the community. After the Babylonian Exile, from the time of Ezra, the Men of the Great Assembly (c. 200 BCE)[65] therefore prescribed a definitive liturgy to be followed at all times. This included the set form of the *Amidah* (known also as *Shemoneh Esreh*, the Prayer of "Eighteen Blessings"), recited three times daily and corresponding to the sacrificial services of the Temple; Sabbath and festival prayers; Grace after Meals; and public Reading of the Law. The Sages incorporated much Biblical phraseology in these prayers and made extensive use of the deep spiritual insights in the Psalms of David, with which everyone could in some way identify. Standard prayers were articulated in the plural form, thus identifying one's personal needs with those of the community for which all were responsible (*Shev.* 39a; Maim. *Tefillah* 1–5).

Although halakhic authorities permitted the introduction of additional, original prayers in suitable places (*Sh. Ar., Oraḥ Hayyim* 119), this practice was not generally followed, apart from the special petition for healing. Prayers were generally recited in a punctilious and uniform manner from the accepted Hebrew text of the *siddur*, according to the various (Sephardi

---

61 וידוי מעשרות
62 ערב ובוקר וצהרים אם אשיך
63 תפילת קבע
64 מצוות אנשים מלומדיו
65 אנשי כנסת הגדולה

and Eastern, Roman and Ashkenazi) rites that took shape, thus uniting Jewish communities throughout the world. Despite the Mishnah's call to innovate in one's supplications (*Ber.* 4:4), the accepted practice was to follow the fixed ritual.[66]

Some additional prayers, devised by Talmudic Sages, were incorporated in regular worship, such as the prayer of Mar bar Ravina, "Guard my tongue from evil",[67] which was added to the *Amidah* (*Ber.* 17a), or the prayer of Rav, "Renew this month",[68] recited on the Sabbath preceding each New Moon (*Ber.* 16b; *Tur Orah Hayyim* 122; *Siddur Ya'avetz, Bet El*).

In the spiritual rapture expressed by pious Hasidim, prayers were often accompanied by a soul-searching melody[69] that reflected a person's inner feelings. The mystical meditations of the kabbalists also contained thoughts that were reflected in the wording of a particular prayer (e.g., Refael Immanuel Ricchi, *Mafte'ah ha-Kavvanot*, Amsterdam, 1740). These kabbalistic devotions are generally ascribed to R. Yitzhak Luria of Safed (16th cent.) and are usually confined to mystical circles having deeper mystical understanding.

Prayer for Knowledge (Honen ha-Da'at)

Intelligence[70] is said to be the natural power with which a person is endowed at birth (Midrash Shemuel). The higher stage, understanding,[71] is developed by one's own efforts through deeper study. However, without a basic grasp of *da'at* (i.e., thorough knowledge of Torah sources), one cannot reach the higher level of understanding (*binah*). The Sages affirmed that if *da'at* is not present, there can be no *binah*.[72]

תפילת קבע	66
אלוקי נצור	67
שתחדש עלינו	68
ניגון	69
דעת	70
בינה	71
אם אין בינה אין דעת	72

In the view of the Sages, the stage of knowledge is reached when one has thoroughly mastered all the teachings of Torah with the traditional interpretations of the Sages. In order to gain this knowledge, one must have the assistance of the Almighty. The power of understanding[73] signifies the mental ability to deduce a new aspect of the law by logical scrutiny of all one's knowledge (Ex. 31:3, Rashi s.v. "*ḥokhmah, tevunah, da'at*"; *Siddur Yavetz*: "*Da'at, binah ve-haskel*").

The Sephardic view – as expressed by Naḥmanides, the achievement of knowledge[74] is that one has discovered all the secret knowledge contained in the building of the Tabernacle and its appurtenances. When God ordered Moses to appoint Bezalel as the Sanctuary's architect, it was because he had achieved all this wisdom (Ex. 31:2, Ramban; *Midrash Shem–uel* by R. Shemuel Uceda; *Avot* 3:23; *Siddur Otzar ha-Tefillot, Etz Yosef*).

Kavvanah in Prayer in Halakha

While the Sages differed as to whether the absence of *kavvanah* in performing the *mitzvot* generally nullified their fulfilment, or whether the mere intention to perform the *mitzvah* would suffice (*Er.* 95b; *Pes.* 114b; *RH* 28b; *Oraḥ Ḥayyim* 60:4), all agreed that prayer must be accompanied by full awareness and attention (*kavvanah*).

The ruling is given by Rabbeinu Yona, at the end of the first chapter of Tractate *Berakhot,* as follows: "Rabbeinu Hai Gaon and many other authorities laid down that the *mitzvot* are fulfilled even where there is no *kavvanah*. This ruling, however, applied only to *mitzvot* in which a particular action is involved, such as taking the *lulav* on the Festival of *Sukkot*; but those *mitzvot* which are performed by word of mouth only, such as reciting the *Shema* or the *Amidah,* whose fulfilment

---

73   בינה

74   דעת

demands an individual's mindfulness and close attention to what he is saying, must be performed with full *kavvanah*".[75]

R. Yosef Caro referred to this difference of opinion among the Sages and maintained that *kavvanah* was essential, particularly in the fulfilment of Torah-ordained *mitzvot*. In his *Shulḥan Arukh,* Caro followed Rabbeinu Yona's interpretation, as well as the ruling of the ROSH in accordance with the teaching of R. Yitzḥak. A man should be modest in prayer; if he is over-confident or unduly insistent that his devoted prayer (*iyyun tefillah*) will be answered, that man's worthiness receives heavenly judgment in the light of his previous transgessions (*RH* 16b).

In one's recital of the *Shema,* the fullest *kavannah* is especially required when reading the first verse, which proclaims man's acceptance of the sovereignty and unity of God (*Sh. Ar., Oraḥ Ḥayyim* 60:45). In one's recital of the *Amidah* prayer, *kavvanah* is particularly essential when reading the first paragraph (*Oraḥ Ḥayyim* 101:1, *Magen Avraham*). In his glossary, REMA follows the ruling of Maimonides (Maim. *Tefillah* 10:1): If such concentration was absent, it is one's duty to repeat that passage with *kavvanah*; since human weakness might, however, make it difficult to attain the desired level of *kavvanah*, even through repetition, we may have to regard a lesser degree as acceptable (*Oraḥ Ḥayyim* 101:1). It was the practice of pious men of olden days – *Hasidim Rishonim* – that they would always spend an hour in reverent meditation before commencing their prayers, clearing the mind of all extraneous thoughts and adjusting it to an awesome awareness of standing in the Divine Presence, as it is written: "Therefore hath thy servant found in his heart [found his heart ready] to pray this prayer unto Thee" (2 Sam. 7:27).[76]

Prayer must be accompanied by complete trust in the love and mercy of God. Throughout the day one's mind should be attuned to that unshaken faith. R. Naḥman of Bratslav, a

---

75 יש מחלקת אם מצות צריכות כונה או לאו
76 על כן מצא עבדך את לבו להתפלל אליך את התפלה הזאת

Hasidic master (Ukraine, 18th cent.), taught that if a man is troubled by depressing thoughts, he should expel them from his mind and make every effort to create a joyful spirit within himself. This he can achieve by simply contemplating the wonders of his own creation, as expressed in the first blessings of the daily Morning Service. Above all, he should somehow arouse a feeling of joy in his heart, since gloomy thoughts have a poisonous effect, leading him to a state of chronic depression. No matter how grave their situation maybe, Hassidic Jews sing and dance in an exuberant manner while they worship the Almighty (*Likutei Moharan*, part 2, 48). The Sages declared that one should not begin praying in a state of anxiety or lethargy, but only when one can feel the joy of performing a *mitzvah* (*Ber.* 31a).[77]

R. Meir Ha-Kohen of Rothenburg (13th cent.) accepted the view of the Tosafot that since, in his troubled times, it was usually hard to maintain proper *kavvanah*, this requirement might be considered of lesser importance (*Haggahot Maimmuniyyot* on Maim. *Tefillah* 4:20). The Rabbis, however, always urged each individual to devise his own way of concentrating his thoughts in prayer. On a weekday, for example, it might be helpful to write a list of things preying on one's mind and then lay it aside before beginning one's prayers. In general it was taught that the recital of any prayer without full *kavvanah* made that prayer akin to a body without a soul (Bahya, *Hovot ha-Levavot*, *Heshbon ha-Nefesh* 3; Yehudah Halevi, *Kuzari* 3:5).

R. Yohanan stated that there are six *mitzvot* which, when fulfilled assure a man of an eternal reward in the World to Come, full *kavvanah* being one of these (*Shab.* 127a). According to R. Amram, it seems impossible for a man to avoid three transgressions: "Contemplation of committing a sin, lack of concentration in one's prayers, and indulging in malicious gossip". Tosafot explained that "concentrating in one's prayers" really means that too great a longing for

---

77   אין עומדין להתפלל מתוך עצבות וכו'... אלא מתוך שמחה של מצוה

those prayers to be answered will result in heartache if one's expectations are not fulfilled. R. Yitzhak taught that when a man is unduly confident that his prayers will be answered, he may later have his own worthiness judged in heaven when the sins he committed are recalled (*RH* 16b; *Ber.* 55a; *BB* 164, *Tos.* s.v *iyyun tefillah*). The Talmud records R. Yehuda's plea: "May my prayers be answered on account of having fulfilled the *mitzvah of iyyun tefillah*" (*Shab.* 118b).

Chief Rabbi Kook identified two categories of *kavvanah*. Firstly, the Sages demanded the worshipper's complete and undivided recognition of how awesome it is to stand in prayer before God. They taught that "one who prays should direct his heart to the Almighty in heaven",[78] as David prayed when he sought God's help for the humble and oppressed: "Thou wilt direct their heart, Thou wilt cause Thine ear to hear" (Ps. 10:17). However, this teaching also refers to another and wider significance of *kavvanah*, by which one pays close attention, to the words one prays and to their meaning. Each individual would be able to attain his personal standard of *kavvanah,* namely, that it makes one pay close attention to the words of the prayer and to their meaning. Every individual can therefore reach his own particular level of concentration (*kavvanah peratit*) and should always strive to do so (Rav A. Y. Kook, *Olat Re'iah*, Vol. 1, p.30).

When reading the *Shema*, at least the first verse (Deut. 6:4), which acknowledges the sovereignty of God and His unity, must be recited with full *kavvanah* (*Ber.* 13b; Maim. *Shema* 2:1; *Orah Hayyim* 61:4). When reciting the *Amidah*, one should have *kavvanah* throughout; but, if it proves difficult to maintain one's *kavvanah*, it must be present at least in the first blessing, *Magen Avot*, since this benediction also proclaims one's faith in the tender sovereignty of God, as recognized by our forefathers. *Kavvanah* is always more effective if the words are clearly expressed, and, particularly in prayer recited in private, when expressed aloud (*Ber.* 34b; Maim. *Tefillah*,10:1; *Orah Hayyim* 101:1, *Magen David, Magen*

Avraham ad loc.).

When fulfilling the duty of reading the Scroll of Esther on Purim, one should read the entire book aloud from the Hebrew text written on a scroll (*megillah*). Reciting it aloud from memory does not fulfil one's obligation, nor will it suffice to read the Hebrew text silently, (*Orah Hayyim* 62:3; 63:4; 690:3)[79] as it is written that the duty to "remember Amalek" is fulfilled by speaking of it (Deut. 25:17).[80] If one copies the text in front of one while reading it aloud, thereby intending to fulfil the *mitzvah*, one has done one's duty (*Meg.* 18a-b; *Orah Hayyim* 690:3, 7, 13).

The Tosafists (12th–13th cent.), who acknowledged their own shortcomings in regard to *kavvanah*, pointed out that the situation of the Jews in a hostile environment had led to a deterioration in their ability to maintain full *kavvanah* even when praying. They asserted that it would be presumptuous for anyone to claim that he had always recited his prayers with full *kavvanah*. They therefore laid down that one's prayers be read as prescribed, even if full *kavvanah* was not attained (*Ber.* 17b, s.v. "*Rav Shesha*"). This view of the *Tosafot* was generally accepted by later authorities, including the Vilna Gaon (*Siddur ha-GRA, Ishei Yisrael*), so that if prayers had been recited without *kavvanah* they need not be repeated in an effort to enhance *kavvanah*, since there is no certainty that another effort would prove more successful (*Orah Hayyim* 101:1, *Tur*, REMA).

A clear case of the need for full mental awareness in a religious act maybe seen in the observant Jew's daily obligation to proclaim his acceptance of God's sovereignty.[81] This declaration is made by reciting the *Shema* passage, "Hear, O Israel, the Lord our God, the Lord is One", together with the paragraph beginning, "And thou shalt love the Lord thy God with all thy heart..." (Deut. 6:4, 5-9). The Rabbis

---

79   אם קראה על פה לא יצא
80   זכור
81   לקבל עליו עול מלכות שמים

were concerned that the declaration should be made with each individual's full understanding, even if this meant reciting it in the vernacular instead of in Hebrew (*Orah Hayyim* 62:2).[82] They therefore interpreted the word *Shema* as an injunction to "understand" rather than simply to "hear".

The Rabbis were also concerned about the level of concentration demanded of an individual and the extent to which it could be maintained. An early *Baraita* stated that the reading of the *Shema* required the full attention of the mind.[83] R. Meir taught that the first sentence of the *Shema*, proclaiming God's sovereignty, called for an exceptional degree of concentration and understanding; the remaining three passages need only be read attentively. Other Sages required full concentration while reading the first two passages of the *Shema*: failure to concentrate obliged one to repeat them, but only if one could be sure of doing so better the second time, for otherwise God's holy Name would be needlessly repeated. All were agreed, however, that the ideal performance of this *mitzvah* required full *kavvanah*,[84] as R. Eliezer ben Tzadok taught: "Perform your *mitzvot* in honour of the One who created them, and recite your words of Torah entirely in their honour" (*Orah Hayyim* 60:4, 61:1, *Mishnah Berurah ad loc.*; *Ned.* 62a).

The authoritative ruling of Rava in the Talmud agreed with that of R. Meir (*Ber.* 13b). Rava declared that if one did not concentrate fully when articulating the first sentence, *Shema Yisrael*, the recital had no meaning (it was "like a body without a soul").[85] In the case of this particular duty, fulfilment involved no action other than a declaration accepting God's sovereignty. The sincerity of that declaration was essentially an act of the mind and had no meaning unless one's mind was fully engaged in thought and *kavvanah*. Rava did appreciate, however, that not everyone could maintain full concentration

---

throughout the performance of each *mitzvah*. Therefore, when it came to other duties in which some physical act was involved, as in some ceremonial duties, he ruled that the fulfillment of such *mitzvot* need not depend on the extent of one's *kavvanah*. Even if it were lacking, the *mitzvah* would still be regarded as fulfilled.[86]

Accordingly, as explained above, Maimonides laid down that if a person had read the *Shema* without full attention in the first sentence at least, he had failed in his religious duty. Nevertheless, for the remaining passages it would suffice to be aware that he was reading the *Shema* prayer, and to recite it with the attention due to passages of the holy Torah (Maim. *Keri'at Shema* 2:1). ROSH also agreed with the view of R. Meir, adding that since this was a statement affirming God's sovereignty in which no physical action was performed, *keri'at Shema* had no meaning unless there was some thoughtful appreciation of what was read (*Ber.* 13b).[87]

Caro ruled likewise (*Orah Hayyim* 60:5). He held, in general, that the performance of every religious duty required k*avvanah* and must be accompanied by the full awareness and intention of fulfilling that *mitzvah* (*Orah Hayyim* 60:4; 61:4).[88] The same requirement applied to reciting the *Amidah*, known also as *ha-Tefillah* – "the intrinsic Prayer". Thus, when the Torah enjoined "to serve Him with all your heart" (Deut. 11:13),[89] the Sages affirmed that "the service of the heart is prayer" (*Ta'an.* 2a).[90] Caro also maintained that while, during the rest of the year, one should recite the *Amidah* quietly (*be-lahash*), on the special days of heavenly judgment, Rosh ha-Shanah and Yom Kippur, one may raise one's voice, so long as this does not disturb the prayer of one's neighbour, since the words of the expanded *Amidah* at those Services are

---

86   תנו רבנן שמע ישראל ה' אלו-הינו ה' אחד עד כאן צריכת כונת הלב דברי ר' מאיר אמר רבא הלכה כר' מאיר

87   קריאה בלא כונה

88   מצוות צריכות כונה לצאת בעשיית אותה מצווה

89   לעבדו בכל לבבכם

90   תפילה איזו היא עבודה שבלב הוי אומר זו תפילה

unfamiliar and their recital aloud could promote the necessary *kavvanah* (*Orah Hayyim* 582:9, *Mishnah Berurah ad loc.*; *Piskei Tosafot*, end of *Rosh ha-Shanah*).

A number of particular spiritual meditations in the recital of prayers and before the performance of all mitzvot were taught by Luria, and were recorded by his pupils, such as Hayyim Vital in his book *Etz Hayyim* (1573), and in the following century in *Sefer ha-Kavvanot* (Venice, 1620). They expressed the mystic striving of integration with the Divine (*devekut*). Particularly in Safed these teachings were enriched with special customs, based on the Sephardi liturgy, and were accepted also in the Ashkenazi, Hassidic practice (*Encl. Judaica*, Vol. 11, p. 577, s.v. Luria, Isaac).

The Lurianic School developed a system of meditative *kavvanot* creating a strengthened bond between the world of man and the heavenly spheres. This was done by a comprehensive exercise in inward meditation. The Eve on the New Moon was treated as "a little Day of Atonement". The time of midnight was devoted to mystical study (*tikkun hatzot*), particularly the nights of Pentecost and *Hoshana Rabbah*. The atmosphere of the Sabbath was pervaded with the mystical unification of man with the upper world, speaking of the Sabbath as the Queen of God's majesty (*Shabbat ha-Malka*), or the Bride of Israel (*lekha dodi*). Solomon's praise of "the virtuous woman" (*eshet hayil*), was expounded as meditations on the man's loving relationship with the *Shekhinah*.

(*Siddur ha-Ari*, as recorded by Hayyim Vital – many editions; and a collection of Sephardi rubrics in the *siddur* of Shalom Sharabi, Jerusalem 1910; Sefer Ta'amei ha-Minhagim, 1912).

These practices were based on the Talmudic teaching that on Shabbat eve R. Hanina used to don his Sabbath clothes and exclaim "Come and let us go forth to welcome the Queen Sabbath", and R. Yannai exclaimed "Come O Bride!, Come O Bride!" (*Shab.* 119a). Based on this tradition R. Solomon ben Moses ha-Levi of the Safed Kabbalist school composed the popular Sabbath eve hymn, *Lekha Dodi*.

Although Maimonides recognized the valid nature of a physically performed *mitzvah*, even where *kavvanah* was absent, he felt that prayer devoid of *kavvanah* had no meaning.[91] Maimonides required that, before beginning to pray, one should wait for a while in order to clear the mind of all extraneous thoughts and experience that one is standing before the Divine Presence. Likewise, if a person was fatigued or distressed, he should wait until his mind was refreshed; if hungry or thirsty, he should eat and drink until he was able to concentrate on his prayer (Maim. *Tefillah* 4:15–16).

In affirming the necessity for complete devotion in prayer, Talmud relates that it was the custom of early pious Jews (*Ḥasidim Rishonim*) who, before starting to pray, would wait a considerable length of time in quiet contemplation until they had freed themselves of extraneous thoughts and attained the required frame of mind that they are standing in prayer before the Almighty; only then would they begin reading their prayers (*Ber.* 30b, *Oraḥ Ḥayyim* 98:1). Due preperation of one's physical and thoughtful condition was expressed by the prophet Amos in the words: "Prepare to meet thy God" (Amos 4:12).[92]

In order to concentrate their mind entirely on their devotions it has been a practice to read a passage of the *Zohar* (*Pataḥ Eliyahu*), describing the mystical approach of man to God. A common practice quoted by the ARI (R. Yitzḥak Luria), is to introduce every recital of prayer and the fulfillment of an ordained ritual with the words "I hereby prepare my mouth to declare..." (*hareini mezamen et pi*). Alternatively it is said, "I am now fully prepared to fulfil the law of..." (*hineni muchan umezuman lekayem...*) (*Siddur Ya'avetz*, Intro. p. 34, 35; Passover Ritual; counting of the *Omer*, etc.; *Siddur Otzar Ha-tefillot*).

The Vilna Gaon wrote that in the recital of one's prayers one must always consider one's action as "appearing before the

Presence of the Almighty" (*Likutei ha-GRA* on Isaiah 112).[93]
Rabbi Moshe Haim Luzzatto quoted the midrashic statement,
that when you stand in prayer your heart must rejoice within
you that you are praying to the one and only God, as the
Psalmist said, "serve the Lord with gladness: come before
his presence with singing" (Ps.100:2),[94] and "Let the heart of
them rejoice that seek the Lord" (Ps. 105:3).[95] Even the most
solemn prayers are accompanied by singing and rejoicing
(M.H. Luzzatto, *Mesilat Yesharim* 19, sect. 2). In Temple times
worship was accompanied by singing and musical instruments
exhilarating the worshippers in their glorification of God. In
a number of David's joyful Psalms praising God he declares,
"for it is good to sing praises unto our God; for it is pleasant,
and praise is comely" (Ps. 147:1).[96] The Palestinian Talmud
relates that David prayed, "may it be thy will, O Lord, that my
songs be sung in synagogues *and Batei Medrashot* (houses
of study), forever" (TJ *Shekalim* 2:5). Although one's own
circumstances maybe anything but happy, one should make
every effort to create in one's self a spirit of joy. Pious men
always endevoured to recite their prayers in this manner (R.
Yehuda ha-Hassid, *Sefer Hassidim,* sect. 18).

To maintain proper *kavvanah,* pious scholars recited their
prayers from the printed page of the *siddur,* reading each word
carefully as though counting it, concentrating on the meaning
of every sentence and directing their thoughts to the service
of God (ARI; Vilna Gaon). Some directed their thoughts to the
words by pointing to each with their finger. Another practice
was to cover the eyes with one's hand while reciting the first
sentence of the *Shema,* so as to avoid any outside distraction,
and to recite the whole text aloud, making sure to read each
of the 248 words contained in the three paragraphs, which
are equivalent to the traditional number of limbs in the body
(*Orah Hayyim* 61:3–5).[97]

התפלה היא ענין כמו ראיית פניו של הקב"ה   93
עבדו את ה' בשמחה באו לפניו ברננה   94
ישמח לב מבקשי ה'   95
כי טוב זמרה אל-הינו, כי נעים נאוה תהלה   96
רמ"ח תאוות כנגד רמ"ח אברים של אדם   97

With regard to the maintenance of *kavvanah*, it is related that the Vilna Gaon made it his practice, especially when reciting the *Shema*, to visualize in his mind's eye the letters forming each word and to read the letters as he saw them (*Siddur ha-GRA, Ishei Yisrael*; Appendix *Orhot Hayyim* by his pupil, R. Hayyim of Volozhin, 41).

Every device that could help sustain one's *kavvanah* was utilized. The Rabbis taught that it was advisable to pronounce each word separately, though quietly, with loving care, like someone counting pearls (*Orah Hayyim* 62:3; 61:25).[98] It was also customary to hold the fringes of one's *tallit* in the left hand while reciting the *Shema*. This heightened consciousness of one's activity was achieved by engaging the senses of sight, speech, hearing and touch at one and the same time. In difficult circumstances, however, it was permissible to recite prayers silently in one's mind (*Orah Hayyim* 62:4).

It is known that some people are better able to maintain their concentration by focussing their mind intently on the prayer and then reciting it quickly while their *kavvanah* is operative. Each person is advised to adopt whichever method best suits his temperament. Some people find that a gentle swaying of the body helps to maintain *kavvanah*, while others prefer to remain motionless in an attitude of thought and humility. Some find it helpful if they fervently walk back and forth to energise their concentration and maintain the momentum of their devotion. The essential achievement must be that their concentration is with full conviction, undisturbed and unbroken.

The Sages warned against the natural propensity to lose one's concentration, as stated by R. Amram in the name of Rav: "There are three transgressions that inevitably confront us every day and which none can escape: evil thoughts,[99] lack of concentration in prayer[100] and slander"[101] (*BB* 164b, *Tos. ad loc.*).

---

98 משמיע לאוזניו
99 הרהור עבירה
100 עיון תפלה
101 לשון הרע

As stated earlier, a *mitzvah* performed physically in the
required manner is valid, even if full *kavvanah* was absent
(*RH* 28b).[102] Prayer is not a physical act, however, apart from
the articulation of the words,[103] and *kavvanah* is therefore
essential, the basic idea of prayer being to direct the heart
(*Ber.* 30b).[104] Fundamentally, according to the Rabbis, prayer
is "the service of God in the heart" (*Ta'an.* 2b).[105] Voicing
one's prayer is thus essential, because mere contemplation in
the mind will not suffice to constitute a positive action that
fulfils a *mitzvah* (*Ber.* 20b).[106]

Kavvanah in prayer entails a realization that the words
of praise or supplication are directed only to the Sovereign
of the universe. Accordingly, the obligation to recite one's
prayers can only be discharged if the words themselves are
understood. In recognition of the difficulty people often
experience in maintaining *kavvanah*, the Sephardi rite added
a special plea (*Shome'a tefillah*) in the closing supplication
of the *Amidah*, "for Thou hearest the prayer spoken by every
mouth".[107] Furthermore, in all rites, the *Amidah* concludes
with the prayer, "May the words of my mouth and the thoughts
in my heart be acceptable before Thee" (Ps. 19:15).[108]

Since, when reciting the *Shema*, it is obligatory to focus
one's mind on every single word,[109] the custom arose for each
individual to chant the three paragraphs of the *Shema* according
to the Masoretic cantillation.[110] This practice, however, was
not insisted upon if it was found that paying regard to the
cantillation lessened one's concentration on the meaning of
the words (*Ber.* 15b, R. Yonah *ad loc.*, *s.v.* "*omerim Shema
Yisrael*"; *Orah Hayyim* 61:24, *Ba'er Heitev ad loc.*).

102 מצוות אין צריכות כונה
103 אין המצוות נעשות
104 כי עיקרא היא כונת הלב
105 איזו היא עבודה שהיא בלב זו תפלה
106 דהרהור לב כדבור דמי
107 כי אתה שומע תפלת כל פה
108 יהיו לרצון אמרי פי והגיון לבי לפניך
109 מדקדק באותיות
110 קורא בטעמים שהם בתורה

Virtually all the earlier authorities agreed that silent contemplation of the words does not fulfil the requirement of enunciating them. This rule is expressed in the axiom, "Thought is not equivalent to speech" (*Ber.* 15a, as R. Yose; *Orah Hayyim* 62:3, *Mishnah Berurah, Bi'ur Halakhah ad loc., s.v. "yatza"*).[111]

Although each individual is duty-bound to recite the central *Amidah* (known as "the Prayer"), when services are held with a quorum of at least ten adult males (*minyan*) it is standard practice for the cantor or "Reader"[112] to repeat the entire *Amidah* aloud after the congregation's silent prayer (*Orah Hayyim* 124:1).

The Sages accepted the ruling of Rabban Gamliel that this repetition of the *Amidah* could absolve a man from his duty if he failed to recite the prayer himself (*RH* 33b).[113] Although leading Geonim expressed differing views, the early commentators accepted the ruling that the cantor's repetition on Rosh ha-Shanah discharged the duty of all those present in synagogue who listened throughout his recital, even though each individual was capable of reading the prayer for himself. Caro, however, excused only someone unable to pray (*Bet Yosef*). The Reader also exonerated those wishing to attend synagogue who were unavoidably absent due to ill health or far distance (*Tur, Orah Hayyim* 591). The early commentators emphasized, however, that this applied particularly to the unusually lenghthened Rosh ha-Shanah and Yom Kippur liturgy; as regards the more familiar daily *Amidah*, only by reciting it himself could each person fulfil his religious duty (*RH* 34b, RAN on RIF, p. 12, Jerusalem Talmud).

Maimonides and Caro both ruled that in normal daily worship the Reader's repetition of the Amidah only absolves those unversed in the prayer who could not discharge their own obligation properly. They must listen closely to every

---

111   הרהור לב כדבור דמי

112   שליח צבור

113   השליח צבור מוציא את הרבים ידי חובתן

word, not allow anything to distract their attention and respond Amen to each blessing (*RH* 33b, 34b; RIF and RAN *ad* loc.; Maim. *Tefillah* 8:9; *Orah Hayyim* 124:1).

Sanctity of the House of Prayer

In every synagogue the sanctity radiated by the fervent devotion of the worshipers and their communion with the Almighty pervades the entire building, even becoming absorbed in its walls, and rendering the structure of the House of Prayer itself sacred. The Sage Rabba, expounding the Biblical verse "Lord, Thou hast been our dwelling place" (Ps. 90:1),[114] taught that the synagogue and houses of learning become the dwelling place of God. Every place of prayer is considered by God as "a miniature Temple", as Ezekiel the Prophet declared, "Although I have scattered them (Israel) among the countries yet have I been to them as a little sanctuary in the countries where they are come" (Ezek 11:16, Jewish Version, JPSA).[115]

King Solomon built the Temple on Mount Moriah in Jerusalem. The priests brought the sacred Ark containing the two tablets of the Ten Commandments testifying to the covenant of God with Israel and placed it in the Temple Sanctuary. He declared: "The Lord, The Almighty, the Creator of all existence, the heavens and highest heavens cannot contain Him, how can this House be His dwelling place in which I may speak with You and address my prayers to You? (Kings 1, 8:27). Isaiah said that the angels declared, "The whole world is filled with His glory" (Isa. 6:3).[116] Yet, the Sages taught that the Almighty, so to speak, compressed His vast presence to rest in the holy place where Israel gathered in devotion to God.[117]

---

114 ה' מעון אתה היית לנו בדר ודור
115 ואהי' להם למקדש מעט
116 מלא כל הארץ כבודו
117 שצמצם יתברך שכינתו בבית המקדש

Because of the sanctity of the building, Jewish law has never permitted the destruction of a house of prayer. The Rabbis recognized that because of changing social and estate conditions it maybe come necessary to change or give up the existing structure. Many rabbinical authorities received inquiries from different communities for halakhic rulings regarding procedure in the case of needed changes in the structure of a synagogue. The ruling in every case was that the demolition of an existing synagogue was basically forbidden. Under certain strict conditions, however, the demolition could take place. An example maybe found in a community where originally only a small gathering of Jews were available to attend prayers but later the number was considerably increased and it was essential to build a larger synagogue, but this could not be done without first demolishing the existing one. In reply to such an inquiry it was stated that the demolishing should not be done until an alternate synagogue had been built to replace it (*BB*, 3b, *Orah Hayyim* 152:1). However, arrangements could be made that the congregation should rent some building which could be used temporarily as a house of prayer. The rental of this place should be guaranteed fully by legal contract. Furthermore, the sum required to build the new structure must first already be in their possession and earmarked for this purpose, so that there should be no fear that they might fail to construct the new building. If the new building was to be on a different site the demolition should not begin at least until after the new foundation had been laid. Even after the compliance with all those conditions no son of Israel himself should actually participate in the demolition of the synagogue (R. Srada Zvi ben Wolf Tannenbaum, Responsa, *Neta Sorek*, No. 3, Munkatz, 1899). Similar rules were given by the Hatam Sofer (Responsa, *Orah Hayyim*, s. 32; R. Moshe Te'umim, Responsa, *Devar Mosheh*, No. 70; and others).

Separation of the Sexes

Even though according to the basic rabbinic law women maybe called to the congregational reading of the Torah even as one of the statutory seven participants (*shiv'a keru'im*), it was the accepted practice that this should not be done, since the failure to find a man capable of doing so would be an affront to the congregation (*mipenei kevod hatzibur*) (*Orah Hayyim* 282:3).

The separation of the sexes during prayer is a well-established practice in Jewish life from earliest time in order to prevent the arousal of immoral thoughts distracting from one's *kavvanah* – *hirhurei aveira*.

In the Talmud and the traditional codes this law is specified particularly while reciting the *Shema*, and extended also to the prayer of the *Amidah* and the study of Torah. Although women are equally obliged to recite the statutory rubric of the prayers (*Ber.* 20b),[118] men are forbidden to do so while confronted with a woman's immodesty in uncovering her hair, or unduly exposing her body in her dress. Even listening to a woman's singing was prohibited because the enticement of her voice could prompt immoral thoughts (*Ber.* 24a).[119] Some Sages explained that this law applied to women, in general but not to one's wife and children. Caro expressed the prohibition in a guarded manner, stating that even the presence of a hand-breadth of revealed flesh of a woman which according to normal custom would be covered, would give rise to the prohibition of reading the *Shema* (*Orah Hayyim* 75:1, *Be'er Heitev, Mishnah Berurah, ad loc.*). In the exposition of the BAH (Joel Sirkes, Poland, 17th cent., *Bayit Hadash*) the restriction did not refer to such parts of the body which were normally uncovered (*Tur Orah Hayyim* 75, BAH. *ad loc.*).

There are other authoritative scholars who held different views, adopting a more lenient attitude in this matter. In his

---

119 קול באשה ערוה, שער באשה ערוה
120 כאוזא חיוורא

commentary on the *Orah Hayyim* the LEVUSH, a contemporary of Caro and Isserles, objected to the blanket prohibition of the mixing of the sexes as pronounced by the *Sefer Hassidim*, and wrote, but in present social circumstances one may not be so strict in this observance because of the normal frequency of the intermingling of men and women, as, for example, at a marriage celebration, the sight of a woman is not considered unusual and therefore need not raise immoral thoughts, since a man would look on a woman merely as seeing something beautiful "as a white swan" (LEVUSH, *Orah Hayyim* 75:1, *ad loc.*).[120]

In general orthodox practice some adhere to the strictest formulation of the prohibition as described above, while others, generally accept the more liberal interpretation of the law; although in the reading of the statutory prayers the separation of the sexes is always followed.

Hearing Is Like Saying – Shome'a ke-Oneh

Despite the general rule that one should at least frame the words with one's lips, the Sages paradoxically accepted the dictum that listening, even without the appropriate response, might be considered a fulfilment of one's duty of reciting the prayer. Their name for this maxim was "hearing is like saying" (*shome'a ke-oneh*), and the reasoning behind it was that the Rabbis defined the essence of a prayer as the thought in a person's heart and the full attentiveness of the petitioner addressing his words to God.

The classic *Tefillah*, the *Amidah*, is recited in a standing position to emphasize the importance of the words. Scripture records that when, after the sin of Baal Peor, Phinehas begged for the plague afflicting Israel to be halted, he "then stood up and prayed" (Ps. 106:30; *Ber* 6b). [121] One should only worship

---

121   ויעמוד פנחס ויתפלל
122   אין עומדים להתפלל אלא מתוך כובד ראש

God in the proper frame of mind, not when distracted by merriment, worry or anger (*Ber.* 30b; *Oraḥ Ḥayyim* 93:2).[122]

Maimonides begins his treatise on prayer with the statement that praying daily is a Torah injunction: "Ye shall serve the Lord your God" (Ex. 23:25).[123] The Sages linked this command with the exhortation of Moses "to love the Lord your God" (Deut. 11:22)[124] and called for a demonstration of that love by imitating His kindness and mercy.[125] Maimonides quotes the teaching of the Sages who referred to the beginning of the second paragraph of the *Shema* in which God required Israel "to love the Lord your God, and to serve Him with all your heart and with all your soul" (Deut. 11:13).[126]

In view of the specific command, "Ye shall serve the Lord your God" (Ex. 23:25),[127] how (the Sages asked) does one serve Him "with all one's heart"? Moreover, in addition to obeying God's laws, there was a duty to love Him with all one's heart. They explained that this signified the daily obligation to pray to God in one's heart (*Ta'an.* 2a).[128] Naḥmanides rejected the view of Maimonides that the duty to pray was a Torah law, recognizing only the specific laws of the *Shema* and grace after meals. He maintained that the laws governing prayer were an institution of the Sages (*mi-de-Rabbanan*).

Maimonides held that details concerning the *manner* of prayer were laid down by the Sages. Thus, after the destruction of the First Temple and the termination of sacrificial services, Ezra and the Men of the Great Assembly[129] (4th–3th cent. BCE) ruled that the *Amidah* prayer should be recited in place of the daily sacrifices.[130] This practice was alluded to by the prophet Hosea when he called for Israel to repent: "Take with

---

123 ועבדתם את ה' אל-והיכם
124 ואהבת את ה' אל-והיך
125 הוא רחום ואתה תהי רחום, הוא גומל חסדים ואתה גומל חסדים
126 לאהבה את ה' אל-והיכם ולעבדו בכל לבבכם ובכל נפשכם
127 ועבדתם את ה' אל-והיכם
128 איזו היא עבודה שבלב הוי אומר זו תפילה
129 עזרא ואנשי כנסת הגדולה
130 הקרבנות

you words, and return unto the Lord; say unto Him: 'Forgive
all iniquity... and we will render as bullocks the offering of our
lips'" (Hos. 14:2–3).[131]

The Sages also referred to the story of Hannah, who entered
the Sanctuary and prayed for God to bless her with a child:
"Now Hannah spoke in her heart; only her lips moved, but her
voice could not be heard" (1 Sam. 1:13).[132] Eli, the high priest,
assumed that she was drunk, but when Hannah told him that
she had "poured out her soul before the Lord", he asked God
to favour her petition (1 Sam. 1:17). From this R. Hamnuna
deduced that one must pray from the heart with *kavvanah* and
form the words of one's prayer with the lips (*Ber.* 31a).[133]
Such was the procedure followed when the priest sought
guidance from the Urim and Thummim (*Yoma* 73a, Rashi).[134]
Maimonides therefore ruled: "One should not only use the
mind in prayer but frame the words with one's lips, so that
they can be perceived even silently" (Maim. *Tefillah* 5:9).[135]

According to the Scriptural account, Rachel complained
to Jacob that whereas Leah had already given birth to four
children, she herself remained barren. Jacob told her that the
ability to conceive was determined by the Almighty. After
Leah's seventh child was born, God hearkened to Rachel's
prayer and enabled her to conceive.[136] The Torah makes no
actual mention of Rachel's prayer, but God knew, of course,
that the blessing of children was what she craved. The
Aramaic Targums (Onkelos and Yonatan) supply the missing
information: "The Lord hearkened to her prayer and gave
her children" (Gen. 30:22). Rachel prayed inwardly and her
prayer was accepted as an act of Divine worship. Such prayer
was described by the Sages as *avodah she-ba-lev*, "the service

---

131 ונשלמה פרים שפתינו
132 וחנה היא מדברת על לבה, רק שפתיה נעות וקולה לא ישמע
133 מכאן למתפלל שיחתוך בשפתיו
134 יוציא בשפתיו מה הוא שואל
135 ולא יתפלל בלבו אלא מחתך הדברים בשפתיו ומשמיע לאוזניו בלחש
136 ויזכור אלו-הים את רחל וישמע אליה אלו-הים ויפתח את רחמה

of the heart",[137] and this is the sense of their ruling (*Ta'an.* 2a;
Maim. *Tefillah* 1:1).[138]

The Amen Response

The Sages emphasized the importance of making the Amen
response when one heard anyone invoke the Name of God in
a prayer or benediction (Shab. 119b). This response should be
made clearly and audibly. When the kohanim (priests) standing
before the congregation proclaim, "The Lord bless thee and
keep thee...",[139] all the words must be uttered with a loud voice
(*be-kol ram*) and the congregation must respond Amen to each
of the three blessings. A congregant thus includes himself in
the blessing when he says Amen, which means "I believe this
is true" and "May this be His will" (*Ket.* 66b; *Sot.* 39b; Maim.
Tefillah 14:3; Orah Hayyim 127:2, 124:6).[140]

Amen is used in three ways: to confirm an oath, to accept
an instruction and to confirm one's belief. In each instance the
declaration of assent must be clearly expressed. The Sages
affirmed that Israel's Amen response is of inestimable value: "it
prolongs life" (*Ber.* 47a.), "a man's sins will be forgiven" and
"the gates of Paradise will open to him" (Shab. 119b). Through
the Priestly Benediction chanted by the *kohanim* (Num.
6:24–26), God bestows a plentiful blessing on His people, but
that blessing rests only on a person who wishes to receive it
and believes in its efficacy. Each individual must therefore
acknowledge the blessing and proclaim his belief that God's
words are true, a belief expressed in his response of Amen.

We are told that Amen is no less important than the Priestly
Benediction itself or any other prayer to which it responds.
Thus, while interrupting one's silent *Amidah* is in general

---

137   עבודה שבלב
138   איזו היא עבודה שבלב הוי אומר זו תפילה
139   יברכך ה' וישמרך
140   כן יהי רצון

forbidden, responding Amen is permitted and each individual thus receives the blessing (Num. 6:23–27; Deut. R. 7:1). Likewise, after each paragraph of the Kaddish, the reader invites worshippers to respond Amen, thereby identifying themselves with the public glorification of God. However, making the Amen response to a blessing of one's own is obviously pointless, as it would merely repeat the original declaration (*Ber.* 7a; *Orah Hayyim* 124:6).

The Shema – The Name of God and its Significance

Recited every morning and evening, the *Shema* is Israel's historic declaration of faith in God, "Hear, O Israel: the Lord is our God, the Lord is One" (Deut. 6:4; *Ber.* 13b,14a – RV "The Lord our God is one Lord"; Jewish version JPSA. "the Lord God, the Lord is One").[141] When reciting this first verse, Jews bear witness to their faith in the Almighty, who alone created the universe and forever maintains the existence of all His creatures.

The four-letter Divine Name in the Hebrew Bible, YHWH – *Yod-Hei-Vav-Hei* – or "Jehovah", also called the Tetragrammaton, is the personal Name of the God of Israel. He first made Himself known to Moses as "I am that I am" (Ex. 3:14–15, Rashi and Nahmanides *ad loc.*).[142]

Israel addressed Him as their ancestral God, the all-powerful and eternal Ruler of the world. The early Israelites heard the name *Elohim* ("Lord and King") applied to the various heathen deities worshipped in Canaan and used this name also for the true God; the Decalogue, however, proclaimed: "I am the Lord thy God... thou shalt have no other gods before Me" (Ex. 20:2–3, Rashi, Sforno).[143] Israel called the true God by the name of YHWH.

---

141   שמע ישראל ה' אל-הינו ה' אחד
142   אהיה אשר אהיה זה שמי לעולם
143   אנכי ה' אל-היך... לא יהיה לך אל-הים אחרים על פני

The ineffable Divine Name (YHWH) was not articulated indiscriminately. It was pronounced distinctly by the high priest once a year only, on the Day of Atonement, when he recited the Priestly Blessing (Mish., *Yoma* 6:2, *Sot.* 7:6). This sacred Name was also pronounced by specially designated *kohanim* when they gave the Priestly Blessing in the Temple, but this practice ended after the death of Shim'on ha-Tzaddik, Simon the Just (Maim. *Guide* 1:5, 61–62).

The Sages ruled that apart from this special usage, the Name of God was not to be pronounced as it is written, *Yod-Hei-Vav-Hei*, but according to the letters *Aleph-Dalet-Nun-Yod*, pronounced *Adonai* (*Kid.* 71). In everyday use this pronunciation was changed to *Ha-Shem* ("The Name") or, less correctly, *Adoshem*. Other substitutes were *Ha-Kadosh Barukh Hu* ("the Holy One Blessed be He") or, occasionally, *Ha-Shekhinah*, "the Divine Presence" (Mish., *Sanh.* 4:5; *Avot* 3:1–2). It could be that this type of circumlocution results from the stern commandment, "Thou shall not take the name of the Lord thy God in vain", although that law refers specifically to the prohibition of taking a false oath (Ex. 20:7, Sforno and Rashbam *ad loc.*).

While Israel proclaims its faith in the opening sentence of the *Shema*, God declares: "I, the Lord, judge your actions each day, and even when judging you I always display My lovingkindness". This idea is expressed in the benediction recited when giving thanks for deliverance from a life-threatening situation: "Who bestows favours on the guilty [or undeserving]" (*Ber.* 54b; 50a; Maim. *Yad* 10:8; *Tur*, *Orah Hayyim* 5:219, *Bet Yosef*). The decrees of Providence we accept as being ultimately for our benefit. Such optimism is reflected in the dictum of R. Akiva: "One should always say that whatever God does, He does for our own good" (*Ber.* 60b).[144]

According to rabbinic tradition, *Hashem* denotes God in His attribute of mercy while *Elohim* does so in His attribute of

לעולם יהא אדם רגיל לומר כל דעביד רחמנא לטב עביד   144

judgment (Gen. R. 33; Ex. R. 3; cf. *Encyclopaedia Judaica*, 7:684). Both Names are used in the *Shema* declaration, "The Lord our God"[145] asserting that the One who judges our thoughts and actions is also the One who exercises love and mercy. These are not twin powers, one creating good and the other fomenting evil. The Lord is One, no matter what providence holds in store for us (*Ber.* 13b;14a).

Scripture relates that Abraham, after his battle with the four kings, was welcomed by Melchizedek, the king of Salem (Jerusalem), with bread and wine. Melchizedek was known as "a priest of God the Most High" (*El Elyon*), and the expression "Most High" is taken to mean "the God above all other gods" (Gen. 14:18, Nahmanides *ad loc.*).[146]

The expression El Elohim is usually interpreted as "the most mighty of the gods". Joshua records that the tribe of Reuben assured Moses of their readiness to participate in Israel's battles, declaring that "God, the Lord of gods, knoweth the honesty of their intentions" (Josh. 22:22, RV). The modern Jewish version reads: "God, the mighty One" or simply "God, the Lord, knoweth" (ibid., Jewish Publication Society of America text, Philadelphia, 1917).

The giving of the Ten Commandments on Mount Sinai clearly showed the difference between heathen gods and the Almighty. His first injunction to the people of Israel was "Thou shalt have no other gods before Me".[147] Rabbinic theology negated any use of the term "god" to denote the wood or stone idols of paganism. The Sages therefore had a completely different interpretation of the verse, "Who is like Thee among the gods?" They considered the word elim ("the mighty") a reference to the mighty forces of nature, which are nothing more than the creations of God which serve as His messengers. The Jewish (JPSA) translation of Ex. 15:11 thus reads as follows: "Who is like unto Thee, O Lord, among the mighty?"

---

145   ה׳ אל-הנו

146   כהן לאל עליון

147   לא יהיה לך אל-הים אחרים על פני

The term *Elohim*, meaning a supreme authority, is also used
to denote the judges in a rabbinical court. Thus, while one
of the Psalms apparently declares that "God standeth in the
congregation of God; He judgeth among the gods" (Ps. 82:1,
RV),[148] the Jewish (JPSA) version reads: "In the midst of the
judges He judgeth". All the Rabbinic commentators view this
Psalm as a reminder that Israel's judges are in duty–bound to
execute justice without fear or favour. When they sit in a court
of law, the Almighty is present among them; alternatively,
God sits in His heavenly court and expects mortal judges
to discharge their obligation and enforce judgment.[149] The
Psalmist adds: "How long will ye judge unjustly, and respect
the persons of the wicked?" (Ps. 82:2).

Sincerity and attentiveness in prayer (*kavvanah*) are
demanded in the *Shema Yisrael* declaration's opening words.
The word *Shema* has various nuances. It can mean "listen to
the command in order to obey" or "pay thoughtful attention" as
well as "understand". By listening, a person understands what
is being said and grasps its significance. Such understanding
is a process of thought and an act of the mind. The sincerity
of one's prayer is also a mental process, set in motion when
the words of a prayer are heard. By registering those words in
his mind and repeating them in his own thoughts, the hearer
is likewise engaged in the act of prayer. Speech is only one
sign of a decision reached in the mind; what really matters is
a person's assent to the act.

The *Shema* comprises three Torah passages (Deut. 6:4–8;
11:13–21; Num.15:37–41) that should be read daily, in the
morning and at night, with great devotion and with "fear and
trembling".[150] The first verse especially, "Hear, O Israel", must
be read with the deepest *kavvanah*; otherwise, the *mitzvah* of
reciting the *Shema* has not been fulfilled (*Ber.* 14b; Maim.
Keri'at Shema 2:1; *Orah Hayyim* 60:5, 61:1).

---

148   בקרב אל-הים ישפוט
149   ניצב בתוך פמליא של מעל
150   באימה ובידאה ברטט בזועה

Early halakhic authorities considered whether the *shome'a ke-oneh* rule applied to reciting the *Shema*. *Magen Avraham*, a commentary on the *Shulḥan Arukh*, quotes the view that hearing the *Shema* read by someone else fulfils one's obligation. Abudarham, however, insisted that each person must recite the *Shema* by himself, since the Torah law is worded in the singular: "And thou shalt speak of them" – *Ve-dibbarta bam* (Deut. 6:7; *Oraḥ Ḥayyim* 61:26, *Magen Avraham* 16). Another ruling, opposed to the view of Caro, states that *shome'a ke-oneh* applies to every law of the Torah, including the reading of the *Shema* (R. Ḥizkiyyahu ben David de Silva, *Peri Ḥadash*).

The Amidah

An instructive example of this maxim can be found in the rubric instituted by the Men of the Great Assembly,[151] requiring the congregational Reader to repeat the entire *Amidah* aloud (*Ber.* 60b). Anyone incapable of reciting the prayer in Hebrew could thus fulfil his obligation by listening attentively and following the words of the Reader. His affirmation of that prayer would normally be indicated by the appropriate response. However, when a question was asked in the rabbinic academy as to what law would apply if someone listening to the Reader failed to make a response, R. Ḥiyya bar Abba gave the following answer. The *amoraim* (early Sages) who expounded the law had ruled that someone who heard the prayer without responding had nevertheless fulfilled his obligation.[152] This ruling accorded with the principle of *shome'a ke-oneh* (*Suk.* 38b).

Hallel

This teaching was further illustrated by the congregational

---

151   אנשי כנסת הגדולה
152   שמע ולא ענה מה הוא אומר להוא חכימיא וספריא ורישיה עמא ודרשיה אמרו
שמע ולא ענה יצא

responses made during the recital of *Hallel* (Ps. 113–118). After each psalm of praise is chanted by the prayer leader, congregants respond with "Hallelujah" and repeat certain verses or phrases. However, the Sages ruled that even if a person listened silently to the Reader, "hearing" the recital of *Hallel* would count as that person's response (*Suk.* 38b), but he would need to do more. Unless he gave his undivided attention to the prayer leader's recital, he would not have fulfilled his religious duty (*Tur, Orah Hayyim* 124:1, 4).[153]

If the worshipper was reciting a prayer that may not be interrupted (such as the *Shema* or the *Amidah*), he would not have to make the Amen response but need only listen to discharge his obligation. This ruling conformed with the principle of *shome'a ke-oneh*. Similarly, one who lacked knowledge of the statutory prayers could listen attentively without even making the prescribed response (*Ber.* 21b). Such was the ruling of Rashi, although the Tosafists (who disagreed with him) engaged in a classical type of debate over this issue (Suk. 38b, Rashi s.v. "*hu omer barukh*"; *Ber.* 21b, *Tos.* s.v. "*ad*"; Hai Gaon, *Tefillah* 92).

The Mishnah records the view of R. Yehudah that a person who was ritually unclean, and thus forbidden to voice anything sacred, could recite the words of the *Shema* in his mind.[154] Ravina observed that while prayers should really be said with one's lips, this ruling indicated that saying them mentally could be equivalent to saying them aloud, and on that basis he formulated the principle that "thinking is like speaking" (*Ber.* 20b).[155]

There is a subtle difference between the opinions of Rashi and the Tosafists regarding the efficacy of "listening" in the *shome'a ke-oneh* process. In Rashi's view, "listening" is equivalent to "speaking" and, by directing his thoughts to the prayer that he hears (*meharher be-kavvanah*), a person fulfils

---

153 צריך לכוון לכל מה שאמר השליח צבור מראש ועד סוף ואינו מפסיק
154 בעל קרי מהרהר בלבו
155 אמר רבינא זאת אומרת הרהור הדבור דמי יוצא בשפתיו

his own obligation through the words of the reader and his own *hirhur*, even without responding himself. Rashi maintained that the act of *hirhur* did not constitute an interruption of one's prayers, because "hearing" is another way of "speaking" – *shome'a ke-oneh*. The Tosafists, however, argued that if this were the case – and by "listening" one was considered to be reciting the prayer and thus fulfilling the duty to pray – then doing so in the midst of his own prayer would constitute an interruption (R. Yehezkel Landau, *Tziyyun le-Nefesh Hayyah* [TZELAH], Prague, 1793, on *Ber.* 21b). R. Hai Gaon's ruling was similar to Rashi's, on the basis of *shome'a ke-oneh* (Hai Gaon, *Laws of Tefillah*, 92; *Ber.* 21b, Rabbenu Yonah).

Later Rabbinic authorities applied the rule of *shome'a ke-oneh* to hearing someone recite *Kiddush* at the beginning of a festive meal or read the *Megillah* in synagogue on Purim, as well as to hearing *kohanim* chant the Priestly Benediction. All these authorities accepted the general principle of *shome'a ke-oneh* (*Orah Hayyim* 104:7; Hazon Ish, *Orah Hayyim* 29:3). However, the commentary of R. Yitzhak Ibn Ghayyat maintained that since the hearer is passive and the reader performs the duty for him,[156] he is thus exempt from even making his own response. This would likewise apply when someone heard the Reader counting the Omer aloud in synagogue.[157]

Different viewpoints were similarly expressed as to whether "contemplating" was equivalent to "speaking" (*hirhur ke-oneh*) or "writing" to "speaking" (*ketivah ke-dibbur*). If they were, such actions would constitute an interruption of one's statutory prayer and would therefore be prohibited. The insertion of *piyyutim* (liturgical poems), even in the festival *Amidah*, became prevalent in some communities and gained acceptance in certain rites, despite strenuous objections to this "intrusive" practice. R. Moshe Isserles (Cracow, 1572) declared, however, that reciting these *piyyutim* was lawful and that studying Torah

---

156   השליח צבור פוטרו
157   השליח צבור פוטרו ממצוות האומר

by "contemplating" a written text (*hirhur*) was not forbidden, since one did not rule according to the principle of *hirhur ke-dibbur* (*RH* 34b; *Orah Hayyim* 28:1, REMA).

Kiddush

Differing interpretations of the *shome'a ke-oneh* principle also affect the recital of *Kiddush*. It is a Torah law that one must hallow the Sabbath day by reciting *Kiddush* at the table on Friday night. This law is based on the Fourth Commandment, "Remember the Sabbath day, to keep it holy" (Ex. 20:8).[158] The Sages received the tradition that the Hebrew word *zakhor* ("remember")[159] indicates that one "calls the Sabbath to mind" or "makes mention of it" by pronouncing a special benediction. This, they ruled, takes the form of a sanctification (*Kiddush*) recited over a cup of wine (*Pes.* 106a; Maim. *Shabbat* 20:1; *Tur, Orah Hayyim* 269:1, 271:1–2).

One person may recite *Kiddush* on behalf of all seated at the table, and it is usually the head of the household or the senior participant who does so. He should always bear in mind that he is acting on behalf of the others present (*Orah Hayyim* 269:1; 271:2, *Mishnah Berurah* 5:1; 273:3, 4, 6).

According to one opinion, when a man recites *Kiddush* and those present listen silently, each listener is credited with having recited it himself since "hearing is a form of speaking" (R. Yosef Baer Soloveichik, Responsa *Bet ha-Levi*).[160] According to the Hazon Ish, however, *shome'a* is not an actual form of *dibbur*: the person who recites *Kiddush* does so on behalf of everyone else, which means that they are exempted from doing so themselves.[161]

Some authorities required the other participants to be more actively involved, and to hold their own cup of wine while

---

158 זכור את יום השבת לקדשו
159 זכר
160 שומע כדיבור דמי
161 המברך פוטר את חברו השומע

listening to the recital of *Kiddush* (*Orah Hayyim* 295:1, *Birkei Yosef* 295:5); this, however, is not the general practice (*Hayyei Adam, Shabbat* 6:4, 6).

Counting the Omer – Sefirat ha-Omer

Torah law required that on the day after the first day of Passover each Israelite should bring to the Temple an offering of the first sheaf of barley, known as the *Omer*. With the prescribed blessing one should then count 49 days, a total of seven weeks, culminating on the 50th day in Shavu'ot, the Feast of Weeks (Lev. 23:15-16).[162]

While counting the 50 years towards the Jubilee was undertaken by the Great *Bet Din* or Sanhedrin, counting the Omer was the responsibility of each individual Jew (*Men.* 65b, Rashi *ad loc.*; Maim. *Temidin u-Musafin* 7:11, 22, 24; *Sefer ha-Hinnukh* 306).[163]

Although it is a mitzvah for each individual to count the days,[164] Caro (following RASHBA) determined that a person could fulfil his duty by listening attentively while someone else made the benediction and counted for him. This ruling accorded with the principle of shome'a ke-oneh, i.e., "listening" is itself a form of "saying". As the purpose of counting is to register in one's mind the progress of days following the first day of the Passover towards Shavu'ot, some authorities declare that even writing the number of the days fulfils one's obligation (Tur, *Orah Hayyim* 489:1, *Bet Yosef, Magen Avraham* 2; R. Akiva Eger, Responsa nos. 31–32).

The Shofar

Rosh ha-Shanah is known as *Yom ha-Din*, the Day of

---

162 וספרתם לכם ממחרת השבת
163 שתהי ספירה לכל אחד ואחד
164 מצוה על כל אחד לספור לעצמו

Judgment,[165] when the life of every human being is judged by the Almighty. The *shofar* (ram's horn) is sounded on Rosh Ha-Shanah in order for its piercing blasts to inspire awe and humility in the listeners as they are made aware of being being summoned to judgment in the heavenly court (*RH* 16b, 26a–b; Maim. *Teshuvah* 3:3–4; R. Saadiah Gaon, as quoted by Abudarham; *Tur*, *Ora*ḥ *Hayyim* 585).

The duty to sound the *shofar* is ordained in the Torah, where Rosh Ha-Shanah, the Jewish New Year, is described as "a day of sounding the *shofar*" (Num. 29:1; TJ *RH* 4:8) and as "a memorial proclaimed with the *shofar* blast" (Lev. 23:24; *Tur*, *Ora*ḥ *Hayyim* 585, *Bet Yosef*).[166]

As is the case with all *mitzvot*, a prescribed blessing is made before the action. In this instance, however, the blessing mentions one's duty not "to sound" but "to hear the sound of the *shofar*".[167] The Sages explained that the purpose of the *mitzvah* is to *hear* and be moved by the sound of the ram's horn: the "sounding" is only the means whereby the *shofar* is heard.[168] There is no need to avail oneself of the *shome'a ke-oneh* principle, since the entire *mitzvah* is an act of hearing.[169]

The blessing recited gives thanks to the Almighty for the duty to hear the *shofar* and for the privilege of now fulfilling that duty. It is recited either by the *toke'a* who blows the *shofar*, without which the *mitzvah* cannot be fulfilled ("hearing" is its completion – *gemar mitzvah*), or by the listener standing next to him. One who blows the *shofar* and hears the sound fulfils his own duty; and, provided that it is his intention to do so (*be-khavvanah*), he also discharges those who listen with the express purpose of thus fulfilling their own duty to "hear" the *shofar*.[170] One who intends to discharge a fellow Jew[171] is

---

165 יום הדין
166 זכרון תרועה
167 לשמוע קול שופר
168 לא בתקיעה תליא מילתא
169 שומע בשמיעה תליא מילתא ולא בתקיעה
170 מוציא ויוצא
171 מוציא

himself required to fulfil the law of "hearing the *shofar*".[172]
Thus, if he directs his *shofar* blast into a pit, the sound that he
hears may not be that of the *shofar* itself but simply an echo,
and therefore his own duty will not have been fulfilled (*RH*
27a–b; *Tur, Orah Hayyim* 587:1, *Bet Yosef*, Bah). If the *shofar*
"blower"[173] has already fulfilled his own duty,[174] he is then
able to act on behalf of his "listener".[175]

If the toke'a is not a learned man and, though capable of
blowing the required sounds, does not know how to make
the appropriate blessing, another worshipper may recite it
both for him and for those listening to the shofar (Ber. 45b).
Congregants normally listen to the Reader and say Amen;
but even if they only "listen" in order to fulfil their mitzvah,
they have done their duty because of shome'a *ke-oneh* (*Orah
Hayyim* 594, *Bet Yosef*).

[General Reference: *Encyclopedia Talmudica,* Vol. 4, p.
309 *s.v. 'letotzi et haveiro'*]

A Superfluous Blessing – Berakhah le-Vattalah

The Name of the Lord, being sacred, is only pronounced in
formal worship. Maimonides declared that "whoever recites
a superfluous blessing (*berakhah le-vattalah*) has violated the
prohibition against taking God's Name in vain".[176] This was
considered as grave an offence as swearing a false oath, and
giving the Amen response to such a blessing was forbidden (Ex.
20:7; *Ber.* 33a; Maim. *Berakhot* 1:15; *Orah Hayyim* 215:4).

This prohibition is also based on a positive commandment
(*azharat aseh*): "Thou shalt fear the Lord thy God; and Him
shalt thou serve, and by His Name shalt thou swear" (Deut.
6:13).[177] Reverence for the holiness of God compels us to

---

172 יוצא
173 התוקע
174 יוצא
175 להוציא את חברו
176 כל המברך ברכה שאינה צריכה הרי זה נושא שם שמים לשוא
177 את ה' אל-היך תירא ואתו תעבד ובשמו תשבע

abstain from invoking His Name in an unprescribed blessing, the needless repetition of a prayer, an emphatic remark or, worse still, an expletive used in daily speech (Maim. *Shevu'ot* 12:9). Except when praying, the observant Jew uses substitutes such as *Hashem* (properly *Ha-Shem*, "the Name"), *Adoshem* (an acronym of *Ado-nai* and *Ha-Shem*) or *Elokim*. Any written text including the Divine Name must be treated respectfully and never discarded as refuse matter, but if no longer usable reverently interred (*Yoreh De'ah* 282:10).

Since Jewish tradition considers bareheadedness disrespectful, it has become the standard practice of the Jews to cover one's head during the day, especially when mentioning God's Name in prayers and benedictions, when studying holy lore or on entering a synagogue (*Orah Hayyim* 91:3). By wearing a hat or skull cap (*kippah*), the Jew acknowledges that he is in the presence of God and indicates his submission to a Higher Authority. The arrogant belief that he may substitute his own wishes for those of God leads man to sin; it is only by pursuing higher spiritual ideals that such transgression can be avoided.[178]

The sanctity attached to a blessing which includes the Name of God is so great that its recital is prohibited if it is not required by statutory law (*Ber.* 12a, 33a) and has not been ordained by one of the Sages (*Sot.* 41a, *Ber.* 40a).[179] An unprescribed benediction, however well-intentioned, is therefore condemned as a superfluous blessing (*berakhah le-vattalah*). In the view of one authority, repeating a prayer that was recited without due attention (*beli kavvanah*) might also be questionable and could turn it into a *berakhah le-vattalah* (Vilna Gaon, *Siddur ha-GRA*, appendix to *Orhot Hayyim* 31). Although one should endeavour to recite 100 blessings daily (*Men.* 43b; *Orah Hayyim* 46:3),[180] it is preferable to make one comprehensive *berakhah* and avoid repeating the Divine Name (*Ber.* 40a).

---

178 את ה׳ אל-והיך תירא
179 אין מברכין ברכה שאינה צריכה
180 מאה ברכות

When someone makes a prescribed blessing with the intention that someone listening closely to it will be regarded as having fulfilled the same obligation, the reciter must have the particular hearer or hearers in mind.[181] The hearer must likewise have every intention of participating in the *mitzvah* (*kavvanah la-tzet*). This kind of dual purpose, involving both the active (*motzi*) worshipper and the passive (*yotzei*) one, characterizes *mitzvot* such as blowing the *shofar*, reading the Torah or *Megillah* and reciting *Kiddush*.

However, because one must avoid making a superfluous benediction (*Ein mevarekhim berakhah she-einah tzerikhah*), a problem would arise if someone felt that he was not "covered" by the reciter's benediction. When reciting *Kiddush* over wine, for example, the head of the household makes this blessing with the express intention of absolving others present from the same duty (*Ber.* 45b–46a). Should one person who heard *Kiddush* nevertheless decide to recite it himself, some authorities would consider this a *berakhah le-vattalah* and that person would need to join a second table where he could recite his blessing afresh.

In a case of uncertainty as to whether a statutory prayer has been read in the prescribed manner, it should not be repeated, as that would involve a needless invocation of the Divine Name.[182] Since all the statutory blessings were formulated by the Sages, when in doubt one should take a lenient view and assume that the duty has been fulfilled.[183] This principle governs all laws instituted by the Rabbis (*Shab.* 34a; *Betzah* 3b).[184] Even the most pious individuals can sometimes be mistaken or forgetful: it is said that R. Yosef ben Meir Teomim (18th cent.) kept a record of whatever distracted him from his prayers, so as to avoid repeating them (*Peri Megadim, Orah Hayyim* 137:4, 140:4).

---

181   כונה להוציא
182   ברכה לבטלה
183   ספק ברכות לקולא
184   ספק דרבנן להקל

If, after reciting *Barukh attah Hashem* ("Blessed art Thou, O Lord"), a person realizes that he meant to say the wrong benediction, he should add *Lammedeni hukkekha* ("Teach me Thy statutes") to the opening words. This completes a scriptural verse (Ps. 119:12), the reading of which constitutes Bible study on which there are no restrictions (*Orah Hayyim* 206:6; *Eshel Avraham* 47:5). In daily prayer, especially at the end of the *Amidah*, we repeatedly beg the Almighty to hear what we really meant to say apart from whatever we said: "May the words of my mouth and the thoughts in my heart be acceptable before Thee" (Ps. 19:15).[185]

The *Amidah* was instituted as a replacement for the daily sacrifices offered in the Temple. Complete devotion is therefore required in its recital, just as meticulous care was taken in the Temple service (*Ber.* 30b; *Orah Hayyim* 98:1, 4). Accordingly, because of its central importance in daily worship, if by error or accident one statutory *Amidah* is not recited, the omission maybe repaired by repeating the *Amidah* in the following statutory service (*Ber.* 26b; *Orah Hayyim* 108:1).[186]

If, before praying, someone is not sure whether he had washed his hands or recited the prescribed benediction, he should repeat the action but not the blessing, in accordance with the lenient (*safek berakhot le-kulla*) rule. Even if he realizes that he has not performed his morning ablutions, he should wash his hands but not repeat his prayers (*Orah Hayyim* 41:1, 92:4; *Mishnah Berurah* 13).

[General Reference: *Encyclopedia Talmuica,* Vol. 4, p. 280–285 *s.v. 'berakhah she'eina tzerikhah'*]

The Sheheheyanu Benediction

An exception is made in the case of the *Sheheheyanu* benediction recited when one enjoys some benefit for the first time. It concludes with the words, "Who has kept us alive,

---

185   יהיו לרצון אמרי פי והגיון לבי לפניך
186   תפלה לתשלום

sustained us and enabled us to reach this season".[187] Known also as *birkat ha-zeman,* this blessing is recited on acquiring a new house or moving into a new home (when it is added to the benediction on affixing a *mezuzah*); before wearing a new item of clothing; and on first tasting new seasonal fruits, when it is added to the statutory blessing for fruit of a tree (*Ber.* 58b; Maim. *Berakhot* 10:1–2; *Orah Hayyim* 225:1, 3, *Mishnah Berurah ad loc.*).[188]

The *Sheheheyanu* benediction is an acknowledgment of God's goodness[189] rather than a mandatory blessing. Because of its discretionary status and weaker sanction, anyone who is not sure if he recited this blessing at the appropriate time may repeat it without fear of its constituting a *berakhah le-vattalah.*[190]

In some Jewish communities it is normal practice for a bridegroom standing under the *huppah* (marriage canopy) to don a new *tallit* with the prescribed blessing and to recite *Sheheheyanu* in thanksgiving (*Orah Hayyim* 8:15, *Ba'er Heitev* 18; *Sedei Hemed: Asifat Dinim, Berakhot* 1:18, 2:5; *Orah Hayyim* 225:1, 4). Some authorities maintain that if he cannot tell whether he has recited *Sheheheyanu*, he may repeat the blessing with a declaration to the effect that if he has not previously said it, this recital will fulfil his obligation; but if he has already said it, this will be an optional, voluntary prayer (*Birkei Yosef, Orah Hayyim* 11:29).[191]

[General Reference: *Encyclopedia Talmudica*, Vol. 4, pp. 431–451 *s.v. 'birikat hazeman'*]

A Voluntary Compensatory Prayer –
Tefillat Nedavah

Since the duty to read the *Shema* is ordained by Torah law,

---

187   שהחיינו וקיימנו והגיענו לזמן הזה
188   הבונה בית חדש או כלים חדשים או בגדים חדשים
189   שבח והודאה להקב״ה
190   ברכה לבטלה
191   לשם חובה או לנדבה

someone who is not sure if he had recited *keri'at Shema* is obliged to repeat it. If he has a similar doubt regarding the *Amidah*, the Sages differed as to his proper course of action. R. Elazar maintained that he should not repeat it,[192] but R. Yoḥanan declared that there is no objection to his doing so, as it would surely be commendable for a man to spend the whole day in prayer (*Ber.* 21a., Rashi).

The early code *Halakhot Gedolot* ruled like R. Yoḥanan in the case of such a doubt. R. Yosef Caro also affirmed that he may repeat the *Amidah*, which would be considered a voluntary, non-statutory prayer.[193] Caro stipulated, however, that he may do so only if he is certain that he can recite it with full *kavvanah*; otherwise, his additional prayer will offend the Almighty (*Oraḥ Ḥayyim* 107:1, 4).

According to a later work, R. Avraham Danzig's *Ḥayyei Adam* (1810), modern conditions are unfavourable to maintaining the reading of the prayer with *kavvanah*, since not even one person in a thousand will find it possible to concentrate on every word from start to finish. The rule allowing a worshipper to repeat his *Amidah* is therefore not practicable. Other halakhic authorities, such as the Vilna Gaon (in a supplement to his *Siddur*) and R. Shelomo Ganzfried (in his abridged *Kitzur Shulḥan Arukh* 21:20), concur with this view (*Ḥayyei Adam* 27:17; *Nishmat Adam* 24:21, p. 228, note 11).

Prayer and Study

Before beginning the daily Morning Prayers it is customary to affirm one's determination to fulfil the *mitzvah* of "loving thy neighbour as thyself" (Lev. 19:18; Ari, *Siddur Ya'avetz, Otzar ha-Tefillot, Iyyun Tefillah*).[194]

Following the initial Thanksgivings for the gift and study

---

192 ספק התפלל ספק לא התפלל אינו חוזר ומתפלל
193 תפלת נדבה
194 ואהבת לרעך כמוך

of Torah, a passage from the Talmud is quoted (*Shab.* 127a), listing religious and ethical duties for the performance of which a man is rewarded "in this world and in the World to Come".[195] Such duties include showing respect for one's father and mother, acting charitably, attending synagogue services, offering hospitality, visiting the sick, contributing to the requirements of a bride and honouring the dead. The Mishnaic Sages, however, emphasized the importance of Torah study, which they described as "equal to all the rest". The duty of Torah study is foremost among all other religious duties because it motivates the fulfilment of the entire Torah way of life (*Pe'ah* 1:1; *Ber.*11b; *Kid.* 39b-40a; *Uk.* 3:12; *Zev.* 5a; Abudarham, *Seder Rav Amram Gaon* and *Sh. Ar.*, *Orah Hayyim*; Maim. *Yad*, *Avelim* 14).[196]

The accompanying summation of the overriding value of Torah study indicated that there maybe circumstances (e.g., old age or injury) where a man is no longer capable of performing these social and religious duties, but where Torah study at least may still be possible. The fulfilment of this *mitzvah* then compensates for the non-fulfilment of others.

Whereas most commandments have prescribed measures governing their fulfilment, Torah study has no limitation,[197] as God admonished Joshua after the death of Moses: "This book of the Torah shall not depart out of thy mouth, but thou shalt meditate therein day and night" (Josh. 1:8).[198] A constant awareness of the Torah in one's thoughts will ensure its continuous fulfilment. The Sages taught that a minimum fulfilment of this law requires studying at least one passage of Torah, Mishnah and Talmud respectively.

These three passages, read daily after the blessings for Torah, comprise the Priestly Benediction (Num. 6:24–26), an extract from the Mishnah (*Pe'ah* 1:1)[199] and the Talmud's

---

195 אלו דברים שאדם אוכל פרותיהם בעולם הזה והקרן קימת לו לעולם הבא
196 ותלמוד תורה כנגד כולם
197 אין להם שיעור
198 והגית בו יומם ולילה
199 ואלו דברים

enumeration of a man's duties (*Shab.* 127a). According to the Rabbis, one's daily study should be allocated as follows: one third Torah, one third Mishnah and one third Gemara (*Kid.* 30a, *Tos.* s.v. "*lo tzerikha*"; *Seder Rav Amram Gaon*; *Siddur Ya'avetz*; *Siddur Tzelota de-Avraham*, ed. Y. Werdiger).[200]

In the moralist teaching of Luzzatto it is stated, "It is our duty to consider what was the intention in the 'mind' of the Almighty in His creation of man, even though it is not possible for man to fathom the thoughts of the Almighty, as the Psalmist declared, "How great are thy works, O Lord! Thy thoughts are very deep" (Ps. 92:5).[201] Our only approach to this understanding is by the study of Torah teaching which had been Divinely revealed to man (Luzzatto, *Mesillat Yesharim*, Appendix, *Dereh Eitz Hayyim*).

Maimonides wrote: The true worship of God is only possible when correct notions of Him have previously been conceived (Maim. *Guide* 3:51). However Torah study even without being an act of religious devotion (*shelo lishemah*) should nevertheless be pursued even if it is simply for knowledge's sake, albeit without any intention of being an act of worship. By the act of carrying out the prescribed religious practices and repeating them continually one may eventually, through force of habit, attain a state of human perfection of loving reverence of God (Maim. *Guide* 3:51, 52).

The paramount importance of "learning Torah" is illustrated in the Rabbinic law: "If while one was engaged in Torah study there arose some duty to perform a good deed to a fellow (*mitzvah*), he should continue with his study without interruption, if there was someone else available who could just as well perform it" (*Kid.* 40a; Maim. *Talmud Torah* 3:3, 4).

Although generally we are told to follow the axiom: Whenever one finds the opportunity of performing a *mitzvah* one should do so immediately and one should not delay it (Ex. 12:17, *Mekhilta, ibid.*), but the study of Torah took preference

---

200   לעולם ישלש אדם שנותיו שליש במקרא, שליש במשנה, ושליש בגמרא

201   מה גדלו מעשיך ה' מאד עמקו מחשבתיך

over other opportunities of Divine service. The Sages praised
the virtuous conduct that those who are zealous in their religious
duty do a *mitzvah* as soon as possible (*Pes.* 4a). Zealousness in
fulfilling one's religious duties arises from his deep devotion
to God which overpowers any physical constraint of desire
(Luzzatto, *Mesillat Yesharim*, Ch.7, "*zerizut*").

Above all these religious exhortations the Sages attributed
paramount importance to the duty of Torah Study since such
spiritual love of the Almighty embraced all the forms of
worship.

The study of Torah was always considered an essential
"Divine worship" (*avodat Hashem*), equivalent to daily
prayer. The duty of studying Torah daily, based on the
Torah obligation, "Thou shall teach them to thy children"
(Deut. 6:7),[202] is considered as important as the fulfilment
of all the duties prescribed in the Torah, preceding that of
the construction of the Sanctuary and the Temple sacrificial
service (*Meg.* 3a; 16b; *Eruv.* 63b; *Shuḥan Arukh, Yoreh De'ah*
246; *Ha-ḥinukh,* sect. 419). *Talmud Torah* was traditionally
done with a melody which the individual found to be an
aide to *kavvanah*. Biblical books were read with a specified
cantillation, and the study of the Oral Law was always
accompanied by some soul inspiring melody which energized
the student in his thoughtful devotion to what he was studying.
It is related in the Tosefta that R. Akiva enjoined his students,
"sing it, constantly sing"[203] (*Tosefta Oḥalot* 16:8; *San.* 99a–b).
The passages studied in the Oral Law are still read in melodic
phrases, sometimes following attractive well known melodies
or merely personally inventive rhythms. The Talmud states
that R. Yoḥanan went so far as to say: "He who reads without
melody and studies without a tune is criticized by the prophet
as though he considered his learning as if the Almighty gave
laws that are not good" (Ezek. 20:25; *Meg.* 32a).[204] The

---

202 ושננתם לבנך
203 זמר בתדירה זמר
204 כל הקורא בלא נעימה ושונה בלא זמרה עליו הכתוב אומר וגם אני נתתי להם
חוקים לא טובים

"learning melodies" were also applied to the study of oral commentary and discussion (Abraham Zvi Idelsohn, Vienna, Melodien, 1932, Vol. 8 preface XVII, quotes Isaiah Hurzitz *Shenei Luḥot ha-Berit,* fol. 256b).

Chief Rabbi J.H. Hertz declared in one of his Jews' College Seminary Addresses: "Study of the Law constituted Divine worship. Apart from the direct intercourse of prayer, study of the Torah was to the Rabbis the way of closest approach to God; in Kepler's phrase, 'thinking God's thoughts after Him'. Here, indeed, we have something new under the sun – the formulation of the ennobling ideal of learning for its own sake (*lishemah*) constituting a 'variety of religious experience' for which one may look in vain among any other people" (J.H. Hertz: *Sermons, Addresses and Studies* Vol. 2, *Addresses*, pp. 45, 46, Soncino, London, 1938).

When the Sages discussed the order of importance of the religious duty of Torah study the question was asked, "Which is greater, study or practice?" R. Tarfon replied, "Practice is greater". R. Akiva replied, "Study is greater for it leads to practice". The Elders then all concluded, "Study is greater for it leads to practice" (*Kid.* 40b).[205]

Torah study should always be engaged in as a form of worship rather than simply an intellectual pursuit. In the closing chapter of the *Ethics of Our Fathers,* R. Meir taught, "Whoever occupies himself with Torah study for the pure purpose as a form of worship merits the reward of many things, and furthermore the entire world is indebted to him". The ideal attitude in Torah study is that it is conducted "for its own sake" (*Torah lishemah*), and not for some personal ulterior motive. In another Talmudic statement, however, R. Yehuda taught: "By all means let a man engage in the study of Torah and in the practice of good deeds, even if not for their own sake; eventually he will arrive at the stage of doing good for unselfish purposes" (*Pes.* 50b).[206] Maimonides explained

205   לימוד גדול שהתלמוד מביא לידי מעשה
206   שמתוך שלא לשמה בא לשמה

that even when he studies without the purest motive, by accustoming himself to study as a habit he will eventually attain the ideal of doing so as pure worship of the Almighty.

Torah study was always an essential mode of worship. The communal house of learning (*bet ha-midrash*) usually serves the double function of study and prayer, and is considered of greater religious importance than the House of Prayer (*Bet Tefillah*). The Sages ruled that in the absence of a *Bet Midrash* in a community, a *Bet ha-Kenesset* maybe changed into a *Bet Midrash* but not vice versa (*Meg.* 27a).[207]. The Sages considered the apparent repetition in the Torah verse describing the observance of the Divine covenant with Israel: "If ye walk in my statutes, and keep my commandments, and do them". They expounded the additional expression, "if ye walk in my statutes", to mean that you should always occupy yourselves in Torah study (Lev. 26:3, *Torat Kohanim, ibid.,* Rashi).[208] The daily early morning prayers express our blessing to the Almighty for the privilege of giving us the duty to study Torah (*Meg.* 19b, TUR, *Oraḥ Ḥayim,* 47).[209]. In this form of worship the Almighty finds delight as we thereby unite our souls with the spirit of God. The Revelation on Mt. Sinai is continually renewed as we delve into the meaning of all His laws.

The daily *Amidah (Shemoneh Esreh)* concludes with a prayer for the Almighty to grant Israel peace, the greatest of all bounties, which includes the blessings of life, grace, happiness, mercy, lovingkindness and Torah knowledge.[210] This prayer, *Sim Shalom*, refers to the blessings of peace as the absence of war, but it also has a wider significance: friendship and harmony among the people of Israel themselves. The Sephardi rubric, following the practice of the ARI, associates this prayer with the study of Torah. As R. Elazar said in the name of R. Ḥanina: "Torah scholars increase peace in the world [through their study]"; and as the Psalmist declared: "The Lord will

207   בית הכנסת מותר לעשותו בית המדרש
208   אם בחקתי תלכו...שתהיו עמלים בתורה
209   אשר קדשנו במצוותיו וצוונו לעסוק בדברי תורה
210   שים שלום

give strength unto His people; the Lord will bless His people with peace" (*Ber.* 64a; Ps. 29:11). Targum Onkelos renders this verse (Ps. 29:11): "The Lord will give Torah to His people; the Lord will bless His people with peace". In the Lurianic rite (*nussah Ari*) the closing blessing of the Amidah prayer for peace the words are added "with abundance of strength and peace" (*berov oz ve-shalom*), which is understood to mean a prayer that we maybe granted great knowledge of Torah (*oz*) and inner harmony (*shalom*).

The plain text of the prayer reads, "The Lord will bless His people with peace",[211] with the addition of the words "with an abundance of strength and peace;[212] one may ask: If there is peace, what is the point of "strength"? Does it mean that peace will be enjoyed only if Israel has might at its command? The Sages explain that the term "strength"[213] here means Torah knowledge. Their understanding was that Torah scholars and Torah fulfilment increase peace in the world – for wherever there is sincere Torah study, conflict has no place. Scholars may differ in their interpretations and rulings, but such differences are ventilated in a respectful, harmonious manner. Hence the Sephardi conclusion of *Sim Shalom* indicates that peace and social harmony depend on an abundance of Torah study and goodwill.[214]

That occupation in the study of Torah is considered one of the foremost duties of every son of Israel is illustrated in the teaching of the Zohar: "He who concentrated his mind in the Torah and penetrates its inner mysteries sustains the world. For without Torah the world would be reduced to chaos (*Zohar* 1:184b).

Mystically, the Sages taught that the Torah preceded the existence of the world, and was used by the Almighty as the "blue print" which He followed in His creation (Gen. R. 1:2; *Zohar* 2:161a).[215]

---

211 ה' יברך את עמו ישראל בשלום
212 ברוב עוז ושלום
213 עוז
214 ברב עוז ושלום
215 הקב"ה מביט בתורה ובורא את העולם

R. Benayahu said, "The entire world and all its existence were created for the sake of the Torah" (Gen. R. 1:6).[216] It is related in the Talmud that when Solomon wished to dedicate the Holy of Holies in the Temple which he had built, the gates refused to open for him. The many prayers which Solomon prayed were not answered, and Solomon begged that he should not be put to shame. Finally, when Solomon prayed that God grant his request in reward of the pious deeds of his father David, the gates opened for him. The Almighty said to David that one day of his devoted study of Torah is received by God as a greater spiritual service than the thousand sacrifices offered by Solomon on the Temple altar (*Shab.* 30a).[217]

R. Huna taught that the Almighty could overlook the transgression even of the three cardinal sins, idolatry, sexual immorality, and muder, for which there may sometimes be some extenuation, but He would not pardon the abandonment of Torah study, for which there could be no excuse (TJ *Hagiga*, 1:7, Rashi *ad loc.*).[218]

Freedom from Inner Strife

In reward for Israel's observance of the Torah and continuous devotion to their study, God made this promise: "Ye shall dwell in your land safely. And I will give peace in the land" (Lev. 26:5-6).[219] The Rabbinic commentators explained that in addition to freedom from war, "there will be peace among yourselves when you all live together in harmony, without discord and mutual strife" (Lev. 26:6, Rashi, Ibn Ezra, RAMBAN). Such peace was considered the greatest of blessings (*ibid.*, Rashi).[220]

---

216   העולם ומלואו לא נבראו אלא בזכות התורה

217   טוב יום אחד שאתה יושב ועוסק בתורה מאלף עולות שעתיד שלמה בנך להקריב לפני על גבי המזבח

218   וויתר הקב"ה לישראל על עכו"ם גילוי עריות ועל שפיכת דמים, מאסם בתורה לא וויתר

219   ונתתי שלום בארץ

220   שהשלום כנגד הכל

Recapitulation:

1. One should direct one's mind to the awesome experience of standing in the presence of the *Shekhinah*, as the Psalmist declared: "I have set the Lord always before me" (Ps. 16:8; *Sanh.* 22b; Maim. *Tefillah* 4:16).

2. One should cleanse one's mind of all thoughts other than the duty to revere God, the supreme King of kings. This requires some time for meditation before one begins to pray (Maim. *Tefillah* 4:16; *Oraḥ Ḥayyim* 98, REMA).

3. One should pray earnestly, reflecting on the words used and trying always to discover a new significance in them. Each spoken word should therefore go together with careful thought (Yehudah Halevi, *Kuzari* III, 5; *Ya'avetz*, *Siddur Bet El*, introd., p. 4).

4. Even if they did not grasp the deeper meaning and intention (*kavvanot*) of the words, as true mystics could do, the ARI's Ḥasidic followers derived spiritual satisfaction from prefacing each benediction or prayer with a plea – that it might be acceptable "for the unification of the Holy One, Blessed be He, and His Presence, and in the name of all Israel"[221] – thus making up for the deficiency of their own effort. In voicing this plea, they relied on God's declaration to Samuel: "The Lord looketh on [what is in] the heart" (1 Sam. 16:7; *Zohar, Va-Yikra*, p. 51; SHELAH, *Ha-Otiyyot* 5:100; *Siddur Yitzḥak Baer*; *Seder Avodat Yisrael*, on the *lulav* blessing). However, some authorities considered this an unnecessary distraction from the prayer or blessing itself (R. Yeḥezkel Landau, Responsa *Noda bi-Yehudah, Yoreh De'ah* 93).

5. The overall guiding principle was stated by R. Eliezer to his pupils, "When you pray, know before Whom you stand".[222] In other words, stand in awe and humility before the all-powerful Creator of the universe (*Ber.* 28b;

---

221 לשם יחוד קודשא בריך הוא
222 דע לפני מי אתה עומד לפני מלך מלכי המלכים הקב״ה

Sanh. 22a). It is a traditional practice to place before the worshiper a plaque containing these words, as well as a quotation from the Psalms of David, "I have set the Lord always before me" (Ps. 16:8).[223]

6.   R. Baḥya Ibn Pakuda taught that, when praying, one should be conscious of the tremendous privilege granted to a mere man when he addresses himself to the Almighty (*Hovot ha-Levavot: Heshbon ha-Nefesh* 3).

7.   To maintain one's *kavvanah*, pious scholars advised against reciting prayers by heart and urged that they always be read from the printed *siddur*. This is said to have been the ARI's constant practice (*Magen Avraham* on *Orah Hayyim* 93). The Vilna Gaon likewise held that praying from the *siddur* helped to rid the mind of extraneous thoughts. It was, however, recognized that each individual should adopt whichever method proved most conducive to his own *kavvanah* (*Magen Avraham*, *ibid.*).

8.   The Sages laid down that before a person begins reading the *Amidah* he should say: "O Lord, open Thou my lips; and my mouth shall declare Thy praise" (Ps. 51:17; *Ber.* 4b).[224] The Rabbis asserted that "everything is in the hands of Heaven, except man's fear of Heaven" (*Ber.* 33b),[225] indicating that whether he will serve God is entirely for man to decide. However, the act of praying needs Divine help (*siyyatta di-shemaya*), because man is so dominated by extraneous thoughts that God alone can enable him to overcome them and pray with full *kavvanah*. Thus, in a High Holy Day prayer, we ask God to send us a true answer,[226] since we recognize that "the preparations of the heart belong to man; but the answer of the tongue is from the Lord" (Prov. 16:1).[227] Thus,

---

223   שויתי ה׳ לנגדי תמיד

224   ה׳ שפתי תפתח ופי יגיד תהילתך

225   הכול בידי שמים חוץ מיראת שמים

226   אשאלה ממנו מענה לשון

227   לאדם מערכי לב ומה׳ מענה לשון

before reciting the *Amidah*, we pray for His direction: "O Lord, open Thou my lips; and my mouth shall declare Thy praise". Similarly, in the *Yehi Ratzon* prayer recited on the Sabbath before *Rosh Ḥodesh* (the New Moon), we ask the Almighty to grant us "a life marked by the fear of Heaven and the dread of sin".[228]

9. That it is extremely difficult to maintain full *kavvanah* throughout one's prayer was recognized by the Sages. They affirmed that, among other good deeds, every prayer recited with *iyyun tefillah* – i.e., full *kavvanah* – is assured of a reward both in this world and in the World to Come (*Shab.* 127a, Rashi). At the same time, however, they warned that human frailty allows wanton thoughts and desires to enter the mind, also giving rise to tittle-tattle and lapses in one's *kavvanah* (*ibid.*).

10. It is a widespread practice to close one's eyes or cover them with one's hand when reciting the first verse of the *Shema*, in order to improve one's concentration. Some find that they are more able to concentrate their thoughts by looking intently at the words printed in the *siddur*. A special achievement in reading the *Shema* with one's eyes covered is to visualise the words, particualarly of the first sentence, and read them from what he sees in his mind. As stated above, each person should adopt whichever method is best suited to his own temperament.

11. Despite all the various methods that can help to maintain *kavvanah*, we are still conscious of the need for Divine help in resisting the *yetzer ha-ra* and its power to sway us. After the morning benedictions heading our daily prayers, we therefore add this plea: "May it be Your will [*Vi-yehi ratzon*]... that our evil inclination be made subservient to You" (*Ber.* 60b).[229]

12. The Sages accepted the rule formulated by R. Eliezer that one should not begin to pray unless one's mind is attuned

228   חיים שיש בהם יראת שמים ויראת חטא

229   וכוף את יצרנו להשתעבד לך

to doing so with *kavvanah*.[230] They held that someone
who had not reached a state of attentiveness should wait
before beginning to pray, if he felt sure that he could
retain his *kavvanah* while there was still time for him to
recite his prayers. Otherwise, as in times of stress, the
prayers should be his major consideration (*Orah Hayyim*
101:1; *Mishnah Berurah, Bi'ur*).

13. Like prayer, Torah study is regarded as an important form
of communion with the Almighty. By diligently studying
Torah one invokes the light of Heavenly intelligence and
implants it in one's soul (Rav Kook, *Olat Re'ayah*, vol. 1,
pp. 19-20). Devotion in prayer is also enhanced by one's
diligent application to the study of Torah (SHELAH,
Tamid: Ner Mitzvah, chap. on Prayer).
[General References: R. Yissakhar Jakobson, *Netiv
Binah*, Sinai, Tel Aviv, 1968, vol. 1, introd., chap. 4–6,
pp. 34–53; R. Mosheh ben Yosef of Trani (Ha-Mabbit),
Bet Elohim, Venice, 1576; Warsaw, 1872 ed., *Sha'ar
Tefillah* 1; Maim. *Tefillah* Chap. 5]

C. The Meaning of *Ratzon* (Will) in Rabbinic Thought

Man is judged by the amount of effort he devotes to purifying
his character (Arama, *Akedat Yitzhak*, Lev., *Emor*, p. 192). In
rabbinic literature all manifestations of reason, emotion or
moral character are attributed to man's "heart". The "heart"
receives diverse counsels; it considers, decides and acts in
accordance with its own choice. The "heart" is the director
of man's life. When, therefore, God considers man, He looks
at the "heart" (Schechter, *Aspects of Rabbinic Theology*, p.
255, note 2; Eccles. R. 1:16). The activities of the "heart"
are synonymous with the whole of a man's psychical life

---

230   אמר ר' אלעזר לעולם יאמוד אדם את עצמו אם יכול לכוון את לבו יתפלל ואם לאו
אל יתפלל

(Sa'adiah Gaon, *Emunot ve-De'ot*, part 6, ed. S. Rosenblatt, pp. 235–264).

The human mind or "heart" devises, wills and effects an action, but the action is that of the man as a whole. According to a story related in the Talmud, Emperor Antoninus told R. Yehudah ha-Nasi that both body and soul could escape judgment by claiming that since they had been separated from each other, neither was responsible for transgression, the body lying immobile like a stone in the tomb and the soul flying in the air like a bird. In reply, R. Yehudah told Antoninus a parable concerning two men, one blind and the other lame, who stole from the king's garden. Each claimed that his disability made it impossible for him to have committed the offence. The king made the lame man climb on the blind man's back and he then judged them together (*Tanḥuma, Va-yikra* 6; *Mekhilta* 36b; Lev. R. 4:5; *Sanh.* 91a–b). Body and soul thus constitute one human being in whose actions both are involved (*Tanḥuma, Va-yikra* 6).

Man's urges and impulses are an essential feature of human life. Even the *yetzer ha-ra* can serve a useful purpose, as this "evil inclination" was also part of God's creation: "And behold, it was very good" (Gen. 1:31; Gen. R. 9:7; *Avot de-Rabbi Natan* 9a). The mind visualizes physical pleasures, rationalizes evil desires and confuses man (Schechter, *Aspects of Rabbinic Theology*, p. 267). Yet it is man who harnesses those inclinations for good or evil and who decides which actions to perform (*Tanḥuma, Bereshit* 7). The determination of man's will and the strength or weakness of his resolve do not depend on the strength or weakness of the "heart" as such, but on the amount of energy that man directs to the "heart" in promoting his resolve.

Despite the familiar ascription of independent activity to various organs of the body, the power of man's will (*ratzon*) inspires his every action and desire, and it is man's exclusive prerogative. This finds expression in the Bible: "And thou shalt choose life" (Deut. 30:19).[231] His true and whole personality is not revealed when he follows any and every inclination, but only when he recognizes the good, chooses to perform it and then does so with intelligence and resolve.

According to Baḥya Ibn Pakuda (*Ḥovot ha-Levavot*), manifest physical actions and non-manifest acts of the mind or the will should both be subject to God's laws. Since He commanded us to perform manifest acts that cannot be fulfilled without the participation of the will, He must also have ordained the non-manifest acts which are motivations of the will in the performance of physical actions. Baḥya postulates clear duties of the will, which he terms "Duties of the Heart",[232] and these man is required to obey by directing his will to act in accordance with God's law. The first step must be his determination to act accordingly, and through his will he should "energize" his intention. Once man sets the act in motion, as it were, God helps him complete it, as the Sages affirmed: "When man determines to purify himself, Heaven comes to his aid" (*Shab.* 104a; Song R. 5:3).[233]

Hence the well-known teaching that "God requires the heart" (*Sanh.* 106b),[234] which emphasizes the importance of directing man's will towards the fulfilment of God's law (Baḥya, *Ḥovot ha-Levavot*, introd.; Albo, *Ikkarim* 3:27). Scripture records that when God told Samuel to choose David as the future king of Israel, He declared: "Man looketh on the outward appearance, but the Lord looketh on the heart" (1 Sam. 16:7).[235]

The word *ratzon* stems from the verbal root *ratzah*, meaning "to be willing, pleased with" or "to accept favourably". The noun *ratzon* is used, *inter alia*, as an expression of goodwill, favour and acceptance. It occasionally signifies the "will" or "desire" of God or man. Thus David says, "I delight to do Thy will [*retzonekha*], O my God" (Ps. 40:9)[236] and "Teach me to

---

232   חובות הלבבות
233   הבא ליטהר מסייעים אותו
234   הקב״ה ליבא בעי
235   וה׳ יראה ללבב
236   לעשות רצונך אל-הי חפצתי

do Thy will, for Thou art my God" (Ps. 143:10).[237] A person's "will" or "desire" is likewise expressed in the order given by King Ahasuerus to celebrate the third anniversary of his reign by supplying drink "according to every man's pleasure" (Esth. 1:8).[238]

The sacrificial laws required a man to bring his offering to the Sanctuary "that he maybe accepted before the Lord" (Lev. 1:3).[239] Such is the meaning of the Torah verse given by Targum Onkelos (ad loc.). According to the Sages of the Talmud, however, the words *lifnei Hashem* mean that the offering should be brought to the entrance of the Sanctuary "before the Lord" (*Zev.* 119b). The determining factor in the sacrificial offering is present in the word *li-retzono*, i.e., the offering must be brought with the full consent, knowledge and desire of the suppliant (*Ar.* 21a).[240]

Only the nonfulfilment of a positive commandment (*mitzvat aseh*) could be expiated through a sacrifice, but the Torah emphasized that no offering would be "acceptable" to God if it was brought under duress, without the suppliant's free will.[241] Nevertheless, the Sages detected an element of compulsion in the words *yakriv oto* ("he shall bring it", Lev. 1:3), indicating that, when found liable, one must bring the offering.[242] Even in this case, however, a person's free consent was essential, as the Sages ruled that he might be subjected to physical pressure until he fully agreed to bring the offering (*Sifra*, Lev. 3:15; *Ar.* 21a; Lev. 1:3, Rashi *ad loc.*).[243] Ibn Ezra, commenting on *li-retzono* (*ibid.*), merely observed that the offering would only be "acceptable" if one brought it of one's own free will and not under duress (Lev. 1:3, Ibn Ezra *ad loc.*).[244]

---

237 כי אתה אלו-הי למדני לעשות רצונך
238 כרצון איש ואיש
239 לרצונו לפני ה'
240 עולה צריכה דעת
241 אין מתכפר לו עד שיתרצה
242 יקריב אותו מלמד שכופין אותו
243 כופין אותו עד שיאמר רוצה אני
244 שיקריבנו ברצונו ולא באונס

A problem discussed by the Sages was how the need for a man's free consent could be reconciled with the use of physical pressure until he said: *Rotzeh ani* – "I agree". What point was there in such a declaration if the man clearly felt otherwise? (*Kid.* 50a).[245] This apparent contradiction the Sages explained away by asserting that a declaration of consent maybe obtained by physical force. They compared this to the law of divorce, where the *get* must be executed willingly by the husband and given freely by him to his wife. However, when the *bet din* rules that he is legally obliged to hand her the *get* and he refuses to do so, physical pressure maybe exerted until the man gives way and declares that he is willing to do so (*Kid.* 50a; *Sh. Ar., Even ha-Ezer* 134:5).

Maimonides reiterates the ruling of the Sages that in a case like this the *bet din* may have the recalcitrant husband lashed until he agrees to hand over the *get*.[246] Giving a bill of divorce in this way is not deemed invalid because of the compulsion involved. As Maimonides goes on to explain, every Jew is at heart a loyal son of Israel and wishes to abide by Torah law. At times, however, the evil inclination dominates him and he is then incapable of obeying God's law. Physical punishment is intended to weaken the *yetzer ha-ra* and neutralize its power; once freed from its restraint, the husband agrees to follow the *bet din*'s instructions and gives the *get* with his wholehearted consent (Maim. Code, *Gerushin* 2:20).[247]

Malbim (R. Meir Leibush Malbim, Hungary, 19th cent.), in his Torah commentary, adopts a psychological approach to the problem. He distinguishes between the term "desire", expressed by the verb *hafetz*, and the term "will", expressed by the word *ratzon*. "Desire" refers to the feeling that attracts someone to various desirable pursuits, but "will" is the all-embracing intellectual factor that determines whichever path of action one resolves to follow. This determination is an act

---

245   יקריב אותו
246   כופין אותו
247   ויצרו הוא שתקפו וכיון שהוכה עד שתשש יצרו ואמר רוצה אני

of the mind, overriding whatever emotion or desire maybe felt. A person may thus have a *desire* to do something but not the *will* to do it, since intellectually he decides that he should not. Sometimes, however, the desire exerts such power in one direction or another that it overcomes the intellectual determination of the will. In that case, ordering the will to act correctly maybe possible. Although one cannot change one's emotions by an external command, one can strengthen the power of the will by exhortation so as to overcome the urgency of the original feeling. The eventual choice made by man and his consequent action represent the decision of his will.

Thus, in everyday life, a person may have the desire to excel in knowledge and skill, to be a great Torah scholar, to do good and act charitably, but greed, lethargy or a wish to engage in other endeavours may prevent him from achieving his real aim. When, through forceful exhortation or even physical coercion, a person is motivated to discharge his real obligations, he removes the constraint of the opposing urge and acts according to his true will and intellectual resolve (Malbim, Lev. 1:26).

The foregoing analysis may help us to understand the ruling of the *Halakhah* in regard to sacrifice and divorce, where the *bet din*'s prescription of lashes can subdue a mistaken "desire" and, by freeing a man, enable him to exercise his own true will. This explains why the *bet din* may exert pressure on an individual until he submits and proclaims his readiness to do whatever the court requires of him.[248]

D. Undefined Intention, Retrospective Designation – *Bererah*

Certain laws require a particular intention for their legal sanction. Where the individual is not currently sure of his

intention, but will take a decision later in accordance with
developments at present unknown, we may sometimes assume
that what he will decide in the future is in fact his present
intention, thus making the act effective. This assumption is
based on the concept known as *yesh bererah*, i.e., a future
choice considered as a present decision or condition. The
Talmud presents us with a division of opinion among both
tannaitic and amoraic scholars regarding the acceptability
of this device and the circumstances in which it maybe
applied (*Talmudic Encyclopedia*, vol. 4, pp. 216–246, *s.v.*
"*Bererah*").

Divorce

When a man commissions a scribe to write a *get* for his wife,
the *get* is only effective if his intention in having it written is
to divorce a particular woman (*li-shmah*), otherwise even if
the names in the *get* are his and hers, the *get* is invalid (Mish.,
Git. 24a; *Even ha-Ezer* 131:1). If a man had more than one
wife and ordered the scribe to write a *get* for whichever wife
came out of the house first, such a *get* would be invalid and
he could not claim that she was the one he originally intended
to divorce according to the principle of *yesh bererah*.[249] Here
there was no decision on the man's part as to whom he wished
to divorce; the decision was left open, depending on the
action of another person.[250] The *tanna* of the Mishnah ruled
that even if that man did subsequently reach a decision,[251]
by telling the scribe, for example, "Write a *get* for whichever
one I choose later", such a *get* would still be invalid and the
bererah principle could not be invoked on the assumption
that the man had first acted in accordance with the choice he
subsequently made.

---

249 יש ברירה
250 תלוי בדעת אחרים
251 תלוי על דעת עצמה

In both instances the *amoraim* held different opinions as to the circumstances in which the principle of *yesh bererah* might apply, assuming that what a man thought of later was already in his mind at the outset.[252] However, Caro in the *Shulhan Arukh* invalidated the *get* in either case (*Git.* 25a, Rashi *ad loc.*; *Suk.* 26b; *Even ha-Ezer* 131:4).

An exception would be made in the case of a *get* written by a childless man who was gravely ill[253] and who wished to spare his wife the obligation of *halitzah*. The ruling here is that she would be divorced from him immediately if he did not recover. In this case, although the man cannot know what lies in store for him, and therefore has no intention of divorcing his wife right away, the likelihood of his recovery is known to his Maker. In view of these circumstances, one assumes that the man's previous wish to divorce his wife corresponded to his wish immediately before his death (*Git.* 72a; Ran *ad loc.*; *Git.* 25a).[254] Furthermore, although the divorce was meanwhile suspended and his wife still remained married to him (as an *eshet ish*), in the event of his death the ruling would be in accordance with the principle of *bererah*, i.e., that the divorce had already taken place, as it obviously could not be effected after the man's death (*Git.* 25b; Meiri *ad loc.*; *Even ha-Ezer* 145:2, 5, 80–9; REMA).[255]

Later authorities felt obliged to forestall any uncertainty in marital relationships that might arise from counter-claims regarding intention. They accordingly laid down that in all matters involving divorce restrictive conditions should be avoided. One should follow only what was plainly stated in the *get*, or before witnesses, disregarding any assumption of what might have been intended or any claim in respect of inner thoughts that a person had not clearly expressed (*Arukh ha-Shulhan*, *Even ha-Ezer* 145:30).[256]

---

252 אומרים הוברר הדבר שרצה מעשה ראשונה
253 שכיב מרע
254 הוברר הדבר שמחיים חל הואיל ותלה הדבר בדעת שמים
255 אין גט לאחר מיתה
256 בגטין לא הולכין אחר אומדנא ולא אחרי מחשבות שבלב

The Eruv

In the Sabbath law restricting movement to a distance of 2,000 cubits out of town, there is a provision which allows one to extend that distance by symbolically occupying a point 2,000 cubits outside the town and thereby extending the permitted distance a further 2,000 cubits. Such a procedure is called a "mixing of boundaries" (*eruv tehumin*). For this purpose, the given point must be occupied or "acquired" before the Sabbath commences (*Sh. Ar., Orah Hayyim* 415:4; Maim. *Eruvin* 6:1–2, 24).

If food is left on both sides of the town to symbolize acquisition of the site, one may decide (on the Sabbath) which side to use, even though the decision was not known beforehand and not made prior to the Sabbath. Here, the Rabbis are moderate in their application of the *yesh bererah* rule, which assumes that the decision was made before the Sabbath. This leniency is due to the fact that the *eruv tehumin* provision is itself of Rabbinic rather than Biblical origin (*mi-de-Rabbanan*). The rabbis preferred, however, that the *yesh bererah* rule be applied to facilitate the performance of a *mitzvah*[257] or one's escape from a heathen attack that might come from either direction (*Orah Hayyim* 415:1; *Mishnah Berurah ad loc.; Er.* 36b; ROSH; *Korban Netan'el ad loc.*).

Tithes – Terumah u-Ma'aser

In the case of Torah laws such as *terumah* and *ma'aser*, where it is forbidden to drink wine before it has been tithed,[258] one may not declare, "Those tenths which I'll separate from the wine shall be *terumah u-ma'aser*", on the basis of the *bererah* rule – and then drink from the wine as though it has already been tithed. Drinking such wine is fully prohibited before the

---

tithes have been separated (*Er.* 37a; *Git.* 25b, Meiri; Maim. *Ma'aser* 7:1).

Having summed up all the arguments for and against accepting the notion of *bererah*, Mar Zutra determined in his academy that one should follow the ruling of Hoshayah. This states that in regard to laws of Torah origin (*mi-de-Oraita*), such as defilement by a corpse (*tum'at met*) and divorce (*gittin*), we do not apply this notion, and rule *ein bererah*. In laws of rabbinic origin (*mi-de-Rabbanan*), however, we do accept it and rule *yesh bererah* (*Betzah* 38a; *Git.* 24b; *Er.* 36b).

Jubilee – Yovel

The law of the jubilee (*yovel*) declares that the Land of Israel belongs to God and has been distributed among the twelve tribes as a permanent trust. Accordingly, a Jew who inherited his due portion (*ahuzah*) could not sell any of that land in perpetuity. However, if dire need forced him to sell any of his ancestral landed property, this would only be for a limited period of time and it had to be restored to him, without payment, at the beginning of the jubilee year (Lev. 25:23–28; Maim. *Shemittah* and *Yovel* 11:1; *Hinnukh* 339–340).[259]

On the same principle, whoever bought such land, which could have been sold a number of times, was obliged to return it to its previous occupier in the jubilee year; this process continued until the land reverted to the original owner (Maim. *Yovel* 11:15).

A problem would arise when two brothers inherited land from their father and were obligated to divide the estate between them. The Talmud raises the question of whether the portion of land that each brother now receives should be regarded as the defined part of his inheritance. Alternatively, it could be that the entire estate was bequeathed to them as one

---

259   ויצא ביובל ושב לאחוזתו

parcel of land and that the brothers divided it between them, each acquiring full ownership rights from the other.

According to the first interpretation, both brothers are original inheritors (*yoreshim*), whereas according to the second they are both considered purchasers (*lakohot*) and must return the land to its previous owner in the jubilee year. The solution to this problem turns on the question of *bererah*. If we follow the principle of *yesh bererah*, we may rule that both brothers are inheritors (*yoreshim*); but if we do not and maintain *ein bererah*, both brothers are purchasers (*lakohot*) and must abide by the Torah law requiring the return of the land when the jubilee arrives. The brothers would accordingly return their portions to each other and then redivide the estate between them (*Bek.* 52b, Rashi *ad loc.*, s.v. "*Ha-ahim she-haleku*"; Maim. *Yovel* 11:20).

Those Sages who did not endorse the concept of *bererah* in this instance ("*Ha-ahim she-haleku*") regarded each brother's land as a new purchase, while those who accepted it regarded each of the brothers as an original *yoresh* who owned the land by inheritance. Accordingly, the land need not be returned.

R. Yohanan, who did not accept *yesh bererah*, ruled that the brothers should be considered "purchasers" from each other (*lakohot hen*) and so, in the jubilee year, they would have to return what they bought from each other and could then agree to a new division of the estate. R. Hoshayah, who accepted the concept, ruled that each brother was a *yoresh* in his own right and that the land need not be returned in the jubilee.

This argument continued, Rav maintaining *yesh bererah*, so that the brothers were *yoreshim*, and Shemuel upholding *ein bererah,* so that they were *lakohot*, though not responsible for the seizure of land by a third party.

Maimonides ruled, like R. Yohanan, that the brothers were "purchasers", aquiring from each other the portion due to them.[260] However, for laws defined as *mi-de-Rabbanan* he accepted the principle of *yesh bererah* (*Bek.* 52b, Rashi *ad loc.*; *BB* 106b, 107a, Rashi and Rosh *ad loc.*; Maim. *Yovel* 11:20, *Shekhenim* 2:12; *Ḥoshen Mishpat* 173:3).

Summary of the Law of Bererah

The following summation is given by R. Shelomo Luria in a discourse analyzing all cases where *bererah* may arise (*Yam shel Shlomo* on *Bava Kamma* 5, "*Din Bererah*"):

1. In all Torah-based laws (*mi-de-Oraita*) we do not apply the concept of *bererah*, regardless of whether this results in lenience or stringency (*kulla o ḥumra*) or whether the subsequent outcome depends on one's own choice or that of others.

2. If the action is conditional on something that has, in fact, already been decided (although it is not yet known to us) and the condition is later fulfilled, we accept *bererah* and rule that this subsequent action is consistent with the decision made at the outset.[261] An example of this situation would be if a man took a wife on condition that his father approved of the marriage[262] and it did prove acceptable to the father; the condition would then be regarded as fulfilled at the time of the marriage, which is therefore valid – *mekuddeshet* (*Git.* 25b).

3. In laws of rabbinic origin (*mi-de-Rabbanan*) the *yesh bererah* principle is always upheld – as, for example, in the Sabbath *eruv* law, where allowance is made for the creation of two *eruv* stations beforehand and the use of either one on the Sabbath day. Here the principle can be helpful in meeting the requirements of the law.

4. A different approach to *bererah* is admissible when no division can be specified. There maybe instances where the question of *huvrar le-mafre'a* (retroactive choice) does not arise, since no division ever took place. Here, the Sages used a type of *bererah* concept to solve a

261   אומרים ברירה למפריע
262   אל מנת שירצה אביו

problem even in matters affecting Torah law, such as
that of property. A case in point is where a courtyard
adjoining two houses belongs to two neighbours[263] and,
being smaller than 4 x 4 cubits, is considered indivisible
(*BB* 11a–b). If both neighbors made a vow forbidding any
benefit to each other, the question arises as to whether
either can make use of the common courtyard, since
every part of the yard belongs to both and one would be
using what belongs to his neighbour[264] (Maim. *Nedarim*
5:1; *Shulḥan Arukh, Yoreh De'ah* 226:1). Here, the actual
division of each one's part can not be made and it is not a
case where the division will be made known later, so that
we wish to assume by reason of *bererah* that the part one
uses is in fact one's own.

In this case, although the accepted ruling of the *tannaim*
does not allow the use of *bererah,* R. Eliezer ben Ya'akov
permitted the assumption that the part used is in fact the
part that belongs to one. Thus, it being a joint property,
both neighbors have the right to make use of the courtyard,
particularly for light work that does not inconvenience
the other (*Ned.* 45b, 46b, RAN; Maim. *Nedarim* 7:4; *Tur,
Yoreh De'ah* 226:1).

E. Legal Assumptions

Gud Aḥid and Gud Asik

In certain laws of the Sabbath an area measuring four square
cubits is defined as a private domain (*reshut ha-yaḥid*). Thus,
according to the law that prohibits carrying from one domain to
another, if one threw an object into an area of that size outside
one's domain, it would be considered as grave a transgression

---

263   אין חולקין את החצר עד שיהא ד' אמות לזה וד' אמות לזה
264   שותפין בחצר ונדרו הנאה זה מזה

as moving an object from one domain to another. If the area measured less than four square cubits, it would still retain that size in accordance with the principle of "stretching down" (*gud aḥid*),[265] and the transgression of carrying would remain (*Shab.* 101a, Rashi *ad loc.*; Maim. *Shabbat* 14:16; *Oraḥ Hayyim* 376:2; *Magen Avraham* 1, 346:1).

The principle of *gud aḥid* is also utilized to modify the law, e.g., by placing a hanging partition[266] over a well located between the property of two householders, so that water from either side of the well maybe regarded as belonging to the one who draws it. This obviates the transgression of carrying from one domain to another (*Er.* 86a; Maim. *Eruvin* 3:21; *Oraḥ Hayyim* 376:1).

Tzurat ha-Petaḥ – A "Door Frame"

A similar rule applies in another case of carrying from one domain to another on the Sabbath. If a man's house opens out into an alley which leads to a street and thus belongs to the public domain,[267] he may place a board on either side of the exit and another across it to serve as a door frame. This is then considered to be "stretched", as if it were a solid door, thereby "enclosing" the alley. In that case one has made an *eruv* which incorporates the alley in the private domain, where carrying is permitted (*Er.* 2a; Maim. *Eruvin*, 1:1; *Oraḥ Hayyim* 363:3).

Lavud – "Joining"

This legal fiction is also known by the term *lavud* ("solid, compact"), two parts that are separated by a gap of less than

---

265 גוד אחיד
266 מחיצה תלויה
267 מבוי מפולש

three handbreadths being regarded as joined together.[268] In a *sukkah* the "joining" could reach the roof or the floor (*Suk.* 16b; Maim. *Sukkah* 4:4; *Orah Hayyim* 630:9).

Thus, according to the *sukkah* laws, if the wall is suspended[269] and does not reach the ground but only misses it by three handbreadths,[270] it is considered to be standing on the ground. In accordance with the *gud ahid* principle, a wall matching the requirements of a *sukkah* has thus been made. The same rule would apply to a wall "stretching upward" to the roof of the *sukkah*. Here, the principle is known as *gud asik* (*Suk.* 16a-b; Maim. *Sukkah* 4:4; *Orah Hayyim* 630:9).[271]

Dofen Akumah in the Laws of the Sukkah – An Assumed Wall

The laws of the *sukkah* include certain requirements as to the materials that maybe used for roofing, specifically those which are a product of the earth and not liable to ritual defilement.[272] Only such permitted roofing (*sekhakh*)[273] maybe used, and non-permitted *sekhakh* four handbreadths wide[274] invalidates the *sukkah*. Natural reeds and bamboo are acceptable, but a wide board is considered too solid and therefore unacceptable (*sekhakh pasul*).[275] If, however, the board is less than four cubits wide and is placed on the roof immediately next to the wall of the *sukkah* or a supporting structure, while the rest of the roofing comprises permitted *sekhakh*,[276] the *sukkah* is deemed *kasher*.

268	לבוד
269	מחיצה תלויה
270	שלשה טפחים
271	גוד עסיק
272	טומאה
273	סכך כשר
274	ארבעה טפחים
275	סכך פסול
276	סכך כשר

This provision, known as *dofen akumah*,[277] is accepted by the Rabbis as a traditional "law originating from Mount Sinai" (*Suk.* 4a, 6b, 17a; Maim. *Sukkah* 5:14; *Oraḥ Ḥayyim* 632:1). The rationale of this law is as follows. Although a wooden board of less than four cubits is itself unfit as *sekhakh*, being wider than four handbreadths, we do not regard it as *sekhakh* but as part of the *sukkah* wall, as if the wall also covered the roof and extended to the permitted *sekhakh*. We thus have roofing of permitted *sekhakh* only next to the wall, which legitimizes the whole *sukkah* (Rashi, *Suk.* 4a).

Other early commentators explain this legal contrivance differently. Unlike Rashi, they do not consider the board part of the wall, but regard the wall itself as a covering of the roof under the board that extends to the permitted *sekhakh* (Ran, *Er.* 4b). Rashi, however, argues that this scarcely explains why an open space of three cubits is not thought to close the roof up to the *sekhakh* (Rashi, *Suk.* 17a). One might say that the status of an unaccepted covering can be mitigated by this expedient, but an empty space has no reality[278] to which one might apply it. According to this view, one might say that an empty space of less than three handbreadths is regarded as joined to the wall,[279] "solid and compact" (Rashi, *ibid*; *Oraḥ Ḥayyim* 632:2).

A similar situation would obtain if the normal roof of a house was shattered, leaving an open space in the middle that could be covered by permitted *sekhakh*. We might say that if the side sections of the original roofing were less than four cubits wide, they would not be considered part of the roof but a continuation of the wall according to the notion of *dofen akumah*, thus furnishing a permitted *sukkah* (*Suk.* 17a; *Oraḥ Ḥayyim* 632:1; Maim. *Sukkah* 4:14). Similar considerations would apply to the concepts of *gud aḥid, gud asik* and *lavud*.

---

277 דופן עקומה
278 מציאות
279 לבוד

The Condition of Sekhakh and the Havot Remi Device

According to the *sukkah* laws, roofing (*sekhakh*) should provide more shade than sunlight to conform with the notion of a "dwelling".[280] Where the roofing consists of reeds, but there is a space between two layers,[281] only if the reeds on top are regarded as contiguous with those below will it meet the requirement of "greater shade" (*tziltah merubbah*). Where the space is more than three handbreadths, we utilize the *havot remi* device and regard the top level as having been "pulled down" to the lower one; this fills the space between the reeds and thus constitutes a proper covering (*Suk.* 22a, Rashi *ad loc.*; Maim. *Sukkah* 5:21; *Orah Hayyim* 631:5).

If the space measures less than three handbreadths, we do not need this presumption, since the covering is already "joined" to what lies underneath by the device known as *lavud*. Furthermore, as mentioned above, we can utilize the concepts of *gud ahid* and *gud asik* to fill any space above or under the board. These devices are so alike that they are sometimes interchanged. They are recognized as laws of ancient origin, "received by Moses on Sinai" (Maim. on *Oho.* 12:5).[282]

Offerings – Korbanot

The sanctity of every part of an offering must be preserved so as to be acceptable on the altar. Should any part of the offering be mingled with an unacceptable substance, the entire offering becomes forbidden. However, if water fell into the blood of the offering and the mixture retained its original colouring, it was still deemed acceptable.

A problem arose if the blood of the offering was mixed with wine, since both liquids were red and it was hard to

---

280   צלתה יותר מחמתה
281   קנה עולה יקנה יורד
282   הלכה למשה מסיני

judge the wine's effect on the blood. Here we apply the rule of "assumption", considering the wine to be water, and estimate whether the blood would still retain its full colouring in such a mixture.[283] If not, the blood would then become unsuitable for an offering on the altar (*Zev.* 8:6, *Tosefot Yom Tov ad loc.*; Maim. *Pesulei ha-Mukdashin* 2:22).

A Situation Considered as If It Were Otherwise – Ro'in Ke-ilu

Heathen Wine – Yayin Nesekh

Another problem arose when forbidden heathen wine was added to permitted kosher wine. Owing to the heathen practice of using wine libations in their idolatrous worship the Mishnah law laid down that any wine that had been devoted or even handled by a heathen was considered to be defiled and prohibited for use by an Israelite, since the heathen could have had idolatrous intentions at the time (*yayin nesekh)*. If such wine had been mixed with non-forbidden wine or water, even the smallest amount of *yayin nesekh* disqualified the entire mixture (*AZ* 73a; Maim. *Yad, Ma'akhalot Asurot* 13, 1-4).[284]

A case was considered where the contents of a barrel of heathen wine fell into a large vat of kosher wine, and later a flask of ordinary water fell onto this. R. Ḥizkiyah and R. Yoḥanan differed in their judgment as to whether the total mixture was permitted or defiled. R. Ḥizkiyah ruled that the mixture was forbidden, since the original kosher wine had immediately been defiled when the heathen wine mixed with it, and was therefore added to the amount of the forbidden wine. R. Yoḥanan, however, ruled that it was permitted. He said we assess the situation as the case is brought before us, and not as the law applied stage by stage, where even a small amount of *yayin nesekh* would prohibit the entire mixture. We adjudge the first permitted wine as though it was not

---

283 רואין אותו כאילו הוא מים
284 יין נסך אסור ואוסר בכל שהוא

of the same substance as the wine of *yayin nesekh* – *kemo she'ein ke-mino*, and, therefore, the *yayin nesekh* can be annulled by being less than one sixtieth of the mixture (*bateil beshishim*). The first wine was permitted and the added water was permitted. These two amounts now annul the forbidden wine. The procedure to be followed was that we reckon the permitted wine with the permitted water, and together they annul the forbidden *yayin nesekh* which becomes less than a sixtieth of the total. This procedure was expressed in the term, "we look at the permitted wine as though it was not (of the same substance)" – *ro'in et haheter ke-ilu eino* (*AZ* 73a–b).[285] Such a legal contrivance was often followed by the Sages in order to save the people from a considerable financial loss – *mipnei hefsed gadol* (*AZ* 73a, Commentary *Yefeh Einayim ad loc.*, *Ha-Mordekhai ad loc.*).

The difference in the judgments of these Sages depended on from which angle the matter was considered. R. Yoḥanan said we assess the situation as the case is brought before us now, when we see that the amount of permitted wine overpowers the amount of *yayin nesekh,* and we do not consider the different stages in which it had developed. R. Ḥizkiya judged the case stage by stage and concluded that the resulting mixture was prohibited (*AZ* 73a, Novellae *Yefeh Einayim ad loc.*).

In the above debate we find an example of how the attitude of outlook of different Sages determined their halakhic judgments.

The problem of a questionable mixture of two different kinds arose also in the laws of ritual sacrifices.

Mingling of Different Sacrifices – Irbuv Korbanot

In view of the differing rituals for various types of offering, such as *olah* (where the sacrifice is completely burnt) or *ḥattat* (where portions of the offering are eaten by the priests), a

---

285   רואין את ההיתר כאילו אינו והשאר מים רבין עליו ומבטלין אותו

problem would arise if parts of the different offerings were intermingled. The Sages did not allow such a mixture to be offered on the altar and laid down that it should be removed and destroyed as a spoilt offering. R. Eliezer, however, permitted the whole offering to be sacrificed on the altar. In his opinion, the limbs of the *ḥattat* should be regarded as pieces of wood and, though disqualified as offerings, the mixed parts could then be added to the wood burning on the altar (*Zev.* 8:4; Maim. *Pesulei ha-Mukdashin* 6:20).[286]

F. Distraction – *Hesseḥ ha-Da'at*

In Ritual Purity

Just as the priests had to be in a state of ritual purity[287] before performing any ritual act in the Temple, so was complete *tahorah* required before they ate any part of the sanctified offerings.[288] God's instruction to Aaron was that the *kohanim* must eat the portions allotted to them[289] in a state of purity: "Behold, I have given thee the charge of... all the sanctified offerings of the Children of Israel" (Num. 18:8).[290] This meant ensuring that they were not defiled (Rashi *ad loc.*).

Accordingly, before eating any of the sacred meats, the priest had to make sure that he was ritually clean and that, from the moment of his purification in a *mikveh*, he retained that purity without distraction.[291] This precaution was taken because, in the meantime, some unclean thing might have defiled him. Even if the priest was certain that he had not

---

286 רואה אני בשר החטאת כאילו הוא עצים
287 טהרה
288 קדושים
289 מתנות כהונה
290 הנה נתתי לך את משמרת תרומתי
291 הסיח דעת

been contaminated, but had allowed his mind to wander from the sacrifice, a further immersion was required. The Rabbis observed that a person's hands are always active and may unwittingly touch some source of defilement (*Talmudic Encyclopedia*, vol. 9, pp. 547–586; Maim. *Avot ha-Tum'ah* 13:1–3; *Pes.* 34a).

Possible causes of distraction:
1. If a priest in a state of cleanness had been prevented from eating sanctified meat[292] because he was in mourning for the dead,[293] he would need to undergo ritual immersion before eating such meat. The period of mourning had diverted his attention, resulting in *hesseḥ da'at*,[294] and he would not realize that he had been defiled (Maim. *Avot ha-Tum'ah* 12:15; 13:3).
2. Since a person had to be ritually clean when eating the paschal lamb, the question asked was whether, if he fell asleep during the meal, this should be considered an unwarrantable distraction. The accepted view of R. Yose was that it would not constitute *hesseḥ da'at* (*Pes.* 120a–b; Meiri *ad loc.*; RAVAD on Maim. *Ḥametz u-Matzah* 8:14; ROSH on *Ta'an.* 1:14).
3. In the purification ceremony of the Red Heifer,[295] the officiating priest is required to devote his complete attention to the sacrifice until it is completely burnt and reduced to ashes. Thus, when slaughtering the beast, he is forbidden to kill another animal at the same time.[296] Rav derived this law from the Biblical injunction, "It shall be slaughtered in his [Eleazar's] presence" (Num. 19:3), which shows that Eleazar, who was responsible for the Red Heifer's preparation, could not allow his attention to be diverted from it throughout the ceremony.[297]

---

292 קודשים
293 עינות
294 הסיח דעת
295 פרה אדומה
296 לא ישחט אחרת עמה
297 שלא יסיח דעתו ממנו

Performing another, simultaneous *shehitah* was therefore prohibited (*Yoma* 42a–43a).

Because of this requirement, it was laid down that if the celebrant engaged in any other activity while conducting the service, he thereby disqualified the Red Heifer (*Parah* 4:4).[298] When the officiating priest had to focus his mind on a particular ritual, any distraction would impair his *kavvanah* and invalidate the ceremony (Maim. *Parah Adummah* 4:17-18).

4. Similarly, when storing the ashes of the Red Heifer for use as "water of sprinkling"[299] and purification from sin,[300] constant attentiveness was a vital requirement (Num. 19:9; *Yoma* 42a; *Git.* 53b, *Tos. ad loc.*; Maim. *Parah Adummah* 7:1; 10:5).

5. Every priestly service in the Temple necessitated a ritual washing of the hands and feet, with scrupulous ritual purity inside the Temple area and no *hesseh da'at* (*Zev.* 20b; Maim. *Bet ha-Mikdash* 5:1–5).

In Ablutions – Netilat Yadayim

1. Before eating bread at a meal, one must perform a ritual ablution by washing the hands[301] and subsequently make sure that one's hands do not touch anything unclean. If a person is remiss about safeguarding the hands from defilement,[302] he must wash them again before eating another piece of bread (*Pes.* 115b, Rashi *ad loc.*; Maim. *Berakhot* 6:1, 17; *Orah Hayyim* 158:1, 164:1).

2. At the Passover *Seder* meal, one should first wash the hands before eating the green *karpas* vegetable,[303] to

---

298 פוסלין אותה (הפרה) במלאכה
299 למשמרת למי נדה
300 מי חטאת
301 נטילת ידים
302 הסיח דעת
303 כרפס

remove any uncleanness, and (as usual) once again before the meal. The reason for the second ablution is that a person's mind has been focused on the lengthy recitation of the *Haggadah* and, in the meantime, his hands could have been defiled by touching the body or some unclean object (Maim. *Hametz u-Matzah* 8:6; *Pes.* 115b).

3. Opinion is divided regarding the procedure to be followed on a Sabbath, if one washes the hands before reciting *Kiddush*[304] over wine and then eats bread (after reciting *Ha-motzi*). The recital of *Kiddush* might be regarded as a form of interruption between washing the hands and eating the bread which would constitute *hesseh da'at* (*Pes.* 106b, Rashbam *ad loc.*; *Orah Hayyim* 271:12, 179:1).

In Grace after Meals

1. In view of the requirement to say Grace after Meals as soon as one has finished eating,[305] both the Rabbis and earlier authorities had differing views as to what would constitute an interval[306] at the end of the meal, resulting in a distraction (*hesseh da'at*) before Grace. Maimonides ruled that the meal ended once a person made up his mind not to eat or drink anything else.[307] If he had no such intention, even a lengthy gap would not discontinue the meal after the blessing made at its commencement. Scholars who wrote commentaries on Maimonides discussed views opposed to his ruling (Maim. *Berakhot* 4:7; RAVAD, *Kesef Mishneh*, *Lehem Mishneh ad loc.*; *Orah Hayyim* 178, 179:1–3). All agreed that once a person lifted the cup of wine to recite Grace, the meal was concluded (*Orah Hayyim* 179:3).

---

304   קדוש
305   ברכת המזון
306   הפסקה
307   גמר בלבו שלא לאכל ולשתות

2. The *amoraim* differed as to whether moving from one house
    to another in the course of a meal should be considered
    an interruption, and whether a fresh benediction was
    needed before eating in the second house. Early halakhic
    authorities likewise reached different conclusions (*Orah
    Hayyim* 178:1–4).
3. However, interrupting the meal for the purpose of reciting
    statutory prayers was not considered a break (*hafsakah*)
    amounting to *hesseh da'at*, since Divine worship accords
    with the sanctity of the table (as an altar), whereas reciting
    Grace definitely marks the end of the meal (*Orah Hayyim*
    178:6).

In the Amidah

R. Yohanan stated that if, during his recital of the *Amidah*,[308]
when no interruption is permitted, someone realized that he
had unwittingly omitted a passage and stepped back from his
place, that action would be considered a *hafsakah*[309] marking
the end of his prayer. He would then be obliged to start all
over again and recite the entire *Amidah* from the beginning.
If, however, he did not step back, there was no discontinuity
(*hesseh da'at*) and he could begin praying from that section
of the *Amidah* in which the omission occurred (*Orah Hayyim*
104:5; TJ *Ber.* 5:3; TB *Ber.* 29b).

In the Priestly Service

During the high priest's service (*Avodah*)[310] on Yom Kippur,
the gold plate that Aaron wore on his forehead was endowed
with a special prayer which enabled him "to bear the iniquity
committed in the holy things" (Ex. 28:38). The gold plate

---

308 עמידה
309 הפסקה
310 עבודה

would remove any uncleanness[311] that might have defiled the offering, regardless of whether the source of that impurity was intentional or not.[312] Since the *tzitz* was ordained to be "always [*tamid*] on his forehead", this implies that the *kohen gadol* had to remain ever conscious of its presence, as the gold plate only functioned when he was aware of its purifying effect. Accordingly, *tamid* signifies that there must be no *hesseh da'at* (*Yoma* 7b; Maim. *Pesulei ha-Mukdashin* 1:34; Rashi and *Tos. ad loc.*).

G. Intention and Defilement – *Tum'ah*

Intention as to the future use of an object can effectively determine its status according to the ritual law of defilement (*tum'ah*).[313] This law states that articles normally used by a human being are liable to become ritually "unclean",[314] whereas those used for animals do not,[315] unless they are transferred to human use. Normally, the use of an article can only be changed by modifying the article itself, but a person's intention regarding its use can also make it "unclean". Thus, a nose ring used for an animal cannot become *tamei* unless it is decided to use it for a person.

The power to change by intention is, however, limited. Once the use of an article has been changed intentionally, rendering that article susceptible to defilement, it cannot revert to its original state (of animal use) unless the change is created by a physical action (e.g., modifying the article for the purpose of its new use), since the first intention cannot be revoked merely by a subsequent intention.

These conditions are expressed in the law of the Mishnah

---

311 טומאה

312 הציץ מרצה בין בשוגג בין במזיד

313 טומאה

314 כל תכשיטי האדם מקבלין טומאה

315 כל תכשיטי הבהמה וכלים אינן מקבלין טומאה בפני עצמן

which states that "all objects can enter a state of 'uncleanness' through a person's intended use, but cannot leave a state of 'uncleanness' by a change of intention, only by some change in the object itself" (*Kel.* 25:9).[316] An intention can effect a change, but cannot alter a previous intention or, to be sure, a previous action (Maim. *Kelim* 8:6–10). The law of defilement governed an object's suitability for the sacred rituals of the Temple (Maim. *Tum'at Met* 1:1).[317]

Torah law decreed that seven types of material that could be fashioned into containers were subject to pollution if brought into contact with a dead body, a reptile, a leper or a sexual emission. These materials included earth, metal, wood, animal hides and clothing. Stone or products of the sea were excluded (Lev. 11:32; Maim. *Kelim* 1:1). Nor were raw materials susceptible to *tum'ah*; but once they had been fashioned into some type of vessel,[318] they were (Maim. *Kelim* 2:1).[319]

Although a wooden beam intended for use as a seat could become defiled, an ordinary piece of wood on which a workman might occasionally sit was not subject to *tum'ah*. If a wooden beam had its top hollowed out so that it could be used as a vessel,[320] the matter of its "cleanness" depended on how the cavity was made. Thus, if someone made the hollow so that it could be used as a container,[321] it would become *tamei*; but if he found that there was already a hollow in it, what he had in mind would prove decisive. If he thought that it would make a good vessel, it would be subject to defilement, the act of his mind having given it an "unclean" status.

For such an effect, however, the individual concerned had to be endowed with mental capacity, being neither a minor nor mentally deficient (Maim. *Kelim* 25:11). An item of furniture

---

316 כל הכלים יורדין לידי טומאתן במחשבה ואין עולין מידי טומאתן אלא בשינוי
מעשה
317 המת מטמאת במגע ובמשא ובאוהל טומאת שבעה
318 כלי קיבול
319 פשוטים טהורים ומקבליהן טמאים
320 קלונסאות החקיקין
321 אם החקקן לדעת

that was unserviceable, such as a table with broken legs, would not be subject to *tum'ah*. If, however, someone found that the table top could still be used, this would again make it susceptible to *tum'ah* (*Kel.* 22:1-2; Maim. *Kelim* 6:10). Produce such as wheat or barley could also be affected if, after harvesting, water was poured on it (Lev. 11:38).[322] This only applied when the food or produce had been soaked or was intended to be moistened by the owner,[323] in which case it became susceptible to impurity (Maim. *Tum'at Okhalim* 1:1–2).

If someone hung a dish on a wall so that it might be washed by rainwater, any food or fruit that he placed in the wet dish would become polluted through contact with something defiled, since the wetting of the dish had been performed with a specific intention.[324] If, however, the vessel was only meant to protect the wall underneath, and not to hold water, that would not be considered an intentional wetting of the vessel and food placed inside it would not be susceptible to *tum'ah*.[325]

As mentioned above, ritual defilement applies only to manufactured articles which a person intends to utilize. If the production of such an article is still incomplete, the law of *tum'ah* does not yet apply; nor can a person's intent change the situation (*Zev.* 4b).[326]

However, the use of an article can also be changed by a conscious decision. Should a person decide to use it just as it is, this thought gives it a new status[327] and it will become subject to "uncleanness". Likewise, if someone consecrated the article as a sacrifice, thus making it holy, that would elevate its status and enhance its importance. His intention would thus introduce a change, rendering the article subject to *tum'ah*.[328]

---

322 וכי יותן מים על זרע
323 ברצון בעלים
324 ברצון הוחשוו המים שבא
325 אינו מכשירין
326 אין מחשבה מטמאת
327 כיון דאחשבה
328 דאחשבה פסלה

Some accompanying act of dedication was also required by various Sages (*Zev.* 13a).

H. Unintentional Transgression – *Davar she-ein Mitkavven*

Throughout the Talmud there is a basic difference of opinion between two authoritative Sages as to whether a forbidden act performed unintentionally incurs guilt.[329] This question arises both in the Sabbath laws, where "purposeful action"[330] is needed for culpability, and in prohibitions as a whole (*Shab.* 29b). Although it may appear that guilt is established only in an intended transgression, this is not the opinion of all the Sages.

The difference of opinion is first expressed by R. Shim'on: "A man wishing to move a bed, stool or bench on the Sabbath may drag it on the earthen floor, even though by doing so it may make a groove in the floor, which would be forbidden 'work' associated with 'ploughing', provided he has no intention of making a furrow".[331] R. Yehudah, on the other hand, ruled that no objects maybe dragged on the floor because of the likelihood of making a furrow, except for something like a child's wagon, the wheels of which could make an impression on the floor but not a furrow. R. Yehudah's ruling accorded with the principle that forbidden "work", even unintentional, is prohibited (*Betzah* 23b).

The reasoning behind these two different opinions is not clearly given, but when the issue was debated by later Sages, the difference of opinion had to do with objects like a chair that can be lifted easily and larger ones, such as a bed, that cannot. R. Shim'on held that since making a furrow was not intended, the action was permitted. R. Yehudah, however, maintained

329 פליגי תנאים בדין דבר שאינו מתכון מלאכת מחשבת
330 מלאכת מחשבת
331 גורר אדם מטה כסא וספסל, ובלבד שלא יתקון לעשות חריץ

that particularly because a small object could be lifted by hand
to avoid making any groove,[332] dragging it was forbidden
even if there was no intention of making a furrow.[333] Thus,
R. Yehudah laid down that even an unintended transgression
incurred guilt, because it could easily have been avoided
(*Shab.* 29b, Rashi *ad loc.*).

The *amoraim* were similarly divided: Rav, for example,
accepted the opinion of R. Yehudah while Shemuel followed
that of R. Shim'on (*Shab.* 22a).

In the law forbidding one to cut a growing plant on the
Sabbath as prohibited "work", certain distinctions are made
concerning an unintended violation of the law. If someone
merely intended to "lift" a plant already cut, which was not
forbidden, but accidentally cut a plant that was growing, he
would be free from guilt. If, however, he intended to snip one
that was already cut, but mistakenly snipped one that was
growing, the Sages had differing views. Rabbah considered
him guiltless; Abbaye maintained that since cutting was
forbidden on the Sabbath, he was guilty even though he did
not intend to cut the plant. Rabbah, explaining his view, stated
that whereas in most cases an unintended transgression made
one liable for a sin-offering, this did not apply here. For a
violation of the Sabbath, liability was only incurred by a
"purposeful action", which did not apply in this case.[334] His
ruling was based on the fact that the person concerned had not
done what he really intended.[335]

This Sabbath law must be distinguished from an
unintended violation of *kashrut* (e.g., by eating forbidden fat)
or the morality code.[336] In cases such as these, even though
a transgression may not have been intended, the body derives
gratification from the act (*Shab.* 72b, *Tos.* and R. Ḥananel *ad
loc.*; Maim. Code, *Shegagot* 2:7).

---

332   כיון דאפשר
333   אסור
334   בשאר מצוות שגג בלא מתכון חייב, אבל בשבת שגג בלא מתכן פטור, דמלאכת
       מחשבת אסרה תורה
335   דלא נעשה מחשבתו
336   המתעסק בחלבים ועריות

Another case where a distinction is made in the law has to do with an apparent, though unintended, transgression of the commandment prohibiting idolatry – one of the three cardinal sins that must not be committed even if the alternative is martyrdom (*Sanh*. 74a). If, for any reason, someone bowed down before an idol or the statue of an emperor and claimed that he did so out of fear or respect,[337] but only revered God in his heart,[338] Rava held that since this person had maintained an inward devotion to God, he was not guilty of idol worship. Abbaye, however, condemned him for performing an idolatrous act: whereas the man's forbidden action could be seen, whatever he had in mind could not be determined (*Sanh*. 61b; Rashi and *Tos. ad loc*.).

All the above considerations refer to ritual offences, but the law of torts is different. The tannaitic Sages laid down that a person is always responsible for physical damage and injury, even if this occurs by accident, unintentionally or while he is asleep (*BK* 26a; Maim. *Hovel* 1:11; *Sh. Ar., Hoshen Mishpat* 421:3).[339]

Following various discussions in the Gemara, the Sages agreed with the view of R. Shim'on that for an unintentional violation of the Sabbath law a person is not liable to bring a sin-offering (*Shab*. 22a, RIF, ROSH, Maimonides; summarized by Caro in *Bet Yosef, Orah Hayyim* 337:1).[340] In the finalized ruling of the *Shulhan Arukh* (337:1), R. Yosef Caro states that an unintended infringement of the Sabbath laws (e.g., "dragging a bed, chair or stool", whether large or small, even though a furrow may then be made) is disregarded, always provided that one never intended to do so. The only exception to this rule would be in a case where the action (such as dragging a heavy object) was bound to result in a violation of the law. This involved neglect and should have been foreseen.[341]

---

337 מאהבה ומיראה
338 לבו לשמים
339 אדם מועד לעולם
340 הלכה כרבי שמעון בגרירה
341 והוא שלא אהיה פסיק ראשיה

The Rule of Pesik Resheih – Inevitability

The expression *pesik resheih* (lit., "cut off its head")[342] stems from the popular adage that "you can't cut off a chicken's head without killing the fowl": in other words, no one can claim that he only wanted the head and never meant to kill the chicken. Similarly, if a robber beheads a man, he cannot plead that he only wanted to rob him and is therefore not guilty of murder (*Shab.* 133a, R. Ḥananel *ad loc.*).

In a case involving some forbidden action by reason of *pesik resheih*, Abbaye and Rava agreed that R. Shim'on would deem it prohibited. Yet even here the commentators gave different interpretations of R. Shim'on's view. The *Tosafot* maintained that if there was no need for the man's action and he had no interest in the result,[343] no liability would be incurred. Rashi insisted, however, on the man's guilt, even if the result was not what he had anticipated (*Shab.* 75a, *Tos. ad loc.*, *s.v.* "*tefei*").

In another discussion we find that Shemuel held generally, like R. Shim'on, that the unintended infringement was permitted;[344] he would nevertheless agree that if it involved *pesik resheih*, it was forbidden, unless no gratification was derived from the result.[345] Where there was satisfaction and a wish to achieve it, R. Shim'on held (like R. Yehudah) that the person concerned was liable for his transgression.[346]

Thus, in the case of a Sabbath cauldron, if someone poured out the hot water[347] and immediately refilled it with cold water so as to lower the temperature of what remained, R. Shim'on declared that although he was thus heating cold water on the Sabbath (an act normally forbidden), this would be permitted, since it was his intention to cool the hot water and not to heat the cold. However, as someone objected, pouring cold water

---

342   פסיק ראשיה
343   אינו צריכה לגופה
344   דבר שאין מתכוון מותר
345   לא ניחא ליה
346   אם צריכה לגופו חייב
347   מיחם שפונה ממנו מים

into the hot cauldron would inevitably harden the metal and thus upgrade the cauldron, an act forbidden on the Sabbath.[348] Shemuel therefore declared that since a benefit was derived, even though no such wish or purpose lay behind the action, R. Shim'on would consider it a violation of the Sabbath, as it was a case of both *pesik resheih* and *niḥa leh* (*Shab.* 41b, *Tos. s.v. "meiḥam"*).

According to R. Yehudah, any such act involving *pesik resheih* and performed on the Sabbath incurs a Torah prohibition,[349] even if it is not a "purposeful action" (*melekhet maḥashevet*). R. Shim'on would also have maintained this opinion, except where the act was both "undesired"[350] and "inessential",[351] in which case he would not have deemed it reprehensible (*Tos. ad loc., s.v. "meiḥam"*).

Among the early commentators, one view maintained, according to the *She'iltot* of Aḥai Gaon, that the Sages accepted the ruling of R. Shim'on – that an unintended violation of the Sabbath laws did not incur guilt[352], while the reverse was true of all other prohibitions.[353] According to the ROSH, however, R. Shim'on's lenient ruling[354] extended to all other prohibitions (*Shab.* 110b; Rosh, *Shabbat* 14:9, discussing various cases).

From all of these discussions it appears that the Sages were divided throughout in their view of the extent of liability, as were the authoritative commentators who followed them. It would therefore be worthwhile to record the opinion of Maimonides with reference to the Sabbath laws, as stated in his Code (chap. 1).

---

348 והלא מצרפו
349 אסור מדאוריתא
350 לא ניחא ליה
351 מלאכה שאין צריך לגופו
352 דבר שלא מתכון מותר
353 אסור
354 מותר

The Ruling of Maimonides

Maimonides sets forth the normal rule concerning the prohibition of "work" on the Sabbath,[355] namely, that if such forbidden acts are performed unintentionally,[356] the offender is obliged to make a sin-offering.[357] When, however, someone undertakes a form of work that is permitted on the Sabbath,[358] but may thereby cause forbidden "work" to be done (e.g., dragging a bed or stool across an earthen floor, thus making a furrow in the ground, which is forbidden, although his only concern is to move that item), such an action is permitted.

This ruling of Maimonides accords with the principle of R. Shim'on[359] that the performance of a lawful action, even if this may involve an unintended forbidden one, incurs no blame and is permissible (Caro, *Orah Hayyim* 337:1). However, if in the course of a permitted action a forbidden one will inevitably take place, even if the author does not intend to violate the law, he is held culpable, since "one cannot cut off a chicken's head and then say that one did not mean to kill it" (*pesik resheih*). As it should have been obvious that the action would lead to an offence, the person involved was negligent and is held liable even for the unintended transgression (Maim. Code, *Shabbat*, 1:5–6; *Shab.* 75a, 150a).

Where an action forbidden on the Sabbath was in fact intended, but its object was not direct but secondary (i.e., the particular transgression was not intentional), one cannot plead that the offence was committed unintentionally. That would be like extinguishing a lamp, not to turn off the light (which would involve prohibited "work"), but in order to save the oil.[360] For so doing one would be held liable (*Shab.* 29b).[361]

---

355 מלאכה
356 בשגגה
357 חטאת
358 דברים המותרים בשבת
359 דבר שאינו מתכוון מותר
360 מלאכה שאינה צריך לגופו
361 המכבה את הנר...כחס על הנר כחס על השמן כחס על הפתילה חייב

Since "work" forbidden on the Sabbath is defined as "purposeful work" (*melekhet mahashevet*), the ruling is that if one's intention was to cut grain already reaped (which is permitted), but in the course of doing so one accidentally cut unreaped grain (which constitutes forbidden "work"), one would not be held liable. This only applies to "work" performed on the Sabbath. In general, offences committed unintentionally (*bi-shegagah*) obligate a person to bring a *hattat* sin-offering (Maim. Code, *Shabbat* 1:8; *Shab.* 73a, according to Rava but not Abbaye).

Error – Shegagah

If by mistake[362] one transgresses a negative commandment of the Torah punishable by "excision" (*karet*),[363] on becoming aware of the unintentional offence one is required to bring a sin-offering (Lev. 4:27–28; Maim. *Shegagot* 1:1). This affords an opportunity to atone for an unwitting transgression; but where neglect is involved, no such opportunity is available.

A person's guilt would be lessened, however, if his mind had been occupied with the fulfilment of a religious duty (*mitzvah*). If that was the purpose of his action and, while performing it, he had committed the transgression, no sin-offering was required[364] as he had been engaged in a lawful act.[365] Furthermore, his mind had been focused on the precept that he was anxious to fulfil.[366]

A standard case of error involves the obligation to circumcise a boy on the eighth day following his birth. The circumcision (*berit milah*) must be performed on that day even if it happens to be a Sabbath, when such "work" is otherwise forbidden. If two children were due to be circumcised, one on the Sabbath

---

362 בשגגה
363 כרת
364 פטור מחטאת
365 מפני שעשה ברשות
366 שהיה טרוד בדבר מצוה

and the other on Friday or one on the Sabbath and the other on Sunday, and the *mohel* became confused and circumcised them both on the Sabbath (thus violating a Torah law in one instance), the *mohel* would be exempt from a sin-offering. The reason is that, in the case of one child, the "work" prohibition had already been suspended and it was lawful to perform the circumcision in fulfilment of a *mitzvah*; circumcising the other child is therefore not considered a neglectful transgression (*Pes.* 72a; Maim. *Shegagot* 2:8).

Other examples of unwitting transgression in the course of performing a religious duty[367] are a mistaken violation of the laws governing marital relations (*Yev.* 34a) or of the Sabbath law on "carrying" when one seeks to fulfil the *mitzvah* of *lulav* (*Suk.* 42a).[368]

There are occasions when a transgression of a rabbinically, or even scripturally, ordained prohibition maybe regarded less gravely. As an example of common conduct which maybe contrary to the ritual law, it is recorded that R. Ḥanan bar Rava asked his teachers if it is the accepted rule that any "work"done on the festivals should be performed differently from the usual (*kamah d'efshar leshanu'yei meshanin*), except where no change of procedure was possible. It is also stated that one may not beat the breast, or some other demonstration of grief (*evel*) on the festivals, and similarly one may not dance with music on the festivals, being an additional precaution (*shevut*) in case one might forgetfully do a forbidden "work" of repairing his instrument on the festival. "Yet", said R. Ḥanan, "we see that there are many religious women who were lax in these matters, and you do not rebuke them in any way" (*Betz.* 30a). Likewise, even though it was scripturally ordained that on the eve of the Day of Atonement one must begin fasting during the afternoon, some while before the Day actually commences, yet we see women, busy caring for the needs of

---

367   טעה בדבר מצווה
368   פטור שהוציא ברשות

the household, eat and drink until it is dark, and we do not rebuke them (*Yoma* 81b).[369]

In both the above cases the Sages ruled: "Let our people be" (*hanah lahem leyisrael*). "Do not overdo it with our good people, Israel. Do not demand of them more than they can manage doing. If they cannot help doing otherwise, and in any case they are likely to continue with their normal conduct, it is preferable that they do so in ignorance (*bishegagah*) rather than deliberately (*bemezid*), and therefore we do not rebuke them" (*ibid.*).[370]

I. Evasion – *Ha'aramah*

An evasive device maybe within the law (*ha'aramah be-hetter*)[371] or utterly forbidden (*ha'aramah be-issur*)[372] – in other words, a deceitful act (*Talmudic Encyclopedia*, vol. 9, p. 697).

Firstborn Animal – Bekhor Behemah

A classic example of evasion for one's own benefit which is nevertheless within the law[373] has to do with the firstborn animal (*bekhor*),[374] which must be dedicated entirely to the priest (Num. 18:17; Lev. 27:26). Since the law comes into force only after the firstling's birth, while it is still in its mother's womb the owner may declare that should the issue be a male (to which the law of *bekhor* only applies), it will be dedicated as a peace-offering.[375] The firstling can then serve

---

369 והאידנא דקא חזינן דעבדן הכי ולא אמרינן להו ולא מידי
370 אלא הנח להם לישראל מוטב שיהיו שוגגין ואל יהיו מזידים
371 הערמה בהיתר
372 הערמה באיסור
373 הערמה באופן מותר
374 בכור
375 שלמים

to discharge a prior sacrificial obligation, thereby avoiding one's duty to give a *bekhor* to the priest. Here we have an example of an evasive artifice (*Tem.* 5:1).

Since the obligation to sanctify the firstling applies only to that of a Jew, if he sells or gives part of the unborn animal to a non-Jew (who then becomes its joint owner),[376] the law of *bekhor* no longer applies. As it is no longer possible to fulfil the law by giving the animal to a Temple priest, the Rabbis advise that some portion be sold to a non-Jew, even though it is understood that the *bekhor* will remain in the Jew's possession. Such an artifice is permitted and recommended (*Bek.* 2a; *Yoreh De'ah* 320:6).

Removal of Leaven before Passover

Since all leaven must be removed from one's property before Passover,[377] one may fulfil this requirement by making a present of the *hametz* to a non-Jew or by selling it to him (*Pes.* 21a, *Mish.*). However, in view of the considerable financial loss that destroying or abandoning *hametz* may involve, it has become standard practice to arrange the sale of one's *hametz*[378] to a non-Jew for a nominal sum and, after Passover, to buy it back from him. Although both parties know that the sale is a temporary one, this legal fiction[379] is permitted. Owing to the strict prohibition of *hametz* on Passover, rabbinic authorities insist that the transaction be made in accordance with all the laws of sale (*Orah Hayyim* 448:3, *Ba'er Heitev* and *Mishnah Berurah ad loc.*).[380]

---

376 שותף
377 ביעור חמץ לפני פסח
378 מכירת חמץ
379 הערמה
380 מכירה גמורה

Vows – Nedarim

In case of an emergency, a simple device is permitted. Thus, if a man has vowed to forgo any benefit from his neighbour and happens to be without food, that neighbour may give food to a third person from whom the first man can take it; or he may declare it ownerless[381] and the food can then be taken by the vower. An obvious evasion is not, however, allowed. Thus, the neighbour may not stipulate that the third person give such food to the first person, as that would constitute a blatant evasion of the oath (*Ned.* 43a, RAN and *Tos. ad loc.*; *Yoreh De'ah* 221:9).

Work on a Festival

Generally speaking, work on a festival is forbidden. In exceptional cases, however, the law permits any work required for the preparation of food (Ex. 12:15).[382] Accordingly, the ritual slaughter of an animal[383] to be eaten on the festival is permitted. A different law prohibits the slaughter of a mother and its young on the same day (Lev. 22:28).[384] If a mother and its young fall into a pit, one may not pull them out on the festival, as this constitutes work aimed at saving one's property. However, since it is allowed to do whatever is necessary to prepare food, one of the animals could be taken out of the pit and slaughtered; but the *oto ve-et beno* prohibition would apply to removing both for the purpose of *shehitah* (*Yoreh De'ah* 16:1).

The strict law can nevertheless be evaded, and both animals removed, through use of the following device. A person might say that the first animal was needed and take it out, then say

---

381   הפקר
382   אוכל נפש
383   שחיטה
384   אותו ואת בנו

that he had changed his mind, preferring the second, and take that one out. Such a ruse was permissible (*ha'aramah be-ofen muttar*), particularly to save the beasts from suffering (*Betzah* 37; *Orah Hayyim* 498:10; Maim. *Yom Tov* 2:4).[385]

Cooking on a Festival

The law governing "work" allows one to prepare whatever food is required in order to fulfil the *mitzvah* of "rejoicing on the festival".[386] Otherwise, any "work" forbidden on the Sabbath is likewise forbidden on a festival (*yom tov*), except for the prohibition against "carrying" from one domain to another (*Orah Hayyim* 495:1).[387] Should it be necessary to prepare food for the Sabbath that immediately succeeds a festival, one must arrange a symbolic "mixing" of prepared food (*eruv tavshilin*) before the festival in order to prepare food on *yom tov* for the next day. This involves "mixing" food for the Sabbath (e.g., a hard-boiled egg) with food cooked on the festival; otherwise, such "work" is prohibited (*Orah Hayyim* 527:1 *ff.*).

J. Appearances – *Mar'it Ayin*

In the view of the Sages, one should avoid performing an action that may in itself be permitted, and where it is clear that no transgression is involved, if there is a danger that an observer may surmise that a transgression is involved (Meiri on *Yoma* 38a).

Even appearing to commit an offence should be avoided. The Sages alluded to actions of this type when they urged one to "keep far away from evil" (e.g., *Hul.* 44a).[388] Those

---

385   צער בעלי חיים
386   שמחת יום טוב
387   הוצאה מרשות לרשות
388   הרחיק מן הכיור

collecting charitable donations should be aware of outward appearances (*mar'it ayin*) and take care not to be suspected of abusing their trust. If they have collected a large amount of small change and there are no poor folk to whom this can be distributed immediately, they may ask another person to exchange the coins of low value for higher denominations, but must not do so themselves in case people suspect them of taking unfair advantage (*Pes.* 13a). Even the most upright collectors of charity and holders of public trust are expected to render an account of the sums collected (*Yoreh De'ah* 257:2, REMA).

Similarly, a priest entering the Temple in order to clean the Sanctuary and collect the half-shekels placed on the table (Lev. 6:3)[389] was forbidden to make personal use of them for fear of "appropriating the sacred" (*me'ilah*). He was to be searched when entering and leaving, and kept under observation while he worked. This supervision was undertaken not because the *kohen* was actually suspected of embezzlement, but in case he became rich or poor at some time in the future, thereby incurring a suspicion that this was due to some offence that he had committed in the Sanctuary.

This law was based on the idea that a man should be seen to be free from guilt,[390] as enjoined in the Torah: "Ye shall be clear before the Lord, and before Israel" (Num. 32:22).[391] A priest therefore had to wear loose open garments in the Sanctuary, so that no one would gain the impression that he was hiding some sacred item in the folds of his clothing (*Tos.*, *Shek.* 3:2). Even Moses, whom one would assume to have been above all suspicion, was careful to wear such a plain garment (*Ta'an.* 11b).

For that same reason, the Temple's expert manufacturers of incense[392] would not allow a bride leaving their home to wear

---

389   לתרום את הלישקה
390   צריך לצאת ידי הבריות
391   והייתם נקיים מד' ומישראל
392   קטורת

any perfume, lest anyone believe that they were using scent from the *ketoret* (*Yoma* 38a). This is reflected in the Biblical exhortation: "So shalt thou find favour and understanding in the sight of God and man" (Prov. 3:4).[393]

Forbidden Foods

Fish Blood — Dam Dagim

Whereas blood from an animal or fowl is forbidden (Lev. 7:26), the prohibition does not extend to blood from a fish (*Ker.* 21b). However, a person seeing fish blood (*dam dagim*) at a meal would not necessarily realize what it was; he might well take it to be animal blood and regard those eating it as transgressors. Accordingly, the Sages ruled that *dam dagim* should likewise not be eaten on the grounds of *mar'it ayin*, unless it contained fish scales, which would indicate its origin (*Ker.* 21b; *Yoreh De'ah* 66:9).

Meat with Almond Milk — Basar be-Halev Shekedim

The prohibition against mixing milk and meat refers to the milk obtained from a "kosher" animal (Ex. 23:19). If, at a meat meal, a person wished to serve almond milk (which resembles the milk derived from animals), the Sages required him to place some almonds next to it, so that people would not be confused and suspect him of violating the "milk and meat" prohibition (*Yoreh De'ah* 87:3).[394] On the same basis, when a non-dairy milk substitute (coffee whitener) is served at a meat meal, it should be clear from the packaging that this is rabbinically approved.

---

393   ומצא חן ושכל טוב בעיני אלו-הים ואדם
394   משום מראית העין

Working on the Sabbath

Contract Work – Kablanut

Torah law forbade various categories of "work" on the Sabbath, including work performed by one's non-Jewish servant (Ex. 20:10). The Sages extended this prohibition to include any non-Jew hired to do certain jobs on the Sabbath, although a non-Jew is under no religious obligation to refrain from work on the seventh day. The law, however, is different if one contracts a non-Jew to work for a fixed price, without specifying on which days the work should be done. In that case, the employee remains independent of the employer while discharging his commission and the employer pays an agreed sum for the work contracted (*be-kablanut*). Furthermore, it is not the employer's concern if the non-Jewish employee wishes to speed up the completion of his job.

This is based on the Talmudic principle that the non-Jewish farm tenant or lessee of a mill or public bath works for his own benefit (*AZ* 21b, *Tos.* ad loc.).[395] Such contract work maybe performed by the non-Jew on a Sabbath or festival, provided it is not done openly and in a manner that would lead a passerby to assume that it has been undertaken on the specific instructions of the Jewish employer. The casual onlooker would have no way of knowing that the work had been ordered by contract.

It is therefore laid down that a person may not contract a non-Jew to build his house, if it is obvious that this work is being done for him on the Sabbath. A transgressor is then forbidden the use of the house (*MK* 12a; *Orah Hayyim* 243, 244:1–3; *Tur, Orah Hayyim* 244, *Bet Yosef, s.v.* "Israel").[396]

---

395   אריסא אריסותיא עביד
396   משום מראית העין

Working on a Festival

Contrary to the law governing "work" on the Sabbath, the law regarding festivals permits one to carry an object needed that day into a public thoroughfare, just as any "work" required for the preparation of food is specifically authorized (Ex. 12:16).

Likewise, according to the ruling of Hillel, one may move a ladder needed to reach a dovecote in an open place so as to remove a bird that can be used for food;[397] if necessary, one may also move a stepladder from place to place within one's home. The Sages, however, forbade moving a large, heavy ladder outside the house, as a passerby might imagine that one was doing so in order to repair the roof,[398] which was a type of "work" prohibited on *yom tov* (*Betzah* 9a–b; *Orah Hayyim* 518:1, 4).

R. Yehudah declared in the name of Rav, the leading (3rd cent.) Babylonian authority, that this prohibition included not only a public place but wherever the Sages forbade an act on the grounds that a passer by might assume that an offence was being committed.[399] Such an action was also forbidden in the privacy of one's own room (*Betzah* 9b, *Tos. ad loc.* s.v. "*mai*").[400]

This prohibition governed any action that might itself be permitted, but which might nevertheless give rise to suspicions that it was forbidden. That would cast an unjustified aspersion on the performer's religious character or, conversely, induce the bystander to follow his example and then do something that was in fact prohibited. In such a case, the action was forbidden even in private, where there were no onlookers, since a man could become used to doing so behind closed doors and absentmindedly do the same in public (RAN on *Betzah* 9a, *s.v.* "*u-mihu*" on RIF 4b).

---

397   מוליכין את הסולם משובך לשובך

398   להטיח גגו הוא צריך

399   שאסרו חכמים מפני מראית העין

400   אפילו בחדרי חדרים אסור

Idolatry – Avodah Zarah

If, during a time of anti-Jewish persecution,[401] one is compelled to stand before an idol and then ordered to bend down for the purpose of loosening the straps of one's boots or picking up scattered coins (thus giving the appearance of bowing down to the idol), it is forbidden to do so because of *mar'it ayin,* i.e., giving the impression that one has kneeled before a heathen image. This rule does not, however, apply to a life-threatening situation (*Yoreh De'ah* 150:1, REMA *ad loc.*).

Ritual Slaughter – Shehitah

The Sages ruled that if, after a cow had been slaughtered, a live calf – even one fully grown (*ben peku'ah*) – was found in its womb, the calf did not require separate *shehitah*: anything within the cow was included in its slaughter (*Hul.* 74a).[402] They nevertheless determined that such a calf should also be slaughtered in case a bystander (unaware of the exceptional circumstances) thought that an animal was being prepared for table without *shehitah* (*Hul.* 75a, Rashi *ad loc.*; Rosh, *Hul.* 4:5; *Sh. Ar., Yoreh De'ah* 13:2, TAZ 4).

Slaughter of Sanctified Animals

Only sanctified animals[403] might be slaughtered within the Temple precincts (*Kid.* 57), but unsanctified animals could be slaughtered anywhere outside. Such *shehitah* did not require any particular *kavvanah* (*Hul.* 12b; Maim. *Shehitah* 2:11). However, if in the course of an animal's ritual slaughter there was any "contemplation" of idol worship, that thought would disqualify the *shehitah* (*Hul.* 39a).[404]

---

401 בשעת השמד
402 שחיטת אמו בטהרתו
403 קודשי מזבח
404 מחשבת עכו"ם פוסלת את השחיטה

If, outside the Temple, a person slaughtered a beast that was normally acceptable as a sanctified offering and declared it to be such, although it had not been sanctified, he inserted a forbidden "intention" in the act of slaughter. The *shehitah* was accordingly disqualified and the meat forbidden.[405] According to the strict law, as the animal had not been sanctified, it did not fall under the prohibition against slaughtering a sanctified beast outside the Temple.[406] However, the Sages ruled that since a bystander might assume that he was violating the prohibition, any meat from this *shehitah* was forbidden because of *mar'it ayin* (*Hul.* 41b, Rashi *ad loc.*; Maim. *Shehitah* 2:17, *Maggid Mishneh ad loc.*).

The Paschal Lamb – Korban Pesah

The offering of the paschal lamb, on the 14th day of the month of Nisan, had to be performed within the Temple precincts (Ex. 12:3, 24; *Mekhilta ad loc.*; Maim. *Korban Pesah* 1:1, 3).[407] In view of the prohibition against slaughtering a sanctified animal outside the Temple, the Sages ruled that when preparing meat for the Passover festival a man should be careful not to say, "This meat is for the Passover,"[408] in case it led others to suspect that he was intending to eat the sanctified meat of a paschal lamb that had been slaughtered outside the Temple.[409] Such meat was now prohibited because of *mar'it ayin* (*Pes.* 53a; *Orah Hayyim* 469:1).[410] Likewise, when reciting the *Haggadah* at the Passover *Seder*, one should not raise the roasted shankbone for fear of giving the impression that it comes from the sanctified paschal lamb (*Pes.* 116b).[411]

---

405 שחיטתו פסולה
406 שחיטת חולין בחוץ
407 בעזרה
408 בשר זה לפסח
409 שחיטת חולין בחוץ
410 מראית העין
411 קרבן פסח

Family Law

Divorce

According to Biblical law, a wife is released from her marriage bond when the husband writes or authorizes a bill of divorce (*get* or *sefer keritut*) and hands it to her (Deut. 24:1). By means of this *get* she acquires her freedom (*Kid.* 13b). He may write the *get* in his wife's absence and have it conveyed to her by an appointed messenger (*shali'ah*). Once it enters her possession, the divorce becomes effective. The messenger is required to testify before the *bet din* that this *get* was executed legally in his presence (*Git.* 2a; TJ *Git.* 6:1; *Even ha-Ezer* 12:1, 140:1, 142:1).

When the *get* was written before a court within the Land of Israel, it was assumed that the signatures attached to it could be confirmed by the *bet din* receiving the document. If the *get* arrived with a messenger from outside the borders of Israel, where the witnesses might not be known, the document's reliability depended entirely on the evidence of the messenger. In that case, the Sages ruled, although the *get* enabled the woman to remarry (since the *bet din* accepted the messenger's testimony), the *shali'ah* himself was not allowed to marry her. The reason given is that evidence of her divorce rests only on the word of the messenger, who might be suspected of having given false testimony in order to marry a woman who was still another man's wife. Any suspicion of immorality had to be avoided (*Yev.* 25a, Rashi *ad loc.*).

On that basis, later authorities declared that the *mar'it ayin* rule is applicable in all circumstances, even in the same town (*Tur, Even ha-Ezer* 141, quoting ROSH, *ad loc.*).[412] This does not mean that the witness is actually suspected of wrongdoing (his evidence is, in fact, accepted), but every effort must be made to ensure that other people do not gain a wrong impression.

This even applied to the Sage who was called upon to judge the effect of a certain vow and who, on the strength of that vow, ordered the husband to divorce his wife. Though fully dependable, the Sage himself was forbidden to marry the divorcee because people might then suspect that he had dissolved the marriage for his own selfish purposes (*Yev.* 26a, Rashi *ad loc.*; *Even ha-Ezer* 12:2).[413]

Forbidden Marriages

Those whom it is forbidden to marry, in accordance with Torah law or by extension to secondary degrees (*sheniyyot*) according to the Sages, include the wife of a man's father, even though she is not his mother (Lev. 18:8). Marrying his wife's mother is likewise prohibited (Lev. 20:14). However, there is no law forbidding him to marry a different wife of his father-in-law, i.e., a woman who is not his wife's mother (*Yev.* 21a). Permission to marry a father-in-law's divorced wife or widow is thus granted by R. Yosef Caro (*Sh. Ar., Even ha-Ezer* 15:24).[414] Nevertheless, other authorities, such as ROSH and MAHARIL, forbade such a marriage on the basis of *mar'it ayin*, since people unaware of the true circumstances might think that the person concerned was actually marrying his wife's mother (*Yev.* 21a, *Tos. s.v.* "*U-muttar*"; TJ *Yev.* 2:4; *Even ha-Ezer* 15:24, TAZ 15).

Harvesting the Corner of the Field – Pe'ah

Torah law requires that, when harvesting the produce of a field, one should leave the corner for the poor and the stranger (Lev. 19:9).[415] The Sages quantified "the corner" as one-sixtieth of the field. This unharvested corner should be left at

---

413   משום חשד ורננה
414   מותר אדם באשת חמיו
415   לא תכלה פאת שדך לקצר

the end of the harvested field, so that poor folk know where to find it. Although the farmer might quite properly leave it at the beginning of his field, it is especially required to be at the end so that passersby may see that it has indeed been left. Otherwise, they might suspect that he would falsely claim that the due amount had been left at the beginning and that the poor had already gathered it. This is another example of a special regulation designed to avoid suspicion (TJ *Pe'ah* 4:3).[416]

A similar possibility of evasion could be found in the harvesting law which stated that when the owner was in his field while the sheaves were gathered, and later he found that some sheaves had been forgotten, he is forbidden to return to take them, but must leave them to be collected by the poor – *shikehah* (Deut. 24:19).[417] The same law applied, likewise, to the collection of odd droppings during the cutting and in grape harvesting – *leket, o'lel* (Lev. 19:9)[418] (Maim. *Mishneh Torah, Matenot Ani'im*, chaps. 1–5).

Mixed Species – Kil'ayim

In regard to the prohibition against sowing a field with "diverse seeds" (Lev. 19:19),[419] culpability depended on there being a minimum quantity of each seed; but even if the measure was less, a person had to remove the odd seeds before harvesting the remainder. Even if he himself had not sown or wanted them there, they must be removed; if he allowed them to sprout, other people might conclude that he intended having "diverse seeds" in his field.[420] If, however, it was clear that he had never intended to sow them, the offending seeds could be left in the ground (Maim. *Kil'ayim* 1:1; 2:1, 7–8).

---

416 מפני מראית העין
417 ושכחת עומר בשדה
418 ולקט קצירך לא תלקט, וכרמך לא תעולל
419 כלאים
420 מפני מראית העין

Usury – Ribbit

Biblical law forbade a Jewish borrower to pay interest on a loan made by a fellow Jew (Deut. 23:20, Rashi *ad loc.*).[421] The Torah likewise forbade a Jew to charge interest on a loan made to a fellow Jew (Lev. 25:37).[422] In a further development of this law, if money belonging to a gentile was deposited with a Jew on the gentile's responsibility, that money could be lent to a Jew on interest, as such interest would be required by the gentile (*BM* 70b). However, the Sages also forbade a Jew to charge interest on this loan, since other people, unaware that the money belonged to a non-Jew, would suspect that interest was being taken from a fellow Jew (*Sh. Ar., Yoreh De'ah* 169:22).[423] Nevertheless, if it is generally understood that this money is not the Jew's personal property,[424] as is largely the case in modern finance, charging interest on the loan is permitted, since the fear of *mar'it ayin* is no longer applicable (*Yoreh De'ah* 169:23, REMA *ad loc.*).

K. Covetousness

A moral injunction restraining human behaviour, "Thou shalt not covet" stands at the end of the Ten Commandments and is expressed in two different forms: *Lo taḥmod* – "Thou shalt not covet" (Ex. 20:14)[425] and *Lo tit'avveh* – "Thou shalt not desire" (Deut. 5:18).[426]

The Sages regarded these as two different laws. The first simply meant that one should not appropriate the object coveted; the second was an exhortation not to harbour

---

421 לא תשיך לאחיך נשך
422 את כספך לא תתן לו בנשך
423 ואם הם באחריות העו'ג מותר אבל אסור לעשות כן מפני מראית העין
424 אם הדבר מפורסם לרבים מותר
425 לא תחמוד
426 לא תתאוה

covetous thoughts. Such thoughts might lead one to acquire the object by devious means, which would violate the *Lo taḥmod* commandment,[427] or even to rob the owner, a violation of the *Lo tigzol* commandment (Lev. 19:13; *Mekhilta*, Ex. 20:14).[428]

Maimonides explained that the law against coveting,[429] does not simply mean wishing to have a desirable object, which is a natural urge that should be kept under control. It refers to the desire for something that belongs to another person ("his wife, his servant, his ox or his ass") and which the owner wants to keep for himself. Because of his burning "desire", the covetous person endeavours to secure it by guile or exerts undue pressure on the owner to accept payment in return. The final act of appropriation completes the man's offence, since no payment of money will reconcile the owner to his loss (*BM* 5b). When a covetous person takes the desired object in this way, he has transgressed a precept of the Decalogue and is obliged to make the necessary restitution (*Mekhilta*, Ex. 20:14; Maim. Code, *Gezelah* 1:9; *Sefer ha-Ḥinnukh* 38).

Maimonides regarded the law "Thou shalt not desire" (*Lo tit'avveh*) (Deut. 5:18)[430] as a separate prohibition. It was a moral injunction forbidding a man to have "a yearning desire" or craving for some item that belonged to another person and which would only be available if the owner agreed to sell or give it to him, which he had no wish to do. As stated above, harbouring any such desire could impel a man to acquire it by guile or pressure, which would violate the *Lo taḥmod* commandment and might even involve robbery (Mic. 2:2).

The act of "desiring" in *Lo tit'avveh* gives vent to an emotional state, whereas the act of "coveting" in *Lo taḥmod* gives practical expression to man's acquisitiveness (*Mekhilta ad loc.*; Maim. *Gezelah* 1:10, *Sefer ha-Mitzvot* 266; *Ḥinnukh*

---

427   לא תחמוד
428   לא תגזול
429   לא תחמד
430   לא תתאוה

38). Most offences are traceable to a craving for possessions or sexual gratification, and these illicit desires can end in wholesale transgression of the Ten Commandments. According to the Sages, one who covets another man's possessions will lose his own and have to endure the fate of exile (Targum Yonatan on Ex. 20:14).[431]

In his Torah commentary, Ibn Ezra raises an interesting question: Since it is natural for a man to desire things that attract him, how can he be ordered not to desire them? Ibn Ezra explains that one may consider something delightful, but know very well that it is out of reach. A shepherd may gaze admiringly at a beautiful princess, yet realize that he has no more chance of marrying her than of sprouting wings and flying through the air. In the same way, a man will not dream of marrying his own mother, however beautiful she maybe. Such thoughts do not occur to him, because he has always known that they are far beyond the realms of possibility.

A man should therefore realize that whatever life has in store is predetermined by the Almighty.[432] As the Sages affirmed, "the gifts of children, long life and sustenance" are allocated to man by God and a person can only obtain what has been ordained for him.[433] Accordingly, a sensible man will not indulge in foolish desires and long for things that he can never possess. He will not covet his neighbour's wife, realizing that she is not meant for him. He will be content with his lot[434] and have faith in Divine providence (Ibn Ezra on Ex. 20:14).

As previously indicated, Maimonides distinguished between a "yearning desire" for someone else's property[435] and "coveting" it.[436] In the latter case (*Lo tahmod*) a person

---

431   וגלותא אתיא על עלמא
432   כאשר חלק לו ה׳
433   בני חיי ומזוני לא בזכותה תליא מילתא אלא במזלא
434   ישמח בחלקו
435   לא תתאוה
436   לא תחמוד

incurs guilt only when he appropriates the object; and even though he paid for it, his forceful methods are comparable to theft, transgressing the *Lo tigzol* commandment.

Leading commentators observe that the prohibition begins with the phrase: "Thou shalt not covet thy neighbour's house". Since a house falls under the category of landed property, the accepted rule is that "land cannot be stolen" (*Suk.* 31a; *BK* 117b).[437] Thus, while "lifting" a movable object violates the law against theft,[438] wrongfully occupying land does not, since land is "immovable property" that cannot be taken away and cannot be stolen. An illegal occupier (squatter) must pay for any loss or damage incurred,[439] but trespassing does not amount to theft.

According to basic *Halakhah*, therefore, if someone went into another person's empty house and occupied it without the owner's knowledge or permission, and if the house was not available for rent or sale, the occupier would not be liable to pay rent as the owner had incurred no loss through the benefit gained by the occupier.[440] He would only have to make restitution for any damage that he had caused (*BK* 21a). Later rabbinic development of the *Halakhah* would, of course, lay down other penalties for trespassing. Legally speaking, in this instance, the trespasser has not committed theft, but he is guilty of violating the law against covetousness (Maim. Code, *Gezelah ve-Avedah* 3:9; NETZIV, *Ha-amek Davar* on Ex. 20:14).[441]

---

437 קרקע אינה נגזלת
438 חייב בלא תגזול
439 חסרון ממון
440 זה נהנה וזה לא חסר
441 לא תחמוד

L. Designation (Right of Choice) and *Tovat Hana'ah*

Biblical law ordained that every landowner should give a portion of his annual harvest to a priest of his choosing. Such gifts were called "tithes" and "heave-offerings".[442] The amount of produce to be given depended on the owner's character: a generous man would give one-fortieth, a mean person one-sixtieth and the average man one-fiftieth. When making his allocation, the owner had the right to choose the *kohen* who would receive it and in return he received the priest's thanks – *tovat hana'ah* (Num. 5:10, *Sifrei* 3-4; *Kid.* 58b, ROSH *ad loc.*).[443]

The concept of *tovat hana'ah* is rooted in Biblical law: "Every heave-offering of all the holy things of the Children of Israel, which they present unto the priest, shall be his" (Num. 5:9).[444] The *Sifrei* notes that the expression "shall be his" (*lo yiheyeh*) means that the satisfaction derived from presenting the gift was the owner's.[445] The *Sifrei* goes on to explain that this right to choose was a moral benefit that could also have monetary value, depending on how much one might be willing to pay for this satisfaction. According to those who maintained that *tovat hana'ah* had a monetary value, the owner could allow someone else to give *terumah* on his behalf, in return for payment, thus enabling the other man to enjoy that *tovat hana'ah* (TJ *Dem.* 6:2).

The Sages even considered whether the use of such monetary value could fulfil the requirement of the *kesef kiddushin* that a man gave his bride when betrothing her (Num. 5, *Sifrei: Naso* 34; *Hul.* 133a; Maim. *Terumot* 12:15; *Kid.* 58a). They concluded that this type of benefit had no intrinsic worth[446]

---

442 מעשר ותרומות
443 טובת הנאה
444 לו יהיו
445 טובת הנאה ליבה עליה
446 כולי עלמא טובת הנאה אינה

and could not be used for the purpose of *kiddushin*, which required something of actual "value" (*kesef mammon*). It was nevertheless agreed that the satisfaction derived from making the gift could be of financial value to the donor (*Ned.* 85a; *Pes.* 46b; *Kid.* 58b).

What would the position be if the landowner appointed an agent to give *terumah* on his behalf, and who would have the right to choose the priestly recipient – the landowner or his agent? After all, it is the giver of the *terumah* who wins the *kohen*'s appreciation and this is of value to him, like the satisfaction derived from making a charitable gift.[447] The Sages ruled that one who gives *terumah* from his own produce while acting as an agent for someone else is entitled to choose the recipient, as when giving *terumah* on his own.[448] This is, of course, a privilege that the agent himself can exercise, and he thus gains the benefit of the *tovat hana'ah* (*Ned.* 36b; Maim. *Terumot* 4:1–2 *Kesef Mishneh ad loc.*; *Yoreh De'ah* 61:1 ,7; see *He-Arukh, s.v.* "*Tov*", "*Tovat Hana'ah*").

The Sages also considered whether an individual might be prepared to pay something for the benefit of *tovat hana'ah*, even if its value was merely that of the smallest coin.[449] If so, one might claim that "the right to choose" possessed a monetary value. The Sages determined, however, that the only benefit was an emotional one, lacking substance, and this was not worth money.

The differing views had many halakhic ramifications. If, for example, the agent acted without the owner's consent, had he deprived him of something of value and would he therefore be guilty of stealing? Or, alternatively, was it not even worth a *perutah*,[450] to which the liability for "stealing" did not extend? A similar question would arise if the *kohen* took the produce for himself, without the knowledge of the owner, because the owner's *tovat hana'ah* was worth less than a *perutah* (*Kid.*

---

447   הכהן יחזיק לו טובה
448   התורם משלו על שאינו שלו טובת הנאה שלו
449   שווה פרוטה
450   פחות משווה פרוטה

58b; _Hul._ 133a; Maim. _Terumot_ 12:15). The theft of _tevel_ produce due to the priest raised another issue: whether the thief should be charged with stealing the owner's produce or merely with depriving him of the _tovat hana'ah_ that he might have enjoyed (_Ned._ 84b–85a).

If someone took a vow that no priest or Levite should receive any benefit from him, would the priestly due be regarded as already in the _kohen_'s possession, since it had been given to him by Torah law and was therefore excluded from the oath? Another question that the Sages discussed was whether the _kohen_ also deprived the man of his _tovat hana'ah_, which (if of financial value to him), would have been included in his oath (_Ned._ 84b). According to later responsa (MAHARAM), if any dispute arose over the ownership of a _tovat hana'ah_, one could not be required to swear an oath in regard to one's claim, as it had no substantial recognized value.[451]

If, however, a man sold his field to another person, but reserved his own right of _tovat hana'ah_ on the _terumah_ due from its produce, that could be something of value to be excluded (_Yad Ramah, BB_ 4:27). Later authorities ruled that _tovat hana'ah_ cannot be acquired by _kinyan_,[452] since it is not a material object attainable by "lifting".[453]

[General Reference: _Talmudic Encyclopedia_, vol. 19, pp. 99–148, _s.v. "Tovat Hana'ah"_]

M. Intention to Give Charity – _Tzedakah_

Reaching a decision in the matter of charity has an enhanced significance. When a man resolves to give a particular sum to _tzadakah_ and says to himself, or to someone else, that he will donate such-and-such an amount, his intention is considered

---

451   דררא דממונא
452   קנין
453   אי אפשר להקנות במשיכה

a sacred vow to the Almighty. The sum offered no longer belongs to him and it has, as it were, already been conveyed to the holy Temple.

Fulfilling this *mitzvah* is thus comparable to bringing an offering to the Temple. Once a man designated something "holy to the Lord", it no longer remained in his possession (*Ned.* 29b).[454] The sacredness of a vow was emphasized in the Torah: "That which is gone out of thy lips thou shalt observe and do; according as thou hast vowed freely unto the Lord thy God…" (Deut. 23:24).[455]

Some authorities ruled that the *bet din* may even compel one to do so. Others held that a person was not bound by what he had merely thought of doing. Had he expressed such intentions to himself, or to others by word of mouth, only then would he be obligated (*Sh. Ar., Yoreh De'ah* 258:13, REMA; *Sh. Ar., Hoshen Mishpat* 212:8).

N. Custom in Jewish Ritual Law

In commercial law it is ruled that contracts must be interpreted by the usage of the country. The common usage of the country has the binding force of law, according to the rabbinic principle, "all procedures must follow the practice of the country, and one cannot change from the local practice." (*BM* 7a; *Tosefta BM* 5:6; *Ber.* 55a)[456]

But this rule applies exclusively to matters of civil and commercial law (*mamon*), but not to matters of religious and moral law (*issur*). Whereas in rabbinically ordained ritual prohibitions, if a doubt arose as to whether the action had involved a transgression in a particular case, the decision would be in favour of leniency (*Shab.* 34a; *Eruv.* 5b).[457] In

---

454 אמירתו לגבוהא כמסירתו להדיוט
455 מוצא שפתיך תשמור ועשית כאשר נדרת לה' אלו-היך נדבה אשר דברת בפיך
456 הכל כמנהג המדינה - אין משנין ממנהג המדינה
457 ספק דרבנן לקולא

financial disputes, however, the decision would follow a stringent view, so that where the value of both claims cannot be determined neither party is given more credit than the other, and the object in dispute is divided equally between them (*Yev.* 37b; *BK* 35b; *BM* 2b; *BB* 93a).[458] A labourer engaged to work for the day may rely on the local custom of what hours he is obliged to work. The Book of Psalms described the existing rule: "Man (at the rising of the sun) goes out to his work and to his labour until evening" (Ps. 104: 22–23). But in a particular locality there was a shorter working day, and despite the employer's intention, the labourer was entitled to the more favourable shorter day; and the *Halakha* would maintain his claim. The *Mishna* stated: "The employer may not compel them to work longer hours where the custom is not to begin early and work late" (*BM* 7:1). This rule works in favour of the defendant according to the principle; the burden of proof rests on the claimant (*BK* 35b).[459] (M. Elon, *Jewish Law*, vol. 1 p. 132, 135 *ff.*)

The Binding Power of Custom

The scriptural source for the binding force of custom is attributed by the Sages to the verse: "Thou shalt not remove thy neighbour's landmark, which they of old time have set" (Deut. 19:14).[460] It is stated in the Responsa of R. Sherira Gaon that this is the source of the law that the practice of custom can become the established law (R. Sherira Gaon, quoted in TUR, <u>Hoshen Mishpat</u> 368).[461] Another source is found in the saying of Proverbs: "Hearken to thy father that begat thee; and despise not thy mother when she is old" (Prov. 23:22; *Ber.* 54a, Rashi *ad. loc*).[462]

---

458   ממון המוטל בספק חולקין

459   המוציא מחבירו עליו הראיה

460   לא תשיג גבול רעך אשר גבלו ראשונים

461   מכאן דמנהגא מילתא היא

462   ואל תבוז כי זקנה אמך

In a halakhic judgment of MAHARAM of Rothenburg, (Germany, 13th cent.) he stated: "In all matters on which the leading authorities differ, I rule according to the stringent opinon, except ... when the lenient view has been accepted pursuant to earlier custom" (Responsa, ed. Berlin, No. 386).

Jacob Moellin (Germany, 15th cent.) ruled that despite the Torah prohibition of taking interest (see Chap. 6, sect. M) the custom of lending out orphans' money even at fixed interest (*ribit ketzutzah*) was justified because of the *mitzvah* of caring for orphans (Responsa, MAHARIL, No. 37).

Custom as an obligation – *Ḥiyyuv mi-Minhagah*

There are many ritual laws that are observed in different communities which have no obligatory sanction (*midina*), even as a rabbinic institution, but are performed as augmented as a pious practice *(mi-minhaga)*.

There are circumstances in ritual law in which no law of prohibition obtains (*ein hiyyuv mi-dina*), but it is the practice in some communities to follow a prohibition which is stricter than the law requires. These are described as an obligation dictated by custom (*hiyyuv mi-minhagah*) (TAZ, *Sh. Ar., Yoreh De'ah* 242:13). Some of these customs are observed with particular meticulousness.

The following are but two examples of the binding power of custom in ritual law:

a) *Prohibition of Pulse as Leaven – Kitniyot*

The Sages of the *Mishnah* stated the five species of grain with which a man can discharge his obligation of eating unleavened bread *(matzah)* on Passover (Deut. 16:3). These are defined as wheat, barley, spelt, maize and oats. These same species, when they are not duly supervised from contact with water can be leavened (*ḥametz*) (*Pes.* 35a)[463]. The Sages of the

---

463   אלו דברים שאדם יוצא בהן ידי חובתו בפסח - בחיטים, בשעורים, בכוסמין,
ובשיפון, ובשיבולת שועל

Mishnah did not agree with the view of Rabbi Yoḥanan ben Nuri that rice is a species of corn, and thus they excluded if from producing leaven (*ibid.*).

Maimonides legislated according to the *Mishnah*, and added that legumes such as rice, mustard seed, poppy seed, sesame seed and grain pods, do not produce *ḥametz,* and therefore are not prohibited on Passover (Maim. *Yad, Ḥametz u-Matzah*, 5:1,2). Caro in the Shulḥan Arukh likewise excluded rice and other types of pulse (*kitniyot)* from any prohibition of *ḥametz* and permitted their use on Passover. The Code of the TUR states the same law, but adds that there are some authorities who forbid the use of rice and other species of pulse because of the possibility of a forbidden grain being mixed with it.

The REMA, however, follows the view of those who forbid the different forms of pulse, and states that the practice in Ashkenazi communities is to follow this stricter ruling, and in Ashkenazi communities one should not depart from this practice. This custom of the prohibition of the use of pulse on Passover is now strictly observed by all Ashkenazi Jews on the level of an ordained law, and they scrupulously refrain from any form of *kitniyot* on the Passover. Legally, the majority exclusory view would be followed, but this punctiliousness is a cautious attitude of mind in fear of transgressing a basic Torah law.

b) *Duty to Rise before the Open Ark –*
Amidah Li-khevod ha-Torah

Biblical law stated: "Thou shalt rise up before the hoary head, and honour the face of the old man, and thou shalt fear thy G-d; I am the Lord" (Lev. 19:32).[464] Based on this ordinance the Sages taught that it is the duty to stand in the presence of a Torah scholar; and they further ruled that "if such respect is

---

464   מפני שיבה תקום והדרת פני זקן ויראת מאלוקיך אני ה'

due to a scholar of Torah how much more so before the Scroll of the Torah itself!" (Kid. 32–33:).[465] Maimonides specified that it was particularly the duty to stand while the Sefer Torah was carried before him (Maim. *Yad, Sefer Torah* 5:7; 10:9).[466]

Caro in his Code particularised further: "All must stand until the one who carries the Scroll arrives at the place where the Scroll is laid, or until it has been carried out of view" (*Sh. Ar., Oraḥ Ḥayyim* 282:2; SHACH *ibid.* sect. 2).

Thus, on the Day of Atonement during the closing *Neila* Service when it is the custom to leave the Ark open, the congregation remains standing throughout. The *Neila* prayers at the close of the day "when the sun is already setting" are the final plea for forgiveness before the heavenly judgment on our lives is determined, and "the gates of prayer are closed" (TJ *Ber.* 4:1).[467] At this time prayers are offered with heightened fervor, marked by the Ark remaining open throughout the service (Ha-Ḥida, *Birkei Yosef, Yom Hakipurim* – Ḥayim Yosef David Azulai, Jerusalem Italy, 18th cent.).

An inquiry was addressed to R. Moshe Feinstein (a modern Talmudic authority, New York, 20th cent.) whether it was likewise necessary to stand for the lengthy period when the Ark was open and the Scrolls, although resting in their normal place, were visible to all. He replied that it would appear from the above rabbinic sources that the law applied only when the Scroll was carried before him, but not when it rested in its place in the Ark. Nevertheless, it was the accepted custom that the congregation always stood whenever the Ark was open and the Scrolls were visible. Despite the fact that standing for such a long period at the end of a day of fasting might entail physical hardship, the custom of standing was faithfully observed, excepting, of course, by the sick and elderly, as a mark of respect before the Ark.

---

465 קל וחומר מפני לומדיה עומדין מפניה לא כל שכן
466 כל הרואה ספר תורה כשהוא מהלך חייב לעמוד מפניו עד שיתכסה מעיניהם
467 נעילת שערי שמים

The 17th century Talmudic authority R. David ben Shmuel Halevi (TAZ) stated that this was the general practice although it was not obligatory in law (*Sh. Ar., Yoreh De'ah* 242:2, TAZ S.13).[468] R. Feinstein elaborated that although the TAZ meant that this was not a halakhic ruling (*ein ḥiyuv mi-dina)*, nevertheless, this custom had become embedded in the law since one is generally obliged to observe recognized pious practices as having the authority of law (Responsa, *Iggerot Mosheh, Oraḥ Ḥayyim* part 5, chap. 38 sects. 1–4). [469]

In all such cases the mind of the individual relied on the propriety of the accepted practice, rather than submitting it to detailed legal analysis. Thus, the practice becomes obligatory by reason of custom. The general principle was followed that "the practice of our fathers is as Torah teaching" (*minhag avoteinu torah hi)*[470] when one is uncertain regarding the correct law on a particular matter, one should follow the Rabbinic adage which states: "Go out into the street and see how the public practice, and act accordingly" (TJ *Peah* 7:5)[471] (Daniel Sperber, *Minhagei Yisrael,* p. 235 quoting *Maḥzor Vitri,* p. 627; *Minhagot* of R. Asher ben Shaul of Lunel).

The Invalidity of Custom Founded on Error – Minhag ta'ut

The multiplicity of customs, particularly local customs were found to need a measure of control. At times a custom maybe founded on an error, or develop unreasonably or illogically in a certain direction, or maybe even in conflict with substantive and fundamental principles of Jewish law. The halakhic scholars found it necessary to declare that such a custom was

---

468   ואין חיוב בדבר
469   חיוב ממנהגא
470   מנהג אבותינו תורה היא
471   צא וראה מה הציבור נוהג ונהוג

founded on error and discredited that particular custom. In the Jerusalem Talmud a rule is laid down by R. Abun that "custom founded on error maybe set aside particularly if the scholar had not been aware that the matter was permitted, and by error had he forbidden it. A distinction was made between a befitting minhag – *minhag yafeh* – and a mistaken minhag or "bad custom" – *minhag ta'ut* (TJ *Pes.* 4:1 – *korban ha'eidah ad loc.*).

In a dispute over a custom concerning the erection of a partition that should be erected between two courtyards so that neither neighbour may observe the other; a custom of erecting a partition smaller than the Talmudic requirements was a bad custom which should not be followed. R. Tam held that some customs are not to be relied upon, even though it has been said, "all is in accordance with custom" (*Tos.*, *BB* 2a sv. *begil*). R. Tam likewise discounted some ritual customs which he considered as entirely illogical, and were even contrary to Talmudical law (*Tos. Ber. 48a veleit hilkheta*)[472] (M. Elon, *Jewish Law* vol. 1; *Encycl. Judaica,* vol. 12, p. 23 sv. *"minhag"*).

Chapter 4

Repentance – *Teshuvah*

4 Repentance – Teshuvah

A. The Meaning of *Teshuvah*

The literal meaning of the Hebrew word for repentance, *teshuvah*, is "return". Man, at the time of his creation, was without sin, which alienates him from his Maker. If, after sinning, he returns to God by means of *teshuvah*, he reverts to his original condition, i.e., he returns to his roots. In this way he heals his own ills. A third-century sage, Ḥama bar Ḥanina, declared: "Great is *teshuvah* for it brings healing to the world"; the entire earth benefits. When an individual is cured of his evildoing, the *teshuvah* that brings him back to God helps to reduce the amount of sin on earth and to save the world from destruction (*Yoma* 86a).[1] R. Yonatan also maintained that *teshuvah* "hastens the final redemption" (*Yoma* 86b; MAHARAL, *Kitvei Maharal mi-Prag*, ed. Avraham Kariv, p. 245).[2]

The attainment of *teshuvah* not only heals, but also prolongs man's life. As Elazar ben Dordia related in his own self-examination, the first step towards that healing process is to acknowledge that the remedy can come from no source other than oneself: "It all depends on me" (*AZ* 17a).[3] Moreover, if we only make a determined effort, the Almighty will help us to move forward and attain complete purification (*Shab.* 104a; *Yoma* 38b).[4]

God's supreme holiness does not engender fear and trembling in man, as one might suppose from the Bible's description of the Revelation at Mount Sinai: "And all the

---

1 גדולה תשובה שמביאה רפואות לעולם
2 גדולה תשובה שמקרבת את הגאולה
3 אין הדבר תלוי אלא בי
4 בא ליטהר מסעיין אותו

people perceived the thundering and the lightning, and the sound of the trumpet, and the mountain smoking; and when the people saw it, they trembled and stood afar off" (Ex. 20:18). It was the turbulence of nature that frightened the people, not the Divine Presence, as a further account of the Revelation indicates: "And the appearance of the glory of the Lord was like devouring fire on the mountaintop in the eyes of the Children of Israel. And Moses entered into the midst of the cloud, and went up into the mount" (Ex. 24:17–18). Here there is no mention of the people trembling at the presence of God among them.

Furthermore, we are told: "Then went up Moses, and Aaron, Nadab, and Avihu, and seventy of the elders of Israel; and they saw the God of Israel... and upon the nobles of the Children of Israel He laid not His hand; and they beheld God, and did eat and drink" (Ex. 24:9–11). Only after Israel has sinned (by worshipping the golden calf), and when Moses returns to the people after receiving the Decalogue a second time, it is stated that "when Aaron and all the Children of Israel saw Moses, and behold, the skin of his face shone, they were afraid to come nigh him" (Ex. 34:30). Commenting on these verses, R. Shim'on bar Yoḥai observed: "See how great is the potency of transgression! When, before they had sinned with the golden calf, the glory of God appeared before the eyes of Israel, they were not afraid; but after they had made the golden calf, they so feared God's presence that even the heavenly lustre on the face of Moses terrified them" (Ex. 34:30, Rashi ad loc.).

It is sin that drives a wedge between the spirit of man and the sanctity of the Divine. By preferring to follow his own desires, man renounces his loyalty to God and withdraws himself from being accessible to the company of God. Thus, in prescribing the attachment of "fringes" (tzitzit) to one's garments as a reminder of His laws, the Torah ordains, "that ye may remember and do all My commandments, and be holy unto your God" (Num. 15:40).[5] The Almighty, however, still

yearns for man's return to His presence. The spiritual chasm
that the transgressor has brought about can be bridged by his
own repentance and the ritual of purification. As Malachi the
prophet declared, God tells the sinner: "Return unto me, and I
will return unto you" (Mal. 3:7).[6]

The Sages do not claim that, through transgression, a barrier
is erected between man and his Maker. They speak of man's
distancing himself from God, whereas, on the other hand,
the Almighty longs for man to return. It is his duty to cling
to God, as visualized in the concept of "spiritual proximity"
– *devekut*. While it may be natural for one's physical being to
try to distance itself from the higher spiritual values of which
man is capable, one should always endeavour to remain close
to the pristine holiness of God. As a result of man's sinfulness,
God rebukes man by "covering His face" and withdrawing
His benevolent protection from him.

This idea finds expression in the Torah, where the Israelites
are warned not to break their covenant with God by following
strange gods: "Then My anger shall be kindled against them in
that day, and I will forsake them, and I will hide My face from
them" (Deut. 31:17).[7] Ibn Ezra's commentary runs as follows:
"'If they call upon Me to save them from their troubles, I will
not answer them'; not because God was no longer among
them, but because *they* had withdrawn themselves from Him.
God is omnipresent, 'but I shall ignore them and they will be
left to whatever fate awaits them', He declares" (*ibid.*, 31:17–
18; Ibn Ezra and Sforno *ad loc.*).[8]

Repentance is man's resumption of loyalty to God, and
He accepts man's "return" with compassion. In Biblical
language this is expressed concisely: "He that covereth his
transgressions shall not prosper; but whoso confesseth and
forsaketh them shall obtain mercy (Prov. 28:13).[9] Isaiah
likewise affirmed: "Let the wicked forsake his way, and the

---

6 שובו אלי ואשובה אליכם
7 ועזבתים והסתרתי פני מהם
8 ואנכי הסתר אסתיר פני ביום ההוא
9 ומודה ועוזב ירחם

evil man his thoughts: let him return unto the Lord, and He will have mercy upon him" (Isa. 55:7).[10]

R. Yehoshua ben Levi said: "Even an iron wall cannot separate Israel from their Father in heaven" (*Sot.* 39a).[11]

To emphasize the weightiness of repentance, the Sages gave the following illustration. "Men asked Wisdom, 'What is the sinner's punishment?' Wisdom replied: 'Evil pursueth sinners' (Prov.13:21). Torah law declared: 'Let him bring a sin-offering and it shall be forgiven him' (Lev. 5:6). But the Almighty said: 'Let him repent, and it shall be forgiven him'" (TJ *Mak.* 2:7; *Pesikta de-Rav Kahana* 158b).[12]

Since God created the evil impulse (*yetzer ha-ra*) in man, He made repentance as the cure before producing the affliction (*Meg.* 13b[13]; *Avot* 4:13[14]). An early Midrash relates, in the name of R. Yishmael, that the world would never have endured if repentance had not been created first (Solomon Schechter, *Some Aspects of Rabbinic Theology*, p. 314). God's acceptance of *teshuvah* is an expression of the Divine mercy with which He created the world, for without His merciful forgiveness the world could not survive (Gen. R. 12:15;[15] *Pirkei de-Rabbi Eliezer* 11).

According to Rabbinic theology, while the *yetzer ha-ra* was itself a Divine creation, man is not powerless in the face of his evil desires. One who consciously chooses the good way restrains his natural impulses, whereas the sinful man is ruled by them (Gen. R. 67:3).[16] In the psychology of the Rabbis (see George Foot Moore, *Judaism*, vol. 1, part 3, chap. 3), the evil inclination is associated with "the heart", where man's wicked thoughts and schemes originate. Hence the Bible asserts that

---

10   וישב אל ה׳ וירחמהו

11   אפילו מחיצה של ברזל אינה מפסקת ביו ישראל לאביהם שבשמים

12   אמר להן יעשה תשובה ויתכפר לו

13   אמר ריש לקישאין הקב״ה מכה את ישראל אלא אם כן בורא להם רפואה תחלה

14   תשובה ומעשים טובים כתריס בפני הפורעניות

15   כך אמר הקב״ה אם בורא אני את העולם... במדת הדין היאך העולם יכול לעמוד

16   הרשעים ברשות לבן... אבל הצדיקים לבן ברשותן

"every imagination of the thoughts of his heart was only evil"
(Gen. 6:5).[17] This statement is reiterated by the Creator: "For
the imagination of man's heart is evil from his youth" (Gen.
8:21).[18] Thoughts and designs prompting evil are generated in
"the heart", where the *yetzer ha-ra* flourishes.

The Brotherhood of Man

The Sages recognized the weaknesses of human nature and
taught that one who fails to behave honestly must not be
rejected. "Love thy neighbour"[19] is a precept that extends to
all mankind. The most inveterate sinner should be respected as
a fellow human being, one created in the image of God. It is,
moreover, one's duty to guide him along the path of "return"
and to love him like a brother.

The Torah laid down a general rule, "that thou hide not
thyself from thine own flesh" (Isa. 58:7).[20] One is similarly
commanded to help another, even one's enemy; when he is
in trouble, "thou mayest not hide thyself" (Deut. 22:3).[21] In
Jewish homes the traditional practice of collecting money in
a special alms box *(kuppat tzedakah)* has long been known
as the "R. Meir Ba'al Ha'ness charity". This term especially
denotes charitable donations to those in need, irrespective of
their character or belief. R. Meir taught that even when Jews
prove disobedient, they are still called "children of the Lord
your God" (Deut. 14:1).[22] R. Yehudah said, "You are His
children when you conduct yourselves like His children", but
R. Meir declared: "Whichever way you behave, you are still
called His children" *(Kid. 36a).*[23]

---

17 וכל יצר מחשבת לבו רק רע כל היום
18 כי יצר לב האדם רע מנעריו
19 ואהבת לרעך
20 ומבשרך לא תתעלם
21 לא תוכל להתעלם
22 בנים אתם לה' אל-היכם
23 בין כך ובין כך אתם קרואים בנים

The Opposing Impulses

According to the Sages, however, man is endowed with two
opposing impulses, one good and the other bad. He can always
rouse his good impulse against the evil one and succeed in
overcoming it.

Rabbinic tradition also speaks of two "kidneys" in man.
One advises him to do good, the other to do evil. It would be
reasonable to assume that the good one is located on his right
side and the evil one on his left, as it is written: "A wise man's
heart is at his right hand; but a fool's heart at his left" (Eccles.
10:2; *Ber.* 61a).[24] When the "kidneys" provide their advice,
"the heart" considers, the tongue and mouth give expression
and the other parts of the body – lungs, liver, gall bladder and
stomach – are activated in accordance with the decision of
"the heart" (*Ber.* 61a).

The Sages elucidate this doctrine of the twin impulses in
their exegetical comments on the Biblical account of man's
creation, where it is stated: "Then the Lord God formed man
of the dust of the ground" (Gen. 2:7).[25] The unusual spelling
of the Hebrew word *va-yitzer* ("formed") with a double *yod*
points to the twin *yetzer* impulses, one good (*yetzer ha-tov*)
and one evil (*yetzer ha-ra*). A similar kind of interpretation is
given to the words of Moses: "And thou shalt love the Lord
thy God with all thy heart..." (Deut. 6:5).[26] Noting the double
letter *bet* in the word *levavekha* ("thy heart"), the Sages again
linked this with the *yetzer ha-tov* and *yetzer ha-ra*, inferring
that even the evil impulse can be subdued and directed to the
performance of God's work (*Ber.* 54a).

Likewise, in the Creation narrative, God looked upon the
work He had finished "and behold, it was very good" (Gen.
1:31).[27] R. Shemuel ben Nahman, clarifying the emphasis on
"very good", explains that this refers to the evil inclination,

---

24   לב חכם לימינו ולב כסיל לשמאלו
25   וייצר ה' אל-הים את האדם עפר מן האדמה
26   ואהבת את ה' אל-היך בכל לבבך
27   והנה טוב מאד

since man's appetites and passions are (like his good impulses) essential for human existence. The Sages taught that man can control his evil inclination (*yetzer ha-ra*) and direct it to good purposes. Thus, when a man feels the natural urge to marry and have children, he is also prompted to build a home, do well at his job and succeed in all his endeavours, thereby contributing to the advancement of humanity and civilization (Gen. 9:7).[28] In sexual intercourse also, while one's own physical desires are gratified, the *yetzer ha-ra* serves to perpetuate the human race (Moore, *Judaism, ibid.*, p. 484).

Yet both the "good" and the "evil" impulses do not themselves propel man's actions. They give counsel to the "heart" or mind, generating the devices of good and evil, but are not the instruments of their own accomplishment. In the final analysis, any act performed is the action of man. He either yields to the deceitful "evil impulse" or subdues it, and then follows the "good impulse" that leads to righteousness. Man therefore has it in his power to submit to evil or to subdue it.

The wicked are described as being *under* the control of their evil impulses while the righteous have control *over* them (Gen. R. 34:11). Ben Zoma said that the strong man is "the one who masters his evil inclination" (*Avot* 4:1).[29]

To strengthen his control over the evil impulse, it is advisable for man to redouble his Torah study. Resh Lakish (R. Shim'on ben Lakish) taught that a man should constantly incite his good impulse to do battle with the evil spirit within him; he should occupy his mind with Torah and the duty to love God with all his being, and he should also ponder God's final judgment. By concentrating on such thoughts, his mind will resist all temptation to behave wickedly (*Ber.* 5a, Rashi *ad loc.*),[30] since evildoing is any departure from God's revealed legislation (Ps. 4:5; Moore, *ibid.*, p. 486).[31]

---

28 ואתם פרו ורבו שרצו בארץ ורבו בה
29 איזהו גבור הכובש את יצרו
30 לעולם ירגיז אדם יצר טוב על יצר הרע
31 רגזו ואל תחטאו אמרו בלבבכם על משכבכם ודומו סלה

The Sages pictured the Almighty saying to Israel: "It is true that, in addition to man's higher nature (*yetzer ha-tov*), I also endowed him with an evil impulse (*yetzer ha-ra*), but I created the power of repentance as its antidote, thus enabling him to free himself of the sins that he has committed (*Kid.* 30b).[32] Man need not be intimidated by the evil *yetzer*, for although it "lies at the door" and awaits an opportunity to attack him, the Almighty assured Cain – the first violent transgressor – that man has the power to "rule over it" (Gen. 4:7).[33] Through his consistent reversion to good deeds, man's failings are forgiven: "If thou doest well, shalt thou not be accepted?" (Gen. 4:7).[34]

Although neither the amount nor the extent of sin can block repentance, the Rabbis warned that in five cases the sinner loses the chance of being forgiven because his repentance is obviously false. Such transgressors are the one who expresses remorse while repeatedly sinning; one who means to repent later and expects to be forgiven; one who sins, even when everyone around him does not; and one whose offence constitutes *hillul Hashem* – a profanation of the Divine Name (*Yoma* 85b; *Avot de-Rav Natan* 39:1, *Binyan Yehoshua, ibid. ad loc.*).

While an effort is made to repent, even one's prompt decision to give up sinning or sense of shame over past or present behaviour may not be sufficient to prevent a relapse into bad habits. Repentance must be strengthened by one's repeated avoidance of sin when faced with temptations like those one succumbed to in the past. For repentance to succeed, one must undergo a complete change of personality, even to the extent of assuming a new and different name (*Yoma* 86b; Maim. *Teshuvah* 22–4).[35]

The Talmud relates that scrupulously pious men (*hasidim*) who felt the awe of God's presence (*yir'at Hashem*) sought

---

32 בראתי יצר הרע ובראתי לו תורה תבלין
33 ואם לא תיטיב לפתח חטאת רובץ ואליך תשוקתו ואתה תמשל בו
34 אם תיטיב שאת
35 באותה אשה באותו פרק באותו מקום

atonement even for their unconscious transgressions. Bava ben
Buta (1st cent.) went so far as to make a guilt-offering every
day, in case he had committed an offence unknown to him.
The Sages, however, required a sin-offering only when one
was aware of having acted in a way that might be tantamount
to wrongdoing (*Ker.* 25a).[36]

Such perfect *yir'at Hashem* is attained through continuous
engagement in Torah study, just as a king of Israel was
obligated to have a scroll of the Law with him wherever he
went for the purpose of lifelong reading (Deut. 17:19). David
said: "Because He is at my right hand – *ki yemini* – I shall not
be moved (from the way of righteousness)" (Ps. 16:8, Rashi
ad loc.). Each individual is required to study Torah at all times
so as to be ever aware of the Divine Presence "when thou liest
down and when thou risest up" (Deut.6:7; *Mesillat Yesharim*
24–25).[37]

Everyone stands in need of God's help in achieving full
repentance. For that reason the daily Amidah contains the
following supplication and benediction: "Cause us to return,
O our Father, unto Thy Law; draw us near, O our King, unto
Thy service; and bring us back in perfect repentance unto
Thy presence. Blessed art Thou, O Lord, who delighteth in
repentance" (Daily Prayer Book).[38]

Maimonides records, as a general principle, that when
repenting a transgression of any kind and seeking forgiveness,
one must first acknowledge one's sin before God. This act
of confession – *viddui* – is regarded as a separate positive
commandment (*mitzvat aseh*) and included among the
Torah's 613 Commandments (Maim. *Sefer ha-Mitzvot*, *Aseh*,
no. 73).[39] Thus, in the Pentateuchal law that requires the
bringing of a guilt-offering (*asham*) or sin-offering (*ḥattat*)
for a transgression of which one was not conscious at the time
and only later aware, it is stated: "Then they shall confess the

---

36 אמרו אליו על בבא בן בוטא שהיה מתנדב אשם תלוי בכל יום

37 ודברת בם בשבתך בביתך ובלכתך בדרך ובשכבך ובקומך

38 השיבנו אבינו לתורתך... והחזירנו בתשובה שלמה לפניך

39 להתודות לפני ה' מכל חטא שיעשה האדם בשעת הקרבן

sin which they committed" (Num. 5:7).[40] Similarly, it is laid down that the offender "shall confess that wherein he hath sinned", and only then is he commanded to "bring his guilt-offering unto the Lord for the sin which he hath sinned" (Lev. 5:5–6).[41] In every case, confession of the sin must accompany the guilty man's repentance for his wrongdoing, together with a determination never to repeat it (Maim. Code, *Teshuvah* 1:1).

According to Maimonides, confession forms part of the *teshuvah* process and so, if the confession is not fully sincere, the *teshuvah* itself has no value (Maim. Code, *Teshuvah* 2:3).[42] Basically, *teshuvah* stems from a person's wish to correct his sinful behaviour. This desire emerges from the inner strivings of conscience and from the man's urge to repair the breach that he has made between the Creator and himself. The incentive to achieve *teshuvah* must first arise in the individual himself, the Torah subsequently prescribing the manner in which it is effected. However, the wish to achieve *teshuvah* cannot be commanded: it must be a voluntary expression of a person's own will. Although *teshuvah* is a matter of the individual's conscience (*davar she-ba-lev*), the Torah instructs man as to how the process of "returning" to God can be given concrete expression...

After Temple times, with the ending of sacrificial rites, true repentance was considered effective in removing the stain of a character defect and in regaining the Almighty's approval. The Talmud relates an incident involving R. Yosef, who admonished his son, Rava, for arrogantly stating his own opinion before his father's. R. Yosef referred him to the passage, "from Mattanah to Nahaliel; and from Nahaliel to Bamoth" (Num. 21:19 *ff.*), which he then expounded as follows: If he exalts himself in his Torah learning, the Holy One, blessed be He, will cast him

---

40 והתודו את חטאתם אשר עשו
41 והתודה אשר חטא עליה. והביא את אשמו וכו'
42 כל המתודה בדברים ולא גמר בלבו לעזוב הרי זה דומה לטובל ושרץ בידו שנאמר ומנחליאל במות. ואם הגביה עצמו הקב"ה משפילו...ואם חוזר בו הקב"ה מגביהו

down; but should he repent, the Holy One, blessed be He, will raise him up again (*Ned.* 55a).

Penitence

Repentance is essentially a condition of the soul involving a change of heart and a renewal of one's personality. It is in no way a means of propitiating God, whose wrath is assuaged by a sacrifice. The purpose of that sacrifice, as an act of outward worship, was to deepen an inner sense of religious devotion in the mind of the suppliant. Yet an abundance of sacrifices, accompanied by persistent evildoing, was loathsome to God. The Bible records how Isaiah rebuked his fellow Israelites: "To what purpose is the multitude of your sacrifices unto Me? saith the Lord... Put away the evil of your doings from before Mine eyes, cease to do evil; learn to do well ..." (Isa. 1:11, 16–17).[43]

David, in his act of contrition before Nathan the prophet, begged the Lord's forgiveness and declared: "Thou delightest not in sacrifice, else would I give it... The sacrifices of God are a broken spirit; a broken and a contrite heart, O God, Thou wilt not despise" (Ps. 51:18–19).[44]

The prophet Joel knew well enough that men could demonstrate their penitence with such outward signs as "fasting, weeping, and lamentation", but what really mattered was the change taking place within people: "Rend your heart, not your garments, and turn unto the Lord your God" (Joel 2:12–13).[45]

Manasseh, king of Judah, provides another telling example. He committed more grievous sins than any of his predecessors and, after his capture by the Assyrians, was led away in chains to Babylon. As a result of his humble repentance, however,

---

43   הסירו רוע מעלליכם מנגד עיני חדלו הרע
44   זבחי אל-הים רוח נשברה לב נשבר ונדכה
45   וקרעו לבבכם ואל בגדיכם ושובו אל ה׳ אל-היכם

God liberated Manasseh and brought him back to Jerusalem (2 Chron. 33:1–13; *Sifrei*, Deut. 6:5).[46]

There are many Rabbinic pronouncements on the efficacy of *teshuvah*, including one by R. Yonatan: "Great is *teshuvah* for it brings redemption" (*Yoma* 86b).[47] Another, by R. Levi, who affirmed that "penitential prayers can bring one into the presence of the Almighty, since they reach His glorious throne" (*Yoma* 86a).[48] R. Meir even declared that "for the sake of one true penitent, the whole world is granted forgiveness" (*Yoma* 86b).[49]

The decision to undergo *teshuvah* lies within man's capacity to exercise his free will. In view of the fact that many sins derive from attitudes of the mind, ruing proclivities such as wrathfulness, envy, hatred, dishonesty or pride is far harder than repenting forbidden acts such as theft, violence or immorality. An evil disposition becomes ingrained in a man's character and is more difficult to change (Maim. Code, *Teshuvah* 7:3).[50] His freedom to choose a particular course of action is a God-given endowment, just as the basic elements of air, fire and water operate according to the rules laid down by the Creator (Maim. *Teshuvah* 5:4).[51]

Maimonides points out that in addition to a sin-offering, Torah law obligates man to confess his transgressions, specifying the ones he has committed (Num. 5:7).[52] This duty applies to every kind of transgression, major or minor, in action or in thought. It is always mandatory, whether in the Land of Israel or in the lands of Exile (*Galut*), as the Torah lays down: "They shall confess their iniquity, and the iniquity of their fathers" (Lev. 26:40; Maim. *Sefer ha-Mitzvot, Aseh*, no. 73; Maim. Code, *Teshuvah* 1:1; *Yoma* 36b).[53]

---

46 ויתפלל אליו ויעתר לו וישמע תחנתו וישיבהו ירושלים למלכות

47 גדולה תשובה שמקרבת את הגאולה

48 גדולה תשובה שמגעת עד כסא הכבוד שנאמר שובה ישראל עד ה׳ אל-היך

49 גדולה תשובה שבשביל יחיד שעשה תשובה מוחלין לכל העולם כולו

50 שבזמן שאדם נשקע באלו קשה הוא לפרוש מהם

51 אל תלכו אחרי רשעכם והוא מתחלת ברייתו כבר נגזר עליו או תולדתו תמשוך אותו לדבר שאי אפשר לזוז ממנו

52 והתודו את חטאתם אשר עשו

53 והתודו את עונם ואת עון אבותם

A supernumerary *Mishnah* (*Baraita*) affirms that the power of repentance was one of those things that the Almighty created in advance of all His other works, as the Psalmist declares: "Before the mountains were brought forth, or ever Thou hadst formed the earth and the world... Thou turnest man to contrition; and sayest: Repent, ye children of men" (Ps. 90: 2–3).[54]

It is axiomatic in Scripture that Torah wisdom preceded the creation of the universe. In God's eyes the Law was more precious than any other of His works. Wisdom (*hokhmah*, i.e., the Law) thus alludes to its unique pre-mundane existence: "The Lord possessed me in the beginning of His way, before His works of old. I was set up from everlasting, from the beginning, or ever the earth was... While as yet He had not made the earth, nor the fields, nor the beginning of the dust of the world" (Prov. 8:22–23, 26).[55]

The Sages maintained that repentance was coeval with the Law, since the Almighty knew that it was beyond the power of man to observe all His commandments and prohibitions without some backsliding, which could entail severe penalties. Accordingly, they said, one of the seven items essential for man's existence that God created before the world – together with the Torah – was man's capacity for repentance.[56] This mercifully supplied in advance the antidote to future evil and prompted Resh Lakish to declare that the Almighty never inflicts a wound on Israel without first creating the remedy (*Meg.* 13b; Moore, *op. cit.*, "The Efficacy of Repentance", p. 526).[57]

Repentance was created before the world, because the world could not survive without the possibility of *teshuvah*. This concept is graphically illustrated in the Kabbalah: "When God decided to create the world, He first created the Torah

---

54 בטרם הרים ילדו ותחולל ארץ ותבל

55 ה' קנני ראשית דרכו קדם מפעליו מאז... עד לא עשה ארץ וחוצות וראש עפרות תבל

56 שבעה דברים נבראו קדם שנברא העולם...תשובה דכתיב בטרם הרים ילדו

57 אין הקב"ה מכה את ישראל אלא אם כן בורא להם רפואה תחלה

and then used Torah as the plan for Creation. When He was about to create man, the Torah protested, saying: 'Should man be created, then sin and stand trial before Thee, the work of Thy hand will be in vain, as he will not be able to endure Thy judgment'. Whereupon God replied: 'I had already fashioned repentance before creating the world'" (Zohar, *Toledot, Mantua* text, Romm Press edn., Vilna, 134b).

The Sages declared that a man sins when he neglects his religious obligations and forgets that he is ever in the presence of One whose glory fills the universe. Having, as it were, become temporarily oblivious of his relationship with God, he alienates himself from the Divine Presence. Since it was unthinkable that any individual would deliberately wish to separate himself from his Creator, the Sages maintained that no one could sin without having first given way to a spirit of folly (Num. R., *Ba-Midbar* 9:3).[58]

When someone repents, he regains an awareness that God's presence fills the entire universe. Conscience-stricken over his transgression, he now directs his mind to restoring his close relationship with his Maker. Full repentance indicates his yearning to return, step by step, to his former position of closeness to the Almighty (Hos. 14:2).[59]

A scrupulously pious man is "one who fears sin" (*Avot* 2:8, 11),[60] because he always stays on guard against the possibility of transgression. Even a sin committed inadvertently (*be-shogeg*) requires *teshuvah* and penitential prayers, because he has momentarily relaxed his guard and become forgetful of his religious duty.

The accomplishment of *teshuvah* involves two basic elements: remorse for the sin committed (*haratah*) and an undertaking never to repeat it (*azivat ha-het*). By fulfilling these obligations, one may succeed in the quest for atonement (*kapparah*) and thus regain a state of holiness. The Torah

---

58   אינה מזנה עד שיכנס בה השטות. הוי כי תשטה אשתו

59   שובה ישראל עד ה' אל-היך

60   רבי יוסי הכהן חסיד רבי שמעון בן נתנאל ירא חטא

encapsulates *teshuvah* in a phrase, "Thou wilt return to the Lord thy God" (Deut. 4:30),[61] indicating that repentance enables one to reach the Divine Presence. Isaiah described the *teshuvah* process in greater detail: "Let the wicked forsake his way, and the man of iniquity his [evil] thoughts; let him return unto the Lord, and He will have compassion on him... for He forgiveth abundantly" (Isa. 55:7).[62]

B. The Process of *Teshuvah*

Although the basic act of *teshuvah* is an individual's determination of the mind, further steps are required before he obtains atonement for sin (*kapparah*). In some instances, according to the gravity of the transgression, *kapparah* is achieved only on the Day of Atonement or otherwise through due punishment or death. In Temple times the wrongdoer had to bring a sin-offering or guilt-offering and make an open confession of his sin (*viddui*). Thus one condemned to death by the Sanhedrin was first required to confess, so that his death would bring him atonement, and he would then obtain his share in the World to Come (*Sanh.* 43b).[63] It was also the practice for a condemned man to declare: "May my death be an atonement for all my sins" (*Sanh.* 43b).[64]

However, punishment or sacrifice alone would not suffice to gain atonement unless it was preceded by inner *teshuvah*. Through performing *teshuvah* in the heart, one submits to the omnipotence of God and acknowledges that His decree is justified, thereby freeing oneself from sin.

The *ba'al teshuvah*, a sinner who fully masters his evil inclination and repents, was commended by the Sages. They maintained that he is capable of attaining a spiritual height

61 ושבת עד ה' אל-היך
62 יעזוב רשע דרכו ואיש און מחשבותיו וישוב אל ה' וירחמהו
63 כל המומתין מתודין שכל המתודה יש לו חלק לעולם הבא
64 תהא מיתתי כפרה על כל עונותי

which even the perfectly righteous individual, who normally shuns transgression, did not reach. R. Abbahu declared that "where penitents stand, the wholly righteous cannot stand", R. Yohanan, however, asserted that no one reaches higher than the perfectly righteous man who has never sinned (*Ber.* 34b).[65]

Should someone be guilty of a particular sin and confess it, without full repentance determining to exclude the possibility of his renewed sinful action from his mind, his confession has no meaning. He may be compared to the man who bathes in a *mikveh*, to rid himself of impurity, while grasping an unclean reptile in his hand, which automatically retained his impurity.[66] Similarly, he cannot obtain atonement if he has robbed or wronged someone and not made restitution (*Ta'an.* 16a, Rashi *ad loc.*).

The process of *teshuvah* begins with remorse (*haratah*) and continues with a cessation of the guilty act (*azivat ha-het*) – not out of mere reluctance to sin but specifically as a result of contrition. By not repeating his transgression two or three times in like circumstances, the sinner manifests his true act of repentance (*teshuvah*). He has thus changed the thinking which previously led him to sin and is now determined not to relapse into that wrongdoing. Both actions, sin and repentance, originate in processes of the mind that man is capable of redirecting.

Man's instinctive appetites have a decided impact on his behaviour and constantly urge him to transgress. As a general rule, the Bible maintains: "There is not a righteous man upon earth that doeth [only] good and sinneth not" (Eccles. 7:20).[67] The Creator certainly does not wish to destroy His own work and looks forward to pardoning the remorseful sinner. God also helps man to subdue his evil inclination (*Hag.* 12b, MAHARSHA *ad loc.*).[68] As R. Hanina bar Papa said: "If, after

---

65   מקום שבעלי תשובה עומדין צדיקים גמורים אינם עומדין
66   אדם שיש בידו עבירה ומתודה ואינו חוזר בו למה הוא דומה לאדם שתופס שרץ
      בידו שאפילו טובל וכו'
67   כי אדם אין צדיק בארץ אשר יעשה טוב ולא יחטא
68   כי לא א-ל חפץ רשע אתה לא יגורך רע

committing an offence, the sinner repents, the Almighty will promptly forgive him" (*Hag.* 5a).[69]

According to the Sages, repentance for disobeying a positive commandment will bring the sinner God's immediate forgiveness; but grave violation of a negative commandment suspends atonement until Yom Kippur and complete remission of the sin is effected by punishment (*Yoma* 86a; *Hag.* 5a, *Tos.*, s.v. "*Ha-yir'uni*"; *Shev.* 12b). If, nevertheless, someone wrongs his fellow man (e.g., by cheating or stealing from him), repentance and the Day of Atonement will not bring forgiveness unless he has made amends to the injured party (Mish., *Yoma* 8:9; TB *Yoma* 85b).[70]

R. Levi declared that for certain defects of character one is punished more severely than for immoral behaviour. In the former case, a transgressor is less likely to repent because his theft of public funds or property makes the compensation of victims hard to determine; whereas, in the latter case, sexual offenders can atone for their misconduct. Although an extramarital liaison creates an irreparable wrong (Eccles. 1:15),[71] since any child born of such a union would be a *mamzer* ("illegitimate"), *teshuvah* is still possible if the affair produces no offspring (*Yev.* 21a, Rashi *ad loc.*; *Yev.* 22b; Ha-Mabbit, *Bet Elohim* 2, *Sha'ar Tefillah*).[72]

An essential element in repentance is the act of confession (*viddui*), without which there can be no *teshuvah*. It draws its authority from the Bible: "Speak unto the Children of Israel: When a man or woman shall commit any sin that men commit, to trespass against the Lord, and that soul be guilty; then they shall confess their sin which they have done; and he shall make restitution for his guilt" (Num. 5:6–7; *Sifrei ad loc.*).[73]

This confession must be aspoken admission of guilt in the

---

69 כל העושה דבר ומחרט בו מוחלין לו מיד

70 תשובה מכפרת על עבירות קלות... ועל החמורות היא תולה עד שיבא יום
הכיפורים וכו׳

71 מעוות לא יוכל לתקון

72 והאי בר תשובה הוא

73 והתודו את חטאתם

prescribed form: "O God, I have sinned, done iniquity and transgressed before You. I have committed such-and-such a transgression, now regret my action and am shamed of it. I hereby declare that I shall never repeat this offence" (*Yoma* 36b; Maim. *Teshuvah* 1:2).[74]

In Temple times, apart from *teshuvah*, specific sacrificial offerings were prescribed as a means of atonement. After the Temple's destruction and the end of sacrifices, however, it was decreed that the fulfillment of *teshuvah*, when succeeded by the Day of Atonement, brought atonement for all transgressions. The only exception to this rule was an offence involving the desecration of God's Name (*hillul Hashem*), in which case *teshuvah* would bring atonement only on the death of the sinner (Maim., *ibid.*, 1:4).

In addition to remorse, *teshuvah* requires a determination on the sinner's part never to repeat his transgression. This resolve, proclaimed in the confession, is not established until the sinner has faced the same temptation and opportunity to do wrong on several occasions and has unwaveringly abstained from the transgression (*Yoma* 86b; Maim., *ibid.*, 2:1–2).[75] Through *teshuvah* he thus succeeds in abandoning his former waywardness and, as a humble, reformed character, appears before the Almighty (Maim., *ibid.*, 2:4).

This process of *teshuvah* applies to all transgressions against the sanctity of God – *bein adam lamakom*. As mentioned previously, however, offences committed against one's fellow man – *bein adam lehaveiro* – will not bring atonement unless restitution has been made to the wronged party (*Yoma* 85b, 87a; Maim., *ibid.*, 2:9).[76]

Although Maimonides enumerates 24 types of apostate who are denied a share in the World to Come, that punishment is only inflicted on those who fail to repent before their death. Maimonides concludes with the ruling of R. Yehoshua ben Korha: even the most obstinate sinners who denied the

---

74   כך היה מתודה חטאתי ועויתי ופשעתי לפניך אני וביתי

75   כגון שבאת לידו דבר עבירה פעם ראשונה ושניה וניצל הימנה

76   עבירות שבין אדם לחבירו אין הכיפורים מכפר עד שירצה את חבירו

existence of God (*koferim ba-ikkar*) will regain their portion in the World to Come if they at least secretly repent (*AZ* 7a–b; Maim., *ibid.*, 3:14 and *Lehem Mishneh ad loc.*).[77]

Rabbinic lore contains the story of how a great *tanna*, R. Elisha ben Avuyah, lost his faith as a result of having delved too deeply into the Creation mysteries and became a heretic known as Aher ("Another"). When urged to repent (Jer. 3:14),[78] he stated that even if he did so, his *teshuvah* would never be accepted because he had heard a voice proclaiming from heaven: "All can repent, except Aher". R. Meir, his devoted follower in Torah learning, constantly begged him to repent, assuring him that he would be forgiven, since the *Halakhah* (Jewish law) is governed by legislative deliberation and not by some "heavenly voice". As Elisha lay dying, R. Meir recited a verse from Psalms: "Thou turnest man to destruction; and sayest: Return, ye children of men..." (Ps. 90:3).[79] On hearing these words, Elisha wept and his soul departed. R. Meir then affirmed, "I believe that he died in a state of *teshuvah*", and reputedly saved his old teacher from punishment in the World to Come (TJ *Hag.* 2:1; TB *Hag.* 15a–b, *Tos. ad loc.*, "*Shuvu banim*").[80]

This episode confirms the teaching of R. Yehoshua ben Korha, that the prophet's call for repentance, "Return, ye backsliding children" – *Shuvu banim shovavim* (Jer. 3:22) – applied even to the most hardened transgressor, whose *teshuvah*, although unspoken, was accepted by the Almighty (Maim. *Teshuvah* 3:4, *Kesef Mishneh ad loc.*).

Mediaeval Moralist Teaching

According to Rabbenu Bahya (*Hovot ha-Levavot*, *Sha'ar Teshuvah* 4), the process of *teshuvah* consists of four elements:

---

77 בין כך ובין כך כך מקבלין
78 שובו בנים שובבים נאום ה' כי אנכי בעלתי בכם
79 תשיב אנוש עד דכא ותאמר שובו בני אדם
80 תלמיד חכם אע"פ שסרח יש לו תקנה.

1. *Haratah* – remorse for transgressing the word of God.
2. *She-ya'azvem* – refraining immediately from reversion to sin, and making restitution to the one wronged.
3. *Viddui* – confessing the sin committed and praying for forgiveness.
4. *She-yekabbel al nafsho* – resolving that one's conscience will never allow one to repeat the sin, in recognition of the fact that one's life depends on the mercy of the Creator.

The process of *teshuvah* is described by Isaiah: "Let the wicked forsake his way, and the evil man his thoughts; let him return unto the Lord, and He will have mercy upon him, and to our God, for He will abundantly pardon" (Isa. 55:7).[81] This is a recurring theme in the Bible: "He that covereth his transgressions shall not prosper; but whoso confesseth and forsaketh them shall obtain mercy" (Prov. 28:13).[82]

Remorse consists of heartfelt regret for having transgressed the word of God, fear of the consequences and humbling oneself before God in thought and conduct. This feeling of contrition is summarized in the words of the Psalmist: "Mine eyes run down with rivers of water, because they observe not Thy law" (Ps. 119:136).[83]

Full *teshuvah*, which includes all of the elements mentioned above, is accepted by the Almighty even in one's final moments, since it demonstrates a new attitude of obedience to the will of God. Having become a different person in His sight, one is no longer condemned for past wrongdoing and receives the Almighty's forgiveness. Man should therefore never despair of gaining atonement, even after a lifetime of transgression (*Hovot ha-Levavot, Sha'ar Teshuvah* 10).

In his ethical treatise, *Sha'arei Teshuvah*, R. Yonah Gerondi describes *teshuvah* as a process comprising many elements, all of which need to occur in the mind or, as the Bible phrases it, in the heart of the penitent. He enumerates these elements in great detail:

---

81   יעזוב רשע דרכו ואיש און מחשבותיו וישוב אל ה׳ וירחמהו וכו׳

82   מכסה פשעיו לא יצליח ומודה ועזוב ירוחם

83   פלגי מים ירדו עיני על לא שמרו תורתך

1. _Haratah_: Sorrow for having acted without consideration for others and regret for having thoughtlessly endangered one's own life by opposing the will of the Creator.

2. Azivat ha-het: Abstaining from the transgression and resolving with all one's heart never to repeat it. This step (as previously mentioned) is delineated in various Biblical passages: "Let the wicked forsake his way, and the evil man his thoughts; let him return unto the Lord..." (Isa. 55:7);[84] "He that covereth his transgressions shall not prosper; but whoso confesseth... shall obtain mercy" (Prov. 28:13).[85]

3. _Ha-yagon_: Profound grief over one's abandonment of God's ways. This should be a tearful, heartbreaking experience.

4. _Ha-tza'ar ba-ma'aseh_: A feeling of remorse to which the Psalmist gives the following expression: "The sacrifices of God are a broken spirit; a broken and a contrite heart, O God, Thou wilt not despise" (Ps. 51:19);[86] "Mine eyes run down with rivers of water, because they observe not Thy law" (Ps. 119:136).[87]

5. _Ha-da'agah_: Fear and trembling over the punishment due for one's sin. As King Solomon observed: "A wise man feareth, and departeth from evil" (Prov. 14:16).[88]

6. _Ha-bushah_: The sense of mortification which is an integral feature of the _teshuvah_ process: "Surely after that I was turned, I repented, and after that I was instructed, I smote upon my thigh; I was ashamed, yea, even confounded, because I did bear the reproach of my youth" (Jer. 31:19).[89]

7. _Ha-keni'ah be-khol lev_: Humble submission to God and recognition of one's utter insignificance before Him. Man's striving for atonement is reflected in King David's

---

84 יעזוב רשע דרכו ואיש און מחשבותיו
85 מכסה פשעיו לא יצליח ומודה ועוזב ירוחם
86 זבחי אל-הים רוח נשברה לב נשבר ונדכה אל-הים לא תבזה
87 פלגי מים ירדו עיני על לא שמרו תורתך
88 חכם יראה וסר מרע
89 בושתי וגם נכלמתי כי נשאתי חרפת נעורי

contrition when the prophet Nathan rebuked him for his shameful appropriation of Bathsheba (2 Sam. 11:2-12:23; *Sha'arei Teshuvah* 1:23). His self-abasing quest for *teshuvah* constitutes the theme of Psalm 51, where he prayed for Divine mercy: "Be gracious unto me, O God". He was fully aware of his guilt: "My sin is ever before me". Like all men, he had given way to his inborn evil impulse: "Behold, I was brought forth in iniquity"; and so he begged the Lord to help him reform: "Create in me a clean heart, O God". Finally, David emphasized that his sincere penitence was more meaningful than any burnt-offering: "The sacrifices of God are a broken spirit; a broken and a contrite heart, God, Thou wilt not despise" (Ps. 51:3, 5, 7, 12, 19; cf. Saadiah, *Emunot ve-De'ot* 5).[90]

8. *Ha-hakhna'ah*: Humility and a lack of arrogance in one's behaviour.
9. *Shevirat ha-ta'avah*: The repression of one's physical desires through abstemious living.
10. *Le-hetiv pe'alav*: Converting one's aptitude for sin into an eagerness to perform meritorious deeds.
11. *Hippus derakhav*: Self-examination with the aim of discovering where precisely one went wrong.
12. *She-yahkor godel ha-onesh*: Gauging the extent of one's punishment.
13. *Hashivut shel averot kallot*: Realizing the gravity of "lesser" sins and never underestimating the magnitude of different transgressions.
14. *Viddui*: Openly confessing one's wrongful acts.
15. *Tefillah*: Praying for the Almighty's forgiveness.
16. *Tikkun ha-ta'ut*: Striving to mend one's ways.
17. *Ma'asei hesed*: Engaging in the practice of good deeds.
18. *Heyot hattato le-negdo*: Being ever conscious of past transgressions.

C. *Teshuvah* and Free Will

Maimonides (*Teshuvah* 5:1–3) states that the basic principle of all Torah teaching is that man was endowed with free will by the Creator. Man can therefore choose whether to do good or evil. His conduct as a righteous man (*tzaddik*) or a wicked person (*rasha*) is not predetermined by God, but the result of his own decision. It was God's wish that man should be free to act on his own responsibility, and so he is not prevented from making up his own mind, even if this leads him to sin. The Torah accordingly proclaims: "See, I have set before thee this day life and good, death and evil, in that I command thee this day to love the Lord thy God, to walk in His ways, and to keep His commandments... Therefore choose life, that thou mayest live, thou and thy seed" (Deut. 30:15, 19).[91]

Man is under no Divine compulsion to sin or to obey; the remedy lies in his own hands: "Out of the mouth of the Most High cometh there not evil and good?... Let us search and try our ways, and return unto the Lord" (Lam. 3:38, 40).[92] The Midrash also affirms: "God does not determine in advance whether a man will be righteous or wicked; that He leaves to man himself" (*Tanḥuma*, *Pikkudei* 3).

The Talmud records a statement by R. Ḥanina: "Everything is in the power of Heaven except man's fear of Heaven, as it is said in the Torah, 'And now, Israel, what doth the Lord thy God require of thee, but to fear the Lord thy God... with all thy heart and with all thy soul'" (Deut. 10:12; *Ber.* 33b; *Meg.* 25a).[93]

Since man, in obeying or disobeying the Torah, does so of his own free will, one who acts righteously deserves his reward whereas one who sins deserves the penalty for his transgressions. It is therefore appropriate for a man to regret what he has done and mend his ways, a process constituting his *teshuvah*.

---

91 החיים והמות נתתי לפניך הברכה והקללה ובחרת בחיים
92 מפי עליון לא תצא הרעות והטוב ..... נחפשה דרכינו ונחקרה ונשוב עד ה'
93 הכל בידי שמים חוץ מיראת שמים

The infliction of Divine punishment on the sinner is justified only because he acted of his own free will; otherwise, if his action was already determined by God, he would not be guilty, having had no choice in the matter. For as Abraham contended: "Shall not the Judge of all the earth do justly?" (Gen. 18:25).[94] Maimonides adds that the notion of Divine prescience raises issues which demand consideration, but they are beyond human understanding (Maim. *Teshuvah* 5:5),[95] as the Torah declares: "For man shall not see Me and live" (Ex. 33:20).[96]

The justice of God's punishment is unequivocal, resting on the Biblical principle that "every man shall be put to death for his own sin" (Deut. 24:16),[97] unless he is safeguarded by his own *teshuvah*. Moses likewise proclaimed an unshakable belief that "all His ways are justice... just and right is He" (Deut. 32:4).[98]

D. The Attainment of *Teshuvah*

The person who manages to overcome his inclination to sin, attaining full *teshuvah* and remaining its master (*ba'al teshuvah*), is highly regarded by the Sages, as his moral improvement brings him into an intimate relationship with God (Maim., *ibid.*, 7:6).[99] The *ba'al teshuvah* deserves every respect and honour, for only *teshuvah* will ensure the final redemption of the Jewish people (*Yoma* 86b; *Sanh.* 97b).[100] The Sages commended the general confession of sins on the Day of Atonement, stating that "*teshuvah* brings healing to the world" (*Yoma* 87b, 86a; *Sh. Ar., Ora*ḥ *Hayyim* 607:1).[101]

94	השפט כל הארץ לא יעשה משפט
95	אין דעתו של אדם יכולה להשיג דבר זה על בוריו
96	כי לא יראני האדם וחי
97	איש בחטאו ימות
98	כי כל דרכיו משפט
99	גדולה תשובה שמקרבת את האדם לשכינה
100	גדולה תשובה שמקרבת את הגאולה
101	גדולה תשובה שמביאה רפואות לעולם

The act of repenting one's sins is often thought to be simply a matter of regretting the error of one's ways, saying "I'm sorry" and asking for forgiveness. In reality, however, repentance is a complex procedure requiring much thought, determination and strength of will.

By committing a sin, transgressing the word of God, a man has to that extent distanced himself from the Almighty's presence. The significance of *teshuvah* – "returning" – is that this procedure enables him to redeem himself and be restored to the company of God (Rabbi A. Y. Kook, *Iggeret Teshuvah*). A sin against God is a sin against the Divine order touching human life, just as any sin against righteousness is a sin against God (I. Epstein: *Judaism*, Penguin Books, London, 1959, p. 67).

The prophet Ezekiel enumerated the Biblical laws on social justice which many of his generation were transgressing, and declared that each individual bore full responsibility for his actions and the inevitable punishment for his sins (Ezek. 18:20).[102] However, when a sinner repents and pursues justice and righteousness, the ways of God, "he shall surely live, not die" (Ezek. 18:21)[103]; furthermore, "he shall save his soul alive" (Ezek. 18:27).[104] By repenting, a sinner can create in himself "a new heart and a new spirit", a new direction in the conduct of his life, which is the Lord's wish and expectation, so that he may live out his life in happiness (Ezek. 18:31–32).[105]

The Almighty Himself longs for man's return to the path of repentance and waits patiently for him. God's hand is always outstretched to receive the penitent (*Pes.* 119a). According to the Sages, if man is willing to start by opening a tiny keyhole of repentance, even one no wider then the point of a needle, the Almighty will open gates of access for him that are wide enough for chariots to enter (Song R. 5:2).[106]

---

102 הנפש החוטאת היא תמות

103 והרשע כי ישוב מכל חטאותיו אשר עשה... חיה יחיה לא ימות

104 ובשוב רשע מרשעתו...הוא את נפשו יחיה

105 ועשו לכם לב חדש ורוח חדשה

106 פתחו לי פתח אחד של תשובה כחודה של מחט...

Repentance does not mean that a man should spend the rest of his life bewailing his past transgressions. It certainly enjoins remorse for the sins he committed, but need not involve unending sadness and contrition. True, the penitent must always be on his guard, knowing that he has previously succumbed to temptation, as David testified: "My sin is ever before me" (Ps. 51:5).[107] Yet like every other human being, he has been endowed with the ability to establish a new order in his life and transform his behaviour. The very realization that he is now able to utilize the Divine gift of free will can engender in him a feeling of delight and self-respect.

After a person acknowledges that he has done wrong, evincing remorse (*haratah*) and shame (*bushah*) for his transgression, he is geared to repent by humbly confessing his sin (*viddui*). Scripture imposes a sin-offering on one who has unwittingly become defiled: "When he knoweth of it, then he shall be guilty... and he shall confess that wherein he hath sinned" (Lev. 5:3–5).[108] Since that person alone was responsible for the offence, only he, by his own resolve, can improve his behaviour. When he has in fact done so, rejecting evil (*tikkun*) and performing good and kindly acts (*hesed u-tzedakah*), he can now pray for atonement and declare: "I am no longer the man who committed those wrongs, but an entirely different person (*ani mishtaneh*), and I seek God's blessing". As Jeremiah said, "After that I was turned, I repented" (Jer. 31:19, Kimhi *ad loc.*).[109] For such repentance the Almighty yearns, and the penitent is assured of His compassion (Jer. 31:20).[110]

The determined exercise of man's free will in overcoming the evil impulse gained the Sages' approbation. Whereas R. Yohanan, the great *tanna*, regarded a life of unbroken piety as the acme of human behaviour, Abbahu – a later Sage who faced

---

107   וחטאתי נגדי תמיד
108   ונעלם ממנו והוא ידע ואשם
109   כי אחרי שובי נחמתי
110   רחם ארחמנו נאום ה'

the rise of Jewish sectarianism – contended that a perfectly righteous man could not attain the spiritual heights of a *ba'al teshuvah*: "Where penitents stand, the wholly righteous cannot stand" (*Ber.* 34b; Maim. *Teshuvah* 7:4).[111]

Since this complete *teshuvah* seems virtually impossible for one to achieve, we pray daily for God to help us repent: without His aid we feel incapable of succeeding (Daily Prayer Book: *Amidah*, 5th Benediction).[112]

The Sages relate that God said to Israel, "Return unto me, and I will return unto you" (Mal. 3:7), but the people of Israel replied that they could not do so without His help. "It is in Your hand" (*be-yadekha*), they said; "first You must bring us to repentance and then we will be able to repent". Hence the Book of Lamentations concludes: "Turn us unto Thee, O Lord, and we shall be turned" (Lam. 5:21; Lam. R., *Eikhah, Petihta*; *Torah Temimah*, Lam. 5:21).[113] [See also: Maim. *Teshuvah* 2:1-2; Saadiah, *Emunot ve-De'ot* 5:5; Bahya, *Hovot ha-Levavot* 7:4; Yonah Gerondi, *Sha'arei Teshuvah*; Yitzhak Aboab, *Menorat ha-Ma'or*; S. Schechter, *Aspects of Rabbinic Theology*, pp. 293–343.]

According to R. Moshe Trani, known from his acronym as Ha-Mabbit (*Beit Elohim* 2, *Sha'ar Teshuvah*), the essence of *teshuvah* is what takes place in the sinner's mind. His feeling of remorse should be accompanied by the resolve never to repeat his transgression, which makes him a true *ba'al teshuvah*.

The Sages exemplified this teaching from the *Halakhah* which states that if a betrothal took place on the understanding that the bridegroom was a completely righteous man, the marriage is valid even if he proves to be a transgressor. Should he then wish to divorce his wife, the statutory *get* would be required. This law follows the principle that the groom may conceivably have performed *teshuvah* in his mind, thereby cleansing himself of sin (*Kid.* 49b).[114]

---

111 מקום שבעלי תשובה עומדין צדיקים גמורים אינם עומדין
112 סלח לנו אבינו כי חטאנו
113 השיבנו ה' אליך ונשובה
114 על מנת שאני צדיק אפילו רשע גמור מקודשת

When teshuvah is performed on the deathbed, it should still include a resolve not to repeat transgressions, even though the sinner may no longer have the strength to do so. To heighten the significance of his *teshuvah*, man is urged to subdue his evil inclination and then repent in the prime of life, rather than wait for his old age when the temptation to sin is weaker. Thus, according to Rav's interpretation, "Happy is the man that feareth the Lord" (Ps. 112:1)[115] denotes someone who performs teshuvah while in the full vigour of manhood, before declining into senility (*AZ* 19a, Rashi ad loc.; Ha-Mabbit, *loc. cit., ibid.*).

Avoiding any reversion to a particular sin is highly commended and judged to be on a par with fulfilling a religious obligation. The Sages declared that a man who unwaveringly resisted the temptation to sin would be rewarded like one who fulfilled a precept. Indeed, they affirm, there is no *mitzvah* greater than this (*Kid.* 39b, Rashi *ad loc.*; Ha-Mabbit, *loc. cit.*, 3).[116] R. Yohanan maintained that no one stands higher than the lifelong *tzaddik*, for of the wholly righteous it may be said: "Neither hath the eye seen a God beside Thee" (Isa. 64:4; *Ber.* 34b, Rashi *ad loc.*; Ha-Mabbit, *ibid.*, 4).[117]

The question is raised as to whether formal *teshuvah* on the Day of Atonement has any value if, after that holy day, one relapses into transgression. According to the Sages, "One who says, 'I'll sin and repent, sin again and repent', will be given no opportunity to do so. As for the man who says, 'I'll sin and on the Day of Atonement I'll repent', Yom Kippur will bring him no forgiveness" (Mish. *Yoma* 8:9; TB *Yoma* 85b).[118] However, if he is genuinely determined not to sin but later falls victim to the same temptation, we conclude that *teshuvah* was certainly intended for the first sin and that his new offence is due to the evil inclination, which accompanies man from his birth (Gen. 4:7; Ha-Mabbit, *ibid.*, 6).

---

115 אשרי איש יראת את ה'
116 ישב ולא עבר עבירה נותנין לו שכר כעושה מצוה
117 מקום שבעלי תשובה עומדין צדיקים גמורים אינם עומדין
118 האומר אחטא ואשוב, אחטא ואשוב, אין מספיקין בידו לעשות תשובה

Although full *teshuvah* requires both remorse for the past (*haratah*) and avoidance of sin in the future (*azivat ha-het*), it is maintained that sincere fulfillment of even one part can remit one's punishment. This emerges from the Biblical episode where Elijah, having first rebuked King Ahab for treacherously robbing Naboth of his vineyard, threatened to destroy Ahab's entire house. The king then humbled himself before the Lord and, despite other sins that he committed, the remorse he displayed over this particular transgression averted God's severe decree (1 Kings 21:29).[119] When the Ninevites similarly faced destruction because of their wickedness, they obeyed their king's order to repent and desist from robbery with violence. According to R. Yohanan, however, they returned only what they had on them – not whatever they had already appropriated, as true remorse (*haratah*) would have required. For this partial *teshuvah* (limited to *azivat ha-het*), God nonetheless revoked the evil decreed against them (Jonah 3:10; TJ *Ta'an.* 2:1; Ha-Mabbit, *ibid.*, 12).[120]

Even a virtuous man's proclivity to fall back into sin is recognized in the Bible: "For there is not a righteous man upon earth that doeth good and sinneth not" (Eccles. 7:20).[121]

Rabbenu Yonah Gerondi's detailed analysis of *teshuvah* and its components has already been mentioned. True repentance calls for a great deal of mental and spiritual effort to achieve a successful outcome in the penitent. Essentially, he must confess to having been the slave of his desires, following his animal instincts; he has tarnished his good name and become "like the beasts that perish" (Ps. 49:21).[122]

Isaiah described the efficacy of *teshuvah* in a memorable passage: "Seek ye the Lord while He may be found, call upon Him while He is near; let the wicked forsake his way, and the evil man his thoughts; let him return unto the Lord, and

---

119   יען כי נכנע מפני לא אביא הרע בימיו
120   וירא אל-הים את מעשיהם כי שבו מדרכם הרע, וינחם אל-הים...
121   כי אדם אין צדיק בארץ אשר יעשה טוב ולא יחטא
122   נמשל כבהמות נדמו

He will have mercy upon him, and to our God, for He will abundantly pardon" (Isa. 55:6–7).[123]

The Sages declared that if even the most hardened sinner repents, the Almighty will show mercy and forgive him (*Pesikta de-Rav* Kahana on Isa. 55:6–7).[124] For the prophet Isaiah, Israel's ingratitude in forsaking God made them lower than brute beasts: "The ox knoweth his owner, and the ass his master's crib; but Israel doth not know, My people doth not consider" (Isa. 1:3).[125]

Teshuvah calls for much resolve in the penitent's mind. To be certain of God's forgiveness, he must display genuine remorse and confess his sins (Prov. 28:13),[126] mend his ways and resist all further temptation (Isa. 55:7).[127] As we have seen, Isaiah ordered the people of Israel to choose repentance and return to God: "Seek ye the Lord while He may be found, call upon Him while He is near" (Isa. 55:6).[128]

The *ba'al teshuvah* must exercise constant vigilance, lest he again be seduced into wrongdoing. That thought informs the Scriptural verse: "Happy is the man that feareth always; but he that hardeneth his heart shall fall into mischief" (Prov. 28:14).[129] Hillel's advice was: "Put no trust in yourself until the day you die" (*Avot* 2:5);[130] and on his deathbed R. Yohanan ben Zakkai warned disciples: "May your fear of Heaven be as strong as your fear of flesh and blood!" (*Ber.* 28b).[131]

Humility

A humble spirit is an essential prerequisite for *teshuvah,*

---

123   דרשו ה׳ בהימצאו, קראוהו בהיותו קרוב: יעזוב רשע דרכו ואיש און מחשבותיו
וישוב אל ה׳ וירחמהו ואל אל-הינו כי ירבה לסלוח
124   אפילו מי שכופר בעיקר
125   ידע שור קונהו וחמור אבוס בעליו, וישראל לא ידע, עמי לא התבונן
126   מודה ועוזב ירוחם
127   יעזוב רשע דרכו ואיש און מחשבותיו וישוב אל ה׳ וירחמהו
128   דרשו ה׳ בהימצאו, קראוהו בהיותו קרוב
129   אשרי אדם מפחד תמיד, ומקשה לבו ייפול ברע
130   אל תאמין בעצמך עד יום מותך
131   יהי רצון שיהי מורא שמים עליכם כמורא בשר ודם

and this frame of mind should be cultivated energetically. In the Almighty's exalted presence man should be ever aware of his lowly station and eschew the vainglory prompted by his wayward heart. A declaration by one of Israel's prophets states that the Lord only requires man "to do justly, and to love mercy, and to walk humbly with thy God" (Micah 6:8).[132] Before Him no mortal can boast of his wisdom, strength or riches. Man can only take pride in his understanding of God's supreme grandeur and in demonstrating his own kindness, justice and righteousness (Jer. 9:22–23).[133]

Here Jeremiah condemned telltale features of arrogance such as man's boasting of his wisdom, strength and wealth. If these characteristics are abhorred by God, humbling oneself in *teshuvah* can facilitate the expiation of sin. An arrogant man becomes the captive of his own nature and God then holds him in contempt: "Everyone that is proud in heart is an abomination to the Lord" (Prov. 16:5).[134]

Maimonides lists the sin of haughtiness as one of the most serious defects in man, tantamount to repudiating the Creator, as Moses warned Israel: "Lest thy heart then be lifted up, and thou forget the Lord thy God..." (Deut. 8:14; Maim. Code, *De'ot* 2:3; *Sot.* 5a).[135]

In contrast to the evil of sinful pride, self-correcting penitent humility gains the reward of forgiveness. Scripture relates that King Ahab did more to provoke God's anger than any ruler of Israel before him (1 Kings 16:30). Yet responding to Elijah's severe castigation, Ahab humbled himself before God: "He rent his clothes, and put sackcloth on his flesh, and fasted... and went softly". Then God told Elijah: "Because he humbleth himself before Me, I will not bring the evil in his days" (1 Kings 21:27–29).[136]

---

132 והצנע לכת עם אל-היך
133 אל יתהלל חכם בחכמתו... כי אם בזאת יתהלל השכל וידוע אותי
134 תועבת ה' כל גבה לב
135 ורם לבבך ושכחת את ה' אל-היך
136 יען כי נכנע מפני

Self-denial

The process of *teshuvah* obliges one to strive for the repression of evil desires. The penitent can subdue his passions and avoid excess by cultivating self-denial, but whatever scoundrels have is never enough: "The righteous eateth to the satisfying of his desire; but the belly of the wicked shall want" (Prov. 13:25).[137] The tendency of self-indulgent people to rationalize their sins and justify their mistakes is depicted by the moralist: "Every way of a man is right in his own eyes; but the Lord weigheth the hearts (Prov. 21:2).[138]

Self-examination

Teshuvah also obliges a man to scrutinize his behaviour and detect any shortcomings. Such introspection will make him aware of his faults and lead to self-improvement, a course of action which the Bible recommends: "Let us search and try our ways, and turn again to the Lord" (Lam. 3:40).

Knowing how he has transgressed, a person should strive to conduct himself in the opposite way. A haughty man, for example, should endeavour to behave modestly (Maim. Code, *De'ot* 2:2).[139] In general, an offender must recognize the depths to which he has sunk: "See thy way in the valley, know what thou hast done" (Jer. 2:23).[140] The Sages warned against making light of "petty" transgressions, on the basis that one should fulfil a "minor" mitzvah as carefully as a "major" one (*Avot* 2:1).[141]

---

137   צדיק אוכל לשובע נפשו, ובטן רשעים תחסר

138   כל דרך איש ישר בעיניו ותוכן לבות ה'

139   אם היה גבה לב ינהיג עצמו בביזיון

140   ראה דרכך בגיא, דע מה עשית

141   והווה זהיר במצוה קלה כבחמורה

Confession – Viddui

The essential requirement for the atonement of all sins is prescribed in the injunction: "He shall confess that wherein he hath sinned" (Lev. 5:5).[142] The basic component of *viddui* is a declaration of profound regret, "But indeed we have sinned" (*Yoma* 87b; Maim. Code, *Teshuvah* 2:8).[143] The confession of sins, though ideally specified, need not be detailed or spoken aloud. It may be confined to the rueful admission, "But indeed we have sinned".[144] According to Maimonides, "the most important part of confession, which all Israel adopted, is this statement". It is also the one followed in the Ashkenazi prayer rite (Maim. Code, *Teshuvah* 2:8; *Sh. Ar., Orah Hayyim* 207:2).

In cases where a man knows that his parents or ancestors likewise transgressed, he should voice his determination to rid himself of those transgressions by stating in his *viddui*: "But we and our fathers have sinned". The son thus prays on his father's behalf for a remission of sins. The efficacy of such a prayer is based on the principle that "a son can bring merit to his father" (*Sanh.* 104b).[145]

The Torah uses a similar expression: "And they shall confess their iniquity, and the iniquity of their fathers" (Lev. 26:40).[146] This reflects and calls to mind the second commandment of the Decalogue (Ex. 20:5).[147] In Daniel's prayer for the ending of the Babylonian Exile, he begged forgiveness "for our sins, and for the iniquities of our fathers" (Dan. 9:16). This may appear to contradict a principle of the Torah: "The fathers shall not be put to death for the children, neither shall the children be put to death for the fathers; every man shall be put to death for his own sin" (Deut. 24:16).[148]

---

142 והתוודה אשר חטא עליה
143 אבל אנחנו חטאנו
144 אבל אנחנו חטאנו
145 ברא מזכה אבא
146 ויתוודו את עוונם ואת עוון אבותם
147 פוקד עוון אבות על בנים
148 לא יומתו אבות על בנים

The Sages explain, however, that children suffer for their parents' misdeeds if they persist in copying them (Rashi on Lev. 26:39; Ber. 47a; *Sha'arei Teshuvah* 1:40).[149]

According to the ritual adopted by the Lurianic school of Kabbalah (*nusah ha-Ari*; 16th cent.) and followed by the SHELAH (R. Yeshayahu Horowitz) in his ethical work, *Shenei Luhot ha-Berit*, the personal *viddui* should always declare: "But we and our fathers have indeed sinned".[150] To this the Eastern Sephardi rite adds, "And [so have] the members of our family" (R. Akiva Eger in note on *Sh. Ar., Orah Hayyim* 607).[151]

Whereas Maimonides ruled that a man's confession should be expressed by the words of his mouth (*Teshuvah* 7:1), Nahmanides adds a note on this ruling (*ibid.*) which states that if, for some reason, he is unable to express the repentant words orally, he should do so in his heart. In that case, he should give a mental account of the transgressions for which he seeks atonement.

Apart from the confession on a deathbed, known simply as *viddui*, a similar confession is also made on the Day of Atonement, particularly at the end of its concluding (*Ne'ilah*) service. It is also customary to recite the formal *viddui* each day after the morning and afternoon *Amidah* prayer, especially on Monday and Thursday mornings (Sephardi rite prayer book). When reciting the *Shema* before going to sleep, it is incumbent on one to think back and repent any habitual shortcomings in one's daily life (*Sh. Ar., Orah Hayyim* 239, note by *Ba'er Heitev*). Some people follow the practice of reciting the full *viddui* together with the nightly *Ha-Mappil* prayer at bedtime, out of a conviction that one never knows which day will be one's last and that one should depart this life with a purified soul. The *viddui* also forms part of the kabbalistic "midnight vigil", *Tikkun Hatzot* (ARI), but this practice is not generally

---

149   כשאוחזין מעשה אבותיהם בידיהם
150   אבל אנחנו ואבותינו חטאנו
151   ואנשי ביתנו

followed and it is not prescribed in the *Shulḥan Arukh* (*Sedei Ḥemed, Dinim* 1, p. 2026; *Birkei Yosef* 581:2; *Eliyahu R.* 239:3).

Everyone is required to make a full confession of sins on his deathbed, just as a condemned man is asked to confess before his execution, thus ensuring one of a place in the World to Come (*Yoma* 36b; RIF and Maim.; *Sh. Ar., Yoreh De'ah* 338; *Ba'al ha-Turim* on Num. 5:7).[152] Maimonides lays down that since man bears responsibility for all of his actions, he should endeavour to repent all of his sins by declaring aloud his remorse and confession so that, when departing this life, he will be in a state of teshuvah and thereby merit life in the World to Come (Maim. Code, *Teshuvah* 7:1; *Shab.* 32a; *Sanh.* 43b; *Yoreh De'ah* 338:1).[153]

From the Biblical account of the murder of Abel it appears that Cain's jealousy of his brother lay at the root of this first violent crime. Both Cain and Abel had brought offerings to God, but Abel's offering was accepted whereas Cain's was rejected. The violent impulses of envy and anger led to a horrifying murder and to the guilty man's effrontery in imputing his own crime to the Almighty (Schechter, *Aspects of Rabbinic Theology*, p. 281).

The Sages delved deeper into the sources of human strife and found three causes for murder (including fratricide). These causes are, firstly, strife over possessions, Cain and Abel having argued about how the world's riches should be divided; next, strife over religion, each brother having insisted that the holy Temple should be within his domain and that he serve as its priest; and thirdly (though not necessarily the least important factor) sexual passion, tradition having it that each man claimed the right to Abel's twin sister, who was the only woman available at the time (Gen. 22:17).

While Cain was still consumed with bitter jealousy, God offered him salvation through repentance and self-

---

152 והתוודו: רמז שכל המומתים מתוודים בעת יציאת הנפש

153 וישתדל אדם לעשות תשובה ולהתוודות בפיו

improvement: "If thou doest well, shalt thou not be forgiven?
And if thou doest not well, sin croucheth at the door" (Gen.
4:7).[154] Eventually, Cain did repent and his repentance was
accepted (*Pesikta de-Rav Kahana*, ed. Solomon Buber, 163a–
b).

The Rabbis expounded "sin crouching at the door" to
mean that the impulse to sin is initially weak; if not rejected
at the start, however, it gains immeasurable strength. In the
beginning it looks as flimsy as a spider's web, but later it
becomes as strong as a towrope. R. Yitzhak maintained that
sin begins unpretentiously, like a guest at the door, and then
brazenly takes possession of the house (Gen. R. 22:11).

The duty to confess is mentioned as being part of the
supplication for atonement in respect of four transgressions
listed in the Torah: defilement of the Sanctuary or its sacred
appurtenances;[155] failure to bear witness as to the veracity of
an oath given in evidence which one had heard;[156] and failure
to abide by one's own oath.[157] In each case, if the sinner has
forgotten his transgression[158] but later becomes aware of it
and regrets what he has done, that person is required to bring
a sin-offering (*hattat*) and to confess his specific transgression
over the animal's head (Lev. 5:1–6; Targum Yonatan *ad loc.;*
Sifrei, Lev. 14:1, 7; Num. 5:7, *Sifrei ad loc.*).

Although the *viddui* obligation is meant to be part of the
sin-offering, the Sages regarded *viddui* as a separate law.[159]
Thus, even if no sacrifice is brought, the duty to confess
remains in force at all times and for all sins, great or small
(*Mekhilta*, Num. 5:5; *Sifrei*, Num. 5:5; Maim *Teshuvah* 1:1;
Sefer ha-Hinnukh 364).

Since the Temple and its sacrificial rites no longer exist,
teshuvah of itself can bring atonement (Maim. Code, *Teshuvah*

---

154   לפתח חטאת רובץ
155   מטמאי מקדש וקדושיו
156   שמיעת קול
157   ביטויי שפתיים
158   ונעלם ממנו
159   מצווה בפני עצמה

1:3, 2:5). Sacrifices would in any case be meaningless without the personal *teshuvah* of confession. Just as the traditional *Shema* proclamation of faith is recited aloud, so should one's confession be made orally, as speech reveals the inner thoughts of the mind. In so doing, the transgressor acknowledges that all his acts are seen by God and vows that he will never repeat his misdeeds. Only such repentance is acceptable before the Lord.

The Almighty's response to penitence and prayer on account of some offence against Him is unreservedly favourable. After a private transgression,[160] God does not insist on demanding forms of repentance but graciously accepts the offender's verbal confession and is reconciled with him. The prophet Hosea equated verbal repentance with sacrifices on the altar: "Take with you words, and return unto the Lord; so will we render as bullocks the offering of our lips" (Hos. 14:3).[161]

Regarding the question as to whether confession should be made aloud, in public or in private, the Sages declared that offences against one's fellow man[162] must be confessed publicly, specifying the wrong, so that one feels ashamed. In the case of a religious transgression, however, the offence is confined to a violation of God's law; confession may therefore be made privately, since it does no honour to God for every infringement of His law to be made public (*Yoma* 86b, Rashi *ad loc.*).

Maimonides accordingly ruled that sins affecting relations with one's fellow man[163] should be confessed in public, specifying the wrong done to the injured party and expressing remorse and repentance. In the case of sins affecting relations between man and God,[164] confession should be made privately, as it would be unseemly to publicize such an offence. In a gloss on the ruling of Maimonides, however, R. Avraham ben

---

160 עובר עבירה בסתר
161 קחו עמכם דברים ונשלם פרים שפתנו
162 בעבירות שבין אדם לחברו
163 בין אדם לחברו
164 בין אדם למקום

David of Posquières (RAVAD) concluded that if the religious offence is already public knowledge, it should rightly be confessed inpublic (Maim. Code, *Teshuvah* 2:5; RAVAD and *Kesef Mishneh*, *ad loc.*).

Despite these rulings in favour of an audible confession, Rabbinic commentators chose to discuss the legality of a silent (private) confession – *viddui ba-lev*. This appears to be at variance with the contractual principle that unexpressed intentions are legally invalid.[165] A sale made with certain mental reservations by either party would, for instance, not be voided if these unexpressed conditions were not realized. The Talmud illustrates this point with a special example, where one might expect that greater consideration would be given to a party's intention. Thus, if a man sold his property only because he intended to fulfil the *mitzvah* of immigrating to Israel, but no such stipulation was made and he was ultimately prevented from doing so, he could not claim that the sale was invalid on the grounds that the condition which he had in his mind was not fulfilled. The contract would therefore be enforceable (*Kid.* 49b, RAN *ad loc.*; Maim. Code, *Mekhirah* 11:9).

A departure from this general rule occurs, however, in the law pertaining to conditions in marriage (*kiddushin*)[166] and the required betrothal procedure, as we shall now explain. That a betrothal is only valid when it has the woman's consent is clearly set forth in the Talmud and embodied by Maimonides in his code.[167] The Sages elucidated the Mishnaic expression, "a woman is acquired",[168] as indicating that the marriage contract depends on her consent, namely, that she allows herself to be "acquired" (*Kid.* 2b; Maim. *Ishut* 4:1).[169]

This is comparable to the law of sale, where a sale is legal only

---

165   דברים שבלב אינם דברים
166   תנאי בקידושין
167   אין האשה מתקדשת אלא לרצונה
168   האשה נקנית
169   האשה נקנית מדעתה כן, בלא מדעתה לא

when the vendor gives his consent.[170] In the case of marriage, the bride conveys to the groom any legal rights that he may have over her (*Kid.* 45a, Rashi ad loc.), hence *kiddushin* may be regarded as a form of transaction. In the law of transactions, if any condition is stipulated, the transaction is only valid when that condition has been fulfilled; otherwise, there is no meeting of minds in the agreement's transaction, as every contract requires. This law applies wherever conditions are stipulated, whether in a sale or, generally, in financial transactions (*dinei mammonot*), in marriage (*kiddushin*) or in divorce (*gerushin*).

Thus, if in contracting a marriage one adds a special condition that it be in accordance with the recognized formalities of the manner of stipulating a condition (*Kid.* 61a),[171] the validity of the *kiddushin* depends on the fulfillment of that condition; for in every contract the full intention and agreement of both parties must be established. Accordingly, the enactment is as follows: "Where a man effects a betrothal on some condition, the woman is legally betrothed if the condition is fulfilled; if it is not, she is not betrothed" (Maim. Code, *Ishut* 6:1).[172]

When a realistic condition is formally laid down for the *kiddushin*, the validity of the marriage depends on the fulfillment of that condition. If, for example, he says, "I betroth you on condition that you give me the sum of 200 *zuz*" (one *zuz* equals one fourth of a shekel), the marriage will only be valid if and when the bride gives that sum to her husband. If he betroths her on condition that she fulfils some requirement of a reasonable nature (*al tenai*), and she knowingly accepted the condition but does not fulfil it, she has deceived him. The *kiddushin* would then be invalid and no marriage would have been performed.[173] If, however, he merely deceived himself, mistakenly presuming the woman to be someone other than she really was, and there had been no deceit on her part,

---

170 דעת המקנה

171 כתנאי בני גד ובני ראובן

172 המקדש על תנאי, אם נתקיים התנאי, מקודשת, ואם לאו, אינה מקודשת

173 הטעתה אותו

the *kiddushin* remains valid and the marriage has full legal standing (*Kid.* 49b, 62a; Maim. *Ishut* 8:2, 6, *Mekhirah* 1:1).

Furthermore, the Sages taught that if a man enters a marriage having assured his bride that he is rich, whereas he is in fact poor or not considered wealthy by his fellow townsmen, the woman can claim that he misled her and the *kiddushin* would then be invalid (*Kid.* 49b).[174]

A similar case discussed by the Sages was especially problematic. The *kiddushin* had been performed on the understanding that the groom was a righteous man,[175] but we then find him in possession of stolen property and know that he can only obtain atonement after returning the goods to their owner. We can therefore dismiss his claim to be righteous. Nevertheless, it was commonly ruled that the marriage had not been nullified by a false assurance and remained valid (*mekuddeshet*) or, as Maimonides ruled, it had to be treated as a possible marriage (*safek mekuddeshet*).

This ruling would appear to contradict those made in earlier cases discussed by the Sages. They explained, however, that even while retaining possession of the stolen goods, the man might conceivably have repented his transgression and determined in his mind that he would return the property to its owner. One could therefore presume that he was now of good character and that he had not been guilty of misrepresenting himself (*Kid.* 49b).[176] That presumed mental act of repentance would result in his status of being married to this woman and that she was a married woman – *eshet ish*, and all that that implied.

The Integrity of Repentance

Teshuvah is itself an act of the mind requiring total will and consent (*li-retzono*), just as the sin-offering had to be made

---

174   הטעה אותה
175   על מנת שאני צדיק
176   שמא הרהר תשובה בדעתו

with complete will and intention (*Ker.* 7a, Rashi *ad loc.*; *Kid.* 49b; Maim. Code, *Ishut* 8:5; *Sh. Ar.*, *Even ha-Ezer* 38:31, *Ba'er Heitev*).

Sefer ha-Ḥinnukh, an exposition of the Torah's 613 Commandments largely following Maimonides (first ed. Venice, 1523), outlines the laws of *teshuvah* (in section 364). In his learned commentary on this work, *Minḥat Ḥinnukh*, R. Yosef Babad considers the implications of the above case where, in his *kiddushin*, the man stipulated that he was righteous. From the Sages' apparently unchallenged ruling in this matter it is possible to elucidate the rabbinic understanding of confession as a part of *teshuvah*. R. Babad points out that this case involved a silent, unexpressed act of repentance (*ibid.*, 364). The *Ḥinnukh*, in its extensive dissertation on the law of *teshuvah* (*ibid.*), quotes the early *Mekhilta* as determining that confession of sins (*viddui*) was an independent law that had to be fulfilled in its own right[177] and was not identical with the separate law of repentance. Thus, *Minḥat Ḥinnukh* explains that although the law of *viddui* requires oral expression, the law governing *teshuvah* is different, for here sincere repentance performed only in the mind would be acceptable to the Almighty and bring one atonement.[178]

This interpretation is supported by the previously mentioned enactment of the Sages, namely, that if a man's betrothal was dependent on his being righteous, even if he gave the opposite impression, it could be that the man had repented inwardly (in his mind), thus becoming righteous and fulfilling the legal condition (*Kid.* 49a). Just as the penitent's sin-offering must be accompanied by a mental determination with his total will and consent (*li-retzono*), so must that repentance be an earnest act of the mind – *li-retzono* (*Ker.* 7a, Rashi s.v. *"ella al ha-shavin"*; *Bet Yosef* on *Even ha-Ezer* 38:31).

When a person wishes to fulfil his duty to repent, he must first show remorse for his transgression. His mental decision

---

177   מצווה בפני עצמה
178   לעניין כפרה על העבירה שעבר נתכפר בתשובה בלב

should be expressed verbally, before the one whom he wronged, in the following words: "I have done such and such, which I regret, and I am ashamed of my conduct". He is then required to declare before God: "But we have surely sinned" (Maim. *Teshuvah* 1:1, 2:8).[179]

The primary obligation of *teshuvah* is illustrated in the sounding of the *shofar* (ram's horn) on the New Year festival, Rosh Ha-Shanah. This ceremony, performed at intervals during worship, is a "Day of Judgment" call for each individual to repent before the Sovereign of the Universe. The sounding of the *shofar* recalls Abraham's total acceptance of God's will, to the extent that he was even ready to sacrifice his son Isaac, although the Almighty had prepared a ram, unknown to him, to be offered up in Isaac's place (*akedat Yitzhak*). Hence this festival is also called "a remembrance [day] of blowing the *shofar*" (Lev. 23:24; Num 29:1).

The Sages emphasized that the purpose of sounding the shofar was to awake all slumberers and rouse them to their duty (Maim. Code *Teshuvah* 3:4).[180] Fulfillment of the *shofar* injunction takes place in the mind – *ba-mahashavah* – as one hears the *shofar* blasts. The ceremonial benediction on performing this mitzvah declares that we bless God for the duty "to hear the sound of the *shofar*".[181] The essential act is not so much blowing the shofar as hearing it and responding to its call in one's consciousness (*Sh. Ar., Orah Hayyim* 585:1, 5:1).

E. Some Modern Views

According to Solomon Schechter (*Aspects of Rabbinic Theology*, p. 334 *ff*.), returning from one's evil ways signifies a keen

---

179 אבל אנחנו חטאנו
180 עורו ישנים משנתכם
181 לשמוע קול שופר

resolve to break with sin. The Sages had said that one who embarked on a course of repentance, but did not abandon his transgressions, was likened to the man who entered a ritual bath (*mikveh*) to cleanse himself of Levitical impurity while still grasping the reptile which was, and continued to be, the cause of his impurity (*Yoma* 5b; *Ta'an.* 16a; *Tos. Ta'an.* 1).[182]

As we have seen, repentance begins in one's mind and should continue with a verbal acknowledgment of sin: "He that covereth his transgression shall not prosper; but whoso confesseth and forsaketh them shall obtain mercy" (Prov. 28:13).[183] The duty to repent is also an affirmative Biblical precept (Num. 5:6–7).[184] As long as a man lives, the Almighty hopes and waits for his repentance.

Although even a deathbed repentance is accepted by God (*Kid.* 40b), R. Eliezer told his disciples: "Repent one day before your death". When they asked, "How does any man know which day he will die?" the Sage answered: "All the more reason for him to repent today, lest he die tomorrow; he should therefore engage in repentance every day of his life" (*Shab.* 153a; Maim. *Teshuvah* 7:2).[185]

It is the universally accepted rule that nothing stands in the way of the penitent. Even if his misdeeds cannot be rectified, he should still put his trust in God and strive for repentance, since the Almighty awaits it (*Pes.* 119a). Likewise, in regard to the profanation of God's Name (*ḥillul Hashem*), where only death can bring atonement, *teshuvah* is still required (*Yoma* 5b).

The Rabbis enunciated the perpetual availability of *teshuvah* as follows: "The gate of repentance is as wide as the sea. Although a ritual bath is sometimes open and sometimes closed, the sea is always open for one to be cleansed in it. When a man wishes to bathe in the sea, he can do so whenever he likes. So it is with repentance: whenever a man wishes to

---

182   הטובל ושרץ בידו

183   מכסה פשעיו לא יצליח, ומודה ועוזב ירוחם

184   והתוודו את חטאם אשר עשו

185   שוב יום אחד לפני מיתתך

repent, God will receive him, as the Bible states: 'For what
great nation is there, that hath God so nigh unto them, as the
Lord our God is whensoever we call upon Him?'" (Deut. 4:7;
Lam. R. 3:35; *Pesikta de-Rav Kahana* 157a; *Midrash Tehillim*
65:4).[186]

Furthermore, although the gates of prayer are sometimes
closed and sometimes open, so that when praying we ask (like
David) for our petition to be received at an acceptable time (Ps.
69:14),[187] the gates of *teshuvah* always remain open. R. Anan,
however, added that the gates of prayer are also never closed
and that God is near us whenever we call to Him (Deut. 4:7;
Deut. R. 2:7; Lam. R. 3:35).[188] On the basis of these teachings,
a medieval authority once prescribed a course of repentance
even for cardinal transgressions such as idolatry, adultery and
homicide, for which it was ruled that no forgiveness could be
expected (Responsa of R. Yosef Trani [Ha-Mabbit] 2:8).

The Sages affirmed that one should never despair of
achieving repentance, for with Divine help man's smallest
effort will be endorsed and amplified. They portray God
saying to Israel: "My children, open a keyhole of repentance
for Me, even one as narrow as the point of a needle, and I will
open gates of access for you that are wide enough for chariots
to enter" (Song R. 5:3).[189]

True repentance is received by God as the most sacred form
of Divine worship. R. Yehoshua ben Levi asked: "Whence can
it be proved that one who repents is regarded like a man who
went up to Jerusalem, built the Temple and altar, and offered
up all the sacrifices mentioned in the Torah? From this phrase:
'The sacrifices of God are a broken spirit'" (Ps. 51:19).[190]
Even a criminal facing execution is urged to acknowledge his
sins, as confession and death will secure him a place in the
World to Come (*Sanh.* 43b).[191]

186   בכל קוראנו אליו
187   ואני תפילתי לך ה׳ עת רצון
188   בכל קוראנו אליו
189   פתחו לי פתח אחד של תשובה כחודה של מחט
190   זבחי אל-הים רוח נשברה
191   יש לו חלק לעולם הבא

The Path of Repentance

According to Rabbi Samson Raphael Hirsch (*Judaism Eternal*, ch. 79), the way to recovering one's purity lies through (1) confession, (2) reparation, (3) contrition and (4) repentance. He offers the following advice:

1. **Confession** *(viddui)*: If you admit to having sinned, enter the Almighty's presence and say: "O God, I have erred and sinned, I have been disobedient before You, I have done such and such; I regret what I have done, I am ashamed and will never do it again." In confessing when the Temple still stood, you could (if your error was unintentional) express this submission to God by means of a sacrifice. With the Temple's destruction the altar has vanished, but in your mind's eye you can picture yourself submitting to God at the altar, so that you may be restored to life again by His hand. Acknowledge this feeling verbally, making your submission a permanent frame of mind that can bear fruit in practical conduct.

2. **Reparation** *(hashavah)*: If you have wronged your neighbour, if you have caused any injury to his person, his honour or his property, make haste to restore what the law demands of you and endeavour to obtain his forgiveness.

3. **Contrition** *(haratah)*: Let deep remorse for the offence you committed take root in your heart. Realize how far you have gone astray; and let the power of your resolve to do better match the depth of your contrition.

4. **Repentance** *(teshuvah)*: The most heartfelt remorse will prove unavailing if you cannot draw from it the strength of mind to renounce transgression and keep your future life more blameless than your past. Complete *teshuvah* is achieved when you have the opportunity to repeat a sin with the same impulse, means and vigour as before, but refrain from doing so because you recognize the wickedness of that action and now wish to reform.

However, even in old age on your deathbed, if at last you realize the gravity of your offence, you may still repent and hope for forgiveness. Even if, throughout your life, you have never walked with God, you are still one of His creatures and may return to your Father like a lost child.

5. The path of true repentance is not an easy one, and it requires a great effort of the will to pursue it, but anyone who does so in earnest will never fail. Prayer is the mainstay of life. When praying, declare unreservedly how you feel about your behaviour and the goals you are striving to attain. Through prayer you can find the strength to overcome temptation and egotism. If you wish to reform, approach this task energetically and with renewed vigour each day, reminding yourself that you seek to become a different person. Never for one moment imagine that you are too weak to succeed. Whatever God demands of you, He gives you the strength to achieve. We all stand in need of *teshuvah*, for who can claim that he has never sinned? The duty to confess on the Day of Atonement applies to us all.

F. Irremediable Sins

Since reparation is an essential part of *teshuvah*, certain transgressions that cannot be rectified are beyond atonement. Such misdeeds include the embezzlement of public funds (where one cannot know to whom restitution should be made), murder and adultery (when an irreversibly illegitimate child has been fathered). The Sages laid down that there can be no remedy for these crimes (*Sanh.* 7a; *BB* 88b).[192]

R. Yitzhak Alfasi (RIF) lists 24 acts enumerated by the Sages which prevent one from attaining teshuvah (RIF on *Yoma* 8, 6a; Maim. *Teshuvah* 4).[193] These include habitual

---

192   לא היה לו תקנתא

193   עשרים וארבע דברים מעכבים את התשובה

slander, anger, evil thoughts, and associating with wicked and lascivious behaviour. They are so prevalent that one hardly regards them as sinful. If, however, a person mends his ways and takes care not to repeat such transgressions, he will be assured of a place in the World to Come.

G. Turning to God in Prayer

A prayer for Divine help in the effort to attain *teshuvah* was included in the Eighteen Benedictions of the *Amidah*, as redacted by the Great Sanhedrin in Rabban Gamliel of Yavneh's lifetime (first century CE).[194] This petition is recited after the one for knowledge,[195] since only a man fully aware of his actions will repent of his sins. The process is described by Isaiah: "Make the heart of this people fat... lest they, seeing with their eyes, and hearing with their ears, and understanding with their heart, [then] return and be healed" (Isa. 6:10; *Meg.* 17b).[196]

In our quest for *teshuvah* we should seek the aid of Torah study, hence we pray, "Bring us back to Your Torah[197] and draw us near to the fulfillment of Your laws",[198] thus cleansing our minds of evil thoughts. Then we pray, "Make us return before You in perfect repentance".[199] Here the expression "before You" (*lefanekha*) means that our repentance should be complete, not only for ourselves but also in the eyes of God, as it is known only to the Creator.

A prayer for Divine help in mastering our *yetzer ha-ra* is included in the daily service, just after the early morning blessings. It reads: "Let not the evil inclination dominate us".[200]

---

194 החזירנו בתשובה שלמה לפניך
195 חננו מאיתך דעה בינה והשכל
196 ולבבו יבין ושב ורפא לו
197 השיבנו לתורתך
198 וקרבנו לעבודתך
199 והחזירנו בתשובה שלמה לפניך
200 ואל תשלט בנו יצר הרע

As stated in the *Amidah*, we appeal directly to God for the granting of atonement, because He Himself desires our repentance[201] – "The Lord taketh pleasure in them that fear Him, in those that wait for His mercy" (Ps. 147:11).[202] This Divine wish for man's repentance is enunciated by the prophet Ezekiel: "As I live, saith the Lord God, I have no pleasure in the death of the wicked, but that the wicked turn from his way and live" (Ezek. 33:11; cf. Ezek. 18:23).[203]

Man's ability to achieve repentance was bestowed on him from the moment of his creation. R. Yishmael declared: "The world could never have existed but for the fact that repentance was created first, and the Holy One, blessed be He, stretches out His right hand to receive penitence every day" (*Pes.* 54a; *Pirkei de-Rabbi Eliezer* 11).

The essence of *teshuvah* is man's "turning away" from sinful acts of the past and "turning towards" the path of righteousness. In this way man has the power to reshape his destiny. As far as atonement is concerned, the Sages relate: "Wisdom was asked, 'What is the sinner's punishment?' Wisdom replied: 'Other sins will follow', as it is written: 'Evil pursueth sinners' (Prov. 13:21).[204] Prophecy declared: 'The soul that sinneth, it shall die' (Ezek. 18:4).[205] Torah stated: 'He may bring a sin-offering and then receive forgiveness' (Lev. 5:6).[206] When the Almighty was asked, He replied: 'Let him [the sinner] repent and he will be granted atonement'" (TJ *Mak.* 2:7, 31d).[207]

In Temple times, certain offences (mainly unintentional and involuntary as well as "ritual" transgressions) could be erased if the offering of a sacrifice was accompanied by repentance. Communal sacrifices, notably the red heifer – *parah adummah*

---

201 הרוצה בתשובה
202 רוצה ה' את יראיו, את המייחלים לחסדו
203 אם אחפרץ במות הרשע כי אם בשוב רשע מדרכו וחיה
204 חטאים תרדף רעה
205 הנפש החוטאת היא תמות
206 וכיפר עליו הכהן מחטאתו... והביא את אשמו לה' על חטאתו אשר חטא
207 יעשה תשובה ויתכפר לו

(Num. 19:2) and the scapegoat – *Azazel* (Lev. 16:5–10, 21), would even atone for the sins of private individuals within the community. After the Temple's destruction and the halting of sacrifices, various forms of atonement are mentioned by the Rabbis. These spiritualized sacrifices include repentance, the Day of Atonement, bodily deprivations such as fasting, charitable gifts, kindly deeds, prayer and Torah study.

Chapter 5

Ethics – *Middot*

5 *Ethics* – Middot

A. Introduction

The distinctive features that constitute the innate dispositions of human beings vary considerably. Different people are endowed with different impulses, according to the balance of natural forces within the minds and bodies with which they are born, and an individual's basic character and behaviour are formed accordingly. Man is in the first instance fashioned genetically, but is also subject to environmental and educational influences. The environment imparts instruction to the mind, but the type of environment can be chosen by the individual. Likewise, the quality of the mind can be determined by study and self-education. Ideally, one should exercise self-control to ensure moderation in all things, so that each inherent quality can be harmonized and given a balanced form of expression. The form that a person's outlook eventually assumes depends on the decisions reached and followed by the individual. Jewish ethics require man to be constantly aware of his responsibility in achieving the required moderation.

The teachings of the Bible and the interpretative guidance of the Sages are offered to man as the best means of achieving a balanced and pious life. To attain this result one must ensure that the duty to follow these practices is embedded in one's natural way of life, and one must always be conscious of the responsibility attached to everything one does (Maim. *De'ot*, 1:1–7).[1] One should compel oneself to love one's neighbor, despite all feelings to the contrary. We must refrain from hating our fellow man, even when condemning his behaviour. This way of life can only be achieved by the individual's own

efforts. The duty to love one's fellow man is eternalized in the
Biblical ordinance: "Thou shalt love the neighbour as thyself"
(Lev. 19:18).[2]

This ethical teaching was described by R. Akiva as the
basic principal in the entire Torah (TJ *Nedarim* 9:4; Sifra, Lev.
19:18; Gen. R. 24:8).[3] In the experience of the whole of life
one must be governed by the law of "love thy neighbour". In
an early teaching of Rabbi Eliyahu (*Tana de-Rabbi Eliyahu*) it
is stated "Thus the Almighty said to Israel, 'My dear children,
there is nothing that I need to ask of you other than that you
should show consideration to each other and honour each
other'." The sage Ben Nanas expounded the verse further
stating that on examination it will be found that all the moral
teaching of the commandments of the Torah are contained in
this precept (R. Avraham Sofer, *Derashot, Shabat Hagadol*
p. 308). A normal person is created in such a way that he is
endowed with the power to make this effort, and he must
choose to do so himself. This is entirely an act of free will, and
the Almighty will help such a person to lead a virtuous life, as
King Solomon urged in the Book of Proverbs: "In all thy ways
acknowledge Him, and He will direct thy paths" (Prov. 3:6;
Maim. *De'ot*, 3:3, 6:1–6; Maim. *Teshuvah*, 5:1, 3).[4]

Human will – *ratzon* – may be distinguished from human
intelligence – *sekhel*. The use of our intelligence enables
us to understand the nature of what exists, or the nature of
creation, as formulated in science or philosophy. Human will
is the creative force by which man fashions the way we live,
determining our social behaviour and our ethical and religious
thought. In this respect, David prayed for Divine help in
turning to and attaining the ideal of God's law, described as
repentance (*teshuvah*): "Create in me a clean heart, O God"
(Ps. 51:12).[5]

---

2   ואהבת לרעך כמוך
3   רבי עקיבא אומר זה כלל גדול בתורה
4   בכל דרכיך דעהו והוא יישר אורחותיך
5   לב טהור ברא לי אל-הים

In Biblical terms the inner will is mostly denoted by the Hebrew word *lev* ('heart'). The guidance offered to man by his Creator, as expressed in the *Shema*, is that he should govern his will through the instruction of Torah. This is the religion taught in Scripture: "And these words, which I command thee this day, shall be upon thine heart" (Deut. 6:6; Sforno).[6]

Although man is given the freedom to make his own choice, we pray that our actions may accord with the will of our Creator. Thus David prayed: "Let the words of my mouth and the meditation of my heart be acceptable in Thy sight" (Ps. 19:15).[7] At the conclusion of every statutory prayer, in the daily *Amidah*, and frequently elsewhere, the Sages repeated these words, praying that the thoughts entertained by man should accord with the wishes of God and be acceptable before Him (*Ber.* 4b; *Sh. Ar., Orah Hayyim* 122:2; Daily Prayer Book).

In Judaism the activities of both the will and the intelligence need to be developed and coordinated, since the requirements of life and society call for the attainment of an appropriate balance in the pursuit of both. Maimonides stated this clearly: "One can love the Almighty only through the knowledge that one gains from Him by learning to know Him. Through such knowledge one will gain His love, depending on whether one's knowledge is small or great". Maimonides concludes that "man must therefore make every effort within his power to understand God, through the various branches of wisdom that can give him knowledge of the Divine and through an understanding of the depths of Torah knowledge" (Maim. *Teshuvah*, 5:1–5).[8]

Jeremiah described the ideals of Judaism in the following succinct way: "Let him that glorieth glory in this, that he understandeth and knoweth Me, that I am the Lord who exercise

---

6   והיו הדברים האלה אשר אנכי מצוך היום על לבבך

7   יהיו לרצון אמרי פי והגיון לבי לפניך

8   רשות לכל אדם נתונה להטות עצמו לדרך טובה... ואם רצה להטות עצמו לדרך רעה

lovingkindness, judgment and righteousness in the earth, for in these things I delight, saith the Lord" (Jer. 9:24).[9]

Micah summed up the principles of ethical social conduct thus: "He has shown thee, O man, what is good; and what doth the Lord require of thee, but to do justly, and to love mercy, and to walk humbly with thy God" (Micah 6:8).

The Torah's description of the human power available to man when he follows this course of serving God was enunciated by Moses: "For this commandment which I command thee this day, it is not too hard for thee, neither is it far off... The word is very nigh unto thee, in thy mouth and in thy heart, that thou mayest do it" (Deut. 30:1:11–14; Maim. *Guide* III, 52, 54).[10]

Judaism requires the search for God, which includes observance of the ritual laws (such as those governing the Sabbath, Festivals, purity and worship), as well as the practice of justice and equity in daily life. The commandment to observe the laws of the Torah was intended to educate man through continuous training in obedience to God's teachings and so to develop within him a deeper knowledge of God and the sublimation of his own human will.

The Sages expressed this aim in an adage: "The Almighty's purpose in giving this law to man is more especially to refine the lives of his creations and man's will, and to raise the level of man's conduct" (Gen. R. 44:1).[11] The Torah declared this to be the whole purpose of the commandments and the Sages added: "The laws of the Torah were ordained so that man could live by them" (Lev. 18:5; Maim. *Yad, Yesodei ha-Torah*, 5:1).[12]

Human activity has its origin in the instincts, material needs and intellect that fill and animate the soul. The purpose of ethics is to assign definite boundaries to all the instincts

---

9   כי אם בזאת יתהלל המתהלל השכל וידוע אותי כי אני ה' עושה חסד ומשפט
וצדקה בארץ

10 כי המצוה הזאת אשר אנכי מצוך היום לא נפלאת היא ממך ולא רחוקה היא... כי
קרוב אליך הדבר מאד בפיך ובלבבך לעשותו

11 לא נתנו המצות אלא לצרף בהם את הבריות

12 ושמרתם את חוקותי ואת משפטי אשר יעשה אותם האדם וחי בהם, אני ה'

clamouring for satisfaction, to create order among conflicting demands and to harmonize the opposing claims that arise in social intercourse.

In Judaism ethical rules produce new ideas that are loftier and nobler than man's original impulses. Jewish ethics teach that upon the natural world's foundation there should arise a spiritual and ideal structure – the moral world. The basis of this moral world can be found in the narrative and ordinances of the Bible, which have an extended application in the ensuing Rabbinical literature.

The ethical life draws its sustenance from the spiritual ideas of the Torah, not simply from the physical requirements of man or the gratification of his desires. Ethics are not some product of nature; they refine nature and use human forces to serve their own purpose. The Sages encapsulated this view in their adage: "The Ark of the Covenant bore its bearers; it was not the priests who bore the Ark" (Ex. R. 36).[13]

The Torah laws governing property, marriage and inheritance, as well as criminal behaviour, deeply affect the private and social life of man. The concept of "the good" is equivalent to that of "good will"; and good will accords with Torah law and study. Obeying the law and the symbols of religious practice constitute an ethical disciplinary measure.

An early Sage, Simeon the Just, declared that the order of the world desired by the Torah, which upheld its ideal existence, could be said to rest on three foundations: "The Law, Divine service and the practice of charitable deeds" (*Avot* 1:2).[14] A man's strength is demonstrated by the choice he makes, when necessary, to reject the urges of his own nature which would lead him astray by satisfying only his own desires and indulging his own love of pleasure. The Sages portrayed the strength of will needed by man in choosing the way of the Lord and doing what He requires in this saying: "Who is the mighty man? – He who masters his instincts" (*Avot* 4:1).[15]

---

13   הארון סבל את סובליו, לא הכהנים סבלוהו
14   על שלשה דברים העולם עומד על התורה ועל העבודה ועל גמילות חסדים
15   איזהו גיבור הכובש את יצרו

The importance of exercising self-control emerges from
the prophetic description of God's choice of Abraham as one
suitable to become the founder of the Jewish people: "Thou
art the Lord God who didst choose Abram, and broughtest him
forth out of Ur of the Chaldees, and gavest him the name of
Abraham; and foundest his heart faithful before Thee" (Neh.
9:7–8).[16]

The Sages deduced from Torah teaching that in addition to
prayer, acts of charity, and the practice of righteous ways, there
are other things that can change man's fate (*shinui ma'aseh*)
including a change of name (*shinui shem*) and a change of
abode (*shinui makom*). Once all of these changes were made
by Abraham, he became a different person from the son of
Teraḥ who had grown up in a family of idol worshippers. For
that reason he was ordered to leave his father's house in Ur of
the Chaldees and move to the land of Canaan.

However, Nehemiah added that one thing more was required
of Abraham, namely, his own determination to follow only the
way of God; and in this he proved faithful. Abraham chose
to create himself anew and become fit to be chosen by God.
He left his ancestral environment and changed his name, but
it was only when he changed his entire lifestyle to continue
serving the Lord that he became a new person – someone
quite different from the old Abraham – worthy of having
been chosen to introduce the wisdom and worship of God to
humanity (Gen. 12:1).[17] In the same way, the possibility of
"returning" to God – *teshuvah* – lies within the power of every
individual, if he chooses to exercise it (Neh. 9:78; *RH* 16b;
Ya'avetz, *Siddur*: Morning Prayers, "*Va-yevarekh David*").

From the Jewish perspective, it is fundamental that man
should heed the laws of science and logic in all his technical
and creative activity and comprehend the world in which
he lives, including the ideas of truth, fitness and beauty. In
Talmudic literature this is summed up in the phrase, *yishuv*

16 ושמת שמו אברהם, ומצאת את לבבו נאמן לפניך
17 ויאמר ה' אל אברם לך לך מארצך וממולדתך ומבית אביך אל הארץ אשר אראך

ha-olam – "the needs of man's earthly existence" – in contrast
to one who spends his time gambling on dice (Eccles. R. 1:14–
15; *Sanh.* 24b).[18] Beyond all of this natural and intellectual
endeavour, the notion of "the good", as revealed in the Torah's
ethical system, constitutes the true, ultimate nature of man.

Here we also need to understand the psychological effect of
moral activity deriving from individual manifestations of our
physical and intellectual nature. The aim of moral activity is
the perfection of life. Fulfilling this ideal by ourselves achieves
a continuation of the Divine work of creation (*Mekhilta*, Ex.,
Yitro, Ch. 2; *Shab.* 10a).[19]

All the laws of the Torah – ceremonial, social and moral
– were ordained by God to help man attain the highest virtue;
but attaining this ideal norm of living depends on the way man
exercises his own moral autonomy, for it is that which finally
determines his mode of life.

Side by side with the sublime teachings of Torah, there are in
man's heart countless tendencies toward evil that clamour for
expression. In order to help man resist these evil inclinations
and make correct moral choices, he has been given laws of
righteousness and justice. By following these Torah laws he
is enabled to refine the thoughts arising in his mind. The sole
object of the law is to benefit man, "for our good always, that
He might preserve us alive" (Deut. 6:24).[20]

Maimonides, in discussing the purpose of the *mitzvot*,
wrote: "Every one of the six hundred and thirteen precepts
serves to inculcate some truth, to remove some erroneous
opinion, to establish proper relations in society, to diminish
evil, to train us in good manners or warn against bad habits"
(Maim. *Guide*, III, 31:322; trans. M. Friedlaender, Routledge,
London, 1910; I. Epstein, "The Ceremonial Laws", in Leo
Jung, *The Jewish Library*, First Series, Macmillan, 1928, p.
366 *ff.*).

---

18   המשחק בקוביא מאי קא עביד... לפי שאין עוסקין ביישובו של עולם
19   נעשה שותף של הקב"ה במעשה בראשית
20   לטוב לנו כל הימים לחיותנו כהיום הזה

The Sages refer to certain proclivities in man which necessitate firm control and suppression on his part. They realized, however, that it is often hard to reverse an evil tendency such as indolence, sensuality or avarice, and they therefore recommended being "inventive" and even "crafty" to overcome such a weakness in one's moral disposition. A person might think of some diversion that would help him to discharge his moral obligations. They used the expression, "Be cunning to help you fulfil the precepts" (*Ber.* 17a).[21] The craftiness often employed for material gain can thus be put to a higher use, to devise some mental stratagem whereby the individual tricks himself, as it were, into performing *mitzvot*.

Judaism lays so much stress on the performance of *mitzvot* that even if this is done without proper care and understanding, the essential thing is that they are performed. The Sages even turned this idea into a general rule (*RH* 28b).[22] They also declared that any transgression or failure to do one's moral duty must be an act of folly (*Sot.* 3a).[23]

B. Creating a Different Person

Conversion – Gerut

The notion of a complete change of personality in pursuit of the good is also found in the halakhic law of proselytisation – *gerut*.

By undertaking to belong to the Jewish people and give up his own, fully accepting the laws of Judaism, the proselyte becomes an entirely different person – *ish aher*. Now considered to have been born anew, he or she starts life afresh. Having the status of a newly born child, the proselyte enters

---

21   מרגלא בפומיה דאביי לעולם יהא אדם ערום ביראה
22   רבא אמר לצאת לא בעי כוונה לעבור בעי כוונה
23   אין אדם עובר עבירה אא״כ נכנס בו רוח שטות

a new family, and all his previous family relationships are dissolved (*Yev.* 22a, 97b).[24] In the laws of inheritance, a son born to him previously is no longer reckoned as his firstborn and is not entitled to the double inheritance usually given to the son (Deut. 22:17; Maim. *Nahalot*, 2:12).[25]

Prior to his conversion (*giyyur*), the conduct of the non-Jew was held to be governed by the seven Noachide Commandments. By his conversion to Judaism he is absolved of guilt for past transgressions, since he is no longer the same person who committed them; but he now carries full responsibility for the observance of all the ordained laws of Judaism (*Yev.* 97b; *Sanh.* 56a).[26]

As a "newly born child" his previous name is changed and he becomes "the son of Abraham, our father". It was the custom to call the proselyte after the name of the first Jew who knew his Creator, calling him "Abraham the son of Abraham". The proselyte who chooses to enter into the covenant of Abraham and place himself under "the wings of the Shekhina – the Divine Presence". He or she becomes a pupil of our father Abraham, and all of them are members of his household. In their prayers they may truly say, "our God and the God of our father". In the love of God there is no difference between a proselyte or one born a son of Israel. A proselyte being obliged to observe all the precepts that bind Jews to the Torah as stated in the law of the Paschal Lamb, "There shall be one law for the citizen and the stranger (proselyte), that dwelleth among you" (Ex. 12:49; Mekhilta, *Pisha*, 15).

Because of the new immense responsibility resting on a proselyte, the Sages took the greatest pains in examining the sincerity of every applicant for conversion before he is formally accepted. The sincerity of his intention is challenged by being told that the Sages taught that being a righteous follower of God by any other faith is considered of a higher standard than

---

24 וגר שנתגייר כקטן שנולד דמי
25 היו לו בנים כשהיה עכו״ם ונתגייר אין לו בכור לנחלה
26 תנו רבנן שבע מצוות נצטוו בני נח וגו׳

a non-observant son of Israel. When a prospective proselyte comes to be converted the burdensome difficulties which he will have to undertake are explained to him. He is asked, "What is your objective? Is it perhaps a social or personal convenience? Is it not known to you that the people of Israel have endured exile and constant suffering at the hands of their oppressors only because of the stubbornness of Israel's faith?" The Bet Din inform him of the chastisements following the transgression of these precepts, although they also describe the reward of their observance. Much effort is taken to discourage him from pursuing his desire for conversion. This is done in order to test the genuineness of his application. If he says: "I know of this, and I wish to belong to the house of Israel", he is accepted (*Yev.* 47a; *Sh. Ar. Yoreh De'ah* 268:2,3).

By the act of undertaking circumcision and immersion in the ritual bath (*mikveh*), the proselyte's past personality is washed away and symbolically he or she becomes a new person. Jewish law adopted a most admiring attitude towards the true proselyte who is mentioned in the Daily *Amidah* prayer in conjunction with the righteous and pious of Israel (*Meg.* 17b). An infant or minor child may be accepted for conversion on the responsibility of his or her parents that the child will be brought up in the traditions of Judaism. It is understood, however, that on reaching maturity the child is entitled to renounce the Jewish faith if he so wishes, and follow his own choice. Parents who are anxious that the child should then choose to continue in his accepted faith will make sure that he was given by them an appropriate Jewish education, since validity of the conversion depended on such observance (*Sh. Ar. Yoreh De'ah* 268:6,7,8).

The pattern of a true conversion to Judaism is presented by the Sages in the conversion of Ruth. Ruth was a Moabite princess who married the son of Naomi and Elimelekh (Ruth R. 2:9). When she wanted to belong to the Jewish people Naomi endeavored to discourage her. She told her of the stringency of the Jewish law the transgression of which would at times entail corporal or even capital punishment, from which she was hitherto exempt (Ruth R. 2:24). To all of this Ruth replied "Thy people will be my people, and thy God shall be my God" (Ruth 1:16; Ruth R. 2:22, 23).[27] The story of Ruth's religious identification concluded with the Scriptural testimony that Ruth, the proselyte (*geyoret*), became the ancestress of Yishai who was the father of King David, "the sweet singer of the worship of God" (Ruth 4:22; *Ber.* 7b).

Holiness in Mind and Thought

It is not just his actions but particularly his mind, thought and will that the Almighty requires man to uplift and purify, for only by doing so will he become holy. In the third section of the *Shema* the children of Israel are commanded to make "fringes" and attach them to their garments. The reason stated is "that ye may remember and do all My commandments, and be holy unto your God" (Num. 15.40). Wearing these fringes (*tzitzit*) should not be confused with putting on a lucky charm to bring good fortune or an amulet to ward off evil. Seeing and wearing the *tzitzit* reminds us of our duty to observe the *mitzvot*, and through performing God's commandments we are uplifted and purified, making us "holy".

The Sages described the creative force of the ethical decisions made by man. Commenting on the passage, "If ye walk in my statutes and keep my commandments, and do them", R. Ḥanina bar Papa said: "If you keep My law, I will regard it as though you have created yourselves by physically completing your creation" (Lev. R. 35:6; cf. *Tanḥuma, Ki-Tavo* 1, on Deut. 4:14).[28]

The Torah's injunction, "Ye shall be holy",[29] implies more than the commandment that all of one's actions should be holy, which would apply to all the laws of the Torah. Every human

---

27   עמך עמי, ואל-היך אל-הי

28   אמר להם אם שמרתם את התורה הריני מעלה עליכם כאילו עשיתם עצמכם

29   קדושים תהיו כי קדוש אני ה' אל-היכם

being is holy by virtue of his creation, in the sense of having been made in the image of God. This special law means that if in all of one's actions one is conscious of the obligation to be holy, one will indeed become holy. Thus *kedoshim tiheyu* is a command to "become holy", i.e., by making oneself holy (Lev. 19:2; *Sh. Ar. Orah Hayyim*). In the light of this teaching, we may grasp the full meaning of the Talmudic expression, *Rahmana libba ba'ei* ("God requires man's heart").[30] This is intended to give further meaning to the exhortation promulgated in the *Shema – Ve-ahavta et-Hashem Elohekha –* which insists that the heart be filled with loving faith in God. There is, however, a preliminary requirement before the love of God can be attained. The Sages said that the Almighty's basic requirement concerns the will of man, expressed as *lev*, enjoining that he first direct his will to fulfilling God's law. From this would follow obeying the law to the utmost of his ability (Deut. 6:5, 13, RAMBAN, Ibn Ezra, Sforno, *ad loc.*; Albo, *ha-Ikkarim*: 3. sect. 31).[31]

Ahithophel was the most learned Israelite in all spheres of religious knowledge (Num. R. 22:7), and King David held Ahithophel's advice to be like a Divine oracle. He called him his teacher in Torah law (*Sanh.* 106b). Yet this great scholar misused his wisdom, giving Absalom evil advice and making him rebel against his father (2 Sam. 17:1–4). Ahitophel's display of wisdom in Torah was only in his learned speech, but was deprived of any inner belief, like that of Do'eg the Edomite who misled Saul (1 Sam. 21:8; 22:9–13; *Sanh.* 106b, Rashi)[32]. In the end, Ahithophel perished dishonorably, taking his own life, and the Sages declared that he had no share in the World to Come (*Sanh.* 108A; Num. R. 22:7).[33]

Ahithophel proved a failure, because he did not choose to utilize his vast knowledge for the purpose of obeying the laws

30 הקב״ה ליבא בעי
31 את ה׳ אל-היך תירא ואותו תעבד
32 אין תורתו של דואג אלא משפה ולחוץ
33 שני חכמים עמדו בעולם אחד מישראל ואחד מאו״ה, אחיתופל מישראל ובלעם
מאו״ה ושניהם נאבדו מן העולם

of God. The Almighty requires that man first direct his heart to serving Him with devotion. Furthermore, the Sages declared categorically that the Lord wishes man to take this first step, which will gain him admission to the hall of God's presence. In order to gain entry, however, one must first step through the outer court. Man's initial resolve to serve God faithfully is the key to that first entrance (*Avot* 4:21).[34]

C. Deceit – *Sheker*

An act of deceit results from an individual's secret decision to deceive his fellow by concealing or preventing the truth for some ulterior purpose.

The Biblical law forbids deceit as equivalent to stealing and exemplifies this deception in a case where a borrower receives a loan and then denies that he had received it, or falsely claims that he had repaid it. Scripture states: "Ye shall not steal; neither shall ye deal falsely nor lie one to another" (Lev 19:21).[35]

Falsehood is particularly forbidden in oaths, of evidence or in legal testimony (*Shev.* 21a). The Psalmist denounced deceit in the following description: "They speak vanity everyone with his neighbour; with flattering lip, and with a double heart, do they speak" (Ps. 12:2).[36]

The Sages condemned deceit in financial transactions as even a greater transgression than overreaching by charging exorbitant prices (*B.M.* 58b).[37]

In the moralistic teaching of R. Akiva it was taught that whereas truth endures on a firm foundation (*yesh lah ragla'im*) falsehood has no firm foundation, and eventually will certainly

---

34 התקן עצמך בפרוזדור כדי שתכנס לטרקלין
35 לא תגנבו ולא תכחשו ולא תשקרו איש בעמיתו
36 שוא ידברו איש את רעהו, שפת חלקות, בלב ולב ידברו
37 גדול אונאת דברים מאונאת ממון

be overthrown (Otiot de R. Akiva).[38] In the end the truth will always triumph. "Truth remains firm but falsehood can not stand."[39] This teaching is graphically portrayed in the letters of the Hebrew alphabet. The word 'falsehood' (*sheker*) rests on one base, but the word 'truth', (*emet*), on two bases (*Shab.* 104a, Rashi *ad loc.* '*ehad kare'a*'; Prov. 12:19, Rashi *ad loc.*). Truth alone carries the irrevocable seal of the Almighty (*Shab.* 55a; Deut. R. 1:17).[40] Scripture states further: "The lip of truth shall be established forever but a lying tongue is but for a moment" (Prov. 12:19).[41] "Deceit is in the heart of them that devise evil" (Prov. 12:20).[42] The prophet exhorted Israel: "Speak ye every man the truth with his neighbour" (Zecharia 8:16).[43]

The inherent nature of a person may incline him normally to opportunism or deceitfulness, in which case the greatest self-control must be exerted in order to reverse that characteristic. Of the characters of the two sons of Isaac the Bible states that Esau was a "cunning hunter" who knew how to deceive and trap his prey, (which the Sages referred to any unwitting victim of his evil purpose), but Jacob was "a plain man" without any hidden contrivance, an honest man who spoke only what was truly in his heart (Gen. 25:27).[44]

D. Envy – *Kine'ah*

A feeling of envy of another's possessions or advantages is an attitude of mind in which one resents that someone else had achieved that which one wishes oneself to possess. Such envy creates a sense of discontent and jealousy which hurts one's

---

38	אמת יש לה רגלים – שקר אין לו רגלים
39	קושטא קאי שיקרא לא קאי
40	חותמו של הקב״ה אמת
41	שפת אמת תכון לעד, ועד ארגיעה לשון שקר
42	מרמה חורשי רע
43	דברו אמת איש את רעהו
44	ויהי עשיו איש יודע ציד איש שדה ויעקב איש תם יושב אהלים

own feeling and can lead to the sin of covetousness. A generous attitude of mind in witnessing the pleasure of another rather than resenting it is a noble quality, whereas the concentration of one's eye on seeking only one's own personal gain and advantage over one's fellow is a feeling of self-centered greed and selfishness. Love is expressed by "giving" rather than by "receiving".

The feeling of good will and generosity is described by the Hebrew term *nedivut*, meaning to offer love to one's fellow, and experience joy in his success. The attitude of jealousy arises from narrowness and meanness in one's own thought which is called *tsarut ayin*, literally "the closure of one's eye", producing a feeling of discontent at another's gain or benefit. A person with "a narrowed eye" resents any benefit to another making him miserly and ungenerous in his social relationships.

The Ethics of the Fathers teaches in the name of R. Eliezer that the most evil attitude which everyone should take care to avoid is the attitude of the "evil eye"; but the admirable disposition which one should develop is that of the "good eye" of generosity and good will (*Avot* 2:9).[45]

Joseph's brothers believed that Joseph's dreams of his coming superiority over all his older brothers was not just the result of his day dreaming which arose from his own ambitions, but was a prophetic message from heaven. They were jealous of this Divine promise to Joseph, and were driven by jealousy to obstruct the realization of his dream. This envy culminated in Israel's slavery in Egypt (Gen. 37:11, Commentary of *Or ha-Ḥayim*, *ad loc.*).[46]

The Sages warned that a disposition to jealousy, lust and aggrandizement ruin a man's life (*Avot* 4:21).[47]

Solomon reached the conclusion that "love is strong as death, jealousy is cruel as the grave" (Song of Songs 8:6).[48]

---

45 איזו היא דרך ישרה שידבק בה האדם ר' אליעזר אומר עין טובה... איזו היא דרך רעה שיתרחק ממנה האדם... עין רעה

46 ויקנאו בו אחיו

47 הגאוה, התאוה והכבוד מוציאין את האדם מן העולם

48 עזה כמות אהבה, קשה כשאול קנאה

R. Ila'i said a man's character can be recognized by his conduct in three things: "his cup, his purse, and his anger"(*Er.* 65b).[49]

The duty to love one's fellow man is eternalised in the Biblical ordinance: "Thou shalt love thy neighbour as thyself" (Lev. 19:18).[50]

This ethical teaching was described by R. Akiva as the basic principle in the entire Torah (Sifra, Lev. 19:45; Gen. R. Ch. 24b–28; TJ *Ned.* 9:4).[51]

The Sage Ben Nanas expounded the verse further, stating that on examination it will be found that all the moral teachings of the Torah are contained in this precept (R. Avraham Sofer, *Ketav Sofer*, Address on Shabbat Hagadol p. 308).

E. Generosity and Gratitude

Generosity

Doing acts of kindness to one's fellow man – *gemilut hasadim* – is considered of greater merit than simply giving charity to the poor (*Sukkah* 49b). The Sages said that doing *gemilut hasadim* is on a level of fulfilling all the laws of the Torah – *shakul keneged kol hamitzvot* (TJ *Pe'ah* 1:1). They set out a list of Divinely ordained services in human relationships which will be rewarded in the World to Come, as well as in the person's lifetime. Included in this list are such deeds as charity, hospitality, helping the sick, providing the needs of a bride, and the burial of the dead (*Shab.* 127a). Hassidic teaching directed that when performing any act of brotherly kindness one should have in mind that he is the messenger chosen by God to do that kindness, as the human agent of the Almighty, and therefore carry out that privilege with the

---

49   בג׳ דברים אדם ניכר בכוסו ובכיסו ובכעסו

50   ואהבת לרעך כמוך

51   ר׳ עקיבא אומר זה כלל גדול בתורה

fullest fervour – *hu sheliaẖ Hashem be'olam hazeh* (Judah
Arye Leib Alter of Gur, *"Sefat Emet"*, *Ḥayyei Sarah*).

Ethical commandments are distinguished from ritual laws,
such as Passover observance, Sabbath, circumcision, offerings,
where the procedure of their fulfilment is precisely ordained.
In the practice of ethics the quality of their conduct depends on
how the actions are inspired by the individual's inner attitude
of mind. A natural generosity of character results in liberality
of outlook and freedom from any meanness. In the laws of
pe'ah, *leket*, *shikeẖah*, the action required by the law is stated,
and its purpose taught, but no measure of its liberality is
enforced, only the minimum amount is stated (*Ḥag.* 7a). Torah
law ordained: "And when ye reap the harvest of your land,
thou shalt not wholly reap the corners of your field – *pe'ah*,
neither shalt thou gather the gleaning of thy harvest – *leket*,
thou shalt leave them for the poor, and for the stranger" (Lev.
23:22).[52] Although it appears that this law could be fulfilled by
leaving the smallest amount of the corner of the field and only
a few grains left for gleaning, the Sages recommended that a
suitable amount would be one sixtieth of the field, according
to the liberality of all gifts to the poor (Maim., *Matenot Ani'im*
1:1, 15; *ha-Ḥinukh* s. 216). It is likewise ordained: "When
thou reapest thine harvest in thy field, and hast forgotten a
sheaf in the field – *shikeẖah* , thou shalt not go again to fetch
it; it shall be for the stranger, for the fatherless, and for the
widow" (Deut 24:19; Maim., *Matenot Ani'im* 5:1; *ha-Ḥinukh*
sect. 592–3).

The prohibition of taking the forgotten sheaf did not apply
to sheaves in his field which he had not yet reaped, and their
existence had been forgotten. Such sheaves were termed,
"What was before him". The law applied only to what had been
left *after* he had passed it during his reaping – "What is behind
him", since the Torah law had stated; "Thou shalt not return
to fetch it".[53] Furthermore, the law applied to a single normal
sized sheaf, but not to a large bundle of sheaves. Although the

---

52 לא תכלה פאת שדך בקצרך ולקט קצירך לא תלקט, לעני ולגר תעזב אתם
53 ושכחת עמר בשדה לא תשוב לקחתו

Sages suggested what was an appropriate size, the decision whether to leave it or not was still left to the discretion and generosity of the farmer (Maim., *Matenot Ani'im* 5:18).

Another law which depended on the generosity of the owner was that which required the giving of part of one's first harvest to a priest, *terumah* (Num. 18:11, 24). Here, again, no particular measure was specified by the Torah, so that giving even one grain could be considered a fulfilment of the law. The Sages, however, required that a larger amount should be given, and they said that the size given by one of average generosity would be one fiftieth of his harvest; even a mean person could give one sixtieth, while a very generous person would give one fortieth. Giving less than one sixtieth does not fulfil the law of *terumah*. Whichever measure one gives it should be of the best of his produce (*Shul. Ar., Yoreh Deah* 331:52). The Sages wished to enlarge the liberality of one's outlook which should become part of his natural character (*Hul.* 137b; Maim., *Terumot* 3:2; *ha-Hinukh* sect. 507).[54]

One should be benevolent in giving charity to the poor and to the needy. The Torah ordained the duty of everyone to give charity to the poor. This duty of readily giving assistance to one in need is a positive command of the Torah in which it is stated: "Thou shalt surely open thy hand unto him", and further, "Thou shalt surely give him, and thy heart shall not be grieved when thou givest unto him" (Deut. 15:8,10).[55]

The amount of charity that one gives should be according to the measure of his own wealth. Charity should always be given generously with a good heart according to the extent of the recipient's needs and to avoid embarrassing him. The needed assistance should be given where required and even repeatedly. The ideal form of almsgiving is where it is given secretly with the identity of each party being unknown to the other. The amount of charity to be given is co-ordinate with the giver's liberality of mind. The practice of giving charity

---

54   תרומה עין יפה אחד מארבעים

55   נתון תתן לו ולא ירע לבבך בתתך לו

is so deeply established in Jewish life that it has never been
known that any Jewish community would fail to maintain a
communal charity fund, *kupah shel tzedakah* (Maim., *Matenot
Ani'im* 7:1; *Sh. Ar.*, *Yoreh De'ah* 247:1; 249:1; *ha-Ḥinukh* sect.
478).

Here again the amount of charity it is our duty to give is not
defined; it is left to the extent of one's charitable disposition;
even the smallest amount a *perutah*, given by a parsimonious
person could still be considered strictly as a fulfilment of
the Torah commandment. The Sages gave a clear direction.
Everyone is duty-bound to give some charity, even a poor
person who himself seceives *tzedada*. Ideally, one should
give as much as the poor need, but one fulfills his *mitzvah* by
giving up to one-fifth of his income. Giving less than that, ten
pecent, represents one of medium generosity, but giving less
than one-tenth indicates a mean character. Nevertheless, the
Sages added that one should not give away as *tzdakah* more
than one-fifth of his possessions (*Sh. Aruch, Yoreh De'ah*
247:1; 248:1; 249:1, REMA).[56]

The community was entitled to exert on the individual to
give his appropriate amount. The regular observance of these
laws would help in forming a generous outlook and producing
a worthy quality in one's character.[57]

Gratitude

Apart from the supplicatory psalms and those celebrating
the majesty of the Almighty, a distinctive feature of a large
number of psalms are songs of thanksgiving. The daily prayers
are replete with expressions of gratitude to the Almighty
for the abundant kindness that he has bestowed on us. The
daily morning blessings after thanking God for His various
personal gifts of life and renewed strength conclude with

---

56 עד חומש נכסיו מצוה מן המובחר ואי מעשרה מדה בינונית ואל יבזבז אדם יותר
מחומש

57 בית דין כופין אותו מכת מרדות עד שיתן מה שאמדוהו ליתן

the summarizing blessing thanking the Almighty for all His kindness to us. These introductory prayers continue with the statement "Therefore it is our duty to give praise and thanks to Thy name".[58]

Our giving thanks to the Almighty for his beneficent gifts to us is not just a matter of 'politeness', it is a devotional act in the service of God, uniting us with the sanctity of our Maker. The individual's own sense of gratitude for the benefit that he had received would prompt him to bring a special thanks-giving offering to God, *Todah*. The enjoyment of this offering is joyfully shared by the votary with his Creator (Lev. 7:11, 15).[59]

The entire Psalm 100, *Mizmor letodah*, is an acknowledgement of the debt of gratitude which we owe to the Almighty. The Sages said: "Even if in some day to come all our prayers will be superfluous but prayers of gratitude and thanksgiving will never cease". This psalm was sung with great gladness during the Temple service at the time when the Thanksgiving offering was brought to the altar; and is now included in the Daily morning service to inculcate in us the duty of expressing thanks, gratitude and appreciation in our daily conduct (Ps. 100:1,2).[60]

The first expression of personal thanksgiving as we begin each day is the blessing of God for having formed man in such a wondrous manner that the human anatomy is created with its function to provide health, stability, and survival (*Sh. Ar. Orah Hayyim* 6:1, REMA).[61]

The acknowledgement is expressed by the words "I thank Thee for each of these gifts... Blessed art Thou... who mercifully restores my soul". The first utterance on rising each morning is "I give thanks to Thee, O Sovereign of the universe who mercifully restores my soul". For this gift I had confidently prayed when I laid down to sleep, and You have

58   לפיכך אנחנו חייבים להודות לך... ולתת שבח והודיה לשמך
59   ובשר זבח תורת שלמיו ביום קרבנו יאכל
60   עבדו את ה' בשמחה... כי טוב ה' לעולם חסדו
61   שמפליא לעשות במה ששומר האדם בקרבו

faithfully fulfiled my prayer. I thank Thee now for my life-restoring wakefulness and happy momentum to begin a new day.[62]

This is followed by the *Asher yatzar* prayer giving thanks for the wondrous anatomy of the human body. The prayer continues, "So long as the soul is within me I give thanks unto Thee".[63]

At the end of the central *Amidah* prayer we say "And all living beings thank Thee continuously, for to Thee all our thanks are due".[64]

The Sages said that in normal life one could find one hundred occasions for giving thanks to the Almighty (*Men.* 43b).[65]

The Almighty commanded: "Thou shalt not abhor an Egyptian, because thou was a stranger in his land". Although the Egyptians persecuted the Israelites with enslaved labor and they had cast all their male children into the river, it was still necessary to appreciate the fact that Israel had first received friendly hospitality in their land in their time of need, when there was famine in Canaan (Deut. 23:8, Rashi; *Ber.* 63b).[66]

Furthermore, the Torah stated "Thou shalt not abhor an Edomite", not only because "He is thy brother", but also because, unlike the Ammonites, they assisted Israel bringing them bread and water. Such a token of friendship and hospitality had been shown to Abraham by Melchizedek the king of Salem when, on Abraham's return from battle, Melchizedek "brought forth bread and wine" (Gen.14:18).

Although Moses had been commanded to inflict the ten plagues on Egypt, when he demanded their liberation, he did not carry our the first two plagues himself. The plague of turning the water of Egypt into blood, and of producing the plague of frogs was performed by Aaron. Moses could

---

62 מודה אני לפניך... שחזרת בי נשמתי בחמלה
63 כל זמן שהנשמה בקרבי מודה אני לפניך
64 כל החיים יודוך סלה... ולך נאה להודות
65 חייב אדם לברך מאה ברכות בכל יום
66 שהיו לכם אכסניא בשעת הדחק

not strike the river of Egypt in appreciation of the river's protection of him when he had been placed in the bulrushes (Ex. 7:19, Rashi; Ex.8:1, Rashi).

The prophet Jeremiah declared that the Almighty would withhold complete punishment for Israel's wrong doings because He expressed gratitude for the love of G-d shown by Abraham, Isaac and Jacob, and the trust of Israel in following Moses through the wilderness for forty years. "I remember for thee the kindness of thy youth, the love of thine espousals; how thou wentest after me, in the wilderness in a land that was not sown (Jer. 2:2, David Kimhi *ad loc.*).

In his final exhortation to Israel Moses reprimanded his people that even though they had themselves experienced the wonders of God's deliverance from their enemies and saw how God lovingly carried them through the wilderness, as a father carried his child, they still did not have faith in God's love for them. The Rabbi's taught that where there is no sense of gratitude even the event of heavenly miracles would not succeed in bringing about faith in God (Deut. 1:31, 32).[67] (Rabbi Elyahu Dessler, *Mikhtav me-Eliahu*, Vol.1, p.142, London, 1955)

F. Forgiveness

Although Judaism stresses the duty to love one's fellow man, the presence of good and evil inclinations within us makes it impossible to avoid some form of insult or injury on the part of those with whom we come into contact. Religion and morality therefore insist on our duty to refrain from harbouring grievances and resentment against others and to cultivate the virtue of forgiveness.

Anger bars the way to forgiveness and is condemned as senseless behaviour: "For anger resteth in the bosom of fools"

---

67   ובמדבר אשר ראית אשר נשאך ה' אל-היך... ובדבר הזה אינכם מאמינים בה'
אל-היכם

(Eccles. 7:9). According to the Sages, a man's sustained fury is one of three things by which his character may be judged by his conduct "in his cup, in his purse and in his anger" (*Er.* 65b, Rashi).[68] A man's character is thus revealed in his financial transactions, his drinking habits and his ability to control his temper. While allowances are permissible in each case, an individual's true nature may be gauged from the way he behaves under pressure.

On the other hand, Akavya ben Mahalalel believed that contemplating these three realities would help a person to refrain from sin: "Know from where you came [i.e., the manner of your creation], and where you are going [into the grave], and before Whom you will have to give a final reckoning – before the Supreme King of kings, the Holy One, blessed be He" (*Avot* 3:1).[69]

An awareness of these three things is bound to affect a person's outlook, giving rise to a sense of his own inadequacy and making him acknowledge the fact that there is no reason why he should feel superior to any other human being.

At the same time, we should realize that each of us is capable of attaining the highest standard of an Abraham, Moses, Aaron or David. Accordingly, we should determine how and why our efforts to reach that standard have failed. By practising these virtues we may reach a state of tranquillity and avoid anger or strife with our fellow man.

G. Vengefulness

The Torah lays down that if someone is upset over a wrong done by his fellow, it is his duty to reprimand that person for the offence. This is a positive commandment: "Thou shalt surely rebuke thy neighbour, and not bear sin because of him". Nevertheless, the wronged party would commit a sin if the

---

68 בג' דברים אדם ניכר בכוסו ובכיסו ובכעסו

69 דע מאין באת ולאן אתה הולך ולפני מי אתה עתיד לתן דין וחשבון

manner of his rebuke injured his neighbour's self-respect or if, by withholding a reprimand, he was left bearing a grudge that made him nurse a hatred for the neighbour. Such an action would transgress the all-embracing rule: "Thou shalt not hate thy brother in thy heart" (Lev. 19:17).[70]

Resh Lakish emphasized that one who raises his hand menacingly against another is deemed a wicked character (*Sanh.* 58b),[71] while R. Ḥanina declared him to be guilty of a transgression (ibid.). Striking another person is always forbidden, and whoever wounds someone else is liable to pay full monetary compensation (*Sh. Ar., Hoshen Mishpat* 420:3).[72]

Anyone putting his neighbour to shame is deemed a wicked person, and for shaming a righteous man he "forfeits his portion in the World to Come". Should a physical injury be inflicted on someone, the perpetrator – in addition to defraying medical expenses – must pay compensation for the shame and distress resulting from the injury (*Sh. Ar. Hoshen Mishpat* 420:39–40; *BK* 83b).[73]

A furious outburst on suffering an injury may be unavoidable, but it should be kept under control. Retaining animosity towards the offender may give birth to cold-blooded thoughts of revenge. This is explicitly forbidden by the Torah: "Thou shalt not take vengeance, nor bear any grudge against the children of thy people" (Lev. 19:18).[74] That injunction refers to a person's inner state of anger and is associated with the teaching: "Thou shalt not hate thy brother in thy heart" (Lev. 19:17).[75]

The Sages observed that most people have an inclination to tell tales or slander their fellow men. There are, they said, three sins which few people avoid committing every day, the

---

70 לא תשנא את אחיך בלבבך הוכח תוכיח את עמיתך ולא תשא עליו חטא

71 המגביה ידו על חבירו אע״פ שלא הכהו נקרא רשע

72 החובל בחבירו חייב בחמשה דברים נזק צער רפוי שבת בושת

73 אין לו חלק לעולם הבא

74 לא תקום ולא תטור את בני עמך

75 לא תשנא את אחיך בלבבך

most prevalent being slander – *leshon ha-ra* – in one form or another. It may just take the form of gossip, a subtle outlet for envy or vengefulness through depriving someone of his good name. The Psalmist urged: "Keep thy tongue from evil, and thy lips from speaking guile" (Ps. 34:14; *BB* 164b). The Sages relate that Moses was so afraid of displaying jealousy towards Joshua, his successor, that he confessed: "Better to die a hundred times than live one's life with envy in the heart" (Deut. R. 9:5).[76]

Forgiveness is one of the thirteen attributes of the Almighty. He is described as "forgiving iniquity and transgression" against Him (Ex. 34:7).[77] Just as God is ready to pardon man, so must man forgive his fellow man; and, in the light of that forgiveness, he begs God to forgive his own sins. The most holy day in the Jewish year was specifically designated *Yom ha-Kippurim* – the Day of Atonement (Lev. 23:27–28; *Yoma* 85b).[78]

On the eve of the Day of Atonement, before commencing the prayers for their own forgiveness, it is customary for Jews to approach friends and neighbours and ask them to pardon any offences that they may have committed against each other during the year. One must likewise approach the Almighty with a heart cleansed of anger or the desire for revenge (*Yoma* 86b; *Sh. Ar. Orah Hayyim* 606:1 and *Mishnah Berurah ad loc.* 1, 2).

H. Consideration for Others

(1) *For the Sake of Peaceful Relationships – Mi-penei Darkhei Shalom*

The Sages declared that showing consideration for the needs of one's fellow man is the virtue most appreciated by God. A popular saying of R. Hanina ben Dosa's ran: "When a person's

---

76   מאה מיתות ולא קנאה אחת

77   נושא עון ופשע וחטאה

78   עבירות שבין אדם למקום יום הכיפורים מכפר

fellow creatures take delight in him, the Omnipresent also takes delight in him" (*Avot* 3:11).[79] This does not mean that he follows the current fashion, but that he behaves in accordance with the Torah's ethical teachings, which will endear him to his fellow men. The Sages gave further expression to this doctrine: "Whoever honours the Torah is honored by his fellow men" (*Avot* 4:6).[80]

Many regulations governing a variety of practices were instituted by the Sages in the interests of social justice and harmony. Though not actually ordained by Torah law, these measures accorded with the spirit of Torah, since all its teachings are based on "the ways of peace" (Prov. 3:17; Mish., *Git.* 5:8-9; TB *Git.* 59a–62a).[81] The guiding principle of all Torah is to "seek peace, and pursue it" (Ps. 34:16, R.V. 14; *Ber.* 6b).[82]

The principle of *mi-penei Darkhei Shalom* calls on man to forgo what is legally due to him, or normally his right, in order to cultivate peaceful relationships (literally, "for the sake of peace"). One should therefore act generously, beyond whatever the law requires, so as not to disrupt friendly association with other people, both Jewish and Gentile.

There is a pearl of wisdom in Abbaye's axiom that a man should always strive to make peace with everyone – within his own family, with his neighbour and with a fellow Jew or even a heathen in the market place – so that he may be liked and respected by others (*Ber.* 17b).[83] Many adjustments to the law were made "in the interests of peace". Normally, the people of Israel were instructed to avoid any association with pagans and pagan festivities or worship; it was nevertheless decreed that occasionally, for the sake of peace and good will, Jews might exchange greetings with idolaters even on one of their festivals (*Shev.* 4:3).[84]

---

79   כל שרוח הבריות נוחה הימנו רוח המקום נוחה הימנו

80   כל המכבד את התורה – גופו מכובד על הבריות

81   אלו דברים אמרו מפני דרכי שלום

82   בקש שלום ורדפהו

83   שיהא אהוב למעלה ונחמד למטה ויהא מקובל על הבריות

84   שואלין בשלומם מפני דרכי שלום

Though forbidden to undertake any kind of labor in his field during the Sabbatical year or to benefit from any of its produce, the Israelite is permitted to encourage a Gentile doing such work at the time – all "in the interests of peace" (*Shev.* 4:3).[85] A Gentile has no obligation to desist from agricultural work in the seventh (*Shemittah*) year of the Hebrew calendar, but a Jew is not allowed to benefit from the non-Jew's work. He is, however, permitted to hire a field from a Gentile, even if the latter has already ploughed it, and may use it himself in the following year. Such permission was granted *mi-penei darkhei shalom* – for the sake of peaceful relations with the non-Jew.

(2) *Considerate Behaviour – Mi-shum Derekh Eretz*

Numerous instructions in proper behaviour, more especially social intercourse, are collected in two minor tractates of the Babylonian Talmud, *Derekh Eretz Rabbah* and. *Derekh Eretz Zuta*. There it is stated as a general rule that one should not act differently from other people (*Derekh Eretz Zuta* 5:5), nor should one deviate from the customs of one's friends or from society (*Derekh Eretz Rabbah* 7:7).

The Sages also ruled that it is one's duty to act in accordance with the accepted practice of the community in which one lives. In Hillel's words, "Do not separate yourself from the community" (*Avot* 2:4, 4:7).[86]

Legal decisions are frequently based on the principle of *derekh eretz* – "considerate behaviour". Literally, this Hebrew expression means "the way of the land" or "the accepted practice". *Derekh eretz* enjoins consideration for the needs of one's fellow man in order to ensure the well-being of society.

There are three parts of righteous conduct: following the teachings of the Bible, and observing Rabbinic Mishnaic law,

---

85 מחזיקים כושיים בשביעית - מפני דרכי שלום
86 אל תפרוש מן הצבור

and complying also with the practice of *derekh eretz*. This three-ply cord is sure to hold one to the true way of life. Having none of these qualities excludes a person from belonging to human society (*Kid.* 40b).[87] The Sages taught, further, that in all one's efforts to fulfil Torah law, ethical conduct, prayer and social integrity, one needs mutual support and the help of heaven (*Ber.* 32b).[88]

In popular usage this term chiefly denotes good manners, politeness and courtesy, etiquette and respectful behaviour in general. It can also signify maintaining proper conditions to safeguard one's health.

The Sages gave an illustration of proper etiquette, quoting the Torah: "One should not, for example, speak to one's friends without first gaining their attention" (*Yoma* 4b; *Git.* 70a).[89] Hence it is written: "The Lord called unto Moses, and spoke unto him out of the tent of meeting, saying ..." (Lev. 1:1), i.e., God first drew his attention, calling him by name, and then he spoke to him (*Yoma*, ibid.; *Git.*, ibid.).

Derekh eretz requires that one's social conduct should go beyond mere conformity with the rules of etiquette. A person's actions should always be thoughtful, unselfish and considerate toward others. The way a man conducts himself in society will largely depend on his own understanding and relationships.

This receives further expression in a teaching of the Sages. A man's outlay on food should always be less than he can afford, but his budget should be stretched to provide for his wife and children. He should remember that they depend on his generosity; whereas he himself must rely on Divine providence (*Hul.* 84b).[90]

---

87   כל שישנו במקרא ובמשנה ובדרך ארץ לא במהרה הוא חוטא שנאמר והחוט
המשולש לא במהרה ינתק וכל שאינו לא במקרא ולא במשנה ולא בדרך ארץ אינו
מן הישוב
88   ת"ר ארבעה צריכין חזוק ואלו הן תורה ומעשים טובים תפילה ודרך ארץ
89   למדה תורה דרך ארץ שלא יאמר אדם דבר לחבירו אלא אם כן קראהו
90   ויכבד אשתו ובניו יותר ממה שיש לו שהן תלויין בו

(3) Judging a Law Suit More Leniently than Required by Strict Law; Equity – Lifnim mi-Shurat ha-Din

It is a principle of Judaism that one should always give consideration to the feelings, dignity and needs of one's fellow man. The ethical spirit of Jewish life required, as circumstances warranted, that a person should not be over-insistent on his legal rights. It was a special virtue to deal leniently with an opponent in a dispute, especially if a strict legal judgment would inflict severe hardship on the defendant. In accordance with the higher standard of morality, one should agree to a settlement representing less than the full measure of the law would provide. This is popularly known as "acting generously, going beyond the strict letter of the law" (*lifnim mi-shurat ha-din*).[91]

The halachic decisions made in particular circumstances "beyond the strict letter of the law" ensured the maintenance of peaceful, harmonious relations. This *derekh eretz* concept applied to good manners and etiquette, as well as to the smooth running of family life and society. It also embraced those commercial disputes in which a severe judgment might give rise to extreme hardship.

R. Yoḥanan is quoted as having said: "Jerusalem was destroyed only because people based their judgments on the strict letter of the law". In doing so, we are told, people failed to go beyond the law's requirements (*BM* 30b).[92]

Rabbah bar bar Ḥannah once hired some porters to bring him barrels of wine. As they were doing so, the barrels fell and were broken and the wine was lost. Since Rabbah considered that the damage had been caused by their negligence, he decided to recoup his loss by seizing their garments. The porters demanded that he return them, and they brought their complaint before

---

91   לפנים משורת הדין

92   א״ר יוחנן לא חרבה ירושלים אלא על שדנו בה דין תורה... שהעמידו דיניהם על
דין תורה ולא עבדו לפנים משורת הדין

Rav, the leading Babylonian scholar and head of the Sura Academy. Rav ordered: "Give their clothes back to them". Whereupon Rabbah asked: "Is that the law? Surely the porters are liable for the damage they caused!" Rav replied: "Even so, in fulfillment of the teaching, 'That thou mayest walk in the way of good men'" (Prov. 2:20). Rabbah accordingly returned their garments. The porters had a further complaint: "We are poor men," they said, "we have worked all day and need money. Are we to receive no pay?" Rav then ordered Rabbah to pay them their wages. Rabbah again asked, "Is that the law?" and Rav replied: "Even so, for the teaching further states, 'And keep the paths of the righteous'" (Prov. 2:20). Rabbah paid the men and received no compensation (*BM* 83a; *Sh. Ar. Ḥoshen Mishpat* 304:1, *Arukh ha-Shulḥan* ibid.).

Maimonides enunciated the general principle that whoever seeks to follow the right and proper way adopts a higher standard than the one stipulated by law (Maim. *Yad, Gezelah ve-Avedah*, 11:7).[93]

(4) *For the Benefit of Society – Mi-penei Tikkun ha-Olam*

Certain laws enacted by the Sages were based on the pressing demands of society (*Git.* 40b). To quote one example, the Biblical law ordaining the release of all debts in the Sabbatical year had the result of inducing wealthy men to refrain from giving loans to those who needed them. The Sages therefore sanctioned a device known as the *prosbul*. They adopted a system in accordance with the law's requirements, whereby the debts were transferred to the *bet din*, from where they could be collected, since they were no longer the debts of an individual as Torah law had prescribed (*Git.* 36b; Mish. *Sheviit* 10:4).[94]

---

93   הרוצה לילך בדרך הטוב והישר עושה לפנים משורת הדין
94   ראה הלל שנמנעו העם מלהלוות זה את זה עמד והתקין פרוסבול

Furthermore, despite the paramount duty to ransom captives, the Sages decreed that exorbitant sums demanded by the captors should not be paid, since this would only encourage those holding the prisoners to kidnap more Jews (*Git.* 36a–b, 40b).

Social stability was one of the factors that the Sages took into account when making their legal decisions.

(5) *Judging People Benignly – Dan le-Khaf Zekhut*

According to the Sages, when faced with the problem of judging the actions of a person whose intentions or moral standards were unknown (and whose acts could be viewed as either good or bad), one should always accept a favorable interpretation of his deed.[95] If, however, the person had already been identified as a transgressor,[96] it would be right to suspect him of malicious intent and to judge him accordingly (*Avot* 1:6, R. Ovadyah Bertinoro *ad loc.*).

As a general rule, it is stated in the name of Hillel: "Do not judge the next man until you find yourself in his place".[97] This cautions a person wielding communal authority to judge the transgressor with compassion and to reflect: "Had you been in his situation, would you have been able to withstand such pressure?" (*Avot* 2:5, *Tiferet Yisra'el ad loc.*).[98]

(6) *A Worldly Occupation; Respect, Polite Behaviour – Derekh Eretz*

The expression *derekh eretz* is popularly used to refer to a person's good manners as are expected in social conduct

---

95 הוי דן לכף זכות
96 רשע
97 אל תדין את חברך עד שתגיע למקומו
98 שפוט אותו בחמלה

(*Yoma* 64b).[99] It denotes courtesy and respect, as in the Biblical ordinance: "Thou shalt rise up before the hoary head, and honour the face of the old man" (Lev. 19:32).[100] The duty to be polite and well-mannered in one's dealings with others, especially those older or less fortunate than oneself, is a preeminent, universal obligation. To emphasize the importance of this *mitzvah*, the Sages declared that just as the teaching of *derekh eretz* had precedence even over the Torah in God's creation (Lev. R. 9:3), so should man always give it priority. The respect due to one's parents must likewise be shown for Torah scholars, and the greatest care must be taken in deferring to them (Maim. *Talmud Torah*, 5:1 *ff.*, 6:1 *ff.*).[101]

In a further sense, *derekh eretz* is employed as a euphemism for sexual intercourse, particularly between husband and wife. "They might derive the Torah law of marital faithfulness from the dove, which mates only with his regular partner, and from the cock, which usually entices the hen by bringing her some gift to please her before they engage in mating" (*Er.* 100b).[102]

Derekh eretz also means earning one's livelihood through trade or some other worldly occupation. The Sages laid particular emphasis on the need to combine a gainful occupation with daily Torah study. They maintained that it was praiseworthy to engage in both, since the combined effort helps one to overcome sinful temptation. They even declared that Torah study without regular work is valueless and leads man to sin (*Avot* 2:2).[103]

The teaching of the Sages quoted above about the importance of *derekh eretz*, meaning etiquette and considerate behaviour (2. *Mishum derekh eretz*, note '85), was applied also to the need to occupy himself in some daily labour. Working

---

99   למדה תורה דרך ארץ

100 מפני שיבה תקום והדרת פני זקן

101 כשם שאדם מצווה בכבוד אביו ויראתו כך הוא חייב בכבוד רבו

102 דרך ארץ מתרנגול שמפייס ואח״כ בועל

103 יפה תלמוד תורה עם דרך ארץ שיגיעת שניהם משכחת עון וכל תורה שאין עמה
     מלאכה סופה בטלה וגוררת עון

for secular pursuits, such as agriculture, industry, commerce, or medicine is a necessary activity for everyone. They said: He who is versed in Bible, Mishna, but not engaged in secular pursuits – *derekh eretz*, does not belong in civilisation (*Kid.* 40b).

They further said: Just as the observance of Torah and *mitzvot* require effort and determination, so the pursuit of secular work providing for the needs of society, must have one's full effort and mutual support in all of which one needs heavenly support (*Ber.* 32b).

R. Elazar ben Azaryah taught that if a person does not study Torah, he cannot lead an honest life; but equally, if he does not have a gainful occupation, his Torah study is nullified (*Avot* 3:21).[104] An individual who does not play a useful role in society, but indulges in gambling and games of chance, will prove to be insolent and untrustworthy. According to R. Yoḥanan, the testimony of someone who does not engage in a worldly occupation is disqualified (*Kid.* 40b–41a).[105]

Earning one's daily bread from manual work is an essential part of human life (Ps. 128:2). On the one hand, according to the Sages, God instructed Joshua that Torah study should be his constant occupation, as it is written: "This book of the law shall not depart out of thy mouth, but thou shalt meditate therein day and night..." (Josh. 1:8). If, on the other hand, man's activities were confined to study of the Torah, how would he manage to receive God's blessing of rain, "that thou mayest gather in thy corn, and thy wine, and thine oil"? (Deut. 11:14)[106] The work of man's hands provides for his basic needs, and it is therefore his duty to engage in manual labour as well as Torah study (*Ber.* 35b).[107]

---

104 רבי אלעזר בן עזריה אומר אם אין תורה אין דרך ארץ אם אין דרך ארץ אין תורה

105 כל שאינו לא במקרא ולא במשנה אמר רבי יוחנן ופסול לעדות... דרש בר קפרא
רגזן לא עלתה בידו אלא רגזנותא... שנאמר ובמושב לצים לא ישב מושבו מושב
לצים

106 לפי שנאמ' לא ימוש ספר תורה הזה מפיך יכול דברים כתבן ת"ל ואספת דגנך
הנהג בהן דרך ארץ

107 יפה תלמוד תורה עם דרך ארץ שיגיעת שניהם משכחת עון וכל תורה שאין עמה
מלאכה סופה בטלה וגוררת עון

I. Inconsiderate Behaviour – *Kofin al Middat Sedom*

The law normally requires that when two brothers inherit a field from their father, the field is divided equally and each half is assigned by lot. A case is discussed, however, where one brother owns a field adjoining the land he inherited. He therefore requests that, for the sake of convenience, his half of the inheritance be contiguous with that field rather than assigned by lot, since both halves are of equal value. If the other brother refuses this reasonable request, the court will uphold the applicant's claim and order that the field be so divided. This ruling accords with the right of contiguity (*BM* 108a).[108]

Similarly, if the field must be divided into three parts, and the firstborn son is entitled to a double portion (Deut. 21:17), he may request that his two-thirds of the land be contiguous. The court is empowered to enforce such a division if the other brother refuses to agree. And were he to suffer no loss by accepting this division, his refusal would incur the judges' grave displeasure as a mean-spirited lack of consideration for the needs of others. Such behavior was categorized as *middat Sedom* – the reprehensible moral standard of Sodom (Gen. 6:18) – for the Torah insists (Deut. 6:18): "Thou shalt do that which is right and good in the sight of the Lord" (*BM* 108a).

A guiding principle in ethical conduct was "always to adopt a pleasant disposition in one's relationship with people" (*Ket.* 17a).[109] It was, likewise, taught that one's speech with one's fellow should always be in a kindly manner (*Yoma* 86a).[110]

If two brothers inherited a field, or bought a field in partnership, or received one as a gift, it must be divided. If, by dividing a plot of land, each half measures less than four

---

108 נהרדעאי אמרי אפי׳ משום דינא דבר מצרא מסלקינן ליה משום שנאמר ועשית
    הישר והטוב בעיני ה׳
109 לעולם תהא דעתו של אדם מעורבת עם הבריות
110 לעולם יהיה דיבורו של אדם בנחת רוח עם הבריות

cubits or less then a productive size, or if the inheritance were an article such as a coat that can scarcely be cut into two, one partner should sell his half to the other and thus solve the problem by mutual agreement. Should one party reject this solution, the other may say to him: "Either you state a price for your half and I'll buy it, or I will state a price and you will then buy it!" (*BB* 11a; *BB* 11a, 12b, 13a, *ad loc.*; Rashi; *ad loc.*; *BM* 108a, 35a; *Sh. Ar. Hoshen Mishpat* 171:3, 6; 289:1; 174:1; Maim., *Shekhenim*, 1:2, 5; 2:10).[111] Should the other party reject this proposal, the court may force him to comply with the request, because his refusal to do so was unreasonable. It would be yet another instance of *kofin al middat Sedom* (*Sh. Ar. Hoshen Mishpat* 174:1; Maim., *Shekhenim*, 12:1).[112]

J. Acts Known Only to the Heart – *Davar ha-Masur la-Lev*

The formation of man's moral character begins when he first perceives "the good" and acknowledges it as the standard that will determine his actions. Man's ethical behaviour is characterized by freedom of action, and his moral character is revealed in exercising his freedom of choice. That choice reflects his own conception of the extent to which a particular duty is, for him, a categorical imperative.

These inner workings of the mind are, however, not perceptible to one's fellow man. Artfulness may be concealed by pious speech or appearances and, if revealed, can always be denied. Hence the Rabbis taught: "All precepts whose fulfillment is known only to the inner workings of the heart are accompanied in Scripture by the words: 'Thou shalt fear thy God'".[113] One who fears God will realize that He knows

---

111   אין בהן כדי לזה לזה וכדי לזה מהו רב יהודה אמר אית דינא דגוד או אגוד

112   וכופה אותו על זה שעיכוב בדבר זה מדת סדום היא

113   וכל דבר המסור ללב נאמר בו ויראת מאל-והיך

man's hidden thoughts and that no deceptive words will mislead man's Creator (*BM* 58b; *Kid.* 32b).

The Torah prohibits taking advantage of someone's deafness and cursing him in the knowledge that the other man cannot hear; nor should one "put a stumbling-block before the blind". These Torah laws contain a special, additional injunction: "But thou shalt fear thy God; I am the Lord" (Lev. 19:14).[114]

Another case of possible deception involves the duty to show respect for the aged, which could be shirked by pretending not to notice such a person (Lev. 19:32; *Kid.* 32b).[115] Concern for the welfare of the poor is a moral obligation, and charging interest on loans (usury) is accordingly forbidden; this precept is likewise reinforced by the command to fear God (Lev. 25:35–37).[116]

According to Biblical law, when a person acquired a slave, the way he treated him may not have been known to others. A slave's work had therefore to be regulated out of consideration for his human dignity: "Thou shalt not rule over him with rigour, but shalt fear thy God" (Lev. 25:43).[117] All these ethical obligations, as well as the ceremonial laws, give man the opportunity to practice moral autonomy. The Torah's ethical laws, in particular, constitute an effective mechanism for man to express his capacity to govern himself from within (I. Epstein, "The Ceremonial Laws", in Leo Jung, *The Jewish Library*, First Series, Ch. 12, p. 367, Macmillan, 1928).

Wronging someone by deceitful speech is a worse offence than committing a felony, since the latter offence can be indemnified whereas the former cannot (*BM* 58b).[118] This would also apply if the guilty act caused no material loss. Misleading a person with dishonest advice falls under the prohibition: "Thou shalt not put a stumbling-block before

---

114   לא תקלל חרש ולפני עור לא תתן מכשל ויראת מאל-היך אני ה׳

115   והדרת פני זקן

116   אל תקח ממנו נשך ותרבית ויראת מאל-היך וחי אחיך עמך

117   לא תרדה בו בפרך ויראת מאל-היך

118   גדול אונאת דברים מאונאת ממון שזה נאמר בו ויראת מאל-היך... זה ניתן
להישבון וזה לא ניתן להישבון

the blind" (Lev. 19:14; cf. Deut. 27:18).[119] In such misdeeds, being hard to trace, the Torah warns man: "Thou shalt fear thy God" (*Kid.* 32b; *BM* 58b; Lev. 19:14, *Torat Kohanim* and Rashi *ad loc.*).[120]

K. Wrongful Speech

Hurting Another's Feelings – Ona'at Devarim

The offence of hurting another's feelings by words that wound his sensibility is greater than wronging another in some financial matter; for the latter could be corrected, but a wound to his self-esteem cannot be erased (*BM* 58b).[121]

The Sages went so far as to say one who publicly puts his fellow to shame is deprived of any portion in the World to Come (*Avot* 3:1).[122]

Even in the act of rebuking one's fellow for his wrongdoing one must take care to avoid hurting his self-respect. The Sages said that in fulfilling the Torah obligation of "thou shalt rebuke thy neighbour" (Lev. 19:17)[123] one should guard oneself from the transgression of wronging one's neighbour (*Ara.* 16b).

Misleading Advice – Eitzah She'einah Hogenet

The Sages forbade making deceitful statements or giving misleading advice based on the Torah prohibition, "Thou shalt not put a stumbling-block before the blind" (Lev. 19:14; Midrash *Torah Kohanim*, ibid.).[124]

---

119 ולפני עור לא תתן מכשול ויראת מאל-היך
120 לפני הסומא בדבר לא תתן עצה שאינה הוגנת לו – ויראת מאל-היך לפי שהדבר הזה אינו מסור לבריות לידע אם דעתו שלזה לטובה או לרע
121 גדולה אונאת דברים מאונאת ממון
122 המלבין פני חברו ברבים אין לו חלק לעולם הבא
123 הוכח תוכיח את עמיתך
124 לפני עור לא תתן מכשול

It is always one's duty to seek the good for his neighbour, and refrain from tale-bearing and slander (*rekhilut ve-lashon hara*). The moral failure in every malicious action is due to one's yielding to the temptation of the evil inclination (*yetzer hara*) which needs to be opposed by strengthening one's determination to observe the admonition of "love thy neighbour as thy self" – *ve'ahavta le're'akha kamokha*. This is the basic ordinance of Torah law (Gen. R. end 24).

The most powerful achievement of man is to overpower the *yetzer hara* as it is stated in the Ethics of the Fathers, "Who is the mighty man? He who subdues his evil *yetzer* (Avot 4:1).[125]

In its purest form virtuous conduct constitutes opposition to self-centredness and faithfulness to the duty of allegiance to God and man (Luzzatto, *Mesillat Yesharim*, 11).

The Talmud related that R. Netunia was asked, "By what particular virtue have you achieved the gift of old age?" To which he replied, "Because I never sought honour for myself in the shame of others".

L. Humility – *Anavah*

The antithesis to pride is humility. As self pride is an attitude of the mind so humility in conduct is a result of one's manner of thinking. Therefore, in order to attain humility one should accustom oneself to divert one's thought into such an attitude of not being worthy of greater esteem, or that his achievements deserved special praise, thus developing in himself a normal character of humility (Luzzatto, *Mesillat Yesharim*, Chap. 22).

The Ethics of the Fathers taught in the name of R. Levitas: "Keep yourself of an exceedingly humble spirit (*Avot* 4:4).[126]

---

125 איזהו גבור הכובש את יצרו
126 מאד מאד הוה שפל רוח

Humility, however, did not mean a spirit of meek subservience. Maimonides described it as a middle position between pride and self-abasement (Maim. *Sanhedrin, Shemoneh Perakim*).[127]

The Torah writes "Now the man Moses was very meek, above all the men which were upon the face of the earth" (Num. 12:3).[128]

In the ethical teaching of Rabbeinu Baḥya it is recognized that it is difficult for one to command the thoughts in one's mind, and therefore he described humility as a control of personal conduct, accustoming oneself by acting in a humble fashion and thus eventually attaining a mental attitude of humility (Baḥya, *Kad Hakemah*, sect. 2, "*Anavah*").

R. Israel Salanter likewise taught that the character of humility was contrary to natural inclination and could only be attained by special effort and force of will-power (Israel Salanter, *Even Israel, Derashot* Ch. 2).

Luzzatto wrote, "For the attainment of *anavah* a combination of two things are needed – the manner of action, and the manner of thought.[129] By conducting one's self in the manner of *anavah* as an unbroken habit, eradicating all thoughts of self-interest one will establish in his mind the natural virtue of humility. Nevertheless it must be remembered that there is no one who is entirely free from sin (Eccles. 7:20; Luzzatto, *Mesillat Yesharim*, Ch. 23, "*Anavah*").[130]

M. The Biblical Prohibition of Usury – *Ribit*

Concern for the well-being of the poor is a moral obligation, therefore lending at interest (usury) is forbidden. This finds support in the injunction to fear God (Lev. 25:35).[131] Biblical

---

127 הענוה ממוצעת בין הגאוה ובין שפלות הרוח
128 והאיש משה ענו מכל האדם אשר על פני האדמה
129 הענוה תלויה במחשבה ובמעשה
130 אין צדיק בארץ אשר יעשה טוב ולא יחטא
131 אל תקח ממנו נשך ותרבית ויראת מאל-היך וחי אחיך עמך

law states: "And if thy brother be waxen poor, and his hand fail with thee; then thou shalt uphold him: as a stranger and a sojourner [i.e., though he be a stranger or a sojourner] shall he live with thee" (J. H. Hertz, *Pentateuch ad loc.*). "Take thou no usury of him or increase, but fear thy God; that thy brother may live with thee. Thou shalt not give him thy money upon usury" (Lev. 25:35–37; Ex. 22:25; Deut. 23:19).[132]

This prohibition applies both to the lender and to the borrower. The lender is forbidden to take interest from a fellow Jew, and the Jewish borrower is forbidden to pay it. The charging of interest is compared to the criminal behaviour of a thief, whose testimony in a court of law is declared inadmissible. The Sages affirmed that taking interest from a needy person was like the bite of a poisonous snake: initially, the borrower feels no discomfort, but gradually the pain becomes unbearable (Ex. 22:24, Rashi *ad loc.*; Ex. R. 31:6).[133]

An existential problem arose, however, during the Middle Ages, when the dominant society barred Jews from engaging in normal business transactions. Their very survival as an autonomous people was then endangered, yet the Torah stated: "Ye shall therefore keep My statutes, and My judgments, which if a man do, he shall live by them: I am the Lord" (Lev. 18:5).[134] The Sages taught that the words "live by them" implied "not die by them" (*Yoma* 85b),[135] so the very fact that Jews observed Torah law ought to ensure their survival. A way of overcoming this moral dilemma had therefore to be found.

During the Amoraic period (fourth century CE), it transpired that the Sages of Nehardea in Babylonia had discovered that the law against taking interest on loans was incompatible with the economic needs of the Jewish community (*BM* 104a). They accordingly sought ways to legalize transactions which apparently fell under the prohibition. To that end they

---

132 לא תשיך לאחיך נשך כסף נשך אוכל
133 למה הרבית דומה למי שנשכו נחש
134 וחי בהם
135 וחי בהם ולא שימות בהם

converted the transaction into a form of partnership contract
in which it was possible for both sides to derive benefit. The
person lending capital would be the silent partner and the one
borrowing it would be the active partner who conducted the
business. According to the laws of partnership, both sides
shared the profits and any losses incurred. A contract was
drawn up, specifying the amount due to each, which could
enable the lender to gain a stipulated advantage from the use
of his capital. In Rabbinic parlance, such a contract was known
as a "business permit" – *hetter iska* (*BM* 104b; 69a; Mish.
5:4; 8:7, *Piskei ROSH*; Maim. *Malveh*, 4:9; Maim., *Sheluhin*
6:23; *TUR* 176:28; *Sh. Ar.*, *Yoreh De'ah* 173:18, REMA; *Sh.
Ar. Yoreh De'ah* 177:6).[136]

The halakhic jurists concluded that a business corporation,
or a "limited company" owned by many shareholders, could
not be considered as "an individual", but as having its own
juristic existence. The personality of such a company was
not that of a natural individual, as referred to in the Biblical
expression "thy brother" (*ahikha*), to which the prohibition
of usury applied. Thus in such situations the law of *ribit* did
not obtain. Modern business transactions with banks charging
interest were accordingly exempt from that proscription.

This facility, however, was only available for business
transactions. In the case of an individual who required money
for his personal needs, all the prohibitive laws were strictly
applied (*Betzah* 30b). Any artful utilization of this device,
exploiting a Jew or Gentile in distress, was completely
forbidden.

If one endeavors to conceal one's real intention, the Sages
reminded man that it was stated in the Biblical prohibition:
"I am the Lord," as the Psalmist declared: "Shall not God
search this out? For He knoweth the secrets of the heart" (Ps.
44:21).[137]

136   היתר עיסקא
137   כי הוא יודע תעלמות לב

The religious teaching imparted by the Torah is entirely ethical, addressing itself exclusively to the will of man, which, it is affirmed, has an essentially moral character.

The prohibition not to exact interest from one's fellow did not prevent an Israelite from lending money to a necessitous brother without the expectation of any profit in return. "If the poor man was to derive any real assistance from the loan granted him, it was absolutely indispensable that no more was required of him than the actual amount the had been lent" (H. Adler). This prohibition led to the establishment in every organized Jewish community of a *gemilut hassadim* society, for advancing loans free of interest to the poor (J.H. Hertz, *Pentateuch*, p. 536, 848).

Chapter 6

Offerings – *Korbanot*

6 Offerings – Korbanot

A. The Concept

The basic concept of Jewish faith and worship is expressed by King David in the Psalms (73:28): "The best thing for me is nearness to God".[1] The pinnacle of Jewish ritual was the joy experienced by Israel through the establishment of the Sanctuary in their midst, where, the Almighty declared: "I shall dwell among them" (Ex. 25:8; 29:45).[2] The Temple on Mount Zion in Jerusalem was exclusively sanctified as the abode of the Divine where Israel and all nations, through prayer and sacrifice, could be reunited in harmony with the sacred presence of God (Ps. 78:68–69, 135:21; 132:13; 1 Kings 8:13, 16).[3]

Any deviation from God's law reflected an estrangement from God by the individual and resulted in withdrawal from His Presence. Committing a sin is tantamount to a self-inflicted distancing from God; and as the gravity of sin increases, the union with God is dissolved and the Divine Providence is finally removed from the sinner, who then suffers physical and spiritual destruction (Ps. 73:27). Moses summed up the blessing of observing the laws of God in the words, "And ye who cleave to the Lord your God are all alive today" (Deut. 4:4; 30:20).[4] But since the urge to sin is a known and innate element of human nature, expressed by the term 'evil inclination' (*yetzer ha-ra*), the Almighty gave man the opportunity to close the breach and to regain his closeness with the Divine by

---

ואני קרבת אל-הים לי טוב	1
ושכנתי בתוכם	2
בנה בניתי בית זבל לך מכון לשבתך עולמים... לא בחרתי מעיר מכל שבטי ישראל	3
לבנות בית להיות שמי שם	
ואתם הדבקים לה׳ אל-היכם חיים כולכם היום	4

means of the ritual of the sacrificial offerings in the Sanctuary. The act of returning to the Presence of God is indicated in the Hebrew word for "offering" – *korban* – from the root *karav*, "to come near". Thus the Temple offering is not mainly "sacrifice" or "penalty" or "propitiation", but simply, "coming near" or returning to the closeness of God's Presence, and through the Temple ritual of the offerings Israel's closeness to the Divine is preserved. Moses expressed this concept in the words, "For which great nation is there whose God is so close to it as the Lord our God whenever we call on Him" (Deut. 4:7).

The need for man's reconciliation with the Higher Power of the Divine lies at the heart of all religion. The antiquity and universality of sacrifices testify to the deep-rooted sacrificial instinct in the human heart which seeks to respond to the claims of God upon man.

In ancient mythology the anger or envy of the gods had to be propitiated by man by bringing sacrifices to them. In Israel these crude ideas characterizing man's approach to God were transformed into ritual with a spiritual-ethical content. Such sacrifices were instituted in the Torah as the effective means of reconciling man with his Creator, guiding him to achieve harmony with his God and raising him to a state of perfection.

The Biblical sacrifices were not intended to satisfy the needs of the Almighty, who lacked nothing, but the needs of man. The sacrifices were not a bribe, nor reparation for man's sins. God required of man "only to do justly, love mercy, and walk humbly before thy God" (Mic. 6:8), and as the prophet taught, "For I desire mercy, and not sacrifice; and the knowledge of God more than burnt-offerings" (Hos. 6:6; Arama, *Akedat Yitzhak* 57, beginning of Leviticus). Their aim was essentially man's spiritual regeneration and perfection. They were designed to foster in the mind of the worshipper a sense of the awfulness of sin in general and of the transgression of the religious and social precepts of the Torah in particular. The Sages declared that all the ritual laws of the Torah were given with the single aim of ennobling mankind and bringing about this perfection (Gen. R. 44:1).[5]

The ritual of the sacrifices was intended to bring home to the offender the seriousness of his transgression of any of the religious precepts, both social and ritual, ordained in the Torah.

Maimonides, in his discourse on the purpose of the sacrificial rituals, explained that the object of all these ceremonies was to impress on the mind of every sinner and transgressor the necessity of continually being conscious of his sin in order not to sin (Maim. *Guide*, 3:46, in Friedlaender's translation).

The reasons for the specific forms of sacrificial ritual as ordained in the Torah defy our understanding and must be regarded as Divine statutes (*hukkim*) intended to elevate man to spiritual perfection (Maim. *Yad, Me'ilah*, 8:8; *Guide*, 3:26, 29).

All the ritual laws are firmly entrenched in Israel's belief in the Torah as the expression of the benevolent will of God and the psychology of human conduct (Nahmanides, Torah Commentary on Lev. 1:9).

B. The Sacrificial Ritual

By the commission of grave sins man brings on himself the judgment of God. The execution of justice calls for his due punishment and retribution. An offering is a ritual which is a part of the process of atonement and reconciliation. Other elements are confession, contrition and prayer. The Sages said that God was grieved that Israel's sins had brought about their suffering in exile, for He Himself felt some responsibility for their sins by virtue of the fact that He had created the Evil Inclination in them *(Suk. 52b)*.

The Sages explained that, through his various transgressions, man defiled the soul-element of his life and deserved to

forfeit his life. But the Almighty had compassion because of
man's innate frailty and He therefore endowed him with the
opportunity to cleanse his soul through sincere repentance.

The Ramban (Nahmanides), in his exposition of the
sacrificial ritual (Nahmanides' Torah Commentary on Lev.
1:1, 9), rejected Maimonides' sociological approach and
explained how rapprochement with the Divine is achieved.
He disapproved of Maimonides' philosophical interpretation
(Maim. *Guide*, 3:26, 32), but followed rather his symbolic
interpretation (*Guide*, 3: 46–47).

Since the Sanctaruy was filled with the Divine Presence
– "and the glory of the Lord filled the Sanctuary" (Ex. 40:34)[6]
– the priests, in the first place, were commanded to preserve
the Temple from any defilement, which would cause the
departure of the Divine Presence. If such defilement took
place, it was their duty to atone for it by a carefully ordered
ritual of supplication and the contrition engendered by the
offering of "sacrifices" on the altar (*korbanot*).

The Ramban maintained that atonement before God
required the reformation of a man's entire conduct. Every
human action, he explained, is composed of thought, speech
and action. Thus, in bringing a "sacrifice", he is first required
to perform the act of "laying his hands" on the offering,
as though to merge his being with that of the animal; his
"confession" by speech atones for his transgression, and the
subsequent "burning" of the sacrifice and the destruction of
all its physical and mental faculties is intended to impress
on the transgressor the gravity of his sin, for which his own
blood deserved to be shed, but by the grace of God – *be-hesed
Hashem* – the blood of the animal was accepted in his place.
Scripture stated: "And he shall lay his hand upon the head of
the burnt offering; and it shall be accepted for him to make
atonement for him" (Lev. 1:4).[7] In this way the sinner becomes
conscious of the full weight of his own guilt and is humbled
into undergoing sincere repentance, which would then be

---

6   וכבוד ה׳ מלא את המשכן

7   וסמך ידו על ראש העולה ונרצה לו

followed by complete atonement (Lev. 1:4, 5, Ramban, *loc. cit.*; *Men.* 93b; *Zev.* 33a).[8] The Sages ruled that while he was fully conscious of the gravity of transferring his own life to the head of the sacrifice by his "laying of hands", the blood of the animal was immediately shed before his eyes.

Some Sages were troubled by the sacrifice of animals as a means of obtaining man's atonement. It was reported that when King Saul was ordered to slay the Amalekites he asked, "If man has sinned, in what way has the animal sinned?"[9] – but the heavenly response was "Do not be over-righteous" (Eccles. 7:16).[10] The animal's life is sacrificed to achieve a higher purpose – the regeneration of man (*Yoma* 22b).

The ritual of a Temple sacrifice involved four separate actions: 1. slaughtering the animal or bird, each in its prescribed way (*shehitah*); 2. receiving the blood of the offering in a Temple vessel (*kabbalat ha-dam*); 3. carrying the blood to the appropriate place (*holakhah*); and 4. sprinkling the blood on the appropriate place on the altar (*zerikat ha-dam*).

A fault in any of these actions rendered the sacrifice unfit – *pasul* (Mish., *Zev.* 1:4, TB *Zev.* 13a; Maim. *Yad, Pesulei ha-Mukdashin*, 13:4).[11]

The meal-offering comprised four similar procedures: 1. "taking out the handful of the meal-offering" (*kemitzah*), comparable to the *shehitah* of the animal; 2. "putting the meal into the Temple vessel" (*netinah bi-kheli sharet*), comparable to receiving the blood of the animal; 3. "bringing the handful of meal near the altar" (*holakhah*), as in an animal sacrifice; and 4. "burning the meal-offering on the altar" (*haktarah*), comparable to *zerikat ha-dam* – sprinkling the animal's blood on the altar (Mish., *Men.* 1:3, TB *Men.* 11b–12a; Maim. *Pesulei ha-Mukdashin*, 13:6).

Each of the four actions had to be carried out by the officiating priest with full intention that it was being done

---

8   סמך שחיטה לסמיכה ללמדך שתיכף לסמיכה שחיטה
9   אם אדם חטא בהמה מה חטאה
10   אל תהי צדיק הרבה
11   הזבח נפסל בארבעה דברים, בשחיטה, ובקיבול, ובהילוך, ובזריקה

according to the prescribed ritual for the sake of the particular
sacrifice. If any of these actions was done not for its own sake
but for some different purpose, the sacrifice was disqualified
– *pasul* (Mish., *Zev* 1:1, 1:3, TB *Men.* 2a; 12b).

There were three types of wrongful intention which
disqualified the sacrifice:[12]

1. Where the intention at the time of the sacrifice was not
   for the particular type of sacrifice for which the offering
   had been brought.[13]
2. When any of the required actions were intended to be
   done not in the proper place assigned for the ritual.[14]
3. When, in the performance of any of the required actions,
   it was intended that the subsequent ritual should be done
   at a time not prescribed by the laws of ritual – *piggul*
   (Mish., *Zev.* 2:2, 3; TB *Zev.* 28a; Maim. *Pesulei ha-
   Mukdashin*, 13:1).[15]

These laws were based on particular instructions given in
the Torah for the purpose of atonement, as it was stated: "And
the priest shall make atonement for him as touching his sin
that he hath sinned, and he shall be forgiven" (Lev. 4:35).[16]

The detailed ritual differed according to the type and purpose
of the offering, which could be described as belonging to two
main categories: propitiatory or dedicatory. The propitiatory
sacrifices were the sin-offering (*hattat*) and the guilt-offering
(*asham*). The main dedicatory sacrifices were the burnt-
offering (*olah*); the meal-offering (*minhah*); the libation-
offering (*nesekh*); the peace-offering (*shelamim*); the freewill-
offering (*nedavah*); and the votive-offering (*nedarim*).

Commenting on the statement that the burnt-offering
"shall be accepted to make atonement for him" (Lev. 1:4),[17]
Nahmanides quotes the Midrash (Lev. R.) as follows. R.

---

12 שלש מחשבות הן שפוסלין את הקרבנות
13 מחשבת שינוי השם
14 מחשבת המקום
15 מחשבת הזמן
16 וכפר עליו הכהן על חטאתו אשר חטא ונסלח לו
17 ונרצה לו לכפר עליו

Shim'on bar Yoḥai said: "The sacrifice of the burnt-offering (*korban olah*) is brought to atone for the evil thoughts in a person's mind that incite him to commit a transgression".[18] This is in contrast to a sin-offering, which is brought for an actual transgression; whereas the term *olah* (literally, "rises") points to an evil thought that spontaneously arises in the mind. R. Shim'on ben Lakish further exemplified this teaching by quoting Job, who brought many offerings on behalf of his sons, declaring that they might well have sinned in the course of their festivities by profaning God in their hearts (Job 1:5; Lev. 7:3).[19]

In the case of an offence committed unwittingly (*bi-shegagah*), Naḥmanides explains, a person is not aware of its gravity, which is known only to God. Therefore, when that individual becomes aware of a possible sin, the burnt-offering is entirely consumed on the altar as a complete sacrifice to God,[20] and so the offering is accepted by Him as full atonement (Lev. 1:4).[21]

[General reference: *Encyclopaedia Judaica*, 14:599–615, "Sacrifice"]

Expiation of Sin – Ritzui Hashem

That bringing an animal as a sacrifice to God effects the expiation of sin is generally asserted in the Torah. However, "It shall be accepted to make atonement for him" (Lev. 1:4; Rashi *ad loc.*) really means that its propitiatory effect is severely limited. The sacrifice of a burnt-offering (*olah*) does not atone for grave transgressions that make one liable to "excision" (*karet*), "execution by order of the court"[22] (*mitat*

---

18   אין העולה באה אלא על הרהורי עבירת הלב

19   אולי חטאו בני וברכו אל-הים בלבבם

20   כולה כליל לשם

21   ונרצה לו לכפר עליו

22   מיתות בית דין

bet din), the "death penalty inflicted by heaven"[23] (*mitah bi-yedei shamayim*) or the penalty of "lashes" (*malkot*). The punishment for such offences is always meted out as the Torah prescribes, according to whether they were or were not committed intentionally.[24]

Rashi states that the sacrifice of an *olah* can bring atonement only for the non-fulfilment of a positive commandment (*mitzvat aseh*), where no punishment is prescribed, or for violating "a prohibition that incorporates a positive remedy"[25], which appears to be a lesser offence. An example of this is the law that forbids "taking the mother bird with its young"; one should first release the mother bird, and then take the eggs or fledglings (Deut. 22:6–7).[26] Similarly, with regard to the meat of an offering, "Ye shall let nothing remain until the morning; but whatever is left the next day ye shall burn with fire" (Ex. 12:10; cf. Lev. 19:6).[27]

Nahmanides (*ibid., ad loc.*) points out that although no punishment is laid down for the transgressions specified by Rashi, such acts are nevertheless unacceptable to God.[28] The voluntary sacrifice of a burnt-offering will therefore gain Divine approval (*ritzui Hashem*) and provide atonement (*kapparah*), even though the actions were performed knowingly.[29] Where violating a Torah prohibition will incur the penalty of "excision" (*karet*), if the act was unintentional (*be-shogeg*), its form of atonement is clearly prescribed – obliging the transgressor to make a sin-offering, in accordance with the full ritual of repentance, so as to obtain forgiveness and regain Divine favour.

---

23 מיתה בידי שמים
24 במזיד או בשוגג
25 לאו שניתק לעשה
26 שלח תשלח את האם
27 והנותר ממנו עד בוקר באש תשרופו
28 שאינם רצויים לפניו
29 מזידים שאינם רצויים לפניו

The Guilt-Offering (Asham) and Sin-Offering (Ḥattat)

Shedding its blood and burning an animal on the altar were key elements in the sacrificial system. The consumption of all animal blood was strictly forbidden: as the source of life, it belonged only to God, and its sacred purpose was to make atonement for man's sins (Lev. 17:11).

When an Israelite realized that he had unwittingly transgressed in the matter of "holy things" or the "rights" of his fellow and then repented, he was obliged to make full monetary reparation, with an added payment of one-fifth of the amount, and to bring the prescribed *asham* guilt-offering (Lev. 5:15–26; Maim. *Shegagot*). Offerings were also brought in a number of cases requiring *tohorah*, "ritual purification" (Maim. *Meḥussarei Kapparah*, 1).

Someone who unknowingly violated Torah-ordained prohibitions that incurred the penalty of "excision", and who later became aware of his transgression, was required to seek atonement for his sin and bring a *ḥattat* sin-offering (Lev. 4:27–28). The term used for this sacrifice, *ḥattat* (from the root *ḥata*, "to miss the mark"), indicates that although the sinner's act was unintentional, it nevertheless "deviated" from the true path, and through his sin-offering he could make atonement (Maim. *Shegagot*, 1–7).

Exceptionally, in the case of a Sabbath violation, an unwitting offence does not make one liable for a sin-offering if the action or object involved was other than that intended. This is due to a particular feature of the Sabbath laws which categorizes a forbidden activity as "purposeful work", but guilt is not attached if it had not been intended (*Shab.* 72b; Maim. *Shegagot*, 2:7, 11).[30] The requirement of a *ḥattat* sacrifice is further relaxed when someone claims to have been under the impression that what he did was lawful, although it actually violated the law (*omer mutar*) (*Pes.* 72b; Maim. *Shegagot,* 2:8).[31]

Naḥmanides (commenting on Lev. 5:15) points out that although two different offerings, the *ḥattat* and the *asham*, are brought to expiate sins committed unwittingly, both are really sin-offerings, even if they have different requirements. The prescribed *asham* (guilt-offering) is a two-year-old ram worth two *shekalim* (Lev. 5:15, Rashi *ad loc.*), while the prescribed *ḥattat* (sin-offering), brought as *shegagah*, is a female lamb or kid of much lower value (Lev. 5:6). His explanation of the reason for two kinds of sin-offering is as follows: The *asham* is applicable to a grave sin for which the offender merits destruction, as signified by the root *asham* ("to destroy"), whereas the sin-offering bespeaks a "deviation" from the true path, as stated above. The Hebrew word "*asham*" may be associated with two root meanings: 1. *Asham* – to commit an offence, to be guilty of an offence; 2. *Shamam* – to be desolated, appalled (Lev. 26:31; Ezek. 33:28).

[Refrences: Brown, Driver and Briggs: *Lexicon of Old Testament* s.v. *asham, shamam*]

Ibn Ezra (ibid.) differentiates between the two offerings: in the case of *ḥattat*, the transgressor did not at first realize that his action was forbidden, but he later became aware of this. In the case of *asham*, he knew that it was forbidden, but momentarily forgot and only later became aware that he had done wrong.

The Doubtful Guilt Offering – Asham Talui

When, *post factum*, a man is not sure whether he has sinned, he still bears guilt for his want of attention during the act and is required to bring a "doubtful guilt" offering (*asham talui*) for the purpose of atonement (Ibn Ezra, Lev. 5:17). Discussing this type of *korban*, the Rabbis note that in the case of a regular guilt-offering (*asham vaddai*) the sacrifice brings atonement (*kapparah*), but someone who has doubts as to whether or not he transgressed is unable to show full repentance (*teshuvah*), although he still requires atonement for his possible offence.[32] Hence the sacrifice is incomplete and only brings partial *kapparah*, with full atonement "suspended" (*Yoma* 85b).[33]

This type of situation may arise when a man who had two pieces of meat, one containing permitted fat (*shuman*) and the other forbidden lard (*ḥelev*), is not sure which he ate, since one piece has vanished or been eaten by a dog. Owing to the doubt as to whether he has sinned, he cannot gain atonement for an unwitting transgression (*shegagah*), since this only applies when he becomes aware of having actually sinned. Some guilt remains attached to him, however, and bringing an *asham talui* "suspends" his atonement until the unwitting offence has been verified. At that stage he may bring the prescribed sin-offering and completely atone for his transgression (Lev. 5:17–18; Maim. *Shegagot*, 8:4).

As mentioned above, the sacrifice prescribed for an unwitting transgression was a lamb or a kid that might be worth as little as a *danka* (one-sixth of a *dinar*); in the case of poor folk this could even be reduced to a tenth of an ephah of fine flour. For an *asham talui*, however, the prescribed offering was more costly – a full-grown ram valued at two *shekalim*. The Sages explained the reason for this greater cost: since the man was not sure of his guilt, it would be more difficult for him to repent. God would know if he had sinned and, if he had, it was incumbent upon him to make atonement (Lev. 5:17–18; Ramban on Lev. 5:15; Maim. S*hegagot*, 8:4).

The Burnt-Offering – Olah

The Sages made it clear that the sacrifices did not absolve a man of his transgressions, nor were they meant to pardon

---

32   והכפרה כתיבה לאשממתו
33   כפרה גמורה

his offence. The punishment for grave violations of the law was set forth in the Torah, and the penalties of "excision" (*karet*), "lashing" (*malkot*) and execution (*mitah*) could not be remitted.

As stated earlier, the burnt-offering (*olah*) brought atonement only for the neglect of a positive commandment, where no punishment or atonement was prescribed, or for violating "a prohibition that incorporates a positive remedy", such as the law against taking the mother bird with its young[34] (Deut. 22:6 –7; Lev. 1:4, Rashi *ad loc.*).[35] A transgression of a prohibition which may be repaired by a succeeding act (*lo ta'aseh shenitak le'aseh*) (*Yoma* 85b, 86a). Naḥmanides, quoting the Midrash, pointed out that an *olah* was also brought for the sin of harbouring evil thoughts and intentions.[36]

The Burnt-Offering and Sinful Thoughts – Hirhurei Averah

The Talmud associates the bringing of a tribute by Israel after the war against Midian with their plea for forgiveness on account of immoral thoughts. Having captured the Midianite women and taken their ornaments, the Israelites felt guilty of unlawful desires: "We have brought an offering for the Lord, what every man hath found, gold jewels, anklets and bracelets, signet-rings, earrings, and girdles, to make atonement for our souls before the Lord" (Num. 31:50). R. Naḥman observed that although they had not committed any offence, they avowed, "We were free from sin, but not from sinful thoughts" (*Shab.* 64a; Num. 31:50, Rashi *ad loc.*).[37]

Lewd habits, such as ogling women and harbouring salacious thoughts (*hirhurei averah*), are rigorously

---

34   שלח תשלח את האם
35   לאו שניתק לעשה
36   אין העולה באה אלא הרהורי הלב
37   אם מידי עבירה יצאנו, מידי הרהור לא יצאנו

condemned. The Sages warned that they could lead a man to perdition *(Gehinnom)*: even if he were otherwise just as pious and learned as Moses, he would not escape punishment for such offences[38] (Mish., *Kid.* 4:14, *Tiferet Yisrael*, end of 77, on how Moses overcame his natural sinful tendencies; *Ber.* 61a; cf. *Even ha-Ezer* 21; *Ber.* 16b). In this sense some prayer book texts have added to the daily prayer of R. Yehudah ha-Nasi a plea for deliverance from *Gehinnom* (*Otzar ha-Tefillot, Nusaḥ Sefarad*).

Mistakes Made while Fulfilling a Precept – Tarud be-Mitzvah

The Sages differed as to whether a person should be exempted from bringing a *ḥattat* sin-offering if he mistakenly transgressed while fulfilling a *mitzvah*.[39] They quote an instance where a man sacrificed his paschal lamb on the Sabbath, which was in itself particularly permitted, but failed to mention what it was and simply brought it as an unidentified offering, thus violating the Sabbath. R. Eliezer considered him liable for a sin-offering, because of his mistaken desecration of the Sabbath (*ḥillul Shabbat*). R. Yehoshua exempted him, however, because the mistake occurred as a result of his preoccupation with the fulfilment of a religious duty,[40] and he had never suspected that he might be guilty of a transgression. In these extenuating circumstances, the man was not culpable of any misdemeanour (*Pes.* 71b, 73b; Maim. *Shegagot* 2:12;[41] *Yev.* 34a).[42]

---

38   אפילו יש בידו תורה ומעשים טובים כמשה רבנו לא יינקה מדינה של גהינום
39   טרוד לדבר מצווה
40   לר׳ אליעזר טועה בדבר מצוה פטור
41   טעה בדבר מצוה פטור
42   הפסח ששחטו שלא לשמו בשבת

C. Appropriate Intention

A wrong intention invalidates the sacrifice only if the thought is actually expressed. Maimonides summarizes the three laws concerning a wrong thought which invalidates an offering, i.e., by changing the name of the offering, its proper place or its proper time,[43] as well as the four sacrificial procedures described above – *shehitah* and receiving, conveying and sprinkling the blood.[44]

According to Maimonides, the officiating priest could render the offering invalid by merely having a wrong thought. Rashi and the *Tosafot* make it clear, however, that the offering was only *pasul* if the *kohen* expressed his thought verbally,[45] which meant some demonstrable action on his part, and not if there was simply an unexpressed thought in his mind[46] (*BM* 43b, Rashi and *Tos. ad loc.*, "*mahashavah*"; *Zev.* 41b; *Men.* 30a; *Men.* 3b; *Zev.* 4b, *Tos. ad loc.*; Maim. *Pesulei ha-Mukdashin*, 13:1, *Mishneh la-Melekh* on 13:1). This was also the case with a pledge that had been wrongfully appropriated (Ex. 22:10),[47] where he would only be judged culpable on the basis of a clearly expressed intention (*BM* 43b, Rashi and *Tos. ad loc.*).

Once a sacrifice had been given a specific designation, e.g., for a burnt-offering, it retained its holy status (*kedushah*) even if the ritual was performed with no special intention *vis-à-vis* that particular sacrifice.[48] It was considered valid (*kasher*), as if the ritual had been performed for an *olah*, because the sacrifice already possessed the holy status designated.

The Sages of the Mishnah declared that even if the ritual's *shehitah* was performed with another aim in mind,[49] such

---

43 שינוי שם, מקום, זמן
44 שחיטה, קבלה, הולכה, זריקה
45 צריך הוצאה בפה
46 מחשבה בלבו
47 השולח יד בפקדון
48 עבד העבודה סתמא
49 חשב שלא לשמה

as slaughter for a different sacrifice,[50] it remained valid. According to this view, expressed by R. Yehoshua, any beasts slaughtered for a different sacrifice were still acceptable.[51] The Sages meant that, even after such improper *shehitah*, one could proceed to the rituals of "sprinkling the blood" and "burning the special parts on the altar",[52] and also eat those portions that were intended for consumption (*ha-ne'ekhalim*). Nevertheless, this offering was not regarded as one fulfilling the votary's sacrificial obligation (*Zev.* 2a and Rashi *ad loc.*).[53]

A different conclusion was, however, reached if the *shehitah* was meant for a wholly non-sacred purpose. Here improper slaughter did not invalidate the sacrifice, which was considered to fulfil the votary's obligation. The reason for this apparently strange ruling was that the votary had no other aim in view, such as a different type of sacrifice, i.e., he had not imbued the sacrifice with an extraneous sacrificial intention. The offering thus retained its original *kedushah*,[54] as if it had been designated for the required sacrifice, because the non-sanctified purpose intended[55] (*le-shem hullin*) did not clash with the ritual or its requirements.[56] In the case of the sanctified offering, however, any intention to perform a different sacrifice rendered it invalid.[57]

If the sacrifice was made with both a correct and an incorrect intention,[58] the effect of the latter negated that of the former (*Pes.* 60b.). Rava accordingly ruled (ibid.) that the intention of the latter (*she-lo li-shmo*) effectively neutralized that of the former (*li-shmo*).[59] Thus, if the *shehitah* of a particular sin-offering was intended by the priest to make atonement for

---

50　שנשחטו לשם קרבן אחר
51　שנזבחו שלא לשמה כשרים
52　הקטרת
53　שלא עלו לבעלים לשם חובה
54　אינה פוסלת
55　לשם חולין
56　עלה לשם לחובה
57　מחשבת שלא לשמו פוסלת
58　לשמה ולא לשמה
59　לשמה

the donor's offence and also to serve a different purpose,[60] the effect of *she-lo li-shmo* would cancel the fulfilment of *li-shmo*. This was not due to a lack of "holiness" (*kedushah*) in the sacrifice,[61] as it was sanctified in both cases, but because one wrong intention[62] ("thought") disqualified the offering.[63] Nevertheless, if the *kohen* performed *sheḥitah* for non-sanctified use (*le-shem ḥullin*), without introducing any foreign intention, the sacrifice would be deemed valid.

In the case of a sin-offering or guilt-offering, there is a special requirement which distinguishes them from the other sacrifices. It is specifically mentioned in the Torah: "The priest shall make atonement for him as concerning his sin that he hath sinned, and he shall be forgiven" (Lev. 4:35).[64] Accordingly, the sacrifice is effective only if it is brought for that particular offence (*Zev.* 46b; Maim. *Pesulei ha-Mukdashin*, 15:4).

A concrete example of this law's application is where a man and his son both took the vow of a Nazarite; when their period of *nezirut* ended, each was required to bring a sin-offering. If the father earmarked his sacrifice, but died before offering it, and the son inherited his father's property, he could not use his father's offering as his own, as it had been reserved for the father's obligation (*Naz.* 30b, Rashi *ad loc.*; Maim. *Nezirut*, 8:15).

A similar requirement applied to the paschal lamb (*korban Pesaḥ*), which had to be brought for that specific purpose and only for those individuals named as participants. This ruling was based on the Torah law, "Thou shalt sacrifice the Passover offering unto the Lord thy God" (Deut.16:2, 12:27), which the Sages interpreted to mean that all the rituals had to be performed for that specific purpose (*Zev.* 7b; Maim. *Pesulei ha-Mukdashin*, 15:11).[65]

---

60   שחיט לשמו ושלא לשמו
61   לקדושת קרבן
62   מחשבת שלא לשמו
63   מחשבתו שלא לשמה פוסלת את הקרבן
64   וכיפר עליו הכהן על חטאתו אשר חטא, ונסלח לו
65   שיהו כל עשיותיו לשם פסח

The halakhic regulation of the Mishnah states that "all sacrifices not slaughtered in their own name (*she-lo lishmah*) are valid". Thus, if the *kohen* slaughtered an animal as a burnt-offering while he had another designation in mind for it (e.g., a *ḥattat* sin-offering or a *shelamim* peace-offering), that sacrifice was still considered valid if its specified ritual requirements were performed correctly after *sheḥitah*.

Although the *sheḥitah* was considered faulty if it had not been performed for the offering specified or for its owner, the *korban* itself remained acceptable as a freewill-offering (*nedavah*). It was not accepted, however, to fulfil an individual's vow (*neder*), since a *neder* had to be fulfilled completely: "That which is expressed by thy lips thou shalt observe and do, according as thou hast vowed" (Deut. 23:24).[66] Thus, a person would only fulfil his vow if all the rituals were performed for the sake of that particular offering and the owner who brought it.[67]

A particular wrong intention in the performance of *sheḥitah* disqualified the offering, as it was not considered a fulfilment of the particular sacrifice. If, however, no particular "deviation" occurred during the sacrificial act, but all the ritual was performed without any specific intention in mind – neither for that particular sacrifice, nor for another specific offering (*setam*) nor even for non-sanctified consumption (*le-shem ḥullin*) – then the sacrifice would be accepted as fulfilling the requirements of the offering originally intended. Thus, if brought for the purpose of expiation (*le-khapparah*), it would effect the required atonement.[68]

In the case of a particular sacrifice, it had to be offered with a sixfold intention:[69]

1. For the particular sacrifice intended – *le-shem zevaḥ*;
2. For the individual who brought the sacrifice – *le-shem zove'aḥ*;

---

66 מוצא שפתיך תשמור ועשית
67 לשם עולה ולשם בעלים
68 ועלה לבעלים
69 לשם ששה דברים הזבח נזבח

3. As a sacrifice in honour of God – *le-shem Hashem*;
4. As a "fire offering" – *le-shem ishim* – i.e., to burn the special parts on the altar;
5. As "a sweet savour to the Lord" – *le-shem rei'ah*;
6. As a sacrifice "pleasing to God" – *le-shem niho'ah*.

These indivisible intentions were mandatory for an effective sin-offering or guilt-offering that was brought for a specific transgression (Lev. 4:3, 31).[70]

The element of intention in performing a sacrifice brings us to the standard of "holiness" (*kedushah*) required for the offering. Thus, the *kedushah* of "most holy" sacrifices (*kodshei kodashim*), i.e., *olah*, *hattat* and *asham*, exceeds that of "less holy" sacrifices (*kodshei kallim*).[71] The *kodshei kodashim* rituals had to be performed in their special place north of the altar. *Kodshei kallim* offerings had less restrictive laws and their rituals could be performed in any part of the Sanctuary (*Zev.* 47b, 55a; Maim. *Perush ha-Mishnayyot, Zev.* 5:1).

Shim'on, the brother of Azaryah, said: "If the intention in performing a sacrifice was for an offering of a higher standard, although a lower standard was required, the offering was acceptable,[72] but if the intention in performing a sacrifice was for one of a lower standard than that required, the offering was entirely invalid and not acceptable" (*Zev.* 2b, *Tos. ad loc.*, s. v. "*le-shem gavo'ah*").[73] The level of intention required for a lower grade of offering was accordingly not sufficient for one of a higher grade, and for that reason it was disqualified. Conversely, a higher level of intention would meet the requirement of a lower-grade offering.

That the offering had to be brought for that particular sacrifice, and for no other, requires further explanation. Since the votary brought his offering for a specific purpose, and that purpose (the sacrifice) conformed with all ritual requirements, how could any *li-shmo* or *she-lo li-shmo* intention of the priest

---

70   והקריב על חטאתו אשר חטא וכיפר עליו הכהן ונסלח לו
71   קודשי קלים, שלמים, בכור, מעשר, תודה
72   שחטן לשמו גבוהה מהן כשרה
73   לשם נמוך מהן פסולין

(see above) affect it? This law is particularly confusing, since if even a *ḥattat* sin-offering was sacrificed when the priest mistakenly believed that it was for non-sanctified use, that *korban* was deemed not only fit to eat (*kasher*) but also, in Rav's opinion, perfectly valid. This accorded with the ruling that an intended non-sanctified use would not invalidate an offering brought for sanctified use (*Zev.* 46b).[74]

According to the *Tosafot*, Rav determined that although the ritual had not been performed with the right intention (*she-lo li-shmo*), the sacrifice was fully valid and even met the requirement that it fulfil the donor's obligation.[75] R. Zeira held that such offerings were valid and effected atonement (*Zev.* 11b; *Tos., ibid.*, 2a, s.v. "*le-shem gavo'ah*").[76] Maimonides, however, disagreed with the view of the *Tosafot*. He ruled that the sin-offering, though not judged to be defiled, would not effect atonement for the donor (Maim. *Yad, Pesulei ha-Mukdashin,* 15:4).[77]

When a sacrifice was performed with a different one in mind (*she-lo li-shmo* or *le-shem korban aḥer*), a defect in the ritual invalidated the sacrifice. This occurred, for example, when a burnt-offering was intended as a peace-offering[78] or *vice versa*. However, a problem was created by this ruling, which apparently contradicted the law stating that if one offered a particular sacrifice but intended it for no sacred purpose[79] whatsover, it was nevertheless accepted as one fulfilling the obligation for which it had been brought.[80] Exceptions were only made in the case of the paschal offering (*zevaḥ Pesaḥ*) and the sin-offering (*Zev.* 46b, Rashi; Maim. *Pesulei ha-Mukdashin,* 15:3–4, 11).

---

74   אין חולין מחללין קודשים
75   עלו לבעליו
76   כשרין ומרצין
77   כשר ולא עלתה לבעליו
78   ששוחט עולה לשם שלמים
79   ששוחט לשם חולין
80   ועלו לבעלים לשם חובה

The Sages explained that a distinction must be made between intending the *korban* for a different sacrifice (*le-shem korban aher*) and intending it for non-sanctified consumption (*le-shem hullin*). In the former case, the priest officiating introduced a contrary intention and therefore disqualified the offering (*Zev.* 47a).[81] If no different sacrifice was intended, however, there having been no sanctified purpose[82] or special intention, no conflicting purpose would spoil the offering. Here the Sages pointed out that although the required sacrifice had not been performed, the offering itself was valid, since the mental purpose had not been directed to any sacrificial end. To avoid any mistake in intention, they recommended adopting a noncommittal attitude (*Zev.* 46b, Rashi *ad loc.*; Maim. *Yad*, *Pesulei ha-Mukdashin*, 15:4; *Tosef. Korbanot* 1:1).

We find this principle laid down in a further ruling of the Mishnah. If, in the course of the sacrificial ritual, one had opposing intentions – in one case right and in another case wrong (*li-shmo ve-she-lo li-shmo*) – or even if one sacrificed an *olah* as both a burnt-offering and a peace-offering (*shelamim*)[83], the whole offering was *pasul*, invalid (*Pes.* 59b; Maim. *Pesulei ha-Mukdashin*, 13:1 and *Kesef Mishneh*).

What disqualified the sacrifice here was a wrong act of the mind (*mahashavah*) itself.[84] This rule applied when one introduced an intention that related to a different sacrifice; but when one had no particular sacrifice in mind – i.e., if there was no contradictory thought – the sacrifice remained valid (Y. Abramsky, *Hazon Yehezkel, Tosef. Korbanot* 1:1).

In the case of *li-shmo ve-she-lo li-shmo* referred to above, it might appear that since, after all, the correct intention had been present, the sacrifice should be deemed correctly performed and fully valid, while the fact that there had been an extraneous intention could be ignored. Yet it was ruled that if the Passover offering had been sacrificed with a dual

---

81 שאין המחשבה הולכת אלא אחר העובד
82 אינה פוסלת משום דלאו מינה לא מחריב בה
83 לשם עולה ושלמים
84 מחשבתו שפוסלת את הקרבן

intention (i.e., both for *Pesah* and for *shelamim*), the sacrifice was disqualified (*Pes.* 59b).[85] Similarly, Maimonides ruled that one's actions here must be directed entirely to the *korban Pesah* (Maim. *Yad, Pesulei ha-Mukdashin*, 15:3).

Hence the explanation of this law is that the introduction of a contrary thought – an act of the mind, not the physical performance of the ritual – affected the sanctity of the offering and invalidated it. The foregoing account, illuminating the role of thought (*mahashavah*) in the sacrificial system, should make it easier to understand many of the detailed laws relating to sacrifices.

D. The Law of *Piggul* – an "Abominable Sacrifice"

The authorized priest must only have in mind only the appropriate thoughts as he performs the various rituals of sacrifice (*Zev.* 47a).[86] The Torah (Lev. 1:3) lays down that every person offering a sacrifice to God must bring it *li-retzono*. This requirement is explained by Shemuel (*Ar.* 21a), namely, that it must be offered with the knowledge and consent of the donor on whose behalf the offering is brought. The expression *li-retzono* is also interpreted to mean that all the laws of sacrifice must be observed (e.g., as in Lev. 1:3), so that it will be "acceptable" before God (RASHBAM *ad loc.*).

Leviticus 19:5–8 supplements the laws governing the appropriate thoughts that are required to ensure approval of the sacrifice. The Torah firstly teaches that the aim of a sacrifice is not to propitiate the Almighty, but to gain His approval for the donor's action (*Men.* 110a). Accordingly, "*you* shall offer" the sacrifice *li-retzonekhem,* i.e., in a manner that will ensure acceptance "for *you*".[87] Since the purpose of bringing

---

85 הפסח ששחטו לשמו שלא לשמו פסול – כיצד לשם פסח ולשם שלמים
86 שאין המחשבה הולכת אלא אחר העובד
87 עולה זריחת דעת שנאמר לרצונו

a votive offering is to gain Divine favour by this action, the whole sacrifice must be performed in accordance with the laws prescribed by God. A further law requires the votary to bring his own offering for the purpose of atonement or thanksgiving. This requirement is already manifest in Noah's actions prior to the Flood. When Noah was ordered to bring two of every living creature into the ark, God told him that "they will come of their own accord"; but the number of clean animals was greater (seven), and from these Noah would make sacrifices to God when emerging from the ark. He also had to bring them in person (Gen. 6:20, RAMBAN *ad loc.*).

A sacrifice is rejected if it is defiled by some improper intention on the part of the officiating priest, i.e., an intention that conflicts with the procedure laid down for such a sacrifice, so that the offering becomes distasteful and offensive to God, a corruption of Divine worship. The service is invalid and heavenly punishment may be incurred.

Some of the Torah's sacrificial laws are itemized in Leviticus (7:12 *ff.*).[88] The flesh of the offering may only be eaten on the day of the sacrifice or the following day, and anything left over until the third day must be burnt (v. 17); if it is eaten on the third day, the priest's sacrifice of that offering is not acceptable to the Lord.[89] Furthermore, any thought that entered his mind (while he performed the ritual) of eating it on the third day would disqualify the offering and render it *piggul* – defiled and abominable. In short, while the *kohen* performed all four sacrificial rites correctly, an inappropriate thought that entered his mind when he did so invalidated the whole procedure.

One of these wrongful thoughts or intentions[90] was particularly serious. Nor only did it invalidate the sacrifice, but anyone who ate even an olive-size portion (*ke-zayit*) of that offering would incur the penalty of "excision" (*karet*).

---

88   וזאת תורת זבח השלמים אשר יקריב לה׳

89   לא ירצה המקריב אותו

90   מחשבת הזמן

This law applied when, in the act of slaughtering an animal, the officiating priest intended one of the subsequent ritual acts to be performed at an incorrect time. Thus, if the *kohen* had it in mind to perform the "sprinkling of blood" (*zerikah*) after sunset, although sunset was the appointed deadline, or to undertake the "burning" (*haktarah*) after sunrise, which was too late, the meat of such an unfitting sacrifice would be *piggul* and forbidden.

Where the priest's wrongful intention alluded to "burning" a *ke-zayit* on the altar at the wrong time, and he then performed subsequent acts of the ritual or ate a *ka-zayit* of the sacrifice at the wrong time[91] as well, that offering would be considered *piggul*. If, furthermore, he ate such *piggul*, he would incur the penalty of "excision". Both human consumption of the forbidden sacrifice and the altar's consumption of it by fire were termed "eating" – *akhilah* (Lev. 7:18, 9:24, 19:8; Mish., *Zev.* 2:2–3; *Zev.* 27b–29b; Maim. *Pesulei ha-Mukdashin*, 13:1).

Maimonides affirmed that the Torah's use of the verb *yehashev* ("will be imputed") when enunciating the rigorous law of *piggul* indicates an act of the mind. The verse in question reads: "If any flesh of the sacrifice of his peace-offerings be eaten on the third day, it shall not be accepted, neither shall it be imputed unto him that offereth it; it shall be an abhorred thing [*piggul*], and the soul that eateth of it shall bear his iniquity [i.e., *karet*]" (Lev. 7:18).[92]

The Mishnah laid down that while all the essential acts of sacrifice had to be performed by a *kohen*, the actual slaughter (*shehitah*) might be undertaken by any capable person who was not a *kohen* – always provided that, if ritually unclean (*tamei*), he did not transmit his "uncleanness" by touching the sacrifice. Despite this authorization, if some wrong thought entered the slaughterer's mind in regard to the ensuing ritual, the offering was invalid (*pasul*). What made it unacceptable

---

91 חוץ לזמנו
92 לא יחשב לו, פיגול יהיה

was not his non-priestly *shehitah*, but his "inappropriate thought" or wrongful intention (*Zev.* 3:1).[93]

As mentioned previously, the Mishnah states that every sacrifice should be offered with a sixfold intention – for the particular sacrifice; for the individual bringing it; as a sacrifice honouring God; as a "fire-offering"; as "a sweet savour to the Lord"; and as a sacrifice "pleasing to God". Furthermore, a sin-offering and a guilt-offering must only be brought for the specified transgression. R. Yose ruled, nevertheless, that even if the officiating priest had none of these intentions in mind, the sacrifice remained valid (*kasher*). Moreover, if the donor himself had these intentions in mind and the priest conducted the whole ritual with no particular dedication (*setam*), but also without any conflicting intention, the offering was still valid.

The Sages of the *bet din* enunciated a basic principle[94] that all the requirements of intention applied only to what was in the officiating priest's mind.[95] Thus, even if the donor had all the correct intentions, the offering's ultimate validity depended on what the *kohen* had in mind. The accepted view of the Sages conformed with R. Yose's teaching (Mish., *Zev.* 4:6). This rule likewise applied when a wrong intention accompanying the sacrifice led to the *piggul* disqualification *(q.v.)*. Here, too, it was not the donor but the priest who gave rise to the *piggul*, in accordance with the principle laid down by the Sages (Mish., *Hul.* 2:7).[96]

A further complication discussed by the Sages was that of the priest having two wrong thoughts in mind, one after the other. He meant to eat the sacrifice in the wrong *place*, which rendered the offering *pasul*, and to eat it at the wrong *time*, thus making him subject to the law of *piggul* and the penalty of *karet*. According to which law was the offering to be judged?

---

93 לפיכך הן פוסלין במחשבה... השחיטה כשרה בזרים

94 תנאי בית דין

95 אין המחשבה הולכת אלא אחר העובד

96 הבעלים מפגלין

R. Yehudah ruled that the decision depended on the order in which the wrong intentions occurred. If the defect of "time" preceded that of "place", the full law of *piggul* applied. If the defect of "place" preceded that of "time", the offering was simply disqualified and the law of *piggul* (incurring the liability of *karet*) would not apply. The reasoning behind this law was that *piggul* only affected an offering that would otherwise be acceptable; as it had already become invalid, the law of *piggul* did not apply. However, since the *piggul* disqualification had arisen first, an extra blemish would not alter the penalty.

The Sages objected to R. Yehudah's ruling. They maintained that if the offering had been flawed by both wrong intentions, in either order, it was simply disqualified (*pasul*) and the law of *piggul* did not apply. *Piggul* would only be applicable if, in all other respects, the animal was *kasher* but another flaw disqualified it (*Zev.* 29b; Maim. *Perush Mishnayyot, ad loc.*; Maim. *Yad, Pesulei ha-Mukdashin*, 16:1–2).

The *Tosafot* disagreed with the assertion by Maimonides that *piggul* arose from an "inappropriate thought" in the priest's mind. They held that it only took effect when thoughts that he expressed verbally were overheard by witnesses, i.e., for the *kohen* to be guilty of a transgression required some action on his part of which there was first-hand evidence. The *Tosafot* based their view on the law of the "unpaid bailee"[97] (*shomer ḥinnam*). This stated that if a person was entrusted with the care of another man's goods, the bailee became responsible for any loss due to negligence. If the goods held in trust were stolen from him, the bailee had to declare on oath before the court that he had neither appropriated the goods entrusted to him nor failed to take reasonable care of them; he would then be free of liability (Ex. 22:6–8). Similarly, were a "paid bailee" (*shomer sakhar*) to claim that the goods deposited with him had been stolen or accidentally damaged, he could only escape liability by testifying that he had exercised all due care in protecting them (Ex. 22:9–12).[98]

---

97 שומר חינם
98 אם לא שלח ידו במלאכת רעהו

This view of the *Tosafot* requires further elucidation. In their development of the bailment law, the Mishnaic Sages pointed out that in a case where the bailee made up his mind to appropriate the goods entrusted to him, there was a difference of opinion between the Schools of Hillel and Shammai.[99] The Sages ruled in accordance with the view of Bet Hillel: the bailee would not be liable to pay compensation until he had actually appropriated them[100] "lifting" – the goods from their place signified acquisition.[101]

Bet Shammai, however, ruled that by even intending to appropriate the goods deposited with him, the bailee was immediately held culpable of violating his trust, as stated in the Torah: *al-kol-devar-pesha*, "for all manner of trespass" (Ex. 22:8; *BM* 43b). In interpreting the view of Shammai, the *Tosafot* (*ad loc.*, s.v. "*ha-ḥoshev*") explained that he would have required some positive action for liability to be incurred. The expression *ha-ḥoshev* ("having in mind") meant that the bailee actually stated his intention in the presence of witnesses.[102]

As the accompanying Gemara (ibid.) indicates, Bet Shammai taught that liability was incurred by intention, which was no less an offence than an act of appropriation.[103] Rashi (*ad loc.*) likewise explained that the bailee had declared before witnesses that he meant to appropriate the deposit, although he had not yet done so.[104] However, there is some lack of clarity in this explanation, since Rashi interpreted the Shammai school's view elsewhere as indicating that by either expressing his intention or merely giving it consideration, the bailee would be held liable (*Kid.* 42b; see note of BAḤ on *BM* 43b).[105]

---

99   החושב לשלוח יד בפיקדון
100   אינו חייב עד שישלח בו יד
101   קנין במשיכה
102   הך מחשבה הוי דיבור
103   על כל דבר פשע בית שמאי אומרים לחייב על המחשבה כמעשה ובית הלל אומרים אינו חייב עד שישלח בו יד
104   אמר בפני עדים
105   לחייב על המחשבה או על הדיבור

Commenting on the Gemara (*BM* 43b, s.v. "*ha-ḥoshev*"), the *Tosafot* declared that use of the word *ha-ḥoshev* in the bailment law meant that the bailee "had it in mind" and expressed his intention.[106] The same rule applied in the matter of *piggul*, where any intention to make improper use of the sacrifice had to be expressed; it did not mean that the priest just thought of doing so, as this would not suffice to incur liability.[107]

Maimonides, however, differentiated between the two situations. In the case of bailment, he ruled (like Bet Hillel) that Torah law required an act of appropriation. If the bailee only thought of appropriating the goods, but never actually did so, he would not be liable to pay compensation for any loss (Maim. *Yad, Gezelah ve-Avedah*, 3:11). It is therefore apparent that Maimonides drew a distinction between financial claims (*dinei mammonot*), where an act had to be witnessed to incur liability, and spiritual transgressions, where a wrong intention in someone's mind was enough to vitiate an object's sanctity – as in the case of *piggul*.

R. Ḥayyim ibn Attar (1696–1743), in his *Or ha-Ḥayyim* Pentateuch commentary (Lev. 19:8), finds it necessary to explain the apparent severity of the *piggul* law and the penalty that it incurs. Why, he asks, should the Torah decree such punishment if the officiating priest wishes to continue eating the sacrifice on the third day? Why is this a graver offence than eating *nevelah* and *terefah* (Lev. 22:8) or reptiles and invertebrates (Lev. 11:41–43)?

The *Or ha-Ḥayyim*'s esoteric explanation is that whereas sanctified objects possess a vast degree of holiness, the sanctity of an offering has a time limit defined in the Torah. Once that time has elapsed, the offering's sanctity departs and gives way to the power of *tum'ah* (impurity or defilement), which overcomes anyone who partakes of the offering and whose soul is then condemned to "excision" (*karet*). This sanction

---

106　הך המחשבה הוי דיבור
107　בדיבור ולא בלב

does not apply in the case of *nevelah* and *terefah*, which are subject to an ordinary prohibition. The defilement that they cause does not incur the severe penalty of *karet*; it is cleansed by a dose of "lashes" (*malkot*). However, by transgressing the *piggul* law, the *kohen* defiles something "holy to the Lord"[108] and it is thus fitting that "his soul shall be cut off from his people".

A simpler interpretation of this law may be found in the commentary of R. Naftali Tzevi Yehudah Berlin (1817–1893; *Ha-Amek Davar*, Lev. 19:8), who endeavours to explain how and why the *kohen*'s offence "profaned the hallowed thing of the Lord". Eating any part of the offering after the time limit was not in fulfilment of God's command, but merely a way of satisfying the priest's desire to eat meat. Once the proper time had elapsed, this meat became loathsome (*piggul*) in the sight of God, yet the priest was still intent on consuming it for his own enjoyment.[109] The purpose of the votive "peace-offering" (*shelamim*) was to attain a mystical communion with God, but the *kohen* abused that privilege by defiling what should be kept sacred to Him.[110]

Rabbi Berlin's interpretation of *piggul* reflects, to some extent, the much earlier view of RAVAD, who had discussed the question as to whether, by his act of *mefaggel*, the priest was liable to compensate the donor of the sacrifice for his financial loss as a result of his offering's disqualification (Lev. 7:17–18).[111] That wasted effort compelled the donor to bring a replacement sacrifice in order to fulfil his vow.

Maimonides (*Yad, Hovel u-Mazzik*, 7:4) ruled that "priests who wilfully profane the sacrifice by their act of *piggul* are obliged to pay compensation for the loss of the animal, but if this occurred unintentionally they are exempt". His ruling is based on the plain statement of the Mishnah (*Git.* 54b), which gave rise to a discussion (*Git.* 53a) in which R. Yoḥanan

---

108   כי את קדש ה׳ חלל
109   רק להנות
110   כי קדש ה׳ חלל
111   לא יחשב לו

affirmed that, strictly speaking, any damage that could not be ascertained physically[112] – such as an act of "defilement" – did not fall under the category of a tort. If, however, the damage was done wilfully, financial liability was imposed as a safeguard against wanton destructiveness.[113]

RAVAD, who claimed that Maimonides was mistaken, found that in the case of *piggul* (as distinct from that of *metamei*), even when the act was accepted as a tort, the priest would not be liable for damages. His intention had only been to satisfy his craving for meat, not to inflict any loss on the worshipper. Naḥmanides concurred with RAVAD's opinion (*Maggid Mishneh ad loc.*).

E. The Red Heifer – *Parah Adumah*

According to the law of the Red Heifer, a cow that was three or four years old, entirely red, unblemished and never employed as a draught animal, should be slaughtered outside the entrance of the Temple and then burnt to ashes. Its ashes were mingled with water and this mixture was sprinkled on a person who needed cleansing from defilement by a corpse (Num. 19:2*ff*.). The strictest laws applied to choosing an animal for this special ritual. However, whereas in the normal course of animal sacrifices even the slightest departure from the ordained ritual would disqualify the offering, in the case of the *parah adumah* many small infringements could be overlooked.

Normally, as we have seen, an inappropriate intention disqualified the sacrifice and so, if the officiating *kohen* meant to perform the sacrifice at the wrong time or in the wrong place, it was rejected as *piggul* and the meat was forbidden (Lev. 7:18). Such would be the law in regard to a sin-offering,

---

112 היזק שאינו ניכר
113 מפני תיקון העולם

with which the Sages compared the law of the Red Heifer (Num. 19:17 and *Sifrei*, ibid.). Any departure in matters of intention or procedure invalidated the sacrifice.

R. Eliezer, however, taught that the law of the Red Heifer was distinct from that of the sanctified offering. All *korbanot* had to be sacrificed inside the Temple, whereas the Red Heifer was slaughtered outside, and the strict ritual of Temple sacrifices was therefore not applicable (Maim. *Shehitah*, 2:1; *Parah* 4:1, ROSH *ad loc.*). Accordingly, a forbidden intention in the priest's mind did not invalidate the Red Heifer. Thus, even if, when slaughtering the animal, he intended to eat its flesh (which was, of course, forbidden) rather than burn it, the sacrifice was not disqualified, assuming that all the prescribed rituals had been followed. In the opinion of R. Eliezer, there was only one essential requirement: that the *parah adumah* be completely burnt and reduced to ashes. If that requirement was met, anything else that the priest might have had in mind was of no significance (*Parah* 4:3).[114] Maimonides adopted R. Eliezer's view in his Code (Maim. *Parah Adummah*, 4:3).

F. Slaughter of a Beast for Idol Worship

If an animal was slaughtered to provide blood for use in idol worship, the accepted ruling of R. Yohanan was that such an act made the whole animal forbidden.[115] If, however, the beast was not slaughtered for the purpose of idolatry but for the use of an idolater, and with no heathen intent on the slaughterer's part, would the idolater's own thoughts render the animal forbidden? Resh Lakish declared such animals permitted, as their *shehitah* was not in itself a religious act but a preparation for the religious service and the idolater's thoughts were not transferred to the animal. This interpretation of the law

---

114   אין מחשבה פוסלת בפרה
115   השוחט את הבהמה לזרוק דמה לע״א ר׳ יוחנן אמר פסולה

was adopted as a general rule: If one slaughters a beast for a heathen, even if that heathen contemplates using it for idol worship, the *shehitah* performed correctly by a qualified slaughterer renders the meat fit for Jewish consumption (*Hul.* 38b; *Sh. Ar., Yoreh De'ah* 4:3; *Zev.* 47a).[116]

G. Summary of the Laws Governing Intention

Maimonides, in his Code, sets forth the laws governing "appropriate thoughts and intentions" when a sacrifice is performed (*Yad, Pesulei ha-Mukdashin*, chaps. 13–18):

1. Sacrifices are disqualified by an inappropriate thought in three respects: (a) By using a wrong designation, e.g., interchanging *olah* and *shelamim*, or by changing the donor's name; (b) by intending to perform one of the rituals in a place other than that assigned to it in the Torah; and (c) by intending to partake of the offering, or have it burnt on the altar, after the specified time limit. A wrong thought in all three cases will invalidate the offering in any of the four rituals of *shehitah, kabbalah, holakhah* and *zerikah* (*Yad*, ibid., 13:14).

2. The law concerning a wrong thought applies only to the *kohen* who performs the sacrifice, not to the individual who brings it (14:1).

3. Any of the wrong thoughts listed above will invalidate the offering, rendering it *pasul*; but a wrong intention as regards the time set for its consumption will render it *piggul* and incur the penalty of "excision" (16:1).

4. In the case of both *pasul* and *piggul*, a transgression only occurs if one intends to eat at least an olive-size amount (*ke-zayit*) of the offering at the wrong time or in the wrong place (16:2).

---

116 השוחט לכותי שחיטתו כשרה ור' אליעזר פוסל אמר ר' יוסי... הכל הולך אלא אחר השוחט

5. The law of *piggul* only applies to the wrong intention involved in an act that is an essential part of the sacrifice, and which is followed by another completing it (16:4).
6. Any person guilty of a wrong thought that disqualifies sanctified offerings has violated a Torah prohibition (*lo ta'aseh*). It is, however, accepted that a wrong thought does not in itself incur the penalty of lashes (*malkot*), since it is an act of the mind in which no physical action is involved. Nevertheless, if someone deliberately eats an olive-size portion of a defiled offering, he incurs the penalty of lashes (*malkot*). If the *piggul* offence is involved, wilfully eating a *ke-zayit* incurs the more severe penalty of *karet* (18:1–6). The same rule applies to the eating of *notar* ("leftovers"), i.e., meat of an offering for which the lawful period of consumption has elapsed (18:10).
7. The laws of *piggul*, *notar* and *tamei* do not apply in the case of offerings brought by heathens, since a pagan's religious outlook is naturally defective and his thoughts have no effect on the sphere of holiness (18:24).

H. Note on the Priestly Gift (*Terumah*) and Tithe (*Ma'aser*)

The Jew's obligation to offer the *kohen* a proportional gift of his crops (*terumah*) and tithes (*ma'aser*) originally related to produce grown only in the Land of Israel. Later, however, the duty to set these offerings aside was extended to Jews living in neighbouring countries, even after the Temple's destruction (Num. 18:8 *ff*., 21 *ff*.; *Sifrei*, Mish., *Yad.* 4:3; Maim. *Terumot*, 1:1; *Sh. Ar.*, *Yoreh De'ah* 331:1, 19, REMA).

If, when buying such produce, a man intended to eat it, the *terumah u-ma'aser* duty obligated him as soon as he paid for it, but not before – even when he had already made up his mind to purchase it and was choosing whatever he required.

The Sages nevertheless ruled that a pious Jew should hand over the tithe as soon as he decided to buy the produce (*BB* 88a; Maim. *Ma'aser*, 5:1).[117]

I. Summation of Sacrificial Service

Chief Rabbi Dr. J.H. Hertz in his excursus on "The Sacrificial Cult" in his *Pentateuch* (p.562) described the sacrificial institutions as an integral part of revealed religion, having the obligation of statutory law. "Sacrifices are the symbols of man's gratitude to God and his dependence on Him; of the absolute devotion man owes to God, as well as man's confidence in Him" (D. Hoffman).

The sacrificial system was advocated by Ibn Ezra, and to some extent by Naḥmanides. Its essence was described as follows: As a sinner, the offender's life was forfeit to God; but, by a gracious provision, he was permitted to substitute an animal victim to which his guilt was, as it were, transferred by the imposition of hands.

Maimonides declared that the sacrificial cult was ordained as an accommodation to the conceptions of a primitive people, and for the purpose of weaning them away from the debased religious rites of their idolatrous neighbours. The manner of worship in use among the peoples of antiquity was retained, but the worship was now directed towards the One and Holy God. "By this Divine plan idolatry was eradicated, and the vital principle of our Faith, the existence and unity of God, was firmly established". Abarbanel supported the view of Maimonides, that the Hebrews had become accustomed to idolatrous sacrifices while in Egypt, and the Almighty wished to wean them from idolatry, tolerating the sacrifices, but commanding that they be limited to one central sanctuary.

---

117 גמר בלבו לקנותו קנה ונתחייב במעשר... אמר רב הושעיא הכא בירא שמים עסקינן

This view was illustrated in a Midrashic parable of R. Levi, of a king who acted similarly in order to induce the prince from his habit of eating forbidden food (Lev. R. 22:5).

Whether any of these laws of the Torah will ever be abrogated we do not know; but we are sure that in the case of such abrogation taking place it will be done by a revelation as convincing as that on Mount Sinai. Likewise, their revival must be sanctioned by the divine voice of a Prophet. Sacrifices must be preceded by purification of the heart and by earnest resolve to obey the word of God, otherwise they constitute, as the prophets declared, "an increase of sin". The Sages taught that it was because of our sins that we have been deprived of our Temple; the rebuilding of the Temple and the possible restoration of the Sacrificial Service would be the result of our own purification (M. Friedländer, *The Jewish Religion*, third edition, London, 1927, pp. 162, 417). The Musaf Amidah prayer on the Festivals includes the statement that "it was because of our sins that we were exiled from our land – *umipenei hata'einu galienu mei'artzeinu* – and we are now unable to ascend the Temple and fulfil our obligations in Thy chosen house" (Ezra 9:7) (J.H. Hertz *The Pentateuch*, Soncino, London 1938, p. 560 *ff.*, 486).

With the cessation of sacrifices, study of the Torah, Prayer and Beneficence take the place of the Temple Service (*Men.* 110a). Only the feeling of gratitude to God would remain. The Sages said: "In the Messianic era, all offerings will cease, except the thanksgiving offering, which will continue forever" (Lev. R. 9:7).[118] Whereas all the sacrifices were offered because of some transgression, with the exception of the thanksgiving offering which was brought without having committed any sin (Midrash, *Lekah Tov*, Lev. 44; R. Tobias ben Eliezer, 11th cent., ed. S. Buber 1884).

[General reference: *Encyclopaedia Judaica,* Vol. 14, s.v. "Sacrifice"]

---

118   לעתיד לבא כל הקרבנות בטלים וקרבן תודה אינו בטל

Chapter 7

The Sabbath - *Shabbat*

7 *The Sabbath* - Shabbat

A. Introduction

The Concept of the Sabbath

The Sabbath, as a day of rest, was uniquely bestowed on the people of Israel. The Sages declared that God told the lawgiver: "Moses, I have a precious gift in my treasury, it is called *Shabbat*, and I wish to give it to Israel. Go and tell them" (*Betzah* 16a).[1] They also recounted His assurance to Israel: "If you keep the Sabbath, I will consider your merit on a par with observing all the laws of the Torah" (Ex. R. 25:16).

The Sabbath gives man the opportunity to follow the example set by his Creator, who laboured six days to create the world and then ceased work on the seventh day, which He blessed and declared holy (Gen. 2:3). The Sabbath is identified with the seventh day of Creation (Ex. 20:8–11). On this "solemn rest – *shabbaton*, a holy Sabbath to the Lord" (Ex. 16:23; 31:14–15),[2] the Israelites were ordered to abstain from all work, in honour of the Creator and as a mark of devotion to His service. It was likewise forbidden to gather the daily portion of manna in the wilderness, and the Israelites therefore received a double portion in advance, on the sixth day (Ex. 16:22; Ex. 31:13–17).

Freedom from work on the Sabbath day enables man to devote himself to Torah study, thus gaining spiritual refreshment and improving his character. The Sages taught that if God, whose work of Creation demanded no physical effort, thought it wise to rest after six days, how much wiser is

---

1   מתנה טובה יש לי בבית גנזי ושבת שמה
2   שבת לה׳ אל-היך

it for man, who was "born to toil"! (Job 5:7; *Midrash Mekhilta, Yitro* 20:11).[3]

In the view of the Sages, "keeping the Sabbath holy" is equal in importance to observing all of the commandments (TJ *Ber.* 1:5; Ex. R. 25:16; *Midrash Tanḥuma, Ki Tissa* 33).[4] They backed this statement with quotations from the Torah, Prophets and Writings (TJ *Ned.* 3:9). Sabbath observance demonstrates a fundamental belief in God's creation of the universe.[5] The commandment to observe the Sabbath was given in the first Tablet of the Law, which proclaims man's faith in the Unity of God, whereas the laws protecting social order were given in the second Tablet.

Enjoying a complete rest from work on the Sabbath is also a mark of human dignity. No master has us at his beck and call: far from being slaves, as we were in Egypt, we are the free men that God wishes us to be, people who can stop working when we choose to do so (Deut. 5:15).[6] This weekly day of rest should also be granted to our servant, to the stranger and even to the beast of burden, whose needs must be appreciated no less than our own (Deut. 5:14 –15, Ibn Ezra *ad loc.*; Maim. *Guide* (*Moreh Nevukhim*), Part 2, Chap. 31).

Maimonides affirmed the Sabbath's twofold significance: it proclaims that God created the world and it provides man with physical rest and spiritual refreshment. The Torah states that in observing the Sabbath day of rest Israel should recall that God liberated them from perpetual servitude in Egypt, where they were not free to decide when to work and when to rest. Through the Sabbath, however, Israel gained emancipation and sanctified the Name of God (Deut. 5:12–15; Maimonides, *ibid.*).

The Sages described the Sabbath as a precious gift bestowed on Israel, for by hallowing every seventh day as one free from all material pursuits Israel enjoys a

---

3   כי אדם לעמל יולד

4   שקולה שבת כנגד כל המצוות

5   חידוש העולם על ידי הקדוש ברוך הוא

6   וזכרת כי עבד היית בארץ מצרים

foretaste of eternal bliss in the World to Come, which is envisioned as one unending Sabbath (*Tam.* 6:4; *Ber.* 57b).[7] Yehudah Halevi, recording an exposition of Judaism to the king of the Khazars, asserted that the wonderful benefit which Jews gain for a seventh part of their lives is denied even to great rulers, who cannot escape from their daily tasks and concerns (*Kuzari* 3:10).

In life's struggle different people achieve different results, but the Sabbath makes everyone rich. The spirit of *Shabbat* fills the home and even the poorest dwelling is transfigured; all are equal and at peace. The Sabbath is a visible sign of God's "perpetual covenant" with Israel, and keeping it is the hallmark of Jewishness.

It is noteworthy that the Decalogue instituted the Sabbath with a command: "Six days shalt thou labour, and do all thy work". This teaches us that "work during the six days of the week is as essential to man's welfare as is rest on the seventh" (J. H. Hertz, *Pentateuch*, on Ex. 20:9). According to Rabbi Samson Raphael Hirsch, the law forbidding productive activity (*melakhah*) on the Sabbath acknowledges God as the Creator of all that exists. Man, who engages in his work for six days of the week, restores the world to God on every seventh day (Hirsch, *Horeb*, 2:21, trans. I. Grunfeld, pp. 61–78).

A noted Jewish essayist, outlining the Sabbath's key role in Jewish life, wrote: "It is impossible to describe to those who have not experienced it, the feeling of holy joy which is diffused throughout the humblest Hebrew home by the solemn repetition of acts which, in themselves, may be regarded as mere customs. The particular institution in which it is embodied most is that of the Sabbath. It is indeed to the Sabbath primarily, and the other home ceremonials, which embody the Hebraic conception of the holiness of the home, that we can trace the remarkable persistence of the Jewish race through the ages" (Joseph Jacobs, *Jewish Ideals*, London, 1896, p. 13).

Rudolf Kittel, a German Protestant Bible scholar, evaluated Israel's unique religious expression in hallowing the Sabbath as follows: "Anyone who has had the opportunity of knowing in our own day the inner life of Jewish families that observe the law of their fathers with sincere piety and in all strictness will have been astonished at the wealth of joyfulness, gratitude and sunshine, undreamt of by the outsider, which the law animates in the Jewish home". The Sabbath is, as the Rabbis described it (*Shab.* 118b), "a joy of the soul" welling up from "pure and genuine happiness" (quoted by J. H. Hertz, *Pentateuch*, on Ex. 20:11). R. Yehoshua once told a Roman emperor, who enquired about the special flavour of Sabbath dishes, that only those who observe the Sabbath can appreciate its uniqueness (*Shab.* 119a).

Ahad Ha-Am (Asher Ginzberg), the modern Hebrew writer and Zionist philosopher, declared that very idea of Jewish existence throughout the ages without the "Sabbath Queen" was unthinkable: "Far more than Israel kept the Sabbath, the Sabbath has kept Israel" (Ahad Ha'am, *Al Parashat Derakhim*, Berlin, 1920). According to the Rabbis, God lends man an "additional soul"[8] on Friday night which He withdraws at the Sabbath's termination (*Betzah* 16a).

An early Boraita quotes R. Yosi bar Yehuda saying: "Two Ministering Angels, one seeking good and the other seeking bad, accompany a man on his return from the evening prayers on Friday night. On their arrival the good angel blesses the sanctity, joy and serenity that he finds in his home. But if there is discord and lack of Sabbath sanctity the evil angel prays that so may it continue in weeks to come (*Shab.* 119b).[9]

These angels are messengers of the Almighty, and it is customary for the family to greet them with a blessing, and we pray that the "additional soul" which accompanies them

---

8   נשמה יתירה
9   שני מלאכי השרת מלווין לו לאדם בערב שבת מבית הכנסת לביתו

will find only peace in the home throughout the Sabbath day, and leave in peace (*Siddur Yavetz*, Sabbath eve service).[10]

The Sabbath Lights

Before its commencement, the Sabbath is welcomed by kindling two lamps or candles that illuminate the Jewish home. These lights represent the twin terms used in the Decalogue: "*Remember* the Sabbath day" (Ex. 20:8)[11] and "*Observe* the Sabbath day" (Deut. 5:12[12]; *Sh. Ar., Orah Hayyim* 263:1, *Kol Bo*, s. 24).

The Sages differed as to the type of oil that may be used for this purpose. R. Yishmael ben Elisha said that all oils are permissible, but not a flame derived from pitch or tar, as the bad smell that they exude would disturb the Sabbath's joyfulness (Maim. *Shabbat*, 5:10).[13] R. Tarfon maintained that one should only use sweet-smelling olive oil, which produces a clear and steady flame,[14] but the Sages ruled that because there was no choice of oil in some localities, the *mitzvah* could be fulfilled by using any oil, even that made from pitch or tar.

It is worth noting that R. Yishmael, a scrupulously observant high priest, took great care over actions performed on the Sabbath. R. Tarfon, a very rich man, cultivated numerous vineyards and olive trees (*Kallah Rabbati*, Chap. 2; Lev. R. 34:16; *Shab.* 25b). The Sages, however, kept the average man's needs in mind and their ruling enabled every Jew to fulfil his obligation (*Shab.* 24b, 26a; *Orah Hayyim* 264:6).

[General References: M. Friedländer, *The Jewish Religion*, London, 1927, pp. 339–360; S. R. Hirsch, *Essays on Jewish Life and Thought: The Jewish Sabbath*, reprinted in *Judaism Eternal* by I. Grunfeld, Soncino Press, London, 1956, Vol. 2,

---

10 שלום עליכם מלאכי השרת מלאכי עליון
11 זכור
12 שמור
13 אין מדליקין בעטרן מפני כבוד השבת
14 אין מדליקין אלא בשמן זית בלבד

pp. 3–4; J. H. Hertz, *The Pentateuch*, Soncino Press, London, 1938, pp. 297–298]

Prohibition of Work – Melakhah

Only a few instances of work forbidden on the Sabbath are given in the Bible. The prohibition of cooking and baking is mentioned with respect to collecting the manna;[15] and an Israelite was also forbidden to "go out of his place on the seventh day" (Ex. 16:23, 29), i.e., beyond a certain distance.[16] Other laws prohibited kindling fire (Ex. 35:3)[17] and gathering firewood (Num. 15:32)[18] on the Sabbath.

The prophet Amos rebuked those artful traders who could scarcely wait for the Sabbath to end so that they might open their stores of grain and sell wheat, fleecing needy customers (Amos 8:4–6).[19] The Sages believed that the Torah's most detailed list of forbidden work appeared in its account of the Tabernacle's construction and sacrificial services. Even while engaged in this most sacred task, the Israelites were ordered to abstain from all work on the Sabbath day (Ex. 31:13).[20]

S. R. Hirsch maintained that "the laws concerning the prohibition of work on the Sabbath, *melakhah*, are as comprehensive as the entire activity of man" (*Horeb*, trans. I. Grunfeld, Vol. 1, p. 64). A tannaitic statement recognized that many laws governing the Sabbath had no explicit basis in the written Torah, but were inferred by the Sages from the original instructions of the Pentateuch. They admitted that the profusion of these laws was like "mountains hanging on a hair",[21] but still considered them to be as holy as those

---

איסור בישול	15
תחום שבת	16
לא תבערו אש	17
מקושש עצים	18
איסור פרגמטיא	19
אך את שבתותי תשמורו	20
כהרים התלויים בשערה	21

possessing a clear-cut Torah sanction (*Ḥag.* 10a–b, Rashi *ad loc.*).

As defined by the Oral Law, work forbidden on the Sabbath is not merely some task requiring physical exertion, but any purposeful "creative labour", even requiring the lightest effort (Maim. *Shabbat*, 1:1–9).[22] The Torah law applies when man uses his technical skills in a bid to master the world, for he must submit to God Himself, the sovereign Creator.

Certain *mitzvot* supersede the prohibition of work and override the Sabbath laws. They include circumcising a male child when it is eight days old (*berit milah*), irrespective of the actual day of the week; offering the daily and Sabbath sacrifices in the Temple; and doing whatever may be necessary to save a person's life (*pikku'aḥ nefesh*). However, apart from these special laws, no *mitzvot* can take precedence over Sabbath regulations (*Shab.* 132a; 133a; *Yoma* 85a; Mekhilta, *Ki Tissa* 103b).

If obeying the injunction to honour one's parents entailed a violation of the Sabbath, this was clearly forbidden. The sacred task of building the *mishkan* (Sanctuary) was also limited to the working week. In both instances the Torah ordained a two-part composite law: "Ye shall fear every man his mother and his father, and ye shall keep my Sabbaths: I am the Lord your God" (Lev. 19:3; *Yev.* 6a; Maim. *Bet ha-Bekhirah*, 1:12). Likewise, "Ye shall keep My Sabbaths, and reverence My Sanctuary: I am the Lord" (Lev. 19:30). In other words, filial piety and building the *mishkan* did not override Sabbath observance.[23]

Since productive work is only inspired by an individual's consciousness, the law excludes any work performed unconsciously (Maim. *Shabbat*, 1:11).[24] Liability for any transgression of the law would likewise require an intention to achieve the productive end (ibid., 1:8).[25] A number of

---

22 מלאכת מחשבת אסרה תורה
23 בניין בית המקדש אינו דוחה את השבת
24 מתעסק
25 כונה

Sages also held that the individual's activity should effect a direct change in the product itself rather than a secondary, unassociated result.[26] Other Sages, however, included such activity in the prohibition of work. The Rabbinic codifiers were similarly divided on this issue, although they generally prohibited an action that would inevitably result in forbidden work (*Shab.* 29b, 141b, 103a; Maim. *Shabbat*, 1:6–7; *Kesef Mishneh, Maggid Mishneh, Lehem Mishneh, ad loc.; Orah Hayyim* 337:1).

Any task performed in a direct and purposeful manner, not in an indirect and unusual way, constitutes forbidden work (*Shab.* 107b, 153b; Maim. *Shabbat*, 1:8–9).[27] The prohibition against heating anything over fire is one example. According to some of the Sages, it was permitted to use water that had been heated in a pipe flowing through the thermal springs of Tiberias, since the cold water was heated *ki-le-ahar yad* – "offhand" or incidentally (*Shab.* 40b; *Tur, Orah Hayyim* 257:8, 258:1). Forbidden work is essentially useful and not destructive (*Shab.* 105b; Maim. *Shabbat*, 1:17).[28]

The Sages who compiled the Oral Law listed 39 categories of work that are prohibited on the Sabbath. These they derived from various forms of activity linked with the building and rituals of the Sanctuary. Eleven were needed to produce the meal-offering and included ploughing, sowing, reaping, threshing, grinding and baking. Thirteen were involved in producing the hangings and the priestly garments, e.g., shearing, dyeing, spinning and sewing. The preparation of animal sacrifices required nine activities, such as catching the animal or bird, slaughtering it, flaying the carcass and treating the skin, as well as cutting and writing. The construction of the Sanctuary involved building, demolishing and rebuilding; while the altar service required another four types of work: kindling and extinguishing fire, beating with a hammer and

---

26 מלאכה שאינה צריכה לגופה
27 כלאחר יד
28 מקלקל

carrying. In all, they amounted to 39 different activities (*Shab.* 7:2, 73a, b).

To these 39 prime categories of work (*avot melakhah*)[29] the Sages added a wide range of other activities stemming from them (*toladot*).[30] Broadening the concept of change and production, they also forbade carrying or picking up an object that was *muktzeh*, i.e., one that had not been designed or intended for use on the Sabbath prior to its commencement (*Orah Hayyim* 310).

A number of other activities prohibited by the Rabbis in their extension of the law, while not involving production, could indirectly give rise to some type of forbidden work, look like it or simply not be in keeping with the tranquil holiness of the day.[31] On the Sabbath one must not even think about doing a Sabbath prohibited work on an ensuing weekday. Such an action would be "contrary to the spirit of the Sabbath" (*shelo ke-ruah Shabbat kodesh*).

These extensions were meant to place a "fence" (*seyag*) around the strict Torah prohibitions, so as to avoid any likelihood of their infringement. They are also called, generally, *shevut* (rest) (*Betzah* 36b; *Orah Hayyim* 242:1, 301:1, 302:1, 306–310, 339:1 *ff.*, 340:1).[32]

The prohibition against carrying or transferring an article from a closed "private domain" to a "public domain",[33] or transferring it from one "domain" to another (*hotza'ah*), is the subject of many detailed regulations, creating fine distinctions between the "private" and "public" domains, since "carrying" is one of the prohibited acts specifically mentioned in the Torah (Num. 15:32; *Shab.* 2a *ff.*; *Orah Hayyim* 301, 303, 345, 352, 353).[34]

אבות מלאכה	29
תולדות	30
מעשי חול	31
שבות	32
מרשות היחיד לרשות הרבים	33
מקושש עצים	34

The prohibition of "carrying from one domain to another"[35] made it hard for observant Jews to lead a normal life on the Sabbath. Accordingly, the Rabbis found it advisable to institute a special device (elucidated in Tractate *Eruvin*) that extended one's own "domain" and thereby facilitated movement to another or shared "domain". Through this arrangement a number of individuals place items of food for a meal in a central position and that "domain" is then shared by all (*Er.* 6a, 7b; Maim. *Eruvin*, 1:1–7; *Orah Hayyim* 345:395).[36]

The Biblical law restricting a person's movements to 2,000 cubits beyond his domicile is also given special attention. By placing food before the Sabbath at the outer limit of the permitted 2,000 cubits, or even *intending* to live at this location, one acquires a new residence and may walk a further 2,000 cubits[37] from the spot. This law is based on the injunction, "Let no man go out of his place on the seventh day" (Ex. 16:29; Mish. *Er.* 4–5, *passim*, TB *Eruv.* 51a; Maim. *Eruvin*, 6–8; *Orah Hayyim* 397*ff.*, 408–416; for a more detailed exposition see below).

The self-restraint shown by the observant Jew in desisting from his weekday labours and observing the Sabbath laws is a rare example of devotion to man's Creator. Resting on the seventh day gives expression to the "perpetual covenant" (*berit olam*) between the Almighty and His people (Ex. 31:16). God enjoined Israel to keep the Sabbath day holy, because "it is a sign between Me and the Children of Israel for ever; for in six days the Lord made heaven and earth, and on the seventh day He ceased from work and rested" (Ex. 31:17).

Despite all its halakhic minutiae, the Sabbath has never been wearisome and oppressive to the observant Jew. On the contrary, in Jewish life it has proved to be an island of tranquillity amid a sea of troubles. The Sabbath's joyful spirit was conveyed in these words of the prophet Isaiah, calling

---

35   הוצאה
36   עירוב חצרות
37   עירוב תחומים

for the hungry to be fed and the downtrodden to be freed: "If thou turn back thy foot, because of the Sabbath, from doing business on My holy day; and call the Sabbath a delight and the holy of the Lord honourable; and shalt honour it – not following thy wonted ways, nor pursuing thy business, nor speaking thereof. Then shalt thou delight thyself in the Lord, and I will make thee to ride upon the high places of the earth, and I will feed thee with the heritage of Jacob thy father; for the mouth of the Lord hath spoken it" (Isa.58:13–14).[38]

Whatever losses the Jew may have incurred by observing the Sabbath, its holiness remained intact throughout the generations, in agriculture, commerce and industry, as the Torah commanded: "Six days thou shalt work, but on the seventh day thou shalt rest; in plowing time and in harvest thou shalt rest" (Ex. 34:21).

In Jewish thought, which the *Halakhah* reflects, virtue and vice constitute not only what men do but also the interplay of their thoughts and intentions with their acts. A man's intention can transform a simple act into a sin or prevent it from becoming one. In the following exposition of the Sabbath laws, as indeed in many other laws of serious consequence, the thought in a person's mind may itself determine the halakhic result of his action. An intention can also have the effect of an action, either positively or negatively.[39]

[General references: S. R. Hirsch, *Horeb*, trans. I. Grunfeld, Vol. 1, Part 2, *Edoth*, Chap. 21, pp. 61–67; Hirsch, *A Book of Essays*, "The Sabbath", in *19 Letters*, p. 199; *Encyclopaedia Judaica*, "Sabbath", 14:55–574; Maim. Code, *Hilkhot Shabbat, passim*; Caro, *Orah Hayyim, Hilkhot Shabbat, passim*; J. H. Hertz, *Pentateuch*, pp. 297–298, 766–767]

---

38   וקראת לשבת עונג
39   מעשה המחשבה

Extended Definition of Rest – Shevut

The fourth commandment of the Decalogue instituted Sabbath observance in two forms: "*Remember* the Sabbath day, to keep it holy" (Ex. 20:8)[40] and "*Observe* the Sabbath day, to keep it holy" (Deut. 5:12).[41] The Sages later established a number of prayers and family rituals (e.g., the *Amidah, Kiddush* and *Havdalah*) to fulfil the duty to "remember", praising the Lord for his gift of the holy Sabbath. The duty to "observe" was chiefly fulfilled by hallowing the day of rest and abstaining from weekday labour.

The Sages itemized 39 categories of "work" that this injunction prohibited (see above). Moreover, they taught that every effort must be made to safeguard the law. Additional "laws of strict rest" (*shevut*)[42] were therefore enacted to take account of other possible infractions. These rules prohibited any activity on the Sabbath that was thought incompatible with the holiness of the day or that might inadvertently result in its violation. They were meant to serve as a "fence around the law" (*seyag la-Torah*; cf. *Avot* 3:13) that would prevent any transgression, however unintentional, and R. Yoḥanan warned against taking them lightly (*Ḥag.* 16b).

The Sages mentioned certain actions prohibited on Sabbaths and festivals under the law of *shevut*. As a preventive measure, climbing a tree is forbidden, lest one pluck the fruit; similarly, riding a horse or donkey is forbidden, lest one cut off a tree-branch for use as a whip. Even the *mitzvah* of betrothing a wife is prohibited on the Sabbath, as it would involve the drawing-up of a marriage contract. Dedicating something to the Temple, another meritorious act, was likewise forbidden on the day of rest (*Betzah* 36b).[43]

The *shevut* rules did not, however, apply to any act performed in the statutory service of the Temple, e.g., the daily

---

40 זכור
41 שמור
42 שבות
43 לא עולין באילן ולא רוכבין על גבי בהמה... ולא מקדשין... לא מקדישין

sacrifice, because the fulfilment of a specific Torah law could not be impeded by a Rabbinic ruling that was itself designed to protect the law (*Pes.* 65a).[44]

The Sages differed as to how far these restrictions were operative. Some claimed that every occupation Rabbinically (but not Biblically) forbidden was also banned at twilight on a Sabbath eve, when the exact time for Sabbath prohibitions to commence might be in doubt. Others maintained that the *shevut* rule governed the period of twilight before the Sabbath's commencement (*Er.* 30b, 35a, 78b). Like the Sages, R. Yosef Caro ruled that the law of *shevut* did not prohibit the making of an *eruv* during twilight (Mish. Shab. 2:7, TB *Shab.* 34a; *Oraḥ Ḥayyim* 393:2).[45]

Perfect Rest – Shabbat Shabbaton

The prohibition of "work" on the Sabbath was far more comprehensive than lighting a fire or any other creative effort might suggest. As indicated above, it even affected the sacred task of building the Sanctuary (*mishkan*), because the Sabbath was designated *Shabbat shabbaton* – a day of "complete (or "strict") rest" (Ex. 35:2, Rashi *ad loc.*).[46]

In addition to banning specific categories of "work", the Torah called for other measures to preserve the Sabbath as a day of physical rest and spiritual refreshment. This *shabbaton* requirement does not refer to particular actions or activities, but obligates the Jew to maintain a pervasive *Shabbat* atmosphere throughout the day.

Naḥmanides pointed out that, by adding the term *shabbaton* to *Shabbat*, the Torah requires us to refrain on Sabbaths and festivals even from activities that do not constitute a forbidden *melakhah*. It is therefore permitted to move kitchen

---

44 אין שבות במקדש
45 מערבין אותו בין השמשות
46 שבת שבתון

utensils, barrels of wine or measures of grain, because of their normal use on the Sabbath, but not to perform these actions all day long – because the Sabbath spirit calls for *shabbaton*, an atmosphere of restfulness, and physical exertion would conflict with that ambience. Such an environment is hard to determine in a code of law, and each person must thus rely on his own notion of the Sabbath as a day of spiritual rest and relaxation (Ramban, commentary on Lev. 23:24; Maim. *Yad, Shabbat*, 24:12–13).

Sabbath observance primarily demands a correct standard of behaviour (i.e., not performing a *melakhah*); but to maintain the *Shabbat* spirit one's proposed actions must also be consistent with Torah values. This axiological concern is not just a requirement of special piety,[47] but an integral part of Torah conduct. Certain activities, though not mentioned specifically in the *Halakhah*, are considered inappropriate for the Sabbath.[48] Their objections show that the Sages fully appreciated the underlying values of Torah.

B. Set Aside – *Muktzeh*

Introduction

Since the main emphasis of the fourth commandment is on refraining from work in order to hallow the Sabbath day, great importance was attached by the Sages to preventing any infringement of the law by forbidden "work". While Torah law decreed a prohibition, "In it thou shalt not do any manner of work" (Ex. 20:10),[49] it also enacted a positive duty: "On the seventh day thou shalt rest" (Ex. 23:12).[50]

---

47   מידת חסידות
48   אין רוח חכמים נוחה הימנו
49   לא תעשה כל מלאכה
50   וביום השביעי תשבות

Fulfilling the commandment to "rest" involves more than simply avoiding productive work. As we have seen, the law is stated in two forms: *zakhor* – "remember" (Ex. 20:8) and *shamor* – "observe" the Sabbath day (Deut. 5:12). Normally, the Torah is satisfied if all of its laws are "observed"; but Sabbath observance also calls for "remembering", i.e., being conscious of the Sabbath's holiness throughout the day, in one's speech and all of one's actions (*Midrash Halakhah: Torat Kohanim, Be-Hukkotai* 26:3).

In accordance with Isaiah's previously mentioned reference to Sabbath observance (Isa. 58:13–14),[51] Maimonides declared that many activities which neither resemble forbidden "work" nor lead to its performance are nevertheless banned on the Sabbath. One should therefore keep away from places where business is conducted and never discuss transactions that one intends to engage in after the Sabbath terminates, as Isaiah phrased it: "Not following thy wonted ways, nor pursuing thy business, nor speaking thereof" (Maim. *Shabbat*, 24:1).

The Sages affirmed that the laws expounded by Israel's prophets had the same religious and moral authority as Torah legislation. Divinely inspired, these teachings complemented those of Moses and were also known as "laws handed down by tradition".[52] Thus, many basic rules of Judaism which had not been clearly stated in the Torah – notably the system employed to determine festival dates in the Jewish calendar – derive from such traditional law (*Rosh Hashana* 7a, *Tos.*, "*mi-divrei kabbalah*"; *Rosh Hashana* 19a; *Hul.* 137a, Rashi, "*anan*").

Similarly, the prohibition of *muktzeh*[53] is nowhere mentioned in the Torah. It was a law enacted by the Sages[54] and based on prophetical teaching (*Ber.* 4b; [55]*Pes.*

---

51 אם תשיב משבת רגלך, עשות חפצך ביום קודשי, וקראת לשבת עונג לקדוש ה'
    מכובד, וכיבדת מעשות דרכיך ממצוא חפצך ודבר דבר

52 דברי קבלה

53 מוקצה

54 מדרבנן

55 איסור דין מוקצה אין לו שורש מן התורה

30a, *Tos.*, *lishehinhu*). Any object that had been mentally "set aside" (*muktzeh*) in advance, as neither wanted nor intended for the Sabbath or a festival, could not be used or handled on that day (*Ora*h *Hayyim* 308:1 *ff.*).

The Sages differed as to whether the extensive *muktzeh* rule had binding authority. R. Shim'on rejected the validity of the prohibition, while R. Yehudah affirmed it (*Shab.* 45b).[56] Later Sages followed the one or the other. An even more basic divergence of opinion emerged after R. Shim'on held that if a man's forbidden "work" had not been part of his intention, he was not guilty of an offence,[57] whereas R. Yehudah held that he was. Later halakhic authorities generally adopted the view of R. Shim'on (*Betzah* 32a, *Tos.*, "*mi-le-mattah le-ma'alah*").

Muktzeh relates to a state of mind with some purposeful association. If someone does not intend to make use of an object on the coming Sabbath or festival, it is (so to speak) banished from his mind and no longer available to him. Various household items are normally handled on a Sabbath or festival, but the object defined as *muktzeh* is excluded from use. It does not fall under the rubric of "preparation"[58] and may not be utilized or handled.

This law prohibiting in advance the use of any object not required on the Sabbath, and therefore dismissed from a person's mind, has a large number of correlated features. Maimonides and the codes provide numerous examples of items and actions which, for different reasons, qualify as *muktzeh* and are thus Rabbinically forbidden. These prohibitions reflect the spirit of Torah law (Maim. *Shabbat*, 1:1–4) and were always intended to minimize the possibility of a Sabbath violation.[59]

In the case of Rabbinic prohibitions, where an infringement of the Sabbath was ruled as *pattur*,[60] it meant that the offender did not incur the severe punishment which Torah law

---

56   רבי שמעון לית ליה מוקצה, ורבי יהודה אית ליה מוקצה

57   דבר שאין מתכוון מותר

58   הכנה

59   הרחקה מן המלאכה

60   פטור

prescribed (i.e., the death penalty, *karet* or a sin-offering), but a prohibition (*assur*)[61] remained in force. An infringement could make one liable to physical punishment for defying the will of the Sages.[62] Where no Rabbinic prohibition applied, the Sages used the term *muttar* ("permitted") (Maim. *Shabbat* 1:3).[63]

Twelve forms of *muktzeh*, all based on various Talmudic references, are exemplified in the Codes:

1. An object that someone does not wish to use, because that may result in a financial loss which he is anxious to avoid.[64]

2. Something of no value or unusable in its present state (e.g., broken china),[65] unless someone has already expressed a desire to make use of it.

3. Food rejected as unfit for human consumption because it is either unripe or putrid.

4. Something that one could never expect to be of use, due to other Sabbath "work" prohibitions, such as a house in a state of disrepair.[66]

5. Something not fully available prior to the Sabbath, e.g., fruit still attached to the tree, which it is now forbidden to pick.[67]

6. Something that did not exist prior to the Sabbath but came into existence (*nolad*) on that day, such as an egg laid on a Sabbath or festival, or a vessel which an artisan completed or repaired on the Sabbath.[68] The egg should already have been formed on a weekday (*Betzah* 2b; *Orah Hayyim* 513:1).

אסור	61
מכות מרדות	62
מותר	63
מוקצה מחמת חסרון כיס	64
דלא חזי למדי	65
שאינו מקווה להתירו	66
מוקצה דהכנה	67
מוקצה דנולד	68

7. Something that provides a base for a *muktzeh* object, such as candlesticks, the tray on which they stand, or a purse containing money – *muktzeh me-hamat issur* (*Shab.* 12a; *Orah Hayyim* 309:4, REMA, *Mishnah Berurah*).[69]

8. Something already designated for a *mitzvah* to be performed on a Sabbath or festival, such as a lamp kindled as the "Sabbath light"[70] or the "*menorah*" kindled on Hanukkah"[71] (*Shab.* 45a; *Orah Hayyim* 638:1).

9. Something prepared for an activity that is forbidden on the Sabbath, such as wooden planks intended for heating or construction, or raw wool for spinning[72] (*Betzah* 30b; *Orah Hayyim* 308:20).

10. Any article or instrument used for prohibited "work".[73] Using cutlery or kitchen tools to prepare and eat food is therefore permitted (*Shab.* 124a; *Orah Hayyim* 308:17).

11. Anything rejected as fetid, such as a grimy lamp, or loathsome, such as a dead animal – *muktzeh me-hamat mi'us* (*Shab.* 45a; *Orah Hayyim* 310:1).[74]

12. Something which, in normal use, is permitted but which is now intended for some other use or merely for storage (*Shab.* 124a; *Orah Hayyim* 308:4).[75]

[General references: *Mishnayyot Shabbat, Tiferet Yisrael,* Introd.]

---

69 מוקצה מחמת בסיס
70 נר של שבת
71 מוקצה מחמת מצווה
72 מוקצה מחמת איסור שבגופן
73 מוקצה מחמת איסור מלאכה
74 מוקצה מחמת מיאוס
75 מוקצה שלא לצורכו

Preparation – Muktzeh de-Hakhanah

According to the law of *hakhanah* (preparation),[76] anything used or consumed on the Sabbath should have been available and ready for use beforehand. This law was based on the Torah passage referring to the gift of manna: "It shall come to pass on the sixth day that they shall prepare that which they bring in" (Ex. 16:5, *Torah Temimah*; *Pes.* 47b, Rashi *ad loc.*, Meiri *ad loc.*; Ramban, *Milhamot*, beginning of *Betzah*).[77]

In their exposition of this law the Rabbis drew up certain rules. Fixing a loose shutter or a window so that it can be closed, or a bolt on a door, may fall either under the category of "building"[78] or of "handling".[79] If, however, an article was prepared *before* the Sabbath to close the window, it may be used for that purpose on the Sabbath as it is no longer *muktzeh*. A regular hinged door is always ready for use and may be shut to enclose a room, whereas an unattached board may not be fitted on the Sabbath to make such an enclosure (*Shab.* 125b, Rashi; *Orah Hayyim* 313:1).

The forbidden *melakhah* of "hunting" (*tzedah*)[80] may apply in the case of a bird that flies into a house through an open door. If someone shuts the door to prevent its escape, he may be held liable for that "work". The Sages, however, ruled that if he only closes the door to shut out the cold or to prevent the entry of strangers (without intending to catch the bird), his action is permitted. Only that individual can tell if his act was a transgression, according to whatever consideration he had in mind. If a stray animal entered the house, shutting the door on it would inevitably constitute "hunting", in accordance with the rule of *pesik reisheh*.[81] Where a person's domestic animals

---

76 הכנה
77 והיה ביום השישי והכינו את אשר יביאו
78 בנין
79 אסור טלטול
80 צד
81 פסיק רישיה

are involved, this rule does not, of course, apply (*Shab.* 106b; *Orah Hayyim* 316:1, *Mishnah Berurah* 5).

Another case of *muktzeh de-hakhanah* would be the following. Since one may prepare food on *yom tov* (a festival), the slaughter (*shehitah*) of an animal should be permissible. However, *shehitah* also involves covering the blood with earth (Lev. 17:13)[82] and this raises the question of such loose soil being available. The Schools of Hillel and Shammai differed as to whether someone might turn up ground for this purpose, as "digging"[83] is associated with the forbidden "work" of "ploughing".[84] Bet Shammai determined that if no earth was available, someone could dig it up in the legitimate process of preparing food. Bet Hillel ruled otherwise: if earth was not already available, *shehitah* could still be performed, as there were presumably some ashes in the stove that might serve to cover the blood. This would also depend on whether the fire had been lit before *yom tov* and not on it, for that would make the ashes a newly created object. This supply of ashes could be regarded as a preparation (*hakhanah*), even if no one had thought of using it for that purpose. *Shehitah* was therefore permitted to enhance the "joy of the festival" (*Betzah* 2a, 7b–8a; *Tos. ad loc.*).[85]

Hillel and Shammai also disagreed about the act of preparing an animal for use on the festival. Bet Shammai maintained that one should "handle" the beast prior to the festival, thereby indicating one's intended course of action. Bet Hillel ruled that merely *stating* that one's intention to use the animal would be a sufficient *hakhanah*. The Sages were generally agreed that stating one's intention would meet the *hakhanah* requirement. Both Maimonides and Caro ruled accordingly: the fact that a person had set his mind on it[86] would suffice (*Betzah* 10a; Maim. *Yom Tov*, 2:5; *Orah Hayyim* 497:10).

---

82 ושפך את דמו וכסהו בעפר

83 חפירה

84 חרישה

85 שאפר כירה מוכן הוא

86 מפני שדעתו עליהן

Some of the Sages restricted the liability of *muktzeh* (as R. Shim'on did) to cases where one had personally and actively set the object aside, excluding it from Sabbath use. For example, if someone placed grapes, figs or other fruit on the roof to dry in the sun, only intending to eat them when they were dried, and meanwhile considered them unfit for consumption, such fruit would then be forbidden to him as *muktzeh*. If they became edible before *yom tov*, he was free to eat them on the festival if he so wished; otherwise, they would remain forbidden as *muktzeh*. If they were only half-ready, some people considering them edible and others not, he would have to make it known before the Sabbath or festival that he thought them fit to eat,[87] thereby fulfilling the requirement of *hakhanah* (*Betzah* 26b, Rashi; *Orah Hayyim* 310:4–5).[88] If, on the other hand, he had figs available which he simply never thought of using at the time, such an absence of intention would not render the fruit *muktzeh* (*Betzah* 11a, RAN *ad loc.*)

Although the laws of forbidden "work" apply equally to Sabbaths and festivals, Rabbinic concern that the laws of *yom tov* should not suffer in comparison with those of *Shabbat* led at times to an even stricter *hakhanah* requirement for the festival than for the Sabbath (Maim. *Yom Tov*, 1:17–18). On the Sabbath, any food in one's possession might be used, even without previously designating it for the day of rest.[89] For use on a festival, however, it had to be so designated in advance, even by a mental determination to eat it during *yom tov*. Thus, although a milch cow was not usually kept for its meat, it would be considered "prepared" for this by deeming it a beef animal prior to the festival. Likewise, an ox normally reserved for ploughing or breeding could be used for its meat on *yom tov*, if one stated that intention beforehand (*Orah Hayyim* 308:26,

---

87 הזמנה
88 אזמין גלי דעתיך
89 הכל מוכן לשבת

311:8, REMA). Generally speaking, in the case of animals or birds not previously intended for consumption on the festival, one was required to state in advance that such use would be made of them (*Betzah* 2b, Rashi, s.v. *"ve-hekhinu"*).[90]

According to certain authorities, the prohibition of *muktzeh* even affected the action of a Gentile who brought a gift to a Jew on one of the the festivals. If such an item was normally attached to the ground or to its source,[91] had to be collected (e.g., fruit, vegetables, fish or fowl) and was not available before *yom tov*, such a gift might not be used by the Jew until the festival's termination. If, however, the gift's appearance clearly showed that it had been ready before the festival, its use would be permitted. Later Sages extended this lenient ruling still further, determining that if it had been available even to a single person, it would be regarded as an accessible item not governed by the law of *muktzeh*. The act of mental exclusion was subject to fine distinctions that had to be considered liberally (*Ora<u>h</u> <u>H</u>ayyim* 310:2, REMA, *Magen Avraham* and *Kol Bo*).

In general, the Sages ruled that the *muktzeh* law did not apply to a Gentile, who could not be expected to mentally exclude an item from use on a Jewish festival (*Ora<u>h</u> <u>H</u>ayyim* 310:2, REMA, *Magen Avraham* and *Kol Bo*; *Betzah* 24a; Maim. *Yom Tov*, 2:10; *Ora<u>h</u> <u>H</u>ayyim* 526:1).

Various opinions were expressed about the *hakhanah* requirement, as to whether an item should be "actively" set aside or just mentally chosen for use. A case in point involved someone who cut the dried branches of a palm tree for fuel, but then changed his mind and decided to use them for a seat.[92] According to one view, since the branches had been meant for fuel, any change of purpose required some deliberate act before the Sabbath (e.g., tying the dried branches together to make a seat) which would indicate that person's real intention.

---

90   והכינו בדיבור פה

91   מחובר

92   כריות של דקל שגדרן לעצים ונמלך עליהן לישיבה

The Sages, however, accepted R. Shim'on ben Gamliel's view that he only needed to say that he had changed his mind.[93] Shemuel declared that the mere thought of doing so beforehand was sufficient "preparation" (*Shab.* 50a, RAN *ad loc.*).[94]

Another aspect of mental preparation had to do with a beehive, which may not be handled on the Sabbath to remove the honey; using such honey is then forbidden as *muktzeh*. Since a beehive is regarded as a parcel of land, removing the honey is akin to "harvesting",[95] a category of forbidden "work", and this renders the hive itself *muktzeh*. The Sages ruled, however, that one may place a mat over the beehive to protect it from the sun or rain, provided one does not intend to trap the bees inside, an act that would constitute "hunting" (*Shab.* 43a; *Uk.* 3:10; for a further discussion, see Chapter 8 below).[96]

Another problem involved keeping cooked food warm on the Sabbath. To maintain the temperature required, on Sabbath eve it was permissible to wrap wool, clothing, cotton wool, straw and the like around the pot. If the wrapping material could be used for prohibited "work", it was forbidden to handle it on the Sabbath.[97] The food could be used, however, by raising the lid of the pot and allowing the material to fall off on its own (*Shab.* 49; Maim. *Shabbat*, 4:1).

The question debated was whether the pot might also be wrapped in pelts. If the skins belonged to a tanner, he would not want them damaged and would never think of using them to keep food warm. They were therefore *muktzeh* and could not be handled on the Sabbath. If the skins belonged to a private person, handling them was permitted, as it would not bother him if they were stained and he would readily designate them as a covering (*Shab.* 49a, Rashi; *Orah Hayyim* 259:1).[98]

93 גלי דעתיה דלישיבה קיימי
94 שמואל אמר חושב
95 קצירה
96 צד
97 טומנין בגיזי צמר, ואין מטלטלין אותן
98 ומנין בשלחין ומטלטלין אותן – של בעל הבית דלא קפיד דלא עליהו

[General references: *Talmudic Encyclopedia*, Vol. 9, s.v. *"Hakhanah"*; Vol. 8, s.v. *"Hazmanah"*; Vol. 4, s.v. *"Basis li-Devar ha-Issur"*; also in a forthcoming volume, *"Muktzeh"*; *Tiferet Yisrael, Seder Mo'ed*, Introd., *"Muktzeh"*; *Hayyei Adam*, Chap. 65, *"Muktzeh"*]

Rabbinic Prohibition – Muktzeh me-hamat Issur

Further distinctions concerning the *muktzeh* law were made by the Sages. If someone deliberately placed coins on a sofa or cushion before the Sabbath, intending them to remain there over the following day, it was (of course) forbidden to touch the coins themselves, nor might one handle the object on which they rested, since they were *muktzeh me-hamat issur* ("on the basis of a rabbinic prohibition").[99] If someone forgot that he had put them there before the Sabbath or happened to find them on the Sabbath, he could shake off the coins and use the cushion. If, however, it had already been excluded from use, touching the cushion was forbidden even if the coins fell off, as it had also been "set aside"; and the *muktzeh* rule applied throughout the Sabbath.[100]

This law would also apply to someone who had not placed coins on the sofa or cushion but discovered the money there and considered it forbidden to him (*Shab.* 47a, Bertinoro; *Shab.* 44b, *Tos.*, s.v. *"lo hini'ah"*, *"yesh aleha"*; *Orah Hayyim* 310, 309:4, REMA).

[General reference: *Hayyei Adam* 65, s.v. *"Muktzeh"*]

A lamp kindled in honour of *Shabbat* or *yom tov*[101] may not be moved on the Sabbath, even after the flame has gone out, because it has been excluded from any use other than fulfilling the *mitzvah*. This mental act of exclusion remains in force throughout the Sabbath or festival (*Shab.* 44a; *Orah*

---

99   מוקצה מחמת איסור
100 מאחר שנעשה בסיס לדבר האסור למקצת שבת אסור כל השבת כולה
101 נר מצוה

Hayyim 279:1, _Mishnah Berurah_ 3).[102] Some of the Sages distinguished between a large lamp, which could be expected to burn the whole day, and a small lamp, which would not burn for long. A person might conceivably have intended to move the small lamp after the flame went out, not intending to exclude its use and possibly anticipating its removal before the Sabbath (_Shab._ 44a, Rashi, s.v. "_be-zutta_").[103] The codifiers would not accept such a distinction, however, because the infringement of a Sabbath law might be involved (Maim. _Shabbat_, 25:10; _Orah Hayyim_ 279:1).

Muktzeh le-Mitzvato

R. Yohanan stated that, in R. Shim'on's opinion, the oil of a Sabbath lamp was excluded from any other use, as the householder intended it to fulfil his duty to "kindle the Sabbath light". Only when the oil is burning can the _mitzvah_ be fulfilled; once it has ceased burning, the _mitzvah_ is terminated and the _muktzeh_ prohibition no longer applies. Thus, the duration of the lamp's _muktzeh_ status coincides with the amount of oil burnt in fulfilment of the _mitzvah_,[104] and the _muktzeh_ law forbidding one to handle the lamp only applies while the oil is still burning (_Shab._ 45a, Rashi, s.v. "_ke-ein shemen_").[105]

Once the prohibition has applied during the Sabbath day, the prohibition remains in force for the whole of that Shabbath. Thus candlesticks in which there had been a burining light on the Sabbath, such as the Sabbath candlesticks, are not to be moved until after the end of that Sabbath.

Since, according to R. Shim'on, this law only applies if one has excluded the oil from use by some indicative action, there is no prohibition against using the surplus oil after it has ceased burning (_Shab._ 42b, _Tos._, s.v. "_ve-ein nei'otin_"; _ibid._ 45a).

102	הקציה לכולי יומא
103	בנר זוטא דדעתיה עלויה
104	הואיל והוקצה למצוותו הוקצה לאיסורו
105	שמן שבנר בשעה שהוא דולק

The basis of the prohibition against handling the lamp while the flame remains alight is that the lamp itself is a substructure of the forbidden flame and thus an accessory of "fire" (*esh*). Like "fire", it is therefore prohibited (*Shab.* 47a, Rashi, s.v. "*le-davar ha-assur*").[106]

C. Taking Medications on the Sabbath

Apart from the three cardinal prohibitions (of idol worship, murder and sexual depravity), all other commandments are set aside when a person's life is in danger. Any "work" normally forbidden on the Sabbath may be performed in an emergency, since "the duty to save human life overrides Sabbath laws" – *pikku'ah nefesh doheh et ha-Shabbat* (*Shab.* 132a; *Yoma* 85a). This means that any treatment needed for a person who is critically ill must be provided on a Sabbath or festival.[107] In the case of minor ailments, however, the general rule is that one should not take medications on the Sabbath, as their ingredients may have to be crushed or ground, which is prohibited.[108] One of the 39 forbidden "work" categories, "grinding",[109] was required to produce flour or spices for the Temple service or dyes for its furnishings (*Shab.* 73a–b, Rashi s.v. "*ha-ofeh*"; Maim. *Shabbat*, 7:1, 21:22; *Orah Hayyim* 328:1–2, *Tur, Bet Yosef*; *Arukh ha-Shulhan, Shabbat*, 328:17).

Some authorities claim that in view of modern pharmaceutical conditions, where all medications are available ready-made, this precautionary law is no longer justified and the prohibition should be annulled.[110] Others maintain that an ordinance affecting all Jews cannot be repealed on the grounds of *battel ha-ta'am* (Responsa *Binyamin Ze'ev*, no. 222).[111] Others again point out that the original measure

---

106 בסיס לדבר אחר הרי הוא תפל לו ואסור במוקצה
107 חולה שיש בו סכנה
108 שחיקת סממנים
109 טחינה
110 בטל הטעם בטל האיסור
111 בטל הטעם

was obviously not intended for our modern industrialized society, where the likelihood of such forbidden "work" does not exist. One might therefore determine that a precautionary law enacted on the basis of an existing situation would not be applicable if that situation no longer obtained (*Minhat Shabbat* 91:9; R. Yehoshua Neuwirth, *Shemirat Shabbat ke-Hilkhatah*, Chap. 21:20, s.v. *"Dinei holeh"*; RADBAZ, Responsa, Part 4, 1147; *Orah Hayyim* 328:37, REMA, *Mishnah Berurah* 121; *Ketzot ha-Shulhan* 134; R. Eliezer Yehudah Waldenberg, *Tzitz Eliezer*, Jerusalem, 2nd ed., 1985, Vol. 8, Chap. 15: 14–17, Vol. 12, Chap. 45:7).[112]

Extenuating Circumstances

Some authorities believe that if a person feels unwell,[113] though not seriously ill, and stays in bed,[114] he should take the necessary medication on the grounds that the Sages never intended their precautionary law to be applied in such a case (REMA). If illness confined him to bed, the Sages did not invoke the prohibition.[115] Others ruled that this law might only be suspended for a person who was critically ill (TAZ). If he was able to carry on as usual, however, all the authorities agreed that he should not take any medication on a Sabbath day because of the Rabbinic prohibition against "grinding spices" (*Orah Hayyim* 328:1, 37, REMA, TAZ, *Mishnah Berurah* 121).[116]

This precautionary law did not mean that the Rabbis had any objection to medical remedies. On the contrary, they asserted that regard for human life (*pikku'ah nefesh*) and its preservation[117] was embodied in the commandment, "Take

---

112 בגזרות חז״ל בטל הטעם בטל הגזירה

113 בעל מיחוש

114 נפל למשכב

115 דבחולה גמור לא גזרו משום שחיקת סממנים

116 שחיקת סממנים

117 שמירת הנפש

heed to thyself, and keep thy soul diligently"[118] and its repetition,[119] which all must obey (Deut. 4:9, 15; *Ber.* 32b; Maim. *Rotze'ah̲ u-Shemirat Nefesh*, 11:4; *Sh. Ar., Yoreh De'ah*, 336:1; Shelomo Ganzfried, *Kitzur Shulh̲an Arukh*, ed. David Feldman, Manchester, 5th ed., 1951, 190:2–3, 192:3–4).

As a general rule, any internal complaint that makes a person feel sick is considered "a danger to life".[120] If necessary, Sabbath laws may be disregarded to alleviate the patient's condition; and relief should be administered promptly, without waiting for a rabbi's permission (*Orah̲ Hayyim* 328:3). This may be done at the patient's own request, without asking for a second opinion, if a serious illness is diagnosed (ibid., 328:11, 239:1).

If the patient is suffering from an external ailment, the doctor's instructions must be followed to the letter. Any medicament that he prescribes should be carefully prepared and administered. Sabbath regulations are promptly waived if treatment is being given for an eye infection, burns or severe wounds caused by a sharp instrument, a rabid dog or a venomous snake (ibid., 329:1). In most cases, whether a person had violated the Sabbath would depend on his honest interpretation of the Rabbinic ruling.

An example of this subjective attitude is given in the Talmud. The law that forbids one to take medications on the Sabbath should also apply to any food or drink taken for medicinal purposes.[121] However, if healthy people considered such items edible, they would be permitted despite their therapeutic effect (*Ber.* 38a; *Shab.* 109b; Maim. *Shabbat*, 21:21–23). This permission would therefore depend on the sick person's intention – to treat those items as food[122] and not as remedies (*Orah̲ Hayyim* 328:37, *Mishnah Berurah* 121).

---

118 רק הישמר לך ושמור נפשך מאוד
119 ונשמרתם מאוד לנפשותיכם
120 חולה שיש בו סכנה
121 לרפואה
122 גברא לאכילה קא מכוין

Another condition would be that the food was part of a normal healthy diet[123] and would not be rejected by a fastidious individual. The culpability of an action was therefore determined by a person's outlook, and his conscience would alone decide whether or not he had committed an offence, depending on his eating habits and the food's acceptability. If most people considered the food agreeable,[124] he would be permitted to eat it (*Ber.* 38a, *Tos.*, s.v. "*ve-i*", "*ve-ha*"; *Arukh ha-Shulḥan*, *Shabbat*, 328:48–49).

Sick People and Women in Labour

When a woman gives birth on the Sabbath day, any action required for the successful delivery of her child may be performed.[125] The Sages ruled that it is one's duty to profane the Sabbath on that woman's account. All the ritual laws are set aside in a life-threatening situation,[126] and permission to do so would be granted here even if the action itself was not essential for the preservation of life (Maim. *Shabbat*, 2:1, 14; *Oraḥ Ḥayyim* 330:1).

According to the accepted rule, one's duty to attend to a sick person's needs overrides the law prohibiting "work" on the Sabbath. Furthermore, it is a paramount obligation to do whatever is required for that person's recovery (Maim. *Shabbat*, 2:1–6; *Oraḥ Ḥayyim* 328:2).

The early codifiers disagreed about the nature of this permission. Some held that Sabbath laws were only relaxed to cater for the needs of the sick[127] but otherwise remained in force (Maim. *Shabbat*, 2:1–2). Others maintained that these prohibitions were completely disregarded once the sick had to be cared for; any service

---

123 מאכל בריאים
124 גברא לאכילה קא מכוין ורפואה ממילא קא הויא
125 יולדת היא כחולה שיש בו סכנה
126 פיקוח נפש
127 עושין לו כל צרכיו בשבת

required, such as cooking, was then no different to work performed on a weekday. Surplus food could thus be eaten by other people without restriction (ROSH, *Yoma* 8:14; cf. RAN, *Betzah* 17b, s.v. *"u-mihu"*).[128]

One may profane the Sabbath on behalf of a woman in labour, even if she does not say "I need it" (commentary of ROSH). The reason for this annulment of the law is that a woman's belief that all steps will be taken to ensure a safe delivery sets her mind at rest, whereas her fear that this may not be so presents a real danger to life (*Shab.* 128b, *Tos.*, s.v. *"ka mashma lan"*; Maim. *Shabbat*, 2:11; *Orah Hayyim* 330:1).

D. Work Performed by a Non-Jew – *Amirah le-Nokhri*

The Sages endeavoured to provide relief for an individual who needed to have some simple "work" performed without violating the Sabbath. A Jew could thus ask a non-Jew to do it for him, and rules were formulated as to what might or might not be done (*Orah Hayyim* 307:5).[129]

The comprehensive prohibition of Sabbath "work" is enunciated in the fourth commandment: "The seventh day is a Sabbath unto the Lord thy God; in it thou shalt not do any manner of work, thou, nor thy son, nor thy daughter, nor thy manservant, nor thy maidservant, nor thy cattle, nor thy stranger that is within thy gates" (Ex. 20:10).[130]

From the wording of this precept the Sages understood that "stranger" referred to a non-Jew. He, the Gentile, is obviously under no obligation to keep the Sabbath and is then free to do any work that he chooses. However, the fact that a Gentile is forbidden to work for a Jew on the Sabbath was maintained

---

128   השבת הותרה – כאילו עשהה בחול

129   אמירה לעכו״ם

130   לא תעשה כל מלאכה אתה ובנך ובתך עבדך ואמתך ובהמתך וגרך אשר בשעריך

by the Sages in their exposition of another law regarding the Passover festival. In its account of the first and last days of that "holy convocation" the Torah states that "no manner of work shall be done in them" (Ex. 12:16).[131] The *Mekhilta* commentary, which records decisions by the early *tannaim*, expounds the law as follows: "Nor shall a Gentile do your work on the Sabbath".[132] This ruling was derived from the passive form of a verb in the Hebrew text, indicating that the prohibition extended to a non-Jew: "Your work should not be done for you by anyone". Scholars argued that if this law applied to festival observance, it would surely have a stricter application to the Sabbath (*Mekhilta* on Ex. 12:16, *Parashah* 9:60).

Naḥmanides (commenting on Ex. 12:16), observed that the Torah nowhere prohibits work by a Gentile on either Sabbaths or festivals. Only the Sages laid down that a "stranger" (i.e., a non-Jew) should not perform such work for a Jew. Since this type of work is evidently permitted by the Torah, the Sages found support for their ruling in the passive (*nif'al*) form of *yei'aseh* – "shall be done".[133]

Going one step further, the Sages forbade a Jew to ask any Gentile to work for him on the Sabbath. This was a wholly Rabbinic enactment, as stated in the Talmud (*Shab.* 150a; *Er.* 67b),[134] Maimonides declaring that its aim was to safeguard Torah law (Maim. *Shabbat*, 6:1). It applied directly to the Sabbath and, by extension, to the major festivals (*BM* 90a, *Tos.*, s.v. "*aval*"). The Sages adopted this measure for fear that the original prohibition would seem less important because it was easy to circumvent (Maim. *Shabbat loc. cit.*).[135]

The codifiers followed the ruling of the Sages that in case of necessity, where the prohibition itself was only of Rabbinic origin,[136] some way to relax the *amirah le-nokhri* law should

---

131 כל מלאכה לא ייעשה בהם
132 לא יעשה נכרי מלאכתך
133 בודאי היא אסמכתא בעלמא שבאו לאסור מדבריהם
134 אמירה לנכרי שבות
135 שלא תהי שבת קלה בעיניך
136 שבות

be found. There was thus no disputing the fact that when a Jew died on *yom tov*, members of the burial society could ask a non-Jew to perform the interment (*Betzah* 6a).[137]

Other rulings by the codifiers stated that if a non-Jew performed tasks on his own initiative, such as kindling light in a darkened room, the Jewish householder could benefit from this. In cases where Sabbath "work" was urgently required, a Jew could ask a Gentile to perform it. Such tasks might include working for the benefit of sick people (even if they were not critically ill),[138] guarding someone's personal effects,[139] averting a grave financial loss and enabling someone to perform a religious duty (*mitzvah*), e.g, carrying the instruments required for a circumcision or bringing hot water for a baby (*Er.* 67b; Maim. *Shabbat*, 6:9; *Orah Hayyim* 307:5).

If someone required the help of a non-Jew in having "work" done for him, but the law of *amirah le-nokhri* prevented him from making a direct request, he could not even drop a hint to the Gentile on the Sabbath. After the Sabbath's termination, however, he could explain what was required so that the non-Jew would understand how to proceed on the following Sabbath without asking for instructions (*Orah Hayyim* 307:2). Furthermore, to enhance honouring the Sabbath (*li-khevod Shabbat*) and enjoying it (*oneg Shabbat*), one might ask a non-Jew to kindle a lamp in one's room and light a fire to warm the house, as severe cold was identified with an illness – *holi* (*Orah Hayyim* 276:2–3).

It became standard practice to make a long-term arrangement, whereby a particular non-Jew undertook this "work" on Friday night and Saturday. In European (Ashkenazi) communities, such a helpful Gentile was affectionately known as a "*Shabbes goy*". Rather than ask for lights to be kindled in the late afternoon, many pious Jews would have this chore delayed until nightfall, prior to the Sabbath's termination (*Orah Hayyim* 276:2, *Ba'er Heitev* 5, *Mishnah Berurah* 24).

---

137   מת ביום טוב ראשון יתעסקו בו עממין

138   מקצת חולי

139   בהול בממונו

E. The *Eruv*

(1) *Amalgamation of Boundaries – Eruv Teḥumin*

Introduction

According to the laws of Sabbath observance, walking a considerable distance is forbidden. The Sages had to gauge the distance permitted and its point of demarcation. The Torah's account of the manna, and of how it should not be gathered on the Sabbath, includes the following expression: "Abide ye every man in his place, let no man go out of his place on the seventh day" (Ex. 16:29).[140] In this context the law did not mean that a person should sit at home all day, but simply that he should not go out to collect the manna.

One Aramaic version of the text interprets it to mean that one should not "leave town" (Targum Onkelos; Ibn Ezra *ad loc.*).[141] Another version (Yonatan ben Uziel) makes the law even clearer: "A man should not walk more than 2,000 cubits[142] out of his town on the seventh day". The Rabbis limited one's movement on the Sabbath to no more than 2,000 cubits in any direction beyond the confines of the town. They formulated a precise way of measuring this distance, which is roughly equivalent to 2,000 paces or 1,000 metres (*Er.* 42a; *Oraḥ Ḥayyim* 397:2).

Rashi (*ad loc.*) assumed from the text (Ex. 16:29) that this 2000-cubit limit was meant to become the "Sabbath boundary" (*teḥum Shabbat*).[143] He further maintained that the ordinance was not a Biblical law but one instituted by the Sages.[144] In view of the fact that most authorities do not consider the *eruv* to be a Torah-mandated law

---

140   שבו איש תחתיו, אל יצא איש ממקומו ביום השביעי

141   לא יפוק אנש מאתריה

142   אלפים אמות

143   תחום שבת

144   אלו אלפים אמה של תחום שבת, ולא במפורש שאין תחומים אלא מדברי
סופרים

(*mi-de-Oraita*) but a protective Rabbinical enactment (*mi-de-Rabbanan*), a lenient rather than severe approach would allow greater freedom of movement, particularly in fulfilling a *mitzvah*.[145]

Many *halkhic* authorities ruled according to the view of R. Shimeon bar Casna that the Torah law limit was 12 miles outside of his town, which was the extent of the Israelite encampment in the wilderness (TJ *Er.* 3:4; Torah Commentary, *Torah Temimah,* Ex. 16:29 n. 45).[146]

According to Maimonides, the Sages credited the Torah with establishing a "Sabbath boundary" of 12 miles, but the 2,000-cubit perimeter that they decreed was the recognized limit of a town's "outskirts" (Maim. *Shabbat*, 27:1). This had been the view of his mentor, R. Yitzhak Alfasi (RIF), who regarded movement beyond the 12-mile limit as a violation of the *Torah de-Oraita*. Other halakhic authorities maintained, however, that the Torah law was specifically aimed at the gathering of manna on a Sabbath, and that the restricted distance was wholly imposed by the Sages (ROSH, s. 4:8, *Mordekhai* s. 499, RASHBA, RAVEN *ad loc.*).[147]

The *Tur* and *Shulhan Arukh* codes did not accept the view of Maimonides. They ruled that all laws governing the "Sabbath boundary" (*tehum Shabbat*) were Rabbinic prohibitions (*Tur, Orah Hayyim* 397, "*Perishah*"; Sh. Ar., *Orah Hayyim* 397:1–2).[148]

Effect of Intention in the Law of Eruv

If a person happened to be outside a town when the Sabbath was about to commence, he could place food where he was before the Sabbath and designate that place as his residence, the new base of his Sabbath limit.[149] If it was in a rural area and totally enclosed by a wall, fence or hedge (*bik'ah*), the

---

145   הלכה כדברי המיקל בעירוב
146   שנים עשר מיל כמחנה ישראל
147   אפילו חוץ משנים עשר מיל דרבנן
148   מדברי סופרים
149   קובע שביתה

entire enclosure was considered his personal residence, i.e., a living space of four cubits.[150] He would then be allowed to walk the 2,000-cubit distance outside the enclosed area. If he was heading for a town, and the place where he found himself lay within its border, he could determine in his mind that his residence was in the town. He could walk all the way to that town, the whole of which would then be his base residence (*Er.* 45a; *Oraḥ Ḥayyim* 409:11).[151]

On the same principle, it was ruled that from wherever an individual found himself he could mentally locate his residence at a distant tree, house or hedge within his Sabbath limit. That designated spot would then constitute his base and within its radius he could proceed for another 2,000 cubits (*Er.* 49b). Furthermore, while standing in his own home, he could determine that some location (such as a tree) should now be his residence and make it his new point of departure. In a further relief measure authorized by the Sages, a person could have food sufficient for two meals deposited at the far end of his Sabbath limit – even by someone acting on his behalf – and in this way acquire a new residence, which would become the next base of his 2,000 cubits.[152] It was specified that for a group of 18 people there must be a portion of food with the bulk of six eggs, which would give each person an amount of food equivalent in size to a dried fig (*Er.* 82b; Maim. *Eruvin*, 1:9).[153] This complicated procedure was known as *eruv teḥumin* – an "amalgamation of boundaries" (Maim. *Eruvin*, 7:1–2; *Oraḥ Ḥayyim* 409:7–8).

The straightforward way to create an *eruv*,[154] as described above, was to proceed before the Sabbath as far as the boundary permitted, to deposit enough food there for the two obligatory Sabbath meals[155] and then to establish one's residence at that

---

150	ארבע אמות
151	קונה שביתה
152	היה מכיר אילן או גדר
153	כגרוגרת
154	עיקר עירוב תחומין
155	מזון שתי סעודות

spot, appropriating it as one's "domicile" (*koneh shevitah*). One could either remain there or return to one's home, going back to that spot on the Sabbath and then proceeding a further 2,000 cubits in any direction.

If someone went there before the Sabbath but failed to designate it as his new "domicile", it would not be clear if he had really intended it to be such or whether he had left and dismissed it from his mind, never having meant to give it that designation (*Er.* 51b, Rashi).[156] If it transpired that he had left the requisite food there, even without designating it as his abode, this must have been done for a purpose and his *eruv* would therefore be valid (*Er.* 49b, *Tos.* s.v. *Ve'amat*).

Regarding the question as to how a traveller would know just where the the next town's Sabbath limit was to be found, Rabban Gamliel is quoted as saying that he had his own method of determining this. By locating the top of a tower whose height he knew and looking at it through a hollow reed, he could work out mathematically the distance to the town from where he stood (*Er.* 41b, 43b).

While journeying to a town, someone might lie down to rest and wake up to find that the Sabbath had already commenced but that he happened to be within the town's Sabbath boundary (*tehum Shabbat*). Since he had not been aware of the need to establish a residence there,[157] he could not "acquire" it on the Sabbath because effecting a transaction is prohibited. R. Yehudah, however, would have allowed him to enter the town, as he obviously intended to reside there (*Er.* 45a; Maim. *Shabbat*, 27:10; *Orah Hayyim* 400:1).

Consent

An *eruv tehumin*[158] must have the knowledge and consent of the person for whom it is made. Whereas the creation of an *eruv hatzerot* (see below)[159] does not require the participant's

---

156   עקר דעתו לקנות שם

157   קונה שביתה

158   ערוב תחומין

159   ערוב חצירות

specific knowledge, since it is entirely for his benefit, establishing a new Sabbath residence through the "amalgamation of boundaries" has different legal requirements. Normally, it is possible for A to acquire something for B without B's knowledge, but this is only the case if the acquisition is in B's interest. Establishing an *eruv*, the designated spot that must be "acquired", will give a person access to one side of the town, but this may not be to his advantage as he may prefer access to the other side, which is now excluded. Here we follow the rule that one has no authority to act on another person's behalf, committing him to some undesirable move, unless one obtains his prior consent (*Er.* 81b; Maim. *Eruvin*, 6:18; *Ora<u>h</u> <u>H</u>ayyim* 414:1; *Er.* 82b, Rashi and ROSH *ad loc.*).

Lack of Consent – Force Majeure

A case may arise where someone is forced to go beyond the Sabbath limit and then is brought back to the permitted area. He may have been taken there by hostile non-Jews or he may have had a fit of insanity (which the Sages likened to abduction by an "evil spirit"), not being aware of what he did. Once this person returned, he was treated like someone who had never left and so continued to enjoy the right to move within his original "domain" (*Er.* 41b).

Assumption of Consent

As a rule, one person may deposit food for the *eruv te<u>h</u>umin* on behalf of all the town's residents, who are then permitted to make use of the *eruv*. However, an individual may only do so if he knew about it before the Sabbath and then decided to use it. If he knew about the *eruv*, but only decided to use it after the Sabbath's commencement, the ruling was that since he had knowledge of the *eruv* before the Sabbath, his later decision to avail himself of it had presumably been contemplated in advance. The facilities granted by the *eruv* were therefore available to him.

The Sages based their lenient ruling on the principle that one may accept a choice made later as having been originally intended but not expressed.[160] In legal matters relating to the conveyance of property, this principle would not be accepted. In the case of a Rabbinic institution, however, if someone knew during the day that the *eruv* had been set, a later decision might be held to confirm a prior decision retrospectively (*Orah Hayyim* 413:1, 414:1; Mish., *Er.* 8:1, R'AV, *Tiferet Yisrael, Tosefot Yom Tov ad loc.*).

If the *eruv* had been duly set and some fault occurred in it, or if the proper amount of food had been reduced, it was permissible to make an adjustment without informing the others, as they had already agreed to participate in the *eruv*. However, any new participant would have to be informed so as to obtain his consent (*Er.* 80b; *Orah Hayyim* 368:1–5).

Eruv Stipulations

Although the Sages differed as to whether an *ex post facto* choice could be accepted as one made at the outset,[161] there was general agreement that a lenient ruling should be issued when any condition was attached to an *eruv* (*Er.* 36b).

[General references: *Talmudic Encyclopedia*, Vol. 4, p. 217, "*Bererah*"; *Kesef Nivhar* 33, s.v. "*Bererah*"]

The Sages accordingly permitted a man to attach a stipulation to his *eruv* – namely, that its exact direction would be chosen on the Sabbath, depending on circumstances at the time. The man in question might wish to meet a Torah scholar arriving from another town, but so far had no idea which way to go in order to welcome him. Alternatively, he might need to avoid thugs coming from either end of the town. In the former case, he was permitted to set his *eruv* on both sides and to stipulate that whichever proved correct would be the side intended for his *eruv*, the place where he had "acquired" his residence (*koneh shevitah*).

---

160   בערוב דרבנן יש ברירה
161   אם יש ברירה או אין ברירה

Although a person is only allowed to "acquire" his new domicile by means of an *eruv* set in one direction, the Rabbinic principle validating a retrospective choice[162] enables us to assume that the side he required was the one that he originally intended. A further concession makes it possible to assume that the choice was in fact determined not by the local man but by the visiting scholar (*Er.* 36b, Rashi, *Tos.* s.v. *"lo"*; *Orah Hayyim* 413:1).[163]

If two people needed to use the *eruv* together, one of them could choose and designate its direction while the second relied on and was included in that choice, rendering his consent automatic.[164] Thus, if two people were travelling together and one could identify the particular tree or hedge where he wished to "acquire" his Sabbath domicile, but the other could not, the latter was entitled to surrender his own right of domicile to the former, so as to share his residence. In that case, the former would designate the spot as jointly theirs (*Er.* 49b, 51a, Rashi; Maim. *Eruvin*, 7:7; *Orah Hayyim* 409:11–12).

If someone travelling home before the Sabbath found himself beyond the 2,000-cubit limit, but recognized a certain tree within his own limit and that of the town, he could designate that tree as his residence and thus complete his journey home. In order to designate a particular place that he "acquires" as that of his "new domicile" and *eruv* (*koneh shevitah*), a person must specify its exact location and not refer vaguely to "somewhere" within his Sabbath limit. If he wishes to designate the place as being located under a certain tree or within a certain cave, where there is a space of at least eight cubits (i.e., twice the area of his own *"dalet ammot"*), his *eruv* will not be effective unless he specifies the exact location of his intended residence, e.g., to the north or south of that place, in front of the tree or behind it.

162　ברירה
163　תולה בדעת אחרים
164　סומכין עליו

If a festival immediately preceded or followed a Sabbath and an individual wished to journey east one day and west on the next, an *eruv* would be required for the festival just as it would be for the Sabbath and he would need one on either side of the town. He could not rely on a single *eruv* and mentally transfer its application from one side to the other, because the festival has a sanctity of its own no less than the Sabbath (*Er.* 38a, Rashi, R'AV; Maim. *Eruvin*, 8:4).[165]

The place designated as a Sabbath residence must be suitable for that purpose. A gravestone would not be appropriate, least of all for a *kohen*, nor would a shaky tree-branch be acceptable (*Er.* 34b; *Oraḥ Ḥayyim* 409:1, 3). An *eruv* is meant for people walking on dry land, not sailing on ships. When a ship docks, one's 2,000-cubit allowance begins at the disembarkation point. This also applies to airline passengers and crew (*Oraḥ Ḥayyim* 404:1).

Mental Capacity of the Messenger

When the Sages ruled that a person could send his *eruv* food to the designated place by messenger, they required the *shali'aḥ* to understand the purpose of his mission: in other words, he should not be a minor, a heathen (to whom this law is not applicable) or a mental defective.[166] Acquiring a place of residence is a legal act (*kinyan*) which becomes valid only if the acquirer understands what he is doing and does it properly.[167]

Nevertheless, if the person concerned observed such a messenger delivering the food as required, the *eruv* was considered valid. The Sages added that even if he used an elephant or an ape to convey food to its designated place, and saw it was delivered there, the *eruv* would be valid.[168]

In the case of a normal adult messenger, the *eruv* would be valid even if the man did not see his food delivered at the specified place, in accordance with the standard presumption that "a messenger discharges his mission".[169] This principle was considered a vital interpretation of the Torah law regarding the sheaf of new wheat offered on the altar (Lev. 23:10–11).[170] General use of new wheat was only sanctioned after the priest had offered the first sheaf on the altar. Although this service was not witnesssed publicly, it was assumed that the *kohen*, as the people's emissary, had duly performed his task (*Er.* 31b–32a, Rashi, *Tos.* s.v. "*kan*"; *Orah Hayyim* 409:8; *Mishnah Berurah ad loc.*).

(2) *Amalgamation of Domains – Eruv Hatzerot*

"Carrying" from a private domain (*reshut ha-yahid*)[171] to a public domain (*reshut ha-rabbim*) or vice versa on the Sabbath was forbidden by Torah law, as was "carrying" in a public domain for a distance of more than four cubits. The Sages based this ordinance on the prohibition of "gathering firewood" on the Sabbath (Num. 15:32). The exact definitions of a "private" and "public" domain were given in the Oral Law (Tractate *Eruvin* and Codes).

In ancient times, a number of houses were built around a common *hatzer* (courtyard) in the form of a square enclosure. Each house was a "private domain", whereas the courtyard area, though normally accessible to all, was not the personal possession of each householder. As carrying something out of one's own property was forbidden on the Sabbath, this law prevented general use of the courtyard.

Although joint ownership of the courtyard afforded each householder some entitlement, no portion could be demarcated

---

169 חזקה שליח עושה שליחותו

170 הקרבת העומר

171 רשות היחיד

separately and each householder had a shared right of ownership, which meant that they were all prevented from carrying on the Sabbath. To resolve this problem, the Sages created a legal device that enabled people to make common use of the *hatzer*. It transformed the whole courtyard into an extension of each house, which thus acquired an extended "private domain". Each of the residents contributed a share of the food (in cash or kind) made available to all and deposited in one of the houses. At the same time, each resident conceded his right of ownership in the courtyard to all those participating in the amalgamated ownership, thus making the whole area a single domain that could also be extended from one *hatzer* to another (Maim. *Eruvin*, 5:6).

Through this symbolic act, permission to carry objects from one house to another or over the courtyard was granted and readily utilized. The Sages based their approval of such a device on the fact that, according to basic Torah law, the prohibition would not have applied to a jointly owned courtyard. However, they extended it as a protective measure designed to avoid a more serious act of "carrying", and thereby made "a fence around the law".[172] The Sages were thus empowered to modify their own institution (Maim. *Yad*, *Eruvin*, 1:1–2).

The entrance to the courtyard or alley[173] was symbolically "closed" by erecting a pole and crossbeam at the entrance. In an extended form, this *eruv hatzerot* technique is also used to "enclose" an entire neighbourhood or town by means of a wire stretched over poles around the area. This particularly facilitated the use of wheelchairs and perambulators within that area on the Sabbath and is known simply as an *eruv* (*Sh. Ar.*, *Orah Hayyim* 366–368).

The minimum amount of food required for an "amalgamation of domains" was a whole loaf of bread, even a small one, which would be edible on the following Sabbath (Maim. *Eruvin*, 1:8). Prior to the Sabbath's commencement,

---

172   סיג לתורה
173   מבוי

one man collected a loaf from each participating household, put all the loaves in a container placed in one of the houses and recited the prescribed blessing. He also made a declaration that the purpose of this *eruv* was to allow carrying from one domain to another on the Sabbath (Maim. *Eruvin*, 1:16; *Orah Hayyim* 366:1–14). In accordance with a later practice, some grain might be collected or purchased and from the flour one whole loaf was baked, often in the shape of unleavened bread (*matzah*)[174] which retained its freshness. This was kept safe in the synagogue over Passover and remained valid for a year (*Shab.* 6a; Maim. *Eruvin*, 1:6–7; *Orah Hayyim* 366:1).

Since the *eruv* food had to be permissible, anything forbidden as *tevel* ("untithed")[175] was not accepted. If, however, it was conceivable but not known for certain[176] that the priestly due had been taken, the food could still be used. This was because of the Sages' concern for needy folk who wished to partake of the food, as was generally the case when *demai* was needed by the poor.

If, on the Sabbath, one had to use food that had not been tithed (the process of tithing required "work" forbidden on the Sabbath),[177] one could nevertheless utilize the following procedure. By looking at one portion and determining that it would constitute the tithe to be separated after the Sabbath's termination, one was permitted to eat the remainder.[178] The lesser stringency of Rabbinic additions to the *eruv* law made it possible to adopt a more flexible approach and use legal fictions to ease compliance. Tradition has it that participating in an *eruv hatzerot* was a custom instituted by King Solomon (*Er.* 21b; 31a; TJ *Er.* 3:2; Maim. *Eruvin*, 1:15).

The process of "amalgamation" would not be effective unless all the residents participated, so that no part of the courtyard was excluded from the common domain. The Sages

---

174 מצה
175 תבל
176 דמאי
177 תיקון מעשר ותרומה
178 כיצד יעשה נותן עיניו במקצתו ואוכל את השאר

might even compel a recalcitrant housholder to participate, since this did not involve him in any expense and his refusal to do so was a manifestation of wicked obstinacy – *middat Sedom* (*Er.* 49a).[179] If, nevertheless, one of the residents persisted in excluding himself, the legal fiction would not apply and the entire *eruv* would be ineffective.

If one resident left home before the Sabbath to visit a friend in another courtyard, and thus failed to participate in his own *eruv*, the Sages ruled that one must decide whether such non-participation indicated that he refused or did not need to use the *eruv*. That conclusion, involving a possible transgression by all the householders, depended on whether he intended to return home during the Sabbath, in which case his failure to participate would invalidate the *eruv*. If he never meant to return on the Sabbath, having left to stay with his daughter or to remain all day in another town, he would not be considered a resident and his absence would not invalidate the *eruv* (*Er.* 86a–b; Maim. *Eruvin*, 4:13; *Orah Hayyim* 371:1–2; *Er.* 62b).[180]

If a resident forgot to participate in the *eruv*, he could save it by declaring that he relinquished the ownership of his home to the other participants.[181] This would grant all of them the right to use the courtyard,[182] just as if they had all participated in the *eruv*. The Sages were divided as to whether a formal relinquishment[183] could take place on the Sabbath. Bet Shammai regarded such an act as a conveyance (*mikneh*), which was forbidden; Bet Hillel considered "abandonment" merely a surrender of ownership (*hefker*) and not a conveyance, which was therefore permitted. Maimonides and Caro followed Hillel's ruling in their codifications (*Er.* 69a–b; Maim. Mishnah commentary (*Perush ha-Mishnah*), on *Er.* 69b, s.v. "*anshei hatzer*"; Maim. *Eruvin*, 2:1; *Orah Hayyim* 380:1–2).

---

179   כופין על מידת סדום
180   שכבר השיאה מלבו
181   שיאמר רשותי מבוטלת לכם
182   חצר
183   ביטול

The accepted rule was that in all matters concerning the Rabbinically instituted law of *eruv ḥatzerot*, the lenient interpretation should be followed wherever possible (*Er.* 46a, 62a, *Tos.* "*ve-Rabbi Yoḥanan*"; *Er.* 80a).[184]

If someone regularly participated with his neighbours in the alley,[185] but failed to do so on one occasion, the neighbours could take the required share from his house, even without his knowledge, as one would assume that he intended to participate (*Er.* 80a–b, *Tos.* s.v. "*ma'aseh*", "*ragil*"; ROSH; Maim. *Eruvin*, 5:2; *Oraḥ Ḥayyim* 67:1).

A jointly owned courtyard that is enclosed on three sides, leaving the fourth side open, can be used as one domain for the purpose of carrying if some type of board is firmly attached to each side of the open entrance[186] and another is placed over and across the two side-posts. This creates a symbolic door, thereby producing an enclosure.[187] The board must already be in place prior to the Sabbath and its use for this purpose must also be recognized.[188] If it stood in place "of itself"[189] (i.e., it had not been put there with the Sabbath in mind), then according to Rava, it would not be considered a valid side-post for the purpose of an *eruv*. The law required a symbolic enclosure to have originally been made for that purpose; if it already stood there, the board had to have been meant for use as an *eruv* enclosure prior to the Sabbath (*Er.* 15a, Rashi; Maim. *Shabbat*, 16:19, 22; *Oraḥ Ḥayyim* 363:11).[190]

As it has been seen above, the domains of two adjacent courtyards belonging to different owners may be enclosed by positioning a board before the Sabbath began to complete the enclosure, or some other form of joining, according to the device of the *eruv*. Rav Huna ruled that if during the course of

---

184   הלכה כדברי המקל בעירוב
185   שיתופי מבואות
186   לחי
187   צורת פתח
188   ובלבד שיסמכו עליו מערב שבת
189   לחי העומד עליו
190   בלבד שיסמכו עליו מערב שבת

the Sabbath some of the structure collapsed, invalidating the enclosure, the carrying from one courtyard to the other was nevertheless permitted. Since permission of this condition had already been approved, the permissibility continues until the day is concluded, although it would be forbidden on future Sabbaths. In these circumstances the general rule was laid down: "As for the law of the Sabbath, once the Sabbath restriction had been removed it remains removed throughout that Sabbath day" (*Er.* 93b, 17a).[191] It is similarly stated that if it had been on any condition of permissibility on the first part of the Sabbath, and then during the course of the day the condition entitling the dispensation was broken, the permissibility remains in place throughout the whole day of that Sabbath (*Er.* 70b).[192]

This apparent leniency in what normally required the strict observance of the Sabbath law may be understood on the principle that the very concept of the sanctity of the Sabbath is itself an act of the mind. The institution of the *eruv,* likewise, is not something factual, but a conception of the mind. Thus, once before the restriction of the Sabbath commenced, the individual had already established in his mind that the requirements of the *eruv,* removing the prohibition of carrying, were duly in place, that condition remained throughout the Sabbath day.

(3) *Amalgamation of Prepared Foods –* *Eruv Tavshilin*

As a general rule, all types of work prohibited on the Sabbath are also prohibited on major festivals. Torah law distinguished each festival day as "a holy convocation" – *mikra kodesh* (Ex. 12:16; Lev. 23:7–8, 21, 35–36), also designating both Rosh ha-Shanah and Yom Kippur as "a day of solemn rest" (*shabbaton*) when no work should be performed (Lev. 23:24,

---

191   שבת כיון שהותרה הותרה
192   זה הכלל כל שמותר למקצת שבת הותר לכל השבת

32). The same expressions are used to forbid work on the
festivals and on the Sabbath (Ex. 12:16, Lev. 23:3).[193]

The aim of these work prohibitions was to free men
from their everyday concerns, enabling them to ponder the
miraculous events associated with each festival day and give
praise to God (Hinnukh 297). However, Torah law made
one significant exception in the law governing festivals:
"No manner of work shall be done in them, save that which
every man must eat, that only may be done" (Ex. 12:16).[194]
The provision of food thus made it lawful to "carry" and to
"make fire" by transferring a flame that was already alight
for the purpose of cooking and baking. The Sages laid down,
however, that preparatory work such as harvesting and milling
flour should be undertaken before and not on the festival (Orah
Hayyim 495:1–2).[195]

Since leave to prepare food was restricted to the needs
of the festival itself, a difficulty arose when yom tov was
immediately followed by Shabbat. Because of the Sabbath
prohibition, it was normal practice to cook Sabbath food on
the previous day; but if that day happened to be a festival,
cooking yom tov food was alone permissible.

The Talmud records a Mishnaic teaching that dealt
specifically with this problem. Since food cooked before the
festival that was left over on yom tov might be eaten freely
the next day, the Sages recommended preparing a special dish
in advance that was intended for a meal after the festival. This
might be a portion of bread and some cooked dish. A legal
fiction was then applied to establish a "mixture of eatables"
that made other food prepared on yom tov itself an extension
of the pre-festival cooking. In order to validate this legal
process, it was essential for the special dish to be designated
part of the food that would be lawfully cooked on the festival.
Any food needed for the Sabbath but cooked on the festival
was thus "left over" from the yom tov items that had begun

---

193   כל מלאכה לא תעשו
194   אך אשר יאכל לכל נפש הוא לבדו ייעשה לכם
195   קצירה וטחינה ובצירה וסחיטה וצידה אסרום חכמים

cooking prior to the festival. This "amalgamation of cooked food" was known as eruv tavshilin (*Betzah* 16b, Rashi; Maim. *Yom Tov*, 6:1–2; *Orah Hayyim* 527:1, REMA).[196]

The law banning the preparation of food on the Sabbath is linked with the daily supply of manna which, the Israelites were told, would not be available on the Sabbath. They were therefore commanded to gather a double portion of manna on Friday and to prepare their food before the Sabbath: "Bake that which ye will bake, and seethe that which ye will seethe" (Ex. 16:23).[197]

In their clarification of this law, the Sages issued the following guidelines. Although it is not permissible to cook food required for the Sabbath on *yom tov*, if a festival happens to occur on a Friday, one may prepare a dish for the Sabbath before the festival actually begins and (as noted above) consider it the basis of any Sabbath food that will still be cooked on the festival itself. Any subsequent cooking on *yom tov* would complete the pre-festival preparation, that first dish making all the remainder permitted Sabbath food.[198]

This "mixing of eatables" was created by deliberately setting the basic dish aside as the *eruv*. The Sages extended the beneficial effect of this procedure by ruling that one person may prepare the *eruv tavshilin* for whoever wishes to avail himself of it (*Betzah* 15b; Maim. *Yom Tov*, 6:1–2; *Orah Hayyim* 527:1–2). There are two essential requirements: the *eruv* dish prepared before the festival must be specially "designated" as food cooked for the Sabbath (*matneh alav*); and whoever creates the *eruv* must fully understand the purpose of his action and recite the benediction on fulfilling his religious duty – *le-shem mitzvah* (*Betzah* 16b; Maim. *Yom Tov*, 6:7–8; *Orah Hayyim* 527:9).

---

196   ערוב תבשילין
197   את אשר תאפו אפו ואת אשר תבשלו בשלו
198   לא יבשל בתחילה מיום טוב לשבת, אבל עושה תבשיל מערב יום טוב וסומך עליו לשבת

Although it was halakhically permissible to eat festival leftovers on the Sabbath, cooking food on *yom tov* with the specific intention of eating it on the Sabbath was forbidden unless one adhered to the *eruv* procedure. Whatever someone had in mind when the food was cooked thus rendered his action either permitted or prohibited. The Sages ruled that if he acted deceitfully by cooking a double portion of food on *yom tov*, although he knew full well that only one portion was required for the festival and that the other portion was intended for the Sabbath, or if he dishonestly claimed that the extra food might be needed for unexpected guests, any surplus he would be forbidden to eat on the Sabbath (*Betzah* 17a; *Orah Hayyim* 527:24, *Mishnah Berurah ad loc.*).

In communities outside Israel each festival lasts for two days, the only exception being Yom Kippur, the Day of Atonement (*Pes.* 52a; *Orah Hayyim* 496:1). The reason for this two-day observance is that Judaism uses a lunar calendar system. In ancient times, the exact date of each festival could only be determined after evidence based on physical observation of the New Moon had reached the Sanhedrin, which then proclaimed Rosh Hodesh (the New Moon). News of the Sanhedrin's proclamation often took time to reach Jews living far away and, whenever doubt arose, they kept one extra day of *yom tov* as a precaution. Although all dates have long been calculated in advance, the "second festive day of Diaspora communities"[199] is still observed outside the Holy Land. An exception was made for the Day of Atonement (10 Tishri), because the date of the New Year (1 Tishri) had already been ascertained and to prevent the hardship of a 48-hour fast.

When *yom tov* occurred on Thursday and Friday, the *eruv* for *Shabbat* was prepared on Wednesday. In that case, if someone forgot to set his *eruv* before the festival and later, on the first day, realized his mistake, he was permitted to correct it on that first day with a reasoned stipulation,[200] as follows: If the first day is the holy one[201] (i.e., two days before the Sabbath), no *eruv* is required; but if the second day is holy, the first is a "pre-festival" working day,[202] and so the *eruv* requirement is now fulfilled (*Betzah* 6a, Rashi *ad loc.*; Maim. *Yom Tov*, 6:11; *Oraḥ Ḥayyim* 527:22).

Summary of the Laws of Eruv

In Jewish teaching, a thought can have the effect of an action and determine the (halakhic) result in a positive or negative way, so that one fulfils a religious duty or commits a transgression. Acts of the mind play an important part in making various facilities available on the Sabbath through the establishment of an *eruv*. The *eruv* procedure itself is an act of the mind.

Amalgamation of Boundaries – Eruv Teḥumin

Walking more than 2,000 cubits (about 1,000 metres) beyond one's town was prohibited on the Sabbath. By establishing a new residence outside the town, however, one could walk a further 2,000 cubits from that point. This required the making of an *eruv*, where an adequate amount of Sabbath food was placed in advance. If necessary, one could establish the new Sabbath residence by determining in one's mind that it would be located there.

If, before the Sabbath's commencement, a traveller found himself some way from his destination but recognized a landmark within the town's Sabbath boundary, he could mentally locate his new "domicile" at that spot, which would make the rest of his journey permissible.

Although a person's *eruv* might be created by someone else, the acquisition of a new "domicile" required his own prior knowledge and consent. If he was not sure of the direction in

---

which he intended to walk on the Sabbath, he could establish his *eruv* on both sides of the town. Whichever side he chose on that day was then assumed to be the one he had originally intended.

Amalgamation of Domains – Eruv Hatzerot

As defined by Torah law, work forbidden on the Sabbath involves technical skill and is intended for a specific purpose. In some instances, only the person concerned would know if this meant that he had violated a Sabbath regulation. Since the need for an *eruv* was an institution of the Rabbis to safeguard the prohibition against "carrying" on the Sabbath, various acts in a participant's mind were endorsed by the Sages, who modified the law in certain cases.

One resident of a "housing complex" built around a courtyard (*hatzer*) who had secured his fellow residents' agreement could thus declare a loaf of bread joint property. That had the effect of combining all the separate "domains", which meant that the courtyard area and the houses surrounding it were now one common "domain". This legal device made carrying on the Sabbath day permissible within the whole complex.

The *eruv hatzer*ot was not effective, however, unless all of the residents participated. If any one of them refused to amalgamate his "domain" with the *eruv*, the legal fiction would not apply and anyone who carried objects outside his private "domain" would be guilty of a Sabbath violation.

If one resident left home before the Sabbath and did not participate in the *eruv*, its validity would depend on whether he meant to return during the day, in which case his non-participation made the *eruv* null and void. If he had no intention of returning on the Sabbath, there was no need to consider him a resident and his absence would not affect his neighbours' *eruv*.

A resident who meant to participate but forgot to do so could preserve the *eruv* by formally declaring that he "relinquished" the ownership of his home to the other householders, which would enable them to use the *hatzer*. If someone who regularly participated in the *eruv* did not do so on a particular *Shabbat*, his neighbours were entitled to assume that he meant to participate and they could take the requisite share of food from his home.

Amalgamation of Prepared Foods – Eruv Tavshilin

Permission to cook food on a festival enables one to prepare whatever is required for *yom tov*, but not for the following day. If the next day happens to be a Sabbath, the *eruv tavshilin* procedure (creating a "mixture of prepared foods") offers a solution to the problem. One takes a dish of food cooked before *yom tov*, "designates" it for the Sabbath and then considers it the basis of all other cooking or baking for the Sabbath that may continue during the festival.

By having in mind the purpose of this *eruv* and by "designating" two food supplies as one, the housewife is permitted to cook food on the festival and serve it on the following (Sabbath) day.

F. Intention

Intended and Unintended Results – Tzerikhah le-Gufah

The Sages ruled that work producing a result that had neither been required nor intended[203] was not blameworthy.[204] According to some opinions, therefore, one who dug a pit on the Sabbath (an act that fell under the 39 categories of forbidden "work"), but whose sole aim was to procure the earth dug out, would not be held culpable.[205] The Sages, however, considered this a type of manual labour that was

---

203   מלאכה שאינה צריכה לגופה
204   פטור
205   אמר רבי אבא החופר גומא בשבת ואינו צריך אלא לעפרה פטור עליה

explicitly forbidden (*Shab.* 73b; Maim. *Shabbat*, 1:7).[206]

One of those 39 *avot melakhah* is extinguishing a flame.[207] R. Yose ruled that a man who did so to preserve the clay lamp in which the flame burnt, or to spare the oil or the wick (i.e., for some purpose other than extinguishing the flame), would be exempt from punishment (*patur*). All agreed, however, that one who did so for the purpose of turning burnt material into charcoal would be held guilty (*hayyav*), because he had engaged in productive work (*Shab.* 29b, 31b; Maim. *Shabbat*, 1:7).[208]

R. Yose also taught that the prohibition of "building and demolishing" only related to the demolition of a structure in order to make way for a new one. Thoughtless destruction (see below)[209] was not what the Torah defined as productive work.[210] The intention behind the work performed would determine whether it incurred liability (*Shab.* 31b; Maim. *Shabbat*, 1:7).

Inevitable Transgression – Pesik Reisheh

The Sages distinguished between an action generating unintended work and one that inevitably resulted in forbidden work. While no prohibition had been violated if the work was not intentional,[211] even a harmless act would be illicit if it inevitably generated forbidden work. This type of situation is known as *pesik reisheh* (see Chapter 3 above).[212]

A typical case involved someone who wished to obtain the blue dye used in the making of *tzitzit* ("ritual fringes") and who crushed a *hillazon* mollusc from which the *tekhelet* colour was extracted. If he did this on a Sabbath, he would have

---

206 חייב
207 המכבה
208 כחס על הנר כחס על השמן כחס על הפתילה, רבי יוסי פוטר בכולן חוץ מן הפתילה מפני שהוא עושה פחם
209 מקלקל
210 סותר על מנת לבנות
211 דבר שאין מתכוון
212 פסיק רישיה

committed an offence. Crushing the mollusc was not in itself forbidden, although "taking life" is prohibited, but destroying the creature was incidental to the *tekhelet*'s extraction: even if a better dye could be obtained from a live mollusc, this action was forbidden on the Sabbath.

The Sages regarded it as an exemplary case of *pesik reisheh* ("You can't cut off a chicken's head without killing the fowl").[213] The dye hunter might think that he only needed the blue secretion, not seeking to kill the mollusc, but (despite his professed intention) the creature's death was unavoidable. Similarly, killing wild animals for sport would violate the prohibition of "taking life"[214] under the category of "hunting" (*Shab.* 75a; Maim. *Shabbat*, 1:6).[215]

"Squeezing" water out of a garment on the Sabbath was also forbidden,[216] as a form of washing clothes;[217] and if a person only used a sponge to wash his body, this too would make "squeezing" (*sehitah*) inevitable. In these instances even R. Shim'on, who advocated *davar she-ein mitkavven muttar* (see above), would rule that it was forbidden as a case of *pesik reisheh* (*Shab.* 75a; *Shab.* 111b, commentary of R. Hananel, "*modeh Rabbi Shim'on*"; Maim. *Shabbat*, 1:6).

A different *pesik reisheh* situation might arise if whoever performed the action, far from being concerned about the inevitable result, felt happier if it did not occur. Nowadays, for example, if blood is needed for a transfusion, it is best obtained from a living donor.[218] Although this does not involve the shedding of blood, human or animal, R. Shim'on would agree that such an action broke the law against "taking a life" (*Shab.* 75a, Rashi and *Tos.* s.v. "*tefei neha*").[219]

If someone had no interest whatsoever in an unavoidable

---

213   פסיק רישא ולא ימות

214   נטילת נשמה

215   הצד

216   סחיטה

217   מכבס

218   דכמה דאית בה נשמה טפי ניהא לה

219   נטילת נשמה

result, such as uprooting grass while walking on it (*pesik reisheh*), he would still not be held liable for the *melakhah* of "uprooting" (*akirah*)[220] or "reaping" (*kotzer*).[221] The "work" of *akirah* might have taken place, but the reverse was also possible.[222] In that case, R. Shim'on would consider the action permitted – *muttar* (*Orah Hayyim* 336:3).

Another exemplary case is where a person finds a wooden splinter in his hand and needs to have it removed with a needle. Piercing his skin with the needle is bound to produce a cut (*pesik reisheh*), which falls under the category of "wounding."[223] Since his only concern is to avoid further pain, and inflicting a wound is not his intention, even in R. Yehudah's strict view the splinter's removal would be permitted. This accords with the principle that a resulting "work" that was not intended, and for which the author himself has no use, is permissible (*Shab.* 107a, *Tos.* s.v. "*u-mimeni*"; *Sanh.* 84a; *Shab.* 103a, *Tos.* s.v. "*lo tzerikhah*").[224]

Constructive and Destructive Results – Mekalkel

As stated earlier, R. Yose ruled that an action resulting in "work" that was neither intended nor required[225] – as in the case that he cited[226] – should not be considered a violation of the Sabbath. This was not, however, the unanimous opinion of the Sages. R. Yehudah, for example, maintained that the "work" had been performed in spite of any different intention and made the performer liable (*hayyav*) for his action. The "I did not mean it" plea in ritual matters was accepted by some and rejected by others (*Shab.* 29b, 31b).

Maimonides followed the opinion of R. Yehudah rendering

---

220 עקירה
221 קוצר
222 אפשר בלי פסיק רישא
223 חובל
224 מלאכה שאינו מכוון ואינה צריכה לגופה מותר
225 אין צריך לגופו
226 כחס על הנר

the performer liable for his action (Maim. *Shabbat*, 1:7).
However, all the Sages, including R. Yehudah, agreed that if
an action had been entirely destructive,[227] such "work" was
not culpable. Thus, if someone dug a hole in the ground and
his purpose was not to make a hole but to damage the field,
this did not fall under the category of "constructive work" and
was therefore not blameworthy (*Shab.* 73b; Maim. *Shabbat*,
1:17). The commentators pointed out that although such an
action might be legitimate (*patur*), it should not be performed
(*assur*), as any exhausting labour conflicted with the spirit of
Shabbat (*Betzah* 8a, *Tos.*).

"Tearing"[228] falls under the category of prohibited "work".
Nevertheless, if someone in a fit of temper destructively
tore his clothing or broke a vessel, he was (according to the
Mishnah) not guilty of a forbidden "work". If, however, he
tore the neckband of his garment to make it less constricting,
he would be guilty of productive "work"; but if he gained no
benefit from tearing it and the act was entirely destructive, he
would not be held liable.

Some of the Sages declared that if one's action resulted
in personal injury, one could not escape blame for violating
the Sabbath.[229] Others claimed that if the action was purely
destructive, one would not of course be liable for constructive
"work"[230] but for damages. Later authorities, however,
rejected the "no liability" decision and ruled that tearing one's
clothes in anger *did* make one liable. This was the view of
Maimonides, who explained that it was not a simple case of
"destructiveness" (*mekalkel*). Tearing his clothes releases a
man's anger and relieves his state of mind, a constructive act
for which he is held liable (*Shab.* 105b; Mish. *Shabbat* 13:3;
Bertinoro *ad loc.*; Maim. *Shabbat*, 1:17).[231]

Maimonides adopted the principle that not every destructive

---

227 מקלקל
228 קורע
229 חץ מחובל ומעביר
230 מלאכת מחשבת
231 מפני שדעתו מתישבת וחמומו משתפר... הוא דומה למתקן

act makes one a Sabbath violator. As in the case mentioned above, he ruled that if someone destructively tore a hole in the ground, he would not be held guilty of flouting a Sabbath prohibition (*Shab*. 105b; Maim. *Shabbat*, 1:17).

The foregoing discussion refers to culpability for a wilfull Sabbath violation that may incur grave spiritual punishment (*karet*), which one should avoid at all costs (Maim. *Shabbat*, 1:1). In practice, the Sages ruled that in view of the supreme importance of keeping the Sabbath, which they regarded as equivalent to fulfilling all Torah laws, *no* kind of work or reference to it was permissible on that day. Apart from the time needed for one's prayers and Sabbath meals, one should only engage in the study of Torah, which was even held to be the main purpose of Sabbath and festival observance (TJ *Shab*. 15:3).[232] A similar ruling was adopted by the Codes (Maim. *Shabbat*, 30:15; *Orah Hayyim* 307:17, 290:2, 285:1).[233]

Error – Shegagah

Only "work" performed as originally intended is forbidden on the Sabbath. If it was done by mistake, the ordained punishment would not be incurred, but one would have to bring a sin-offering[234] (Maim. *Shabbat*, 1:9; Maim. *Shegagot*, 1:1).[235]

For a transgression committed in error, "if anyone sinned unwittingly",[236] the Torah prescribed different kinds of sacrifice and atonement to be made by the high priest, by the nation as a whole, by the king or by an individual (Lev. 4:2 ff.).[237] There were also different levels of responsibility, according to the offender's awareness or unawareness of

---

232 לא ניתנו שבתות וימים טובים אלא לעסוק בהן בדברי תורה
233 אסור ללמוד זולת בדברי תורה
234 חטאת
235 מלאכת מחשבת אסרה תורה
236 נפש כי תחטא בשגגה
237 נפש כי תחטא בשגגה אשר נשיא יחטא

his mistake. In regard to an individual, the Torah stated: "If anyone of the common people sin through error, in doing any of the things which the Lord hath commanded not to be done, and be guilty; if his sin, which he hath sinned, be made known to him, then he shall bring his offering... and the priest shall make atonement for him, and he shall be forgiven" (Lev. 4:27–31).[238]

The Sages distinguished between the following cases:

If someone deliberately performed an act forbidden on the Sabbath in the mistaken belief that it was not the Sabbath day, that act was deemed an "error" (*shegagah*)[239] and he was obliged to bring a sin-offering (*Ker.* 19b–20a).

If a person meant to do something that was permissible on the Sabbath, but mistakenly performed some forbidden "work", he was not liable to bring an offering for the *shegagah*, since everyone knew that the act he intended to perform was not prohibited.

To clarify this second ruling, the Sages gave an illustrative example. It is forbidden to "cut" a growing plant on the Sabbath, as this falls under the category of "harvesting".[240] If someone meant to take a plant that was already detached from the soil, which is permitted, but while doing so inadvertently cut one growing in it, he would not be guilty of an offence. Abbaye explained that this person had never intended to "cut" the plant, but only to pick one no longer in the ground. If, however, he had meant to pick one already detached from the soil and inadvertently cut a plant still rooted in it, his intention to "cut" was all that mattered. He would have engaged in a forbidden action by mistake and was therefore liable to bring a sin-offering for his *shegagah* (*Ker.* 19b., Rashi, *Tos.*; Maim. *Shegagot*, 2:7; 72b, Rashi, *Tos.*, "*mitkavven*").

A further distinction was made by Shemuel. If someone meant to pick one particular fig from a tree (which was forbidden), but mistakenly picked a different one, or if he

---

238   ואם נפש אחת תחטא בשגגה מעם הארץ... והביא קרבנו

239   שגגה

240   מלקט

intended to pick figs and absentmindedly picked grapes, it might be argued that his act was at variance with his intention and did not fall under the category of "purposeful work".[241] One might, however, argue that he had violated the law in either case, had meant to do so and should therefore be held culpable. Here the Sages ruled in accordance with the view of R. Yehoshua: since the action that he performed was not what he had actually intended, and the "work" in question was inadvertent, he would be acquitted of liability, having neither achieved his real purpose nor fulfilled his intention.[242] In halakhic terms, such an offence is known as *mit'assek* (*Ker.* 19b; Maim. *Shabbat*, 72b, Rashi and *Tos.* "*nikavin*").[243]

Assumed to be Permissible – Omer Muttar

Where a transgression is committed by mistake, unwittingly or unintentionally, the pertinent laws are finely distinguished, according to the extent of the mistake and liability in each case. These unintended actions have separate designations – *shegagah*, *mit'assek*, *be-shikhehah* and *be-omer muttar*.

In the cases mentioned above the "error" occurred in the performance of the action (*be-shogeg*). However, a person might sincerely but mistakenly "believe that his action was permitted" (*omer muttar*).[244] Such a mistake could occur in the form of an action (*shigegat melakhot*) or of a failure to realize that it was a Sabbath day and that certain precautions must be taken (*shigegat Shabbat*).

The Sages differed as to whether the "error" of *omer muttar* was or was not culpable. If someone performed forbidden "work" on the Sabbath, being under the impression that his action was permitted, he would be regarded as one who had transgressed "in error" (*be-shogeg*). Rava held that a case of

---

241 מלאכת מחשבת אסרה תורה
242 לא נעשתה כוונתו ומחשבתו
243 מתעסק
244 אומר מותר

omer muttar was subject to the *shegagah* rule and thus exempt from punishment (*patur*). His colleague Abbaye, however, insisted that *omer muttar* approximated to a deliberate offence[245] and was therefore *ḥayyav*, culpable (*Mak.* 7b).

A distinction could be made here as follows. If someone knew that certain actions were forbidden on the Sabbath,[246] but thought that a particular one was not forbidden or else forgot that this was so,[247] he would not incur the penalty ordained, as this was a case of *shogeg*. However, he would be obliged to bring a sin-offering (*ḥayyav ḥattat*), which would afford him atonement (*Shab.* 64b; Maim. *Shegagot*, 2:6).

A case involving the prohibition of idolatry is discussed in the Talmud. The act of worshipping a false god is one of the three cardinal sins that a man dare not commit even if the alternative is martyrdom (*Sanh.* 74a; see also Chapter 3). Strict obedience to all admonitions against this offence was demanded of Israel: "Thou shalt have no other gods before Me... thou shalt not bow down unto them, nor serve them" (Ex. 20:3–5).[248] Whereas, generally speaking, one is not held responsible for transgressions committed under duress (by *force majeure*), since preserving life is a foremost consideration (Lev. 18:5),[249] one may not submit to idol worship even when threatened with death. Obedience to this law is known as *kiddush Hashem*, "sanctifying God's Name" (*AZ* 54a).[250]

This principle was laid down by the Sages: "Whoever engages in idol worship, willingly and knowingly [*be-mezid*],[251] faces the death penalty in the last resort. It makes no difference whether a person serves or sacrifices to an idol, offers incense, makes libations, prostrates himself before it or says 'You are my god' to the image" (*Sanh.* 60b; Maim.

---

245 קרוב למזיד
246 ידע מעיקר שבת
247 הכיר ולבסוף שכח
248 לא תשתחווה להם ולא תעבדם
249 וחי בהם
250 קידוש השם
251 במזיד

Avodat Kokhavim, 3:1, 3).[252]

In view of this statement, a question was raised as to what was meant by the expression "whether a person serves it". Abbaye held that the law declared him guilty in all circumstances, even if he bowed down to the idol "through love or fear of the one commanding him" – because of his respect for the ruler or belief that his life would be forfeit if he did not prostrate himself before a human being or a statue – even though the thought of recognizing a false god never entered his mind.[253] Rava, however, maintained that if a person violated the law out of fear for his life (*Sanh.* 74a), he would not be considered guilty of idol worship (*Sanh.* 61b).

With reference to the "unwitting sin" (Lev. 4:2), a distinction was made between unawareness of the prohibition (or ignorance of the fact that a certain action involved the prohibition)[254] and performance of the forbidden action by mistake (*bi-shegagah*). The Sages ruled that an action was culpable only if both conditions obtained (*Hor.* 7a; *Sanh.* 62a; Maim. *Shegagot*, 15:3).[255]

Accordingly, if someone prayed in a heathen temple, not realizing where he was, it would be a case of "unwitting transgression". If, on the other hand, he knew where he was and prostrated himself there, intending to worship the true God and none of the heathen images, or if he felt that he was only paying respect to the governing power, it would be deemed "a transgression committed in error" – *be-shogeg* (*Sanh.* 61b–62a, Rashi *ad loc.*).

Another case of "unwitting transgression" might be as follows. The *bet din*, for some strange reason, mistakenly ruled that it was not forbidden to prostrate oneself before an idol, or to carry on the Sabbath or to disregard the length of a wife's ritual "impurity". In such instances the court's ruling would have voided an unambiguous Torah law: this would

252 העובד עכו"ם אחד העובד ואחד המזבח
253 העובד מאהבה ומיראה
254 העלם דבר
255 העלם דבר עם שגגת מעשה

not be considered a mere "oversight" in regard to that law,[256] but a case of sheer basic "forgetfulness" (*shikhehah*).[257] Where a mistaken ruling was given by the Bet Din,[258] and then realising their mistake they corrected it, the culpability of a transgressor would depend on the circumstances. If the person left the country after the first ruling, and acted on the mistaken first ruling, he would be free of guilt; or, according to R. Elazar, be liable for a "doubtful-offering" – *asham taluyi*, since we don't know whether he relied on the Bet Din's ruling or followed his own opinion for which he would have been liable for a sin-offering – *hattat*. If he had remained in the country he would certainly be liable for a *hattat,* since every Jew is expected to be aware of the Torah's specific injunctions and realize that the ruling had been a mistake (Mish. *Hor.* 1:1–3; TB *Hor.* 3b, Rashi *ad loc.*; Maim. *Shegagot,* 14:1–2; *Kesef Mishneh ad loc.*).

If someone never knew that such an act was forbidden or, having grown up among Gentiles, was completely unversed in Jewish religious law,[259] the Sages held different opinions. Some ruled that once his offence was made known to him, he would have to bring a sin-offering. Others declared that the unusual circumstances had obviously made it impossible for him to observe the law[260] and he was therefore free of guilt (*Shab.* 68, Rashi, *Tos.*; Maim. *Shegagot,* 2:6, *Kesef Mishneh* and *Lehem Mishneh ad loc.*).

Another case of *omer muttar* involved a landowner who caught sight of a person bending down to lift an object and, mistaking the man for a stray animal, shot him dead with an arrow. The landowner was well aware that killing a person is forbidden,[261] but mistakenly believed that he was killing an animal, which is permitted.[262] Here it was ruled that the

---

256   העלם דבר
257   שכחה – הורו בית דין לעקור את כל הגוף
258   שגגת הוראה
259   תינוק שנשבה
260   אונס
261   רציחה

man had unintentionally committed homicide,[263] for which he would be exiled from his home (*goleh*) but protected in a city of refuge (*Mak.* 7b, 9a; Maim *Rotze'ah*, 5:1).[264]

Under the prohibition of murder (Ex. 20:13), killing *anyone* is forbidden. Even if a person truly believed that he was entitled to kill an unrepentant sinner or a disobedient slave, he would be judged guilty of homicide. His mistake might have been in a wrong understanding of the law, but he still had to answer for his crime, which meant banishment as an exile (*goleh*) to a city of refuge (Maim. *Rotze'ah*, 5:1, 3; 4:11). The prohibition of homicide was only waived in a life-threatening situation, where a person might kill his attacker in self-defence (*Sanh.* 72a; Num. R. 21).

In the view of Rava, unintentional homicide by someone who knew that murder is prohibited would invariably be considered a type of negligence close to a premeditated act,[265] although the perpetrator would not bear full guilt and would be granted protection in a city of refuge. Only if someone had been completely unaware that the law prohibited homicide would he be considered "unavoidably prevented from obeying" (*anus*)[266] and so exempt from liability.

According to Rava, a case of *omer muttar* involved the same level of guilt as *shogeg,* and his penalty for manslaughter incurred exile to a city of refuge. Abbaye disputed this reading of the law and regarded manslaughter as an accidental, unintended occurrence for which a person bore no guilt and was not obliged to suffer exile. In general, however, the Sages adopted Rava's opinion, considering the act one close to an intentional killing – *karov le-mezid* (*Mak.* 7b, Rashi; Maim. *Rotze'ah*, 6:10).

If someone who had witnessed an act withheld evidence,

---

262   כסבור בהמה ונמצא אדם
263   מכה נפש בשגגה
264   גולה
265   קרוב למזיד
266   אנוס

maintaining in court that he had no knowledge of it, he would be guilty of bearing false witness under oath (Lev. 5:1).[267] If, when giving testimony, he forgot that he had witnessed the act and so believed that he knew nothing of it, he would be held guiltless of a false oath. Torah law referred to someone who was fully aware of the facts as *adam*, a "man". If, therefore, he did not recall witnessing the event, he would be free of guilt; but if he later realized his mistake, he brought a sin-offering and was forgiven (Lev. 5:18; *Shev.* 26a).

The Sages taught that the law of "error" (*shegagah*) in regard to Sabbath observance was rather different from the laws governing other prohibitions. In some ways the Sabbath law was more stringent, in other ways less so. Rava declared that if a person mistakenly believed that his action was not forbidden on the Sabbath (*omer muttar*), he would be exempt from liability.[268] Others, however, maintained that this was true only if he made a more basic mistake, i.e., he was not aware of any prohibition (*Shab.* 72b, Rashi, *Tos.* s.v. "*be-omer muttar*"; Rava, *Mak.* 7b, *Tos.* s.v. "*ella*"; Maim. *Shabbat*, 1:18).[269]

The Talmud discussed a fundamental difference of opinion among the early Sages. Rav and Shemuel both maintained that a person was held liable if he had known the law and forgotten it.[270] This even included *tinok she-nishbah*, "a captive child raised among Gentiles",[271] i.e., someone who had never had an opportunity to know the law, but who was obliged to bring a sin-offering once the law became known to him. On the other hand, R. Yoḥanan and R. Shim'on ben Lakish contended that only a person who knew the law and subsequently forgot it would be liable; a *tinok she-nishbah* did not fall under this category and bore no guilt whatsoever. Distinctions were thus made in the extent of a person's guilt – between one who

---

267 שבועת העדות
268 פטור לגמרי
269 השוכח עיקר שבת
270 היודע עיקר שבת ולבסוף שכח
271 תינוק שנשבה

never knew that there were laws prohibiting certain acts on the Sabbath and one who knew that there were such laws but forgot them[272] or who mistakenly believed that his action was not prohibited (*Shab.* 68b, *Tos.* "*aval*").

A further insight into Rabbinic psychology may be gained from an analysis of the law's interpretation by major halakhic commentators.

Rashi's view followed that of Rav and Shemuel. When someone never knew that an action was forbidden and honestly believed that it was permitted (*omer muttar*), his situation was comparable to that of the "captive child" for whom the entire law did not exist.[273] If he ate food on Yom Kippur or leaven on Passover, in the mistaken belief that they were normal weekdays (*omer muttar*) when no such prohibitions were in force,[274] he would be regarded as one "unavoidably prevented from obeying the law" (*anus*) and thus free of guilt (*patur*). If he *was* aware of the law but it escaped his mind, he would have transgressed "in error" (*be-shogeg*) and was thus liable to a sin-offering (*Ker.* 2a, Rashi, s.v. "*ve-al lo hoda*"). This accorded with the opinion of Rava.

Abbaye ruled that the *omer muttar* transgression was little less than intentional (*mezid*), and undoubtedly so if a person knew but forgot the law, which was "close to intentional" (*karov le-mezid*). This accorded with the view of R. Yoḥanan and Resh Lakish (*Sanh.* 62a, Rashi, s.v. "*omer muttar*").

If, while a man was unloading a quantity of stones, another person sat below and was killed, the first man would not be held responsible and guilty of homicide. Likewise, if one of the rungs broke suddenly while he was climbing a ladder and he fell on someone below, killing that person, he would not be held responsible for the accident. If, however, the man climbing the ladder was known to be ill-disposed towards the victim, he would not receive protection in a city of refuge,

---

272   היודע עיקר שבת, הכיר ולבסוף שכח
273   עוקר כל הגוף
274   עוקר כל הגוף

as this type of case was specified in the Biblical law (Num. 35:20–21). If a person was suddenly attacked in an alleyway and, thinking that in self-defence he was entitled to kill his assailant (*omer muttar*) did so, the slaying was termed "close to intentional" (*karov le-mezid*): although the *sin* of killing was not intended, the *act* of killing had been. Such a person was guilty of culpable homicide and would not be afforded protection in a city of refuge (*Mak.* 7a–b; Maim. *Rotze'ah*, 6:1–15).

Where the killing was entirely accidental,[275] the slayer was exempt from the ordained penalty, and his own life would be protected in a city of refuge (Num. 35:11). If, however, someone intended to kill A but mistakenly killed B, or if he believed that the victim was someone whom he was entitled to slay, he could not claim "error" as a defence, making him *shogeg* and *patur*. Whereas, in the case of a Sabbath violation, he could plead *shogeg* (because of *omer muttar*), this plea was not tenable in the case of unintentional homicide. Even those Sages who maintained that *omer muttar* was *shegagah* and *patur* would agree that in this instance the man knew that he was killing a person – an obvious transgression of the universal law prohibiting murder, for which he could not claim *omer muttar* as a defence (*Mak.* 7b, Rashi and *Tos.* s.v. "*ella*"; *Mak.* 9a, *Tos.* s.v. "*Ve-Rav Hisda*").

[General references: *Talmudic Encyclopaedia*, Vol. 1, s.v. "*Omer Muttar*"; R. Hayyim Ha-Levi of Volozhin, *Hut ha-Meshullash*, 13: an in-depth study of the *Halakhah*]

Because the law prohibiting work on the Sabbath specified "purposeful work",[276] Shemuel issued the authoritative ruling that any work performed unawares did not make one culpable (*Ker.* 19b; *Sanh.* 62b).[277] Other religious offences would likewise not incur guilt, although in matters of civil law (torts and commerce) the position might be different. An exception

---

275　מכה נפש בשגגה
276　מלאכת מחשבת אסרה תורה
277　המתעסק בשבת פטור

was made in regard to acts transgressing the laws of "prohibited fat"[278] or forbidden sexual intercourse,[279] where the offender would be held liable even if he transgressed "in error" (bi-shegagah), since he had derived physical gratification from the act (Sanh. 62b; Ker. 19b).[280]

The authority for excluding mit'assek[281] from liability for an unconscious transgression was found in the Torah law which states as follows: "If anyone shall sin unwittingly, in any of the things which the Lord hath commanded not to be done... if his sin, wherein he hath sinned, be made known to him, he shall bring for his offering a goat... and the priest shall make atonement for him as concerning his sin, and he shall be forgiven" (Lev. 4:2, 23, 26; Midrash Torat Kohanim ad loc.).

Since the wording of the text indicated that only a sin committed in full awareness incurred guilt, it was accordingly ruled that an unwitting sin would be pardoned if one brought a sin-offering (Sanh. 62b; Hor. 5a). In civil matters and the laws of homicide, much stricter rulings applied to actions performed unwittingly (Mak. 7b; Tiferet Yisrael ad loc., 2:1, Introd.).

Picking fruit from a tree is a type of "work" forbidden on the Sabbath – "reaping".[282] As mentioned above, one case that the Sages discussed involved someone who meant to pick figs but absentmindedly picked grapes or who intended to pick ripe dark figs but picked white ones instead.[283] Since he had not done what he intended, could this be regarded as "purposeful work"?[284] R. Eliezer ruled that since his transgression had been committed "in error", he would need to bring a sin-offering.[285] R. Yehoshua, however, maintained that he was

---

278 חלב
279 עריות
280 המתעסק בחלבים ובעריות חייב שכן נהנה
281 מתעסק
282 קוצר
283 ללקוט תאנים ולקט ענבים
284 מלאכת מחשבת

not liable. As far as Sabbath "work" was concerned, this case amounted to an unintended act in the course of another act. Since he had not meant to transgress, he was not culpable. On the other hand, R. Eliezer argued that although this individual mistook one kind for another, he had intended to pick fruit on the Sabbath, which was forbidden, and his intention had thus been fulfilled (*Ker*. 19b–20a, Rashi s.v. "*ve-ha–batterei*").[286]

Maimonides ruled as follows in a number of similar cases. If a person meant to cut something already detached from the ground, which was permitted, but mistakenly cut something still growing in it, he would not be liable to a sin-offering for his forbidden "work", since he had not done what he intended.[287] It was an action performed by mistake and not one subject to the Torah penalty, which only related to "purposeful work" (*melekhet mahashevet*).

If, however, a man poked some coal on a fire just enough to warm himself, but in doing this made all the coal blaze up, he would be liable for the result, although it was not exactly what he had intended.[288] Even so, he had achieved his original aim – to warm himself (*Ker*. 19b; *Pes*. 25b; *Shab*. 73a; Maim. *Shegagot*, 7:11–12; Maim. *Shabbat*, 1:9).

Liability for "carrying" an object out of a "domain" on the Sabbath[289] depended on whether it had been removed a distance of at least four cubits. If a person had intended to throw something a distance of two cubits only, but it landed four cubits away from him by mistake, the Sages reached different conclusions. Rava determined that this person was not liable, his transgression having been committed in error (*mit'assek*). Abbaye, however, ruled that he was liable (*hayyav*), since the intended act of throwing had been performed.[290] Maimonides accepted Rava's ruling (*patur*), since the offending act had not

---

285 חייב חטאת
286 נעשה כוונתו
287 המתכוון לחתוך את התלוש
288 מלאכה שאינה צריכה לגופה חייב
289 הוצאה
290 חיב דהא קא מיכוין לזריקה

been "purposeful" (*melekhet mahashevet*) as the law required (*Shab.* 73a; Maim. *Shabbat*, 1:8, 9).

In yet another case, if a man took a sack of coins out of his "domain", intending to carry it in front of him, where it would be well protected, but then found that it had shifted onto his back, he would not be liable, since the end result was less than he had intended.[291] Had he first meant to carry it on his back but then carried it in front of him, he would be held liable, as he had done more than he intended. The second case is one of *me-tavekh mahashavto*,[292] whereas the first is considered one of *lo me-tavekh mahashavto,* i. e., the culpability of his actions depended on the fulfilment of his intentions.

Unintended Violation While Engaged in Fulfilling a Mitzvah – Mit'assek bi-Devar Mitzvah

A Jewish father's prime religious obligation is to ensure that his infant son undergoes circumcision (*berit milah*) when he is eight days old, in line with the covenant first entered into by Abraham (Gen. 17:10–12; 21:4; *Kid.* 29a; *Yoreh De'ah* 260:1). This positive duty must be fulfilled on that day, even if it is a Sabbath (*Shab.* 133),[293] when "inflicting a wound"[294] has the appearance of a forbidden activity. However, the *mitzvah* of circumcising a male child on the eighth day overrides Sabbath work prohibitions (Maim. *Milah*, 1:9; 2:6; *Yoreh De'ah* 266:2).[295]

The accepted law, quoted in the Mishnah, states that if a person had two babies in front of him, one born on the Sabbath and the other on the following day,[296] and out of concern to do his duty circumcised the wrong child, he had violated the Sabbath by mistake (*shegagah*) and for this he was required

---

291 המתכוין להוציא לפניו ובאו לאחריו פטור
292 מתוך מחשבתו
293 עושין כל צרכי מילה בשבת
294 חובל
295 מילה בזמנה דוחה את השבת
296 מי שהיו לו שני תינוקות

to bring a sin-offering (*hattat*). Circumcising a child born on
the Sabbath was a lawful act, but for the one born a day later
such an act was premature and amounted to "wounding".[297]
Although he had erred in good faith, this man was still guilty
of a forbidden action.[298]

Where different circumstances prevailed, this law was
disputed. When, for example, one child was due to be
circumcised on Friday and the other the next day,[299] but the
former's circumcision mistakenly took place on the Sabbath,
this involved "work" forbidden on *Shabbat*. Only when the
eighth day fell on a Sabbath was the *berit milah* permissible;
although the *mitzvah* was already applicable on the ninth day,
it could not then override the Sabbath.[300] The significant point
here is that while the individual concerned had zealously but
mistakenly performed "work" forbidden on the Sabbath, he
had nevertheless fulfilled the *mitzvah* of circumcision.[301]

R. Eliezer laid down that for this kind of transgression the
offender was liable to bring a sin-offering – *hayyav hattat*.
R. Yehoshua ruled that, despite his mistaken violation of the
law, he had still performed a *mitzvah* and was neither culpable
nor liable (*patur*). While dealing with one child to whom the
Sabbath prohibition did not apply, he had made the mistake
of thinking that because circumcision was permitted in one
case,[302] it would not be forbidden in the second. At any rate,
he had fulfilled a vital *mitzvah* and should not be considered
blameworthy (*Pes.* 72a–b).[303]

Although later Talmudic Sages followed either R. Eliezer or
R. Yehoshua, Maimonides adopted the ruling of R. Yehoshua
(*Shab.* 137a, Rashi, Bertinoro; Maim. *Shegagot*, 2:8).

Since the Sages had applied certain dispensation of the

---

297 חובל, והיה מתקן באותה חבורה
298 טעה בדבר מצווה ולא עשה מצווה, חייב
299 אחד למול בשבת ואחד למול בערב שבת
300 מילה שלא בזמנה אינה דוחה את השבת
301 טעה בדבר מצווה ועשה מצווה
302 מפני שעשה ברשות
303 טעה בדבר מצווה פטור – הרי נתנה שבת לדחות אצל תינוקות דעלמא

strict observance of the law in special cases it is appreciated that the duty of the restriction had been thus removed from his awareness and the individual might then continue with the same action even though the terms of that dispensation no longer applied. The Sages were prepared to overlook such a transgression quoting the adage that since he is so accustomed to transgress this law, he deems it as legitimate – "since he already trod on it, he continues treading" – *kivan dedash dash* (cf. *Hul.* 4b; *Git.* 56b).

Unintentional "Work" – Davar she-eino Mitkavven

Though normally permitted, certain actions may involve the unintentional performance of forbidden "work". The Sages had to decide whether such actions were in fact permissible, and here R. Yehoshua and R. Shim'on issued different rulings.

If someone poured hot water out of a boiler,[304] he was not allowed to refill it with cold water, as this might have a tempering effect on the metal.[305] Nor was he permitted to add a little cold water to the boiler for heating purposes, as this would be a form of "cooking".[306] However, if the boiler contained hot water, he could add some cold water to lower its temperature, as no specifically forbidden "work" was involved.

According to R. Yehudah, even an unintentional act was forbidden.[307] R. Shim'on did not forbid such an act,[308] maintaining that it was permissible to take the chill off cold water poured into an emptied boiler,[309] since there was clearly no intention to perform any forbidden "work". One might also add some cold water to hot water or hot water to cold, in order

---

304   מיחם שפינה ממנו מים חמים
305   מצרף הוא תולדת מעביר
306   מבשל
307   דבר שאינו מתכוון אסור
308   דבר שאינו מתכוון מותר
309   כדי להפשירו

to adjust the temperature.

R. Shim'on's view was followed in the Codes and enunciated as a principle: *Davar she-eino mitkavven muttar* (*Shab.* 41a–b, *Tos.* s.v. "*Meiḥam*"; Maim. *Shabbat,* 22:6, *Maggid Mishneh* and *Kesef Mishneh ad loc.*; *Sh. Ar. Oraḥ Ḥayyim* 318:12).[310]

Extinguishing a fire on the Sabbath constitutes forbidden "work",[311] but if that fire poses any danger to life, extinguishing it is not only permitted but obligatory.[312] The Sages considered whether it was permissible to extinguish a flaming brand on the Sabbath or a festival if it might endanger the public. According to R. Shim'on, since the object in extinguishing it was not to make the wood available for use (e.g., as charcoal), which the person involved did not require, his action would not be culpable.[313] Maimonides allowed one to extinguish burning metal in these circumstances, as it did not yield any new product; but he maintained the Mishnah's strict prohibition against burning wood (*Shab.* 2:5). R. Shim'on's lenient decision was followed by Caro (*Shab.* 42a, *Tos.* s.v. "*afilu*"; *Sh. Ar. Oraḥ Ḥayyim* 334:27).

The opposing decisions of R. Yehudah and R. Shim'on were also applied to cases of unintended transgression (*davar she-eino mitkavven*) distinct from those pertaining to the Sabbath, and the Sages generally followed R. Shim'on's view.

The Torah prohibition against wearing clothes made of *sha'atnez* (wool and flax)[314] is expressed in two forms: "Thou shalt not wear a mingled stuff, wool and linen together" (Deut. 22:11)[315] and "Neither shall there come upon thee a garment of two kinds of stuff mingled together" (Lev. 19:19).[316] The Mishnaic Sages explained that "wearing" a garment meant putting it on the body to give warmth or to afford protection

---

310 דבר שאינו מתכוון מותר
311 מכבה
312 פיקוח נפש
313 מכבין גחלת של עץ
314 שעטנז
315 לא תלבש שעטנז
316 ובגד כלאיים שעטנז לא יעלה עליך

from the sun or rain; but it was the practice of itinerant dealers to carry items of clothing on their shoulders to display them to prospective customers. A clothier was allowed to sell garments made of *sha'atnez*, but would his practice make him guilty of "wearing" them if he did not intend to use them himself? The Mishnah ruled, like R. Shim'on, that he might carry the garments so long as he had no intention of using them to keep warm or to protect himself from the elements. Displaying clothes for sale was also permitted on the basis of the same principle (*Kil.* 9:5; Maim. *Kil'ayim*, 10:12; *Sh. Ar. Yoreh De'ah* 301:6).[317]

As we have seen, permission to cook food on a major festival only applied to what was required for the holy day itself. The Sages laid down a general rule: on *yom tov* it is forbidden to bake or cook for the following day.[318] They stated, nevertheless, that while cooking food a woman was allowed to fill the pot with meat, even though she might not need all of it the same day, as a dish may improve if it is cooked in a full pot. However, she was not allowed to cook an additional quantity on the pretext that some of it might be required on *yom tov*. Such misuse of the law was forbidden and condemned as a deceitful practice (*Betzah* 17a; *Sh. Ar. Orah Hayyim* 503:1).[319]

Although productive work is forbidden on the Sabbath day, if the action itself is performed beforehand and the ongoing process completes the "work", one may enjoy its benefits on the Sabbath. Accordingly, if on Friday one opens a faucet that continues to run on the Sabbath, thereby watering one's garden, no transgression has been committed. Nets to trap birds or fish may also be spread in advance, even though "hunting" (*tzidah*)[320] takes place on *Shabbat*. If a flame or fire is kindled in advance, the continued light or heat may be enjoyed on the Sabbath. A pot of half-cooked food may likewise be placed on

---

317 דבר שאינו מתכוון מותר
318 אין אופין מיום טוב לחברו
319 דהביא בהערמה
320 צדה

a hot stove or in a hot oven and left there before the Sabbath, to be enjoyed when it is fully cooked on the Sabbath day.

Once the Sabbath begins on Friday evening, no uncooked food may be left overnight on the stove. If such food was put there deliberately (be-zadon),[321] it must not be used; if this occurred by mistake (bi-shegagah), one may eat it after the Sabbath. Biblical law specifically prohibited cooking on *Shabbat*, but the Sages also declared it forbidden to set a pot of uncooked food in the oven beforehand, so that it would be ready on the Sabbath day. They explained that the *shegagah* restriction was imposed in case someone deceitfully claimed that the food had been cooked by mistake – pretending that he had forgotten all about it, although he had been fully aware of what he was doing.[322] Such a relaxation of the law might have been allowed if only a Rabbinic prohibition was involved (*Shab.* 38a, Rashi; Maim. *Shabbat*, 6:23; *Sh. Ar Orah Hayyim* 318:1).

Particular care, pedantic – Kapdanut

Fastidiousness

The prohibition against squeezing water from a garment (*sehitah*) also includes shaking rain or snow off new clothes, an act also associated with forbidden "cleaning" (*Shab.* 147a).[323] While Rashi (*ad loc.*) includes "shaking off dust" in the prohibition, the *Tosafot* and ROSH disagree, omitting any reference to this in the Codes. The prohibition similarly includes "folding a garment" in order to preserve a sharp crease.[324]

A "new garment" is defined as one that a person is anxious

---

321 בזדון
322 הערמה דרבנן
323 כיבוס
324 אדעתא דלכנופי

to keep neat and clean, his nature being such that he will not wear it before making sure that it is free of dust and smartly creased.[325] The Sages recognized, however, that there is a limit to how fastidious a person can reasonably be (*Git.* 79b).[326] In this law we find that the individual's attitude determines whether his action is or is not culpable (*Shab.* 147a, Rashi; *Sh. Ar. Ora<u>h</u> <u>H</u>ayyim* 302:1, *Tur, Bet Yosef, Mishnah Berurah ad loc.*).

Divorce

If a man living under two roofs allocates one space to his wife, who also makes use of the other one at times, and this man delivers a *get* in the second space, it is considered validly delivered in her courtyard (see Chapter 10 below). The Sages declared that although one normally ensures that the boundary of one's own property is not trespassed, here one should not be legalistic and object if the other space is also regarded as her property.[327]

Witchcraft

The Bible forbids the practice of witchcraft and necromancy (Lev. 19:26).[328] This includes superstitious belief in omens and astrology or in divination by reading the entrails of birds so as to decide how to act (Ex. 22:17; *Sanh.* 65b–66a). It was felt that attempts to foretell the future negated Divine providence and encouraged men to seek the guidance of wizards (*Ha-<u>H</u>innukh* 255–256).

In the course of a detailed discussion of sorcery, Abbaye said: "The laws regarding sorcery are like those of the Sabbath; certain actions call for the penalty of stoning; some are exempt from punishment, yet forbidden; while others are permissible". If someone actually produced things by witchcraft (which was

---

325 והוא דקפיד עליהו
326 כולי האי לא קפיד איניש
327 כולי האי לא קפדי אנשי
328 לא תנחשו ולא תאוננו

not considered impossible), he was liable to the full penalty. If, however, he simply created an illusion and performed "magic" by hocus-pocus (although this was also forbidden), he was exempt from punishment. Rav had an example in mind: "I saw for myself how an Arabian nomad took a sword and hewed a camel to pieces; then he rang a bell and the camel got up." Abbaye distinguished between sorcery and conjuring tricks: "A sorcerer needs tangible objects to perform his magic [*kapid aman*][329] while the other does not, because he achieves his effects by sleight of hand" (*Sanh.* 67b).

Irascibility

The Sages used the terms *kapid* and *kapdan* to describe someone who was pedantic or irritable. They urged people to emulate Hillel the Elder, not his more exacting or impatient colleague Shammai (*Shab.* 30b),[330] because Hillel would answer the most ridiculous questions patiently without ever losing his temper (*Shab.* 31a).[331] An irascible person cannot be an effective teacher (*Avot* 2:5) nor a hasty person a judge, since one must be deliberate in judgment (*Avot* 1:1).[332]

Extent of Knowledge of Transgression

Even when someone commits an unwitting transgression, he is held guilty of failing to observe God's law consciously and meticulously. His thought, whether deliberate or careless, is an action of the soul for which he is responsible and any offence, however unintentional, requires atonement ("If anyone sin through error...," Lev. 4:2).[333]

Apart from the guilt that must be expiated, transgression blemishes the soul and this stain must be removed before one can achieve communion with the Almighty. The Torah

329   קפיד אמן
330   ולא היה קפדן כשמאי
331   והלל לא יקפיד
332   ולא הקפדן מלמד, הוו מתונים בדין
333   נפש כי תחטא בשגגה

ordained that if anyone committed a sin without meaning to
disobey the word of God, he could atone for it through a sin-
offering as soon as he became aware of his transgression (Lev.
4:2, RAMBAN *ad loc.*).

If someone committed an offence twice or more often, being
unaware each time that he had transgressed, the extent of his
guilt depended on whether he had been conscious of his sin
between the two acts (*yedi'ah beinatayim*).[334] After his first
offence, he might have discovered that the act was forbidden
and then, owing to a lapse of memory, repeated it. The Sages
considered whether the intervening state of awareness indicated
a new unwitting transgression, so that a sin-offering was
required for each infringement, or whether both acts should be
attributed to the same state of unawareness, which meant that
only one sin-offering was required (Mish., *Ker.* 4:2).

A general rule was laid down regarding three such cases of
involuntary Sabbath violation:

1. If someone completely ignorant of the law performed
numerous acts of forbidden "work" on many Sabbaths, he was
liable to bring one offering only when he became aware of
the law and this would atone for all his offences. The sin-
offering was mandatory not because of any fault on his part,
but because the Torah required it even of a person who never
knew that such a law must be obeyed. A Jew taken captive in
childhood (*tinok she-nishbah*),[335] who had not been informed
of his true identity and religious heritage, would certainly
know nothing of Torah law. Once aware that he was a Jew,
he had to bring a single offering to atone for all the "work"
done while he unknowingly violated the Sabbath law; but
an additional offering was also required for each separate
transgression (e.g., eating forbidden fat or blood)[336] as soon
as he became aware of them (Maim. *Shegagot*, 2:6).[337]

Another issue was the extent of ignorance that might be

---

334   אם היתה ידיעה בינתיים
335   תינוק שנשבה
336   אכל חלב, אכל דם
337   חייב להביא חטאת על כל עבירה ועבירה

classified as "unwitting transgression" (*shegagah*) in the case of a person who knew that something was forbidden, but still knowingly violated the prohibition[338] and then learned that he was liable to the penalty of "excision" (*karet*).[339] Such lack of knowledge justified the acceptance of his transgression as *shegagah*. If he claimed not to have known that a sin-offering was required for the offence that he committed, such lack of knowledge would not be regarded as a *shegagah* offence but as one committed intentionally (*be-mezid*) and thus subject to the full penalty (*Shab.* 69a; Maim. *Shegagot*, 2:2).[340]

2.   If a person was in principle aware of the law and unwittingly performed many acts of forbidden "work" on numerous Sabbaths, he would be liable to an offering for each Sabbath violated.

3.   If someone unwittingly performed many acts of forbidden "work" each time he knew it was the Sabbath, he would be liable to an offering for his Sabbath desecrations under each category of *melakhah*.

Intervening Awareness – Yedi'ot Meḥallekot

Accepting the plea that an offence was an unintentional *shegagah* depended on the type of unawareness and its extent. R. Akiva discussed this issue with R. Eliezer, who stated that if someone claimed *shegagah* on two consecutive Sabbaths, and if his ignorance of the Sabbath was continuous,[341] he would be liable to an offering for each Sabbath. R. Akiva held that he should bring one offering to cover them all. If, however, he knew about the Sabbath laws, he must have had some knowledge of its prohibitions in the course of the ensuing week, which meant that his violation of each Sabbath amounted to a new act of carelessness. Such intervening knowledge, which resulted in a fresh lack of awareness,[342] thus made him liable

---

338   מזיד בעבירה
339   כרת
340   שגגת קרבן אינה שגגה
341   העלם אחת

for each ensuing Sabbath. This ruling was in accordance with the principle that knowledge of the wrong between two offences established new responsibility.[343] In the opinion of R. Eliezer, if someone knew about the Sabbath but was ignorant of particular prohibitions, each case was deemed a separate transgression owing to the principle of *yedi'ot mehallekot*. R. Akiva, however, considered them one and the same type of "forgetfulness" (*Ker.* 16a–b).[344]

As an example of "intervening knowledge" or "continuous unawareness", the Sages discussed the following case in which the principle of *yedi'ot mehallekot* relieved a person of guilt.

Associated with "building", where sections that one joined together had to be marked, the act of "writing" (*ketivah*) was one of the "works" prohibited on the Sabbath (*Shab.* 73a; Maim. *Shabbat*, 7:1). Sabbath law forbade writing an inscription that contained at least two letters of a word (*Shab.* 103a, 75b; *Sh. Ar. Orah Hayyim* 340:4). In the case of someone who, knowing it was the Sabbath day but ignorant of the prohibition, wrote two letters of a word, one on one Sabbath and the other on a different Sabbath, the precise category of this *shegagah* had to be ascertained. The Sages differed as to whether the two acts should be regarded as one full transgression embracing two letters, which (if unwitting) therefore made the writer liable to a sin-offering; or whether the two letters were not connected, which meant that he had not violated the Sabbath.

Certain Sages, following the "disconnected actions" principle, ruled that the intervening period separated the two actions: each thus involved the writing of one letter only and incurred no guilt (*Ker.* 17b, 16b).[345] Maimonides adopted the view of other Sages, ruling in his Code that if a particular transgression was repeated several times because (as in the case above) a man was ignorant of the prohibition from the

---

342 העלם דבר
343 ידיעות מחלקות
344 העלם אחד
345 ידיעות מחלקות

start and thereafter continuously,[346] all the offences must be treated as one act of *shegagah*. He would only need to bring one sin-offering in atonement for all his mistaken actions, which in fact resulted from the same lack of awareness (Maim. *Shegagot*, 5:1). However, a distinction had to be made if, in one state of forgetfulness, a person committed a number of transgressions, each belonging to a different type and each bearing a separate culpability, which rendered him liable for an unwitting transgression (*Ker.* 16b; Maim. *Shegagot*, 4:1).

R. Yosef Caro's *Shulḥan Arukh* did not rule on the above cases, as it only dealt with laws currently applicable, which exclude Temple sacrifices. The question of sin-offerings for *shegagot* is discussed here to show how differing attitudes arose among the Sages regarding the measure of culpability that should be attached to an unwitting offence.

Another example of the *yedi'ot meḥallekot* rule and its application has to do with forbidden sexual relations. If a particular unwitting offence occurred several times, owing to continued unawareness of the law on and between each occasion,[347] all the separate offences were reckoned to be a single involuntary transgression (*shegagah*), making the offender liable for one sin-offering only. If, however, this individual had shown any awareness of the prohibition in the interim, he would have to bring an offering for each separate forbidden act, on the principle that intervening awareness created a new state of forgetfulness.[348] Where there was continued unawareness of the law, as above, the man would be required to make one offering; but if the woman had meanwhile become aware of the prohibition, she would need to bring a sin-offering for each forbidden act. In the reverse situation, however, she would bring only one offering and he would be liable for each offence (Maim. *Shegagot*, 5:2).

The Torah law prescribing liability for a sin-offering was a

---

346   בהעלם אחד
347   בהעלם דבר
348   שהידיעות מחלקות השגגות

concession to the offender, who had not purposefully violated the law. Bringing a *hattat* gave him the opportunity to cleanse himself of the blemish that had corrupted his soul (Ramban on Lev. 4:2). This privilege was only available to him if he had remained completely unaware of his transgression; it was not available if, at any stage, he had known that his act was forbidden. If there was insufficient evidence of guilt, he would be exempt from punishment; but if there had been any awareness of the transgression, he would not be given the chance to atone through a sin-offering.

The rule laid down was that a person could only bring a sin-offering when unawareness characterized his action from beginning to end.[349] If, for example, in violation of the law against moving an object a distance of four cubits from one domain to another (*hotza'ah*)[350] he forgetfully threw something, but then remembered what day it was before the object landed in the other domain, he would not have to bring a *hattat*. Similarly, if he threw a stone that could injure a person or an animal, but immediately afterwards (before it struck its target) remembered that this was forbidden on the Sabbath, his action was not regarded as complete unawareness and he would therefore not have to bring a sin-offering. He would still remain liable, however, for any damage that he caused. Mishnaic law prescribed a sin-offering only when there had been total unawareness on his part throughout (Mish. *Shab.* 11:6, TB *Shab.* 102a; Maim. *Shabbat*, 1:19; Maim. *Shegagot*, 2:1).

Intention and Culpability

With regard to the 39 principal categories of "work" – *avot melakhah* – prohibited on the Sabbath, many details were closely examined in the *Halakhah* (Maim. *Shabbat*, 7:12). One early Sage taught that "pruning a tree"[351] and similar agricultural improvements were no less culpable than

---

349 עד שתהי תחילתן וסופן שגגה
350 הוצאה
351 הזומר

"planting"[352] or "sowing",[353] which fall under the category of prohibited "work", since pruning fosters the growth of a tree (*Shab.* 73b, Rashi).[354]

R. Kahana declared that if someone pruned a tree and then used the wood, he was guilty of two forbidden "works" – "reaping",[355] since his intention was to gather wood from the tree, and "planting" to improve its growth. This ruling was questioned by R. Yosef, who saw a difference between "work" that was intentional (*be-khavvanah*), such as collecting wood,[356] and the likely result[357] of pruning (*note'a*), although any deliberate improvement would constitute the "work" of *note'a* (*MK* 2b, *Tos.* s.v. "*ḥayyav shetayim*", "*ke-marpuyei ar'a*").

The *Tosafot* make a similar distinction elsewhere, noting that the view of R. Shim'on, exonerating a person from guilt when he had not meant to perform a forbidden act,[358] was now generally accepted. If the act itself was intended, even though the obviously prohibited result was not, the ruling might be more stringent (*Betzah* 32b, *Tos.* "*mi-lematta*").[359]

Another ruling in the name of R. Shim'on refers to digging a pit on the Sabbath.[360] If a person dug it as the foundation of a building, he would have purposefully undertaken forbidden "work" (*melekhet maḥshevet*), which made him liable for "building".[361] If he only dug it to make use of the earth,[362] not intending to build there, he would not be held culpable. As far as the field was concerned, one might perhaps argue that digging improved the soil, but here it actually damaged

---

352 נוטע
353 זורע
354 תנא הזורע והזומר והנוטע והמבריך והמרכיב כולם מלאכה אחת הן
355 קוצר
356 קוצר
357 דמיון
358 דבר שלא מתכוון מותר
359 מתכוון לעשות מה שהוא עושה
360 החופר גומא בשבת
361 חייב משום בונה
362 ואין צריך אלא לעפרה

the field; therefore, according to the standard rule that an act which causes damage is not culpable, *mekalkel patur* – he would be exonerated (*Ḥag.* 10a; Maim. *Shabbat*, 1:17–18).

"Work" of Completing a Vessel – Makkeh be-Pattish

One may not complete the manufacture of a vessel on *Shabbat* (e.g., adding a spout to a closed vat), but, if someone has an unopened barrel of raisins and wants to eat some, he may make an aperture to remove or pour out some of the contents, provided that he does not intend the opening to complete the vessel. If raisins, dates or other foodstuffs are enclosed in wickerwork, he may break through it to reach the contents (*Shab.* 146a; Maim. *Shabbat*, 23:2; *Oraḥ Ḥayyim* 314:6, *Mishnah Berurah*).

Subsequent Indication of Original Intent – Yesh Bererah

One may ritually slaughter an animal on a festival (though not, of course, on the Sabbath), provided it is needed for a meal on that *yom tov*. Since whatever may be used on the festival requires preparation in advance,[363] one must know whether the animal was specially designated for that purpose. According to the view of R. Yehudah, *sheḥitah* would be prohibited if, before the festival, it had not been earmarked for *yom tov*. A problem arose over the matter of intention. The Sages explained that cattle were raised either for meat[364] or for breeding.[365] The slaughter of a beast already indicated that it was meant for consumption.[366] R. Yehudah did not agree with this concept (*yesh bererah*),[367] whereas R. Meir accepted it: the action was indicative of the intention (*Ḥul.* 14a; *Betzah*

---

363 הכנה
364 לאכילה עומדת
365 לגדל עומדת
366 הרהור הדבר
367 יש ברירה

4a; Maim. *Yom Tov*, 1:18, 10; *Oraḥ Ḥayyim* 513:1).
[General references: *Betzah* 40a.; *Er.* 36b, 37b; *Betzah* 10a, 37b; *Yoma* 55b; *Git.* 24a; *BK* 69a; *BB* 107a, *Tos.* s.v. "*ve-hilkheta*"; *Oraḥ Ḥayyim* 498:1*ff.*; *Ḥoshen Mishpat* 103:3, 104:1]

Action Indicating Intention

As mentioned earlier, a pot of food may not be placed in a hot oven during the Sabbath, as this involves the forbidden "work" of cooking.[368] If the food was already hot and someone removed it from the oven, he could replace it there if he continued to hold the pot without setting it down, thereby demonstrating his intention to put it back immediately, as though it had remained in the oven without a break (*Shab.* 38b; *Sh. Ar. Oraḥ Ḥayyim* 253:2, REMA; *Sh. Ar. Oraḥ Ḥayyim* 318:1).

Action Resulting in Unrequired "Work"

The prohibition of Sabbath "work" refers above all to purposeful skilled effort (*melekhet maḥashevet*). "Hunting" an animal (*tzeidah*), whether for food or its skin, is therefore banned on the Sabbath. Nor may one kill a reptile, regardless of whether it is identifiably one of the eight unclean "swarming things" (Lev. 11:29; Maim. *Avot ha-Tum'ot*, 4:1)[369] or any other forbidden creature, even though one desires its skin, not its flesh. While "work" for which there is no need is also prohibited,[370] killing a venomous snake is permitted as a safety measure (*Shab.* 107a–b; *Shab.* 3a, *Tos.* s.v. "*ha-tzad naḥash*"; Maim. *Shabbat*, 10:21; R. Ḥayyim Ha-Levi of Volozhin, *Ḥiddushim*: *Shabbat*, "Intention").

---

368 בישול
369 שמונה שרצים
370 שאינה צריכה לגופה

Intention in the "Work" of Carrying Outside – Hotza'ah

Carrying an object outside one's domain (*hotza'ah*) is made up of two actions: "lifting" and "laying down",[371] both of which must be performed deliberately. If an object was meant to be thrown a distance of less than four cubits, which would not constitute a Sabbath violation, but happened to land eight cubits away,[372] the act of "laying down" would have been performed unintentionally and would not count as a purposeful action (*melekhet mahashevet*) unless the person who threw it said, "Let it fall wherever it does". The requirement of purposeful action therefore depends on his intention (*Shab.* 97b, Rashi; Maim. *Shabbat*, 13:21).[373]

Liability for the prohibited act of "carrying outside" (*hotza'ah*) depends on the amount involved, which varies according to the minimum useful size of each object, whether this be wood for cooking, spices for seasoning or material for dyeing wool (*Shab.* 89b).

The Sages ruled that if a person set aside a negligible quantity (e.g., one grain of wheat, which is less than the minimum laid down), either for a sample or for medicinal purposes, and then took it outside his domain on the Sabbath, he would be culpable, as even this tiny amount was all that he required. He had thus achieved his aim[374] and executed a purposeful *melekhet mahashevet*. If, however, someone deliberately changed his mind about using it and then carried it outside the domain without specifying his purpose, he would only be liable if it was of the standard measure: since his change of mind, the item was no longer of special importance to him.[375] If, however, the amount carried outside was essential for the purpose he had in mind, his action was culpable. Anyone

---

371 הוצאה צריכה עקירה והנחה
372 נתכוון לזרוק ארבע וזרק שמונה
373 נתקיימה מחשבתו
374 דבר חשוב לו
375 בטל מחשבתו הראשונה

else, who did not share his intention, would only be liable
if the item was of the standard size (*Shab.* 90b, Mish., "*Ha-
matzni'a*", *Tiferet Yisrael* and Bertinoro; *Shab.* 75b, Mish.,
"*kol ha-kasher le-hatzni'a*").

"Work" for Constructive Purposes – She-tzarikh le-Gufo

If someone extinguished a lamp on the Sabbath,[376] not
because he had no need of the light but because he wanted
to preserve the lamp or save the oil or wick, the Sages ruled
that his "work" was culpable. R. Yose, however, absolved
him from liability, since his act had an extraneous purpose in
mind. This decision was based on the principle that "work" is
culpable only when its intention is to achieve some purposeful
result. An example of such "work", in accordance with the
prohibition of "building", would be demolishing a structure
and then using its material to construct a new one.[377]

As stated in the Mishnah, even R. Yose would agree that
"saving the wick" – *kehas al ha-petilah* – rendered a person
liable, since his action carbonized the wick and facilitated
speedy rekindling. Later Sages declared that in Temple times
a man was not obliged to bring a sin-offering if his "work"
(e.g., extinguishing the light) had been simply destructive. In
general, however, they ruled that any destructive action was
also forbidden on the Sabbath (Mish. *Shab.* 2:5; *Shab.* 29b,
31b, Rashi, Bertinoro; Maim. *Shabbat*, 10:15; 12:2; 1:7–8;
Sh. Ar. Orah Hayyim 275:1, 277:1).

Unintended Forbidden Work – Davar she-eino Mitkavven

Detailed particulars were given in the Talmud regarding the
Four Species used ceremonially on the festival of *Sukkot* (Lev.
23:40).[378] The three twigs of the myrtle had to be closely

---

376 המכבה את הנר
377 סותר על מנת לבנות
378 לולב והדס והערבה ואתרוג

covered by their leaves, and if any twig contained more ripe berries than leaves, it was not acceptable. Although the defect could be eliminated by reducing the number of berries, this was not permitted on the festival, as it would constitute an act of *metakken*,[379] which was similar to the "work" of completing an article.[380]

Nevertheless, if one made the adjustment on *yom tov*, the twig would be deemed acceptable.[381] This ruling obviously required a justification: since the berries were ripe, the person who removed them had done so in order to eat them; hence, according to R. Shim'on, the resulting "repair" had not been the prime intention. In accordance with R. Shim'on's view, the Sages ruled that this action was not culpable, since it did not qualify as "purposeful work".[382] Alternatively, if a person had an extra twig that was ritually fit, one might say that "repairing" the faulty one was not essential and therefore, according to R. Shim'on, not culpable (*Suk.* 33b, Rashi s.v. "*lo tzerikhah*", Tos. s.v. "*modeh Rabbi Shim'on*"; Maim. *Lulav*, 8:5; *Orah Hayyim* 646:2).[383]

A more theoretical case involved a man who had two candles before him, one lit and the other unlit. His intention was first to kindle the one and then to extinguish the other, but he actually did so the other way round – first extinguishing and then kindling. How did this occur? He first blew on the lit candle and with the same breath that extinguished the one transferred the flame to the other: the act of extinguishing thus preceded that of kindling, which was not what he had intended. His aim had been to transfer the flame already lit to the other candle, and since this "work" did not correspond to his intention he would be exempt (*patur*) from a sin-offering, although the Sages declared that any such action was prohibited (*assur*). Later authorities ruled that even if the "work" was not

---

379 מתקן
380 מכה בפטיש
381 כשרה
382 דבר שלא נתכוון מותר
383 דבר שלא צריך לגופו מותר

what he required, he would still have to bring a sin-offering. If the original action was permitted, but resulted in forbidden "work", the man would not be liable.[384] If, in any case, the action that he had performed was forbidden, even though he had no need of the result, he would be liable (*Ker.* 19b–20a; Maim. *Shegagot*, 7:11–12).[385]

[General references: R. Hayyim Ha-Levi of Volozhin, *Hiddushim: Shabbat* 10:17; R. Elhanan Wasserman, *Kovetz Shi'urim*, Part 2, Chap. 33; *Talmudic Encyclopaedia*, Vol. 6, p. 631ff. *Davar she-eino mitkavein*.]

Liability Subject to Intention

The halakhic prohibition of carrying or throwing something from one domain to another, or within a public domain, related to picking up an object (however small) in one place and making it rest in another that was at least four cubits away.[386] If a person threw something a distance of more than four cubits and it was caught by another person or in the jaws of a dog, it would not be reckoned to have landed on the ground and, since he had not completed the forbidden action, that person would not be liable. The Rabbis, however, laid down that such actions should not be performed on the Sabbath.

Another example of liability subject to intention is where an object meant to be thrown a distance of four cubits lands eight cubits away. One might say that because this did not fulfil the original intention, no liability was incurred. The Sages declared, however, that even while flying through the air an object could be held to rest anywhere in its trajectory, which incurred liability for "taking out" (*hotza'ah*). In practice, they ruled against carrying any object on the Sabbath, even over a space of less than four cubits (*Shab.* 97b; Maim. *Shabbat*, 13:16, 21; *Orah Hayyim* 349:5, *Mishnah Berurah ad loc.*).

---

384 מתעסק פטור
385 מלאכה שאינה צריכה לגופה חייב עליה
386 עקירה והנחה

The Place of Thought in Action – Hirhur

Fulfilling one's duty to recite the *Shema* each day (Deut. 6:7)[387] means that it should be spoken aloud, since the Torah uses the expression "hear" (*shema*). The Sages ruled that one should enunciate the words, at least to oneself.[388] However, if some disability or uncleanness prevents one from reciting the words and they are only kept in mind, one's obligation has been fulfilled (*Ber.* 25a–b; *Orah Hayyim* 62:3). This rule of the *Shema*, is explained by the phrase *be-khol levavekha*, "with all your heart",[389] which implies "in your mind"; as the Sages observed: "The intentions of the heart are the words themselves".[390] Thus, whenever a prayer or blessing must be recited, "thinking" of the relevant words is like "speaking" them (*Ber.* 20b, ROSH *ad loc.* 3:14).[391]

In the case of work prohibited on the Sabbath, one's "thought" of doing it is tantamount to its "performance". Here the prophetical exhortation is quoted: "If thou turn away thy foot because of the Sabbath, from pursuing thy business on My holy day; and call the Sabbath a delight, and the holy of the Lord honourable; and shalt honour it, not following thy wonted ways, nor pursuing thy business, nor speaking thereof; then shalt thou delight thyself in the Lord." (JPS Isa. 58:13).[392] The prohibition includes giving verbal instructions for work to be done as well as its actual performance. One should not discuss business affairs or check financial accounts on the Sabbath; but the prohibition does not extend to thinking about such matters, although the Sages favoured a stricter approach (*Shab.* 113a–b, 150a; *Sh. Ar. Orah Hayyim* 306:8).[393]

R. Yehoshua ben Korha also concluded (from the verse

387 ודברת בם
388 צריך להשמיע לאוזנו
389 בכל לבבך
390 כוונת הלב הן הדברים
391 הרהור הוא כדיבור
392 ממצוא חפצך ודבר דבר
393 דיבור אסור, הרהור מותר

in Isaiah) that if someone dropped a hint about working for him without being explicit, he had not violated the law. Thus, although it is forbidden to engage a workman on the Sabbath, if someone were to ask, "Do you think you will be able to join me in the evening?", it would be for the workman to decide what was meant. Such an arrangement only takes place in the mind and does not constitute a forbidden act (*Shab.* 150a, Rashi *ad loc.*; Maim. *Shabbat,* 24:4; *Sh. Ar. Orah Hayyim* 307:7).[394] Nevertheless, the *Shulhan Arukh* gloss of the REMA affirms that even a hint in these circumstances is prohibited (*Sh. Ar. Orah Hayyim* 307:22).

In day-to-day conduct, harbouring thoughts of any forbidden act is also forbidden.[395] The Torah enjoins in the law of "fringes" (*tzitzit*)[396] "that ye go not about after your own heart and your own eyes" (Num. 15:39),[397] and the Sages connected this with hankering after idols and fornication (*Ber.* 12b). It was their belief that a sinful thought is more harmful to man than the sinful act itself (*Yoma* 29a, Rashi *ad loc.*).[398] Whereas sexual intercourse is one aspect of man's animal nature, dwelling on it is a misuse of the God-given faculty of thought (Maim. *Guide,* 3:8).

When someone fulfils a *mitzvah,* the Torah additionally credits him with the determination to perform a meritorious act;[399] but when he commits a sin, punishment is confined to the actual misdeed.[400] As far as halakhic culpability is concerned, man is judged solely by his actions. R. Ashi asserted that if a man intended to perform a meritorious act but was accidentally prevented from doing so, he would be credited with its actual performance (*Ber.* 6a).[401] On the other

---

394   הנראה שתעמוד עמי לערב

395   אסור להרהר בעבירה

396   ציצית

397   ולא תתורו אחרי לבבכם ואחרי עיניכם

398   ההרהורי עבירה קשין מהעבירה

399   מחשבה טובה מצטרפה למעשה

400   מחשבה רעה אין הקב"ה מצרפה למעשה

401   חשב אדם לעשות מצווה ונאנס ולא עשה מעלה עליו הכתוב כאילו עשהה

hand, one forbidden act strengthens a man's propensity to commit further transgressions, for which he will receive due punishment (*Kid.* 40a).[402]

Miscellaneous Laws Subject to One's Intentions

Cooking

In order to avoid the prohibition against cooking (*bishul*) on the Sabbath, a heated stove used to keep food warm during the day must have the coal or wood fire, or heating element, burning before the Sabbath and the food must already be cooked prior to its commencement. Meat that is at least partly cooked and edible before the Sabbath may be kept warm.[403] On the eve of Sabbath, one may place a pot of cooked food on the stove and leave it there for use during the next 24 hours.

A distinction is made between a pot suspended over a fire, where cooking (*bishul*) is forbidden on the Sabbath, and an oven filled with burning coals, where any food placed inside is cooked by the heat from the fire (*hatmanah*).[404] Utilizing the *hatmanah* process from Sabbath eve onwards is permissible if one first removes the burning coals, or at least smothers them with dirt, so that there is no temptation to stir them. Heat remaining in the oven may then be used to keep food warm during the Sabbath. This food may be taken out on the Sabbath, but whether it may also be put back inside is doubtful. Bet Hillel ruled that one may do so, but only if the food is immediately replaced in the oven so as to retain its heat and not constitute a new act of *hatmanah*. If one did not intend to replace it immediately, having decided to stop using the oven, putting food back later would constitute a new and forbidden act of *hatmanah* (*Shab.* 38b, *Tos.* s.v. "*tannur*"; cf. Mish., *Shab.* 2:7; Maim. *Shabbat*, 3:8–10; *Orah Hayyim* 253:1–2).

---

402 כיון שעבר אדם עבירה ושינה בה נעשית לו כהיתר
403 נתבשל כמאכל דרוסאי
404 הטמנה

Carrying Outside (Hotza'ah) an Object of Importance to Him (Aḥsheveih)

The law against carrying an object from one domain to another applies only to an object of a minimum size (shi'ur).[405] An item of food, for example, must have at least the bulk of a dried fig (ki-gerogeret).[406] Any other object should also be large enough to fulfil some useful purpose.[407] A chip of wood must be usable as tinder, and any liquid has to be sufficient for a drink or for use as a salve.

If an object was very small (i.e., less than a shi'ur), but someone put it aside with a certain purpose in mind and then forgot what this was, he would be guilty of violating the Sabbath if he carried it outside his domain, as his original intention had made the object important (aḥsheveh).[408] Another man, who did not consider it useful because it was so small, might "carry" it with impunity. If the item was so objectionable that no one cared to use it or thought of putting it aside, no liability would be attached. The Sages ruled that the law against "carrying" only applied to something that was normally worth keeping: if it was not worth saving, no penalty would be incurred (Shab. 75b; Maim. Shabbat, 18:22).[409]

R. Shim'on ben Elazar extended the rule, maintaining that it applied even to something that was not usually kept but might still be required for some purpose. If another individual who had no use for the item came and took it away, that second man would be liable on account of the importance attached to it by the first (Shab. 76a).

Improper Intention in the Sacrificial Act

The sacrificial laws provide a similar example of one man rendered liable by the thought of another. While performing

---

sacrifices, the *kohen* had to have in mind the purpose for which the animal was slaughtered. This intention was particularly required of the officiating priest, irrespective of whether the owner of the sacrifice had these things in mind. Any distraction or faulty intention on the part of the priest would invalidate the offering (*Zev.* 46b).[410]

Together with R. Shim'on ben Elazar, some Sages held that if, while the *kohen* was performing all his sacrificial rites, the owner of the *korban* had an adverse intention, such as partaking of the meat at the wrong time or place, this would render the sacrifice *piggul*[411] – unfit (Lev. 7:18; Maim. *Pesulei ha-Mukdashin*, 14:1).[412] Another Sage, R. Eliezer, maintained that a similar law would apply to the intention of a heathen. If an animal belonging to a heathen was ritually slaughtered by a Jew (*shehitah*), but the owner tacitly meant it to be in honour of his pagan god, the animal would be deemed unfit for food.[413] By this ruling any improper intention of any participant in the act would render the object unfit (*Zev.* 47a; Maim. *Pesulei ha-Mukdashin*, Chaps. 13–18).

Anxiety and Agitation – Behilut

Extinguishing fire,[414] like kindling fire, is "work" forbidden on the Sabbath, unless one faces a life-threatening situation. Nevertheless, if a fire does break out, it is considered a duty to rescue volumes and pages of Holy Scripture, Talmud and religious literature, as well as prayer books, in respect to their sanctity,[415] ensuring that they are removed to a safe place. If a fire breaks out at home on the Sabbath, but there is no danger to life, one is not permitted to extinguish it; one may, however, save clothing and any food needed that day for members of the

---

410 תנאי בית דין שאין המחשבה הולכת אלא אחר העובד
411 פיגול
412 זה מחשב וזה עובד הויא מחשבה
413 השוחט לעכו"ם רבי אליעזר פוסל
414 מכבה
415 כל כתבי קודש מצילין

household and one's animals,[416] removing them all to safety. The same would apply in the case of flooding or in the danger of an impending attack by robbers.

Someone once asked why a person should not save more than that limited amount, since it was not in itself prohibited "work". The answer was that if a person could legally remove more than the minimum amount, he would try to save all his possessions and, being anxious and alarmed (*bahul*), he might well forget that it was the Sabbath and then put out the fire (*Pes.* 11b).[417]

If fire broke out in the home of any other person, Jew or Gentile, he might save whatever he could, because his anxiety would not be so great and he would not forget that the law prohibited extinguishing a fire on the Sabbath. If fire broke out in his own home, he was allowed to call on a non-Jew to extinguish it (*Shab.* 117b, Rashi on RAN, p. 43; Maim. *Shabbat*, 23:20–21; *Sh. Ar. Orah Hayyim* 334:1–2).

Sabbath Joy – Oneg Shabbat

In order to preserve an atmosphere of Sabbath joy (*Oneg Shabbat*), one should avoid engaging in prayers of intercession so as not to disturb one's peace of mind on the Sabbath. One should not embark on a sea journey less than three days before the Sabbath, so that by the time *Shabbat* arrives the mind will have become adjusted to the new environment and discomfort, thus lowering the risk of anxiety and agitation on the Sabbath (*Shab.* 19a; TJ *Shab.* 24:6; Maim. *Shabbat*, 30:12–13, *Maggid Mishneh ad loc.*).

Even some of the restrictions of "work" on the Sabbath were relaxed by the Sages in order to preserve the spirit of the Shabbath. Every effort had to be made to avoid a feeling of anxiety and distress on the Sabbath whenever possible so as to maintain a sense of the joy of the Shabbath – *Oneg Shabbat*. Despite the law forbidding the extinguishing of fire

---

416   מצילין מזון שלוש סעודות
417   מפני שהאדם בהול על ממונו

on the Sabbath, the Sages of the Mishnah ruled that in certain circumstances such 'work' may be permitted. Thus, according to some views, in the case of a troublesome illness, although not life-threatening, such as migraine or melancholia (*holi she'ein bo sakanah*), certain relaxations of Rabbinically ordained prohibitions are provided, such as extinguishing a disturbing light, no penalty would be imposed since the action was done in order to ease the mind from distress (*mishum tza'arah*).[418] (*Shab.* 29b–30a, Rashi, *ad loc.*; Maim. Mishnah commentary *ibid.*; Maim. *Yad.*, *Shabbat* 1:7, *Maggid Mishneh*).

Summation

The Bible relates that *Shabbat*, the Sabbath, was the seventh and final day of creation, a crowning achievement that completed all the work performed by God on the previous six days (Gen. 2:1–3). By observing the Sabbath man acknowledges God as Master of the universe; but the Sabbath was instituted as a covenant between the Almighty and His people. It is the touchstone through which every Jew's faith in and acknowledgment of God the Creator is tested. In the worship of God the Sabbath was reckoned as of greater importance than the building of the Temple, "for this only is the sign of recognition that I God do sanctify you". Israel was commanded to build a Sanctuary for the Lord, "that I may dwell among them", and through which the whole earth became full of His glory. Nevertheless, it was not the Temple or the altar which sanctified God: it is the Sabbath which has the sanctity of God's covenant. Keeping the Sabbath day holy is the sign between God and Israel of the fathomless love that sanctifies them both (Ex. 31:13:16).[419] Abstaining from work on the Sabbath demonstrates the Jew's homage to God as the Creator and Lord of the world (S. R. Hirsch, *Judaism Eternal*, ed. I. Grunfeld).

---

418   המכבה את הנר... מפני רוח רעה, ואם בשביל החולה שייש פטור
419   אות היא ביני וביניכם לדורותיכם לדעת כי אני ה' מקדשכם

The Decalogue ordains: "Six days shalt thou labor, and do all thy work; but the seventh day is a Sabbath unto the Lord thy God, in it thou shalt not do any manner of work" (Ex. 20:9–10; Deut. 5:13–14). Man is allowed, even urged, to dominate the world by doing everything possible to turn all things in his environment to his own purpose. On the seventh day, however, he is forbidden to fashion anything for his own purpose, thus acknowledging that everything in existence belongs to God the Creator and Master of the world. Even the smallest work initiated by man on the Sabbath day is a denial of God the Creator. The Sabbath is marked out from other days to lay upon man the unique task of ennobling life. By making the Sabbath holy, man upholds the covenant that governs his relationship with God: "It is a sign between Me and you throughout your generations" (Ex. 31:13).[420]

A supreme effort is required to observe all the minutiae of the Sabbath laws. Clearly, at times, one may fall short of perfection and a genuinely pious man will submit his own doubts and hesitations to the judgment of his religious authorities. The *Halakhah* endeavours to ascertain what part his thought played in a given action. On the basis of true facts known only to the questioner, that action may be judged culpable or blameless; and in innumerable situations his state of mind would determine the quality of his action.

Work forbidden on the Sabbath is defined as any creative act involving man's technical skill and undertaken for his own intelligent purpose.[421] This principle governs the entire range of human activity, reflecting the triumph of mind over matter. Should someone unwittingly violate the prohibition of "work",[422] with no thought of challenging Divine sovereignty, he is not deemed a transgressor since his act was performed without conscious intention.[423] If, however, such an act will

---

420 אות היא ביני וביניכם
421 מלאכת מחשבת אסרה תורה
422 מלאכה
423 מתעסק

inevitably (though indirectly) result in forbidden "work", it is forbidden on the grounds of *pesik reisheh*. If, on the other hand, the result of his action is not what he intended, he has not violated the prohibition (*Betzah* 13b).[424]

Even when no strenuous effort is involved, carrying is also prohibited on the Sabbath. Here, the law applies to the transfer of an object from one "domain" to another[425] or from a person in a house to another person outside, however small the object may be (*Shab.* 3a; *Sh. Ar. Oraḥ Ḥayyim* 347:1). This prohibition was extended by the Sages,[426] who created a "fence"[427] to safeguard individuals from an unintended transgression. Other Sabbath laws prohibited the handling of objects associated with forbidden "work" or previously excluded from use but required after a change of mind (*Shab.* 45a; *Sh. Ar. Oraḥ Ḥayyim* 310:1).

"See that the Lord hath given you the Sabbath" (Ex. 16:29) is a statement to which the Midrash adds: "Behold the lovely pearl which I have given you" (*Yalkut ad loc.*). When the Sabbath arrives, it is traditionally welcomed as a queen,[428] and whoever takes her to his heart is a king. One of the *Amidah* prayers recited on a Sabbath morning includes this charming passage: "May all the people who hallow the seventh day be satisfied and delighted with Your goodness; for You favoured the seventh day and hallowed it. You called it "the most desirable of days" in remembrance of the act of creation".[429]

"Had Judaism brought into the world only the Sabbath, it would thereby have proved itself to be a creator of joy and a promoter of peace for mankind" (Hermann Cohen, *Die Religion der Vernunft*, 1919).

"Nothing can be simpler than... to rest on the seventh day after six days of work, yet no legislator in the world hit

---

424 מלאכה שאינה צריכה לגופה

425 הוצאה

426 שבות

427 סייג

428 שבת מלכה

429 חמדת ימים אותו קראת

upon this idea! To the Greeks and Romans it was an object of derision, a superstitious custom; but it removed with one stroke the contrast between slaves who must labour incessantly and their masters who may celebrate continuously" (Benno Jacob, *The Decalogue*, 1923). One cannot understand the make-up of a practising Jew without knowing what the Sabbath has meant to Jews throughout the ages. As Aḥad Ha-Am observed, it has, to a great extent, ensured the survival of Israel.

Chapter 8

Festivals – _Haggim_

8 Festivals – Ḥaggim

A. Work on Festivals

Preparation of Food

As the previous chapter indicated, any "work" needed to prepare meals for a major festival is permitted, but only for the actual *yom tov* (festival) requirements. Once the process of cooking has begun, however, one may add more food than one needs for the day, since in any case cooking a full pot will produce a tastier dish and enhance one's enjoyment of the festival. Leftovers may thus be eaten on the following day, and it is likewise permissible to slaughter an animal on *yom tov*, even though not all of the meat is required for that day.

The Sages differed as to whether cooking for *isru ḥag* (the day after the festival) was a transgression. Rava declared that someone who did this would not be held culpable as he might have thought, "I'll prepare extra food in case friends visit us on *yom tov*". If they did not arrive, he could eat some of the food himself. This ruling accorded with the principle of the legal device, "it might just happen" (*ho'il*) is an acceptable reason.[1] R. Ḥisda insisted, however, that there was no justification for saying that "because visitors may arrive, we will cook extra food for them".[2] The codifiers followed the more lenient view, accepting the *ho'il* principle (*Pes.* 46b, Rashi, "*mi-shum hefsed mamono*"; *Betzah* 21a; Maim. *Yom Tov*, 1:9, 15; *Sh. Ar., Oraḥ Ḥayyim* 503:1).

Although permission to lay anything on the fire is restricted to the cooking of food, Rabban Gamliel also authorized the

---

 1   אמרינן הואיל
2   לא אמרינן הואיל

placing of incense on burning coals so as to inhale the aroma, which he compared to the enjoyment of food.[3] The Sages were inclined to forbid this, however, since burning incense was not a common practice but one in which only pampered folk indulged (*Eduy.* 3:11, Bertinoro, *Tiferet Yisrael*).[4]

The law governing "work" on a festival only allows one to prepare whatever food is needed that day in order to fulfil the *mitzvah* of "rejoicing on the festival".[5] Otherwise, any "work" forbidden on the Sabbath is likewise forbidden on *yom tov*, except for the prohibition of "carrying" from one domain to another (*Sh. Ar., Orah Hayyim* 495:1).[6] Should it be necessary to prepare meals for a Sabbath that occurs on the following day (see Chapter 7 above), a symbolic "amalgamation of prepared food" (*eruv tavshilin*) is required before the festival to permit cooking on *yom tov* for the next day, otherwise such "work" is forbidden (*Sh. Ar., Orah Hayyim* 527:1ff.). If some of the food needed on the festival is left over, even if an excessive amount was cooked, one may eat it after *yom tov* and in this case the *eruv tavshilin* procedure would not be necessary.

The Sages, however, prohibited any deliberate and deceitful evasion of the law. Thus, when everything had been cooked, no one was allowed to make a second pot "in case I need it today" when they really intended it for the next day. That kind of deception (*ha'aramah*) was absolutely forbidden (*Betzah* 17b, Rashi *ad loc.*; *Sh. Ar., Orah Hayyim* 527:24). The Sages condemned such an evasion of the law because of its deceitfulness and even banned consumption of the extra food after *yom tov*.

This rigid prohibition is all the more surprising as extra food prepared even intentionally (*be-mezid*) during normal cooking may be eaten after the festival as explained above. Here the Sages argued that when a person commits a deliberate transgression, he is aware of his sin and may then repent,

---

3 מניחין את המוגמר ביום טוב
4 שאינו אלא למפונקים ביותר
5 שמחת יום טוב
6 הוצאה מרשות לרשות

whereas the *ha'aramah* leads him to believe that he was permitted to do such "work" and that he need not do penance for his action. In the case of such a *ha'aramah*, therefore, the transgressor was subjected to a further penalty (*kenas*) by having the extra food banned after *yom tov* as well (*Betzah* 17b, Rashi s.v. *'sha'anei ha'aramah'*; Maim. *Yom Tov*, 1:11; *Sh. Ar., Orah Hayyim* 527:24).[7]

Use of Firewood

Although the use of an open fire to cook food is permitted on a major festival, and one may add any wood or other fuel needed to keep the fire burning, such firewood must be ready before *yom tov* for possible use on the *yom tov*. One may not chop wood from timber intended for building purposes and not stored as firewood,[8] since this would render it *muktzeh*. Similarly, one may not use a shattered beam or plank unless it was broken before the festival. If someone required the beam for firewood, he was not allowed to cut it with an axe or saw, as that would involve excessive weekday "work",[9] but only to use a household butcher's cleaver.[10] However, because of uncertainty as to the exact shape of this implement, later codifiers only permitted the use of a knife (*Suk.* 31a–b, Rashi; *Sh. Ar., Orah Hayyim* 501:1; Maim. *Yom Tov*, 2:12).

Fishing and Hunting

The *muktzeh* rule applies equally to fish and fowl, which should first be caught in their natural habitat. Since all types of hunting (*tzidah*) are forbidden on *yom tov*, whatever has

---

7   שאני הערמה דאחמירו בה רבנן טפי ממזיד
8   אינו מוכן
9   טרחה יתירה
10   קופיץ לאו למלאכת אומן הוא

not been taken already is excluded (*muktzeh*) from all thought of use.

Domestic poultry and pigeons are readily available, however, and these may be taken, slaughtered and prepared on the festival. By the same token, fish kept in a small pond may be collected with a fishnet, since this does not involve "hunting", whereas catching fish in a river or lake is forbidden. The halakhic requirements are satisfied by the common practice of storing live fish in a tank of water.

If, prior to the festival, a flowing stream was partly diverted to create a small lake,[11] fish might be caught there and removed on *yom tov*, since no "hunting" was involved. Such fish were permitted on the basis that they were available before the festival (see "*Hazmanah*" below) and one might well have thought of using them (*Betzah* 23b, Rashi; *Betzah* 25a, Rashi, "*bah*"; *Sh. Ar., Orah Hayyim* 497:1, 5; *Shab.* 106b).[12]

The culpable nature of a *melakhah* depends on whether someone performed the forbidden act intentionally. Thus, as indicated above ("*Muktzeh de-Hakhanah*", Chapter 7), if a deer or other stray animal entered the house and a person shut the door to prevent its escape, this might constitute "hunting" (*tzidah*). If he positioned himself to block the animal's escape but did not seal off the exit, and the arrival of a second person did so and prevented the animal from escaping, whether that second person was culpable would depend on his intention when he blocked the exit, i.e., if he sealed it off deliberately, with *kavvanah* (*Shab.* 106b; RIF, *Shabbat*, p. 38, RAN *ad loc.*, s.v. "*ha-sheni hayyav*"; *Sh. Ar., Orah Hayyim* 316:5).[13]

Because hunting is a prohibited category of "work" on Sabbaths and festivals, a problem arises if one wishes to cover a beehive to protect it from the sun or rain. The beehive itself cannot be moved, since "handling" a *muktzeh* object is forbidden. According to the Sages, on holy days one may

---

11 השוכר אמת מים

12 אבל צדין חיה ועוף מן הביברין

13 צבי שנכנס לבית ונעל אחד בפניו חייב

spread a mat over the beehive to protect it from the rain in wet weather or to shield it from the heat of the sun.[14]

A further halakhic problem would then arise, however, since the covering might imprison the bees in the hive, which would also constitute "hunting". The Rabbis therefore permitted use of a covering only if there was no intention to trap the bees inside[15] and an exit was left open so that the bees would be able to fly out of the hive. Their permission was thus subject to the purpose that the owner had in mind (*Betzah* 36a-b, Rashi, *Tos.* s.v. "*ella*"; Maim. *Shabbat*, 25:25).

B. *Muktzeh, Hakhanah* and *Hazmanah*

The Firstborn Animal – Bekhor Behemah

Every male firstling of "clean" (permitted) animals, cattle, sheep or goat, was automatically sanctified from birth, destined for sacrifice on the altar and therefore excluded from any non-sanctified use (Ex. 13:2, 12). Of "unclean" animals, an ass could be redeemed by exchanging it for a lamb (Ex. 13:13; *Sh. Ar., Yoreh De'ah,* 306, 321). In Temple times the firstling had to be given as an offering to a priest, one of the 24 "gifts" reserved for *kohanim*.

An animal that was perfect, without blemish, had to be offered on the altar and the statutory portions could be eaten by male priests in Jerusalem. If it proved unfit for the altar, it still belonged to the priest who had received it and could be eaten by that priest and his family or given to anyone he chose. These laws applied to all firstborn animals, whether in or outside the Land of Israel (*Bekh.* 3b, 4b; *BK* 110b; Maim. *Bekhorim,* 1:1, 5).[16]

---

14 פורסין מחצלת על גבי כוורת דבורים בשבת
15 ובלבד שלא יתכוון לצוד
16 בכור בהמה טהורה והבכורים אלו אינן נאכלין אלא בירושלים

Following a firstling's birth, the owner was expected to attend to its needs for 30 days, after which he had to give it to a priest (if one was available). Should the firstling remain in his care, he had to protect it from injury and watch out for any blemish that might disqualify it as an offering, but not necessarily make it *terefah* (forbidden for consumption) under the laws of *kashrut*.

A Further Muktzeh Problem

The Sages discussed the case of a firstling that fell into a pit on *yom tov* and which, it was feared, might die if left there. The animal might not have sustained an injury that rendered it *terefah*, and ritual slaughter would then make it acceptable as food. The owner wished to slaughter it before it died, when the animal would become prohibited *nevelah* (carrion). However, in view of its sanctity as a *bekhor behemah*, it could only undergo *shehitah* if it already had some blemish prior to the festival.

R. Yehudah maintained that an expert in *Halakhah* could go down and inspect the animal. If, in his judgment, a blemish had already marred it before the festival, the owner could bring it up from the pit, have it lawfully slaughtered and prepare *yom tov* food from the meat, on the assumption that it would not be declared *terefah* (*Betzah* 25b). R. Shim'on thought differently, asserting that because the animal's condition was not known before the festival, it must be excluded from use (*muktzeh*) and forbidden as "not prepared" (*eino mukhan*). This prohibition stemmed from the *muktzeh me-hamat issur* rule: since the animal was deemed forbidden beforehand, using its meat had never been contemplated (*Betzah* 25a, *Tos.* s.v. "*bekhor*")[17] as it was simply not available (*Betzah* 25b–26a, Rashi).[18]

---

17   לאו דעתיה עלויה מאתמול
18   אין זה מן המוכן

R. Yehudah insisted, however, that any blemish would have made it available prior to *yom tov*, because the owner of a firstling always expected some defect to appear. No matter whose rule was followed, the animal must always be rescued from the pit *mi-shum tza'ar ba'alei hayyim* – to prevent needless suffering (*Betzah* 26a, Rashi s.v. *"ya'aleh ve-yishhot"*). The Sages agreed with R. Yehudah's ruling, but in later generations it was felt that one could no longer rely on discovering his type of halakhic expertise (*Yoreh De'ah* 306:5; 309:1).

Designation – Hazmanah

The *muktzeh* prohibition can be avoided by some form of preparation or designation (*hakhanah* or *hazmanah*). The Sages were divided over the issue of form when they considered the views of Bet Hillel and Bet Shammai on preparing the earth needed after ritual slaughter (*shehitah*) on a festival. According to one view, loose earth had to be immediately available for "covering the blood" (*kissui ha-dam*); according to the other view, if one simply thrust a shovel into the ground before *yom tov*, that would be enough to demonstrate one's intention.

They also differed over the question of slaughtering a bird from the dovecote. Some ruled that one must actually take hold of the pigeon before *yom tov* to show what was intended on the following day.[19] Others maintained that one only had to stand next to the dovecote and say, "I'll take this one or that one".[20] According to a third view, mere thought – without any expressed intention – would suffice. It thus appears that *hazmanah* could be achieved by a clear act of preparation (*ma'aseh*), by speech (*dibbur*) or by thought (*mahashavah*). The codifiers laid down that a person only had to say, "I'll take these and these" (Maim. *Yom Tov*, 2:5; *Sh. Ar., Orah Hayyim*

497:10), without necessarily holding the pigeon he meant
to eat, but his intention had to be expressed verbally. They
ruled that an intention expressed in thought but not in speech
was insufficient (*Betzah* 9b–10a, Rashi, *Tos.*, "*Bet Shammai
omerim*").

The law against using some *muktzeh* object on a festival
coincides with the requirement that whatever one intends to
use then must be designated for that purpose and ready for
use when the festival begins. This preparation of an article in
advance is known as *hakhanah*, being "ready for use".

The act of setting an item aside for a particular use is itself
regarded as a type of "work" (*melakhah*) forbidden on *yom tov*.
This ruling was derived from the Sabbath injunction, "Thou
shalt not do *any manner of* work" (Ex. 20:10).[21] Furthermore,
the Biblical law governing the collection of manna stated
that any food eaten on the Sabbath must be taken from the
double portion received a day earlier: "And it shall come to
pass on the sixth day that they shall prepare that which they
bring in" (Ex. 16:5; *Pes.* 47b, Rashi). The Torah describes its
preparation in this way: "Bake that which ye will bake, and
seethe that which ye will seethe" (Ex. 16:23).[22]

Later Sages pointed out that "baking or boiling" food
was obviously prohibited on the Sabbath, which shows that
the need for preparation referred to making some type of
sign (*reshimah*) that indicated what a person meant to use.
Alternatively, in the view of others, he merely stated his
intention to use part of it on the festival.[23]

Some authorities went even further in their lenient
interpretation of the law and permitted the mental act of
"looking" at whatever an individual wished to use and then
making up his mind to do so. This form of preparation could
indicate a mental resolve to use one particular sheep in his
flock or certain fruits in his possession. The entire preparation

---

21   לא תעשה כל מלאכה
22   את אשר תאפו אפו, ואת אשר תבשלו בשלו
23   הזמנה בפה

would thus be made only in that person's mind (*Betzah* 2b, *Tos.* s.v. "*ve-hayah*", Rashi s.v. "*ve-hekhinu*"; *Sh. Ar., Orah Hayyim* 495:4, REMA, *Mishnah Berurah* 21–22, *Bi'ur Halakhah*).

Some Questions of Hakhanah

If, on Friday, someone cut branches from a palm tree with the intention of using them as fuel, which may not of course be set alight on *Shabbat*, he would also be forbidden to handle them on the Sabbath. If, however, someone intended to use the wood as a chair, an action that is not forbidden, such use of the branches would be permitted as due *hakhanah* for the Sabbath day (*Sh. Ar., Orah Hayyim* 308:20; *Sh. Ar., Orah Hayyim* 310: laws of *muktzeh* on the Sabbath).

Since *hakhanah* is needed before the festival, any item requiring but lacking it would be prohibited on *yom tov*. If someone put an article aside only on the festival itself, it would be prohibited on the following day, if that was a Sabbath, because its use on *Shabbat* required *hakhanah* on a weekday. Similarly, any preparation for a festival must be carried out on a foregoing weekday. This rule, first enunciated by Rabbah, actually became known as "the *Hakhanah* of Rabbah" (*Betzah* 2b, Rashi).[24]

An Egg Laid on a Festival

The Sages differentiated between two occurrences on a festival: the preparation of an object by an individual and an object's becoming available through a process of nature. Such a case would be that of an egg laid on *yom tov* which had obviously not existed beforehand.[25] Most of the Sages held that Rabbah's rule likewise applied to anything created

---

24 הכנת רבה
25 ביצה שנולדה ביום טוב

in a natural fashion, as it had not been prepared before the festival. Others maintained that Rabbah's prohibition affected something available but not prepared, rather than something newly created on the festival over which a person had no control (*Betzah* 2b, 3b, 4a). Early halakhic authorities were also divided on this question. Some felt that Rabbah had never meant to include anything created by nature on a festival (RASHBA, Meiri, ibid.). Moreover, they said, an egg was already complete the day before it was laid.[26] However, the codifiers applied the *hakhanah de-Rabbah* to every situation (*Betzah, ibid.*, RIF; Maim. *Yom Tov*, 1:19, Rashi).

Covering Blood from Shehitah

Since preparing food for *yom tov* was permitted on the festival itself, one could also perform all the rites governing slaughter (*shehitah*), which included "covering the blood" of a beast or bird[27] with earth (see also "*Muktzeh de-Hakhanah*", Chapter 7 above). This ritual act was ordained by the Torah in connection with the hunting of any permitted beast or fowl: "He shall pour out the blood thereof, and cover it with dust" (Lev. 17:13).[28]

Torah law regards the blood of an animal or bird as the carrier of life, which is why eating blood was strictly forbidden. Even the flesh of a permitted animal may not be eaten until all of its blood, the life force, has been drained and removed from one's sight: "Only be sure not to eat the blood: for the blood is the life; and thou shalt not eat the life with the flesh..." (Deut. 12:23–24; Lev. 17:13–14; *Ha-Hinnukh ad loc.*). The blood of a slaughtered animal should first be poured on to loose earth (lit. "dust"), which soaks it up, and then covered with more loose earth.[29] This must be prepared before *shehitah* takes

---

26 כל ביצה דמתיילידה האידנא מאתמול גמרה לה
27 כיסוי הדם
28 ושפך את דמו וכיסהו בעפר
29 וכיסהו בעפר

place, so that the blood is concealed "in the ground" (*be-afar*), i.e., earth made ready for that purpose (*Hul*. 83b; *Sh. Ar., Yoreh De'ah* 28:1, 5).

No earth could be prepared on a festival, however, because digging was a forbidden category of "work". If, for some reason, the necessary earth had not been prepared before *yom tov*, no meat from the slaughtered animal could be supplied. If, nevertheless, *shehitah* was performed on a festival, the meat had to be set aside (as *muktzeh*). It could not be used on *yom tov* or the following day, if that day were a Sabbath, as food for *Shabbat* had to be cooked on a preceding weekday, in line with the *Hakhanah de-Rabbah* (*Betzah* 2b, Rashi).

The Sages felt that this requirement would cause hardship and mar the "joy of the festival". They therefore ruled that one might not only use earth for "covering" purposes, but other substances resembling it as well. "Covering the blood" could be done with any type of "earth" that produced vegetation, which included sand, gravel and dust. Bet Hillel decided that ashes could be used, since "ashes" in Hebrew (*efer*) resembled the word *afar* ("earth" or "dust"). The use of ashes was found to be a convenient practice (*Hul*. 88b; *Sh. Ar., Yoreh De'ah* 28:24). Burning the material needed to produce ashes had to be completed before the festival began, after which any ashes remaining in the stove satisfied the *hakhanah* requirement.[30] If, however, the fire only started to burn on the festival, no "designation" of the ashes could have taken place, as they had still to be produced. Nevertheless, some of the Sages tended to permit the use of these ashes as well, especially if they retained sufficient heat for cooking, because the "joy of the festival" principle overrode the *muktzeh* prohibition (*Betzah* 8a, *Tos.*; *Betzah* 15b; *Pes*. 68b; *Sh. Ar., Orah Hayyim* 498:14–15).[31]

---

30 אפר כירה מוכן הוא
31 שמחת יום טוב מצוה היא

Preparation of Tefillin

According to Jewish law, if an object is made or set aside for religious purposes, it is considered to be sacred and may not be put to ordinary secular use. The question then arose as to whether an object would likewise be deemed sacred if a person had only designated it in his mind for some holy purpose.

Specific requirements were laid down from ancient times for the making of *tefillin* (Ex. 13:9; *Shab.* 79b; *Men.* 32a; *Sh. Ar., Orah Hayyim* 32:7). The law states that the leather boxes of the *tefillin* must be made from the skin of a ritually clean animal and the tanning process must be undertaken specifically for the making of *tefillin* (*Sh. Ar., Orah Hayyim* 32:37).[32] The boxes and straps should therefore be made by a pious Jew who believes in their sacred function and not by a heathen or an apostate. The same law applies to the handwritten Torah passages housed in the boxes as to the writing of a complete Torah scroll (see below; *Shab.* 28b, 108a; *Git.* 45b, *Tos.* "*ad*"; Maim. *Tefillin*, 1:11, 18; 3:1; *Sh. Ar., Orah Hayyim* 32:37).

R. Shim'on ben Gamliel declared that the *tefillin* were fit for use (*kasher*) only if the leather had been made with *tefillin* specifically in mind (*ibbud li-shmah*). Others believed, however, that in general the Sages permitted the use of *tefillin* for which the skin had been tanned with no such intention.[33] The *Tosafot* held that the Sages' final ruling accorded with that of R. Shim'on ben Gamliel,[34] because specific preparation (*hazmanah*) was required (*Sanh.* 48b, Rashi, *Tos.* "*af al pi*").

Other Problems Resolved

In view of the sanctity accorded to anything (such as a shroud, grave or tombstone) that was meant for a person's burial, such

---

32 עור בהמה טהורה כשרות לתפילין. עור הבית צריך להיות מעור בהמה חיה ועוף
הטהורים... צריך שיהיה מעובד לשמו

33 כשרות אף על פי שלא עיבדן לשמן

34 צריך עיבוד לשמן

items were considered to belong to the dead. The Sages ruled that even things intended and designated, though not specially made for that purpose took on a degree of holiness and might not be used for any non-sacred objective.[35] Abbaye maintained that designation alone would suffice to confirm the proprietary rights of the deceased, and that any living person's use of the designated item would infringe the rights of the dead.[36] Rava, on the other hand, claimed that *hazmanah* without a formal declaration in the course of *hakhanah* was not sufficient to bestow rights on the deceased.[37]

The Sages accepted Rava's view and determined that intention alone would not suffice to confirm the rights of the dead until some action had been performed in connection with those objects for that purpose.[38] Since the dead were thought to "acquire their place", every acquisition required *kinyan*, which only some action could establish[39]. This ruling upheld the general view that mental intention is not effective (*Sanh.* 47b–48; Maim. *Avel,* 14:21; *Sh. Ar., Yoreh De'ah* 349:1).[40]

When a *tallit* (prayer shawl) was made, for example, the woolen threads of the *tzitzit* (fringes) had to be spun with that religious purpose in mind, and before the spinning took place one had an obligation to declare that this work was undertaken specifically for the making of *tzizit* (*Men.* 42b; *Sh. Ar., Orah Hayyim* 11:1).[41]

The problem of effective "designation" also arose in the Sabbath and festival *muktzeh* law, where previous intention was required for the use of an object on the coming holy day, since otherwise "handling" it was forbidden. The object had to be ready in advance, available for use and specifically designated (by *hazmanah*). In the case of animals, birds or

---

35 הזמנה לתשמיש המת
36 הזמנה מילתא
37 הזמנה לאו מילתא היא
38 שאין הזמנה אוסרת
39 מת מצוה קנה מקומו
40 הזמנה לאו מילתא היא
41 בעינן טוייה לשמה

fish caught in traps, the Sages prohibited taking them on the festival unless one knew that they were already caught before *yom tov* began. If their availability could not be ascertained, the due "preparation" for their use (*hakhanah*) would be lacking. It was permissible to remove animals from special enclosures, but not from nets or traps, because of uncertainty as to when they had been caught (*Shab.* 24a). If, as mentioned earlier, a man diverted the water of a stream into his pond before *yom tov*[42] and discovered fish swimming in it the next day, he might consider such fish to have been available on the eve of the festival, even though he was not aware of their presence, in which case no "designation" was required.[43] If a bird nested in his orchard before the festival, he would have to give it some mark of identification (e.g., by tying its wings) to distinguish it from any similar bird (*Betzah* 25a, Rashi, R. Hananel; *Sh. Ar., Orah Hayyim* 497:1–5).

A Torah scroll was deemed *kasher* only if it had been written by a pious *sofer* (traditional scribe) who devoted all his concentration to preparing it for sacred use.[44] No holiness was attached to a scroll written by a heathen or an apostate; indeed, the unholy thoughts accompanying its production made it a source of defilement that had to be burnt. Idolatrous notions and intentions might well have been injected into the scroll, thus profaning it (*Git.* 45a; Maim. *Tefillin*, 1:13; *Sh. Ar., Yoreh De'ah* 281:1).[45]

The use of a building meant for idol worship or any false cult, even if its operation has not yet begun, is strictly prohibited (*AZ* 47b, *Tos.* "even"; *Sh. Ar., Yoreh De'ah* 139:1).[46] The Sages considered whether a heathen object might be "cleansed" by the nullification of its idolatrous purpose. They stated that a heathen who had projected his own idolatrous thoughts onto the object could reverse them and thus eliminate its pagan

---

42 הסוכר אמת המים
43 לא בעיה זימון
44 כוונה לשמה
45 סתם מחשבת עכו״ם לעבודת אלילים
46 כיון דגלי דעתיה דלעבודה זרה נתכוון נאסרה

significance. A Jew could not do this, however, because he had never entertained idolatrous thoughts; he was therefore bound to destroy the idol. Only a heathen whose mental resolve initiated the false worship had the power to cancel it (*AZ* 52b; Maim. *Avodat Kokhavim*, 8:8–9; *Sh. Ar., Yoreh De'ah* 146:1).

C. Appearance of a Transgression – *Mar'it Ayin*

The Rabbis banned certain actions which, though quite innocent, might be open to misinterpretation. Such acts were and are prohibited *mi-shum mar'it ayin* – "for fear of how they may be viewed by other people".[47]

A typical case involved the ruling that a person may take a bird selected in advance from his dovecote and slaughter it on *yom tov* (*Betzah* 10a). With regard to this act, Bet Shammai declared that "one may not carry a ladder from one dovecote to another on a festival", as it might appear to a bystander the ladder had been taken from the dovecote so that man could plaster his roof (*Betzah* 9a).[48] Bet Hillel claimed that there was no reason to fear *mar'it ayin* in this case, since it would be obvious to anyone that the man needed a ladder to reach the dovecote. In other cases the ruling would depend on whether an action really lay open to misinterpretation by an onlooker (ROSH on *Betzah* 6a).[49]

The Sages taught that if a person's clothes became wet on a festival, he could lay them in the sun to dry. They stipulated, however, that this might only be done in that person's own courtyard and not in some public place. Here, too, objections were raised, insisting that this ought to be prohibited. The Sages eventually decided that drying clothes in public was

---

47 משום מראית עין
48 אין מוליכין סולם משובך לשובך
49 חושד על מעשה איסור

forbidden, because it might be thought that someone had violated the law against "washing" them (*kevisah*). Extending their prohibition, they ruled that a person should not even dry them in his own courtyard on the basis that "wherever the Sages have forbidden an act because of appearances [*mi-shum mar'it ayin*], it is also forbidden in private, even within one's innermost chambers" (*Shab.* 146b; *Sh. Ar., Oraḥ Ḥayyim* 301:451; *Betzah* 9a).[50]

In regard to taking the pigeon for *yom tov* food, however, the Sages adopted the view of Bet Hillel. Seeing that *mar'it ayin* was a Rabbinic precaution, not a strict law, they were inclined to relax it in case its severity detracted from enjoyment of the festival (*Betzah* 9a, B. 10a, Rashi; Maim. *Yom Tov,* 5:4; *Sh. Ar., Oraḥ Ḥayyim* 518:4, 529:2).[51] Early authorities observed that, strictly speaking, the extended prohibition applied only to a law based on the Torah (*mi-de-Oraita*), as in the case of apparent washing, which constituted forbidden "work" (*Ket.* 60a, *Tos. "mema'akhan"*).[52]

A better known instance of *mar'it ayin* reflects the tragic experience of Jews, especially in the Roman era. The Sages ruled that if someone happened to drop coins in front of an idol or statue, he should not bend down and pick them up in case this appeared to be an act of idol worship.[53] If others did not gain such an impression, however, he was allowed to do so. For the same reason, it was thought wrong to drink water from a faucet shaped like a human figure, in case this appeared to be kissing the mouth of an idol (*AZ* 12a).[54] Here, too, the Sages banned such acts everywhere, according to the general rule that whatever is forbidden in public on account of *mar'it ayin* is also forbidden in private (*Ket.* 60a).

---

50 כל מקום שאסרו חכמים מפני מראית העין אפילו בחדרי חדרים אסור
51 בית הלל מתירין מפני שמחת יום טוב
52 כביסה, מלאכת דאורייתא
53 מפני שנראה כמשתחווה לעבודת אלילים
54 לא יניח על פיהם וישתה מפני שנראה כמנשך לע״א

D. Work on *Ḥol ha-Mo'ed*

To maintain an appropriate atmosphere throughout the festival, various "weekday" (secular) activities are prohibited during the intermediate days (*ḥol ha-mo'ed*)[55] of Passover and Sukkot. It is, however, permissible to undertake such "work" if one resorts to the device of *ha'aramah,* i.e., giving the impression that it is specially needed for *yom tov* so that an onlooker will not conclude that this activity has any other purpose in mind.[56] On *ḥol ha-mo'ed* one may therefore prepare, for later use, a beverage made from barley or dates if part of it is drunk on the same day, as though it is required for the festival itself.

Alternatively, the Sages permitted any "work" which, if left undone, would result in a complete financial loss.[57] Such "work" is also permitted if it is undertaken with the aim of fulfilling a religious obligation[58] or of maintaining public services (*Sh. Ar., Oraḥ Ḥayyim* 545:1–10; 544:1–2; *MK* 12b; *Sh. Ar., Oraḥ Ḥayyim* 538:6; Maim. *Yom Tov,* 7:8).[59]

E. The New Year Festival – *Rosh ha-Shanah*

Sounding the Shofar

The Jewish New Year is celebrated on the first two days of Tishri, although Biblical law prescribed one day only, and the spring month of Nisan marks the beginning of a new year in the agricultural cycle. The Torah does not call this religious festival Rosh ha-Shanah ("New Year"), but *Yom Teru'ah* ("a day of sounding the *shofar*"). The basic ordinance reads as

---

55   חולו של מועד
56   אין ערמה זו ניכרת לרואה
57   דבר האבוד
58   לדבר מצווה
59   צורכי רבים

follows: "In the seventh month, on the first day of the month, ye shall have a holy convocation: ye shall do no manner of servile work; it is a day of blowing the [ram's] horn unto you" (Num. 29:1).[60] Rosh ha-Shanah is also called "a memorial proclaimed with the blast of horns, a holy convocation" (Lev. 23:24).[61] The word "memorial" conveys the idea of introspection – examining one's thoughts, words and deeds – and of confessing one's sins and imperfections. It is only through such a process that we can hope to elevate ourselves, cleanse our minds and "return" in penitence (teshuvah) to the Almighty.

In Rabbinic thought the blast of the shofar heralds the Day of Judgment – Yom ha-Din, when all mankind passes before God in the heavenly court (RH 16b). The shofar is not a musical instrument (such as a bugle or trumpet) fashioned by man, but the processed horn of a ritually "clean" animal, usually the curved horn of a ram. Its importance does not lie in the "music" of its notes, but in the harsh sound of its message, which recalls the Akedah and Abraham's submission to God (Gen. 22). The sound of the shofar is meant to pierce one's conscience and arouse one's sense of duty. It comprises a long blast, followed by three "broken" notes and another long blast.[62] The initial blast (teki'ah) is an alarm, a warning that a critical moment has arrived. The "broken" note, staccato (teru'ah) or "wailing" (shevarim), reflects our tremulous realization that every single human action is now being judged on High. The final blast (another teki'ah) reminds all within earshot that they must obey the summons to repent and mend their ways.

In the liturgy of Rosh ha-Shanah, the opening sequence of 30 notes is preceded by a benediction acknowledging that God "has commanded us to hear the sound of the shofar".[63] This indicates that the mitzvah is fulfilled by "hearing" the shofar; blowing ("sounding") it merely enables us to hear the shofar,

---

60 יום תרועה יהיה לכם
61 שבתון זכרון תרועה מקרא קודש
62 תקיעה תרועה תקיעה
63 לשמוע קול שופר

take its message to heart and perform our religious duty. The one who blows the *shofar* (*toke'a*) must direct his attention (*le-hitkavven*) to everyone present and listening, conscious that he is now fulfilling the law on their behalf as well as for himself. Each individual should have the same purpose in mind, otherwise the *mitzvah* is incomplete (Maim. *Shofar*, 1:1, 21:1, 5.; *Sh. Ar., Orah Hayyim* 585:2, 586:1, 589:8, 590:1).[64]

A casual listener who pays no regard to the actual *mitzvah* is not considered to have fulfilled it; if he sets his mind on it, however, he is reckoned to have done so.[65] This is comparable to the situation described when Moses ordered Israel to fight the Amalekites. Seeing the hands of Moses raised in prayer to God, the Israelites also put their trust in Him and defeated their enemy; but when Moses lowered his hands, they did not share his faith in God and started to lose the battle (Ex. 17:11; *RH* 27b, 29a, 33b; *Sh. Ar., Orah Hayyim* 589:8).[66]

If a *toke'a* only blew the ram's horn for his own musical entertainment, even though he happened to produce the requisite notes, this would not be accepted as a valid "sounding of the *shofar*". The same applied to hearing someone practice the notes (*le-hitlammed*). The Sages differed as to whether the performance of a *mitzvah* was valid if it lacked the proper intention.[67] They quoted the example of R. Zeira, who asked his servant to blow the *shofar* for him. "Take care", he said, "to blow it in fulfilment of the *mitzvah*", for only then would he (R. Zeira) fulfil his own duty "to hear the sound of the *shofar*". Since that *mitzvah* depended on "hearing", with no physical action of his own involved, what R. Zeira had in mind was clearly essential (*RH* 28a–b, 29a; RAN *ad loc.*, 7b).[68]

The codifiers ruled that the sounding of the *shofar* was only valid if the proper intention was maintained by the *toke'a* and

---

64 נתכוון להוציא ונתכוון לצאת חובתו
65 אם כיוון לבו יצא, ואם לא לא יצא
66 והיה כאשר ירים משה ידו וגבר ישראל
67 אם מצוות צריכות כוונה
68 אמר ליה רבי זירא לשמעיה איכוין ותקע לי

the listener.[69] Many halakhic authorities decided, however, that since people are not all capable of grasping the significance of this *mitzvah*, performing it is what counts, even if someone lacks a full measure of understanding (Maim. *Shofar*, 2:4; *Sh. Ar., Orah Hayyim* 589:8; RAN on *RH* 28a). Because the need to hear and understand what one heard was essential here, and anyone with a handicap would not find this possible, the Sages exempted a deaf person, a minor or someone mentally incapacitated[70] from the obligation to "hear" the *shofar*. If any such persons attended synagogue when it was blown, however, they were credited with a meritorious act (*RH* 29a; *Sh. Ar., Orah Hayyim* 589:20).

If someone took an oath not to accept any benefit from a particular individual,[71] could he listen to that person's sounding of the *shofar* in order to fulfil his personal duty? On the face of it, hearing the *shofar* granted him a satisfaction that he had pledged himself not to receive. The Sages declared, however, that the fulfilment of a *mitzvah* was a religious duty that had nothing to do with enjoyment.[72] True, one could derive satisfaction from the performance of a *mitzvah*, but this was strictly a religious matter and any pleasure that one gained from it was irrelevant. The first man could therefore listen to the second man blowing the *shofar* and thereby fulfil his obligation without breaking his oath (*RH* 28a, RIF *ad loc.*, 7; RAN *ad loc.*, "*aval*"; *Sh. Ar., Orah Hayyim* 598:7).

F. The Day of Atonement – *Yom Kippur*

Fasting

The tenth day of Tishri, the most solemn occasion in the Jewish calendar, is Yom Kippur, the Day of Atonement. The

---

69 עד שיתכוון שומע ומשמיע
70 חרש שוטה וקטן
71 המודר הנאה מחברו
72 מצוות לא ליהנות ניתנו

Torah reserved it for introspection and prayer, confession of sins (*viddui*), heartfelt remorse, penitence (*teshuvah*) and the resolve to lead a better life. Yom Kippur is both a "holy convocation" (*mikra-kodesh*) and "a Sabbath of solemn rest" (*Shabbat shabbaton*) with two paramount injunctions: "Ye shall afflict your souls"[73] and "Ye shall do no manner of work"[74] (Lev. 23:27–28).

The duty to "afflict one's soul"[75] implies the curbing of our physical desires, chiefly by abstaining from any food and drink throughout the period that begins at sunset on the ninth day of Tishri and ends at nightfall on the tenth. By exercising self-control and suppressing his appetites a person demonstrates his remorse and his willingness to repent. Conscious and purposeful disobedience of this law makes one liable to *karet*, "spiritual excision" before God (*Yoma* 73b; *Sh. Ar., Orah Hayyim* 611:1).

Extent of Fasting

As a general rule, eating food the size of "a large date"[76] or drinking a mouthful of liquid[77] constitutes a violation of the fast. The Sages, recognizing human weakness, laid down that the forbidden quantity of food should be twice the amount ordained in standard prohibitions, which refer to the bulk of an olive (*ka-zayit*). Although Jews have always denied themselves the smallest amount of food on Yom Kippur, they are allowed a minimal quantity. According to R. Yehudah, the bulk of "a large date" prescribed as the measure was somewhat larger than that of an egg in the Talmud's reckoning, i.e., more than the amount generally permitted by the Sages. This opinion was based on an estimate by R. Yehudah's school that no

---

73   ועיניתם את נפשותיכם
74   וכל מלאכה לא תעשו
75   עינוי נפש
76   האוכל ככותבת גסה
77   מלוא לוגמיו

less than that amount would satisfy a person's hunger (*Yoma* 80b).[78] The Sages ruled, however, that even food amounting to less than the size of a hen's egg would be sufficient (*Yoma* 73b; 79a, 79b–80a, *Tos.* s.v. "*lomar lakh*").

As regards how much could lawfully be drunk, Bet Hillel ruled that one mouthful would violate the fast. Bet Shammai was more lenient in this instance, permitting a quarter of a *log*, which was equivalent to one and a half eggs or 137 cc (*Yoma* 80a, *Tos.*). The codifiers ruled, however, that only an amount equal to less than "a large date" was permitted, i.e., under a mouthful of liquid. These measurements applied to all Jews, whatever their size and however great their appetite (*Yoma* 80a, *Tos.* s.v. "*hakhei namm*"; *Sh. Ar., Oraḥ Ḥayyim* 612:1, 9). R. Yoḥanan asserted that these measures, as well as the Biblically ordained punishments laid down in the *Halakhah*, derive from the Oral Law which Moses received on Mount Sinai (*Yoma* 80a).[79]

The basis for these rulings was the fact that the Torah nowhere forbids "eating" (*akhilah*) on Yom Kippur, but specifically requires the "affliction of souls" (*innui nefesh*).[80] Had it prohibited "eating" as such, even an "olive-size" amount (*ka-zayit*) would have been forbidden. The extent to which deprivation of food would induce such an "affliction" was calculated in different ways, but the Sages believed that eating less than the volume of "a large date"[81] would not relieve anyone's hunger. Accordingly, partaking of that negligible amount would still count as *innui nefesh*, but eating more was forbidden.[82] The quantity permitted could not be left to a man's own judgment; it was determined by the Sages in line with their understanding of a person's physical needs, some declaring that the amount of liquid should only fill one

---

78 דבהכי מיתבא דעתיה בציר מהכא לא מיתבא
79 אמר ר' יוחנן שעורין ועונשין הלכה למשה מסיני
80 עינוי נפש
81 האוכל ביוה"כ ככתובת הגסה חייב
82 אבל איסורא איכא בכל שהוא

side of the mouth.[83] In normal circumstances, however, even a fraction of the limited measure[84] was prohibited throughout the day (Mish., *Yoma* 8:2, Bertinoro *ad loc.*; *Sh. Ar., Orah Hayyim* 612:1).

The obligation to fast devolves on women as well as men, but pregnant women and nursing mothers can secure exemption. In the normal course of events married women were not required to attend daily services, as the obligations of a wife and mother took precedence over such duties.[85] Wherever possible, however, women endeavoured to participate in the community's religious life ritual while undertaking the special responsibilities of motherhood, a *kasher* home and marital purity – *tohorat ha-mishpahah* (*Sh. Ar., Orah Hayyim* 617:1–2; *Ha-Hinnukh* 313).[86]

Where someone's poor health might worsen if he fasted, anything prescribed by a physician or requested by the patient himself had to be made available. Such a person was encouraged to break his fast, even if medical opinion considered this unnecessary, in accordance with the traditional principle: "Take therefore good heed to yourselves" (Deut. 4:15; *Ber.* 32b).[87] The one overriding consideration must then be whatever in a person's own judgment might seriously endanger his health (Mish., *Yoma* 8:5, Bertinoro *ad loc.*; *Ber.* 31b; *Sh. Ar., Orah Hayyim* 618:1).[88]

Repentance

Fasting is only one obligation to be fulfilled on Yom Kippur. The second major obligation is to complete the process of *teshuvah* (repentance) begun on Rosh ha-Shanah and

---

83	צד אחד בולט
84	בכל שהוא
85	מצוות שהזמן גרמן
86	נדה חלה והדלקת הנר
87	ונשמרתם מאוד לנפשותיכם
88	שומעים לחולה

continued throughout the first ten days of Tishri, which are known as the Ten Days of Penitence (*RH* 16b; *Sh. Ar., Orah Hayyim* 602:1).[89] On this Day of Atonement we are especially required to consider our behaviour over the past year and ascertain our shortcomings. No one is exempt from this task, "for there is not a righteous man upon earth that doeth good and sinneth not" (Eccles. 7:20).[90]

The discovery of our past failings and our sense of remorse must be followed by the public confession of our sins (*viddui*) and by a firm resolve to abandon our evil ways. The Yom Kippur liturgy includes two alphabetical lists of transgressions (*Al Het* and *Ashamnu*) which are constantly recited to help refresh a person's memory of sins he committed. Each individual must consider these offences and decide how to reduce or eliminate them in the future.

Yom Kippur ends with each congregant's proclamation of unswerving belief in the unity and sovereignty of God. A single blast of the *shofar* then marks the termination of the fast and the conclusion of that year's Day of Judgment. Everyone leaves the synagogue with a cheerful, optimistic feeling that he has been granted a fresh start in the year ahead (Tur; *Sh. Ar., Orah Hayyim* 620–623).

Fasting was considered a greater act of self-abnegation than giving charity, since the latter only involved the disbursing of money while the former resulted in a lessening of one's strength (*Ber.* 32b).[91] According to the Sages, however, going without food and drink could be a senseless denial of one's physical needs. Judaism regarded self-mortification as a heathen custom aimed at propitiating some deity. The true purpose of fasting was to arouse one's conscience, make one humble and turn one's mind from sinful to righteous deeds.

The chief lesson taught by the Book of Jonah (read during the Afternoon Service of Yom Kippur) is that the sins

---

89   עשרת ימי תשובה
90   כי אין צדיק בארץ אשר יעשה טוב ולא יחטא
91   גדולה תענית יותר מן הצדקה מאי טעמא - זה בגופו וזה בממונו

of Nineveh, though grave enough to incur the city's total destruction, were eventually forgiven. God pardoned its inhabitants not because of their "sackcloth and fasting", but because they demonstrated their true repentance by forsaking their evil ways and performing kindly acts (Jonah 3; *Ta'an.* 16a).[92]

The prophet Isaiah, speaking in the Name of the Lord, underlined this objective: "Is such the fast that I have chosen, the day for a man to afflict his soul? Is it to bow down his head as a bulrush, and to spread sackcloth and ashes under him? Wilt thou call this a fast, and an acceptable day unto the Lord? Is not this the fast that I have chosen: to loose the fetters of wickedness and let the oppressed go free? Is it not to deal thy bread to the hungry, and that thou bring the poor that are cast out to thy house? When thou seest the naked, that thou cover him, and that thou hide not thyself from thine own flesh?" (Isa. 58:5–7).[93]

The purpose of fasting on Yom Kippur is to elicit introspection and rid oneself of every offence before God. Then, and only then, will He answer our prayers: "For on this day shall atonement be made for you, to cleanse you; from all your sins shall ye be clean before the Lord" (Lev. 16:30).[94]

G. The Four Fasts

Yom Kippur is of unique religious significance, but there are four other fast days recalling tragic events in Jewish history, particularly the destruction of the First and Second Temples. In the Bible they are known as "the fast of the fourth month, and the fast of the fifth, and the fast of the seventh, and the fast of

---

92 לא נאמר בהם וירא אל-הים את שקם ואת תעניתם אלא וירא אל-הים את מעשיהם
כי שבו מדרכם הרעה
93 הכזה יהיה צום אבחרהו יום ענות אדם נפשו...
94 כי ביום הזה יכפר עליכם לטהר אתכם מכל חטאתיכם לפני ה׳ תיטהר

the tenth" (Zech. 8:19). They mark the beginning of the siege of Jerusalem by Nebuchadnezzar on the Tenth of Tevet, 586 BCE (2 Kings 25:1*ff.*); the breaching of the walls of Jerusalem, first by the Babylonians in 586 BCE and then by the Romans on the Seventeenth of Tammuz, 70 CE; the destruction of the First Temple by Nebuchadnezzar and of the Second Temple by Titus on the Ninth of Av (*Ta'an.* 26a; this fast is known as Tish'ah be-Av); and the heartless assassination of Gedaliah, the Jewish governor of Jerusalem, on the Third of Tishri (2 Kings 25:25–26, Jer. 40–41).

In addition, the Thirteenth of Adar, one day before Purim, is observed as the Fast of Esther (Ta'anit Esther). It recalls the three-day fast proclaimed by Queen Esther when Haman planned a massacre of all Jews in the Persian Empire (Esth. 4:16).[95]

All of these fasts begin at daybreak, except for Tish'ah be-Av, which (like Yom Kippur) begins on the previous evening and lasts for just over 24 hours (Jer. 52:12–13; *Ta'an.* 4:6; *Sh. Ar., Orah Hayyim* 549:1–3, 550:1). In his survey of these historic fasts Maimonides affirms that they are observed because of the tragedies that befell Jews on those dates: "The aim of fasting is to direct our hearts to the paths of repentance. These commemorative observances recall the wickedness of our forefathers, whose misdeeds incurred an agonizing punishment, and make us reflect on our own evil ways. Remembering what happened then is conducive to repentance, the forsaking of error and a thorough improvement of one's life" (Maim. *Ta'anit*, 5:1).[96]

The Sages gave a detailed account of the moving public ceremonies held on these fast days, which created an atmosphere of national grief and mourning. The *aron ha-kodesh* (holy ark) was uncovered, brought from the Sanctuary and placed in the open square amid the grieving people. The president and elders of the Sanhedrin were clad in sackcloth and wore ashes on

---

95 וצומו עלי ואל תאכלו ואל תשתו שלשת ימים לילה ויום

96 כדי לעורר הלבבות לפתוח דרכי התשובה

their heads. Their oldest member would admonish the people, urging them to repent, and the entire assembly then joined together in heartfelt prayer and supplication (*Ta'an.* 15a).

H. Passover – *Pesah*

Matzah and Hametz

Passover is also called "the Feast of Unleavened Bread" (Lev. 23:6),[97] a name that derives from the commandment, "Seven days shall ye eat unleavened bread" (Ex. 12:15).[98] This springtime festival, which begins on the eve of 15th Nisan and lasts for a week in Israel (eight days elsewhere), commemorates the deliverance of the Israelites from slavery in Egypt as well as the manner of their departure – for they left Egypt so hurriedly that their dough had no time to ferment and the bread that they baked for themselves was unleavened (Ex. 12:34, 39).

According to ancient tradition, flour milled from one of the Five Species of grain – wheat, barley, spelt, rye or oats – can be used to make "unleavened bread" (*matzah*).[99] This takes the form of thin cakes which are baked immediately after their preparation, leaving no time for the dough to ferment; otherwise the cakes become "leavened" (*hametz*) and thus forbidden. Bread made from any of the five grains enables one to fulfil the precept of "eating *matzah*" (*Pes.* 35a; *Sh. Ar., Orah Hayyim* 453:1),[100] but for normal consumption only wheat is used at the present day.

Violation of the law against eating *hametz* throughout Passover is listed as one of the cardinal sins punishable by

---

97 חג המצות
98 שבעת ימים מצות תאכלו
99 אלו דברים שאדם יוצא בהן ידי חובתו בפסח בחטים בשעורים בכוסמין ובשיפון ובשיבולת שועל
100 דברים הבאים לידי חימוץ אדם יוצא בהם ידי חובתו במצה

"excision" (*karet*) if committed wilfully, and by flagellation or even death if clear warnings had been ignored. So grave is this offence that eating even an olive-size portion of *hametz* is strictly prohibited (Maim. *Hametz u-Matzah*, 1:1).[101] Complying with the law is an acknowledgment of God's merciful protection, and observant Jews have always fulfilled it punctiliously.

Drinks made from fermented grain, such as beer and whisky, are also prohibited. Not only is the consumption of *hametz* forbidden, so is keeping any *hametz* in one's home or possession during the festival. This law is twice emphasized in the Torah: "Seven days shall there be no leaven found in your houses" (Ex. 12:19);[102] and "Unleavened bread shall be eaten throughout the seven days ... neither shall leaven be seen with thee in all thy borders" (Ex. 13:6–7).[103]

To reinforce the injunctions that leaven should "not be found" (*lo yimatzei*) and "not be seen" (*lo yera'eh*) during Passover, the Sages decreed that on the eve of 14th Nisan one should inspect one's home by candlelight to ensure that all *hametz* has been removed.[104] After the house has been thoroughly cleaned, symbolic portions of leaven are collected after dark, a blessing is recited on the performance of one's duty[105] and the *hametz* is burnt out of doors on the following morning (*Pes.* 2a, 6a; Maim. *Hametz*, 1:1–2; *Sh. Ar., Orah Hayyim* 432:1; see below).

The destruction of any leftover *hametz* is expressly ordained in the Torah: "On the first day ye shall put away leaven out of your houses" (Ex. 12:15). The Hebrew verb used here, *tashbitu*, means "put an end to" or "destroy". The Sages laid down that one can "put away" leaven in any effective manner: it may be burnt, broken up and scattered in the wind, fed to the birds or thrown into the sea. Burning, however, is

---

101 כזית חמץ
102 שבעת ימים שאור לא ימצא בבתיכם
103 ולא יראה לך חמץ ולא יראה לך שאור בכל גבוליך
104 ביעור חמץ
105 על ביעור חמץ

the preferred method, as it ensures that the leaven no longer exists (*Pes.* 27b).[106]

The removal of leaven may be performed in either of two ways: by making it cease to exist or by making it cease to be one's property. One could obviously fulfil the law by destroying all *hametz* that was "found" and "seen"; but if one did not see every shred of *hametz* in the house, how could it be destroyed? The Sages ruled that on the night before Passover eve one must conduct a search for leaven in order to destroy it.[107] According to the early halakhic Midrash, *Sifrei*, however, the *tashbitu* injunction could be fulfilled by nullifying the existence of *hametz* in one's mind,[108] and this ruling was followed by Maimonides.[109] The Torah's requirement that all leaven be "destroyed" was thus satisfied by a mental annulment.[110] One may therefore nullify the existence of any undetected *hametz* by determining in one's mind that it is no more than "dust of the earth" (Maim. *Hametz*, 2:2; *Kesef Mishneh ad loc.*).[111]

The *Shulhan Arukh* codification of R. Yosef Caro, which is the authoritative textbook for conducting a "search" and for all other laws concerning *hametz*, ruled that on the night before Passover eve one should inspect every corner of the house where leaven might be found and remove the *hametz* as well as anything with which it could have been mixed (*Sh. Ar., Orah Hayyim* 432:1; 433:3).[112] Since every householder is presumed to have undertaken a thorough "spring cleaning" and to have removed any forbidden scraps, it is standard practice to lay small pieces of bread around the home in advance, so that the "search" will result in their discovery and collection. These pieces of *hametz* are then ceremonially burnt the next morning. Any *hametz* unlawfully retained by a Jew

---

106 תשביתו בכל דבר
107 בדיקת חמץ
108 החמץ שאינו ידוע יבטלנו בלבו. ביטול חמץ
109 ביטול בלב
110 השבתה האמורה בתורה היא שיבטלו בלבו
111 ויחשוב אותו כעפרא דארעא
112 תערובת חמץ – בדיקת חמץ

during Passover is subsequently forbidden to any Jew. For that reason it is customary to arrange the sale of all one's remaining *hametz* to a non-Jew, although it may be repurchased from him after the festival.

The Sages taught that while carefully removing all *hametz* from his sight and ownership, a man should ponder the inner meaning of this act, which is the removal of any fermentation or "sourness" in his character (*hametz* of the soul). Just as he rids his home of leavened food, so should he cleanse his mind of all presumptuous and evil thoughts, remembering that his duty is to serve God with all his heart and soul (*Ber.* 17a; *Orah Hayyim* 431:1; 432:1–2, REMA; 442:1; 445:1; 448:3).

"Guarding" the Matzah during its Preparation

The cakes of unleavened bread made for the festival are called *matzot mitzvah*, i.e., "specially prepared for the *mitzvah* of eating *matza*" on the first night of Passover. The Torah first emphasized that these cakes must be free of all *hametz*: "Whosoever eateth leavened bread from the first day until the seventh day... shall be cut off from Israel" (Ex. 12:15).[113] This was followed by the commandments to "observe the feast of unleavened bread" (Ex. 12:17)[114] and to eat *matzah* from the evening of 14th Nisan until the evening of the 21st (Ex. 12:18).[115]

The verb *u-shemartem* ("ye shall observe") alludes to "special watchfulness" in preparing the *matzot*, i.e., taking great care to avoid moistening the flour with water before they are made, as this would result in its becoming leavened. The dough must be kneaded quickly, using cold water only, to prevent the dough's fermentation. The Sages thus interpreted *u-shemartem et ha-matzot* as an injunction to "guard" the

113 כל אוכל חמץ ונכרתה הנפש ההיא מישראל
114 ושמרתם את המצות
115 בראשון בארבעה עשר יום לחודש בערב תאכלו מצות

unleavened bread for the special purpose of fulfilling the religious obligation to eat *matzah* on Passover.

In Temple times, as recounted in the Mishnah, 30 loaves of unleavened bread accompanied the thanksgiving offering (*zevah todah*), but the Sages ruled that even this sacrificial *matzah*[116] was not acceptable as unleavened bread for the festival. Such *matzah* had to be made with the specific intention of fulfilling one's duty to eat it on Passover (*Pes.* 38b, Rashi; Maim. *Matzot*, 5:9; *Ha-Hinnukh* 10; *Pes.* 12a, RIF). It has long been customary for those producing "handmade" *matzah* to remind themselves of the purpose of their work by repeatedly declaring: "*le-shem matzat mitzvah*" – "This is intended for the ritual of eating *matzah* on Passover".[117]

Taking special care in the production of *matzah* involves not just kneading the dough, an obvious requirement, but also maintaining diligent supervision at every stage, from reaping the wheat to baking the *matzah*. The Sages considered this a separate obligation[118] and ruled: "Guarding is necessary from the beginning of the process to the very end" (*Pes.* 40a, Rashi).[119] Halakhic authorities differed over the extent of "guarding" needed. Some required *shemirah* "from the time of reaping",[120] others "from the grinding"[121] and others again "from the kneading of the dough",[122] so that the *matzah* would be fully kosher. Ideally, the grain should be supervised "from the time of reaping",[123] the final product being "specially guarded" or *matzah shemurah* (*Sh. Ar., Orah Hayyim* 453:4).

The Rabbis called Passover *Zeman Herutenu*, "the "Season of Our Freedom", a name preserved in the liturgy. While eating *matzah* and reciting the *Haggadah*, Jews show they are

---

116 מצה של זבח
117 לשם מצת מצווה
118 השמירה היא מצווה בפני עצמה
119 שימור מעיקרה מתחילתו ועד סופו בעינן
120 משעת קצירה
121 משעת טחינה
122 משעת לישה
123 משעת קצירה

free by leaning on a cushion at the *Seder* table (*Pes.* 108a, Rashi).[124]

The Paschal Lamb – Korban Pesah

While the Israelites were enslaved in Egypt, God commanded them to set aside a male lamb on the Tenth of Nisan, one for each household, to slaughter it at dusk on the 14th day of the month and to eat it that night "roast with fire". The meat had to be entirely consumed and anything that remained was burnt the next morning (Ex. 12:3*ff.*). Since a whole lamb might be too much for one family, the householder and his next-door neighbour could "take one according to the number of the souls; according to every man's eating ye shall make your count for the lamb" (Ex. 12:4).[125] This practice, like the festival itself, was to become a yearly institution: "Ye shall observe this thing for an ordinance to thee and to thy sons for ever" (Ex. 12:14, 24).[126]

The offering of the *korban pesah*, like all sacrifices, could take place only in the Sanctuary, as Moses decreed when he again spoke to Israel about the way Passover should be observed: "At the place which the Lord thy God shall choose to cause His Name to dwell in, there thou shalt sacrifice the Passover offering at even" (Deut. 16:6).[127]

In Mishnaic times, when the Temple still existed, the Sages discussed every aspect of these ceremonies. Although the offering of sacrifices was halted after the Temple's destruction, certain rituals – eating unleavened bread and bitter herbs (*matzah u-maror*) and drinking four cups of wine (*arba kosot*) – are still observed at the traditional *Seder* table, as well as a

---

124   מצה צריך הסיבה
125   איש לפי אוכלו תכוסו על השה
126   ושמרתם את הדבר הזה לחוק לך ולבניך עד עולם
127   כי אם אל המקום אשר יבחר השם אל-היך לשכן שמו שם תזבח את הפסח בערב

piece of roasted meat symbolizing the paschal lamb (*Sh. Ar.,* *Orah Hayyim* 472:8; 473:4, 6–7; 475:1; 477:1).

Participants in the Offering – Ha-Menuyim

The Torah required every Israelite to partake of a paschal lamb. When the head of a household brought it to be slaughtered in the Temple for the festive meal, each family member (and any neighbour included) had to participate in the collective offering. Prior to the animal's slaughter, therefore, one needed to know exactly who was included: those fit to partake of the lamb were then known as the "counted ones" (*ha-menuyim*) or "members of the group".[128] This met the Torah requirement: "According to the number of souls… ye shall make your count for the lamb" (Ex. 12:4; Maim. *Korban Pesah,* 2:1).[129]

The Sages taught that only those already "counted" as participants made the ritual slaughter effective (*Pes.* 61a).[130] Furthermore, each participant had to direct his or her mind to the action involved. Anyone who had not been "counted" in the family group, and who had not meant to be included, was later debarred from eating the paschal lamb (Maim. *Korban Pesah,* 2:1).[131] Every participant had to be aware that the offering was also made on his or her behalf and that they were included in the ritual. Such mental participation was necessary for the offering to be effective in their case (*Pes.* 88a).[132] One naturally took it for granted that the householder's wife and family were participants, since he had an obligation to provide them with food.

In the normal course of events, a newly wedded wife was automatically included in her husband's offering. A complication might arise, however, if she wished to spend the

---

128 ואלו המתמנים על הפסח הם הנקראים בני חבורה
129 איש לפי אוכלו תכוסו על השה
130 אין הפסח נשחט אלא למנוייו
131 אין שוחטים את הפסח אלא למנוייו
132 אין שוחט אלא מדעתן

first Passover after her marriage together with her parents. Not knowing of her intention, the husband would include her in his *korban pesah*; whereas the father, expecting his daughter to join him, was bound to include her in his own offering. The Sages ruled that both "counts" were valid. According to the dictates of her heart, the wife could pick the group in which she chose to be included and then partake of its lamb (*Pes.* 87a; Maim. *Korban Peshah*, 2:11).[133]

Since it was essential for all participants to know and intend that they would be included in the offering, the paschal lamb could only be eaten by those who had consciously joined the group. Although a young wife's inclusion in the offering made by her father was valid during the first year of her marriage, in subsequent years she had to state unequivocally which group she wished to join. Otherwise, she would be assumed to have participated in her husband's offering; and without an unambiguous statement of her intention she could not lawfully partake of her father's offering (*Pes.* 87a, Rashi, s.v. *"ha-ishah tokhal"*).

If the celebrant had any extraneous thought in mind when performing *shehitah*, such an offering would not be a valid paschal lamb. Legally, someone who was deaf and dumb, mentally disordered or a minor[134] was deemed incapable of understanding the sacrificial act and therefore disqualified from performing the ritual for others. The head of the household could, however, include him among those "counted" in his group (*ha-menuyim*), since if a minor had any other intention it would be of no effect (*Hag.* 2b). Adult women were duty-bound to perform the ritual themselves, if they chose not to be included in the family group (*Hag.* 2b, *Tos.* s.v. *"shome'a"*; *Pes.* 88a, Rashi; Maim. *Korban Pesah*, 2:10).

---

133 ולקח הוא ושכנו הקרוב אל ביתו במכסת נפשות

134 חרש שוטה וקטן

I. The Feast of Weeks – *Shavu'ot*

The Omer

The three yearly Pilgrim Festivals, associated with the harvest, began with Passover. Reaping the first sheaves of barley for the Omer took place while the young grain was still rooted in the soil. The "cutting" was performed after sunset on 15th Nisan, i.e., when the first day of Passover ended, as the Torah ordained: "On the morrow of the festive day" (Lev. 23:10–11; *Men.* 65a).[135]

In Temple times, on the night before Passover eve (14th Nisan), messengers sent to the chosen field tied up the ripest standing grain in order to identify them and to simplify the reapers' work two nights later. People from all the nearby towns would gather for the ritual "cutting" of the sheaves, when three *se'ah* measures of barley were ceremonially cut with a scythe. Once brought to the Temple, these were threshed and ground into an *ephah* measure of very fine flour, which was then sacrificed as a "wave offering".[136] No reaping of grain was permitted in the Land of Israel before the Omer had been cut. On the following days, landowners would bring their own first sheaves as Temple offerings (Maim. *Temidin*, 7).

The Two Loaves – *Shetei ha-Lehem*

Shavu'ot, the second Pilgrim Festival, is observed 50 days after the first day of Passover (see below). In Biblical times it was also known as *Hag ha-Katzir* – "the Harvest Festival" (Ex. 23:16), and *Yom ha-Bikkurim* – "the Day of the First Fruits" (Num. 28–26). Celebrations then began with the

---

135   ממחרת השבת
136   מנחת תנופה

whole people's Temple offering, which consisted of two specially shaped square loaves baked from the first sheaves of wheat.[137] All new produce was forbidden until the "two loaves" had been offered in the Temple, after which farmers could proceed with their harvesting. One and a half *se'ah* of grain from the sheaves, thoroughly ground, yielded just one tenth of a *se'ah* of fine flour for each loaf of bread. Since no leaven was prohibited on the altar, the "two loaves" were not burnt there (Ex. 23:16–18, Rashi; Lev. 23:17; *Men.* 66a, 73b, 84b, 94a). Instead, they were eaten on the festival, one by the high priest and the other by officiating *kohanim* (Maim. *Temidin*, 8:1–11).

First Fruits – Bikkurim

The first fruits that each landowner brought to the Temple were not chosen casually. The law required him to check his produce carefully as he sought ripe examples of the Seven Species grown in the Land of Israel – wheat, barley, grapes, figs, pomegranates, olives and dates (Deut. 8:8).[138] He marked the best that he found with a ribbon and declared, "These are my first fruits".[139] The marked produce was brought to Jerusalem, with much ceremony and rejoicing, from all parts of the land. Farmers living close to Jerusalem brought baskets of fresh grain and fruit, while those coming from a greater distance brought dried produce, all these gifts being richly decorated. No one appeared before the Lord empty-handed (Ex. 23:15).[140]

The pilgrims entered Jerusalem in festive processions, with an accompaniment of music and psalm singing. They were joyfully greeted by Temple officials and citizens, who

---

137 ממושבותיכם תביאו לחם תנופה שתים... בכורים לה׳
138 ארץ חטה ושערה וגפן ותאנה ורמון ארץ זית שמן ודבש
139 הרי אלו ביכורים
140 ולא יראו פני ריקם

escorted them up to the Temple Mount. During their stay in Jerusalem, pilgrims knew that warm hospitality would be available (Mish., *Bik.* 3:2–9, *Bik.* 80a; Maim. *Temidin*, 8).

As each individual presented his basket of first fruits, the officiating priest would place his hand under the donor's and, as he waved the offering, set it before the Temple altar. The quantity of *bikkurim* had no fixed measure: it might be large or small, depending on the contributor's feeling of gratitude and economic status. He was expected, however, to give no less than one sixtieth of his produce (*Pe'ah* 1:1).

The Torah ordained that the purpose of bringing first fruits to the Temple had to be expressed clearly, quoting the original Hebrew text (Deut. 26:3–10; *Sot.* 32a). The value of this elaborate ceremonial was contingent on the donor's sincerity and the appreciative thoughts in his mind, which distinguished his offering from any other type of gift (*Ha-Ḥinnukh* 606).

The donor was required to express his thankfulness to God for the bountiful gifts of the harvest which he was now about to enjoy. His declaration to the priest quoted the formula written in the Torah: "I profess this day unto the Lord thy God, that I am come unto the land which the Lord swore unto our fathers to give us" (Deut. 26:3; *Ha-Ḥinnukh* 91, 606).[141] He then confessed that everything he enjoyed was a gift from God and avowed that only the Lord had enabled him to dwell in the land promised to his ancestors. This declaration mentioned Jacob's early experience as a homeless shepherd, subject to the whim of Laban in Syria,[142] and the starvation that later drove his family to settle in Egypt, where the Israelites became so numerous that the Egyptians enslaved them with cruel bondage. However, God delivered the Israelites from Egypt "with a mighty hand, with signs and wonders". It was to this "land flowing with milk and honey" that they finally came. The pilgrim's statement ended with the words: "Now, behold,

---

141   ואמרת אליו הגדתי היום לה׳ אל-היך כי באתי אל הארץ אשר נשבע ה׳ לאבותינו
לתת לנו

142   ארמי אובד אבי

I have brought the first fruits of the land, which Thou, O Lord, hast given me" (Deut. 26:10).[143]

The recital of this declaration was an essential part of the first fruits offering and a confession of faith (*viddui*). The Shavu'ot festivities were not some type of merrymaking but an expression of heartfelt thanks to God, and the validity of a man's offering depended on the sincerity of his confession (Deut. 26:5–10; *Bik.* 2:2).

The Revelation on Mount Sinai – Mattan Torah

After the Second Temple's destruction, when the offering of sacrifices came to an end, Shavu'ot acquired a new significance in Rabbinic literature as *Zeman Mattan Toratenu*, "the Season of the Giving of Our Torah".[144]

This aspect of the festival also had a Scriptural basis: "In the third month after the Children of Israel were gone forth out of the land of Egypt, the same day came they into the wilderness of Sinai... and there Israel camped before the mount" (Ex. 19:1–2). Moses climbed Mount Sinai, where he was instructed to make the Israelites purify themselves so that they might hear the words of God. The Divine Revelation took place as the sound of a *shofar* rang out and the mountain was enveloped in fire and smoke: then God spoke all the words of the Ten Commandments (Ex. 19:10–20, 20:1*ff*.). The anniversary of that momentous event, which traditionally occurred on the Sixth of Sivan (*Shab.* 86b), became the main aspect of the festival, which the Torah had determined as the fiftieth day after the Exodus (Lev. 23:15–16). Since the Omer was brought on the second day of Passover and this festival was observed seven weeks later (Deut. 16:9–10), it is called Shavu'ot, the Feast of Weeks.

---

143 ועתה הנה הבאתי את ראשית פרי האדמה אשר נתתה לי ה׳

144 זמן מתן תורתנו

The Rabbis viewed the Giving of the Law on Sinai as the culmination of Israel's deliverance from Egypt. *Mattan Torah* consummated Israel's union with the Divine, following their betrothal at the Exodus. Much emphasis was laid on counting each additional day of the Omer, which was compared to a future bride's anticipation of her wedding day (cf. Hos. 2:21–22). The commentators likewise associated "the love of thine espousals" (Jer. 2:2)[145] with Israel's bride-like acceptance of the Torah (Kimhi, *Metzudat David*; cf. Song 3:11, Midrash Song R., end 3; Ex. 19:17, Rashi s.v. *"li-krat"*; *Mekhilta ad loc.*; *Pirkei de Rabbi Eliezer* 41; Deut. 33:4; *Ber.* 57a; *Pes.* 49b).

Each night's counting of the Omer felt like a new preparation for *Mattan Torah*. Preceded by a blessing, this ritual was followed by a prayer for the restoration of the Temple and its service, of which the Omer had been part.[146] The solemnity of one's actions had to be accompanied by an earnest desire to fulfil every detail of the Torah law (*Meg.* 20b, *Tos.* s.v. *"kol ha-layelah"*).

Reciting the Ten Commandments – Aseret ha-Dibrot

When Temple sacrifices could no longer be offered, the Sages made the public reading of the Ten Commandments from a Torah scroll (Ex. 20) the central observance of Shavu'ot. After the Morning Service, it is customary for worshippers to stand and listen carefully to each word of the reading, as if they too were present at Sinai. This reenacts Israel's declaration of faith in the Torah's Divine origin (Maim. Commentary on *Sanh.* 10, "Thirteen Principles", 8–9).[147]

---

145 אהבת כלולותיך
146 יהי רצון שיבנה בית המקדש
147 תורה מן השמים

Attuning their minds to the solemnity of the occasion, most observant Jews spend all or part of the night before studying prescribed literature or attending lectures. In the devotional works of two Safed mystics, R. Shelomo Alkabetz and his mentor R. Yosef Caro (16th cent.), a prayer of thanksgiving for the privilege of obeying God's commandments preceded the night's study (*Siddur Ya'avetz 'Beit Ya'akov'*, *Tikkun Leil Shavu'ot*, quoting the *Zohar*; *Sh. Ar., Orah Hayyim* 494, *Magen Avraham*).

The Book of Ruth, also read in synagogue, emphasizes the righteous proselyte's acceptance of the Torah, which took place at this time. Wherever Shavu'ot is mentioned in the festival's liturgy, it is called "the Season of the Giving of Our Torah" (*Sh. Ar., Orah Hayyim* 494:1, *Mishnah Berurah*, quoting the *Zohar*; Mahzor Vitri).[148]

J. Feast of Tabernacles – *Sukkot*

Introduction: The Duty to Rejoice – *Simhah and Sason*

Sukkot, the Feast of Tabernacles, is the third of the Pilgrim Festivals and its week-long observance begins on the fifteenth of Tishri (Lev. 23:34). It is also called *Hag ha-Asif*, "the Feast of the Ingathering" in the Bible (Ex. 23:16), and *Zeman Simhatenu*, "the Season of our Gladness", in the festival liturgy. Sukkot was ordained as a time for celebration: "Ye shall rejoice before the Lord your God seven days" (Lev.23:40)[149] and "Thou shalt rejoice in thy feast" (Deut. 16:14).[150] Maimonides' list of positive commandments also includes the duty to rejoice on this festival (*Sefer ha-Mitzvot, Aseh*, no. 54; Maim. *Yad, Yom Tov*; *Sh. Ar., Orah Hayyim* 529:2).

---

148   זמן מתן תורתנו
149   ושמחתם לפני ה' אל-היכם, שבעת ימים
150   ושמחת בחגך

The Torah laid further stress on this *mitzvah* with the expression *ve-hayita akh same'ah* – "Thou shalt be altogether joyful" (Deut. 16:15).[151] Shemini Atzeret – the Eighth Day of Solemn Assembly (Lev. 23:36; Num. 29:35), was later made part of this obligation (*Suk.* 48a). According to the Vilna Gaon, three *mitzvot* had to be observed during the first seven days: *lulav*, *sukkah* and *simhah* (rejoicing). On the eighth day, however, there was one obligation only – "to be joyful" – and that was implied by the word *akh*, meaning "altogether" or "entirely" (MAHARATZ (R. Tzvi Hirsch Chajes), *Hiddushim*: *Suk.* 48a).

In Temple times, the Water-Drawing celebration from the Pool of Siloam (Shiloah) near Jerusalem gave rise to much public rejoicing (*Suk.* 48a–b, Rashi *ad loc.*).[152] It took place during *hol ha-mo'ed* and involved drawing water for the next morning's libation ceremony over the altar. The Sages, who played a leading part in the celebration, linked it with a verse from the Prophets: "Therefore with joy shall ye draw water out of the wells of salvation" (Isa. 12:3).[153] This alluded to Israel's future deliverance from all the nation's enemies: it would be a complete redemption, leaving no anxiety about the years to come, just as someone drawing water from an abundant well remains joyfully confident that the source will always be available. For such joy Isaiah used the word *sason* (*ibid.*, Kimhi; *Metzudat David, ad loc.*). He foretold the Return to Zion in similar terms: "They shall obtain gladness and joy [*sason ve-simhah*], then sorrow and sighing shall flee away" (Isa. 35:10);[154] "Joy and gladness [*sason ve-simhah*] shall be found therein, thanksgiving and the voice of melody" (Isa. 51:3).[155]

These twin expressions also occur in the Biblical account of Haman's downfall after his genocidal plan miscarried:

---

151 והיית אך שמח
152 ניסוך המים כיצד... תקעו והריעו ותקעו
153 ושאבתם מים בששון ממעיני הישועה
154 ששון ושמחה ישיגו, ונסו יגון ואנחה
155 ששון ושמחה ימצא בה תודה וקול זמרה

"The city of Shushan exulted and was glad. The Jews had light and gladness, joy and honour" (Esth. 8:16).[156] From all the sources quoted here it is evident that *simḥah* and *sason* are two different concepts of rejoicing. There is an allegorical story in the Talmud about two men, one named Simḥah and the other Sason. They conducted a debate as to which of them was the greater, each quoting Biblical passages in support of his claim. While this remained an open question in the Talmud, the Sages implied that there *was* a difference between the two concepts (*Suk.* 48b).

Simḥah can be experienced through outward acts such as feasting and singing, music and entertainment. At *Simḥat Bet ha-Sho'evah*, the Water-Drawing ceremony, lamps and torches lit up Jerusalem, especially the Temple Mount, men performed acrobatics as an entertainment, people sang and danced; and "one who had not witnessed the celebration had never seen rejoicing in his life" (Mish., *Suk.* 5:1). It was, however, the joyous feeling within a person that filled his heart with gladness (*Tosef. Sukkah*; Maim. *Lulav*, 8:12; Maim. *Sefer ha-Mitzvot, Aseh*, no. 54).[157]

According to R. Ovadyah Sforno, "*simḥah* is created by acts that express rejoicing, but *sason* comes from the removal of sorrow and anxiety" (Deut. 16:15, Sforno *ad loc.*).[158] The Vilna Gaon once confessed that having a joyful heart on Sukkot, at a time when he was overwhelmed with cares and troubles, was the most difficult *mitzvah* he ever fulfilled.

As part of the Sukkot, in view of the particularly happy nature of the outstanding "season of our rejoicing", occasion is taken to return our thoughts to the seriousness of life and its frailties. The Book of Ecclesiastes, describing our earthly imperfections, is publicly read on the intervening Sabbath. On the concluding Festival of the Eighth Day of Assembly the closing chapter of the Book of Deuteronomy is read followed

---

156   ליהודים היתה אורה ושמחה וששון ויקר
157   המצוה לשמוח בכל מיני שמחה
158   תהיה שמח בלבך, ובשמחתך לא תיערב עצבון

immediately by the first chapter of Genesis with special honours given to "the Bridegroom" of the Law (*Hatan Torah*) and "the Bridegroom" of the first section of the law (*Hatan Bereishit*). The special readings inspire love for the Torah in both young and old.

The Festive "Booth" – Sukkah

Apart from the duty to rejoice, building and spending at least part of the week in a *sukkah* is the festival's major requirement, as ordained in the Torah: "Ye shall dwell in booths seven days... that your generations may know that I made the Children of Israel to dwell in booths, when I brought them out of the land of Egypt" (Lev. 23:42–43).

The structure and dimensions of the *sukkah* are governed by the requirement to leave one's permanent home and dwell in a temporary one (*Suk.* 2a).[159] Basically, a *sukkah* is a roughly constructed "pavilion" offering "shade by day from the heat of the sun" and "a refuge from storm and rain" (Isa. 4:6). Its temporary nature is indicated by the roofing (*sekhakh*), which consists of material derived and cut from the earth, such as tree branches, straw and bamboo.[160] This roofing must not contain man-made "vessels", anything perishable (such as fruit and vegetables), or anything liable to become "unclean",[161] as defined in the Rabbinic laws of impurity (*Suk.* 11a; Maim. *Sukkah*, 5:1, 3; Maim. *Kelim, dinei tum'at kelim*). Items subject to impurity (*tum'ah*) include food suitable for human consumption and already severed from the place of its growth (Maim. *Tum'at Okhalin, passim*).

The Sages discussed a case where it was evidently uncertain whether a man had cut various fruits or vegetables as food[162]

---

159 צא מדירת קבע ושב בדירת ארעי
160 גידולי הארץ
161 שאין מקבלין טומאה
162 לאכילה

or for the roofing of a *sukkah*.[163] In the words of the Sages, "he cut them with the intention of using them for food, which would of course make them susceptible to impurity and unfit for *sekhakh*. He then changed his mind and decided to use them for covering a *sukkah*."[164] If so, had his original intention been nullified by his change of mind or was it still shackled to the produce that he had cut?

They determined that his original intention to use it for food had already made the cut produce susceptible to impurity and thus unfit for use as *sekhakh*. No change of mind could alter the condition imposed on it by the original intention. The Sages established the principle that only a change caused by a physical act would annul a prior intention.[165] That intention itself has the power to create a stable condition, which can only be altered by a positive action that changes the whole nature and purpose of the object, and not by a change of intention as an act of the mind (*Suk.* 14a, Rashi, s.v. "*ma'aseh mevattel*"; *Suk.* 13b–14a; *Sh. Ar., Orah Hayyim* 629:1).

Another question involving a change of purpose for the material used could be as follows. The law requires a *sukkah* to be no more than 20 cubits (about 30 feet) high so as to indicate its temporary nature, but someone found that his "booth" exceeded the permissible height. He then reduced it by piling cushions and bolsters on the ground in order to raise the floor level. With that aim in mind, he dissociated these articles from their normal use, regarding them as no more than the "dust of the earth", so that they would become part of the floor. This transformation was an entirely mental process, like the nullification of any remaining *hametz* before Passover.[166] He thus determined that these articles were now just another layer of earth, which could be used for the *sukkah*'s interior.

The Sages ruled, however, that this type of expedient was invalid, because anyone could see that the cushions were

---

163   כשר לסכך
164   כגון שקוצצן לאכילה ונמלך עליהן לסיכוך
165   רק מעשה מבטל מחשבה
166   ביטול חמץ

cushions, and the idea that they might be considered "dust of the earth" had no meaning for others.[167] Such an objection did not apply to the annulment of *hametz*, as everyone knows that *hametz* is forbidden on Passover and therefore worthless.

If the same man laid bundles of straw on the ground, explicitly abandoning their use as such, they could be regarded as earth; not being susceptible to "uncleanness", they would make the *sukkah* ritually fit (*kasher*). Some of the Sages declared that a mental nullification of the straw or stones on the floor would suffice, even if it was only intended to last for the seven days of the festival. Halakhic scholars expressed opposing views on this subject (*Suk.* 4a, Rashi, s.v. "*mahaloket*"), but later authorities adopted the more lenient opinion (*Suk.* 3b–4a; Maim. *Sukkah*, 4:13; *Sh. Ar., Orah Hayyim* 633:3, *Mishnah Berurah* 11, s.v. "*u-vittelo*"; *Bi'ur Halakhah, ibid.,*s.v. "*aval setam*").

Roofing (Sekhakh) and its Intended Use

Someone took a bundle of reeds, wove them into matting (*mahtzelet*) and wished to use it as roofing for a *sukkah*. Loose reeds are not susceptible to "uncleanness"[168] and can therefore be used as *sekhakh*; but matting is a serviceable artifact that might be considered a "vessel" (*keli*), which would render it liable to impurity and thus unsuitable for roofing. The Sages differentiated between matting intended for a person to lie on, which made it a *keli* and unsuitable, and matting that was always intended for covering the *sukkah*, which made usable as *sekhakh*. If it had been made with no special use in mind (*setam*), its suitability would depend on how most people thought it could be used. A small mat would probably be used to lie or sit on, whereas a large mat would provide roofing for a *sukkah*, a practice that many found convenient (*Suk.* 19b,

---

167   דבטלה דעתו אצל כל אדם
168   אינו מקבל טומאה

Rashi and ROSH, *ad loc.*; Maim. *Sukkah*, 5:6; *Kelim* 25:13; *Sh. Ar., Ora̲ḥ Ḥayyim* 629:1, 6; *Mishnah Berurah ad loc.*, 14–17; *Sha'ar ha-Tziyyun* 814:26).

Once the *sukkah* had been completed and judged kosher, it was consecrated to festival use only and no wood could be removed from it to serve any other purpose. This Rabbinic law took its authority from the Scriptural verse: "On the fifteenth day of this seventh month is the Feast of Tabernacles for seven days unto the Lord" (Lev. 23:34).[169] The additional word *la-Shem* ("unto the Lord") implied that the Sukkot "booth" was dedicated to God (*Suk.* 9a).

The law forbidding any wood to be taken from its structure throughout the festival might also apply to carpets, pictures, fruits and other decorations that were considered part of the *sukkah*. If before *yom tov*, however, a householder stipulated that items of value (e.g., paintings and tapestries) were intended for daytime use and would be returned to the house in the evening, that was considered permissible. He had not made them part of the *sukkah* itself, which would have resulted in their being "set aside" (*muktzeh*) and therefore usable only as temporary decorations.

Later authorities disallowed stipulations excluding particular articles from the limits of the *sukkah*. They maintained that everything inside belonged to the *sukkah*, was so dedicated for the entire week and should not be removed (MAHARIL; *Betzah* 30b, Rashi; Maim. *Sukkah*, 6:16; *Sh. Ar., Ora̲ḥ Ḥayyim* 6:1–2, REMA).

The Muktzeh Rule Applied to a Citron (Etrog)

If someone decided beforehand not to make use of a particular object on *yom tov*, either because its use then was forbidden or because it was not needed, any intention to use it had been put out of his mind (*muktzeh*) and even handling it was no less prohibited on the festival than on a Sabbath (see Chapter 7 above).[170]

Thus, when someone reserved his *lulav* and e*trog* (palm branch and citron) exclusively for the *mitzvah* of taking the Four Species, any other use of them was forbidden. The *etrog*, though a desirable fruit, might not be eaten during the festival as it had been "set aside" (as *muktzeh*) for the prescribed ritual only. Even on the seventh and last day of Sukkot (observed as the eighth day outside Israel), after the *mitzvah* had been performed, eating the *etrog* was still forbidden until the festival's termination.

The Sages, however, disagreed about this law. R. Yoḥanan maintained that the *etrog* was forbidden throughout the festival, as its consecrated purpose excluded it in a man's mind from any other use during the whole of Sukkot.[171] Resh Lakish claimed that once the blessing was recited, the *etrog*'s purpose had been fulfilled; it was thus no longer *muktzeh* and could be used for any other purpose.[172] Most of the later authorities accepted R. Yoḥanan's opinion.[173] The *muktzeh* rule came into force at sunset on the eve of the festival, since the *etrog* had already been set aside for the *mitzvah* to be performed on the following day and throughout the holiday (*Suk.* 46b, Rashi and *Tos*, s.v. '*etrog*'; *Sh. Ar., Oraḥ Ḥayyim* 665:1, *Ba'er Heitev* 1).

A Palm Branch (Lulav) and its Presumed Ownership

With regard to the Four Species (*arba'ah minim*) taken together ceremonially on the festival of Sukkot, Biblical law states: "Ye shall take for yourselves on the first day the fruit of goodly trees [*etrog*], branches of palm trees [*lulav*], boughs

---

170 אסור בטלטול
171 מגו דהתקצה לבין השמשות יתקצה לכולי יומא
172 למצוותה איתקצה
173 ומגו דאיתקצה לבין השמשות איתקצה לכולי יומא

of thick trees [*hadassim*] and willows of the brook [*aravot*]"
(Lev. 23:40). The Sages interpreted the word *lakhem* ("for
yourselves")[174] as an indication that the Torah emphasized
that these four items should belong "to you". They accordingly
ruled that no one could fulfil his religious obligation on
the first day of Sukkot with a *lulav* belonging to his friend
or neighbour, unless the latter handed it to him as a gift. In
order to facilitate the performance of this *mitzvah*, however,
they also declared that the gift could even be of a temporary
nature, on the understanding that the *lulav* was returned to its
previous owner once the *mitzvah* had been fulfilled (*Suk.* 41b,
Bertinoro; *Sh. Ar., Orah Hayyim* 658:1).[175] If the borrower
failed to do so, it would be considered a stolen *lulav* and
no valid *mitzvah* could be performed with it (*Sh. Ar., Orah
Hayyim* 649:1).

This alleviation of the law was further understood to mean
that even if one took some other man's *lulav* without his
knowledge, it could be assumed that the owner agreed to lend
it to him and expected its return after the borrower had fulfilled
his own *mitzvah*. This presumed consent was based on the
rule that a person derives satisfaction from the knowledge that
a *mitzvah* has been performed with something that belongs
to him, especially since that possession will in no way be
compromised by the waving of his *lulav*. It might therefore be
taken for granted that he would agree to the man's using it for
such a purpose (Mish., *Suk.* 3:13, Bertinoro, *Tiferet Yisrael* 75;
Sh. Ar., Orah Hayyim 649:5, REMA; *Mishnah Berurah* 34).

K. The Festival of Dedication – *Hanukkah*

In addition to the Festivals ordained in the Torah, four
other joyous occasions are celebrated: Hanukkah, Purim,
Tu bi-Shevat and Lag ba-Omer. None of the usual "work"
prohibitions are applicable to these minor festivals. Tu bi-

---

174   ולקחתם לכם
175   מתנה על מנת להחזיר

Shevat, the fifteenth of Shevat, is also called "New Year for Trees" (*Rosh ha-Shanah la-Ilanot*), or "Arbour Day", and marks the commencement of spring in the Land of Israel (Mish., *RH* 1:1). Lag ba-Omer, the thirty-third day of the Omer period (18th Iyyar), commemorates the miraculous end of a plague that afflicted disciples of R. Akiva during Bar Kokhba's tragic campaign against Rome (2nd cent. CE).

When the Hellenizing Syrian tyrant Antiochus IV Epiphanes forcibly imposed idol worship on the Jews under his rule, the priestly Hasmonean family (known also as the Maccabees) raised the standard of revolt and eventually succeeded in recapturing Jerusalem. Yehudah ha-Makkabi ("Judah the Hammer") then set to work purifying the Temple which the Syrians had desecrated. A rededication ceremony took place on the 25th of Kislev in 165 BCE. Priests rekindled the Temple's seven-branched Menorah and held an eight-day festival of thanksgiving to the true God.

The Sages amplified the historical account of these events, declaring that only a single cruse of pure olive oil (enough to keep the perpetual lamp burning for one day) had been found in the Temple, yet this oil miraculously lasted for eight days, by which time a fresh supply could be obtained (1 Macc. 4:59; *Shab.* 21b). Although the Hasmoneans continued to celebrate their military achievements, those loyal to the religious authority of the Sages (the Pharisees) chose to emphasize the prophetic teaching of Zechariah: "Not by might, nor by power, but by My Spirit, saith the Lord of hosts" (Zech. 4:6).[176]

The central theme of the Ḥanukkah festival is the struggle and self-sacrifice needed to preserve Jewish religious values under a heathen oppressor. The Sages reminded Jews that Antiochus had sought to eradicate their faith, which might have led to Israel's disappearance as the people of God; but the Almighty had intervened, overthrowing the evil despot, and had enabled the weak and few to triumph over their powerful enemies.

The *Hallel* songs of praise (Ps. 113–118) are recited each

---

176   לא בחיל ולא בכוח כי אם ברוחי אמר ה׳ צבאות

morning of Hanukkah, as well as Torah verses mentioning the gifts brought for the Sanctuary's dedication in the wilderness (Num. 7). The rekindling of the Menorah symbolized the revival of Israel's spiritual light. On each successive night of the festival, candles or oil lamps are therefore kindled in every Jewish home to reenact the miracle and recall the nature of Israel's survival. These lights may not be used for any other, secular purpose (Daily Prayer Book: *Ha-Nerot ha-lalu*; *Sof.* 20:6, 8, p. 43; *Sh. Ar., Orah Hayyim* 674:1; 676:4).

On *Hag ha-Urim* – the Feast of Lights – as this festival is sometimes called, oil lamps or candles are lit in ascending order: from one on the first night to eight on the last. An auxiliary ninth light, the *shammash* ("servant"), is used to kindle each of the others in turn. The festive *hanukkiyah* or "menorah" housing all these lights is stood on a window ledge or some other prominent place to "publicize the miracle" which they represent.[177] Kindling the lights is not sufficient; watching them burn and recalling their significance is an essential part of the *mitzvah*. Since this can be fulfilled by just looking at them, the head of the household may perform the actual lighting and recite the prescribed blessings while the rest of the family watch the ceremony and direct their thoughts to its wondrous meaning. The lights must be kindled with that sole purpose in mind. They must not be considered to fulfil any other purpose, such as brightening a room, lighting up the dark or even facilitating Torah study (*Sh. Ar., Orah Hayyim* 673:1).

L. The Feast of Lots – *Purim*

The Jewish people's deliverance from the annihilation decreed by Ahasuerus, king of Persia, at the behest of his wicked viceroy, Haman, is celebrated each year on the fourteenth of Adar. That date, which Haman chose by lot for the intended slaughter, was providentially transformed into "a day of feasting and gladness" known as Purim, the Feast of Lots.

The Book of Esther, read in synagogue from a handwritten parchment scroll, describes how Queen Esther, the young cousin and ex-ward of Mordecai, outwitted Haman and saved her people from destruction. It is an obligatory *mitzvah* to hear this dramatic account of a merciful deliverance and to "blot out the memory" of Haman, who was reputedly descended from the treacherous Amalekites (Esth. 3:1; Deut. 25:17–19). Any time devoted to reading the *Megillah* (Esther scroll) can even set aside time reserved for Torah study. The Purim laws require exchanging trays of food, sending gifts to the needy and arranging a festive meal in the late afternoon (Esth. 9:20–22; *Sh. Ar., Orah Hayyim* 687:1–2, 689:1–2, 692:1–2; 694:1; 695:1–2, 4).

Purim is normally celebrated on the fourteenth of Adar, but in Shushan (Susa), Persia's capital, the Jewish battle for survival extended to the fifteenth. Since Shushan was a walled city, the festival is traditionally observed a day later in Jerusalem and other towns fortified by walls since ancient times (Esth. 9:18*ff.*; *Meg.* 2b). A person's location can thus be a matter of some importance. If someone journeys from one town to another on Purim, he should listen to the reading of the *Megillah* wherever he happens to be, even if he means to arrive home the next day. If he intended to be home for Purim, but was unavoidably prevented from doing so, he would have to fulfil the *mitzvah* according to his own town's practice (*Meg.* 19a, Rashi). The way the law is applied therefore depends on a man's original intention rather than his current location. Maimonides adopted the same view in his ruling (Maim. *Megillah*, 1:10; *Lehem Mishnah ad loc.*).[178]

178 אם היה דעתו לחזור למקומו... ונתעכב ולא חזר קורא כמקומו... הכל תלוי במחשבה

Chapter 9

Marriage – *Kiddushin*

9 *Marriage* – Kiddushin

A. Introduction

The permanent nature of the marriage bond was emphasized
by the Sages when they compared the legal effect of
contracting a marriage with contracting the sale of a field. Just
as the conveyance of a field bestows permanent ownership on
the purchaser, so does a mutually agreed marriage establish
a permanent husband-and-wife relationship.[1] The husband
thus "acquires" his wife as an exclusive possession that is
forbidden to any other man. This is exemplified by the use of
similar terminology in the Bible. Commenting on the Biblical
text that relates Abraham's purchase of the field of Ephron,
where payment of the full price conveyed it to Abraham as
his permanent possession, the Sages noted his use of the term
lekihah ("taking") when the payment was negotiated: "Take it
from me" – *kah mimmeni* (Gen. 23:13). In Biblical parlance
the arrangement of a marriage is similarly described as the man
"taking" a wife (Deut. 24:1).[2] The reasoning behind this law
stemmed from the accepted hermeneutical rule of analogy.[3]

Marital Rights and Duties

Among the rights of a wife in relation to her husband are
the following:
1) Dowry – *nedunyah* – property brought by the wife (*Sh.
Ar., Even ha-Ezer* 50:4; 51:1; 66:11; *Sh. Ar., Hoshen
Mishpat* 43, 49; 118:9; *Sh. Ar., Even ha-Ezer* 90:13, 15,
17).

---

1   קנין עולמית
2   כי יקח איש אשה
3   גזירה שווה

2) *Ketubbah* (*Sh. Ar.*, *Even ha-Ezer* 55:1, 61:1, 62:9, 66:7, 13, 18).
3) *Tzon Barzel* (*Sh. Ar.*, *Even ha-Ezer* 77:3, REMA; 85:2, 3; *Sh. Ar.*, *Even ha-Ezer* 85:1, 3; 88:1*ff.*; *Bet Shmuel* 6; 90:14, 15, 17*ff.*, REMA; 96:1).
4) *Melug* – wife's property before marriage and not included in her *nedunya*.
– her marriage gifts.
– gifts that are limited to her use.

The rights and duties of the husband in relation to his wife are also spelled out in the sources (*Sh. Ar.*, *Even ha-Ezer* 69, 80, 83, 85, 90 for rights; 70, 73, 93, 94, 100 for duties; 66, 69, 70, 78, 79, 86, 89, 96 for the *Ketubbah*.)

General References:

Maimonides, *Nashim* 12, 13, 14.
A. Gullack, *Yesodei ha-Mishpat ha-Ivri* III, 3:14-16.
Encyclopaedia Judaica, Vol. 8, p.1120*ff.*, s.v. Husband and Wife.
Encyclopaedia Judaica, Vol. 6, p. 185, s.v. Dowry.
Sh. Ar., *Even ha-Ezer* 69, 80, 83, 85, 90 for husband's rights.
Sh. Ar., *Even ha-Ezer* 66, 69, 70, 73, 78, 79, 86, 89, 93, 94, 96, 100 for husband's duties.
Sh. Ar., *Even ha-Ezer* 43, 49, 50, 51, 55, 61, 62, 66, 77, 85, 88, 90, 96, 118 for wife's rights.
Sh. Ar., *Even ha-Ezer* 66, 69, 70, 73, 78, 79, for wife's duties.
E.E. Scheftelowitz, *The Jewish Law of Family and Inheritance* 5, 6, pp. 86–110

Although the husband has the right of usufruct – *perot* – of his wife's property, he has no right to dispose of any of the property itself.[4] The Sages said that if the husband sold a field which belonged to his wife's mortgaged property, the purchaser would still need the consent of the wife, otherwise the husband's sale was invalid. If he had sold it, either the principal or the usufruct, without her consent, she had the right subsequently to get it back from the purchaser (*BB* 50b.). If she gave her consent, the Sages were divided in their opinions as to whether even such a sale was valid.

In one view, she really would not want to sell, and her consent would be given under duress, since she was afraid of the anger of her husband if she refused; therefore, she would consent only to please her husband.[5] Hence, the sale would be invalid.[6]

The other view was that although the husband has no right of ownership of his wife's property, he is already enjoying the use of her property, to which she does not object; therefore, she cannot claim that she gave her consent out of fear. If she wished to refuse her husband would recognize that only she had the right of disposal,[7] but if she consented her consent would be genuine and it completed the sale. The sale is ruled valid.[8] Maimonides ruled according to the second view,[9] as did Caro in the *Shulḥan Arukh*.

General References:

Bava Batra 49b., Rashi s.v. '*Tanya naḥat ru'aḥ*'.
Ketubbot 80b.
Maim. *Ishut* 22:5, 16, 35.
Sh. Ar., *Even ha-Ezer* 90:16.

Kiddushin is more than the contracting of certain rights and duties; it is the placing of men and women in the bond of marriage.[10] Such a contract may only be terminated through

---

5	נחת רוח עשיתי לבעלי
6	מקח בטל
7	אין לה טענת נחת רוח
8	ממכרו ממכר
9	מכרן קיים
10	קנין הגוף

the Torah-ordained procedure of a get (divorce). The Sages declared that the holiness of such a relationship cannot be changed arbitrarily; it can only be nullified by means of a legally halachically required get, (and from the time of Rabbi Gershon (11th cent.) by a mutually agreed divorce).[11]

Talmudic law states that "a man cannot say to a woman, 'Today you are my wife, but tomorrow you're not.'" Once the marriage has been duly contracted, we must regard the woman's "acquisition" as a permanent arrangement by legal conveyance similar to the purchase of a field (*Kid.* 2a; *Talmudic Encyclopaedia*, Vol. 2, p. 137; K. Kahana, *Birkat Kohen*, p. 27).

B. The Principle of Consent

According to rabbinic law, a woman can only be betrothed with her consent.[12] The Sages never held that a man simply "acquires" his wife, as the Hebrew verb's active form (*ha-ish koneh*) would suggest. Their view is reflected in the Mishnah's use of the passive form (*ha-ishah nikneit*) when describing how "the woman is acquired" through the *kiddushin* procedure. This indicates that she allows herself to be *assigned* to the man as his wife, according to the terms agreed in the *kiddushin* (*Kid.* 2a–b, Bertinoro *ad loc.*; Maim. *Ishut*, 4:1; *Sh. Ar., Even ha-Ezer*, 42:1).

There may be an exceptional circumstance where the man is halkhically obligated to wed a particular woman, and the *bet din* (rabbinical court) orders him to do so, even though it may be against his own wish. Maimonides, when stating: "a woman can only be betrothed with her consent", adds "but there may be a case where a man was forced to betroth a woman against his own will". This case is understood to refer to an occasion when other people used *force majeure* on him to effect the

---

11   קדושת הגוף לא פקעה בכדי
12   אין האשה מתקדשת אלא מדעתה

marriage. RAVED comments that in such a marriage it would only be valid if he also expressed his consent – rotzeh ani, since every marriage required the consent of both parties. [In such a case, pressure will be put on the man until he finally gives way and says "I agree" – rotzeh ani] (Maim. Ishut, 4:1, RAVED ad loc., Hagahot Maimuniot ad loc. sect.1).

In Biblical law the following extreme case is governed by a particular ordinance referring to a man who forcibly raped an un-betrothed girl, and witnesses testified to this; he is termed anas and the girl anusah. He was obliged to pay her father a fine of fifty silver shekels, apart from payment of compensation for the damage inflicted on her (Ket. 39a, 40b; Maim. Na'arah 2:1, 2). Furthermore Torah law obliged him to take her as his wife, even though she may be disfigured and entirely unacceptable to him, and thereafter he is forbidden ever to divorce her. If, nevertheless, he did divorce her the bet din compels him to take her back – kofin oto (Deut. 22:28–29;[13] Ket. 39a, Maim. Na'arah 1:7, Sh. Ar., Even Ha'ezer 177:3).[14]

The violated woman, however, may herself, or her father, object to such a marriage and refuse to marry him, and such refusal would cancel his obligation to marry her, since no marriage can be effected without her consent. The man would still, however, be obliged to pay his fine and the sum of compensation due (Ket. 39b).[15]

By the stringency of this law, the Torah protected the honour of the daughters of Israel that they should not be used as loose women, free for all (Maim. Na'arah 1:3).[16] In practice, in all such cases, in view of the conflict of rulings among the Sages, and the principle that any uncertainty in the validity of the marriage must be avoided, and in order to escape the possibility of a "forced marriage" the bet din always taught

---

13 ולו תהיה לאשה תחת אשר ענה לא יוכל שלחה כל ימיו
14 ואם עבר והוציאה כופין אותו להחזירה
15 היא יכולה למאן
16 התורה חסה על כבודם של בנות ישראל שלא תהיינה כהפקר לכל

her to say that she did not wish to marry him (*Ket.* 40a, Rashi ad loc.).[17]

In later years, when the Rabbis lacked full Rabbinic authority, and especially in view of the growing laxity and confusion in the moral standards of family relations, the *halakhic* authorities agreed that this entire law of compulsory marriage may no longer be implemented (*Sh. Ar., Hoshen Mishpat, Arukh Hashulhan*, 1:1).[18]

As a rule, every contract and agreement made in accordance with tradition can be vitiated by reason of fraud, misrepresentation, error or duress. In *kiddushin*, where the consent of both parties is essential, any agreement may be voided if consent was obtained fraudulently or through non-compliance with the terms agreed. Jewish law regards this defective agreement as "a mistaken transaction".[19]

Maimonides initially quotes the law strictly prohibiting deceitful treatment of one's neighbour, especially in transactions, as the Bible commands: "Ye shall not wrong one another" (Lev. 25:14, 17; *BM* 58b; Maim. *Mekhirah*, 18:1).[20] He goes on to declare that if any item is sold on the basis of misleading information, the sale is cancelled and the seller must return all money received to the purchaser (*BM* 14a; Maim. *Mekhirah*, 19:1–2).[21]

C. Instances of Possible Misunderstanding

(1) Part of the woman's consent to a betrothal is her acceptance of the man's undertaking in her *ketubbah* (marriage contract) to pay her, in the event of their divorce or his death, the amount stipulated in the *ketubbah* – usually 200 *zuz*, or 100 *zuz* if she

---

17 מלמדין אותה לומר איני רוצה
18 דין אונס ומפתה אין דנין בזמן הזה
19 מיקח טעות
20 אל תונו איש את אחיו
21 יבטל המיקח ויחזיר המוכר את הדמים

had been previously married. The legal requirement is that she must feel confident that this obligation will be discharged. Her reliance on this payment is assured by the man's declaration that all his present and future goods are pledged as a guarantee. Shim'on ben Shetaḥ established the rule that the husband must include this guarantee in her *ketubbah*, using a specific formula.[22]

Now that the woman feels easier in her mind, she agrees to the *kiddushin*.[23] It would not suffice if the man simply laid 200 *zuz* on the table and declared that this sum would be available to pay for her *ketubbah*. She might fear that he might spend it in the interim and not have it available at the time of their divorce. Her uncertainty and apprehension might also arouse lasting resentment towards him.[24] Accordingly, to set her mind at rest, he must affirm in the *ketubbah* that all of his property, both present and future, is now mortgaged to her as security for the payment when it falls due (Mish., *Ket.* 80b; TB *Ket.* 82b, Rashi *ad loc.*, s.v. *"u-dekanina"*; Maim. *Ishut*, 10:7; *Sh. Ar.*, *Even ha-Ezer* 66:1, 3, REMA; *Even ha-Ezer* 100:1).[25]

On preparing the *ketubbah* just before the marriage a specific sum of liability is inserted at the instruction of the bridegroom, which he gives to his bride (*tosefet ketubbah*), in addition to the obligatory minimum sum, (*ikkar haketubbah*), which she is entitled to collect in the event of their divorce, or on his decease (from his estate). In the enthusiasm of the happy occasion it occurs that a bridegroom may enter an exaggerated sum, such as a million shekels, which would be beyond his financial ability. Since this was not a realistic sum in his financial circumstances it was not really intended to be a binding undertaking, but only a demonstration of his great affection for his bride, or as a boastful gesture to impress the gathering at his wedding. Since such a contract had been made

---

22 דקני ודעתיד אנא למקני
23 סמכה דעתה
24 דאיכא איבה
25 כל נכסיו אחראין לכתובתה - דקני ודעתיד אנא למיקני

without serious intention, it has been ruled by the Rabbinical Court that, apart from the payment of the statutory two hundred *zuz* or one hundred *zuz*, such an undertaking was not binding. In the event of such a divorce the Court would determine the amount to be paid according to prevailing circumstances.

[Ref. *Encyclopaedia Otzar Yisrael*, s.v. *Ketubbah, Nedunya*]

(2) When such a pledge is entered in the *ketubbah*, as was obligated by the decree of R. Shimon ben Shetaḥ (*Ket.* 82b),[26] we must decide whether it was the bride-to-be's impression that if payment were made in the form of land, she could claim land of the best quality (*iddit*), as when payment is made for an injury, although the Sages ruled otherwise. In order to facilitate the marriage, the Sages ruled that the value could be paid even in land of poor quality – *zibburit* (*BK* 8a; Maim. *Malveh ve-Loveh*, 19:4). If so, did she form a wrong impression at the time of her betrothal and was her agreement a mistake, thus invalidating the *kiddushin*? On this question the Sages maintained, firstly, that it was advisable to reduce the husband's liability so that a man would be more inclined to take a wife;[27] and secondly, that a woman had a greater urge to be married than a man had to take a wife. One might therefore presume that she had nevertheless given her full consent and accepted her suitor's *kiddushin* (*Git.* 49b, *Tos.* "*mi-shum ḥina*"; *Ket.* 84a, *Tos.* "*li-khetubbat ishah*"; *BK* 7b, Rashi, "*u-khetubbat ishah be-zibburit*").[28]

(3) The woman's agreement must be clear and explicit. If, in the *kiddushin*, a man had stated that he was a *kohen* (of priestly descent), but the woman later discovered that he was only a *levi* (Levite), or that he was rich but was in fact poor or vice versa, she would have accepted the *kiddushin* by mistake, rendering it a fraudulent transaction (*mikkaḥ ta'ut*). In these circumstances the *kiddushin* was invalid (*einah mekuddeshet*).

---

26 כל נכסיו אחראין לכתובתה - שישיעבד לה כל נכסיו ... דקנאית ודאקנה

27 משום חינא

28 יותר ממה שהאיש רוצה לישא, האשה רוצה להינשא

The same ruling would apply to any similar declaration that this man falsely or erroneously made about himself.

It might, however, transpire that despite his false claim the woman had no wish to invalidate the *kiddushin*. She might well contend that his deceitful behaviour did not revoke the *kiddushin* which she desired, because she had made up her mind at the time that the man's offer was acceptable, even if he did not prove to be wealthy or a *kohen*. The same difficulty might also occur in reverse, if she made untruthful claims about her own status.

The betrothal was nevertheless declared invalid, because the woman had not explicitly consented, only agreeing to the *kiddushin* in her mind. Since there was no substantiating evidence of that agreement, it remained questionable as she might only have thought of it *ex post facto*. The generally accepted rule was that unexpressed thoughts had no bearing on the terms of any agreement, whether in financial transactions, marriage or divorce (Mish., *Kid.* 49b, *Tos. ad loc.*, "*devarim she-ba-lev*", Bertinoro).[29]

(4) In giving her consent the woman had also assumed that the *kesef kiddushin* (betrothal gift) was worth as much as the man claimed, although something to the value of one *perutah* would have been sufficient in law. Had he written less than the statutory amount in her *ketubbah* (i.e., one *maneh* instead of two), she would have been sufficiently vexed to withhold her consent, and the *kiddushin* would be invalid.[30] Should sexual intercourse then take place, it would amount to fornication (*Ket.* 56b, Rashi).[31] If the man gave her *kesef kiddushin* of indeterminate value, the *kiddushin* would be revoked owing to the woman's misgivings. Accordingly, unless the *kesef* item had a sound official valuation (*shumah*), there was room for doubt about the woman's consent.[32] On that basis the *kiddushin* would be deemed invalid.

---

29   דברים שבלב אינם דברים
30   לא סמכה דעתה
31   בעילת זנות
32   לא סמכה דעתה

In accordance with this ruling, it has become standard practice when the bridegroom gives a ring (as *kesef*) to the bride for the metal content of the ring to be obvious and its value clear to all. The wedding ring must have no gem set in it, as this might be either a precious diamond or a cheap glass imitation. Those witnessing the *kiddushin* are usually required to affirm that the ring is worth at least one *perutah* (*Kid.* 9a, *Tos.* "*hilkheta*"; *Sh. Ar., Even ha-Ezer* 31:2). Symbolically, a ring on the wife's finger is a visual reminder that she is consecrated to her husband (*Sefer ha-Ḥinnukh* 522).

(5) Although the Sages taught that the *kiddushin* procedure requires the man to give his statutory *kesef* to the woman he marries and not vice versa (*Kid.* 5b), they allowed for an unusual case in which the *kiddushin* may be valid, despite the fact that the woman has ostensibly received nothing. A woman asks A to do her a favour: "Give this *maneh* to B, and through it I will become betrothed to you". When A gives the *maneh* to B and at the same time declares to her in the presence of witnesses, "Be thou betrothed to me through this", she does in fact become his betrothed.

The problem here is that A has not given B any *kesef kiddushin*, nor has she received any *kesef*, so how can such a betrothal hold good? The explanation is that by undertaking to comply with the woman's request, A is performing a service for her; if the *maneh* is transmitted to B who is a person of distinction[33] and B accepts the woman's gift, the satisfaction she derives from his acceptance is worth at least the perutah that she should receive from him.[34] In this case it appears that virtually the whole *kiddushin* was a mental process, including the payment and acceptance of *kesef*. Who exactly qualifies as a "person of distinction" is, of course, debatable, but the Sages regarded the *kiddushin* as valid (*Kid.* 7a, Rashi and RAN *ad loc.*; Maim. *Ishut*, 5:21; *Sh. Ar., Even ha-Ezer* 27:9).

---

33   אדם חשוב
34   ובהנאה זו הקנתה עצמה לו

(6) The woman's consent must also be assured after her marriage. Thus, in the event that she lost her *ketubbah*, R. Meir urged the *bet din* to have it replaced, since a man was forbidden to live with his wife unless the *ketubbah* remained in her possession. Once the contents of the lost *ketubbah* were presented in evidence, the *bet din* had a substitute document issued as a replacement, containing all the essential particulars of the original *ketubbah* – *ikar haketubbah*. This document was evidence of the marriage (*shetar kiddushin*), and that the husband had undertaken in the *ketubbah* those particular obligations in case of divorce or death. It certified that the husband had executed the marriage by stating, "Behold thou art betrothed to me". Such a document was one of the three ways in which a marriage could be effected – *shetar kiddushin* (*Kid.* 9a);[35] this substitute document was known as "the lost *ketubbah*" – *ketuba de'irkesa*.[36] Without the security of this document, the woman might fear that its terms would not be discharged, leaving her no peace of mind (*Ket.* 57a, Rashi, *ad loc.*; *Sh. Ar., Even ha-Ezer* 66:3,4).[37]

A ruling by R. Yehoshua ben Levi, approved by the Sages, declared it sinful for a husband to coerce his wife into sexual intercourse, even if he deemed himself to be fulfilling the *mitzvah* of procreation. Conjugal relations may only take place with the wife's full consent (*Er.* 100b, Rashi *ad loc.*).[38] Maimonides enunciates the law explicitly: No man should compel his wife to have sexual intercourse against her will; it may only take place with mutual consent and for mutual pleasure (Maim. *De'ot*, 5:4).[39]

(7) As a general rule, no transaction is complete and legally binding until both parties have conducted some form of acquisition procedure (*kinyan*). A verbal agreement,

---

35 האשה נקנית בשלוש דרכים ... בכסף בשטר ובביאה ... ת"ר בשטר כיצד כתב לו
על הנייר

36 כתובה דאירכסא

37 לא סמכה דעתה

38 אסור לאדם שיכוף את אשתו

39 לא יאנוס אותה והיא אינה רוצה, אלא ברצון שניהם ובשמחתם

though morally binding, is therefore not actionable (*BM* 49a; Maim. *Mekhirah*, 1:1).[40] An exception was made in the case of marriage. After the parents of the bride and groom had concluded their negotiations regarding the dowry that one side would give for the daughter and the other for the son, and once all terms of the marriage (*tena'im*) had been agreed and promptly followed by *kiddushin*, that agreement – though not set down in writing – was now legally binding. R. Gidel taught, in the name of Rav, that in a case like this even the verbal agreement was lawful and enforceable. The Sages, for their part, regarded the *kiddushin* that followed as an act of *kinyan*, since the mental gratification that both sets of parents derived from the marriage of their children was a tangible gain exchanged by *kinyan*, as well as a binding verbal agreement (*Kid.* 9b, Rashi *ad loc.*; Maim. *Ishut*, 23:13).[41]

(8) According to some opinions all names by which the bridegroom and bride are called must appear in the written *ketubbah*, as was required in a bill of divorce (*get*). But this requirement is considered an additional precaution – *humra*, rather than a strict rule; and it is not generally followed (*Sh. Ar., Even ha-Ezer* 32:4, *Arukh Hashulhan* 32:10; RASHBA, Responsa No. 420).

This document was evidence that the marriage had taken place, and that the husband had undertaken in the *ketubbah* certain particular obligations in case of divorce or death. It certified that the husband had executed the marriage by stating: "Behold thou art betrothed to me" (*Kid.* 9a),[42] and detailed the particular obligations undertaken in the *ketubbah*.

The betrothal may be effected by the man giving the bride a document which included a formal statement by the bridegroom, "Behold thou art consecrated to me..." (*harei at mekuddeshet li*),[43] and was handed to the bride in the

---

40   המיקח אינו נקנה בדברים
41   כמלווה על פה
42   שטר קידושין
43   הרי את מקודשת לי

presence of witnesses – *shetar kiddushin*. This procedure of marriage, however, was not customary because of the possibility of doubt whether it had been accepted as such, and any failure in the marriage procedure had to be avoided. "Due consent" means that the *ketubbah* itself must be written with the couple's full agreement. Any uncertainty in the procedure of the requirements of the marriage resulting in a "doubtful marriage" – *safek kiddushin*[44] – was most undesirable, as it often resulted in halakhic complications that only the execution of a divorce would resolve (*Kid.* 9a, Rashi and *Tos. ad loc.*, s.v. *"vehilkheta"*; Maim. *Ishut*, 3:3–4; *Sh. Ar., Even ha-Ezer* 32).

(9) If a man gave a woman one *maneh* and said, "Be betrothed to me with this *maneh*", whereupon she took the coin and threw it into the sea or flung it down on the ground before him, she was not betrothed to the man.[45] Clearly, the very idea of marrying this man disgusted her and so she withheld her consent (Rashi). However, there may have been a different reason for the way she acted. Dissatisfied, perhaps, with the meager sum, she just threw it away – like a beggar who receives far less than he expected. That need not indicate that she rejected the man's offer of marriage. Alternatively, she may have thought, "I'll test him to see if he is easily enraged" (RAN), or "I'm willing to get married, but I do not need your gift".

Similarly, if the man offered her a loaf of bread as *kesef kiddushin* and she said "You can give it to the dog", that could mean one of two things: either the woman refused his offer in disgust or she accepted it with a request: "Give this bread to the dog as it needs to be fed".

Wherever the woman's reaction lends itself to different interpretations, and in order to avoid possible misunderstanding, the Sages made it known that they disapproved of her

---

44   קידושין מספק
45   אינה מקודשת

behaviour. They ruled that the *kiddushin* was invalid and that she was not betrothed. It is a basic principle in *kiddushin* that the woman's consent should always be unambiguous (*Kid.* 8b, Rashi and RAN *ad loc.*; Maim. *Ishut*, 4:3; *Sh. Ar., Even ha-Ezer* 30:7).

(10) According to Biblical law, if an Israelite sold his minor daughter into slavery[46] and received payment for her, it was the owner's moral duty to marry and thus free her, or to give her in marriage to his son. This betrothal was no ordinary *kiddushin*, since the young man declared, "Behold you are *assigned* to me[47] by the payment which my father made to yours". The Sages ruled that although she had been sold as a slave, her consent was essential in any such betrothal (*Kid.* 19a; Maim. *Avadim*, 4:7–8, *Kesef Mishneh ad loc.*; *Kid.* 5a, *Tos.* s.v. "*she-ken*").

(11) In yet another case, a man who owed a woman one *sela* gave it to her saying, "Take this sum which I owe you, and be betrothed to me through it", whereupon she took money without saying a word.[48] If they had just agreed to get married,[49] her silence would indicate that she accepted the *sela* as a betrothal gift, and the *kiddushin* would then be valid. If no such agreement had been reached,[50] however, it would only be valid if she now gave her explicit consent to his proposal.[51] The Sages ruled that this woman's silent acceptance of the money could have meant: "I'm taking the *sela* because it belongs to me, but I don't regard it as *kesef kiddushin*". Were she later to maintain that, despite having said nothing at the time, she really accepted the proposal, her statement would not give legal force to the marriage. Only an unequivocal declaration of consent would validate the *kiddushin* (*Kid.* 13a, Rashi and RAN *ad loc.*; *Sh. Ar., Even ha-Ezer* 28:3; R. Moshe mi-Trani [Ha-Mabbit], Pt. 1, 299).

---

46 אמה עבריה
47 הרי את מיועדת לי
48 נטלתו ושתקה
49 היה ביניהם שידוכים
50 אם לא שידך
51 עד שתאמר הן

(12) Even after divorcing his wife, a man was usually permitted to wed her again, unless she had been married to someone else in the interim (Deut. 24:4; Maim. *Ishut*, 11:1; *Sh. Ar., Even ha-Ezer* 10:1). This remarriage necessitated a second *kiddushin*, performed in the normal manner. The husband could not maintain that since she had agreed to marry him in the first place, her agreement to the reunion should be taken for granted. This second marriage also required her full consent.

The Sages were asked to give a ruling in the following case. At the time of their betrothal a man gave a woman two coins and declared: "With one *perutah* you are betrothed to me this day and, should I divorce you, you are again betrothed to me with the other *perutah*". If she accepted the *kiddushin* as stipulated, was she betrothed to him with no need for any other formality? After some legal discussion the Sages concluded that while the first marriage was valid, the second was questionable.[52] True, the woman might have agreed to the man's stipulation, but (in halakhic terms) divorce made her completely free and independent, so that her consent would be required once again. There may have been some doubt, nevertheless, as to whether in fact she had given her consent retroactively. In view of the possible confusion, such a marriage should not be legalized (*Ned.* 30b; Maim. *Ishut*, 17:14; *Sh. Ar., Even ha-Ezer* 40:7).

(13) When a married Israelite woman (*eshet ish*) fell into enemy hands, it was assumed that she had been ravished by her heathen captor – the usual fate of such prisoners. As a captive woman (*ishah she-nishbeit*), she would have found it impossible to ward off an indecent assault. Normally, a woman who engaged in extramarital relations was considered a harlot (*zonah*). Thus, if the captive's husband happened to be a priest (*kohen*), he was forbidden to jeopardize his priestly status by living with her after her release (Lev. 21:7). This restriction did not necessarily apply, however, to a non-priestly Israelite.

In regard to a captive woman, whether she had been forced to have sexual intercourse was hard to determine. If her captor resorted to violence, she might well have submitted out of fear for her life. The sin of fornication would only apply in this case if she had slept with the man of her own free will and not under duress. Her status could only be determined on the basis of what she had felt at the time of her violation. Although the facts might never be known, it was the Sages' belief that a woman – however much she protested – inevitably derived gratification from sexual intercourse.[53] Accordingly, upon her release, she was thereafter forbidden to a *kohen* and, initially also, to an Israelite husband.

The Sages, however, felt the need for a modicum of leniency. If, therefore, a woman captive had been given a chance to contact her immediate family (due to the captor's expectation of a ransom payment for her release), she might not have been raped, as her will to resist him would have been stronger. Thanks to this consideration, the Sages declared that she would not be forbidden to her Israelite husband, although the ban involving a *kohen* nevertheless remained in force.

The idea that women derived pleasure even from enforced sex was greatly modified in the light of Jewish historical experience. Later halakhic authorities bore in mind the plight of women and girls during riots, wars and pogroms. Compelled to endure sexual assaults, they could not be blamed for submitting to their violators. Even though a woman offered no resistance, because of the danger to her life, it would be wrong to conclude that she had gained pleasure from the brutal act (*Ket.* 26b, Rashi and *Tos.* s.v. "*ve-al yedei nefashot*"; Maim. *Issurei Bi'ah*, 18:30; *Sh. Ar., Even ha-Ezer* 7:11, REMA).[54]

---

53   שמא נתרצית
54   ברצונה נאנסה

D. Some Contractual Problems

The basic rule in contracting a marriage is that the man gives the woman some item of value[55] which she agrees to accept for that purpose (*Kid.* 2a; Maim. *Ishut*, 1:1, 3:21; 4:1). If the two of them understood that they were arranging to be married (*shiddekhu*), and the woman took the *perutah* given to her without a clear statement or indication that she did so for the purpose of marrying him, we presume that her acceptance – albeit in silence (*bi-shetikah*) – is sufficient confirmation of her mental agreement to the marriage, which is accordingly valid. Every transaction, including marriage, requires a "meeting of minds" in regard to whatever is being negotiated, as we may assume to be the case here. This type of *kiddushin* normally forms part of a marriage held under the wedding canopy (*huppah*), during which the bride gives no verbal expression to her consent.

In some instances it appears that a man gave a woman a monetary gift, but this may not have been a genuine part of *kiddushin*. Here two things are uncertain: whether she consciously agreed to the marriage, and whether the marriage is binding.

One such doubt may arise over a question of fact, as in the case where the man previously gave some money to the woman as a loan and now says, "Keep the money as my payment for *kiddushin*" (*Kid.* 46a; Maim. *Ishut*, 5:12, 13).[56] The Sages discussed the uncertainty that she might have felt as regards the genuine nature of this transaction, which would thus render the marriage open to question.

There is, firstly, a difference of opinion among the Sages as to whether the actual sum loaned remains in the borrower's possession or was spent, as she presumably intended. The accepted ruling is that it was meant to be used,[57] and so

---

55 כסף שווה פרוטה
56 המקדש במלווה
57 מלווה להוצאה ניתנה

the woman no longer has the money in her possession. She thus receives no money payable for the *kiddushin*, which is therefore inoperative.

Rav enunciated the rule in simple terms: If a man uses money he had lent, and was due to him, to pay for *kiddushin*, the woman is not betrothed to him (*Kid.* 47a; Maim. *Ishut*, 5:13; *Sh. Ar.*, *Even ha-Ezer* 28:7).[58]

A different problem would arise if the man handed over the item or the cash value of his *kesef kiddushin* as a temporary gift, specifying that it should later be returned to him.[59] Rava held that such a gift bestowed full ownership on the recipient, despite that individual's obligation to return it a later stage. The gift had been made on condition that it was returned and so, if it was not returned, the gift would be cancelled, nullifying his ownership (*Sh Ar.*, *Ḥoshen Mishpat* 241:6). A gift of this nature is accepted in the ritual blessing over the *etrog* (citron) on the festival of Sukkot, whereby the *pro tem* recipient may consider the *etrog* his own and thus fulfil his religious duty (*Sh. Ar.*, *Oraḥ Ḥayyim* 658:4).

R. Ashi, however, thought otherwise. Such a procedure might in general be valid, but it would not apply to the giving of *kesef kiddushin*. Although the woman might derive some virtual benefit from its use, returning it to the lender brought her no material gain (*hana'ah*). She had to receive an outright gift and could not be "acquired" in exchange for a temporary gift, as if this was some kind of barter transaction.[60]

Later Rabbinical scholars, anxious to facilitate marriage in difficult social circumstances (or, perhaps, when no ring was available for the performance of *kiddushin*), moderated this rule by suggesting legal procedures whereby a conditional "giving" might be valid. They held that since *kesef kiddushin* was meant to afford some benefit or enjoyment (*hana'ah*), the

---

58   המקדש במלווה אינה מקודשת
59   מתנה על מנת להחזיר
60   אין אשה נקנית בחליפין

offer of *kiddushin* would please the woman to such an extent that she would readily give herself in marriage, as if this were a gift in kind (*Kid.* 6b–7a; Maim. *Ishut*, 5:22–23; *Sh. Ar.*, *Even ha-Ezer* 29:1.2, REMA *ad loc.*; ROSH, *Teshuvot* 35).[61]

A further development of the case is where a man says, "Be betrothed to me by this sum of one *maneh* (containing 100 *dinar*)", and the woman then finds one *dinar* missing. Do we assume that she has no second thoughts and agrees to the *kiddushin*? Or should we take it that the woman feels uneasy, having expected the full amount, but is too embarrassed to raise any objection, even though this arrangement is not to her liking?[62] Because of the uncertainty about her true feelings, if she now wishes to confirm this marriage, the *kiddushin* will have to be renewed and steps must be taken to ensure that the man pays the full amount (*Kid.* 47a).[63] The validity of the marriage did not depend on what she said now but on what she thought at the time when the *kiddushin* was given.

Another problem involves a man who, on borrowing money from a woman, gives her a pledge and says, "Keep the pledge and be betrothed to me through receiving that item of value".[64] The legal complication here is that whereas a loan can be spent, the pledge is undoubtedly in her possession, since the lender must retain it until the debt is paid but the security is to be returned. Thus, by being allowed to keep the pledge, she does receive an item of value for *kiddushin* and the betrothal would be valid. If the whole pledge is no longer in her possession (e.g., because it was stolen), as long as she still has one *perutah* her receipt of that amount validates the *kiddushin*. If none of the pledge remains, however, she is not betrothed, since it never belonged to her and she has received no *kesef* from the man.

This decision is rather like one mentioned earlier, where

---

61   בהאי הנאה גמרה ומקניה ליה נפשה

62   לא סמכה דעתה

63   התקדשי במנה ונמצא מנה חסר דינר

64   התקדשי לי בפקדון שיש לי בידך

a man betrothed a woman with the money he had previously lent her.[65] Some of the Sages felt that an exception could be made if even one *perutah* of his money remained in her possession. That would suffice, if she agreed, to meet the required payment. They also declared that even if none of the original money remained with her, she still owed him the emotional satisfaction of having her debt cancelled, which would surely be worth a *perutah* (*Kid.* 47a, Rashi *ad loc.*).[66]

A more complicated issue arose when a man, having lent money to a third person, retained the IOU (*shetar ḥov*) and then gave it to a woman saying, "Be betrothed to me by this promissory note, which I make over to you as a legal document".[67] Here she received a benefit that she did not have before, and R. Meir accordingly maintained that the *kiddushin* was valid (*mekuddeshet*). The Sages nevertheless ruled that the *shetar* would not effect her betrothal, since she was not given any real money.[68] Their ruling is generally followed in the codes (*Kid.* 47b; *Sh. Ar., Even ha-Ezer* 28:13).

The Sages also needed to explain the woman's conceivable dissatisfaction with the amount legally transferred to her: another ruling, by Shmuel, raised further doubts. He had maintained the following: If someone holding a promissory note sold it to a third person and subsequently nullified the original debt, he had the power to do so and the debt was cancelled (*Kid.* 48a; Maim. *Mekhirah*, 6:12; *Sh. Ar., Ḥoshen Mishpat* 66:23).[69]

Early Rabbinical commentators shed light on this decision. Maimonides claimed that Torah law made no provision for an IOU to be negotiable. The document had a symbolic value, as it contained evidence of the borrower's obligation to the lender, but otherwise it was no more than a worthless piece of paper. Accordingly, although the Sages had extended the law

---

65   המקדש במלווה
66   מקודשת בהאי הנאה דמחיל ליה גבה
67   התקדשי לי בשטר חוב והרשה עליהם
68   חכמים אומרים אינה מקודשת
69   המוכר שטר חוב לחברו וחזר ומחלו מחול

by permitting the sale and transfer of the *shetar* to someone else, the borrower's moral obligation to the lender still retained force and this he could now cancel if he so wished.

Rabbenu Tam, a leading Tosafist, offered a different explanation. In his view, Torah law did provide for the sale of the *shetar*, but the borrower's personal obligation to the lender was excluded from the sale and the lender could nullify it, thus writing off the debt. That explains why the lender, even after selling the IOU to a third party, was still authorized to cancel the debt (RAN, p. 44, on RIF on *Ket.* 86a, s.v. "*hamokher shetar hov le-havero*"; Maim. *Zekhi'ah u-Mattanah*, 10:2).[70]

Considering that the lender is empowered to nullify the original debt after selling or giving away the *shetar*, one can understand why (in the case of a betrothal) "giving" a promissory note as the requisite *kesef kiddushin* is not acceptable. Since it is a basic rule of *kiddushin* that the woman should fully consent to the marriage, she may feel uncertain in this case as to whether the document will prove worthless, and her nervousness would be sufficient to void the *kiddushin*. On that basis some Sages felt that the woman would not be content with the gift,[71] hence the marriage contract was invalid.[72] Other Sages, however, maintained that it was valid (*mekuddeshet*). They reasoned that since the man had displayed his affection by taking her as his wife, she could rest assured that he would not forgo her interests to benefit someone else and she could therefore rely on the value of his gift (*Kid.* 48a, Rashi *ad loc.*).[73]

---

70 המוכר שטר חוב לחברו וחזר ומחלו, מחול
71 לא סמכה דעתה
72 המקדש במלווה אינה מקודשת
73 סמכה דעתה

E. Consent of Minors

It is a fundamental rule of marriage that the *kiddushin* process
requires the consent and understanding (*da'at*) of both parties.
Since minors are considered to fall short of these requirements,
they do not have the legal capacity to undertake *kiddushin*. Any
marriage contracted by a *katan* (i.e., a boy under the age of 13
years and one day), is unequivocally void (*Yev.* 96b, 112b;
Sh. Ar., Even ha-Ezer 43:1). In the case of a girl under the age
of puberty (12 years and one day), her father has the right to
give his consent on her behalf and to arrange for her marriage
with a man of his choice; once she reaches that age, however,
he must obtain her consent (*Kid.* 41a; *Sh. Ar., Even ha-Ezer*
37:1).[74] The Sages based this prerogative on an incident in
the Bible where a father complained that his minor daughter's
chastity had been impugned by her new husband. "I gave my
daughter to this man as a wife", the father declared, thereby
indicating that he had contracted the marriage on her behalf
(Deut. 22:16; *Ket.* 46b).[75]

This paternal authority remained in force while the daughter
was a *ketannah* under the age of 12 years and a day, or even
a *na'arah* aged 12 years and six months, at which time she
reached full puberty (*bogeret*). During this period the father
could rightfully accept *kiddushin* on her behalf from a man
approved by him, thus legalizing the marriage. He would
sometimes have recourse to this procedure in order to safeguard
her financial interests and protect her from unscrupulous men
(*Kid.* 45b, *Tos.* s.v. "*be-feirush*").[76] The Sages, however,
strongly objected to this practice, as R. Yehudah declared
in the name of Rav: "A father is not permitted to give his
daughter in marriage before she reaches the age of puberty
[*ad she-tigdal*][77] and gives her own consent, stating that this

---

74   האיש מקדש את בתו כשהיא נערה
75   את בתי נתתי לאיש הזה לאשה
76   משום הפקר
77   אסור לאדם שיקדש את בתו הקטנה

is the man whom she wishes to marry" (*Kid.* 41a; Maim *Ishut*, 10:16; *Sh. Ar., Even ha-Ezer* 37:8, REMA *ad loc.*).[78]

A problem would arise if the father, having already consented to his minor daughter's engagement, told no one how he felt about her actual marriage, and then left the country. With her father no longer available to express an opinion, the daughter agreed to be married on her own responsibility. The Court now had to decide whether the girl's father had or had not made up his mind in favour of the proposed marriage (*Kid.* 45b).[79]

The Sages were anxious to determine this girl's status and, by removing any doubts about her marriage, to prevent her from transgressing. Despite R. Assi's objections, Rav pronounced this marriage indisputably valid. Furthermore, if the husband was a kohen, any priestly offerings (*terumah*) that were his due might be shared by her as his wife;[80] but for this purpose she had to be married with the full marriage ceremony (*huppah*), but at that time the father's agreement was not known[81] (*Kid.* 45b), and her eating of the terumah could be a transgression (*Ket.* 57b).[82] If she was not married to a priest she would be treated as "one of the laity" (Lev. 22:12; Num. 18:11, *Sifrei*) and partaking of the sacrifices would constitute a major transgression (*Kid.* 10b, Maim. *Terumot*, 6:3).[83]

In view of these circumstances, the Sages treated the girl as a fatherless child (*yetomah*) and, despite her being a minor, permitted her to marry the man of her choice (*Kid.* 45b, *Tos.*). They argued that although the father's explicit agreement was normally required, in this case he had not previously offered any objection. Had he been present but said nothing (*hishtik*),

---

78 ותאמר בפלוני אני רוצה
79 נתקדשה לדעת אביה והלך אביה למדינת הים, ועמדה ונישאת
80 רב אמר אוכלת בתרומה
81 שמא יבוא אביה וימחה ונמצאת זרה אוכלת בתרומה למפרע
82 אין האשה אוכלת בתרומה עד שתכנס לחופה
83 וכל זר לא יאכל בו

we would presume that he consented to the marriage, and his "silence" therefore validated the union (*Sh. Ar., Even ha-Ezer* 37:11). However, if the father happened to be overseas at the time and his absence made it uncertain whether he objected or agreed, thus giving rise to possible complications, his daughter would then have to obtain a bill of divorce (*get*) or a document stating her "rejection" of the marriage (*mi'un*), so as to remove any possible doubt about her status (*Sh. Ar., Kid.* 44b; *Even ha-Ezer* 37:11). On coming of age, she would be able to accept a new *kiddushin* with the husband of her choice, and the halakhic problem would thus find a solution.

The Sages also ruled that a father could agree to his minor daughter's betrothal on the understanding that the man whom he chose would marry her when she reached puberty (*Ket.* 57b).[84] Although consummation of a marriage was thought possible from the age of three, the Sages considered it improper for anyone to wed a minor by *kiddushin*.[85] If the girl refused to marry him, she was entitled to register her refusal by entering a declaration of *mi'un*. Any consummation *below* the age of three had no significance (*Kid.* 10a; Maim. *Ishut*, 10:16;[86] *Ket.* 57b; Maim. *Ishut*, 11:3[87]).

In the benediction recited at a wedding the celebrant is required to say, "Blessed art Thou... Who has forbidden to us women who are only betrothed[88] and permitted us women whom we marry through the ceremonial wedding canopy (*ḥuppah*) and statutory *kiddushin*"[89] (*Ket.* 7b; *Sh. Ar., Even ha-Ezer* 34:1).

The marriage of a *yevamah* (i.e., that of a widow to the brother of her late husband who died without issue) is governed by a special Torah precept known as levirate marriage (*yibbum*). The surviving brother – or next of kin – is

---

84 פוסקין על הקטנה להשיאה כשהיא גדולה

85 ואין ראוי לעשות כן

86 מיום שתיוולד

87 מבת שלוש שנים ולמטה

88 ואסר לנו את הארוסות

89 והתיר לנו את הנשואות לנו על ידי חופה וקידושין

obliged to marry her so that she may bear children in the name of the deceased (Deut. 25:5–10). According to Torah law, he is obliged to marry her with or without her agreement (*Yev.* 29b), but the Sages ruled that in giving her the enjoined *kiddushin* (known as *ma'amar*) he must obtain her consent (*Yev.* 19b; Maim. *Yibbum*, 2:1; *Sh. Ar., Even ha-Ezer* 166:3).

An orphan girl who is also a minor has the right to decline levirate marriage with her brother-in-law. In this case she should give a clear indication of her refusal (*mi'un*) by simply making it known that she objects to the marriage, and there is no need for her to make an official declaration before the *bet din* (*Yev.* 107a; Maim. *Gerushin*, 13:3–4; *Sh. Ar., Even ha-Ezer* 155:1–5).

F. Unclear Intentions

Problems sometimes arise because the intention in the mind of the transactor is unknown or unclear. In the straightforward type of *kiddushin* a man gives a woman the requisite *kesef* (i.e., a coin worth at least one *perutah* or an item of the same value) and says, "Behold you are betrothed to me with this". Through that act she is immediately betrothed to him. If the man says, "I give you this *perutah* and you will be married to me in 30 days' time", the marriage will become valid after 30 days.

At the time of his *kiddushin*, a man may also lay down a condition in respect of the marriage. He may first require the woman to do something for him, or he may tell her, "You are betrothed to me with this *perutah* if I give you 200 *zuz* within 30 days". If he does give her the money within the specified time, their betrothal will have the force of law.[90] If he does not, no betrothal will have taken place (Mish., *Kid.* 60a).[91] Thus, in the event of a delayed marriage, if a second man offered

---

90   הרי זו מקודשת

91   אינה מקודשת

to betroth her within the 30 days and the woman accepted, she would be deemed fully and unquestionably betrothed to the second man,[92] as the first *kiddushin* was never actualized (Mish., *Kid.* 58b; Maim. *Ishut*, 7:11).

If, when betrothing a woman, a man declared that she was now engaged to him, the betrothal was immediately legalized. However, if he made use of both formulas in his declaration, saying "You are betrothed to me now and in 30 days' time",[93] his intention remains unclear. Did he mean that the betrothal was to take place now and the marriage within 30 days or, after saying "now", had he promptly changed his mind and announced that the betrothal would not take place for another 30 days? If, within the 30 days, a second man betrothed her, was she free to accept another offer or was she already a betrothed woman?

The *tannaim* of the Mishnah ruled that the woman must be considered both betrothed and not betrothed.[94] The situation was so complicated that she would be forbidden to both men. In order to regularize her status, which the possibility of a subsequent forbidden union made intolerable, both suitors would need to give her a bill of divorce (*Kid.* 58b, Rashi *ad loc.*).

Later Sages expressed various opinions about this kiddushin. They differed as to whether the second expression cancelled the first,[95] so that despite having originally said "now", the man did not intend the kiddushin to become effective until 30 days had elapsed; or whether the first expression overrode the second, with a proviso (tena'ah) postponing the actual marriage for 30 days (*Kid.* 59b).[96]

According to Shmuel, the first *kiddushin* held good and would take effect within 30 days, and the second (interim)

92   מקודשת לשני
93   מעכשיו ולאחר שלושים יום
94   מקודשת ואינה מקודשת
95   וחזר ביה — אתי דיבור ומבטל
96   דתנאה הואי

kiddushin would then be cancelled. Rav objected, however, declaring that the woman's status would always remain in doubt.[97] Most of the Rabbinical codifiers followed the latter's ruling: both men would have to release the woman by providing her with a *get* (*Kid.* 59b; Maim. *Ishut*, 7:12, *Maggid Mishneh*; *Sh. Ar., Even ha-Ezer* 40:3).

The wife's consent is required not only in the act of *kiddushin* but also in the subsequent division of her property. In regard to property that she received after her marriage by gift or inheritance, the husband is entitled to all benefits therefrom during her lifetime; in the event of their divorce, he is liable to return her property in its current state.[98] The Sages ruled that "the husband may enjoy its fruits during her lifetime, but the capital itself remains in the woman's possession" (*Yev.* 38a–b).[99]

According to the standard law enunciated by R. Shim'on ben Shetaḥ, the husband and his entire estate were liable (*aḥra'im*) to pay compensation for the wife's marriage portion (*nedunyah*), as recorded in her *ketubbah*. She was entitled to claim the amount specified in the *ketubbah* if he died or divorced her (*Ket.* 82b; Maim. *Ishut*, 61:1, *Maggid Mishneh ad loc.*; *Sh. Ar., Even ha-Ezer* 85:2, REMA *ad loc.*).

The responsibility for handing back a wife's property relates to assets of two kinds. Regarding property that was hers before the marriage and which she brought into the marriage, the husband is liable to restore its full value or, if it still exists, to restore it *in specie* when the marriage is dissolved. Inalienable property (mortmain) is designated "property of iron sheep" (*nikhsei tzon barzel*).[100] Property that the wife acquired after her marriage, by gift or inheritance, falls under a different heading. It is known as "plucked property" (*nikhsei*

97　מקודשת ואינה מקודשת לעולם
98　נכסי מלוג
99　הבעל אוכל פירות בחייה והקרן קיים לאשה
100　נכסי צאן ברזל

melog) and the husband may have its usufruct without being responsible for any loss or gain resulting from such utilization. The principal, however, remains in the wife's ownership and any residual property must be returned to her *in specie* should the marriage be dissolved (*BM* 69b, Rashi; Maim. *Ishut*, 61:1, *Maggid Mishneh ad loc.*; Maim. *Ishut*, 16:2; *Sh. Ar., Even ha-Ezer* 85:2, REMA *ad loc.*, and *Sh. Ar., Even ha-Ezer* 85:7).

[General references: *Encyclopaedia Judaica*, 6:186f., s.v. "Dowry"; also, the detailed account in B.Z. Schereschewsky, *Dinei Mishpaḥah* (1967), pp. 100–105, 153–170, 213–223.]

Unclear Intention in Procedure

As we have seen, the act of *kiddushin* requires the man to give the woman some item (*kesef*) worth at least one *perutah*. The woman's consent is likewise essential, as the Sages explain at the beginning of Tractate *Kiddushin* in the first Mishnaic law the expression, "a woman is acquired in marriage"[101] (i.e., allows herself to be bound in marriage), rather than "the man acquires her" teaches us that acquisition through *kiddushin* takes place only with her consent. The purpose of giving the intended bride at least one *perutah* is to reassure her that she is not to be treated as someone's "public property"(*hefker*) that a man can just take for himself (*Kid.* 2a–b, 12a).

Situations may arise in which doubt is cast on the one *perutah* sum and its acceptance as *kesef kiddushin*. Similarly, doubts may be raised when the man's intention and the woman's consent are not clearly expressed. The Talmud presents the following case: A man gave a small fruit to a woman and said, "Be betrothed to me with this date".[102] He then gave her another date saying, "Be betrothed to me with this one".[103] Here, a technical issue arises as to whether he satisfied the law requiring him to give a *perutah*. The operative phrase, "Be

---

101   האשה נקנית
102   התקדשי לי בתמרה זו
103   התקדשי לי בזו

betrothed to me" (*hitkaddeshi li*), was recited twice, possibly because the man thought that his first offer was not valid and decided to make another.

The Sages ruled that in view of the fact that two separate statements were made, the combined value of the two dates could not be gauged. They had to decide whether each time the man said "*hitkaddeshi li*", the date he offered was worth a perutah. If, as seemed likely, it did not possess that value, the *kiddushin* would have no binding force; yet elsewhere, perhaps, one date might be worth a *perutah*. The case might have been simpler had the man offered three dates and used the "*hitkaddeshi* li" formula only once, saying "with this one and this one and this one".[104] The Sages could then have assessed the value of all three together and, if they were worth a perutah, the kiddushin would have been valid.

In the first case, where the man repeated "*hitkaddeshi li*", the problem faced by the Sages was ascertaining his intention each time he betrothed the woman. He may well have made two attempts to perform the *kiddushin*, first with one date and then with the other, but the *kiddushin* would only be valid if either of the dates was worth a *perutah*. In the second case, he made one clear declaration that the *kesef* was meant to have the value of all three dates and, if so, the *kiddushin* would be valid.

In this second case, where three dates were given one after another, we have to decide what was in the woman's mind when she took them. She might have accepted the first date as a snack, not for *kiddushin*, likewise the second date, leaving only the third (which was not worth a *perutah*) for *kiddushin*. The law, however, insisted on the value of one *perutah* at least in all *kiddushin*, even if she was willing to take less (*Kid.* 46a, *Tos.* "*eima*"; Maim. *Ishut*, 5:26–28.; *Sh. Ar., Even ha-Ezer* 31:1).[105]

---

104 בזו ובזו ובזו
105 גמרה ומקניא נפשה

Some authorities laid down that if, when reciting the "You are betrothed to me" formula, a man makes an incomplete declaration (omitting the vital word *li*, "to me"),[106] the *kiddushin* does not take effect[107] as he may have served as another man's agent (*Kid.* 5b, *Tos.* s.v. "*hakha*"; *Kid.* 6a, RASHBA, Meiri *ad loc.*). Others held the legality of this marriage to be dubious (*Kid.* 5b, Meiri). Others again stated that if the couple had already worked out the details of their engagement (*shiddukhin*), the incomplete declaration would still be acceptable. All things considered, they believed that the man had intended to leave nothing undone in his *kiddushin*, relying on the principle that a defective statement is comprehensible when circumstances make the underlying intention obvious.[108]

Two opposing views were held: one maintained that we can only follow what has been stated clearly,[109] while the other declared that, because of our uncertainty, we should follow the stricter view and rule that a marriage did take place (*Kid.* 5b, commentary of MAHARSHA quotes the view of commentary of Mahari ibn Lev; *Kid.* 7a, RAN "*ha'hi iteta*").[110]

Maimonides adopted the stricter view, ruling that when the man told a second woman, "and you also",[111] they were both betrothed to him. Had he only said "and you" (*ve-at*), this would be considered a "doubtful" marriage (*Ned.* 6b; Maim. *Ishut*, 4:2; *Sh. Ar., Even ha-Ezer* 36:9).[112]

Unclear Intention in Terms Stipulated

The entire validity of a marriage can depend on the intention that those parties negotiating the *kiddushin* had in mind. Where

---

106 הרי את מקודשת לי
107 אינה מקודשת
108 הידיים מוכיחות
109 היכא דגלי גלי, היכא דלא גלי לא גלי
110 בקידושין נקטינן לחומרה
111 ואת נמי
112 ספק מקודשת

a clear formal condition was stipulated by the man or the woman, and that condition was fulfilled, the marriage became valid. If it was not fulfilled, no valid marriage took place and the union was voided on account of misrepresentation (Maim. *Ishut*, 6:1, 25:1; *Sh. Ar., Even ha-Ezer* 38:1).

If the man stipulated, "I make this *kiddushin* proposal on condition that you are not bound by any vows", and it then transpired that the woman was bound by one of the three main vows of forbearing to gratify one's normal appetites or desires by self-denial (*innui nefesh*), such as obligating herself to abstain from meat, wine, or adorning herself with coloured garments (Maim. *Ishut*, 25:1), no valid marriage had taken place (*einah mekuddeshet*).[113] It was assumed, however, that the man would not be so concerned about other, less restrictive vows.

If, having made this stipulation when the *kiddushin* took place, the man later consummated his marriage without referring to any such condition,[114] the question that arises is whether this consummation (*nissu'in*) was still based on his former stipulation or whether he now withdrew it and married the woman unconditionally. The valid nature of the marriage would depend on what he had in mind at the time of consummation.

Opposing views were again expressed by the Sages. Rav declared that a marriage had been effected and, if the couple separated, the woman would have to receive a bill of divorce.[115] Shmuel maintained that the husband's mind would still be focused on the stipulation he had previously made, as it worried him so much that he had given formal expression to his wish. Thus the condition still stood, and if it was not fulfilled, the marriage was thereby voided, and no *get* would be required.[116] Shmuel's ruling would still apply if the man

---

113 קידושי טעות
114 כינסה סתם
115 צריכה ממנו גט
116 אינה צריכה גט ממנו

divorced the woman and later remarried her without stating
any condition,[117] as he had already made it clear that he did
not wish to marry her if she was bound by the vows.

Rav, on the other hand, affirmed that anyone who
consummated a marriage would not do so without intending
the bride to be his wife.[118] One could thus assume that he was
prepared to behave like any responsible man who had chosen
his bride (*kiddushin*) and arranged to marry her (*nissu'in*).
He did not intend the consummation to be mere promiscuity
but a genuine unconditional marriage, having abandoned and
thereby nullified his original condition.[119] Rav accordingly
ruled that a valid marriage had taken place and that any
subsequent divorce would require the formal issue of a *get*.
This ruling was followed by Maimonides (*Ket.* 73a; Maim.
Ishut, 7:6, 23; *Sh. Ar., Even ha-Ezer* 39:1).

The law was particularly strict in regard to *ḥalitzah*, ie., the
ceremony in which a deceased man had left his widow without
any child of his, and a brother of his was obliged to marry the
widow as a levirate marriage. If the brother is unwilling to
perform the duty of levirate marriage (*yibbum*), the widow
removes her brother-in-law's shoe in a special ceremony; only
after which she becomes free to marry anyone of her choice,
except a *kohen* (Deut. 25:5–10; cf. Ruth 4:5–10).[120] Even if
the condition which had been stipulated for giving *halitzah*
was not fulfilled, the *halitzah* remained valid and no plea that
a mistake had occurred would be entertained once *halitzah*
had been performed (*Yev.* 106a, ROSH, 12:19).[121]

The transaction of a marriage was originally performed
in one of three ways: a) by payment of money – *kesef*;
b) deliverance of a written deed – *Shetar*; or c) by sexual
intercourse – *bi'ah* (*Kid.* 2a, Rashi *ad.* loc.).[122] The document

---

117   כינסה סתם
118   אין עושה בעילתו בעילת זנות
119   בטל
120   לא תהיה אשת המת החוצה לאיש זר יבמה יבא עליה ולקחה לו לאשה ויבמה
121   חליצה מוטעת כשרה
122   האשה נקנית בשלש דרכים... בכסף בשטר ובביאה

of the ketubbah was something different, since it mainly contained his undertaking of particular financial obligations ensuing from his *kiddushin*. In each of the above procedures the act must be accompanied by his statement that this is done with the intention of marriage. Both the act and the statement must be duly witnessed. Particularly when a man wished to avail himself of the last method he had to declare before two witnesses that by this act he was taking a wife (*Sefer ha-Hinnukh*, 552).

A complicated matter of intention discussed by the Sages involved a father who arranged the betrothal of his under-age daughter and accepted *kiddushin* on her behalf. After marrying this girl, the husband divorced her, but then remarried her while she was still a minor (*ketannah*). The *Halakhah* laid down that once a father had given his daughter in marriage, he no longer exercised any authority over her and was not entitled to receive *kiddushin* on her behalf. Since she lacked the capacity of *da'at*, the second marriage had no validity.

The Sages considered what the husband's intention might have been when the second marriage took place. According to one opinion, while aware that a minor could not accept *kiddushin*, the husband meant their intercourse to be for the purpose of *kiddushin* once she reached maturity, thus consummating a legal marriage.[123] According to another opinion, he might not have been aware of the girl's inability (as a minor) to accept *kiddushin* and, as her father's permission had rendered the first marriage legally valid, he might well have believed that a renewal of the *kiddushin* was unnecessary. The second marriage would thus prove invalid because of a misunderstanding.[124] One further problem had to be tackled in the event of a levirate marriage. If the second contract was not binding, however, no *yibbum* would be necessary.

In all questions to do with the laws of marriage Rabbinic

---

123 גמר ובעל לשם קידושין

124 קידושי טעות

codifiers always followed the stricter interpretation. Only in their effort to free a "tied wife" (*agunah*) from the bond with her missing husband did the Sages of the Talmud, codifiers and later authorities search for every possible measure of relief available in the *Halakhah* (*Git.* 3a; *Yev.* 88a; Maim. *Gerushin*, 13:29; *Ket.* 73b–74a, Rashi *ad loc.*; Maim. *Gerushin*, 7:13; *Sh. Ar., Even ha-Ezer* 173:16).

A different type of problem would arise if, when betrothing a woman, a man failed to say, "I give you this for *kiddushin*", but used some vague phrase implying that it was given to her for that purpose. Such an intimation is known as a "handle" (*yad*) and means, for example, that only by grasping the handle of a jug can one move the whole jug and only by grasping a person's hand can one move his whole body. In this way, an incomplete statement may refer to the whole purpose of an action.

One such case is mentioned in the Talmud. A woman readily accepts a man's *kiddushin* provided that he gives the requisite *kesef* to another woman acting on her behalf, as her agent (*Kid.* 41a; *Sh. Ar., Even ha-Ezer* 36:1). He accordingly gives it to her friend, stating that this is *kesef kiddushin* for his bride, but then tells the woman, "and for you also",[125] whereupon she accepts it. The Sages have to decide whether the second woman is also betrothed to him.

The difficulty created here is the man's additional phrase, which remains unclear. His intention might either have been to betroth the other woman as well or just to ascertain her feelings. Assuming that he meant to say, "If I gave the same to you, would you be willing to marry me?", no second *kiddushin* was intended. The Sages had to decide whether giving *kiddushin* by intimation was acceptable.[126] Such issues were also discussed in other matters of *Halakhah* – the declaration of vows (*Ned.* 2a–b), donations to charity (*tzedakah*) and allocating produce from the corner of one's field (*pe'ah*) to the indigent (Lev.

---

125   ואת נמי

126   אם יש יד לקידושין

19:9–10). The validity of a *get* also hinged on this question (*Git.* 85b; *Ned.* 5b).

It is worth noting that although monogamy was praised in Biblical times (Prov. 5:8, 31:10*ff.*; *Sot.* 2a), there was no law against polygamy (Lev. 18:18; Gen. 29:26–30; 1 Kings 11:3). Accordingly, in the Talmudic era, a Jew was allowed to marry two women at the same time (*Ned.* 6b; Maim. *Ishut*, 4:2). From the mediaeval period onwards, however, bigamy was prohibited under the ban (*ḥerem*) imposed by the distinguished Franco-German authority, Rabbenu Gershom Me'or ha-Golah (Mainz, c. 960-1028).

Another case of uncertainty arose in the following dispute. A mature girl (*gedolah*) empowered her mother to be the agent receiving *kiddushin* on her behalf. The prospective husband accordingly gave his *kiddushin* to the mother. She then claimed that the *kiddushin* had been given to her and that it was the man's intention to betroth her.[127] He immediately protested, saying "It was for your daughter that I gave you the *kiddushin*." His real intention was thus the subject of a dispute. As his marriage either to the daughter or to her mother was now in doubt, both were obliged to receive a *get* owing to the uncertainty (*get misafek*) and further restrictions in terms of family relationship were also applied to them (Mish., *Kid.* 3:11, *Tosefot Yom Yov ad loc.*; Maim. *Ishut*, 9:15; *Sh. Ar., Even ha-Ezer* 48:4, 5; *Kid.* 65a).

Disputed Dowry Claims

It was normal practice for the *ketubbah* to include details of certain possessions which, the bride's father promised, would accompany her in her marriage as her *nedunyah* (dowry). A difficulty would arise if, when the bridegroom (*ḥatan*) and his bride (*kallah*) were already engaged through *kiddushin* and tied to each other in a state of betrothal (*erusin*), the groom

---

127 קידשתי את בתך והיא אומרת לא קידשת אלא אותי

divorced her or died. The *kallah* was then entitled to receive the normal 200 *zuz* stipulated in the *ketubbah* from the groom's estate. If she also claimed the dowry promised to her by her father, the question was whether that promise still needed to be kept, since there had been no complete marriage (*nissu'in*). For his part, the father could maintain that the promise had only been made with the forthcoming marriage of his daughter in view; that wedding (*nissu'in*) had not taken place and so he had no obligation to provide her with the dowry.[128] For her part, the daughter could argue that the dowry was a gift to them both, in order to encourage her fiancé to marry her, and that he had already accepted it prior to the betrothal. Accordingly, after his death she was entitled to claim this property, since the transfer of the dowry to her intended husband had already been effected legally with her father's agreement.

According to one school of thought in the Talmud, it was the Court's estimation (*umdanah*)[129] that the husband had in fact received the promised dowry when he effected the betrothal (*erusin*). The Sages' ruling, however, followed the opinion of R. Elazar ben Azaryah – that in the Court's estimation the father had meant to pass the *nedunyah* to the husband only at the time of the full marriage (*nissu'in*). Thus the husband had never acquired the dowry and she now had no right to it (*Ket.* 47a, Rashi and *Tos.*).

How should the issue be resolved when the bride's father promised to give a certain amount as her dowry, the bridegroom died after their betrothal and the duty of *yibbum* then fell upon the dead man's brother? The brother might well claim the *nedunyah* originally promised, since the bride had already acquired it on the basis of a decision that in a case like this, although the promise had not been set down in writing, even a verbal assurance would suffice to bring about an immediate acquisition.

---

128 דאין דעת האב לתן נדוניא זו אלא על מנת שתהנה בתו ממנה

129 אומדנא

The Sages ruled, however, that such an acquisition by the daughter had not yet taken place because her father only intended to hand over the *nedunyah* when she married one particular bridegroom. The father could now argue that he had promised it to that *ḥatan*, as a token of esteem, but had never meant to give the same dowry to the man's brother. He therefore had no obligation to transfer that sum to the *yavam* (*Ket.* 66a, Rashi, RAN and RIF; *Sh. Ar., Even ha-Ezer* 53:1).[130]

It was required by law that when the payment of a *ketubbah* fell due, any wife who had been a virgin (*betulah*) at her marriage would collect 200 *zuz* or, if previously married, one *maneh*, i.e., 100 *zuz* (*Sh. Ar., Even ha-Ezer* 66:6). If the groom so desired, he could pledge an additional sum (*tosefet ketubbah*) in the contract, even as large as 100 *maneh*, and this would have the same binding effect as the statutory *ketubbah* (*Sh. Ar., Even ha-Ezer* 66:7). However, this additional sum would only be payable if the man had completed his betrothal with the full marriage ceremony (*nissu'in*). If the couple were divorced after their betrothal, the groom would have to pay the basic amount (*ikkar ketubbah*) but would not be liable for the additional sum (*tosefet*).

R. Eleazar ben Azariah taught that the purpose of this man's generous offer was to make the bride a happily married woman. Since it was conditional on the marriage, which had never taken place, his offer was not binding. He had no need to pay anything as he had never committed himself to do so if the marriage was not solemnized (*Ket.* 54b; *Sh. Ar., Even ha-Ezer* 55:6).[131]

G. Effectiveness of Conditions

In principle, any condition, made according to the statutory rules of a stipulation that was inserted in the *ketubbah* has the

---

130   הפוסק מעות לחתנו ומת חתנו... לאחיך הייתי רוצה ליתן ולך אי אפשי ליתן
131   דאין דעת האב לתן נדוניא זו אלא על מנת שתהנה בתו ממנה

same binding force on both parties as the *ketubbah* itself, and is enforceable by the *bet din* (*Ket.* 54b.).[132] Every realizable obligation must be discharged and the validity of the *kiddushin* is subject to that condition's fulfillment (Maim. *Ishut*, 12:1*ff.*; *Sh. Ar.*, *Even ha-Ezer* 69:1*ff.*; *Even ha-Ezer* 38:1–2).

As mentioned above, if a man stipulated that his marriage would be effective only if the woman was not bound by vows that he considered intolerable,[133] the *kiddushin* would not be deemed valid if it was found that such vows had indeed been made, in contradiction to his stipulation.[134] The same law would apply if the man, having stipulated that the woman should have no physical blemishes, discovered them on her when they were married, but which had not been noticeable before the marriage.

The Sages placed limits on the type of vow that would invalidate *kiddushin*. Their ruling was that the law only applied to vows of self-denial which the average husband would find objectionable, such as his wife's abstention from meat or wine and discarding the wearing of handsome coloured garments (*Ket.* 72b, 73a; *Shab.* 64b).[135]

Furthermore, even if no such stipulations had been made in the *ketubbah*, and after the marriage these unacceptable conditions were found to obtain, he had the right to abrogate the *kiddushin*. R. Ashi laid down that this applied to any situation that a man would normally find unacceptable.[136] His ruling made the entire validity of the marriage dependent on what a normal husband would consider intolerable; should disputes arise over the ruling's interpretation, this marriage would be termed doubtful.[137]

The status of the *kiddushin* might also depend on whether, after verifying his situation, the husband promptly refused to

---

132 תנאי כתובה ככתובה
133 קפיד עליהם
134 אינה מקודשת
135 בגדים צבעונים
136 מידי דקפדי אינשי
137 מקודשת מספק

acknowledge the marriage; or whether he first remained silent, having consummated the marriage, and only later registered a protest. Such factors could determine whether the marriage was valid or invalid, raising issues of grave consequence on which the Rabbis expressed different points of view. If no final decision was taken, the marriage would have to be annulled by a *get* (*Ket.* 72b–73a, Rashi and RAN *ad loc.*, *Tos.* s.v. "*lo tema*" and "*umidi de-kapdi inshi*"; *Sh. Ar.*, *Even ha-Ezer* 39:1, 5).

When performing *kiddushin*, a man may tell the woman that he is making a stipulation (e.g., "I give you this *dinar* as *kesef kiddushin* on condition that you give me 200 *zuz*"); the *kiddushin* would then become effective only when she did so. In order to exclude any doubt regarding the seriousness of his intention, the Sages resolved that any stipulation must comply with all the formal regulations governing the imposition of a condition. The first of these rules laid down that a condition should be expressed in a double form,[138] stating first the positive aspect (i.e., "If you give me the 200 *zuz*, this will be your *kiddushin*"), and then the negative aspect ("but if you do not give me 200 *zuz*, this *dinar* will not be your *kiddushin*").[139]

If the condition was not stated clearly and unambiguously, any reservation that the man might have had in mind would be invalid and the condition of no effect (*Kid.* 61a, Rashi and Bertinoro *ad loc.*; Maim. *Ishut*, 6:2–3; *Sh. Ar.*, *Even ha-Ezer* 38:2; *Kid.* 49b, *Tos.* s.v. "*devarim*"; *Pes.* 63a, *Tos.* s.v. "*ha-mitkavven*").[140]

Certain basic requirements are recognized as conditions in the *kiddushin* although they had not been stated, and their non-fulfillment voids the *kiddushin* on the grounds of its being a "mistaken transaction" (*mekah ta'ut*).[141] It was understood, for example, that a man marries a woman to have children and

---

138 תנאי כפול
139 שיהיה הן שלו קודם ללאו ושיהיה התנאי קודם למעשה
140 דברים שבלב אינם דברים
141 מיקח טעות

assure himself of issue. Had he known, therefore, that his wife was barren, unable to conceive (*aylonit*), he would presumably not have married her. It was also accepted that a man did not have intercourse with her merely for sexual gratification, as an act of harlotry.[142] If, therefore, it transpired that his wife was incurably barren, the marriage could be annulled on the grounds that it had been entered into by mistake.[143] If, however, this inability to conceive was known to him before they married, there would have been no mistake on his part and all the usual laws of marriage would apply (*Ket.* 101b).

Similarly, if a levirate marriage was called for on the death of a childless husband, and it then transpired that the wife's infertility had prevented them from having children, the first marriage was declared void, and in this case the law of *yibbum* did not apply. A similar law would be operative if the *yavam*, her late husband's brother, was found to be physically incapable of reproduction – *saris* (*Yev.* 79b, 80b; *Yev.* 2b, *Tos.* s.v. "*o she-nimtze-u aylonit*"; Maim. *Ishut*, 2:1*ff.*; *Sh. Ar.*, *Even ha-Ezer* 172:1– 4, 67:6).

H. Unintended Evidence

In the laws of evidence certain classes of witness were strictly debarred from giving testimony.[144] They include relatives (*kerovim*) of the party involved; those with a personal interest in the case;[145] and women, who were not considered free to give impartial evidence owing to family pressure. Others without legal capacity are deaf mutes, imbeciles, minors and the blind, who are not considered to be responsible for their actions.[146] Also disqualified are those excluded from the

---

142 בעילת זנות
143 קידושי טעות
144 פסולי עדות
145 נוגע בדבר
146 חרש שוטה וקטן

people of Israel (Maim. *Edut*, 10:1*ff.*). Their testimony may provide useful information, but is not usually accepted as legal evidence.

Certain exceptions may nevertheless be made, so that testimony shedding light on a vexed issue can be brought in evidence. Such is the case if the relevant statements were made innocently, in ignorance of their legal weight, and with no thought of giving formal testimony.[147] In these circumstances the court may accept the statements as evidence and act upon them. The exceptions are of vital importance in efforts to help a "tied woman" (*agunah*) seeking evidence that will permit her to marry, and also in establishing the purity of a "captive woman" (*shevuyah*) so that she may be reunited with her husband.

Such evidence would be particularly helpful in determining a wife's status. Thus, if some legally disqualified person made a casual remark that was overheard (to the effect that, as he was walking down the street with Mr. X, the latter collapsed and died), this statement would be accepted as evidence of the husband's death, thus granting her the freedom to remarry. Likewise, if no one could tell if a woman's husband was dead or alive, but her little girl quite innocently remarked that she had once been told by an aunt that her father was dead, this statement would be accepted as evidence of the father's death, thus enabling the mother to remarry. Such evidence would also remove the stigma of illegitimacy (*mamzerut*) from any child conceived at a later date (*Ket.* 27b, *Tos.* s.v. "*bi-mesihah*"; Maim. *Gerushin*, 13:11–14; *Sh. Ar., Even ha-Ezer* 17:5, 7:2; *Yev.* 121b, Rashi, *ad loc.*).

---

147   מסיח לפי תומו

I. Annulment of Vows in Marriage

Torah law strictly prohibited the breaking of a vow (Deut. 23:24),[148] but also empowered a husband – under certain conditions – to annul a vow made by his wife (Num. 30:13).[149] After their marriage, a husband could annul his wife's vows of self-denial (Num. 30:9),[150] known later as "vows of self-affliction".[151] This annulment would be effective even if she had not been told about it (Maim. *Nedarim*, 12:1).

During the period of betrothal or engagement (*erusin*), the husband-to-be may advise his fiancé that all the vows she intends to make up to the day of their marriage (*nissu'in*) are immediately annulled. He has the right to do so, even if the vows are not made in his presence (Maim. *Nedarim*, 12:1; 13:9).

The right to annul his wife's vow accompanies the husband's obligation to provide for her maintenance (*mezonot*). From that time onwards, to maintain domestic harmony, she must submit to her husband's wishes and her vows will require his consent.[152] According to R. Papa, whenever a woman makes a vow, she tacitly and mentally accepts the overriding authority of her husband.[153] It is recorded that R. Pinhas quoted this principle in the name of Rava, thereby demonstrating that it was generally accepted (Num.30:14; *Ned.* 67b, 72b, 75a, 76b; Maim. *Nedarim*, 11:21, 12:1, 13:1; *Sh. Ar., Yoreh De'ah* 234:2).

J. Unexpressed Intention

The inadmissibility of a mental reservation in the *kiddushin* procedure is shown in the case of a man who stipulated that

---

148 מוצא שפתיך תשמור
149 אישה הפרם וה׳ יסלח לה
150 אשר אסרה על נפשה
151 נדרים שיש בהם עינוי נפש
152 על דעת בעלה
153 כל הנודרת על דעת בעלה היא נודרת

his marriage would depend on the woman's fulfillment of certain conditions. When she failed to do so, he claimed that his intention had always been to proceed with the marriage, even if his conditions were not fulfilled. The Sages ruled that his *kiddushin* was invalid, since a clear stipulation is not abrogated on the basis of a mental reservation.

Rava declared that intentions which someone had in the mind, but never expressed when a contract was made, have no legal validity (*Kid.* 49b).[154] The general rule laid down in the Talmud and Codes states as follows: Any condition stipulated in the *kiddushin* procedure, whether by the man or the woman, and which is not fulfilled (even unintentionally), will invalidate the *kiddushin* (*Sh. Ar.*, *Even ha-Ezer* 38:1).

This rule obtains even if the man defaulted and the woman still wished the marriage to take place, affirming in her mind that she had resolved to be the man's wife, even if he failed to discharge his undertaking; or, alternatively, if the man wished the marriage to take place, even though his undertaking had not been fulfilled. Accordingly, if the couple now wished to be legally married, they would require new *kiddushin*. The Sages ruled that an unstated intention[155] gave neither party the right to abrogate the condition laid down,[156] even if one had reason to believe that this was the true objective (*Kid.* 50b, *Tos.* RID *ad loc.*; Maim. *Ishut*, 8:2; *Sh. Ar.*, *Even ha-Ezer* 38:24).

Nevertheless, the Sages did allow for an exceptional case where *kiddushin* might be effected by an unexpressed intention, as we shall discover. At the betrothal ceremony, two qualified witnesses must be present and the man must give the woman some item of value, even a coin of small value[157] or its equivalent.[158] He is then obliged to make a formal declaration, "Behold you are sanctified to me by this token", to which he

---

154 דברים שבלב אינם דברים
155 דברים שבלב
156 לאו כל כמינה דעקרא לתנאיה
157 כסף פרוטה
158 שווה פרוטה

adds: "according to the laws of Moses and of Israel" (*Kid.* 2a, 5b; *Sh. Ar., Even ha-Ezer* 27:1).[159]

In the case before us, the prospective husband did not make the statutory declaration. Immediately before the *kiddushin*, while this man and his intended bride were discussing the arrangements for their marriage,[160] he gave her the requisite gift without saying a word (*bi-shetikah*) and later claimed that what he had given her was meant for *kiddushin*. The Sages ruled that a proper marriage had been contracted.[161] In this instance, they explained, evidence that he had acted specifically for the purpose of *kiddushin* was indisputable, i.e., "the situation was sufficient proof".[162] Here, an act of the mind was definitive in legalizing the marriage (*Kid.* 6a, cf. *Kid.* 2a, Rosh; *Sh. Ar., Even ha-Ezer* 27:1).

In the case of a sale, any transaction complying with the legal requirements is final, and it makes no difference whether one entered into it whole-heartedly or half-heartedly. In the case of an unsolicited gift (*mattanah*), however, where the recipient's acceptance may be presumed, there is no need to depend on "a meeting of minds". Since the gift is voluntary, what we require is the donor's full consent; if it is in any way lacking, this indicates that he has not really made up his mind and the gift is then voidable (*Sh. Ar., Hoshen Mishpat* 207:4, REMA; ROSH on *Ket.* 97a, s.9).[163]

When a man makes a vow that seems to indicate a resolve to abstain from something, although his words also lend themselves to a different and more cautious interpretation, the Sages recognize that what he claims to have really had in his mind will determine the true meaning of his statement and negate the vow, since a vow (unlike some contract between two parties) is a unilateral undertaking.

---

159 הרי את מקודשת לי בזה כדת משה וישראל
160 על עסקי קידושין
161 הווי קידושין
162 ידים מוכיחות
163 שלא גמר בדעתו

One example was quoted by the Sages: "If a man vowed, 'My wife shall henceforward receive no benefit from me', we accept his explanation that the reference was to his first wife, whom he had divorced". Similarly, if he said, "My wife is like my mother to me", we accept his explanation that this should not be taken to mean that she was forbidden to him sexually under the laws of incest; it simply meant that he loved her. Accordingly, we release him from what might have been construed as an oath (*Ned.* 20a; Maim. *Nedarim,* 2:12).

K. Adultery

All forbidden sexual relations are termed "uncleanness" (*tum'ah*).[164] A woman who willingly had intercourse with someone other than her husband was an adulteress and the penalty for her offence was capital punishment: "The men of her city shall stone her to death ... so shalt thou remove the evil from thy midst" (Deut. 22:21).[165] The adulterer likewise was put to death (Lev.20:10).[166] Masturbation was also forbidden, and every effort of the will must be made to subdue it (Maim. *Issurei Bi'ah,* 21:19). Immorality was condemned in general as well as specific terms: "The Lord thy God walketh in the midst of thy camp ... therefore shall thy camp be holy; that He see no unclean thing in thee, and turn away from thee" (Deut. 23:15). Before they sinned, the *Shekhinah* (Divine Presence) rested on all the people of Israel, but after they abandoned themselves to immorality the *Shekhinah* departed from them (*Sot.* 3b).[167] As the Psalmist declared, "Evil shall not sojourn with Thee" (Ps. 5:5; *Nid.* 13b).[168] R. Yitzhak asserted that

---

164   טומאה
165   ובערת הרע מקרבך
166   מות יומת הנאף והנאפת
167   כיון שחטאו נסתלקה שכינה מהם
168   לא יגורך רע

whoever transgresses in secret drives away the *Shekhinah* (*Hag.* 16a, R. Hananel *ad loc.*);[169] while Isaiah remonstrated with Israel as if quoting the Almighty Himself: "I cannot endure iniquity along with solemn assembly" (Isa. 1:13; JPSA translation).[170]

Adultery is committed in secret to ensure that no one witnesses this particular transgression: "The eye also of the adulterer waiteth for the twilight, saying, 'No eye shall see me'... " (Job 24:15).[171] Though concerned about the opinion of other men, the adulterer pays no regard to the judgment of the Almighty. The Sages felt that this demonstrated a heretical belief that God's knowledge does not extend to the hidden actions of man (Num. R. 9:1).[172] "What I do in secret is concealed even from the eyes of Heaven", the offender maintains.

Strictly speaking, adultery means having sexual relations with another man's wife, a cardinal offence prohibited in the Decalogue (Ex. 20:13),[173] and many other social evils are traditionally subsumed under the law (Lev. 20:10–21). Maimonides lists 37 different offences that were envisaged by this prohibitive commandment (Maim. *Issurei Bi'ah*, Introduction, 1:1).

The Sages believed that men and women had different sexual urges. Normally, if someone committed an offence against morality under duress (*ones*), he or she was not charged with transgression. If, as mentioned previously, a married woman had been coerced into an adulterous relationship, she would be free of guilt. Any sexual gratification that she might have derived from such enforced intercourse was ascribed to her innate libido.[174]

---

169   כל העושה עבירה בסתר כאילו דחק רגלי שכינה

170   לא אוכל און ועצרה

171   ועין נואף שמרה נשף לאמר לא תשורני עין

172   הוא סבור לפי שעושה מעשיו בחשך שהקב״ה לא ידע בו... הם חושבים שהקב״ה לא יראה במעשיהם

173   לא תנאף

174   מפני שיצרה ניתגבר עליה

If, however, a married man claimed that he had been forced into an adulterous relationship against his will, he would be liable to pay the penalty ordained for his transgression. The Sages ruled that he could not excuse his immoral behaviour on the grounds of coercion.[175] Sexual intercourse could not have taken place without his own participation, and he must surely have derived pleasure from the act. Had this offender exercised greater self-control, he might well have kept clear of any involvement (*Yev.* 53b; Maim. *Issurei Bi'ah*, 1:9).[176]

A successful husband-and-wife relationship is built on mutual trust. When that confidence is destroyed, the marriage bond no longer exists and sexual intercourse between the man and woman can only be viewed as fornication.

If someone told a man that his wife had committed adultery, the testimony of a single witness provided insufficient grounds for divorce, since the law required no fewer than two witnesses.[177] The Sages ruled, however, that if the husband fully believed this witness's evidence, any continued relationship with his wife would be immoral and he would be compelled to divorce her. Similarly, if his wife told him that she was involved in an extramarital relationship, the law would depend on whether he believed her or not: she might have invented the whole story to prod him into giving her a *get*, so that she could marry another man. If he did believe what she said, he would be obliged to divorce her (*Kid.* 66a; *Ned.* 90b–91a; Maim. *Issurei Bi'ah*, 18:8; Maim. *Ishut*, 24:17–18).[178]

From the time of Rabbenu Gershom's *ḥerem* (ban) (11th cent.), however, Rabbinical authorities followed the rule that in almost every situation a wife might not be divorced without her consent. If the *get* had been duly executed, the divorce was final, however "unintended" or "unavoidable" it

---

175 אין אנוס לערוה

176 שאין קישוי אלא לדעת

177 אין דבר שבערוה פחות משנים

178 הואיל וסמכה דעתו לדבר זה שהיא אמת

may have been; thereafter, the court would entertain no plea of duress.[179] Any uncertainty regarding the wife's status had to be accounted for; otherwise, she might be left "chained" (*agunah*) without redress (Maim. *Gerushin*, 9:8; *Sh. Ar., Even ha-Ezer* 144:1).

The "Bitter Waters" Ordeal

In the Talmud's discussion of the Biblical procedure followed when a wife suspected of adultery (*sotah*) by her husband had to undergo the ordeal of the "bitter waters" (*hamayim hame'ararim*) (Num. 5:12–31),[180] there is an instructive division of opinions among the Sages.

According to R. Shim'on, the suspect wife brought a meal-offering (*minhah*) to the Temple and the priest burnt her sacrifice on the altar. He then ordered her to drink the "water of bitterness" prepared for her, and the resulting effect proved whether her sworn denial of transgression was truthful.[181] The general view of the Sages was that she drank the water[182] prior to making the sacrifice; the ordeal that followed would then indicate any drastic physical change in the woman.[183] They maintained that the sanctity of her offering tested the woman's faithfulness to her husband.

The Sages adhered to the plain text of the Torah, but R. Shim'on contended that after the water filled the suspect wife's body, the burnt sacrifice had the effect of recalling all the transgressions that she had committed. In that sense the Torah calls her sacrifice *minhat zikkaron*, "a meal-offering of remembrance" (Num. 5:15; TJ *Sot.* 3:2).[184] Following the

---

179   אין אונס בגיטין
180   המים המאררים
181   מנחה היא שהיא בודקת
182   המים בודקין
183   המים הן בודקין אותה
184   מנחת זכרון מזכרת עון

Sages, Maimonides ruled that the priest first made her drink the water and then took the meal-offering that she held before him. This he set on a Temple vessel (*keli sharet*) and, after placing his hand beneath hers, ritually "waved" the offering from side to side (Mish., *Sot.* 3:1, 19a; Maim. *Sotah*, 3:15).

The water used was clean holy water from the Temple laver (*min ha-kiyyor*), and the scroll quoting applicable texts ("curses") was soaked in it. R. Tarfon, who accepted R. Shim'on's explanation of the test, asserted that the offering recalled all the woman's transgressions as well as the present charge of adultery (*mazkeret avon*). R. Akiva differed, however, maintaining that the effect of the sacrifice was to recall the woman's meritorious deeds and bear witness to her faithfulness. The normal purpose of bringing a meal-offering was to help the petitioner with his or her defense and secure atonement, not to impute blame. Here also, the "offering of remembrance" was intended to serve as the woman's defence counsel.[185] All her meritorious deeds were weighed against the sum of her transgressions, enabling her to secure a just release from the "bitter waters". Hence the Torah made two statements – *minhat zikkaron* for her good and *minhat avon* for her guilt. The difference of outlook among the Sages shows how different their views were in regard to the woman's psychology and the effect each stage of the ordeal was meant to have on her (TJ *Sot.* 3:4, "*korban ha-edah*" *ad loc.*).

It may be noted that this entire ordeal to which the suspected wife was submitted (*sotah*) was practiced only when the Temple ritual was available, after which it was no longer administered.

---

185 לימוד סניגוריא

Indulging in Lewd Thoughts – Hirhurei Averah

Expressions used in the Bible and by the Sages to denote man's evil inclination (*yetzer ha-ra*) suggest that it is thought of as a genuine entity, one that is perpetually seeking to mislead human beings. This "accuser" besets man daily and instigates all of his wrongdoing. Though present in man from birth, the *yetzer ha-ra* is opposed by an impulse to do good, the *yetzer ha-tov*. When praising the merciful Lord who "hath not dealt with us after our sins, nor rewarded us after our iniquities", the Psalmist affirms: "He knoweth our nature."[186] In the Targum translation "nature" (*yetzer*) is rendered "the evil impulse that causes man to sin" (Ps. 103:14).

The Rabbis lost no opportunity to warn against sexual immorality, which they termed "the prevailing sin" (*averah – yitzrah de-averah*). In becoming the ruler of Egypt, Joseph was rewarded for his strength of mind: despite enormous temptation, neither his body nor his thought was contaminated by immorality (Gen. R. 90:1).[187]

Man is described, metaphorically, as possessing two hearts, one bad and the other good (i.e., the *yetzer ha-ra* and the *yetzer ha-tov*). King David's exhortation to his son, Solomon, ran: "Know thou the God of thy father, and serve him with a perfect heart and with a willing mind; for the Lord searcheth all hearts, and understandeth all the imaginations of the thoughts" (1 Chron. 28:9).[188]

The evil *yetzer* is identified with Satan ("the adversary"), whose business it is to lead man astray. He induces man to sin, then accuses him of sinning and deprives him of his soul. Resh Lakish declared that "Satan, the *Yetzer ha-Ra* and the Angel of Death are one and the same" (*BB* 16a).[189] Quoting the Torah's admonition "that ye go not about after your own heart and

---

186 כי הוא ידע יצרו

187 גופו שלא נגע בעבירה... מחשבה שלא חשבה בעבירה

188 כי כל לבבות דורש ה' וכל יצר מחשבות מבין

189 אמר ריש לקיש הוא שטן הוא יצר הרע הוא מלאך המות

your own eyes, after which ye go a-whoring" (Num. 15:39), the Sages added that "the eyes and the heart are the agents of sin" (TJ *Ber.* 1:5; Num. R. 17:6, Rashi *ad loc.*).[190] In other words, the eye sees, the heart lusts and the body commits the transgression. They stated, furthermore, that "after your eyes" refers to having lewd thoughts (*Ber.*12b).[191] The heart itself is not especially depraved, but its functions render it more liable to serve the evil *yetzer* (S. Schechter, *Some Aspects of Rabbinic Theology*, p. 260).

The Holy One, blessed be He, tells man: "I created the *Yetzer ha-Ra*; take care that he does not make you transgress; but should he succeed, hasten to repent and then I will forgive your sins" (*Midrash Tehillim* 57:1).

The Sages give a few examples of situations that should be avoided in case they arouse lewd thoughts. Thus, "whoever follows a woman along the road or across a river loses his share in the World to Come. Any man who walks behind a woman, even his own wife, and looks at her figure is guilty of indulging in lewd thoughts". Similarly, "a man is forbidden to count coins into a woman's hand so as to look at her face. Even if the man himself is a Torah scholar and as faithful as Moses to Torah law, he will not be saved from punishment in Gehenna". The term 'Gehenna' (properly *Gei ben Hinnom*, a valley outside Jerusalem) designated purgatory, hell or the nether regions, where a man's soul endured punishment for his sins (*Ber.* 61a, *Tos.*, MAHARSHA, Melo ha-Ro'im, *ad loc.*; cf. *Sot.* 4b, *Kid.* 81b, *Er.* 18b–19a).

The Sages considered the harbouring of unchaste thoughts an even graver sin than immorality itself, because whereas a sexual offence may be regretted and atoned for, a lewd thought is not taken seriously since no physical action was involved (*Yoma* 29a, Rashi *ad loc.*).

The usual sacrifice brought to atone for an offence was a sin-offering (*ḥattat*), which was not completely burnt on

---

190 הלב והעינים הם סרסורין לגוף שהם מזנין את הגוף
191 אחרי עיניכם זה הרהורי עבירה

the altar. For unchaste thoughts, however, an entirely burnt offering (*olah*) was made: while the offender might not have been aware of his transgression, the Almighty knew that it had been committed and so the offering belonged entirely to Him (Lev. 1:4, Rashi, *Siftei Hakhamim* and Ramban *ad loc.*).

L. Forbidden Relationships

In *Sifrei*, an early Midrashic work, we learn that of all the commandments given to Israel at Sinai the most difficult one for them to accept was the prohibition of incest – *gillui arayot* (Lev. 18:6-18). The Torah relates that when they complained about their monotonous diet of manna, "Moses heard the people weeping, family by family" (Num. 11:10).[192] The Sages taught that this prohibitive commandment was the reason for their tears, basing that conclusion on the words "family by family" (or "throughout their families").[193] The Israelites wept because marriage with a close member of one's family had been decreed incestuous (*Yoma* 75a.; *Sifrei*, Num.11:10).

On the strength of this Midrashic tradition, Maimonides concluded his treatise on forbidden marriages by stating: "No law in the Torah was harder for most of the people to observe than the law defining the extent of forbidden marriages. That objection was at the root of all their complaints in the wilderness".

Surrendering to one's baser urges is a familiar aspect of human nature.[194] One therefore needs to exercise a great deal of self-control, dismissing impure thoughts from the mind and avoiding improper contact with the opposite sex. Drunken

---

192 וישמע משה את העם בכה למשפחתיו

193 למשפחתיו

194 דעתו של אדם קרובה אצל עריות

and loose behaviour is also condemned, since it often leads to promiscuity. Failure to keep one's desires under control is thoroughly reprehensible (Maim. *Issurei Bi'ah*, 22:17–21).

Chapter 10

Divorce – *Gittin*

10 Divorce – Gittin

A. Introduction

The Jewish concept of marriage, as expressed in the Bible, embraces the dual purpose of companionship and procreation. The basis of this idea is found in the following verses: "It is not good that man should be alone; I will make him a help meet for him" (Gen. 2:18);[1] "Therefore shall a man leave his father and his mother, and shall cleave unto his wife, and they shall be one flesh" (Gen. 2:24); and "Be fruitful, and multiply, and replenish the earth" (Gen. 11:28).[2]

Marriage is intended as a permanent relationship, but when that relationship is no longer tenable owing to hatred and strife or if its basic purpose is not fulfilled, the marriage may be terminated by divorce (*get*).

Divorce may be effected by mutual consent. Both the husband and the wife have the right to ask for a divorce on the grounds of physical or moral incompatibility. Should the husband become loathsome to the wife, if he proves to be impotent or refuses to give her children or to have sexual relations with her, she is entitled to demand that the marriage be revoked on the grounds of misrepresentation,[3] making the contract of marriage invalid as a "mistaken agreement".

Similarly, if it transpires that the wife was incapable of bearing children (*aylonit*) when the couple were married, the husband may divorce her by *get*, although the marriage itself is deemed valid. The early tannaitic Sages ruled, in general terms, that if the wife proved unable to conceive, the marriage itself would be invalid, having been entered into by mistake.[4]

עזר כנגדו 1
פרו ורבו 2
מיקח טעות 3
קידושי טעות 4

No *get* would then be required and (as indicated in the previous chapter) the wife would not be entitled to receive the amount stipulated in her *ketubbah* (*Yev.* 2b, *Tos. s.v. "o she-nimtzeit aylonit"*, ROSH *ad loc.*).

Maimonides ruled, however, that if at the time of the marriage the husband knew of his wife's physical disability, i.e., that she had all the symptoms of a barren woman (*aylonit*), but he only later complained about this, the *kiddushin* was fully valid as there had been no misrepresentation. Divorce would require a *get*, and the wife would be entitled to all the benefits of her *ketubbah*.

The Sages described the symptoms of a woman's infertility (*Nid.* 47b; Maim. *Ishut*, 2:6). In his *Shulḥan Arukh* code, R. Yosef Caro stated that the *kiddushin* would be invalid only if she was unquestionably barren – *aylonit vadda'it* (*Sh. Ar., Even ha-Ezer* 44:4). If her disability became apparent after the marriage, resulting from an illness that prevented conception, the husband was duty-bound to provide for his wife's medical requirements (Maim. *Ishut* 12:2; *Sh. Ar., Even ha-Ezer* 69:2; *Ket.* 100b; *Yev.* 2b; *Ket.* 72b).[5]

Later commentators raised questions about the *aylonit*: was her condition irremediable or was it susceptible to a cure? They determined that each case must be regarded as doubtful (*safek*), thus rendering the marriage valid. As stated by Maimonides, this ruling might be explained on the basis that continuing advances in medical knowledge increase the possibility of a wrong diagnosis (*Bet Shemuel* 55).

The Jewish law of divorce closely follows the Biblical ordinance: "When a man taketh a wife, and marrieth her, then shall it be, if she find no favour in his eyes, because he hath found some unseemly thing in her, that he shall write her a bill of divorcement and give it in her hand, and send her out of his house. And when she departeth out of his house, she may go and become another man's wife..." (Deut. 24:1–2).

The Sages derived all their divorce laws from the ten statements contained in this passage (Maim. *Yad, Gerushin,* 1:1–3; *Tiferet Yisrael, Gittin,* introd.).

The essence of the bill of divorce (*get pitturin*) is the husband's statement: "You are now free to marry any other man" (Mish., *Git.* 85a; Maim. *Yad, Gerushin,* 1:4. Maim. *Yad, Gerushin* 4:12 supplies the full text of a *get*).[6]

Once the valid *get* has been received by the wife, the divorce is final. She has been relieved of any obligation to her former husband and may enter into any other permitted marriage; her freedom from him is now permanent. This complete abrogation of the marriage is stated in the *get*: "From this day and for ever" (Maim. *Yad, Gerushin,* 8:9).[7]

The act whereby the husband or his agent hands the prescribed *get* to the wife is the only way for the marriage to be terminated, apart from the death of either party. An appeal may be made to the *bet din* (rabbinical court) so as to ensure that the *get* is served, but the court itself is not empowered to execute a divorce. It can only ensure the validity of the *get* or persuade both parties to act in accordance with the court's rulings.

The complete breakdown of a marriage as a result of obvious disharmony provided sufficient grounds for the execution of a divorce. Improper conduct, or defects in either husband or wife, could make the court decide that a *get* was necessary to terminate the marriage. The *bet din* was not required to establish responsibility for the breakdown of a marriage; it had to acknowledge the fact that marital harmony was no longer possible since "domestic peace" (*shelom bayit*) no longer existed. Nevertheless, the break-up of a marriage was greatly deplored by the Sages: "If a man divorces his first wife, the very altar sheds tears for him" (*Git.* 90b).[8]

In exceptional cases, the authority granted to the Sages could serve to annul a marriage altogether. Every marriage

---

6   גופו של גט הרי את מותרת לכל אדם

7   מן יומא דנן ולעולם

8   אפילו מזבח מוריד עליו דמעות

solemnized by *kiddushin* is understood to be a vow contingent on their rulings (*Git.* 33a; *Ket.* 3a, *Tos. s.v. "ada'ata"*).[9] The marriage vow obligates both parties to follow the traditional laws of marriage enacted by the Rabbis. In Jewish wedding ceremonies this obligation is emphasized in a special formula: "You are betrothed to me with this ring *according to the laws of Moses and of Israel*" (*Sh. Ar., Even ha-Ezer* 27:1, REMA; Alshekh, 104).[10]

[General reference: *Encyclopaedia Judaica*, "Divorce", 6:126; "Agunah", 2:433]

In Biblical times a husband could divorce his wife when she no longer appealed to him – "if thou have no delight in her" (Deut. 21:14).[11] And when outlining the laws of divorce, the Torah implicitly restricted the grounds for divorcing a woman to improper behaviour on her part – "if she find no favour in his eyes, because he hath found some unseemly thing in her" (Deut. 24:1).[12]

The Sages had differing views as to what might be considered grounds for divorce in accordance with their interpretation of the words *ervat davar* – "some unseemly thing".[13] On the basis of the former verse (Deut. 21:14),[14] R. Akiva declared that a man only had to find a woman who was more attractive than his own wife. As far as such a husband was concerned, the bond of marriage with his wife had already been severed. However, Bet Shammai (the school of Shammai) adopted a restrictive view of the text, claiming that it meant "*only* if he found some unseemly thing in her", such as proven immoral conduct. Bet Hillel (the school of Hillel) took an intermediate position, affirming that there would be grounds for divorce if she went out of her way to annoy him (e.g., by serving burnt food) (Mish., *Git.* 9:10, TB *Git.* 90a).

---

9   כל המקדש אדעתא דרבנן מקדש
10   הרי את מקודשת לי בטבעת זו כדת משה וישראל
11   אם לא חפצת בה
12   אם לא תמצא חן בעיניו כי מצא בה ערות דבר
13   ערות דבר
14   אם לא חפצת בה

R. Meir generalized, stating that just as one person's fastidiousness over hygiene can differ from another's, so may the notion of a wife's "unseemly" behaviour vary from one husband to the next in accordance with his wise or warped judgment.

The concluding opinion of the Talmud was enunciated by a Babylonian Sage, R. Papa. If none of the grounds mentioned above were applicable, a man should not divorce his wife; but if he had nevertheless done so, the *get* was valid. R. Papa himself was anxious to preserve domestic harmony, believing that every husband should evince the greatest respect for his wife and her wishes. He is quoted as saying, "If your wife is short, bend down to hear her whisper" (*BM* 59a; *Git.* 90a; *Torah Temimah* on Deut. 24:1, note 14; Maim. *Gerushin* 1:1; *Sh. Ar., Even ha-Ezer* 119:3).

Maimonides and subsequent codifiers ruled in accordance with the teaching of Hillel, which paid regard to the feelings of a normal husband in matters concerning the proper behaviour of a Jewish woman (*Git.* 90a; Maim. *Peirush ha-Mishnayot, ad loc.; Sh. Ar., Even ha-Ezer* 119:4).[15]

B. Intention

Sincerity of One's Intention

The apparent facilitation of divorce in R. Akiva's ruling was based on the generally accepted concept of the sanctity of marriage. Once a man had made up his mind to divorce his wife, for whatever reason, it was improper for him to continue living with her as if they were still happily married. It is shameful to deceive her by ostensibly maintaining the husband-and-wife relationship, since she relies on his good faith and "dwells securely" with him (Prov. 3:29).

That also explains why the Sages forbade a man to marry a woman whom he already planned to divorce (*Yev.* 37b).[16] Such an intention can only pull them apart even before the divorce is executed, and engaging in sexual intercourse with the woman is like going to bed with a whore if this man has already negated the marriage in his mind.

According to Shammai, if a man wrote a *get* or had it written for him and then changed his mind, the very intention to divorce his wife blemished the marriage and sullied the couple's relationship. Such a damaged marriage had "the smell of a *get*",[17] emitted by the thought in the man's mind (*Yev.* 52a). It came so close to a *get* that the wife was thereafter debarred from marrying a *kohen* (priest), to whom a divorced woman was forbidden (*Git.* 81a).[18]

Bet Hillel did not agree with Shammai's moralistic stand, ruling that only the divorce procedure's completion – in line with all requirements of the *bet din* – could validate such a disqualification. Nevertheless, the teaching of Shammai evidently expressed the Sages' dissatisfaction with such duplicity by the husband (*Git.* 81a).

Tractate *Gittin* (on the laws of divorce) concludes with a statement urging men to desist from divorcing their wives. R. Elazar quoted the prophet Malachi (2:14): "If a man divorces his first wife, the very altar sheds tears, 'Because the Lord hath been witness between thee and the wife of thy youth, against whom thou hast dealt treacherously, although she is thy companion and the wife of thy covenant'" (*Git.* 90a–b;[19] Maim. *Gerushin* 10:21, *Maggid Mishneh ad loc.; Sh. Ar., Even ha-Ezer* 119:1–3, REMA).[20]

The Sages strongly disapproved of any man who capriciously sought a replacement for his wife. If, however,

---

16   לא ישא אדם אשתו ודעתו לגרשה
17   ריח הגט
18   כתב לגרש אשתו ונמלך פסלה מן הכהונה
19   אמר רבי אלעזר כל המגרש אשתו ראשונה אפילו מזבח מוריד עליו דמעות
20   ה' העיד בינך ובין אשת נעוריך

he accused her of grave misconduct – *ervat davar* – it was his duty to divorce her. According to early law he should do so even without obtaining her consent; but in later law in the case of his marriage to his first wife he should not hurry to divorce her unless she agreed to be divorced. If there was strife between them on these particulars, the *bet din* should determine what his duty was. Malachi's exhortation remained apposite: "Therefore take heed to your spirit, and let none deal treacherously against the wife of his youth" (Mal. 2:15; *Tur. Even ha-Ezer* 119, "*Perishah*" *ad loc.*).[21]

Avoidance of Uncertainty

At the climax of a divorce procedure the husband gives his wife the statutory Bill of Divorce, the *get*, and declares: "This is your *get* and you are now permitted to marry any man". The standard text also concludes with this declaration (*Git.* 78a; Maim. *Gerushin* 1:11; *Sh. Ar., Even ha-Ezer* 154:101).[22]

Although a *get* can be made contingent on some future action (*Sh. Ar., Even ha-Ezer* 143:1–2), the intention of the *get* itself must be a complete and unqualified rescinding of the marriage bond. Thus, if instead of ending the sentence with "you are now permitted to marry any man", the husband adds "except for so-and-so",[23] the *get* arouses uncertainty and becomes invalid. An exclusion that was intended as a normal proviso might be acceptable, e.g., "on condition that you marry so-and-so" or even "that you do not marry so-and-so". This would be a recognized form of condition (*al menat*).

However, the Sages laid down that for the *get* to take effect, the divorce itself must be complete and on no account exclusionary. They therefore ruled that when the man used the words "except for so-and-so", his statement was ambiguous.

---

21   ובאשת נעוריך אל תבגוד
22   הרי זה גיטך והרי את מותרת לכל אדם
23   הרי את מותרת לכל אדם אלא לפלוני

He might have meant "to marry this one in particular" or "anyone except for this man". We would therefore be entitled to assume that he had imposed a limitation on his *get*, declaring that it applied to any man except for that person. This would restrict the intention of the *get*, and any such exclusion would deprive it of validity (*Git.* 82b; Maim. Mishnah commentary *ad loc.*; Maim. *Gerushin* 8:16, 18; *Sh. Ar., Even ha-Ezer* 137:1).[24]

Another problematic situation involved a husband and wife who were making arrangements for the giving of his *get*; in the midst of their discussion he handed it to her without making the statutory declaration. Here the ruling of R. Yose was accepted that the intention and seriousness of his purpose to divorce his wife was obvious, the *get* that he handed her was valid. The same rule would apply, in like circumstances, to negotiating the manner of *kiddushin* for a marriage (*Kid.* 6a, Rashi; *Sh. Ar., Even ha-Ezer* 136:2; Maim. *Gerushin* 1:11, *Ishut* 3:7–8).

Clear Understanding of Someone's Intention

As stated, a basic rule in effecting a *get* is that when the husband gives it to his wife, he must say "This is your *get*".[25] If he placed it in her hand while she was asleep, and on waking she realized that she had the *get*, it would have no validity unless he said to her when she was awake, "This is your *get*". If he told the witnesses, "See, I am about to give this *get* to my wife", and then, instead of saying, "This is your *get*", he wrongly declared to her, "Receive this bond of debt",[26] that might (in some opinions) constitute a divorce, but its validity would be doubtful. He should therefore hand the *get* to his wife

24   וחכמים אוסרין... דהא שייר בגט
25   הרי זה גיטך
26   כנסי שטר חוב זה

once again, this time with the correct declaration.[27] According
to another opinion, by saying "Take this bond of debt", no
divorce had been effected, and she remained his wife.

There had to be a clear understanding in the woman's mind
that she was receiving her *get*; in this case, however, she might
well have believed that what she received was merely a bond
of some debt owing to her husband. The authoritative rule is
as follows: on receipt of her get, the wife must be fully aware
that it is a bill of divorce terminating her marriage. This rule
is implied in the Torah prescription for divorce in which it
is stated, "that he shall write her a bill of divorcement, and
give it in her hand". This law is understood to mean that the
get must be given to her, clearly and specifically, as a bill of
divorce (Deut. 24:1[28], *Sifrei ad loc.; Git.* 78a., *Tos. "eino get"*;
Maim. *Gerushin* 1:9; *Sh. Ar., Even ha-Ezer* 138:3–4).[29]

If a man divorced his wife by means of a *get* and then lodged
overnight with her at an inn,[30] where, in their accustomed
intimacy, they presumably had sexual intercourse, the question
that arises is whether by this act he had remarried her. In the
opinion of Bet Shammai, their intercourse was not intended to
have the effect of a marriage, and the man was simply acting
promiscuously, "as some men are wont to do".[31] Accordingly,
no marriage had been effected and, if the man wished to
preserve his divorce, no second *get* was required. However,
Bet Hillel maintained as a general rule that when a man had
intercourse with a woman with whom he was intimate, he did
not do so frivolously but for the purpose of consummating
a marriage.[32] Through their intercourse – or intimacy in the
presence of witnesses – (*yihud*) he had thus remarried her
and, if he now wished that she be divorced from him, he was

---

27 ספק מגורשת
28 וכתב לה ספר כריתת ונתן בידה
29 שיתן אותו בתורת ספר כריתות
30 לנה עמו בפונדקי
31 אדם עושה בעילתו בעילת זנות
32 אין אדם עושה בעילתו בעילת זנות

obliged to give her a second *get*.[33] The two schools differed in
their understanding of what this man had in mind at the time.
If Bet Hillel's interpretation was correct, his prior divorce
would be superseded by his later marriage and the woman
was no longer free to marry another man (*Git.* 81a; Maim.
Gerushin 10:17; *Sh. Ar., Even ha-Ezer* 149:1–2).

The general rule is that a husband when ordering the scribe
to write a get for him must give clear instructions, saying:
"Write and give a *get* from me to my wife".[34] If he only said,
"Write a *get* for my wife" – *kitevu*, he might not have meant
it seriously but just said so in jest, or simply to annoy her, or
to have it prepared for future use. If, however, the man was
in a life-threatening situation, such as being a prisoner facing
execution[35] and hurriedly said "Write a *get* for my wife"
without using the complete formula ("write... and give"), the
document should be written and given to his wife before he
died.

The Sages added that the same law would apply when a
man embarked on a long sea voyage or a hazardous overland
journey, or if he was dangerously ill.[36] This perilous situation
would weigh on his mind and, being in the grip of fear (*bahul*),
he might not manage to find the right expression. Since it was
clearly his intention to give his wife a *get*, even though he was
unable to issue the proper instructions, he would be credited
with having said, "Write and give" – *kitevu u-tenu* (Mish., *Git.*
6:5; *Tosefot Yom Tov ad loc.*; *Git.* 65b; *Sh. Ar., Even ha-Ezer*
141:16).

An Uncertain Intention Clarified Later – Bererah

It is an obligatory requirement, when a man writes a get or

---

33 צריכה הימנו גט שני
34 כתבו ותנו
35 היוצא בקולר
36 אף המפרש והיוצא בשיירא... אף המסוכן

has one written for him, that it be written specifically for the particular woman to whom he is married and whom he is now divorcing. His intention to divorce her must accompany the writing of the *get*, and any failure in that regard will render the *get* invalid (*Git.* 24a, Rashi and *Tos.* s.v. "*le-eizo*"; Maim. *Gerushin* 3:34; *Sh. Ar., Even ha-Ezer* 131:1,4). If, at the time of writing, there was some uncertainty in his mind or that of the scribe as to what he intended, but later he claimed that that was what he had really meant, the Sages debated whether the later decision was really what he had intended in the first place.[37]

The Sages also discussed a case where a man had two wives, both of whom happened to have the same names. He could not therefore order the scribe (*sofer stam*) to insert those names in a *get* intended to be used for one of the wives whom he might later wish to divorce. The ruling in this case invalidated the *get* for either wife's divorce (*Git.* 24b, 25a).

A man who had two wives, both bearing exactly the same name,[38] instructed the scribe to write a *get* on those names intending to use it for the one he would later decide to divorce.[39] The early authority in the Mishnah (*tanna*) ruled that even though this *get* had been intended for this man and his wife, the divorce would be invalid for the divorce of both these wives, since it is not certain that at the time of writing it was intended to divorce a particular wife; whereas the Torah law had stated, "He shall write her a bill of divorcement and give it into her hand" (Deut. 24:1).[40] The Torah stipulated "and he shall write her", meaning specifically for her.[41]

Some Sages of the Gemara assumed that the Mishnaic teaching ruled that we do not accept the principle that the man's

---

37 אם יש ברירה
38 מי שיש לו שתי נשים ששמותם שוות
39 ואיזו שארצה אגרש בו
40 וכתב לה ספר כריתות ונתן בידה
41 לה לשמה

ultimate choice was in fact what he had originally intended at the time of the writing of the *get* (*Git.* 24b).[42] This ruling followed the principle that the authoritative law is always as stated in the Mishnah (*Git.* 81b; *Sanh.* 86a).[43]

Other Sages, however, argued that although the law of divorce was restricted in accordance with the requirement of the Torah teaching, it could be possible to maintain that in other matters, such as the division of an inheritance among brothers, the part which one eventually received was the portion originally given by the testator. The different determination of *bererah* here would determine whether a person was deemed to have received the property as a gift or to have bought it from his brother (*Git.* 25a.; *Kid.* 42b.; *Betz.* 37a).

There may be other instances where one can resort to the principle that when something undefined is later thought suitable for a particular purpose, that subsequent decision counts as the one originally intended. This would be the case when two brothers inherited a portion of land from their father and negotiated a division of their inheritance. In accordance with the principle of *bererah*, it was then agreed that each half represented the half bequeathed by the father (*yesh bererah*). Had this principle not been followed (*ein bererah*), one would have to assume that all the land belonged to both of them, since each piece of land was subject to a partnership that obtained even after the agreed division. One would therefore need to rely on another presumption, that the sons had arranged for the parcels of land they inherited to be sold to each other. This procedure would involve a change in the status of the land, which would also necessitate the return of each portion to its original owner at the beginning of the jubilee year (Lev. 25:28; *Bekh.* 57a).[44]

A similar problem would arise when a partnership was terminated. Did the later division now represent each partner's

---

42   לשמה קמ״ל דאין ברירה

43   הלכה כסתם משנה כרבי מאיר

44   ויצא ביובל ושב לאחוזתו

separate possession? The Sages differed as to whether the principle of *bererah* could be applied here, but the writing of a *get* involved the Torah law concerning forbidden marriages. The Sages therefore agreed that one could not rely on the *bererah* principle, as indecisiveness was unacceptable.

An Outdated Bill of Divorce – Get Yashan

The husband's intention to divorce his wife must be clear at every stage of the preparation and giving of the *get*. He himself must direct the scribe to write the *get* for this purpose and he must ask the witnesses to sign it (*Git.* 71b; Maim. *Gerushin* 2:5). The *get*, which can be written by a scribe or by himself, must be written exclusively for him and his wife for the purpose of terminating the marriage (Maim. *Gerushin* 3:1).

If a man prepared a *get*, not meaning to give it to his wife directly but to keep it in readiness if they failed to become reconciled, and they continued to live together, such a *get* (which had not been written for an immediate divorce) would be invalid; it was an out-of-date *get* – *get yashan*. Likewise, if the man wrote the *get* while fully intending to divorce his wife, but then changed his mind and continued living with her, such a *get* could not be used when he finally resolved to divorce her (*Git.* 18a, Rashi; 79b; Maim. *Gerushin* 3:5). A similar problem might arise if he post-dated the *get* when it was written,[45] although he could stipulate that the correctly dated *get* would not be effective until a specified later time (*Git.* 72a).

In order to avoid future legal problems over issues such as the date of a child's conception, whether it was before or after the passing of the *get*, or in the use of marriage property, it was ruled that the get must be witnessed on the day that it was written. Only in certain contingencies can this regulation be somewhat relaxed (*Sh. Ar., Even ha-Ezer* 127:1–3).[46]

It was usually presumed that the *get* had been delivered to the wife on the day it was written or as soon as possible thereafter. If the *get* was witnessed after the day on which it was written, as recorded in the text, the document was considered "old" or "out of date" (*get yashan*).[47] Bet Hillel refused to accept such a *get* whereas Bet Shammai permitted its use, since it was nevertheless a proper *get* which the husband had every intention of using to divorce his wife (*Git.* 79b).

The rabbinical codes followed Bet Hillel's ruling, although they were ready to accept the validity of this *get* in exceptional (emergency) circumstances (Maim. *Gerushin*, 3:5; *Sh. Ar., Even ha-Ezer* 148:1). Rabbinic legislators (*posekim*) usually exercised wide discretion in their rulings to make sure that the wife did not become an *agunah*, in a state of limbo (*Arukh ha-Shulhan, Even ha-Ezer* 148; Responsa of Rabbi Isaac Ha-Levi Herzog, *Heikhal Yitzhak, Sh. Ar., Even ha-Ezer* 2:43, 45).

Change of Mind

If a husband sent a messenger to give his wife a *get* and then changed his mind, he could make a declaration to that effect before witnesses and, so long as the *get* had not yet been delivered, he could cancel it (*Sh. Ar., Even ha-Ezer* 140:1).

The Sages considered whether, in the case of a man who had apparently changed his mind without saying so explicitly, this mental cancellation would suffice to nullify the *get*. The problem arose because of their uncertainty as to whether he had really changed his mind or kept to his original decision.

Another case involved a man who wrote a *get* for his wife and instructed his agent to deliver it. When the messenger

---

46   שלא יאמרו גיטה קודם לבנה

47   גט ישן

arrived at her home, he found her busy weaving and she said to him: "Go away now, and come back tomorrow". The messenger left, taking the *get* with him. When the husband was informed of this, he declared, "Blessed be the Lord who is good and does good",[48] the benediction recited when one hears good news, implying that he was happy that the *get* had not been delivered.

Rava affirmed that the recital of this blessing indicated how glad the man was that the *get* had not been delivered, since he had changed his mind about divorcing his wife, and the *get* was therefore cancelled.[49] Abbaye, however, maintained that his blessing was commendable as such but did not change the validity of the *get*, which remained in force and could still be delivered.[50]

The point at issue here was whether indicating an intention[51] would be sufficient to alter the validity of the *get*.[52] Abbaye held that a condition or intention formulated in the mind, but not stated verbally, could not be enforced in law.[53] The man's obvious satisfaction over the non-delivery of his *get* or even running after the messenger in an effort to prevent him from delivering it (*Git.* 32a) – these were mere unspoken indications that would not suffice to cancel his *get* in the event of its delivery. Every bill of divorce had to possess finality so that the status of the woman and her future children were not left in any doubt.

This view was accepted by the Sages, who ruled that the *get* retained its force.[54] They laid down the principle that only a further, clearly spoken order could cancel a previous verbal instruction (*Git.* 34a, *Tos.*, RID *ad loc.*; Maim. *Gerushin* 6:25; *Sh. Ar., Even ha-Ezer* 141:62).

---

48 ברוך הטוב והמיטיב
49 הגט בטל
50 הגט לא בטל
51 גילוי דעת
52 אם גילוי דעת בגיטה מילתא היא, או לא מילתא
53 דברים שבלב אינם דברים
54 לא בטל

The importance of ensuring the finality of the divorce is illustrated by the following case. A husband sent a messenger with instructions to deliver a *get* to his wife. After the messenger left, the husband changed his mind and wanted to cancel the *get*. He declared before witnesses that the *get* he had sent was null and void.

Earlier law permitted him to appear before the local *bet din* and cancel the *get*. At a later stage, however, Rabban Gamliel the Elder (first century CE, head of the Jerusalem Sanhedrin) introduced a strict regulation (*takkanah*) whereby the *bet din* rejected such procedure. This rule aimed to prevent the disruption of family life.[55] If the *get* was still in his hands, the husband could obviously cancel it. Moreover, according to Biblical law, if the wife had not yet received the *get*, her husband was free to withdraw it. In that case, prior to her receiving the document, he had already changed his mind and could thus declare that the *get* he had sent was nullified. As a result, there would have been no divorce.

Rabban Gamliel's *takkanah* ruled out an annulment of the *get*, however, and it remained in force. The Sages declared that serious confusion would arise if the woman received such a *get* from the messenger. Believing that she was now divorced, she might remarry, not realizing that her husband had actually voided the *get* and that she remained his wife. This could have tragic results, as any children born of her second marriage would be illegitimate (*mamzerim*).

The new regulation found endorsement in the undertaking by the bride and groom that their *kiddushin* would be contingent on any ruling adopted by the Sages. They had ruled elsewhere that if necessary, for the sake of equity, they were empowered to dispossess a person of his property (*Yev.* 89b).[56] In the present case, for the good of society, they ruled that the amount paid by the man at his wedding was not part of the statutory *kesef kiddushin* but simply a gift to the woman. By thus nullifying the original *kiddushin*, the Sages were able

---

55   מפני תיקון העולם

56   הפקר בית דין הפקר

to declare that the couple had never been married in the first place. Accordingly, receipt of the *get* was meaningless and the woman was naturally free to marry any man. The Talmud's account of this procedure states that "the Rabbis divest him of his *kiddushin*" (*Yev.* 90b, Rashi *ad loc.*).[57]

The Sages were always at pains to rescue a woman from the tragic situation of an *agunah*, "tied" by a marriage that no longer exists because her husband cannot be found or for lack of due evidence of his death. They were even willing to utilize a halakhic procedure to circumvent Biblical law by canceling the marriage *ab initio* or accepting secondary evidence (*Shab.* 145a–b).[58]

C. Conditional Divorce

One may deliver a *get* which is conditional on the fulfilment of a certain requirement and, if the requirement is not fulfilled, the *get* does not take effect. Its validity will depend on the condition being fulfilled precisely as stated (Maim. *Gerushin* 8:1; *Sh. Ar., Even ha-Ezer* 143:1).

A problem might arise if the wording of the condition left some doubt as to what had been intended. For example, a sick man anticipating his own death (*shekhiv me-ra*) wrote a get for his wife with the aim of freeing her, prior to his death, from the tie of a levirate marriage (Deut. 25:5*ff.*). He did not stipulate, however, that the get would be valid only if he died of his illness. The Sages had to decide whether the condition he had in mind was binding or whether the get should be regarded as a straightforward divorce. Mention was made of a case where, having written his get, the man "moaned and groaned" at the thought of divorcing his wife. "Why do you moan?" said she. "If you recover, I will be yours".[59] The Sages ruled that while

---

57 הפקיעו רבנן קידושין מיניה
58 עד מפי עד
59 אי קיימת דידך אנא

he could have attached such a condition to the *get*, she could not do so; her words were merely "said to comfort him".[60] The giving of the *get* is the man's prerogative and only he may attach a condition to it. In this instance he had made no stipulation in his bill of divorce.

One might claim that he intended the get to have that condition attached; or, more generally, that he was prepared to give it in accordance with her own wishes (so that it would have a conditional validity); or that he actually had no condition in mind. Because of these various possibilities, the Sages determined that they must abide by the rule that unless the husband formally stipulated that the get was conditional on his imminent death,[61] it constituted a final act of divorce which could not be retracted (*eino ḥozer*).[62]

The laws of family relationship were so sacrosanct that they could not be governed by a mere mental reservation. In any case, if the man recovered from his illness, effecting a remarriage would present no difficulty (*BM* 66a; *Git.* 72a; 75a,b; *Sh. Ar., Even ha-Ezer* 145:4); although since she had now become a divorcee – gerusha – if the man happened to be a kohen such a marriage would be forbidden (Lev.21:7; *Yev.* 52a; *Sh. Ar., Even ha-Ezer* 6:1).

Another sick man who felt that his death was imminent[63] and, having no children, realized that his wife, would have to contend with difficulties that could arise in obtaining *ḥalitzah* from her deceased husband's brother (Deut. 25:5–10; see below), might wish to divorce her before he died, thereby releasing her from the obligation of *yibbum*. If, in the usual manner, he simply gave her a *get*, she would immediately cease to be his wife (the formal text of the *get* bearing the date and stating, "from this day and for ever").[64] If, therefore,

---

60 פטומי מילי בעלמא הוא
61 הרי זה גיטך אם מתי
62 אם עמד אינו חוזר
63 שכיב מרע
64 מן יומא דנן ולעולם

he meant her to remain his wife in the event of his recovery, when giving her the document he could have said: "This is your *get* should I die from this illness".[65]

This would give rise to a further complication, as the man apparently wanted the get to become effective when he died, whereas the *Halakhah* rules out the possibility of effecting a *get* when one is no longer alive (*Ket.* 3a).[66] His only recourse would be to declare: "This is your *get* from now" or "from today", adding the condition, "if I die from this illness", or, if he traveled abroad, "if I do not return within twelve months", i.e, while he was still alive.[67] If he used an ambiguous expression such as "from now and after my death",[68] this would be open to misinterpretation, since he might first have intended to say "from now", which would be valid, and then changed his mind, saying "after my death", which would be invalid. The problem would then be determining his real intention when he handed the *get* to his wife.

The halakhic definition of "recovering from one's illness" is being able to walk outside one's house with the help of a cane.[69] A further problem might arise, however, if the man's illness went into remission, death occurring at a later stage. If he died childless, his widow would have to perform *ḥalitzah*, but doubts concerning her personal status would prevent her from marrying her late husband's brother.[70] Entering into such a marriage might render her liable to the punishment of "excision" – *karet* (*Git.* 72a, Rashi; *Kid.* 60a; *Sh. Ar., Even ha-Ezer* 145:1).

If a man lying on his deathbed handed his wife a *get*, telling her "This is your *get*" without adding "if I die from this illness", that would be a final and unconditional divorce.

65	אם מתי מחולי זה
66	אין גט לאחר מיתה
67	מעכשיו או מהיום
68	מעכשיו אם מתי
69	אם עמד והלך בשוק במשענתו
70	היא חולצת, ואינה מתייבמת

If he subsequently recovered, the Sages would not allow him to claim that he had only meant the *get* to be effective if he died. They differentiated between a bill of divorce and a gift (*mattanah*) that was made on the assumption that he was dying. The gift could be withdrawn if he recovered, since it was clearly bestowed out of conviction that his life was at an end, but not otherwise (*BB* 151b). The law of divorce was different: a *get* must be final and irrevocable.[71]

The Sages recognized, however, that a man could attach a stipulation to his *get* from the very outset, declaring: "I give it to you now, but I do not intend the divorce to come into effect until such-and-such a time". If, upon giving the *get*, he made both a positive and a negative stipulation in the correct halakhic manner,[72] i.e, in both a positive and negative stipulation, such a condition would be valid and once it was fulfilled the *get* would become legal.

To avoid uncertainty, the codifiers (*posekim*) urged the man give his wife a simple *get*, with no provisos. If his health improved, the couple could remarry.

[General references: *Git.* 72a–b; *Sh. Ar., Even ha-Ezer* 145:1–10]

The following example of a clear condition and a clear fulfilment was given by the Sages. If a man lying sick in bed told his wife, "This is your *get* from today, should I die of this illness",[73] his condition would be sustained and the *get* would accordingly be valid. If, on the other hand, he said, "Should I die of this illness", and he was killed when his house collapsed, the specific condition governing the effectiveness of his *get* would not have been fulfilled and his *get* retained its validity[74] on the principle that a fatal accident cannot invalidate a *get* already delivered (*Git.* 34a).[75] Such an accident was entirely unforeseen and could not have been visualized when the man

71 אינו חוזר
72 תנאי כפול
73 אם אמות מחולי זה
74 הרי זה גט
75 אין טענת אונס בגיטין

added the stipulation about his impending death, and therefore had not been included in the condition that he had made (*Git.* 73a, Rashi *ad loc., Sh. Ar., Even ha-Ezer* 145:6).[76]

The same principle is found in the law of sale, where one man sells his field to another, assuming responsibility for any damage that may come to light in the field. The river then overflows and ruins the purchaser's crops. Since this type of damage goes far beyond normal expectations, it could never have been envisaged by the seller and he is therefore not liable to pay compensation.[77] The Sages, nevertheless, allowed for differences of opinion as to the kind of disaster that might be completely unexpected or just rather unusual, according to the prevailing circumstances (*Git.* 73a, Rashi, *Tos. "etiveh"*, ROSH, *ad loc.*; Maim. *Gerushin* 9:17; *Sh. Ar., Hoshen Mishpat* 225:3).

A similar case of a *get* being valid, despite the condition attached, involved a man who told his wife: "This is your *get* should I not return within 30 days". While making his return trip on that last day, the ferry broke down and he could not reach home in time. This was not an unusual occurrence and the man should have taken it into consideration. He might, of course, plead that he had wished to return within the stipulated time but had not managed to do so because of the accident. The Sages, however, ruled that by failing to return within 30 days he had not adhered to the condition laid down. The *get* was therefore valid and his divorce had taken effect. They accepted the principle, in respect of a *get*, that a man cannot maintain that he did not want the divorce and failed to arrive in time due to a mishap. Once the *get* has been delivered, no such claim, even if the accident had been unavoidable, is admissible (*Sh. Ar., Even ha-Ezer* 144:1).[78]

The exact wording used to express a condition may alter its meaning and produce a completely different result. It may

---

76 אונס שלא שכיח לא עלה על דעתו

77 אונסא דלא שכיח הוא

78 אין אונס בגיטין

be expressed in two ways: "on condition that... " (*al menat*), or "if (*im*) such-and-such occurs". How these two separate wordings affected the validity of the *get* would depend on the Sages' interpretation of whatever the husband had in mind when he made his stipulation.

They taught that giving the *get* "on condition that... " meant that it became valid immediately, as if the husband declared that it would take effect at once (*me-akhshav*); the condition was then dependent on the fulfilment of his or her undertaking. When the *get* was given with an "if" (*im*) condition, however, it only became valid after the condition had been fulfilled.

The following cases were discussed. A man told his wife, "This is your *get* on condition that you look after my father for two years" or "provided that you suckle my child for two years". If, in the event, the man's father or his child died before those two years were up, the condition became impossible to fulfil and no blame could therefore be attached to the wife. Consequently, the effectiveness of the *get* would not be altered by non-fulfilment of the condition and the *get* remained valid.[79] If, however, the condition had been expressed in a different form, "This is your *get* if you look after my father... ",[80] the Sages were not of the same opinion in their ruling.

In R. Meir's view, the *get* had been made subject to fulfilment of the condition, and validation of the *get* would only commence when that condition had been fulfilled. Accordingly, if the full terms of the condition had not been discharged, the *get* was invalid (*eino get*), and no divorce had taken place. The Sages, however, would not permit such uncertainty to affect the status of the *get* and consequently that of the woman. They ruled that whichever term had been used, the validity of the *get* depended on whether or not the condition had been fulfilled.

The early commentators stated that using the phrase "on condition that... " (*al menat*) was equivalent to the husband's saying "the *get* is valid from now" (*me-akhshav*). The *get* would immediately be valid without being subject to fulfilment of the condition or to its expression by the husband in accordance with the statutory formulation (Maim. *Ishut*, 6:1–2, 17–18). If, however, the husband used the term "if" (*im*), the condition's validity would depend on whether he had employed the correct formulation (*Git.* 75b–76a, ROSH 9; Maim. *Gerushin* 9:11, 17–20; *Ket.* 3a, *Tos. s.v. "ikka de-amerei"*).

Some of the Sages made a distinction here between marriage and divorce on the basis of intention. "This is your *kiddushin*, provided that (*al menat*) I give you 200 *zuz*" meant that the *kiddushin* took effect immediately and so the man owed the woman 200 *zuz*. In the case of a *get*, however, its validity was subject to fulfilment of the condition. The difference lay in the man's frame of mind. By proposing marriage, the man intended to show his affection towards the woman; in divorcing the woman, he was impelled by a spirit of animosity[81] and wished her to remain in suspense until he finally gave her the 200 *zuz* (*Git.* 74a, Rashi *ad loc.*; *Git.* 74b, Rashi *ad loc.*).[82]

On the other hand, in the case where a man delivered his *get*, stating that it would be effective only on condition that his wife gave him 200 *zuz*, and then he died before she gave him that amount,[83] the Sages differed as to what had been in his mind when made the stipulation. Some held that he meant the *get* to be conditional on his actually receiving the 200 *zuz*, in which case the condition had not been fulfilled and the *get* was not binding. Others claimed that he intended the *get* itself to be valid and the sum of 200 *zuz* to be his due; in the event of his death, that payment would be assigned to his heirs.[84] Whether the woman's status was or was not that of a divorcee would depend on whatever her husband had in mind when he

---

81 לצעורה קא מכוון
82 גבי קדושין דלקרובה קאתי... גבי גרושין משום דלרחוקה קאתי
83 הרי זה גיטך על מנת שתיתני לי מאתיים זוז, ומת
84 לי ואפילו ליורשי

made his stipulation (*Git.* 74a; Maim. *Gerushin* 8:1; *Sh. Ar.,*
Even ha-Ezer 143:1–2).

D. Divorce on the Basis of a Mistaken Complaint

The case was shown above (A. Introduction) where a man
divorced his wife in the belief that she was permanently
infertile (*aylonit*), without his being aware of that disability
when he married her with *kiddushin*. She subsequently
married another man and bore him children, thus proving that
she was not infertile. The Sages, in accordance with the strict
law, ruled that the divorce had been a mistake (*get be-ta'ut*),
and it was therefore cancelled (*batel*) and the first husband
might reclaim her (*yahzir*).[85]

R. Yehuda held a different view and ruled, that the *get*
was valid. He explained that the man could not claim that the
original marriage itself had been made by mistake. He might
claim also that had he known that his wife could be cured
of her presumed infertility he would never have divorced her
even if someone were to give him as much as 100 *maneh*. He
gave the divorce only on the understanding that if she could be
cured from her complaint he would be happy to have her back,
but if he had known that she may not return to him when she
was cured he would not have divorced her. He would argue
that since his *get* had been given by mistake (*get beta'ut*) it
was therefore invalid. He might also say that his marriage with
an *aylonit* was a marriage by mistake, (*kiddushin be-aylonit*
kiddushei ta'ut hem), and his marriage with her had not been
a valid *kiddushin*. However, it was an accepted rule that it was
not normal for a man to say that he engaged in intercourse
with one to whom he had given *kiddushin* merely as an act of

harlotry. Therefore his sexual relationship with her had been intended as a normal marriage, and the giving of the *get* was a full divorce. This situation, where he might make such claims would cast doubt on the lawfulness of the *get*, and could arouse suspicion as to the subsequent status of the woman and her children according to family law – *hayesh lekilkulah*, and had to be avoided. Accordingly after divorcing her he could not claim that it was a mistake and he wished to take her back (*lo yahzir*). The Sages, however, would accept his claim that the *get* had been given by mistake and was therefore invalid, and he may take her back (*yahzir*).

The final ruling agreed with R. Yehuda (*lo yahzir*) and decreed that whenever a man wished to give a get on the grounds of his wife being an *aylonit* the Court must warn him that if he did so he would not be permitted to change his mind and take her back (*Git.* 46b, Rashi, *Tos. "hamotzi"; Yev.* 2b, *Tos. "o";* Maim. *Gerushin* 10:13; *Sh. Ar., Even ha-Ezer* 10:4–6).

A similar ruling applied in such a case when the man after handing the *get* to his wife, is told that he must pay her the full amount recorded in her *ketubbah*. He then claims ignorance of the law, having thought that an *aylonit* could be divorced without giving her that payment. Had he known of this liability, he would not have divorced her; and, since the *get* had been given by mistake, he now wanted to take her back. He cannot do so, however, for the reasons stated above.

Although the husband is exempt from paying the money to an undoubted *aylonit*, he is liable to give his wife the full amount when she proved capable of having children, and the normal laws of divorce applied. In all cases of this type, the Sages ruled, that every effort must be made to avoid problematic relationships and possible doubts regarding the legitimacy of the second husband's children (*mi-shum kilkulah*). The first husband's claim is therefore disallowed; his *get* is final and he is not permitted to reclaim her.

This kind of situation also faced a woman who had been divorced on the grounds of her having a reputation of immorality (*mi-shum shem ra*)[86] but who later repented and conducted herself as a religiously observant person (ba'alat teshuvah). The ex-husband might seek to cancel their divorce on the grounds that she was now a reformed character, but no such revocation was permitted, and he would never be allowed to take her back[87] (Git. 45b, 46b, Rashi; Mish., Git. 4:8, Bertinoro; Maim. *Gerushin*, 10:3, 12; *Sh. Ar., Even ha-Ezer* 10:3, 117:4).

E. Accusations of Immoral Behaviour

The gravity of the sin of adultery was enunciated in the axiomatic prohibition in the Ten Commandments, "Thou shalt not commit adultery" (*lo tin'af*). After the full legal procedure of inquiry and evidence and a judgement of guilt, the death penalty was inflicted (Ex. 20:13). Torah law specified, "And the man that committeth adultery with another man's wife, even he that committeth adultery with his neighbour's wife, the adulterer and the adulteress shall surely be put to death".[88] Accusations of such a grievous sin were most meticulously examined by the *bet din*, and any charge of such conduct had to be made with the greatest responsibility (Lev. 20:10, Rashi; *San.* 50b, 52b; *Shev.* 47b; Maim. *Issurei Bi'ah* 2:10).

The commission of a transgression, and its ensuing penalty, usually refers to the performance of some forbidden action. An exceptional case in *Halakhah* is that of a person being sentenced to a punishment of lashes, or "stripes" (*malkot*), for something that he had said, without being guilty of some physical action (Maim. *Sanhedrin*, 18:1).[89] This was when a

---

86   שיצא עליה לעז זנות

87   אומרים לו גמור בלבך לגרשה שאין זו חוזרת לך לעולם

88   מות יומת הנאף והנאפת

89   לאו שאין בו מעשה

man slandered his wife, alleging that she had not been a virgin when he married her.[90]

According to Biblical law, "If any man take a wife... and lay wanton charges against her, and bring up an evil name upon her... ", should his charge prove true, she is condemned to death by stoning – *sekilah* (Deut. 22:13–14, 19–21). If it proves false, he is sentenced to a fine of 100 silver coins and to the penalty of flogging (*malkot*). He is also compelled to retain her as his wife, and he will be barred from divorcing her on his own wish at any time even if later there may be good grounds to claim that she had become odious to him. If, however, she does not wish to remain his wife, she may testify that he is now loathsome to her and apply to the Court to order a compulsory divorce. The *bet din* usually advised her to make this petition (Deut. 22:17–18, *Sifrei ad loc.*; *Ket.* 39b–40a, Rashi "*mi-iteih*").

The Sages had to judge a case where a man divorced his wife because of some evil report, after which she married another man and bore him children. Her ex-husband then discovered that the report he had received was malicious: the two men who claimed that she had solicited them proved to be false witnesses. The first husband claimed that he had only divorced her because of his belief that she was promiscuous; had he known that the report was false or that she would become a true penitent (*ba'alat teshuvah*), he would never have considered divorcing her. In these circumstances, he now wished to cancel his *get*.

The former husband maintained that the *get* had been issued conditionally, on the assumption that the accusation was true; but since this was not the case, his bill of divorce was surely void (*ha-get batel*). However, rescinding the *get* was not permitted: if the *bet din* judged that there had been no divorce, the woman would have remained this man's wife and the children of her second marriage would be stigmatized as illegitimate (*mamzerim*). The Court therefore gave notice to the petitioner that once he divorced his wife on the grounds of ill repute (*shem ra*), he could never remarry her (*Git.* 45b–46a; *Ket.* 46a; *Mak.* 2b; Maim. *Gerushin*, 10:12).[91]

To avoid any future serious complications, the Sages always determined that unless clear stipulations had been made at the outset, the issue of a *get* must always be considered final and irreversible. Even when the husband believed he had every reason to give a *get*, and was himself free of any fault, and later discovered that he had been misinformed, he cannot claim that the *get* was issued in error and should therefore be rescinded (*batel*). Any stipulation about the *get* that existed only in his mind, but had not been stated, was deemed ineffective.

F. A Suspect Motive

Torah law states that a woman's husband may annul vows that she has made: "If her husband disallow her on the day that he heareth it; then he shall make void her vow... " (Num. 30:7–9).[92] If he did not annul her vow when he heard it, he cannot do so later and the vow remains binding. She might then change her mind and ask a Sage to annul it, which he is authorized to do if, in his judgment, her rash behaviour needs to be curbed.

If she vowed never to derive pleasure from her husband[93] and he failed to annul her vow, the couple would have to be divorced. If she then asked a Sage to annul her vow and he refused her request on the grounds that he could find nothing to justify such an annulment, that particular Sage was forbidden to marry the woman after her divorce. Otherwise, people might suspect that his refusal to annul her vow had been prompted by ulterior motives (*Yev.* 25b, Rashi *ad loc.*).[94]

---

91   המוציא את אשתו משום שם רע לא יחזיר

92   אישה יניא אותה והפר את נדרה

93   נדרה הנאה מבעלה

94   לא ישאנה משום חשד

G. Obligatory Divorce and Rules of Evidence

The law of evidence required the testimony of two witnesses, particularly when someone was charged with marital infidelity. According to the accepted rule, no such charge could be made on the evidence of a single witness (*Git.* 4b; *Kid.* 66a).[95] If, of course, the husband testified that he had caught his wife in the act, *in flagrante delicto*, no further evidence was necessary. The law then forbade him to continue living with her, and required him to divorce her, since it would be abhorrent to him to retain her as his wife and preserve the marriage bond.

The Sages considered what should be done if a friend or relative of the man, who were normally excluded from being valid witnesses (*pesulei eidut*), told him that he or she had witnessed misconduct by his wife. In legal terms, such evidence was insufficient to prove her guilty. Similarly, if only one witness, male or female, testified against her they ruled that if the man trusted this friend and believed that the evidence was truthful, and accepted it as reliable as the evidence of two valid witnesses, and, as a result, had an aversion to his wife, he was morally obliged to divorce her "for no one can live with a serpent in the same basket", (i.e., never knowing when she would hurt him again) (*Ket.* 72a).[96] The ruling was wholly dependent on his frame of mind – whether he accepted this report or dismissed it as hearsay (*Kid.* 66a, *Shiltei Hagiborim*, on RIF, p. 28 s.4; Maim. *Ishut* 24:17, *Gerushin* 10:22; *Sotah*, 1:9).[97]

The Mishnah records a decision by the early Sages that if the wife herself told her husband that she had committed adultery, he was obliged to divorce her.[98] In view of the fact that her admission was not supported by the evidence of two

---

95 אין דבר שבערוה פחות משנים

96 אין אדם דר עם נחש בכפיפה

97 אי מהימן לך כבי תרי זיל אפקה

98 חייב להוציא

witnesses, as required in all such cases,[99] she would not lose
the sum written in her *ketubbah*. Later Sages, however, thought
that her statement might not be truthful, but simply a ruse
enabling her to marry someone else. They therefore modified
the ruling as follows. If the husband was of a mind to credit
her admission no less than the evidence of two witnesses, he
was bound to divorce her. Even if he did not believe her, he
should be requested – i.e., not obliged – by the court to divorce
her (*Ned.* 90b; *Kid.* 66a).

If only one witness testified that a woman had played the
harlot, and she remained silent in face of the charge, her silence
would be interpreted as an admission of guilt.[100] In the view
of three early authorities, RIF, RAN and RASHBA, the ruling
that her husband was obliged to divorce her on the evidence
of a single witness only applied if she failed to protest her
innocence and remained silent (*shoteket*). If she denied the
charge, he was not obligated to divorce her,[101] but the court
would advise him to do so as a moral obligation[102] (*Kid.* 66a,
RIF *ad loc.*, 29a; RAN and ROSH, *ibid.*; Maim. *Ishut* 24:18;
RASHBA, *Hiddushim* 118, 236; *Sh. Ar., Even ha-Ezer* 115:6–
7, REMA *ad loc.*).

An addendum by REMA to the above law, as set forth
in the *Shulhan Arukh*, quotes the view of a commentator
on Maimonides (*Haggahot Maimoniot*), that since we are
now bound by the proclamation of Rabbenu Gershom (11th
cent.),[103] which prohibits divorcing a woman without her
consent, this man cannot divorce his wife unless there is
evidence of her guilt provided by two reliable witnesses. One
should not trust the man's declared belief in her confession,[104]
since even if he gave no credence to the charge against her,

---

99   אין דבר שבערוה פחות משנים
100 שתיקה כהודאה דמיא
101 אינו חייב להוציא
102 לצאת ידי שמים
103 חרם דרבנו גרשום
104 אם היה מאמינה וסומך דעתו על דבריה הרי זה חייב להוציאה

he might well pretend to believe it out of a desire to marry
some other woman (Maim. *Ishut*, 24:18, note in *Haggahot
Maimoniot ad loc.*; Sh. *Ar., Even ha-Ezer* 178:9).[105]

H. Divorce against the Husband's Wishes

Maimonides lists ten rules for the issue of a *get*. The first rule
states that a *get* may only be effective if it is given freely by the
husband (Maim. *Gerushin* 1:1).[106] This was clearly laid down
by the tannaitic Sages, who contrasted the husband's right to a
divorce with the early rule that a wife could be divorced with
or without her consent (*Yev.* 112b; Maim. *Gerushin* 1:1).[107]

The same Sages, however, also ruled that in a case where
the husband had become loathsome to the wife because of
some disgusting physical condition, the *bet din* might properly
force him to grant his wife a *get* on the basis of her maintaining
that she "cannot endure him". Rav explained: "no one can
live with a serpent in the same basket" (*Ket.* 72a, 77a).[108]
Similarly, if the wife claimed that her husband had turned out
to be sterile or impotent, incapable of fulfilling the *mitzvah* to
"be fruitful and multiply" (Gen. 1:28), while she was anxious
to have children who would support her in her old age, the *bet
din* might compel the husband to divorce her so that she could
marry someone else (*Yev.* 65b; Maim. *Ishut* 15:10; Sh. *Ar.,
Even ha-Ezer* 154:6).[109]

Although the law requiring a man to produce a progeny
does not apply to a woman (*Yev.* 65b),[110] her claim that she
needs help in her old age is accepted. She could say, does not

---

105 חוששין שמא עיניו נתן באחרת
106 שלא יגרש האיש אלא ברצונה
107 אמר לשנים כתבו גט... והוא יגרש בו בכל עת שירצה
108 ואלו שכופין אותו להוציא... מומין גדולים... ועכשיו איני יכולה לקבל
109 כי הא ודאי כפינן
110 האיש מצווה על פריה ורביה אבל לא האשה

a woman like herself require "a staff in her hand and a hoe for digging a grave?" Therefore the *bet din* compels the husband to give her the *get* she demands, as well as to pay her *ketubbah* (*Yev.* 65b).[111]

Since the accepted rule states that a *get* is valid only if it is given freely by the husband, there appears to be a contradiction here, as it is a legal requirement in certain circumstances that the husband should be compelled to grant his wife a *get*. Such a bill of divorce is called "a forced *get*".[112]

R.Naḥman ruled, on the authority of Shmuel, that although a *get* issued under *force majeure* was invalid, one granted on the orders of a *bet din*, imposed in accordance with the *Halakhah* was valid.[113] However, any "forced *get*", other than one halakhically prescribed, was not only invalid but also deficient in the requirements of a proper *get*, not having even the slightest trace of a *get*, and it could not be used to sanction a divorce (*Git.* 88b).[114]

Maimonides, grappling with this apparent inconsistency in the law, offers this explanation. If a man is ordered by the court to divorce his wife but refuses to do so, the *bet din* may sentence him to be flogged until he agrees to obey the court order and writes a *get* for his wife.[115] The husband cannot claim that he acted under *force majeure* (*anus hu*) and that his *get* is therefore invalid. If he was obliged by Torah law to take this action, it is presumed that in his heart he wished – as a loyal son of Israel – to obey the Torah, but his true nature was overcome by the evil impulse (*yetzer ha-ra*) that made him refuse to do his duty. The *force majeure* argument could only apply where no Torah law was involved, such as coercing a man into selling or handing over something that he wished to keep for himself.

---

111 חוטרא לידה ומרה לקבורה
112 גט מעושה
113 גט המעושה בישראל כדין כשר, שלא כדין פסול
114 אפילו ריח גט אין בו
115 מכין אותו עד שיאמר רוצה אני... והוא גט כשר

If, however, the evil inclination had taken hold of this man, urging him to shirk his religious duty,[116] but was then subdued by the flogging, after which he rid himself of its constraint and agreed to follow the court's directive, the *get* which he now delivers is given of his own unfettered free will and therefore valid.[117]

Such pressure may be applied only if it is put on the husband by the *bet din* for a *get* required by the *Halakhah*. Force applied in any other case, such as an obdurate heathen beating a man or threatening his father or child so as to wring a consent from him, would invalidate such a *get*.[118] While subject to duress, the man had only performed a physical action (writing the *get*); but consciously, he had not divorced his wife. The mere fact that he had issued the *get* did not prove that it was the freely given divorce required by *Halakhah*. Only when the court compelled him to perform his halakhic duty, by consenting to divorce his wife,[119] would the *get* be accepted as freely given and binding (*Git.* 88b; Maim. *Gerushin* 2:20; *Sh. Ar., Even ha-Ezer* 134:7).

I. The *Halitzah* Ceremony

According to Biblical law, if a man dies childless, one of his surviving brothers (in order of seniority) fulfils the duty of levirate marriage (*yibbum*) by taking the widow as his wife (Deut. 25:5–6). "Levirate" derives from the Latin word *levir*, meaning "the husband's brother"; he is known in Hebrew as the *yavam* and the widow as the *yevamah*. A simple form of *kiddushin* is held, involving either a document (*shetar*) or a payment (*kesef*), with the "levir" (*yavam*) declaring, in

---

116 מי שתוקפו יצרו הרע לבטל מצווה

117 וכיון שהוכה עד שתשש יצרו ואמר רוצה אני, כבר גרש לרצונו

118 אנסוהו עכו״ם לגרש שלא כדין אינו גט

119 גמר ומגרש

the presence of witnesses: "You are betrothed to me". This form of *kiddushin* is designated *ma'amar*, the final form of the marriage is completed at the time of its consumation (*Yev.* 39b; *Sh. Ar., Even ha-Ezer* 166:2).

A *yevamah* was forbidden to marry anyone other than the *yavam*, unless he freed her by means of *halitzah* – a special type of divorce (Deut. 25:7–10; *Yev.* 13b). If the *yavam* refused to marry the widow, or if she refused to marry him, the *bet din* arranged a ceremony during which *halitzah* – "removal" of the man's shoe by the widow – took place and she was formally released from the levirate bond (*Yev.* 39b, RAN *ad loc.*, s.v. "*amar Rav ein kofin*"; Maim. *Yad, Yibbum ve-Halitzah* 1:1–2, 6).

The Sages were aware that a marriage of the widow with her late husband's brother, conflicted with a basic rule governing forbidden marriages (*arayot*), which prohibits marrying a brother's wife (Lev. 18:16). Torah law, they explained, which normally forbids such a union, gives special sanction to the obligation of a levirate marriage (TJ *Ned.* 3:2). This sanction was given for one purpose only: to make the levir's sister-in-law pregnant and thus "raise up unto his brother a name in Israel" (Deut. 25:7).[120] If such a birth was not physically possible (e.g., sterile, *aylonit* or in the male condition, *saris*) such a marriage would revert to being a forbidden marriage (*Yev* 24a; Maim. *Yibbum ve-Halitza* 6:8).

Abba Sha'ul, a disciple of R. Akiva, had suspicions about the *yavam*'s role: "If his reason for marrying and having intercourse with her was not simply the duty of fulfilling the *mitzvah*, but her physical allure, romantic love or anything else, he would then have violated the marriage prohibitions".[121] Generally speaking, however, the Sages preferred not to examine the *yavam*'s motives and accepted the validity of the marriage. He had, after all, done his duty by marrying his widowed sister-in-law, as the Torah prescribed (*Yev.* 39b, *Tos.* "*uleshum ishut*"; *Ber.* 13a).

---

120 להקים לאחיו שם בישראל
121 הכונס את יבימתו לשם נוי ולשום אישות וכו׳ כאילו פוגע בערווה

Although *yibbum* was theoretically preferable to the alternative of *halitzah*, deteriorating moral standards worked in favour of *halitzah*. Furthermore, social practices in the West often differed markedly from those in the East and, as a result, *yibbum* marriage is not practiced in the modern world (*Ket.* 64a; *Yev.* 39b; *Ber.* 13a).[122]

The basic requirement in *halitzah* is that both the *yavam* and the widow should clearly understand its purpose (*da'at*) and what their intention is in performing it (*kavvanah*) (*Yev.* 102b; Maim. *Yibbum ve-Halitza* 4:16). If such understanding is absent, such as when she is performing her part in the ceremony of removing his shoe, or in any action which he performs, the *halitzah* is invalid (*Yev.* 104b).

Either party may be disqualified by reason of their insufficient age, status as a minor[123] or mental incapacity.[124] One whose only defect is a speech impediment[125] may not be disqualified on that account, as his understanding and mental capacity need not be impaired (Yev. 104b, Ramban and RITVA ad loc.). Even a certifiably insane person may have lucid periods in which he is able to exercise his own consent and intention, and he is not merely acting automatically under instructions (*Yev.* 112b, 113b; Maim. *Yibbum ve-Halitzah*, 4:16[126]; *RH* 28a[127]).

[General reference: *Encyclopaedia Judaica*, "Levirate Marriage", 11:122–130]

---

122 בראשונה שהיו מתכוונים לשם מצווה, מצוות ייבום קודמת למצוות חליצה –
ועכשיו שאין מתכוונין לשם מצווה אמרו מצוות חליצה קודמת

123 קטן וקטנה

124 חרש וחרשת

125 אילם ואילמת

126 או שנתכוון היא ולא נתכוון הוא, או שנתכוון הוא ולא נתכוונה היא, חליצתן
פסולה

127 עתים חלים עתים שוטה כשהוא חלים הרי הוא כפקח לכל דבריו

J. Agency in Divorce

Capacity to Write a Get

The writing of a *get* may be performed by any Israelite, man or woman, who has reached the age of puberty (*Git.* 22b).[128] Those who are mentally deficient (such as a deaf mute) or insane and a minor do not have the capacity to write a *get*. A heathen (idolater – *akum*), and an alien slave (*nokhri – eved Canaani*) would also be excluded, since they did not have the right to contract a marriage or divorce. In the case of an Israelite who had been sold as a slave to a Jewish master, he has the ability, also during the six years of his service as a slave, to contract a valid marriage with an Israelite wife. During the term of his "slavery" the master has the duty to give food and shelter also to his slave's wife and children, fulfilling the normal duty of the slave as a husband, whose responsibility the master had now undertaken; but he would have no such obligation if he married after entering his "slavery", unless he did so with his master's consent (Ex. 21:3, Rashi, Ramban, *ad loc. s.v. 'veyatz'ah ishto imo'*; *Kid.* 22a).[129] (Maim. *Gerushin* 3:15, 16, *Lehem mishneh ad. loc.*)[130] (*Git.* 22b; 23a, Rashi *"bar heterah hu"*; Maim. *Gerushin* 3:15; Maim. *Avadim* 3:4, *Kesef Mishneh*; *Arukh Hashulhan, Sh. Ar., Even ha-Ezer* 123:1, 141:66).[131] A Jewish apostate (*mumar*) is likewise excluded, since such people do not consider themselves bound by any obligation to act in accordance with Jewish law, their writing may be influenced by their own thoughts instead of the required intention needed for the writing of a *get* (*Git.* 23a; Maim. *Gerushin* 3:15; *Sh. Ar., Even ha-Ezer* 123:1, 2).[132]

---

128   לשם האיש המגרש ולשם האשה המתגרשת

129   אם בעל אשה הוא ויצאה אשתו עמו

130   הכל כשרין לכתוב את גט חוץ מחמשה, עכו״ם, ועבד, וחרש, ושוטה, וקטן

131   העבד אינו בתורת גיטין וקדושין

132   עובד כוכבים דלדעתיה דנפשיה עבד

Nevertheless, if any of the aforesaid disqualified individuals happen to write the standard text (*tofes*) of the *get*, leaving blank spaces (*toref*) for the details, the essential particulars can be inserted by a qualified *sofer* (scribe) and the *get* will be fully valid (*Git.* 22b–23a, Rashi, *Tos. "oved kokhavim"*; Maim. *Gerushin* 3:15–20; *Sh. Ar., Even ha-Ezer* 123:1–4).

The husband himself must ask the scribe to write his *get* and he himself must instruct two witnesses to sign it, after which he or his duly appointed agent gives the *get* to his wife.

If he instructs two people to write and sign it, they may do so, but only they themselves are competent to act in this way (Maim. *Gerushin* 2:24). If he requests a constituted *bet din* to perform this procedure, the court may do so, but it cannot instruct a scribe and witnesses to execute the *get* without direct instructions from the husband himself to the scribe and witnesses (*Git.* 66b; Maim. *Gerushin* 2:5; *Sh. Ar., Even ha-Ezer* 120:4).

Specific and General Instructions to the Scribe

The statutory text of a bill of divorce (*get*) may be written in two forms. The standard, traditional form (*get pashut*) occupies 12 lines, under which the signatures of two witnesses are placed (Mish., *Git.* 1:1, *Tosefot Yom Tov ad loc.*; Maim. *Gerushin* 4:12; *Sh. Ar., Even ha-Ezer* 126, 154:101). Another, unusual form was more complicated, as each line of the text was separated by an intervening blank line. Each written line was folded over the blank line, and sewn, a witness signing on the back of each fold, and at least three witnesses were required. Known as a "folded *get*" (*get mekushar*), this complicated form – with its elaborate folding, stitching and signing procedure – was introduced by the Sages to give the husband a "cooling-down period" in which to reconsider his decision (*BB* 160a–b; *BB* 161a: the Soncino Press translation, p. 704, provides an illustration of a "folded *get*"; the *Jewish Encyclopaedia's* "Divorce" entry, Vol. 4, p. 625, includes an illustration of a "plain *get*").

In some communities it was normal practice to write only the standard *get pashut*; in others the folded *get mekushar* was written. The validity of the *get* depended on local usage, *minhag ha-makom* (*BB* 160a, 165a).

The Sages discussed the situation where a man instructed the *sofer* to write him a *get pashut,* but the scribe wrote a *get mekushar*. Opinions were divided, some claiming that the scribe, as the husband's agent, was in duty bound to follow his instructions and, since he had not done so, the *get* was invalid. Others maintained that everything depended on whether the husband was specific (*kappedah*) as to how the *get* should be written or merely asked the scribe to indite it in the usual form.

According to the latter view, if the husband's specific instructions were not followed, the *get* would be invalid; if his request was couched in general terms, it would be valid. The validity of the *get* or the continuation of the marriage depended on what the husband had in mind when he ordered it (*BB* 165a). A similar rule would apply to agency (Maim. *Ishut,* 7:21; *Sh. Ar., Even ha-Ezer* 35:67). If the wife asked her agent to receive the *get* on her behalf in one particular place (*kappedah*), since she objected to having her divorce discussed elsewhere, or the delivery of her *get* by an agent in any other place the agency might be ineffective because of the limitation in her mind. If, however, she just happened to mention a place where the *get* could be received, without particularizing, her *get* would be valid, i.e., not *kappedah* but *mar'eh makom* (*BB* 165a; Maim. *Gerushin* 9:34; *Sh. Ar., Even ha-Ezer* 141:45, 49).

The law required that the husband's instructions to the scribe be given as follows: "Write the *get* and deliver it to my wife".[133] If the husband was in a life-threatening situation, all he needed to say was "Write the *get* for my wife".[134] If, however, the man was in good health or just slightly unwell, a

---

mere request to "write the *get*" would not constitute sufficient authorization, since he might only have intended to vex his wife and not to divorce her in earnest.[135]

The Sages distinguished between a person who was so dangerously ill[136] that everyone around him wished to ensure that he received immediate attention and someone who had just fallen sick and whose close relatives were in attendance (*Git.* 65b–66a; TJ *Git.* 6:7; Maim. *Gerushin* 2:12).[137]

Intentions of Scribe and Husband

As previously indicated, a *get* must be written with the sole aim of effecting a divorce between two specific people.

A *sofer* is allowed to copy the basic text of a *get* as a writing exercise or as guidance for a pupil, but the Sages ruled that no *get* is valid unless it has been written for the man and woman specified in the husband's instructions. If a husband were to find or receive a *get* already prepared for a couple living in the same town, whose names were identical with those of the husband and his wife, such a document might have all the appearance of a specially written *get*, but it could never be used to effect his divorce.

When preparing a *get*, the *sofer* himself must make it clear that he is writing it specifically for these two people; he must also keep that intention constantly in mind as the writing of the *get* proceeds, and the same holds true for the husband. This ruling is based on the Torah law, "He shall write her a bill of divorcement" (Deut. 24:1),[138] which the Sages took to mean, "He shall write it expressly for her".[139]

---

135 רוצה לצחק בה
136 מסוכן
137 במסוכן והוא אדם שקפץ עליו החולי במהרה והכביד עליו חוליו מיד
138 וכתב לה ספר כריתות
139 וכתב לה, לשמה

The entire validity of the divorce and its impact on any future marriage will depend on what the scribe had in mind when he wrote the *get* (*Git.* 20a, 24a–b; Maim *Gerushin* 1:1; *Sh. Ar., Even ha-Ezer* 131:1). In order to show that the entire *get* was prepared without a break, the writing must be continuous.

A problem would arise if the *sofer* wrote the *get* in two columns instead of the usual one, the signatures of the witnesses appearing at the end. Should there be an empty space at the bottom of the first column and one at the top of the second, a break in the writing might be suspected. After instructing the *sofer* to write the *get*, the husband might conceivably have resolved not to divorce his wife, at which point the scribe stopped writing. Later, however, the husband might have changed his mind again and then ordered the scribe to complete the document.[140] In that case, the first part of the *get* had been mentally cancelled and only the second part was authorized, thereby rendering the entire *get* invalid (*Git.* 87b–88a, Rashi and *Tos.*, *s.v.* "*ve-dilma*").

Appointment of an Agent – Shali'ah

The principle of agency was recognized in Jewish law from earliest times, the Sages declaring that "a man's agent is as himself".[141] This doctrine applied in various spheres of *Halakhah*. Apart from commercial law and the laws of sacrifice, it was also recognized in the area of marriage and divorce, an agent being empowered to effect a marriage – *kiddushin* – or deliver a bill of divorce on his principal's behalf.

When a husband has his *get* written before a *bet din*, he can declare that so-and-so, who may not even be present in court, is the agent appointed to deliver this *get* to his wife (Maim.

---

140 ודלמא אמלוכי אימלך וכתב
141 שלוחו של אדם כמותו
142 הרי פלוני שליח

Gerushin, 7:22; *Sh. Ar., Even ha-Ezer* 140:1).[142]

The effectiveness of an agent was, however, subject to some limitation. An agent could normally deputize a second man to perform the same task on his behalf (*Kid.* 41a–b). A distinction was made, however, between transferring to another agent an object entrusted with the first agent for a certain purpose and transferring the verbal instruction given to the agent. In principle it was laid down that a man could hand a written *get* to an agent with instructions to give it to his wife, and this *get* could then be passed on to a second agent.

A complication would arise in the following case. If a man said to two individuals, "Write a *get* for my wife and give it to her", they could write the *get* and effectively deliver it. As agents, however, they could not empower a third individual to discharge their task. Accordingly, they could not instruct a *sofer* to write the *get* on the husband's behalf; were the scribe to follow their instructions, even if they formally witnessed the *get*, no valid divorce would have been effected. The law required that the *get* be written solely on the husband's personal instructions. A duly appointed agent could write the *get* and entrust its delivery to a second agent, since the *get* itself was a transferable object, but verbal instructions lacked actual substance and an agent did not have the power to transmit something insubstantial to a deputy.[143] The ruling in this case was that the agent could not transfer words addressed to himself, as if the second agent had received them from the principal (*Git.* 66b).[144]

A possible reason for this limitation was that while the husband might rely on these individuals to fulfil his request, he might feel embarrassed if his message was passed on to any other individual.[145] Any transfer of the agency to a second person would therefore lack his personal consent. In the case under discussion, the husband had chosen those who should

---

143 מילי לא ממסרן לשליח
144 אין שליח עושה שליח
145 משום בזיון דבעל

write the *get* and no one else; it would thus have been written
without his consent. This ran counter to a basic law of divorce,
and the *get* was therefore invalid (*Git.* 29a, 66b; *Kid.* 41a–b;
Maim. *Gerushin* 9:31; *Sh. Ar., Even ha-Ezer* 141:38, 43).

Capacity of an Agent – Sheliḥut

Both the husband and the wife may, in the presence of
witnesses, appoint an agent to give or receive the *get*. Any adult
Israelite, man or woman, may serve as the agent (*shali'aḥ*) for
this purpose.

The following, however, are excluded: a deaf mute, a
lunatic, a minor, a blind person, a heathen and a Canaanite
slave.[146] Women have the full capacity to act as agents,
though preferably when they are not related to either party;
even if they are related, however, the *get* is valid. A minor
is excluded because he still lacks understanding (*da'at*) and
he is specifically disqualified by the Biblical reference from
which the law of agency derives, requiring a "man" and not
a minor (*Kid.* 42a). A blind person is excluded because he is
unable to identify the parties involved.

Nevertheless, the Sages sought to widen the possibility
of using an agent for a *get*. Neither those who were lax in
their religious observance nor those who might otherwise
be disqualified as witnesses were excluded from *sheliḥut*.
According to some opinions, even a *get* delivered by an
apostate (*mumar*) was valid, since being an Israelite (*ben
berit*) was the essential requirement.

In the case of someone who lacked an agent's capacity
when receiving the *get*, such as a minor, a lunatic or a blind
person, the *get* remained invalid even if the said agent outgrew
or overcame his impediment. The agent had to have the
requisite capacity at the time of his appointment. Any sickness

occurring thereafter would not disqualify him, provided that he was fit when giving or receiving the *get*. In later years it was ruled that a husband could mail his *get* to a suitable *shali'ah*, who would then deliver it for him (*Git.* 23a, Rashi; Maim. *Gerushin* 6:6; *Sh. Ar., Even ha-Ezer* 141:31–34).

Specific and General Instructions to the Agent

The authority exercised by a lawful agent in discharging his commission is no less than that of the principal carrying out the same task (*Ber.* 34b; *Kid.* 41a; Maim. *Ishut* 3:14 and *Terumah* 4:1; *Git.* 62b).[147] Whatever the principal does himself he can do by means of an agent.

The Sages derived this rule from the law of the Paschal lamb, which states: "The whole assembly of the congregation of Israel shall kill it" (Ex. 12:6). One person obviously slaughtered the lamb on the entire congregation's behalf, and such an agency was accepted. The Sages also inferred this law from the Torah's statement concerning divorce, which includes the phrase: "And he shall send her out of his house" (Deut. 24:1).[148] They held *ve-shillehah* ("he shall send her") to be superfluous in the context, understanding – by a play on the words – that its inclusion was meant to imply that the divorce could be effected by an agent, or even a third person to whom the agent delegated his authority, since the husband's only concern was the woman's departure from his home (*Kid.* 41a).[149]

The valid nature of this authority depends, however, on the agent's acting in conformance with his principal's instructions.[150] It is usually assumed that an agent follows the

---

147 שלוחו של אדם כמותו
148 ושילחה מביתו
149 מלמד שהוא עושה שליח – מלמד ששליח עושה שליח
150 עושה שליחותו
151 חזקה שליח עושה שליחותו

directive given to him.[151] If he deviates from this in any way, his actions are not binding on his principal and the agent must accept full responsibility for what he has done.[152]

If the principal asked his agent to contravene a religious law, the agent himself would be responsible for this transgression and could not maintain that he was only acting on someone else's behalf (*Hag.* 10b; *Kid.* 42b; *Mel.* 20a).[153]

[General references: *Jewish Encyclopaedia* (1925 ed.), "Divorce", Vol. 4; "*Get*", Vol. 5; *Encyclopaedia Judaica*, "Agency", 2:349–354; "Divorce", 6:122–136]

The Courtyard as Agent – *Hatzer*

There is a general rule that if an article is placed in someone else's house or courtyard, the recipient acquires it (*Sh. Ar., Hoshen Mishpat* 268:3).[154] Such an acquisition is effected even if the householder was not present at the time and knew nothing about it, as in the case of a stray animal entering his property. However, the courtyard has to be under his direct control and adjacent to his house, not somewhere distant like an open field. The rule applied to a "guarded courtyard",[155] but not to an open, unguarded place (*BM* 11a; *Sh. Ar., Hoshen Mishpat* 243:20).[156]

This form of acquisition, the receipt of an article on one's property, is based on the legal consideration that a woman's courtyard is an extension of "her hand" (Deut. 24:1, *Sifrei ad loc.*; *Git.* 77a–b).[157] The courtyard (*hatzer*) is also considered to be her agent,[158] the Sages deriving this principle from the Biblical law that when a stolen article was found in the hand

---

152 שליח שלא עשה שליחותו

153 אין שליח לדבר עבירה

154 חצרו של אדם קונה לו

155 חצר משתמרת

156 שדהו שאינה משתמרת

157 חצר משום ידה אתרבאי

158 שחצר משום שליחות אתרבאי

of the thief, he had to repay the owner twofold. The wording here is "If the theft be found in his hand" (Ex. 22:3).[159] This, the Sages explained, could not mean only if it was found "in his hand" but must surely also refer to stolen items discovered anywhere on his property, on his roof, or in his courtyard (*BK* 65a).[160]

Now according to early Biblical law, the husband or his agent could deliver the *get* into the woman's possession even without her consent. Thus, if it was thrown into the courtyard of her house while she was there, the courtyard was said to acquire the *get* on her behalf and she was thereby divorced (*Git.* 21a; 77a; Maim. *Gerushin* 5:12; *Sh. Ar., Even ha-Ezer* 139:1; *Arukh ha-Shulḥan, Even ha-Ezer* 139:12).

Later, however, the Sages ruled that according to the interdict of Rabbenu Gershon her consent to receive the *get* was necessary. She had to have knowledge of the giving of the *get*, so that she could decide what was her wish concerning it.

In one particular instance, a *get* which was placed in a woman's courtyard also referred to the conveyance of a gift that the husband wished to give her. According to Biblical law, the *get* was an acquisition through which she had been divorced as soon as it was placed in her *ḥatzer*. But the inclusion of the gift complicated the situation.

The receipt of any gift depends on the willingness of the recipient to accept it. Therefore, the general rule is given that one cannot convey a gift to a person who does not wish to receive it (Maim. *Zekhiyyah* 4:2).[161] Thus, if the wife had no wish to accept her husband's gift, the courtyard could not be regarded as her agent for acquiring the document; and if the courtyard was rejected, it could not receive the *get* on her behalf. Had she accepted the gift, she would have recognized the *ḥatzer* as the agent (*shali'aḥ*) empowered to acquire the

---

159 אם הימצא תימצא בידו
160 גגו וחצרו
161 אין נותנים מתנה לאדם בעל כורחו

get for her, which in turn would automatically effect her divorce. However, since she was entitled to refuse a gift, and had not empowered the *ḥatzer* to acquire it as her agent, the *ḥatzer* could likewise not serve as her agent to acquire the *get*. Consequently, she had not received the *get* and was therefore not divorced (*Git.* 21a, Rashi, "*be'al korḥah leta*"; Maim. *Gerushin* 5:18; *BB* 138a, "*i efshi bahen*"; Maim. *Zekhiyyah* 4:2).

K. Mental Capacity

Mental Illness with Lucid Intervals

The execution of a divorce requires the husband's consent to give the *get*. In basic law it was only the husband's consent that was necessary; but later, by the ordinance of R. Gershom (10th cent.), *ḥerem d'Rabbenu Gershom*, a wife could not be divorced without her consent. The divorce of an insane man or woman is (like marrying them) invalid. However, in the case of one who is only weak-minded, it is valid. Should the husband become insane after the marriage had been duly contracted, he cannot effectively agree to the divorce and is therefore incapable of signing it. Had he already been certifiable when the marriage took place, such a union would be declared null and void. Obviously, in that case, no *get* would be necessary (*Yev.* 112b; Maim. *Gerushin* 2:17, *Ishut* 4:9).[162]

The Sages realized that a husband might simply possess lower than average intelligence[163] without being of unsound mind. That need not prevent him from entering into a marriage or executing a divorce, as the same capacity would be effective in both actions. They also discussed the case of

---

162   מי שנשא כשהוא פיקח ונתחרש ואין צריך לאמר נשתטה אינו מוציא לעולם עד
שיבריא
163   דעתה קלישתא
164   עתים חלים עתים שוטה

an insane individual who had periods of mental clarity.[164] A regulation was enacted, governing the validity of all religious duties (*mitzvot*) which that individual performed. Thus, if it transpires that such a person's mind was lucid when he fulfilled the *mitzvah*, that individual is deemed legally competent, and the *mitzvah* had been fully performed (*RH* 28a; *Yev.* 113a).[165]

In matters of divorce and *halitzah*, both parties must fully understand the significance of their actions. Thus, during one of his lucid intervals, a mentally disturbed person would be capable of giving his own consent instead of merely acting according to instructions given to him (*RH* 28a; *Yev.* 102b, 113a; Maim. *Yibbum* 4:16). Although the Rabbinic codifiers had determined that an insane man or woman could effect neither *kiddushin* nor divorce (*Sh. Ar., Even ha-Ezer* 44:2), the REMA, however, in his annotation (*ibid.*) in the name of Rabbenu Yeruham ben Meshullam, quoting the authority of REMAH (R. Yisrael Meir Halevi) laid down that if the deranged or retarded person's mind had a remission and was lucid, even if it was of low intelligence, during the execution of the *get*, that *get* would be valid, since the Rabbis were anxious to release the wife from unbearable hardship (*Git.* 67b; Maim. *Ishut* 4:9; *Sh. Ar., Even ha-Ezer* 44:2, REMA *ad loc.*; R. Yosef ibn Lev, responsa, no. 11).

Temporary Insanity

The giving of a *get* is valid only if the husband was of sound mind throughout the procedure.[166] If his normally rational mind was disturbed at the time,[167] his action had no meaning.[168]

Although there is no doubt that one who is totally insane (*shoteh*) does not have the capacity to give a *get*, the Sages

---

165   יצא ידי חובתו
166   דעתה צלילותא
167   רוח רעה מבעתת אותו
168   לא אמר כלום

had to reach a decision about someone whose mind was temporarily disturbed – such as by a sudden fit of apoplexy (*kurdikus*), or a temporary unbalance of mind by the onset of a stupor (*tunba*). If he was in a normal frame of mind when he gave instructions for his wife's *get* to be written, but suffered an apoplectic fit before the execution of the *get* had been completed, opinions among the Sages regarding the *get's* validity were divided.

Resh Lakish declared that this man had been fully competent to issue his instructions, and therefore they should be followed and the writing of the *get* completed, as we do in the case of a mortally sick person (*shekhiv me-ra*). In this case his incapacity was only transient, and it may be compared to the case of someone who fell asleep while the writing was being done.[169]

R. Yoḥanan, however, decreed that the writing of the *get* should be postponed until the man recovered from his seizure. The entire procedure was subject to this man's full capacity and understanding, but during the period in question he had been of unsound mind.

The Sages mainly ruled according to the judgment of R. Yoḥanan, as did Maimonides in his code, requiring full mental capacity throughout the *get*'s preparation. A similar incapacity would disqualify an individual who was "blind drunk".[170] Thus, although the instructions given before he took ill were valid, the process of writing and delivering the *get* required a man's full mental competence. Once he recovered from the attack, his instructions remained in force and it would be proper to write the *get* for him (Maim. *Gerushin*, 2:15). The codes also adopted this ruling (*Git.* 70b, *Tos. s.v.* "*ha-tam*"; *Git.* 67b; Maim. *Peirush ha-Mishnayyot*; Maim. *Gerushin*, 2:15; *Tur, Even ha-Ezer* 121, *Bet Yosef ad loc.*).

Anything said by a person during a fit of apoplexy has no

---

169 מדמיי ליה לישן

170 שיכור שהגיע לשכרותו של לוט

171 מי שאחזו קורדייקוס ואמר כתבו גט לאשתו, לא אמר כלום

meaning, since he is held to be incapable at the time.[171] If he gave instructions for the divorce prior to his seizure, but countermanded them during the attack, we comply with his first request and act accordingly. If, after having a stroke and losing the power of speech (*nishtatek*), he was asked whether the *get* should be written and nodded his head in approval,[172] the court would test his mental ability. Three questions would be put to him and, if he replied intelligently each time with a nod of his head,[173] his instructions would be deemed valid. The case of a *nishtatek* is not treated in the same way as that of a *heresh*: see below (*Git.* 67b, Rashi; Maimonides, Mishnah commentary; Maim. *Gerushin* 3:16, *Ishut*, 2:26).

Consent by a Deaf Mute – *Heresh*

The term *heresh* may be applied to someone who is either deaf[174] or dumb.[175] If a completely intelligent person, who was fully able to write and deliver a *get,* later fell victim to being deaf mute (*nishtatek*), he still maintained his full mental capacity (*Git.* 71a, Rashi, *Tos. s.v. "amar Rav Yosef"*, *"katani mi-hat ediyot"*).[176]

The codifiers ruled, according to Rabbenu Gershom that all cases of executing a *get* required the wife's consent, but in certain exceptional circumstances a particular need was met by the helpful adjustment of the law. In early law a deaf and dumb person (*heresh*) was considered to be lacking intelligence and therefore incompetent to give consent. A case which the Sages were asked to decide involved a young deaf and dumb girl (*hereshet*) who had been legally given in marriage by her father. If a divorce was later thought necessary, the Sages ruled

---

172 והרכין בראשו
173 על לאו לאו, ועל הן הן
174 מדבר ואינו שומע, שיכול לדבר מתוך הכתב
175 אילם – שומע ואינו מדבר
176 זה וזה הרי הן כפיקחין לכל דבר

that this mentally handicapped girl could nevertheless receive her *get*.[177] Since Biblical law, had permitted the giving of a *get* without the wife's consent, although the law was later made subject to Rabbinic limitations, the Sages availed themselves of this flexibility in this unusual situation in order to rescue an unfortunate woman from her predicament (Mish., *Ed.* 7:9, Bertinoro and *Tiferet Yisrael ad loc.*; *Git.* 55a, Rashi).

In the course of this law's development it was resolved that deaf and dumb adults, male or female, could be married halakhically and likewise divorced through the use of sign language. The Rabbis understood that such people were not necessarily lacking in intelligence, and that only a tragic defect prevented them from voicing their wishes (*Yev.* 112b; Maim. *Gerushin* 10:23).

Child Marriage

It is an accepted rule that a minor lacks the capacity to change his or her status by independently contracting a marriage (*Kid.* 50b). If such a marriage ever took place, it would be nugatory and no *get* was therefore required for its dissolution (*Yev.* 112b; *Sh. Ar., Even ha-Ezer* 43:1).

Biblical law permitted a minor girl over the age of 12 and up to the age of 12 years and six months and one day (*na'arah*) to be married on her father's authority (*Kid.* 79a; *Sh. Ar, Even ha-Ezer* 37:1–2). Once they reached puberty, however, a boy aged 13 (*gadol*) and a girl above the age of 12 years and six months (*bogeret*) could contract their own marriage. Although a male was obliged to fulfil all precepts from the age of 13 (*bar mitzvah*), the Sages ruled that the duty to marry was incumbent on males only from the age of 18 (*Sh. Ar., Even ha-Ezer* 1:3, *Bet Yosef ad loc.*).

On the basis of a Scriptural passage referring to the marriage of an under-age girl contracted by her parents, the Sages ruled

---

177   אין לה דעת

that a father had the right to give his minor daughter in marriage to a man of his choice (Deut. 22:16; *Ket.* 46b; *Sh. Ar., Even ha-Ezer* 37:1).[178] They were nevertheless opposed to the father's unrestricted right to give his daughter in marriage without obtaining her consent. R. Yehudah declared in the name of Rav: "A father is not allowed to contract such a marriage for his minor daughter until she reaches the age of puberty and expresses her consent, declaring that this is the man whom she wishes to marry" (*Kid.* 41a; *Sh. Ar., Even ha-Ezer* 37:8; see the previous chapter).[179]

According to the Sages, when a minor girl was fatherless (*yetomah*), or the father had left the country, or when his authority had automatically ceased after her first betrothal,[180] the mother and brothers were empowered to effect *kiddushin* for her, provided that she had agreed to the marriage (*le-da'atah*). Without her consent, however, the marriage would be nugatory (*Tur, Even ha-Ezer* 37, BA<u>H</u>, '*ketanah*').[181]

Whether she, as a minor, had the mental capacity to enter such a marriage was debated by the Sages. Did she grasp the significance of her *kiddushin* and was she sensible enough to look after it?[182] If an intelligent minor wanted to reject the man, she could do so by clearly expressing her refusal (*mi'un*). The assumption was that a child under the age of six lacked such understanding and no *kiddushin* would have been effected; she could thus leave the husband even without *mi'un*. Over the age of ten, she was credited with understanding and the statutory *mi'un* would therefore be necessary. Between the ages of six and ten her intelligence would have to be tested (*Yev.* 107b, Bertinoro, *Tosefot Yom Tov ad loc.*; Maim. *Gerushin* 11:7).

Nevertheless, owing to the social and economic conditions of Diaspora life, a father might be hard pressed to find a suitable husband for his daughter. He was therefore encouraged to

---

178 קטנה או נערה
179 עד שתגדל ותאמר בפלוני אני רוצה
180 יתומה בחיי אביה
181 אינה מקודשת כלל
182 יכולה לשמור קידושיה

arrange her marriage with someone of whom he approved, even when the girl was under age, in order to safeguard her interests, protect her from unscrupulous men and prevent her from remaining unmarried or becoming an *agunah* (*Kid.* 41a, *Tos. s.v. "asur"*; *Sh. Ar., Even ha-Ezer* 37:8, REMA).

If a minor girl's father had her betrothed,[183] either he or she could receive her *get*. Whether she herself accepted the *get* depended once again on her ability to grasp its significance and keep it safe.[184] She would not possess that capacity if (for example), after her divorce, she did not understand that she must steer clear of her ex-husband's house; or if she could not tell the difference between throwing away a stone that someone gave her and keeping an edible nut (*Git.* 6:2, Rav, *Tosefot Yom Tov, Tiferet Yisrael ad loc.*).[185]

Even if a minor orphan girl had been given in marriage by her mother and brothers, and she had consented to her betrothal, she was entitled to reject the prospective husband during her minority without the need for a *get*. All that she required was the simple procedure of "refusal" (*mi'un*), whereby her refusal to marry this man was expressed before two witnesses, who made a declaration to that effect in a statutory certificate handed to her (*get mi'un*). She could do so at the very last moment until she reached her puberty (*ad sh'higdilah*) even after her *kiddushin,* and although full arrangements for her marriage [the *kiddushin*] had already been made (*Yev.* 107b–108a; Maim. *Ishut* 4:8, *Gerushin* 11:11, *Maggid Mishneh ad loc.*; *Even ha-Ezer, Arukh ha-Shulhan* 155, sect.10).

The effect of *mi'un* is not divorce, but annulment of the marriage *ab initio*. If the girl had been married without her consent or understanding, the marriage could be annulled even without *mi'un*. If, after her minority, she objected to the marriage and had not previously exercised her right of *mi'un,* she would require a statutory *get* (Maim. *Ishut* 11:6–8; *Sh. Ar.,*

---

183 נערה המאורסה
184 לשמור את גיטה
185 נותנין לה לצרור וזירקה וזירקה אגוז ונוטלה

Even ha-Ezer 155:1–3).

Bar Kappara thought it inadvisable to rely on the decision of a minor and suggested that the need for *mi'un* could be avoided altogether if one waited until she attained her majority (*bogeret*), when the court would then require the husband to give her a *get* (*Yev.* 109a, *Tos. s.v.* "*ve-yitrahaku*").

Prevailing social conditions later induced some later Rabbinic decisors (*posekim*) to sanction an act of "refusal" by a girl under the age of 12. Others, however, felt that relying on the child's common sense and intelligence was problematic. They therefore refused to authorize the cancellation of her legally performed marriage (Maim. *Ishut* 4:7,8; *Sh. Ar, Even ha-Ezer* 155:22).

Although modern Israeli law prohibits the marriage of a girl under the age of 16, the courts enjoy discretion in this matter (*Takkanah* of National Rabbinical Conference, Jerusalem, 1950; Knesset Marriage Age Law, 1950, 1960).

[General references: RITVA, *Sha'ar Efrayim* 112, "*mi'un*"; E. Scheftelowitz, *The Jewish Law of Family and Inheritance in Palestine* (Tel Aviv, 1945); B. Schereschewsky, *Dinei Mishpahah* (1967) pp. 41–51, 431*f.*; *Encyclopaedia Judaica*, Vol. 5, "Child Marriage", p.423]

L. The *Get* Written on a Tablet

The law states that a bill of divorce (*get*) which a man gives to his wife must be a document which belongs to him. Rami bar Hama, an amoraic Sage, raised the following question. A *get* was written on a writing tablet belonging to the woman as she and the man both held it. When the man released his hold, leaving the tablet entirely in her grasp, would that action be regarded as a valid conveyance of his *get* to her?[186]

The problem here was determining whether mentally she

---

186   היו מוחזקין בטבלה של האשה וגט כתוב עליה

had conveyed full ownership of the tablet to him when the *get* itself was in their joint possession, and he then gave it to her as a tablet belonging to him.

The Sages thought it unlikely that she had any conveyance in mind[187] and more probable that she never intended the tablet itself, which might be of some value, to reach him as a gift.[188] Thus, the tablet on which the *get* was written belonged to her and could not be used for the purpose of her divorce. In giving the *get* to his wife it is required that he must utilize a *get* which was his own property, in accordance with the Biblical expression, "he shall give" (*ve-natan beyadah*) (Deut. 24:1). The Sages concluded, however, that since she herself could write the text of her *get* and give it to him, because of her wish for a divorce, it seemed probable that she had indeed conveyed legal ownership to him so as to validate the *get* (*Git.* 20b–21a, Rashi *s.v. "lo yad'ah"*, *Tos. s.v. "ishah" ad loc.*; *Sh. Ar, Even ha-Ezer* 124:7).

M. Precautions on Remarrying after the Death of a Husband

When depositions were needed in cases of marriage, death and divorce, the Sages occasionally modified the rules of evidence which required testimony by two witnesses that might not be available. In order to alleviate a woman's difficult situation (*Yev.* 25a),[189] the testimony of a single witness was accepted.[190]

The halakhic justification for this lenient measure was as follows. Though insufficient in itself, the evidence of one witness is supported by the axiom that a woman makes

---

187 לא ידעה להקנויה ליה
188 לא גמרה ומקנייה ליה
189 בעדות אשה הקלו בה רבנן
190 עד אחד נאמן
191 אשה דייקא ומינסבה

doubly sure of her legal position before she marries.[191] If only one person testified that her husband was no longer alive, the widow, knowing the grave consequences of an unlawful marriage, could be relied on to take great care to verify her husband's death before she remarried. The Sages therefore permitted her to remarry even on the evidence of a single witness.[192]

Mishnaic law deals with the case of a woman whose husband left home and traveled to a foreign land.[193] Subsequently, two or more people arriving from that country told her that he had died there. On the strength of their report she remarried, but her "deceased" husband eventually returned. Both men were required to divorce her: the first, because she had had extramarital relations, and the second, because she was already a married woman. Furthermore, she was penalized (*kenas*) for her action by losing the benefits of her *ketubbah*; and more seriously, the child whom she had borne to her second husband was declared illegitimate – a *mamzer*.

The Sages explained that although according to the halakhic rules of evidence her second marriage by the evidence of two witnesses was a valid marriage, requiring a *get* for its dissolution, the Sages explained that she was penalized because the law relies on a wife's efforts to ensure that the reported death of her husband is accurate. She had acted on her own responsibility, without due care in ascertaining the true facts, and without obtaining the prior consent of the *bet din*, which would have conducted a thorough investigation before sanctioning her remarriage.

The woman's marriage was deemed reliable on the understanding that she had already verified her legal capacity to get married.[194] According to a general rule enunciated by Maimonides, a woman will take good care not to impair her

---

192 הוחזקו להיות משיאין עד מפי עד... ותנן נמי עד אחד

193 האשה שהלך בעלה למדינת הים

194 אשה קא דייקא ונישאת

personal status (Maim. *Gerushin* 12:15; *Yev.* 25a, Rashi, and 87b, Rashi; Rabbi Yehezkel Abramsky, *Hazon Yehezkel* on *Tosefta*: *Yevamot ibid.*).[195]

N. Mental Surrender of the *Ketubbah*

A widow is entitled to be paid the amount written in her *ketubbah* from her late husband's estate. If the heirs are unable to pay the full amount, she is entitled to be duly maintained from the property of his heirs.[196]

If she wishes to continue living in her husband's house, she may do so and the heirs are obliged to provide for her maintenance there in line with the standard and dignity to which she is accustomed. They cannot ask her to leave the house and return to her father's home, or to move to a less expensive place where they would continue to maintain her (Maim. *Ishut* 17:2).

Alternatively, if she does wish to live in her father's house, the heirs must provide her maintenance there. In the meantime, she is still entitled to receive payment of her *ketubbah* from them. If, however, she had not demanded payment of the *ketubbah* for a long time, her failure to do so may perhaps indicate that she had waived her claim and surrendered her *ketubbah* (*mahelah*).

The Sages differed over their interpretation of her thoughts, depending on whether she still lived in her late husband's house or in her father's. They accepted the ruling that as long as she remained in the husband's house, she was entitled to claim her *ketubbah* even though she might not have claimed the payment of her *ketubbah* for a period of 25 years, they assumed that the reason why she had not demanded it from the heirs for that long period might be her reluctance to strain her amicable relations with them; even so, she had never forgone

---

what was due to her and she had always retained the right to receive the full amount of her *ketubbah* and that right would continue to remain hers.

If, however, she lived in her father's house where she would feel no such embarrassment with the heirs, and she had not demanded her *ketubbah* for 25 years, she lost her claim to it. The Sages assumed that her continued silence (*shetikah*) over such a long period of time indicated that, without saying so, she had mentally surrendered it, and therefore her claim was no longer tenable. If she remained with her father and the heirs were assiduous in providing for her and there was no question of ill feeling between them, she might have been embarrassed to make her claim, but that did not mean that she waived it. If, she had retained the deed of her *ketubbah*, that emphasized the continuation of her right, enabling her to produce it as evidence and collect whatever was due to her at any time (*Ket.* 104a, Bertinoro *ad loc.*).

There was a difference of opinion among the Sages on this subject. R. Meir held that so long as she was in her father's house she could always claim her *ketubbah*, but if she was in her late husband's house she could collect her *ketubbah* only if she claimed it within 25 years. The Sages, however, ruled on the contrary that if she was in her husband's house she could always have the right to collect her *ketubbah*, but if she lived in her father's house she could do so only for a period of 25 years. Caro in his code ruled that in her father's house her claim was limited to 25 years, but in her husband's house the period of her claim was unlimited (*Ket.* 104a; *Sh. Ar, Even ha-Ezer* 101:1).

O. Annulment of a Marriage

In order to safeguard family life and prevent undue suffering, the Sages enacted a law empowering the *Bet Din* to nullify a marriage when legal complications made the normal delivery of a *get* impossible.

This process of annulment was unlike the procedure in a divorce, where the *kiddushin* remained valid until abrogated by the *get*, as Torah law enjoined in such cases. Through this new process the original act of *kiddushin* was itself revoked *ab initio*,[197] as if the marriage had never been effected (*Ket.* 3a, Rashi and *Tos.*, "*Hafla'ah*" ad loc. [*Sefer Hafla'ah* by R. Pinhas Ha-Levi Hurwitz]; *Yev.* 110a, Rashi; *Git.* 33a, Rashi and *Tos. s.v. "afke'inhu"*).

The court's ability to apply this sanction is inherent in the original act of *kiddushin*, where the man declares that his *kiddushin* is subject to whatever ruling the *bet din* issues in regard to its validity, affirming that his marriage will be "according to the laws of Moses and of Israel".[198] His *kiddushin* would therefore be contingent on the Sages' approval and, if that condition was not met, no *kiddushin* would have been effected. Such a condition in *kiddushin* was recognized as binding; for example, the man said, "I betroth you on condition that your father agrees to the celebration of our marriage". The effectiveness of the marriage would thus depend on the father's approval.

Rabbinical exegetes felt that the man might seek to evade this ordinance by making a mental reservation to the effect that, from the very outset, he did not intend his marriage to be dependent on the Rabbis' approval and was not bound by such a condition. The Sages declared, however, that they could impose legal sanctions to invalidate the *kiddushin*, such as an expropriation order depriving the man of his *kesef kiddushin* retroactively, on the principle that the bet din could declare an object ownerless, and so this requirement was lacking.[199] Alternatively, they could declare that his intercourse with the woman, by which he intended to consummate the marriage, was simply an act of fornication.[200]

In their humane concern to rescue the woman and her

---

197 הקידושין נעקרין מעיקרן
198 כדת משה וישראל
199 הפקר בית דין הפקר
200 שויוה רבנן בעילתו בעילת זנות

children from the tragic plight that had befallen them through no fault of her own, the Sages resorted to every possible legal fiction that might relieve the woman's distress. Although their enactment apparently contravened Biblical law, the Sages were convinced that such a benevolent interpretation of the law was what the Torah really desired. In practice, both the mediaeval codifiers and all later Rabbinical authorities adopted the same approach.

The man's intent and action were thus overruled. The Sages justified the use of their prerogative to revoke the original *kiddushin* on the grounds that this measure was necessary to save the woman from becoming a "chained wife" (*agunah*), confined to a state of limbo where neither marriage nor divorce would be possible (*Git.* 33a).[201] Since whatever stipulation the husband may have had in mind could not be ascertained, the validity of the get was doubtful. The result would be irreparable suffering for the woman and the stigma of bastardy (*mamzerut*) attached to any children born to her if, in the belief that she was divorced, this woman subsequently remarried. Furthermore, a dissolute woman who chose not to await the court's ruling might hastily marry another man – *mi-shum peritzut* (*Ket.* 3a, Rashi and *Tos.*; *Yev.* 90b, 110a; *Git.* 33a, 73a; *BB* 48a).

An annulment is not the same as a declaration of nullity (*battel*). If it could be shown that the marriage entered into was totally prohibited – due to incest, for example, or some other relationship prohibited by Biblical law, as well as marriage with a non-Jew – the court decreed that no marriage had taken place (Maim. *Ishut*, 1:6–7). The Sages extended this judgment to a further category, that of a Rabbinically prohibited marriage, where the bet din could impose the granting of a divorce at the instance of either party (*Ket.* 77a; Maim. *Ishut* 25:12; *Sh. Ar.*, *Even ha-Ezer* 154:1–2).

---

201   מפני תקנת עגונות

P. Condition in Divorce – *Hamegaresh al tenai*

Just as it is possible under certain circumstances to stipulate some condition when contracting a marriage (*Sh. Ar., Even ha-Ezer* 38:1*ff.*), so it is possible to effect a divorce which is dependent on the fulfillment of certain conditions. When that condition is fulfilled the *get* that he had given her comes immediately into force and she is divorced; if it is not fulfilled no divorce takes place (Maim. *Gerushin* 8:1*ff.*; *Sh. Ar., Even ha-Ezer* 143:1*ff.*). The laying down of such conditions would be governed by the particular halakhic rules prescribed by the Sages (*Sh. Ar., Even ha-Ezer* 38:1–4). By their non-fulfillment the divorce is non-effective. The entire validity of his *get* was contingent on the realization of the condition he had stipulated. If that condition had not been fulfilled he had no intention that there should be any *get*. Thus, a bill of divorce which lacked his will to divorce, had no force, and was null and void (*batul*) (*Sh. Ar., Even ha-Ezer* 143:1, 2).

In all matters concerning a *get* the greatest care is observed to ensure its validity and to protect the wife from future complications. The Sages ruled that a man traveling out of his country on a sea voyage, or joining a caravan traveling into the desert, or anyone whose life is put in danger, is exhorted to give a *get*, or to instruct an agent to give the *get*, on the condition that if he did not return within a certain time the *get* would become effective (*Git.* 65b; *Sh. Ar., Even ha-Ezer* 154:8). The removal of any doubt concerning the validity of such a *get* would be a particularly severe matter in the light of the Rabbinical enactment that a plea of accident (*oness*), such as a failure in the means of transportation or some other unexpected damage, did not avail in divorce. The Sages ruled that if a man gives a *get* to his wife on the stipulation that if he does not return within a particular period of time, that *get* would come into effect and no excuse of any undesired prevention would be accepted (*Git.* 34a; *Sh. Ar., Even ha-Ezer* 144:1).

In view of the various doubts that may arise regarding the compliance with all the regulations concerning a conditional *get*, and the uncertainty as to exactly what had been in his mind at the time when he stipulated his condition, the Sages discouraged the making of such a conditional *get* in any circumstances. In the light of practical experience, however, the *bet din* was sometimes requested to approve the arrangement of a conditional *get* in exceptional circumstances. In times of persecutions when a husband might be compelled to separate from his wife, not knowing whether he may be able to return to her or not, he would wish to adopt the procedure of giving his wife a *get* on the condition that it would be effective if he failed to return.

A Jewish soldier going out to battle and, realizing the possibility of his non-return, would wish to protect his wife from a possible difficulty in obtaining the necessary *ḥalitzah,* according to the laws of a levirate marriage, which would apply if he died without children, but would not apply if she had already been divorced. The halakhic law would require that he gave his wife a divorce before he left. But he loved his wife and had no desire whatsoever to divorce her, but rather to protect her from a difficulty which could prevent her remarriage, since without receiving *ḥalitzah* she would be tied to a brother-in-law who had not fulfilled his duty, and she would not be permitted to marry anyone – *agunah.* In these circumstances the court would agree to grant such a *get* conditionally, to become effective if he did not return within some specified period. If he had thus divorced his wife, and she had not married another husband there would be no impediment to the soldier's remarriage with her, providing that he was not a *kohen* (Lev. 21:7) (*Yev. Tosefta,* 6; *Yev.* 85b; *Git.* 81a). There would be, however, a restriction to remarriage if the court had ruled for some reason of impropriety that she was obliged to be divorced, hence the *get* would have been final as far as that husband was concerned (*Ket.* 74b, Rashi, *Tos.*; *Ket.* 76b).

Even in this exceptional case the halakhic authorities insisted that the terminology of the *get* should contain a statement that the *get* was fully effective from the moment that he wrote the *get* and handed it to her. The husband himself, before leaving was required to state that the divorce is completed now (*me'akhshav*), after which there is no possibility of making any change or condition in the divorce (Maim. *Gerushin* 8:1).

Although R. Judah Hanasi maintained that the words, "on condition that", implied the same meaning as saying "now", the general ruling of the Sages was that the words "on condition that" (*al menat*), did not have the same meaning as saying "now" (*me'akhshav*) (*Git.* 74b, *Tos.* "*ademiflegi*").

In view of the many differences of opinion among the halakhic authorities regarding the legality of each detail of the divorce procedure, it has been generally accepted that the soldier referred to would always give an unconditional divorce taking immediate effect. At the same time, in order to maintain confidence in each other, the couple were encouraged to give a solemn promise to each other, even on pain of a *herem* (ban of excommunication), that when he returned from battle they would both remarry again. The halakhic compilation of the *Mordekhai* (Mordecai ben Hillel, 13th cent.) quotes the ruling of Rabbi Itzhak of Paris that it was advisable that no form of conditional *get* should be entered into (*Gittin* chap. sect. 427); which ruling was followed by the REMA in his gloss on the *Shulhan Arukh* (*Even ha-Ezer* 145:9) (*Mirkevet Hamishnah* on Maimonides *Gerushin* 8:1, *Maggid Mishneh ad loc.*; Shmuel Ehrenfeld, *Hidushei Hatan Sofer,* sect. 22, 1, 14).

The practice of a soldier giving his wife a conditional *get* was based on the historical ruling of the Sages that whoever went out to fight the wars of the House of David, before leaving wrote a *get* to his wife; as it was explained in the incident of David and Uriah, the husband of Batsheva (2 Sam. 11:3,15, Rashi, *ad loc.*; *Shab.* 56a, Rashi *ad loc. s.v. shebikesh Tos. ad loc. s.v. "get keritut"*).[202]

---

202 א"ר יונתן כל היוצא למלחמת בית דוד כותב גט כריתות לאשתו

In general circumstances, in order to save a woman from becoming an *aguna*, rendering her a woman of intermediate status, being both married and not married, the court was authorized to solve her dilemma by cancelling her original marriage altogether. They did this by withdrawing the *kiddushin* that the husband gave her.[203] This was done by forfeiting his original payment of *kesef kiddushin*, so that no *kiddushin* had taken place, according to the principle that the court has the right to forfeit the possession of an individual (*Git.* 36b).[204]

When a sick man said to his wife: "This is your get, if I die from this illness within twelve months",[205] the Sages required that his divorce must come into effect immediately according to the date written in the *get*. When he gave it to her he meant that the divorce would take place just before he died. His intention was to delay the divorce till the last moment of his life. In his mind he thought that so long as he was alive he did not want to be divorced from his wife. The Sages said, however, it appeared that he wanted the *get* to apply only after his death; but once he had died he could not then give her a *get*. They insisted that he had to agree that the get should be fully effective immediately when he gave it to her; and therefore in making his condition he must declare "this is your get from today", or "from now" (*Git.* 72a, 73b, *Tos. 'amar Rabbah'*).[206] If his death was caused not by his illness but by some unusual external accident, such as if his house collapsed on him, or he had been bitten by a poisonous snake, the condition that had been placed on the get on the result of his illness, did not take effect, and the *get* which she had received was an unconditional *get*, and she had thereby been divorced (*Git.*73a).[207] A problem was discussed whether the husband had meant "particularly from this illness", or

---

203   אפקעינהו רבנן קידושין מיניה

204   הפקר בית דין הפקר

205   זה גיטך אם מתי מחולי זה

206   מהיום אם מתי מעכשיו אם מתי

207   אם לא אעמד מחולי זה ונפל אליו הבית הרי זה גט

whether it was only the obtaining circumstances of his illness which had prompted him to give the *get*, but in his mind he had meant if for any reason he had died the *get* should be effective. On the other hand it was maintained that such a particularly exceptional event could not have been part of his thinking at all. Because of such uncertainties it was advised that such a conditional *get* should always be avoided (*Git.*73a, Rashi, *Tos.* *"eitiveih"*; Maim. *Gerushin* 9:16–20; *Sh. Ar., Even ha-Ezer* 145:1–10).

It has been seen that a *get* which was conditional on such an event as the payment of money, or an act, or conduct was dependent on whether it had been carried out by one of the betrothed couple. A further case was considered by the Sages when the condition placed on the marriage in the first place was not subject to their own action but to the agreement of a third person, so that if that agreement had not taken place the marriage would have no effect. The Mishnah ruled as follows: He stated, "I give you this *kiddushin* on condition that my father will agree to this marriage". If his father agreed then the *kiddushin* was effective, but if he objected there was no marriage; so that if the couple wished to part no *get* would be necessary, and if they wished to continue in marriage he would have to give her a new *kiddushin*. If the father died before expressing any objection the *kiddushin* was valid, since the expression "if his father agreed" meant "if his father did not object"; and the father had expressed no objection. If the son died before the father had expressed his consent or refusal, and the opinion of the father was problematic, the validity of the marriage would be in doubt. The Sages, wishing to save the widow from any possible difficulty in obtaining *ḥalitzah*, would then urge the father to declare that he did not approve of the marriage, so that no marriage had taken place. In this case instead of having to rely on the *bet din* adopting some legal device in order to annul the marriage, the marriage was void, *ab initio – batel*, and therefore no *get* was required (*Sh. Ar., Even ha-Ezer* 38:8–10).

Q. Cancellation of *Kiddushin* by the *Bet Din– Afke'inhu Rabbanan lekiddushin mineih*

When the Sages discussed their ruling which prohibited any plea of failure to fulfil the condition they had agreed owing to some unavoidable accident (*oness*), they explained that this rule was intended to avoid a subterfuge pretext endangering the stability of family relationships. They considered the problem, however, that if a *get* was valid according to the Torah law, which accepted the plea of *oness*, on what authority did the Rabbis invalidate the *get,* which could result in a forbidden subsequent marriage of an already married woman. The Sages replied that since every *kiddushin* was made in the first place to be subject to the laws laid down by the Sages, as was declared at the marriage, *kedat mosheh v'yisrael*, the Sages were enabled to cancel the *kiddushin* which the husband had given, declaring that payment which had been intended as *kesef kiddushin* to be only a gift and not an act of *kiddushin*, and thus making a subsequent *get* superfluous. They were even empowered to declare his sexual union as an act of harlotry, and not a marriage (*Ket.* 3a, Rashi *ad loc. "d'medeorita"*).

A further situation may be when the husband sends a *get* to his wife by an agent, which according to Torah law could be canceled by the husband at any time prior to the wife receiving it. The Sages ruled that if the husband canceled it unknown to the wife or agent his cancellation was invalid, and the *get* remained in force. In the light of this halkhic problem the Rabbis forfeited his original *kiddushin* so that she was free to marry according to her choice. Such a remedy was justified in the light of the needs of orderly societal relationships – *mipnei tikun ha-olam* (*Git.* 33a). A similar ruling was given in a case of a dangerously ill man (*shekhiv mera*) who had given his wife a *get* conditionally on whether he died or recovered. Torah law permitted him on his recovery to withdraw the *get*, although the Rabbis forbade any such withdrawal. The legal remedy applied by the Sages was by canceling his original marriage by forfeiting his *kiddushin* resulting in her being an unmarried woman after she had received the *get* (*Git.* 73a, Rashi *ad loc.*).

Rabbinic law required that a woman may be married only with her consent (*Kid.*2b). According to basic law, however, even by the use of *force majure* the *kiddushin* would be valid, even if the man had put her under physical pressure to accept the marriage, such as by dangling her off the ground until she consented.[208] The Sages, however, invalidated such *kiddushin* stating that since he had acted improperly the Sages canceled his *kiddushin* (Maim. *Ishut* 4:1–2).[209] The marriage had originally taken place contrary to the law laid down by the Sages, and therefore Sages invalidated the *kiddushin* altogether (*BB* 48b). Later halakhic authorities, even in the gaonic period, questioned whether the Rabbis after the time of the Talmud also had the power of canceling a marriage by the means of the maxim of *afke 'inhu rabbanan lekiddushin mineih*. The recognized authorities in each country, however, instituted their own regulations regarding this matter, which were binding on all the members of their community (*Otzar ha-Geonim, Ketubot,* sect. 60).

There was another law governing the certification of the death of the husband. Where the Torah law would normally accept the evidence only of two valid witnesses, the Sages recognized the establishment of death even by the hearsay of one witness from another (*Ket.* 3a, RASHBA Part 1, sect. 1162). In exceptional cases of great hardship the Rabbis usually exercised flexibility in their halakhic rulings.

[General references: Maim. *Gerushin* chap. 8; *Shulḥan Arukh, Even ha-Ezer* chap. 143–145; R. Mosheh Sofer, *Ḥidushei Ḥatam Sofer, Gittin* 72a–75b; *Encyclopaedia Talmudica* Vol. 6 *s.v.* "*Gerushin*" sect. 12; *Encyclopaedia Judaica* Vol. 6 *s.v.* "Divorce" p. 133]

---

208   תליוה וקדיש קדושיו קדושין
209   הוא עשה שלא כהוגן ואפקעינהו רבנן לקידושין מיניה

Chapter 11

Oaths and Vows – *Nedarim*

11 Oaths and Vows – Nedarim

A. The Sanctity of Oaths and Vows

The truth or certainty of one's words was attested in ancient Israel by making a statement on oath, either voluntarily or as a court of law required. The oath (*shevu'ah*) was associated with an individual's plea for God to be his witness; it affirmed the truthfulness of his statement as well as his belief in the Creator's integrity. A false declaration (*shevu'at sheker*) would thus revile God's Name, making the perjurer guilty of sacrilege. Biblical law decreed: "Ye shall not swear by My Name falsely, so that thou profane the Name of thy God: I am the Lord" (Lev. 19:12).[1]

The truth of what a person said or meant by his utterance is known to the Almighty, and He judges the veracity of that man's oath. Biblical admonitions often stress man's responsibility before God by adding the words, "I am the Lord" – *Ani Hashem*. This indicates that while an individual's thoughts may be hidden and kept to himself,[2] the Almighty is aware of them (Lev. 19:14, Rashi *ad loc.*; *BM* 58b, Rashi *ad loc.*). "For He knoweth the secrets of the heart" (Ps. 44:22)[3] and, as man's Creator, He perceives anything that enters his mind (Ps. 94:11).[4]

The exhortation not to swear a false oath, and the dire consequences of transgression, are basically embodied in the Third Commandment: "Thou shalt not take the Name of the Lord thy God in vain" (Ex. 20:7; *Shev.* 39a).[5] Even if the

---

1   לא תשבעו בשמי לשקר, וחיללת את שם אל-היך

2   דבר המסור ללב

3   כי הוא יודע תעלומות לב

4   ה' יודע מחשבות אדם

5   לא תשא את שם ה' אל-היך לשוא

Divine Name itself was not uttered, but some kindred epithet (e.g., "the Eternal" or "All-seeing One"), the perjurer would be condemned for blasphemy – *hillul Hashem* (*Ned.* 2a; Lev. 19:12, *Midrash Torat Kohanim*; Maim. *Yad, Shevu'ot* 2:4).[6]

The gravity of this offence is reflected in the Talmudic law stating that perjury could not be expiated by sacrificial offerings or the Day of Atonement, unless it was specifically included in the offender's confession and repentance (*Shev.* 2a).

Anyone legally competent to bear witness in a disputed matter is adjured to give evidence before the *bet din* (rabbinical court). Failure to do so renders that person guilty in the sight of Heaven (*Sh. Ar., Hoshen Mishpat* 28:1). The court would nevertheless refrain from administering an oath to an individual suspected of habitual perjury (*Shev.* 45a; *Sh. Ar., Hoshen Mishpat* 92:3).

The law of Moses has a twofold aim: the well-being of the soul and the well-being of the body. Physical well-being is attained through harmonious relationships, the elimination of injustice and the establishment of healthful conditions that satisfy the material needs of mankind. The well-being of the soul is promoted by high-minded attitudes and opinions that are also imparted to one's fellow men.

Scripture, particularly the Decalogue, conveys the major highlights of those principles which lead to the true perfection of man. It teaches the unity, omniscience and omnipotence of God, and likewise trains man to cherish and express true opinions, thus enabling him to attain perfection (Maim. *Guide* 3:27–28).

While inculcating a belief in God's omnipotence, the Decalogue urges man to concentrate his thoughts on the glorious majesty of God and to regard Him with constant awe and deference. The Third Commandment therefore proclaims that one must never mention the Name of God casually, thoughtlessly or, above all, disrespectfully. According to this law, "Thou shalt not take the Name of the Lord thy God in vain" (Ex. 20:7).[7] The expression "in vain" refers to futile and meaningless oaths (*shevu'ot bittui*) – swearing, for example, that a pillar obviously carved from stone is made of gold or that it is a stone pillar, when no oath to that effect is necessary; or by giving other false or pointless testimony (*Shev.* 29a; Rashi, Ex. 20:7; Albo, *Ikkarim* 3:26).

One should always be mindful of the fact that nothing in the universe is comparable to the everlasting, omnipotent sovereignty of God. Any thought of or reference to His Name should accordingly reflect man's complete awe and reverence. One dare not speak lightly or thoughtlessly of God, as if He were some common topic or on the level of mortal man. The Torah stresses our obligation to revere the Lord in all our thoughts and actions. The injunction not to take His Name in vain makes any such offence punishable by flogging – *onesh malkot* (Ex. 20:7; *Shev.* 21a, 39a).

Associating the Name of God with a declaration that one knows to be false is blasphemy, constituting a denial of His sovereignty and omniscience. Vowing to do something also implies that one's word can be relied upon like a Divine assurance, and non-fulfilment of that vow is therefore a similar impious denial of God's truthfulness and omniscience.

The same risk of committing blasphemy is incurred when a person swears to do or abstain from something that is normally permitted, but which he now associates with a Divine prohibition; or when he undertakes to perform some voluntary act as though it were mandatory. The fulfilment or non-fulfilment of such an oath acquires the sanctity of Divine law. A person is similarly bound if he makes a vow (*neder*) to sanctify an object as Temple property or to forbid himself some item that would otherwise be permitted.

The Sages were deeply concerned about the grave result if one failed to abide by one's vows. R. Yehudah agreed with his colleagues that "it is better not to vow than to vow and not pay", although he maintained that "better than both is one who vows and pays". In R. Meir's opinion, however, "better than both is one who does not vow at all" (Eccles. 5:5; *Hul.* 2a; *Sefer ha-Ḥinnukh* 30, "*she-lo li-shava le-vattalah*").[8]

Torah law decreed that a man is duty - bound to fulfil every oath or vow that he undertakes, whether he voluntarily forbids himself some item or vows to treat something as holy or to dedicate some object as appropriate for the Temple. This law derives from the precept, "That which is gone out of thy lips thou shalt observe and do; according as thou hast vowed unto the Lord thy God, a freewill offering which thou hast promised with thy mouth" (Deut. 23:24).[9] A further basis of this law is the injunction: "When a man voweth a vow unto the Lord, or sweareth an oath to bind his soul with a bond, he shall not break his word; he shall do according to all that proceedeth out of his mouth" (Num. 30:3; Maim. *Yad, Nedarim* 1:4).[10]

Although the Torah basically ordained, "Thou shalt not take the Name of the Lord thy God in vain" (Ex. 20:7),[11] prohibiting false or disregarded oaths, another injunction was added: "Ye shall not swear by my Name falsely, so that thou profane the Name of thy God" (Lev. 19:12). Uttering the Lord's Name or alluding to Him in some vulgar remark was thus likewise forbidden (Rashi *ad loc.*; *Shab.* 120a; *Torah Temimah*, Ex. 20:7; *Shev.* 20b–21a).[12] This extra prohibition shows that the law applies not only to the actual misuse of God's Name using the express name of God, but also to any connotative word or phrase (Lev. 19:12, Rashi *ad loc.*; *Midrash Torat Kohanim ad loc.*; *Shev.* 20b).[13]

The prohibition extends to anything with a sacred implication – vowing that "this is forbidden to me as if it were a Temple sacrifice",[14] for example, or declaring that something

---

8   טוב אשר לא תדור משתדור ולא תשלם
9   מוצא שפתיך תשמור ועשית כאשר נדרת לה׳ אל-היך... נדבה אשר דברת בפיך
10   לא יחל דברו, ככל היוצא מפיו יעשה
11   לא תישא את שם ה׳ אל-היך לשוא
12   לא תשבעו בשמי לשקר, וחיללת את שם אל-היך, אני ה׳
13   לרבות את כל הכינויים
14   הרי עלי קורבן

is forbidden to that person as *konam* (i.e., *korban*) under a vow of abstinence (*Ned.* 2a, 10a; *Sh. Ar., Yoreh De'ah* 207:1).

The law would apply even if someone, far from utilizing any Divine Name, merely said "I undertake to do such-and-such"[15] or "I separate myself from... ". This is considered to be like grasping the handle of an object, and the speaker has accordingly bound himself with a vow. Such expressions are in fact called "handles of a vow" (*yadot*) and the prohibitive law fully applies to them (*Sh. Ar., Yoreh De'ah* 206).

Furthermore, if someone made up his mind[16] to offer a particular sacrifice, even without stating his intention, he is already obligated to fulfil that mental vow (*Shev.* 26b). Likewise, if he meant to give a certain sum to charity and failed to do so, he would incur the disgrace of breaking his word,[17] just as if the sworn promise of a Temple offering had been neglected (*RH* 6a).

In a case where the phrasing of a vow was ambiguous and open to different interpretations, the Sages resolved that the vow should be understood as it was evidently meant to apply when first undertaken.[18] Thus, if a man invited his friend to have a meal with him and the friend refused, vowing that he would not even accept a drop of water from him, he would be permitted to drink some water with the man. Why so? Because he meant to emphasize his unwillingness to partake of a meal with him, and that vow he was bound to fulfil. Likewise, if a man divorced his wife and vowed that she would never derive pleasure from him again, she might still receive some benefit from her ex-husband because he presumably meant to say that he would never remarry her (*Ned.* 63b; *Sh. Ar., Yoreh De'ah* 218:2, 4; *Shach ad loc.* 1).

The Biblical law enunciating the sanctity of a vow reads

---

15   הרי עלי
16   גמר בלבו
17   לא יחל דברו
18   הולכין אחר כוונת הנודר

as follows: "When thou shalt vow a vow unto the Lord thy God,[19] thou shalt not be slack to pay it; for the Lord thy God will surely require it of thee; and it would be sin in thee... . That which is gone out of thy lips thou shalt keep and perform; according as thou hast vowed freely unto the Lord thy God, which thou hast promised with thy mouth" (Deut. 23:22–24). Here, the solemn nature of the obligation is emphasized by its repetition in both positive and negative forms (Rashi *ad loc.*; *RH* 6a).[20]

Jewish Bible commentators (*mefareshim*) drew on human psychology to explain that when someone is bound by an oath, the evil inclination (*yetzer ha-ra*) urges him to disregard it on the pretext that this oath is not binding or that he never meant to fetter himself in that way. According to the Torah, whatever a person vows he must fulfil,[21] since the words issuing from his mouth reflect the thoughts present in his mind, which is equivalent to binding one's Divine soul. The Sages therefore taught that it is best not to make any vow involving a personal commitment,[22] because one runs the grave risk of sinning against God and profaning His Holy Name (Deut. 23:23, Ramban; *Or ha-Hayyim*; *Keli Yakar ad loc.*). The Rabbis even regarded the person making such a vow as a transgressor, even if he fulfilled that vow (*Ned.* 22a; RAN *ad loc.*; *Sh. Ar., Yoreh De'ah* 203:1).

This law is incumbent on men and women at all times (*Sefer ha-Hinnukh* 575). Apart from the moral obligation stated above, a vow becomes *legally* binding only when it is expressed verbally, and when the words accurately reflect the intention in a person's mind (*Sh. Ar., Yoreh De'ah* 210:1).

Every oath is considered to be most sacred. The Rabbis compared the remarkable effect of an oath which an individual imposed on himself to the binding power of a Divine command.

---

19   כי תידור נדר לה׳ אל-היך
20   לא תאחר לשלמו – מוצא שפתיך תשמור – ליתן עשה על לא תעשה
21   מוצא שפתיך תשמור ועשית
22   נדרי ביטוי

Just as the dedication of an offering to God makes that object forbidden to the donor, so does a self-imposed oath have the same effect or create an obligation that the swearer is duty-bound to fulfil. This new obligation becomes mandatory by the Torah law which ordains that "he must not break his word" (Num. 30:3)[23] and "according to all that he has expressed by his mouth he shall do" (*ibid*.).[24]

Stressing the inescapable duty to keep one's word, the Rabbis condemned any resort to some unexpressed mental reservation as a device (*ha'aramah*) to avoid fulfilling one's vow. Such deceitful behaviour was a major transgression of the law: "Keep thy distance from any false matter" (Ex. 23:7).[25]

It is related in the Talmud that a certain non-Jewish woman showed R. Yoḥanan how to prepare the remedy for a skin disease, on condition that he would not reveal the secret to anyone else. She asked him to swear an oath to the God of Israel that he would keep her secret and he swore accordingly, but then taught her method in the Academy. When the Rabbis rebuked him for violating his oath, R. Yoḥanan explained what he had meant: "to the God of Israel" he would not reveal the secret, but to His people he *would* make it known. The Rabbis warned him that such duplicity was forbidden; moreover, even if that excuse was offered to the non-Jewess when he swore his oath, conduct such as his resulted in *ḥillul Hashem*, the profanation of God's Name (*Yoma* 84a).

B. Covenant

Three great covenants were established between God and mankind. Having undertaken to protect His creatures, the Almighty expected man to obey His commands. Each

---

23   לא יחל דברו
24   ככל היוצא מפיו יעשה
25   מדבר שקר תרחק

covenant (*berit*) was accompanied by a dramatic sign which ensured its perpetuation. Man's allegiance to God as Creator of the universe (Gen. 1:1) was associated with *Shabbat*, the seventh day of rest (Ex. 31:15–17), an everlasting reminder of God's sovereignty. His promise that mankind would survive and increase after the Flood was marked by the rainbow's appearance in the sky (Gen. 9:11–16). The unique covenant between God and His people and between Israel and their God was hallowed at the Revelation on Mt. Sinai (Ex. 19:5–8) and ratified at the inception of Hebrew nationhood in the Land of Israel (Deut. 26:16–19).

This third covenant was marked by a solemn declaration of the blessing or curse that God would bestow according to the extent of Israel's obedience to, or violation of, His law. The Sages mentioned three occasions on which Israel entered into this Torah covenant: at Mount Sinai, at Mount Gerizim and on the Plains of Moab.[26] It was confirmed, as the life of Moses was nearing its end, by a further pledge of loyalty to God made by all the people of Israel, great and small, who were then ready to enter the Promised Land. This covenant, Moses declared, was binding on themselves and on all their future generations (Deut. 29:1, 9–14; *Ber.* 48b, Rashi *ad loc.*).[27]

Through an earlier covenant Abraham accepted the rite of circumcision (*berit milah*), demonstrating a steadfast belief in God. It was accompanied by God's promise to multiply Abraham's descendants, who would be given all the land of Canaan in perpetuity: "This is My covenant, which ye shall keep, between Me and you and thy seed after thee; every male among you shall be circumcised" (Gen. 17:6–14).[28]

Another type of compact, between two individuals, was the peace treaty made by Abraham and Abimelech, the Philistine king. It involved a solemn oath and an affirmation that "they two made a covenant" (Gen. 21:22–34).[29] When Abimelech

---

26 תורה ניתנה בשלוש בריתות
27 אתם נצבים היום כולכם לפני ה' אל-היכם
28 זאת בריתי אשר תשמרו ביני וביניכם ובין זרעך אחריך ימול לכם כל זכר
29 ויכרתו שניהם ברית

decided to renew the covenant with Abraham's son, Isaac, he urged: "Let there now be an oath betwixt us and thee, and let us make a covenant... " (Gen. 26:28, Rashi).[30] The Bible also records Joshua's solemn compact with the Gibeonites: "And Joshua made peace with them, and made a covenant with them, to let them live; and the princes of the congregation [representing the people of Israel] swore unto them" (Josh. 9:15).[31]

The idea of a covenant between God and His people is a special feature of the religion of Israel, charging Israel to bear an exclusive allegiance to God and His laws in all matters of faith, morality and observance, and in their adherence to truth and justice, both socially and nationally. Entering into the covenant is demonstrated by an oath of allegiance. At Sinai, where Moses administered the oath to Israel, we are told that "he took the book of the covenant, and read in the hearing of the people; and they said: 'All that the Lord hath spoken we shall do and obey'" (Ex. 24:7).[32]

The compact between God and His people was symbolized by dividing the blood of the sacrifices: one half was dashed against the altar and the other half sprinkled on the people (Ex. 24:6–8). This act represented the "cutting" of the covenant (*keritat ha-berit*). God's promise to Abraham, that he would inherit the Land of Israel, was likewise marked by dividing the sacrificial beasts in half, after which a flaming torch passed between them: "And he took all of these, and divided them in the midst, and laid each half against the other."[33] This ritual sanctified the oath as an inviolable covenant to be fulfilled under all circumstances (Gen. 15:7–10, RAMBAN *ad loc.*).

The Book of the Covenant (*Sefer ha-Berit*), the earliest assemblage of Biblical law, was the constitution governing the daily life of Israel (Ex. 24:7). The sacrificial blood represented

---

30   תהי נא אלה בינותינו בינינו ובינך ונכרתה ברית עמך

31   ויעש להם יהושע שלום ויכרתו להם ברית לחיותם וישבעו להם נשיאי העדה

32   ויאמרו כל אשר דבר ה' נעשה ונשמע

33   ויבתר אותם בתוך ויתן איש בתרו לקראת רעהו

the merger of body and soul in a permanent covenant. The Hebrew word for covenant, *berit*, probably derives from an old Akkadian root meaning "to tether or bind together", as God bound Himself to Israel (Deut. 29:11–12).[34] The permanence of the covenant was marked by the ritual addition of salt, which symbolized its enduring quality (Num. 18:19).[35]

The heart of every covenant is the solemn vow made by the participants; the validity of the covenant rests on the high purpose of those who enter into it and their truthfulness in abiding by it. The covenant at Sinai was put into effect by God's sworn oath to bless and protect the people of Israel, and by Israel's commitment to worship only God and obey the laws that He had commanded them. These solemn undertakings, sealed in a covenant, could not be revoked.

At the Giving of the Law (*Mattan Torah*), non-fulfilment of a vow – even unintentionally – became a punishable offence, and for that a sin-offering (*ḥattat*) had to be brought. "He shall not break his word" was an unconditional imperative. According to the Sages, an oath made of one's own free will incurred this liability, but the oath binding all the Jewish people "since Sinai" was irrevocable; no oath that an individual subsequently wished to attach could affect it (*Ned.* 17a–b).[36]

This concept is reflected in the *Halakhah* (rabbinic law) governing vows. If someone took an oath stating that he would not fulfil a particular *mitzvah*, (e.g., dwelling in the *sukkah*), but actually fulfilled it, he was not liable to bring a sin-offering (*korban shevu'ah*) for breaking his oath, since that oath could not override the one to which he was bound "since Sinai". No oath of his own could abrogate the solemn and perpetual commitment entered into by the whole nation at Mount Horeb (*Ned.* 16b–17a).[37] Accordingly, as the Sages ruled, no Jew can

---

34 ברית ה' אל-היך
35 ברית מלח לעולם
36 מושבע ועומד מהר סיני
37 נשבע לבטל את המצווה ולא ביטל שאין רשות בידו

obligate himself in any way by swearing an oath to transgress precepts of the Torah (*Ned.* 16a–b).[38]

If someone took an oath to abstain from food and then reneged on his word by eating forbidden food such as non-kosher meat (*nevelot u-terefot*), he would be guilty of that specific transgression, but not of violating his oath. In this case his oath was inoperative, since it ran counter to the one taken at Sinai which covered the prohibition of such foods; nor was he entitled to obligate himself with a further prohibition. This was the accepted view of R. Shim'on (*Shev.* 22b, Rashi *ad loc.*),[39] and the Sages affirmed that the man was already bound by his oath "from Sinai" (*Shev.* 23b; *Yoma* 73b; Maim. *Shevu'ot*, 5:5).[40]

Should someone take an oath of his own free will not to violate a *mitzvah* and then transgress it unwittingly (*bi-shegagah*), he would be liable to bring a meal-offering (*korban minhah*) for this offence but not liable for breaking his oath, since he was not empowered to add a sworn (and needless) obligation of his own to the one imposed on him by the covenant at Sinai.

Likewise, if a Nazarite took an oath not to eat grape pips, which were forbidden to a Nazarite by Torah law (Num. 6:4),[41] and then ate some, he would be guilty of breaking his Nazarite vow, but not liable for violating the useless oath he had sworn (*Shev.* 22b; Maim. *Shevu'ot* 5:9).[42]

In his final message, calling upon the people of Israel to ratify their oath of obedience to God's law, Moses admonished them to fulfil their religious obligations. He warned against the pernicious idea that one might inwardly subject an oath to limitations of one's own choosing. Anyone who disregarded the law, claiming that he was not bound to uphold it, was severely rebuked.

---

38 אין נשבעין לעבור על המצוות
39 רב שמעון פוטר דמושבע ועומד הוא עליהן
40 מושבע מהר סיני הוא
41 מחרצנים ועד זג
42 שבועה שלא אוכל חרצן

Even after committing the grievous sin of worshipping false gods, a wily individual might salve his conscience by thinking, "I shall have peace, though I walk in the stubbornness of my heart" (Deut. 29:18).[43] The wilful belief that some inward urge could modify the obligation undertaken in his public oath was mere self-deception (Rashi *ad loc.*). On the one hand, he had vowed to do what God required of him, as the Torah records: "And all the people answered together and said: 'All that the Lord hath spoken we will do'" (Ex. 19:8).[44] On the other hand, he had told himself that the oath depended on what he actually had in mind at the time – that certain things should be excluded. This man stuck to the belief that he could do as he pleased and invalidate any part of the oath that did not suit him.[45] While taking the oath in public, he would cancel it in his own mind (Sforno *ad loc.*). Moses therefore warned such a villain: "The Lord will not pardon him... and all the curse that is written in this book shall lie upon him" (Deut. 29:19).[46]

The words spoken in an oath must be followed to the letter. They cannot be modified by any mental reservation that negates the tenor of one's oath. According to a principle enunciated by the Sages, intentions at the back of a speaker's mind have no legal effect (*Kid.* 49b).[47] The *Halakhah* dealing with vows gives the following example. If someone vowed that he would not eat bread and then ate bread made from wheat, he was guilty of breaking his vow, even though his intention might really have been to forgo other kinds of bread. The point was that he had expressed his vow in general terms, the word "bread" referring to a loaf made from any type of grain. Vows are sacred, thus any mental reservation on his part would be untenable (*Shev.* 23a; *Tos. s.v.* "*dilma*").

There is a spiritual element in human speech and a person's words must always be chosen with care, even when the

---

43   שלום יהיה לי כי בשרירות לבי אלך

44   כל אשר דיבר ה׳ נעשה

45   בשרירות לבי אלך

46   לא יאבה ה׳ סלוח לו

47   דברים שבלב אינם דברים

phrasing of an oath is not involved. The Rabbis underlined the metaphysical power of words in a saying: "God made an unbreakable covenant with man, that whatever issues from his lips will in some way be fulfilled" (*Sanh.* 102a).[48]

Man's creative power in thought and speech was apparent from the very beginning. The Bible relates that "man became a living soul" (Gen. 2:7),[49] and the Targum of Onkelos translates "a living soul" as "a speaking soul".[50] This Aramaic interpretation of the phrase was destined to become authoritative (Rashi *ad loc.*).

Speech has the power to work its own effects. A positive example may be found in the Biblical account of Abraham's journey, at God's command, to sacrifice Isaac: "And Abraham said unto his young men: 'Abide ye here with the ass, and I and the lad will go yonder; and we will worship, and come back to you'" (Gen. 22:5).[51] Abraham thought that only he would return, but his words were fulfilled and Isaac did come back with him (*MK* 18a). A sadly different example can be found in Laban's search for his idols, which were hidden in the saddle of Rachel's camel, and Jacob had told him: "With whomsoever thou findest thy gods, he shall not live" (Gen. 31:32, Rashi *ad loc.*).[52] As a result of that curse, Rachel died on the way to Bethlehem and was therefore denied burial in the family vault of Machpelah (Gen. 35:19, 48:7; Gen. R. 74, sect. 3).

Another example of speech having a negative effect is quoted by the Sages, who recalled Isaiah's warning to the kings of Judah: "Had not the Lord of hosts left unto us a very small remnant, we should have been as Sodom and like unto Gomorrah".[53] These bitter words were actually followed by

---

48   ברית כרותה לשפתים
49   ויהי האדם לנפש חיה
50   נפש ממללא
51   ונשובה עליכם
52   עם אשר תמצא את אל-היך לא יחיה
53   כסדום היינו

the designation of Judah's kings as "rulers of Sodom" (Isa. 1:9–10; *Ber.* 19a).[54]

A traditional saying of the Rabbis was: "Do not open your mouth to Satan" (*Ber.* 19a).[55] One should never refer to the possibility of a dire event, because Satan will gladly seize upon those words in order to fulfil them. This was laid down as a strict rule: A person should never say anything that might give the Evil One an opportunity to cause mischief.[56] If, however, one feels compelled to warn against some likely disaster, a prayerful expression (meaning "Heaven forbid") is often attached, such as "Have mercy and give us peace", "May it not be so" or "God protect us".[57] Words speak and also have their effect.

Despite the exhortation to beware of Satan's guile, one should realize that there is no separate power fomenting evil in opposition to God's beneficent will. Reference to Satan as a personification of iniquity is only a common form of speech and Jewish theology allows for no dual powers ruling the universe. The Sages rigidly excluded any concept of two dominions (*Ḥag.* 15a; Gen. 1:1).[58] God's sovereignty embraces the whole of creation and His Providence governs all (see also Chapter 12, end).

C. Effectiveness of a Vow

A vow of self-denial or imposing a new obligation is only effective when it involves something permitted that has become sanctified, not something that is in any case prohibited by Torah law. The Rabbis quoted the following verse: "When a man voweth a vow unto the Lord, or sweareth an oath to bind his soul with a bond, he shall not break his word".[59]

---

54 קציני סדום
55 אל תפתח פה לשטן
56 לעולם אל יפתח אדם פיו לשטן
57 חס ושלום, חס וחלילה - רחמנא ליצלן
58 אין שתי רשויות
59 איש כי ידור

From this they deduced that his vow would render that object forbidden to him, but they excluded anything like a "firstborn animal", which was already prohibited from its birth (Num. 30:3; *Ned.* 13a).

Na<u>h</u>manides explains that since the Torah regards the vow as "making forbidden",[60] this implies that whoever makes it creates a prohibition, vowing to deny himself something otherwise permitted, like a ritually fit animal that has been sanctified as an offering (*ke-korban*). If, however, the vow of self-denial applies to something already forbidden by the Torah, no prohibition is created and so his vow is not effective. Accordingly, if he said, "This bread is forbidden to me like a firstborn animal [*bekhor*] or pork [*besar* <u>h</u>*azir*]", that would not be a prohibition of his making, since it is already included in the Torah (*Ned.* 13a; *Ned.* 14a, RAN *ad loc.*, *s.v.* "*amar kera*"; Maim. *Nedarim* 1:8).

The *Shul<u>h</u>an Arukh* also considers this type of vow to be effective only if it applies to something otherwise permitted but now sanctified, not to something already forbidden (*Sh. Ar., Yoreh De'ah* 204–205).[61]

D. Interpreting a Person's Intention

As distinct from the mandatory oath sworn before a court of law, the term "oath" (*shevu'ah*) also denotes an individual's solemn undertaking to perform or not to perform a certain action, as if this constituted a Temple prohibition. The term "vow" (*neder*) denotes a person's solemn undertaking to abstain from a normally permitted object or activity, or to derive any benefit from it, were he to say (for example): "I declare this loaf of bread forbidden to me *ke-korban* – just like a Temple sacrifice".

---

60   לאסור איסר
61   שיתפיס בדבר הנדור ולא בדבר האסור

The possibility exists to have his vow annulled. The Sages felt that such an annulment was justifiable if they were convinced that the person taking the vow had done so mistakenly, that there was no act of mind in the words he uttered and that his present regret was not just an afterthought. If, therefore, he asked for the annulment, his regret must be *ab initio* (*Sh. Ar., Yoreh De'ah* 228:7).[62]

When an oath or vow is not clearly expressed, its original intention must be ascertained in view of the precept, "He shall not break his word; he shall do according to all that proceedeth out of his mouth" (Num. 30:3).[63] The meaning of the vow and its intention both depend on what the author had in mind when and as he made it. The extent to which his vow is applicable will be determined by the way that vow would be understood in the everyday language of his own social milieu, even if his words might be interpreted differently elsewhere. In short, when a vow requires interpretation, one follows the meaning of words as they are normally understood (Maim. *Nedarim*, 9:13).[64]

Wherever possible, the Rabbis endeavoured to narrow rather than widen the scope of a vow in order to minimize the likelihood of its non-fulfilment. If, for example, a man's vow prohibited the consumption of meat (*basar*), which was normally understood to mean boiled meat (*mevushal*), it excluded roast meat (*tzeli*) and stewed meat (*shaluk*) as well as meat gravy (*rotev*). If his vow prohibited drinking wine (*yayin*), he was allowed to eat grapes (*anavim*); and if grapes were forbidden, he could drink wine. The same applied to olives and olive oil, dates and date honey.

If the key word was ambiguous, its more stringent meaning would be applicable (*Ned.* 6–8; Maim. *Nedarim*, 9; Mish., *Ned.* 3:7, Rav). However, if someone denied himself any benefit from "what is born" (either *ha-yelodim or ha-noladim* in

---

62   צריך שיתחרט בעיקר הנדר

63   לא יחל דברו, ככל היוצא מפיו יעשה

64   בנדרים הלוך אחר לשון בני אדם לשון בני העיר

Hebrew), both words could also mean "what is already born" or "what will yet be born", i.e, what is in existence or what in the future will exist.[65] Anything of the kind is therefore forbidden, since the terms are interchangeable and the meaning is in doubt. Here, again, the more stringent ruling would apply (Mish., *Ned.* 3:9, *Tosefot Yom Tov*; *Ned.* 9a, 30b, Rashi; *Tur, Sh. Ar., Yoreh De'ah* 217, *Bet Yosef; Ned.* 6:2, R'AV).[66]

If a person set a time limit to his vow of self-denial, the court's ruling takes account of what he probably had in mind. Thus, if he said "until Passover",[67] and it is not clear if he meant up to but not including the festival[68] or until the festival's termination,[69] the court rules that "until Passover" is normally taken to mean "until Passover begins". In any case, it is unlikely that a person would want to have the prohibition extended if this could be avoided (Mish., *Ned.* 8:2, R'AV).

Since making a vow is an act of determination by the mind, even a loosely expressed vow still reflects a person's mental resolve. The Rabbis accordingly ruled that if in his vow of abstinence a person did not equate what he had forgone with the interdiction of a sacrifice (*ke-korban*), but used a synonym (e.g., *konam*) instead,[70] his vow is completely valid.

Furthermore, even if that person never used a replacement term for *korban* in his vow, but merely stated that he would keep his distance from a particular individual, this is considered to be holding only "the handle of a vessel",[71] though really holding all of it, and regarded as a legitimate vow (Mish., *Ned.* 1:1, *Tosefot Yom Tov* and *Tiferet Yisrael ad loc.*).

If someone denied another person any benefit from him and then found an item which that person had lost, he may

---

65	הנודר מן הילודים... אותם שעתידים להיולד
66	ספק נדרים להחמיר
67	עד הפסח
68	עד ולא עד בכלל
69	ועד בכלל
70	כינוי נדרים
71	ידות נדרים

return it,[72] because it was never the intention of his vow to ban the fulfilment of a *mitzvah*, such as returning a lost object to its owner – *hashavat avedah* (Deut. 22:1–3). The same would apply to visiting the sick – *bikkur holim* (Mish., *Ned.* 4:2, 4; *Sh. Ar., Hoshen Mishpat* 259, 265).

Similarly, if a man divorcing his wife vowed that she would never enjoy any benefit from him again, one assumes that he actually had sexual relations in mind, not other possible benefits (*Ned.* 63b, Rashi and ROSH). As indicated above, since the Rabbis were anxious to prevent unwitting transgression and to minimize the adverse effects of a vow, they felt that it should be interpreted according to the circumstances in which it was made and the way in which it would usually be understood (Mish. *Ned.* 3:9, *Tosefot Yom Tov*; *Ned.* 63b, RAN *ad loc., s.v.* "*ha-omer le-havero*"; Maim. *Nedarim* 9:1.).[73]

In the same spirit R. Akiva determined that annulling part of a vow would result in the entire vow's annulment. Such would be the case if a man chose to interdict a whole group of people, but then discovered that his father was among them; this had never been his real intention.[74] Since Torah law declared that a person must fulfil "*all* that is expressed by his mouth" (Num. 30:3), when part of the vow was justifiably annulled, what remained was held to be inoperative (Mish., *Ned.* 9:6–7, RAN; *Sh. Ar., Yoreh De'ah* 229).

People sometimes make casual use of an expression, including a vow, to emphasize an opinion. Seeing how an animal lies helpless on the ground, for example, a person may claim that it will never get up, saying "I'll be a Nazarite if it stands on its own four feet!" Then someone lifts the poor beast and it manages to stand upright. The question arose as to whether that person's remark committed him to the vow of a Nazarite (Maim. *Nezirut*, 2:1, 8).

Bet Shammai (the school of Shammai) argued that he must be held responsible for what he said: using the term *Nazir* was

---

72 מחזיר לו את אבדתו
73 בנדרים הלך אחר לשון בני אדם
74 הותר מקצתו, הותר כולו

like making a vow to the Sanctuary, and he was thus forbidden to partake of the animal (were it to become an offering), just as a Nazarite was forbidden to drink wine. He did not have to become a *Nazir* in the full sense, but was forbidden to eat any flesh of the animal. *Bet Hillel* (the school of Hillel) on the other hand, maintained that he was neither a *Nazir* nor forbidden to partake of the animal, unless he used a formal term of consecration such as *konam* (*Naz.* 10a).

Bet Shammai adhered to the principle that "one does not express words meaninglessly".[75] *Bet Hillel* disagreed, however, stating that one may follow what the words implied – that the animal would not get up on its own unless someone lifted it, which is what occurred. Furthermore, the consecration of an object would be subject to use of the proper procedure. Likewise, if someone undertook a Nazarite's vow in regard to figs or dates instead of (genuinely forbidden) wine, the prohibition would in no way apply to him (*Ned.* 9a; Mish., *Naz.* 2:1, R'AV *ad loc.*). The circumstances in which a vow was taken also had to be considered. If, for example, someone was offered a goblet of wine, knew that he might drink to excess and therefore replied, "I am a *Nazir* as far as that is concerned", what he said did not amount to a Nazarite's vow but simply emphasized his objection to drinking the wine (*Naz.* 2:3, R'AV *ad loc.*).

If someone vowed to be a *Nazir* on the strength of a mistaken impression, his Nazarite vow would not apply. Although *Bet Shammai* declared that even one made in error was binding,[76] *Bet Hillel* ruled that neither a vow nor a consecration made in error had any effect;[77] the words spoken by a person must always coincide with the intention in his mind.[78] Maimonides followed *Bet Hillel*'s ruling (Maim. *Nedarim* 4:2).

The Sages of the Mishnah relate that when the Jews returned to Jerusalem after their captivity and found the Temple

---

75   אין אדם מוציא דבריו לבטלה
76   הקדש טעות הקדש, נזיר, בטעות נזיר
77   הקדש טעות אינו הקדש, נזיר בטעות אינו נזיר
78   פיו ולבו שווים

destroyed, Nahum the Mede asked those who had taken the vow of a *Nazir*, "Had you known of the Temple's destruction, would you still have become Nazarites?" "No", they replied, and on that basis he cancelled their vows (*Naz.* 5:1, R'AV).[79]

As a young man, R. Akiva was a shepherd employed by the wealthy Kalba Shebu'a when Rachel, the latter's daughter, fell in love with him. Annoyed that she had chosen to marry an *am ha-aretz* (ignoramus), Kalba Shebu'a vowed to cut them off without a penny. Rachel, however, urged her husband to immerse himself in Torah study and, after a period of 24 years, Akiva had become a renowned *tanna* (Sage). When Kalba Shebu'a begged for the annulment of his vow, R. Akiva asked: "Had you known that your son-in-law was destined to become a great Torah scholar, would you have made such a vow?" Kalba Shebu'a replied that he would not have done so, and on that basis his vow was annulled (*Ned.* 50a).

If, in view of a terrible storm, a person declared, "These trees are consecrated as an offering [*korban*] if they are not blown down",[80] and they remained standing, the consecration would take effect and an offering would have to be bought with the redemption money. The man's words are regarded as a definite commitment, not as an over-statement of his belief that the trees would fall down.[81] Although he might really have hoped that they would not be consecrated, his inner thoughts[82] would carry no weight here, only the vow that he actually expressed (*Ned.* 3:5, R'AV and ROSH; *Tosefot Yom Tov ad loc.*).

E. Annulment of Vows

The sanctity of a vow, undertaking, or promise is enunciated, as we have seen, in the precept: "That which is gone out of thy

---

79   טעות בנולד

80   הרי נטיעות אלו קרבן

81   נדר זרוז

82   דברים שבלב

lips thou shalt observe and do" (Deut. 23:24).[83] Although this
verse enjoins that whatever has been devoted to God must be
offered "according as thou hast vowed freely... [and] promised
with thy mouth",[84] the verse was understood by the Rabbis to
mean that any utterance, promise or intention has the binding
force of a vow sacred to God. Strictly speaking, the precept
refers to a vow invoking God's Name (Ibn Ezra, Deut. 23:24),
but the Rabbis also considered "that which thou hast promised
with thy mouth" to be the promise of a gift to charity (*Ned.*
7a).

A more comprehensive purport of the law is expressed
in another Biblical verse (Num. 30:3), which lays down that
whenever a man is under a vow to God or binds himself with an
oath, he may not break his word.[85] Whatever he has voiced he
must do.[86] This form of vow includes a person's undertaking
to deny himself a certain commodity or else to act or not act in
a certain way. The Torah law thus embraces two kinds of vow:
those that offer something to God[87] and those that express a
personal commitment (RAMBAN on Torah, *ibid.*).[88] Although
the Biblical prohibition strictly refers to an utterance in the
form of a vow, the Rabbis treated any person breaking his
word in any circumstance as a "reprobate".[89] This castigation
extended the judicial directive, "Keep thee far from a false
matter" (Ex. 23:7),[90] to include anyone going back on his
word (*Sefer ha-Ḥinnukh* 407).

In his list of the Bible's positive commandments, Maimonides
includes the duty to fulfil whatever one has undertaken by
word of mouth, whether in the form of an oath (*shevu'ah*),
a vow (*neder*), a charitable offering (*tzedakah*) or a Temple

---

83   מוצא שפתיך תשמור ועשית
84   אשר דברת בשפתיך
85   לא יחל דברו
86   ככל היוצא מפיו יעשה
87   נדרי גבוה
88   נדרי ביטוי
89   פשוטי נפש
90   מדבר שקר תרחק

sacrifice (*korban*). He bases this law on the precept referred to above (Deut. 23:24).[91] This, he states, is an injunction to fulfil anything that a man has obligated himself to perform, and it is repeated in the phrase, "According to all that proceedeth out of his mouth he shall do" (Num. 30:3; Maim. *Sefer ha-Mitzvot, Aseh* 24).[92] Maimonides also lists as a positive commandment the provision for annulling vows (*hattarat nedarim*), but he emphasizes that this is not a mandatory law to be followed in all circumstances.

The Torah makes specific provision for the annulment of a vow only in the case of vows made by an unmarried woman, which her father can revoke, and by a married woman, which her husband can annul, provided that he does so "in the day that he heareth" (Num. 30:2–17; see below).

The Rabbis, however, developed an elaborate system based on ancient teaching[93] that gave permission in certain instances for the absolution of an oath or a vow (*hattarat nedarim*). Maimonides conceded that this type of annulment had no solid foundation in the Bible, and that the rabbinical provisions seemed to be "flying in the air".[94] His statement reflects the tannaitic traditions of the Mishnah (*Hag.* 10a).[95] Rashi (*ad loc.*) had already explained that these rules governing the annulment of vows were transmitted to the Sages through the Oral Law.[96]

R. Yehoshua (*ibid.*), who disagreed, is quoted in a *baraita* as expressing the opinion that these laws of annulment *did* have a Biblical basis (TJ *Ned.* 3:1). This sanction he found in the words, "that I swore in my wrath" (Ps. 95:11),[97] implying that a vow made in anger did not reflect one's genuine intention since it was not undertaken with a clear mind. A person might

---

91   מוצא שפתיך תשמור
92   ככל היוצא מפיו יעשה
93   באה בקבלה
94   פורחים באוויר
95   היתר נדרים פורחים באוויר ואין להם על מה שיסמוכו
96   מסור לחכמים בתורה שבעל פה
97   אשר נשבעתי באפי

thus claim that the vow misrepresented his thoughts; now that he realized how mistaken his vow had been, he could justifiably ask for a re-examination of his true intent, which would enable the *bet din* to cancel his vow (Rashi *ad loc.*).

The task of determining his real intention is not entrusted to the applicant, who would almost inevitably reach a decision favourable to himself. The Torah therefore ruled *lo yaḥel devaro* ("he shall not break his word", Num. 30:3), meaning that *he* cannot annul the vow, but *others* may do so (*Ḥag.* 10a).[98] It is emphasized, however, that his claim to have made an erroneous vow must refer to his state of mind at the time,[99] and not to a change of heart resulting from its consequences (*Sefer ha-Ḥinnukh* 406).

[General references: *Sh. Ar., Yoreh De'ah* 228:5; *Talmudic Encyclopaedia*, Vol. 11, pp. 333–391; Maim. *Shevu'ot* 6; Mish., *Ned.* 4:11–13]

A matter of grave concern to the Rabbis was the possibility that a vow unfulfilled would violate a basic law of the Decalogue, "Thou shalt not take the Name of the Lord thy God in vain" (Ex. 19:7), as well as the injunction not to break one's word (Num. 30:3).[100] With this danger in mind, they made every effort to find some way of justifying a man's release from his vow (Maim. *Shevu'ot* 6:1–10). Obviously, no Sage was empowered to cancel a vow once it had been properly made, but he could ascertain whether the man realized the full implications of his vow when he made it. If not, the Rabbis could simply declare it null and void.

This they tried to do by showing that the manner in which the vow was worded did not reflect the author's actual thoughts at the time. When someone was perplexed because of his inability to fulfil a vow, the Rabbis endeavoured to release him from his obligation by satisfying themselves that the vow had not been made with his full intention or sound judgment,

---

98 הוא אינו מוחל אבל אחרים מוחלים

99 חרטה דמעיקרו

100 לא יחל דברו

thus proving that his words were not a true expression of his mind. Taking a vow was not a physical action but a moral undertaking, which required an act of the mind. Without such a mental commitment, or if mind and speech were not in harmony, the vow had no binding force. However, such a release would only be effective if the individual replied truthfully to the questions put to him by the Sages, and he could obviously not presume to rely on his own judgment of the issue (*Ned.* 64b, Rashi *ad loc.*).

Although the *tannaim* held that such an annulment could only be executed by an ordained rabbinical authority,[101] it was later accepted that when such an expert was unavailable, the annulment could be effected by any three respected members of the community (Mish., *Bekh.* 5:5, *Tosefot Yom Tov ad loc.*).[102]

The *geonim* of Babylon, in a subsequent ruling (6th cent.), differed as to whether the Sage himself should suggest possible interpretations of the vow that the author would reject, thereby invalidating the vow. According to the widely accepted view of one *amora*, R. Naḥman, the Sage might propose that an individual express regret for his vow,[103] and that Sage might well be disappointed if he failed to gain such a response (*Ned.* 22b, RAN *ad loc.*). Maimonides ruled that even if a person had invoked the Divine Name and then regretted it, he should ask the Sage to annul his vow (Maim. *Shevu'ot*, 6:10; *Sh. Ar., Yoreh De'ah* 228:7; *Ned.* 64a, Rashi and *Tos. ad loc.*).

If, when making his vow, a person stipulated that he fully committed himself to the public understanding of what the vow entailed, rather than his own judgment (*Bekh.* 46a),[104] any quest for the vow's real intention by sounding public opinion would be futile. There was accordingly no way of having it annulled. Exceptionally, however, this ruling could

---

101 מומחה
102 שלש הדיוטות בני הכנסת
103 פותחים בחרטה
104 על דעת רבים

be set aside if adhering to the vow obstructed the performance of a religious duty (Maim. *Shevu'ot*, 6:9; *Git.* 36a; *Bekh.* 46a; *Sh. Ar., Yoreh De'ah* 228:21, REMA *ad loc.*, examples of *devar mitzvah*).[105]

[General reference: *Talmudic Encyclopaedia*, Vol. 11, p. 349, *s.v.* "*Ḥaratah*"]

Limitations on Annulment

The *tannaim* differed as to the kind of situation that would justify their efforts to make someone renounce his vow (Mish., *Ned.* 9:1–4, R'AV; *Sh. Ar., Yoreh De'ah* 228:11). In R. Eliezer's opinion, the Sage might reprimand him by pointing out that making such a vow was iniquitous and that such conduct would dishonour his parents. If he then replied, "Had I been aware of this, I would never have made the vow", the Sage would accept his apology and have just cause for annulling the vow.

The Rabbis decreed, however, that the man's fear of disgracing his parents would make him nullify his vow – out of consideration for them rather than genuine regret. One might just as well tell him what he already knew, that vowing in general is an affront to Divine law and to God Himself. Such a reprimand would not lead him to withdraw his vow, but might induce him to give an untruthful answer (Mish., *Ned.* 9:1; *Sh. Ar., Yoreh De'ah* 228:11).[106] The same ruling would apply if the Sage invoked the honour of this man's teacher (*Ned.* 64a, ROSH *ad loc.*).

Likewise, if something unusual occurred after he made his vow which had a bearing on the words expressed and caused him to regret them, this would not prove that he never intended to make such a vow in the first place. Only proof of a different intention would substantiate his regret

---

105 לדבר מצווה
106 חיישינן שיתבושש וישקר

(*haratah*), as he would mostly have no reason to expect an unusual occurrence (*Ned.* 9:2; *Sh. Ar., Yoreh De'ah* 228:12). Nevertheless, if he volunteered a regretful declaration in such a case – i.e., had he anticipated such a development, he would not have made the vow to begin with – this might be accepted as "essential regret" (*Sh. Ar., Yoreh De'ah* 228:13, REMA and TAZ *ad loc.*).[107]

If a person originally conditioned his vow in a way that was generally understood,[108] the Sage could not annul this man's vow unless his community gave its consent (*Sh. Ar., Yoreh De'ah* 228:21). By making the vow *al da'at rabbim*, he had submitted his own thought (*da'at*), an essential element in the vow, to the interpretation and discretion of his community. Thus, having waived the right to interpret his own vow, he could no longer claim that fulfilling the vow was never his intention. The community had, as it were, made this vow and their intention provided the "mental element" (*da'at*) rendering it effective. In some instances that stipulation was essential (Mish., *Yoma* 1:5, *Tosefot Yom Tov*).

On Yom Kippur (the Day of Atonement), elders of the *bet din* made the High Priest vow that he would not depart/diverge from the prescribed Temple ceremony. This vow was binding on him specifically, as the court understood (*Yoma* 1:5, *Tosefot Yom Tov*).

A community is likewise empowered, by a majority decision, to impose a new regulation which is binding on the entire membership as a vow undertaken by all. That vow permits no annulment for an individual, unless the whole community agrees to suspend the regulation (*Sh. Ar., Yoreh De'ah* 228:25).[109] The community may, however, exercise its own discretion and revoke such an enactment (*Shev.* 29b, *Tos. s.v.* "*Ki*"; *Sh. Ar., Yoreh De'ah* 228:25).

---

107 חרטה מעיקרה
108 על דעת רבים
109 נדרי ציבור

In the case of an attestation before a court of law,[110] the oath is always administered explicitly as it is understood by members of the *bet din*, and any mental reservation on the part of an individual is excluded (*Ned.* 25a.; Maim. *Shevu'ot*, 2:15–16; *Sh. Ar., Hoshen Mishpat* 87:20).

F. Invalidating a Future Vow

In common with the decision providing for the annulment of past vows, allowance was also made for the annulment of future vows, as in the *Kol Nidrei* declaration recited during the Yom Kippur eve service.

The Talmudic basis for this provision is as follows. The Mishnah (*Ned.* 23a) quotes a teaching of R. Eliezer ben Ya'akov: before undertaking a vow, one can declare: "Every vow that I make in the future shall be null and void". Any subsequent vow would thus be invalid, provided the man taking it was aware of his previous declaration. R. Eliezer, we are told, was not referring to all vows, but to a vow of "inducement" (*zerizut*),[111] such as one designed to hasten a friend's visit by vowing that if he did not come for a meal, the host would forgo any benefit from him. Due to this previous declaration, however, the author's vow would not really be effective (*Ned.* 20b).

The Gemara (*ad loc.*) expanded the teaching of R. Eliezer to include a broader spectrum: "He who desires that no vow of his made during the year shall be binding, let him stand at the beginning of the year and declare: 'Every vow that I make in the future shall be nullified'".

The *amoraim* Rava and Abbaye (*ad loc.*) differed in their interpretation of R. Eliezer's proviso, as regards the function of the mind in this type of vow and remembering a previous

---

110 שבועת הדיינים
111 נדרי זריזות

declaration when the vow was made. According to Abbaye, the new vow would only be annulled if its author was not conscious of his earlier declaration; if he was aware of it and still made a new vow, he thereby cancelled his previous declaration. Rava, on the other hand, maintained that being aware of his declaration, the author now made his vow on the same understanding[112] and the vow was therefore ineffective.[113]

In Rava's opinion, the effectiveness of the annulment was would depend on whether the man remembered his previous declaration when he made the new vow.[114] If he was not aware of it, the limitation would not be operative and so the new vow would take effect. In general, the Rabbis based their decisions on the view of Rava (*Tos. ad loc.*; RAN *ad loc.*; Maim. *Nedarim* 2:4–5).

Rava, however, was concerned that such an easy release from one's vows might lead to their being treated too lightly. He therefore ruled that steps be taken to ensure that this law was not taught incautiously to the general public (*Ned.* 23b).[115]

Public Annulment and the Kol Nidrei Declaration

Based on this provision for the annulment of future vows (*Ned.* 23a), it became the practice on Yom Kippur eve, when the whole community gathered in the synagogue, for the *sheli'ah tzibbur* (cantor) to recite a solemn declaration three times, whereby "all vows" (*kol nidrei*), past or future, that a congregant had made rashly were annulled. Similarly, on the eve of Rosh ha-Shanah, individuals nullified their earlier vows by making such a declaration before three scholars acting as a *bet din*.

---

112   על דעת הראשונה אני נודר
113   נדרי לית ביה ממש
114   זכור בשעת הנדר
115   שלא ינהגו קלות ראש בנדרים

Rabbenu Tam objected to the idea that past vows could be revoked by such a declaration instead of by the recognized annulment procedure. Accordingly, he excluded "all vows made from last Yom Kippur until this Yom Kippur"[116] but retained "from this Yom Kippur until next Yom Kippur",[117] thus nullifying only vows made in the coming year. Furthermore, it was generally agreed that this *Kol Nidrei* declaration only applied to vows affecting the individual;[118] it did not cover vows made to someone else, those imposed by a rabbinical court or specially enacted communal regulations (*takkanot*).

Despite the reservations of Rabbenu Tam, it was widely accepted from early times[119] that the text of *Kol Nidrei* also referred to the annulment of vows made "since last Yom Kippur", thus enabling people who had not fulfilled their vows to escape punishment. The recital or chanting of *Kol Nidrei* gave each member of the congregation an opportunity to express his or her own remorse and to beg forgiveness for any violation of an undertaking.

Although R. Saadiah Gaon favoured the use of this text, R. Natronai Gaon stated that *Kol Nidrei* was never recited in his Babylonian academy and that he firmly opposed its introduction (as did R. Hai Gaon). Some communities adopted their view or the modification by Rabbenu Tam, but *Seder Rav Amram Gaon* (c. 860) includes the full text of *Kol Nidrei*, which is widely followed today (Rosh on *Yoma*, end of chap., 8:28).

G. Vows Not Meant Seriously

Since a vow becomes legally binding only when its wording correctly reflects the intention in the author's mind, certain

---

116 מיום כיפור שעבר
117 מיום כיפורים זה עד יום כיפורים הבא עלינו לטובה
118 בינו ובין עצמו
119 כמנהג הקדמונים

vows made in a burst of excitement are high-flown words rather than genuine undertakings. They were never meant seriously, have no binding power and require no formal annulment.

The *tannaim* list four such types of vow (*Ned.* 20b). They are called vows of "inducement" (*nidrei ziruz*), "exaggeration" (*nidrei havai*), "error" (*nidrei shegagot*) and "duress or accident" (*nidrei onesin*). The following examples of an ineffective vow are given:

(1) A vow of "inducement" (*ziruz*) is simply intended as a form of persuasion. When a merchant, for example, wishes to impress on a customer that the price he is asking for some item is the lowest possible, he may declare: "Even a piece of bread won't pass my lips if I lower the price". The customer may then vow to do the same if he ever pays more than he offered. They eventually reach a compromise. The vows made in the course of bargaining were never meant to be taken seriously; their aim was to make the other side give way and they have no validity. Likewise, if someone invited a friend to dinner and said, "If you don't come, I swear I'll never speak to you again", this was merely a form of persuasion, not a serious vow.

(2) A clear case of "exaggeration" (*nidrei havai*) would be someone vowing in the course of table talk: "May I never partake of this again if the crowd I saw was not as large as that of the Israelites leaving Egypt"; or "if that wall did not tower up to heaven"; or "if the snake I found was not as thick as a wooden beam".

(3) A typical vow made "in error" (*nidrei shegagot*) would be a man swearing, "I'll never eat bread again if I've had anything to eat or drink all day", having forgotten that he did eat something. Had he remembered this, he would not have made such a commitment. Similarly, if a man declared, "I'll have nothing more to do with my wife because she stole my wallet", and it turns out that she did nothing of the sort; or if he vowed not to marry a woman because she was said to be ugly, and he then found her attractive. Two other examples are cited: Feeling sure that

Mr. X would not attend a certain event, a man pledged 100 *zuz* to charity if he turned up, and Mr. X was there; or if someone vowed never to do something, being under the impression that it was religiously prohibited, only to discover that it was in fact permitted. All these mistaken vows (*nidrei ta'ut*) are non-binding (*Ned.* 3:2, 9:10).

(4) Examples of a vow made "under duress or by accident" (*nidrei onesin*) are also given. Someone promised to visit a friend and have a meal with him, but was prevented from doing so because he fell ill or because heavy rain made the road impassable; similarly, when a person undertook to discharge a certain responsibility, but was prevented from doing so by a governmental decree. Likewise, when a man was compelled to undertake a vow because someone threatened to kill or injure him. In such circumstances which are beyond the vow-maker's control, the vow had no binding effect (*Ned.* 20b, 24b, 25b, 27a–b; *Sh. Ar., Yoreh De'ah* 232).

Instances of Limitation

One normally follows the rule that in vows, as in contracts or marriages, a mental reservation differing from what was expressed has no validity (*Kid.* 50a).[120] In the cases listed above, however, no deception was involved, as it is quite obvious that the vow was not meant seriously.[121]

The Rabbis allowed a person to take a false or deceptive oath in order to save himself from physical violence or extortion by the hands of an oppressor. It was accordingly laid down that one might resort to these deceptions when heathens threatened one's life and property.[122] In such cases of *force majeure* a false oath was permitted, despite the general rule

---

120 דברים שבלב אינן דברים
121 שאנן סהדי שאין דעתו לכך
122 נודרין להרוגין ולחרומין ולמוכסין

that an oath accompanied by a mental reservation had no validity (*Kid.* 50a).[123]

That permission did not apply, however, to oaths and vows made under a just legal authority, Jewish or non-Jewish, where a mental reservation was no excuse for non-fulfilment. Such a legal authority had to be obeyed without question or deception; violating one's pledged word, especially where a non-Jewish authority was concerned, amounted to the desecration of God's Name (*hillul Hashem*). Apart from legitimate self-defence when Jews faced an attack, there was no justification for depriving even a heathen of what rightfully belonged to him, in accordance with the principle that theft from a Gentile is no less forbidden than theft from a fellow Jew (*Ned.* 28a, RAN *ad loc.*; *Sh. Ar., Yoreh De'ah* 232:14, REMA; *Sanh.* 57a; *BK* 113a, MAHARSHAL, *Yam shel Shelomo, ad loc.*, 20; Maim. *Genevah* 7:8).[124]

H. Vows and Sacrifices

The general rule governing sacrifices is that a person must bring the exact type of offering he vowed, and the best of that type. Should he be uncertain about the exact type, he is obliged to offer one of each. However, the Rabbis laid down that if he did know the specified type (e.g., a burnt-offering), but could not remember whether he spoke of an ox or a calf, he should always bring the larger offering – in this case an ox (*Men.* 107a; Maim. *Ma'aseh ha-Korbanot* 16:9).

Another decision concerned a man who vowed to bring a sacrifice, declared that it would be a *minhah* meal-offering of the flat-pan type (*be-mahavat*), but mistakenly brought one of the deep-pan type (*be-marheshet*). Since the offering must be as specified, his *minhah* was apparently unacceptable. Despite

---

123   דברים שבלב אינם דברים
124   גזל עכו״ם גזל

the fact that this man did not fulfil his vow to the letter, it was in any case his intention to bring a meal-offering; his *minḥah* would therefore be regarded as a separate freewill-offering, which was acceptable (*Men.* 102b, Rashi *ad loc.*; Maim. *Ma'aseh ha-Korbanot* 17:2).

I. Validity of a Woman's Vow

As soon as a girl (*ketannah*) reaches the age of 12 years and a day, she attains her majority (as a *gedolah*) and her vows are valid and binding. However, her father is entitled to annul her vows or oaths "in the day that he heareth them", since she is considered to be under his authority (*bi-reshuto*). As a result, she cannot be held accountable for the non-fulfilment of her vows. The father's jurisdiction is limited to a period of six months, after which she reaches her maturity (as a *bogeret*); thenceforth, she is not subject to her father's authority and has a personal liability for all her vows. Once married, she is released from her father's jurisdiction; even after returning to her father's house as a widow or a divorcee, she remains bound by any vow that she subsequently made (Maim. *Nedarim* 11:6–7; Num. 30:4–6, 10, Rashi *ad loc.*).

Torah law grants a husband the right to annul any vow made by his wife, provided he does so on the day that he hears it; otherwise, her vow remains binding. If the husband annuls her vow, God pardons her for its non-fulfilment (Num. 30:13).[125] In the case of a betrothal (*erusin*) that takes place before marriage (*nissu'in*), such authority is exercised jointly by the father and the groom (Num. 30:7, Rashi *ad loc.*; *Ned.* 67a).

The Rabbis justify this dispensation on the grounds that a wife's rash vow may counteract her husband's wishes and undermine his authority, provoking marital strife. The Torah is thus prepared to overlook the non-observance of her vow, which would normally entail Divine disfavour, in order to safeguard domestic harmony (*shelom bayit*). Such indulgence brings to mind the case of a "suspect wife" (*sotah*), where God permits His Name to be erased from a written text in order to restore marital harmony (*Ned.* 22b, Rashi *ad loc.*, s.v. "*Konam ishti*"; Num 5:23; *Sot.* 20a).

In legal terms, the woman's vow is initially subject to the approval of her father or husband[126] since she is powerless to act unless they give their consent; otherwise, her vow does not take effect (*Keli Yakar*, Num. 30:3). R. Pinḥas enunciated the general rule that every vow made by the wife is subject to her husband's approval (*Ned.* 73b, Rashi and *Tos. ad loc.*; Maim. *Nedarim* 11:20; *Sh. Ar., Yoreh De'ah* 234:2, 35).[127]

The husband's annulment of her vow was effective even if she assumed the vow of a Nazarite – lashes or "stripes" (*malkot*) usually being prescribed for the violation of that undertaking. If, however, the woman's husband had already annulled her vow, even without her knowledge, she was released from her commitment and not liable to punishment, since his action had prevented the vow from taking effect (*Naz.* 4:3).

If, for any reason, the husband remained silent throughout the day on which he heard of the vow, this implied that he had no objection to it. The vow therefore remained binding on his wife (Num. 30:15, *Torah Temimah ad loc.*, 83; *Ned.* 79a, RAN *ad loc.*; Maim. *Nedarim* 12:18).

Mental Confirmation or Active Annulment

A woman is basically responsible for her own vows, and (as indicated above) their annulment is a special provision. Once

---

126   על דעת אביה או אישה
127   כל הנודרת על דעת בעלה היא נודרת

her vow has been confirmed by the father's or husband's agreement, neither of them can annul it; to do so would require the authorization of a Sage (*hakham*). Likewise, once either the father or the husband has annulled her vow, he is not entitled to confirm it thereafter (*Sh. Ar., Yoreh De'ah* 234:21 and 23, REMA). Either man's confirmation of her vow need not be expressed in so many words: his silence would in fact indicate that he does not object. This is automatically regarded as an act of confirmation,[128] and the woman remains liable for the fulfilment of her vow. Its nullification by her father or husband must be clearly expressed: no mental reservation[129] will suffice to annul it (*Ned.* 79a, RAN *ad loc.*, based on Num. 30:15; *Torah Temimah ad loc.* 83).

Another form of annulment would be through a subsequent (not necessarily verbal) measure by the father or husband, forcing the woman to counteract her vow (Maim. *Nedarim* 13:3; *Yoreh De'ah* 234:24). Mere mental consent was thus effective in confirming a vow, and the father or husband could not subsequently annul it. If either man, however, only had annulment in mind and never made a formal statement, that would be of no effect; but he could later confirm it, if he so wished (Maim. *Nedarim* 13:19).

The binding sanctity of a woman's vow emerges from the rule that no more than an act of the mind is necessary to confirm it, whereas a positive act of expression is required for its annulment, which is then irreversible (*Ned.* 79a; Maim. *Nedarim* 13:19).

Annulment on the Sabbath

A question discussed by the Rabbis was the permissibility of annulling a wife's vow, or any vow, on the Sabbath. In the

---

128 קיים בלבו
129 הפר בלבו

case of a general vow, the Sage was required to give a legal judgment, which Sabbath laws prohibited as an active form of "work" (*melakhah*).[130] In the case of the wife's vow, however, where any annulment had to be performed on the same day and the termination of *Shabbat* would rule out such a possibility, an annulment by the husband was permitted (*Shab.* 157a).[131]

According to RAN's explanation, although a husband confirming his wife's vow may do so in his mind, by mere thought,[132] a mental annulment lacking clear expression is not effective, and so he cannot explicitly annul her vow on the Sabbath. He may, however, oblige his wife to do something that negated whatever she had vowed, and that would be the equivalent of an annulment by the husband. If, therefore, she vowed not to eat bread, he could say, "Take this slice of bread and eat it", thus nullifying her vow. The *tannaim* accordingly ruled that a husband may annul his wife's vow on the Sabbath (*Ned.* 77a, RAN *ad loc.*).[133]

J. Capacity of a Minor

The normal age of responsibility for making oaths and vows is 13 years and one day for males and 12 years and a day for females. In certain circumstances, however, the age of competence may be lowered by one year. Thus, if a boy aged 12 years and one day made an oath or a vow (*she-nishbe'u o naderu*), that oath or vow would be effective if a thorough examination proved that he realized the significance of the Divine Name which he had invoked. In this case, the boy (though still under age) was credited with special intelligence as well as his approaching majority (Maim. *Nedarim* 11:4).[134]

---

130 אין דנין בשבת
131 מפירין נדרים בשבת
132 קיים בליבו קיים
133 מפירין נדרים בשבת
134 מופלא סמוך לאיש

The younger age was reserved for females because they were considered to possess keener intelligence than males of the same age (*Nid.* 45b, as R. Ḥisda). Before they turned 12, however, even if they had a proven understanding of the Divine Name's significance, their vows were not recognized. The same applied to oaths and vows in general, as well as to consecrated Temple offerings (*Nid.* 45b, Rashi *ad loc.*; Maim. *Nedarim* 11:4; *Sh. Ar., Yoreh De'ah* 233:1–2).

K. Grave Exceptions

As a rule, the court would inflict the penalty of a lashing only when the breach of a prohibition involved some physical act; if no such action was involved, "stripes" were not imposed.[135]

Three exceptions to this rule, however, are given by R. Yose ha-Gelili: if someone took a false oath, maintaining (for example) that he had not eaten a certain item when in fact he had; if he sacrificed an animal in place of the one already consecrated for the altar; or if he invoked God's Holy Name when cursing another person.[136] Such mendacious behaviour, though restricted to words, incurred due punishment and a lashing was imposed (*Mak.* 16a; Maim. *Sanhedrin* 18:2).

---

135   כל לאו שאין בו מעשה אין לוקין עליו
136   חוץ מן הנשבע, ומימר ומקלל את חבירו בשם

Chapter 12

The Evil Eye – *Ayin ha-Ra*

12 The Evil Eye – Ayin ha-Ra

A. Introduction: Psychological Considerations

Psychiatric research has confirmed that the human body may undergo a variety of changes in response to nervous tension. Emotional stress or conflict can give rise to psychological problems, and psychiatrists mostly deal with the effects of these conditions. Psychosomatic disorders may result in incapability or even death.

Leaving aside the investigations of psychoanalysis, it is known that various forms of emotional stress – anger, fear, jealousy, hate, lust, aggression and anxiety in general – can have a serious effect on the gastrointestinal tract, as well as the cardiovascular system and the metabolism. This harmful reaction or "poison" was widely believed to have its own baleful effect when directed at some other person by the "evil eye" (*ayin ha-ra*).

Parapsychology records experiments demonstrating the fact that people can communicate with each other outside the normal sensory channels. Impressive studies in telepathy show how thoughts can be transferred from an agent's subliminal mind to a percipient's consciousness. While no consensus about telepathy yet exists, psychologists are generally agreed that a change in the electrical properties of the human body does take place in response to emotional stimuli.

This psychogalvanic action of certain emotions is reflected in Biblical and Talmudic literature, including a belief in the objective power of one person's mind to affect that of another.

[Selected references: *Encyclopaedia Britannica*, "Psychiatry"; Bain, "The Emotions and the Will", in *Mind*,

Vols. 9, 11; David Wechsler, "The Measurement of Emotional Reactions" in *Archives of Psychology*, No. 76 (1925); H. G. Wolff and George Wolf, "Studies on the Nature of Certain Symptoms Associated with Cardiovascular Disorders" in *Psychosomatic Medicine* (1946); Walter B. Cannon, *Bodily Changes in Pain, Hunger, Fear and Rage*, 2nd ed. revised (1929); F. Dunbar, *Emotions and Bodily Changes* (1935). *Psychosomatic Diagnosis*: R. R. Grinker and J. P. Spiegel, *Men under Stress* (1945); Sigmund Freud, *New Introductory Lectures on Psychoanalysis* (1933)]

B. Subjective Aspects

Maimonides states that just as everyone is born with a different physical constitution, so temperaments vary from one person to the next. A person's temperament may be gauged on a scale of (higher or lower) values, and any deficiency must be compensated. An ideal nature is one that strives to attain the golden mean, avoiding the dangers inherent in either of two extremes. Generosity (*nedivut*) thus stands midway between stinginess and extravagance. Courage (*gevurah*) is similarly the mean point between foolhardiness and cowardice; humility (*anavah*) between arrogance and self-abasement; and tolerance (*sovlanut*) between indifference and bigotry.

It is man's basic obligation to control his natural impulses and guide them towards the acceptable mean. This achievement is within the grasp of every man, since it is the ability to perfect himself that raises him above all other creatures, as the Almighty declared at the time of creation: "Behold, the man is become as one of us, to know good and evil" (Gen. 3:22).

All human beings are endowed with varying temperaments: in some these characteristics may be superior, in others inferior. The inferior traits, such as lust, pride, anger, cruelty or greed, alienate man from his Creator. Hence the Sages taught: "The gift of prophecy rests only on one who is wise, strong and rich" (*Shab.* 92a).[1] This meant that the capacity to serve as God's prophet would only infuse one whose mind was pure, who controlled his desires and who was content with what he possessed.

The more a person succeeds in mastering his imperfections, the closer he comes to the holiness of God. A person's nature may be determined by genetic factors, but the resolute exercise of his free will can outweigh any defect in his character (Maimonides, Introduction to *Avot*).

It is clear, from his legal and medical works, that Maimonides recognized the psychosomatic effect of human emotion and its influence on the bodily functions, whether in giving rise to sickness or in effecting a cure (Maim. *Hanhagat ha-Beri'ut*). In his code he set forth his views on the promotion of mental health, and in his medical writings he diagnosed psychosomatic illness and indicated possible remedies (Maim. *De'ot* 1–3; Introd. to *Avot*; *Hanhagat ha-Beri'ut*).

Maimonides alludes to rabbinic teachings about the harmful effects of negative emotions and quotes the following pronouncements: "R. Yehoshua said: 'The evil eye, the evil inclination and hatred of one's fellow men drive a person out of the world' (*Avot* 2:16).[2] "R. Elazar Ha-Kappar said: 'Envy, lust and ambition drive a man out of the world'" (*Avot* 4:21).[3]

The Maharal (R. Yehudah Löw ben Betzalel) of Prague attributes a wider sense to these dicta in his commentary on *Avot*. It is in man's best interests to avoid the sinful propensities mentioned here, as King Solomon affirmed: "Eat not the bread of him that hath an evil eye" (Prov. 23:6).[4] The evil inclination (*yetzer ha-ra*) is likewise a negative proclivity and a source of danger to man. Misanthropy and antisocial attitudes are personality disorders endangering one's mental

---

health. Since the Almighty created the world "for good" (Gen. 1:31), everything that exists should have a positive purpose and anyone who submits to these evil propensities excludes himself from God's creation plan. In the words of the Sages, they "drive him out of the world" and bring about his destruction (MAHARAL, *Derekh Hayyim ad loc.*).[5]

The Sage's admonition concerning the *ayin ha-ra* (*Avot* 2:11) implies that one who gives way to his evil inclination and looks on his fellow with an "evil eye" exposes himself to the wholesale dangers of emotional upset and psychic disorder. Giving free rein to antisocial attitudes will create obsessions and guilt feelings that ultimately remove a person from normal society ("the world").

The Sages warned against yielding to envy, jealousy and passion, or to an excessive pursuit of honor and glory, which also have the effect of "driving a man out of the world" (*Avot* 4:28). R. Elazar Ha-Kappar's dictum forewarns a person consumed with envy or passion that he runs the risk of contracting a psychosomatic disease which may prove fatal.

The Bible affirms that "envy is the rottenness of the bones" (Prov. 14:30).[6] An inordinately jealous person's mind is tormented by grudges and frustrations that will deprave his mind. According to the Talmud, whenever Rav visited a cemetery he was able to ascertain the disease to which each person buried there had succumbed. Rav declared that out of every hundred, all but one had given up the ghost because of his "evil eye" (*BM* 107b).

How one person was consumed with these vices is related in the Talmud. Jeroboam ben Nebat, the first ruler of Israel's northern kingdom, persistently followed his evil inclination by worshipping idols. Nevertheless, the Holy One, Blessed be He, assured Jeroboam that if he now repented his misdeeds he would walk in *Gan Eden* (Paradise) together with David the son of Jesse. Jeroboam asked, "Who will go first?" – *Mi*

---

5   מוציאין את האדם מן העולם
6   ורקב עצמות קנאה

ba-rosh? When told that David would go first, he replied, "In that case I won't repent",[7] and he did not return from his evil ways (*Sanh.* 102a).

The Talmud also quotes the saying in Proverbs that an envious heart makes the bones rot, whereas an even temperament ("tranquil heart") keeps a person healthy (*Shab.* 152b). The following adage occurs in the Apocrypha: "Jealousy and sickness shorten a man's life; anxiety makes him old before his time" (*Wisdom of Ben Sira* 30:28).[8]

R. Yehoshua spoke of three proclivities that are especially baneful and destructive to one's health: envying another man's possessions and begrudging his happiness – *ayin ha-ra*; giving way to one's evil desires – *yetzer ha-ra*; and hating one's fellow men – *sin'at ha-beriyyot* (*Avot* 2:11). R. Yehoshua took *ayin ha-ra* in this instance to mean stinginess (*kamtzanut*) as opposed to generosity (*ayin tovah*). He also distinguished it from the active type of malevolence also known as the "evil eye" (*ayin ha-ra*).

Mediaeval Jewish scholars echoed this teaching. Solomon Ibn Gabirol, for example, taught that jealousy is a vice to be given a wide berth, since it brings in its wake recurrent vexation and weariness of spirit.[9] Commenting on *Avot* 4:28, R. Yitzḥak Aboab stated that a man prone to jealousy exhibits feelings of anger and hatred which give rise to physical sickness and his own downfall (*Menorat ha-Ma'or* 1).

In regard to the other saying (*Avot* 2:11),[10] Rabbenu Yonah Gerondi drew a distinction between *ayin ha-ra* and *ayin ra'ah*, the spite from which R. Eliezer said a man should distance himself (*Avot* 2:9). The "evil eye" denoted by the term *ayin ra'ah* refers to egoism and meanness of spirit (*middat ha-kilut*): this may not actually lead a person to sin, but it will prevent him from doing good deeds.[11] Commenting on the

---

7 אי הכי לא בעינא

8 קינאה ודווי יקצרו ימים, ובלא עת תזקין דאגה

9 ייסורים ממושכים ויגיעת נפש

10 עין הרע ויצר הרע ושנאת הבריות מוציאין את האדם מן העולם

11 איש בליעל במידות טובות

vices mentioned by R. Elazar Ha-Kappar in *Avot* 4:21 ("Envy, lust and ambition drive a man out of the world"), Rabbenu Yonah argued that these propensities are not wicked in themselves, as they can be utilized for good ends. Jealousy of a man who has distinguished himself in Torah study and the fulfilment of *mitzvot* can thus prompt someone to emulate those achievements. This praiseworthy attitude inspired a Talmudic maxim, "Envy [i.e., competition] among scholars increases wisdom" (*BB* 21a).[12]

On the other hand, jealousy can also evidence chagrin over someone else's success, particularly if the other man has greater achievements to his credit. Such jealousy arouses heartache, melancholy and bitterness of the soul, like a poison infecting the body and causing irreparable damage.

Passionate desire (*ta'avah*) can likewise fulfil virtuous aspirations when it promotes marriage or a yearning to excel in Torah knowledge and the service of one's Creator, as David affirmed: "O Lord, all my longing is to be in Thy presence" (Ps. 38:10).[13] Similarly, an ambitious craving for honour (*kavod*) may serve to glorify the Torah and its upholders; or it may be no more than a selfish pursuit of fame and grandeur.

In his discussion of basic Jewish principles, Maimonides summarized moralistic doctrine regarding the human temperament (Maim. Code, *Madda* 1–3). He declared that human beings possess different characteristics according to their physical and genetic constitution. Each characteristic has its purpose in life, but any excess is injurious and can bring about a man's destruction. The Sages had already emphasized the baneful effects of jealousy, sensualism, acquisitiveness and ambition (*Avot* 4:21).[14]

Though seemingly opposed to one another, these traits can foster exemplary moral behaviour. Thus, being proud or humble, hot-tempered or phlegmatic, mean or generous,

---

12 קנאת סופרים תרבה חכמה

13 ה׳ נגדך כל תאוותי

14 הקנאה והתאוה והכבוד מוציאין את האדם מן העולם

greedy or content, each in its proper place, can be virtuous; when taken to an extreme, however, such qualities are not only unethical but a danger to mental health. It should therefore be one's ideal to seek the golden mean in all things.

Maimonides followed the teaching of R. Yehoshua ben Levi, that man is required to shun evil and exercise moral restraint, in accordance with the verse: "And to him that ordereth his way aright will I show the salvation of God" (Ps. 50:23).[15]

Finally, in his code (*De'ot*, 3:3), Maimonides dismisses belief in the power of the "evil eye" as mere superstition. He exclusively relates mental health to the functioning of the human body and its appetites, each individual's self-control governing his quest for the middle road between indulgence and asceticism. The approach of Maimonides is both ethical and religious; faithful service of the Almighty was taught by King Solomon: "In all thy ways acknowledge Him, and He will direct thy paths aright" (Prov. 3:6).[16]

[General reference: *Encyclopaedia Judaica*, "Evil Eye", 6:997–1000]

C. Objective Aspects

Among ancient peoples there was a widespread belief that someone possessing an "evil eye" could have a baleful effect on others merely by looking at them. In post-Talmudic literature the "evil eye" reputedly contained an element of fire that spread destruction (Maharal, *Netivot Olam* 107d). Envy, malice, anger or resentment directed against another person could bring to life a sinister angel who inflicted harm on the person targeted (Manasseh ben Israel, *Nishmat Hayyim* 3:27).

Folk tradition had it that countering the menace of an "evil eye" required self-restraint on the part of the one casting it

---

15   ושם דרך אראנו בישע אל-הים
16   בכל דרכיך דעהו והוא יישר ארחתיך

and protective measures by the person endangered to avert or escape its malignant effect. Such measures included wearing a lucky charm around the neck or an amulet (*kamei'a*) containing Scriptural verses or mystical combinations of Hebrew letters forming the Divine Name (*Encyclopaedia Judaica, loc. cit.*).

It is widely acknowledged by physiologists that the human eye is capable of influencing another person – especially through the effect of hypnotism, which can induce a trance or render someone controllable by hypnotic suggestion. Psychologists, however, have different opinions about animal magnetism and mostly give little credence to the belief that some magical power in the eye can adversely affect a victim (*Encyclopaedia Britannica*, Vol. 18, "Psychiatry").

European literature of the pre-modern era reflects a widespread belief in the destructive power of the "evil eye". Thus, in Shakespeare's play, *Henry V* (Act 5, Scene 2), when the English and French kings sign a peace treaty after the battle of Agincourt, Queen Isabel of France describes the hatred hitherto visible in the eyes of the English as "fatal balls of murderous basilisks". She trusts that "the venom of such looks" is now a thing of the past and that the meeting of reconciliation "shall change all griefs and quarrels into love".

In Midrashic literature the danger of the *ayin ha-ra* is a prevalent motif, and early Sages linked its effect with a number of Biblical narratives. Thus, Sarah was represented as having been jealous of Hagar when she conceived a child by Abraham and, as a result of Sarah's "evil eye", Hagar miscarried. For this discreditable act Sarah herself was punished (Gen. R. 45:8 on Gen. 16:4).

The Sages also relate that Joseph's dreams made his brothers cast an "evil eye" on him, but to no effect, since Joseph was endowed with a miraculous resistance to the *ayin ha-ra* – a virtue that his descendants reputedly inherited. Like Sarah, Joseph's brothers incurred punishment. His special power is said to have derived from Jacob's blessing: "Joseph is a fruitful bough, a fruitful bough by a fountain; his branches run over the wall" (Gen. 49:22).[17] The Sages interpreted the words *ben porat alei-ayin* ("a fruitful bough by a fountain") to mean that his power exceeded that of the "evil eye" (Gen. R. 84:10 on Gen. 37:8; *Ber.* 55b on Gen. 49:22).

Before instructing Israel to build the Sanctuary, we are told, God gave them the Priestly Blessing (Num. 6:22–27) as a talismanic protection from the "evil eye", which had brought about the shattering of the first stone tablets inscribed with the Decalogue. In later Jewish tradition it was accepted that the words of the Priestly Blessing might serve as a protective device against the *ayin ha-ra* (Num. R. 12:4 on Num. 7:1).

Some extreme examples of the "evil eye" inflicting mortal injury are given in the Talmud. With one look R. Yoḥanan is said to have killed a man who disparaged Jerusalem (*BB* 75a). R. Shim'on bar Yoḥai had the same magical power: in one instance, he "cast his eye" on an abusive old man, who then died.[18] On another occasion, he looked at a wicked man and "transformed him into a heap of bones" (*Shab.* 34a).[19]

When Joshua divided the land of Canaan among the Israelites, the tribes of Ephraim and Manasseh complained that they had a large population and needed more land. Joshua urged them to go into the forest and mask their numbers, so that no "evil eye" would fall on them.[20] Ephraim and Manasseh then told him that they did not fear the "evil eye", since they were descendants of Joseph and immune to the poisonous effect of the *ayin ha-ra*. As mentioned earlier, Jacob had blessed Joseph as "a fruitful bough by a fountain",[21] which meant that his power surpassed that of the "evil eye" (Josh. 17:14–18; *BB* 118 a–b, Rashi *ad loc.*, on Gen. 49:22; *Ber.* 55b).

The Sages transmitted a number of moralistic ideas about avoiding harmful effects of the *ayin ha-ra*. Merchants selling large bundles of wicker canes were urged to beware of the

---

17 בן פרת יוסף עלי עין בנות צעדה עלי שור
18 יהב ביה עיניה ונח
19 נתן בו עיניו ועשהו גל של עצמות
20 שלא תשלוט בכם עין רע
21 בן פרת עלי עין

"evil eye", since people might begrudge their abundant stock
(*Pes.* 50b). R. Abbahu said, a man should also keep away
from his neighbour's field when it is full of standing corn,
in case the sight of it made him jealous and his "evil eye"
then damaged the produce (*BM* 107a, Rashi *ad loc.*). Even an
expression of admiration such as 'Your child is so beautiful'
may sometimes bring the "evil eye" to result in harm, and
therefore it is customary that such a possibility be immediately
excluded (*beli ayin ha'ra*). Thus, when Miriam and Aaron
complained that Moses had married the daughter of Jethro
she was described as uncomely of dark colour, (*ishah kushit*)
instead of, as the Sages explained, they meant that she was a
beautiful woman (Num. 12:1, Rashi, *ad loc.*).

When reciting Grace after Meals at a banquet, one should
only offer the cup of blessing to someone who has "a kind
eye".[22] Even birds were said to recognize mean-eyed people
and to refuse crumbs from their table. One should therefore
avoid food provided by a mean individual, in accordance with
the saying: "Eat not the bread of him that hath an evil eye"
(Prov. 23:6).[23] The commentary of MAHARSHA explains
that a person deemed miserly (*tzar ayin*) embitters the soul of
anyone who partakes of his bread; he will be left with a sour
taste in his mouth and must vomit the food he has eaten (*Sot.*
39a, MAHARSHA *ad loc.*; Ibn Ezra on Prov. 23:7).

The Sages held that Hananiah, Mishael and Azariah
(Shadrach, Meshach and Abed-Nego), the three righteous
men who refused to bow down before the idol set up by
Nebuchadnezzar and who miraculously escaped death in the
fiery furnace, perished later as a result of the "evil eye" cast by
onlookers gazing in astonishment at their deliverance (*Sanh.*
93a, Rashi *ad loc.*, on Dan. 3:24–27).

Expounding the Biblical verse, "And the Lord will take
away from thee all sickness" (Deut. 7:15),[24] Rav declared that

---

22   אין נותנין כוס של ברכה לברך אלא לטוב העין
23   אל תלחם את לחם רע העין
24   והסיר ה' ממך כל חולי

the source of all ailments is the "evil eye" (*BM* 107b, Rashi *ad loc.*).

D. Protection from the Evil Eye

Prayer

The Sages often referred to invisible baneful spirits that endeavour to harm man and from which he needs to be protected. According to R. Yehudah, three require special protection – a sick person, a bride and bridegroom, and a midwife at the delivery of a child (*Ber.* 54b, Rashi *ad loc.*).[25] R. Yitzhak suggested the best means of defense available to a person going to sleep at night: "Whoever reads the *Shema* at his bedside is like one holding a two-edged sword in his hand; the evil spirits will flee from him" (*Ber.* 5a, Rashi *ad loc.*). R. Yehoshua ben Levi stated that even if someone has already said the *Shema* in his evening prayer, he should repeat it at his bedside as an additional safeguard (*Ber.* 4b; *Sh. Ar., Orah Hayyim* 239:1).

Tannaitic teachers noted that whenever an addition to the city of Jerusalem and the Temple precincts was consecrated by the Sanhedrin, "two thanksgiving hymns and a special song" were required.[26] The Sages explained that the latter was "a song of protection from harm".[27] Rashi (*ad loc.*) considered this to be *Yoshev be-seter Elyon* – "He that dwelleth in the shelter of the Most High..." (Ps. 91:1),[28] which Moses traditionally recited at the dedication of the Sanctuary (Ex. 39:43; *Shev.* 14a, 15b).

Rabbenu Yonah, commenting on the same passage of Talmud, observed that when Ezra rededicated Jerusalem,

---

25 שלשה צריכין שמור ואלו הן, חולה, חתן וכלה וחיה – במתניתא תנא חולה חיה
26 בשתי תודות ובשירה
27 שיר של פגעים
28 יושב בסתר עליון

the people marched around the city and sang this Psalm with musical accompaniment to repel evil spirits (Rabbenu Yonah on RIF, *Ber.* 3a *s.v.* "*shir*").

R. Yehoshua ben Levi is said to have adopted the practice of reciting *Yoshev be-seter Elyon* every night before he went to sleep. The Sages asked how it was that he relied on this Psalm when he himself had banned the use of Torah verses as a prophylactic.[29] R. Yehoshua ben Levi replied that he had condemned using them as a magical cure for sickness; but reciting verses from the Torah to protect oneself against evil spirits was legitimate (*Shev.* 15b).

The Sages declared it proper to add, immediately after the thanksgiving benedictions of the Morning Service, two special petitions for God's help in strengthening our devotion to His Law and keeping us away from temptation and sin. This practice is based on their instruction to amplify the last blessing, "Who removes sleep from my eyes,"[30] with a personal petition for Divine aid in obeying His commandments.[31] The prayer books of R. Amram Gaon, R. David Abudarham and Ya'avetz follow this text.

Also included here are the words, "Keep us far from an evil person and an evil companion".[32] Though unidentified, the author of this prayer is thought to have been Rav (*Ber.* 60b; *Sanh.* 107a). Maimonides refers to a similar petition (Maim. Code, *Tefillah* 7:4; cf. Seligmann Baer's *Seder Avodat Yisra'el*, Rödelheim, 1868). This is followed by *Yehi ratzon,* another petition, quoting the special prayer which R. Yehudah Ha-Nasi recited after the daily *Amidah* (*Ber.* 16b), but now added here. It invokes God's protection "from brazen men and from arrogance, from an evil man, an evil companion and a bad neighbour, from any mishap and from a harsh opponent..." (lit., "the satanic destroyer").

---

29 אסור להתרפאת בדברי תורה

30 המעביר שינה מעיני

31 שתרגילני בתורתך ודבקני במצוותיך

32 מאדם רע ומחבר רע

R. Yosef Caro's *Shulḥan Arukh* lays down that one should read the *Shema* and Psalm 91 before going to sleep at night (*Sh. Ar., Oraḥ Ḥayyim* 239:1, *Magen Avraham ad loc.*). The *Tur* codification, which gives the same Talmudic text as the one quoted in *Siddur Rav Amram*, notes that the worshipper may attach to this prayer any additional requests that he desires (*Tur, Oraḥ Ḥayyim* 46).

The prayer book of the Sephardi rite contains an extended plea for God's protection from various evils that endanger man. After "Deliver me from... any mishap", the following additions occur: "from an evil eye (*me-ayin ha-ra*) and a wicked tongue (*lashon ha-ra*), from slander, false evidence and misanthropy, from libel, unnatural death, tormenting sickness and calamities". Kabbalistic tradition enjoins praying for deliverance from seven types of adversity. This reflects the answers given by disciples of R. Yoḥanan ben Zakkai to a question that he asked: "Which is the evil way that a man should avoid?" They replied that one must avoid above all "an evil eye; a bad friend; a wicked neighbour; one who borrows and does not repay; and an evil heart" (*Avot* 2:14).

Belief in the power of witchcraft and malign spirits dominates kabbalistic literature. According to the *Zohar*, when a man goes to bed at night he should recite the *Shema* and entrust his soul to the keeping of Heaven, thus protecting himself against demons (*shedim*) and disease. When Aaron turned his rod into a serpent, Pharaoh's magicians resorted to witchcraft and did the same, although their wizardry was less powerful (*Ber.* 11a; *Zohar, Va-era* III, 28a).

Amulets

The use of amulets (*kamei'ot*) to ward off of evil spirits became widespread in mediaeval Spain and Eastern Europe, and later among the kabbalists of Safed (*Encyclopaedia Judaica*, Vol. 2, "Amulet").

Maimonides condemned the use of amulets bearing mystical arrangements of the Divine Names (*shemot*) and any belief that they afforded miraculous protection against harm. Charms and incantations were useless, he declared, and no rational person should believe in such heathen superstitions. Utilizing sacred texts for the purpose of healing a physical complaint was, moreover, a negation of the Torah. Maimonides subsumed these idolatrous beliefs under the prohibitions of magic and witchcraft (Ex. 22:17; Deut. 18:10–12),[33] and forbade the use of Torah verses in a bid to cure sickness when a medical remedy should be applied. He also took this stand in his critique of Roman speculation about planetary influences (Maim. *Perush Mishnayot, Avodah Zarah*, 4, 54a; Maim. *Guide* 1:61–62; cf. *Tur, Yoreh De'ah* 179; Maim. Code, *Avodat Kokhavim* 11:12, *Tefillin* 5:4; *Tur, Yoreh De'ah* 179).

Caro agreed that scriptural verses should not be applied in the treatment of a physical illness, but differed with Maimonides over their talismanic use in repelling evil spirits (*shedim*) and averting demonic mischief. Such charms might only be used, however, if they had already proved effective in warding off a contagious disease. Here Caro followed the ruling of RASHBA, who likened this case to one in which the Sages permitted women to wear such amulets on the Sabbath because of their protective value (*Sh. Ar., Yoreh De'ah* 179:9–10; *Sh. Ar, Orah Hayyim* 301:24, 305:17).

Caro does follow Maimonides in denouncing the futile use of incantations (*lehashim*) as an antidote to snake venom, since an incantation has no curative effect and the bite requires prompt medical treatment. An incantation would be permitted, however, if it eased the patient's mind (*Sh. Ar., Yoreh De'ah* 179:6).[34]

The Vilna Gaon rejected Maimonides' wholesale condemnation of these practices. There are, he argued, numerous passages in the Talmud indicating that the Sages

---

33 מאונן ומכשף
34 שלא תיטרף דעתו עליו

themselves utilized charms and incantations combined with the Divine Name and that particular Biblical verses were recited. He believed that the Sages understood their deeper meaning. The Vilna Gaon also referred to passages in the Talmud (e.g., *Sanh.* 67a–68a) showing that certain magical acts were permitted. Each Friday night, for example, R. Ḥanina and R. Oshayah engaged in practical Kabbalah, producing a three-year-old calf which they ate at their Sabbath meal (*Sanh.* 65b).

In a further passage (*Shab.* 66b), Abbaye recalls his mother's advice that incantations for the sick should be repeated several times, always including the name of the patient's mother. It is related elsewhere (*Shab.* 81b) that R. Ḥisda and R. Huna outwitted a Roman lady whose incantation had tied up their boat: they then invoked the Divine Name to release it from her spell. The Vilna Gaon recognized that these strange accounts have a deeper, esoteric meaning which was revealed to initiated mystics, not skeptical philosophers (Eliyahu ben Shelomo Zalman Gaon, commentary on *Sh. Ar.*, *Yoreh De'ah* 179:6, n. 13).

E. Satan

As the embodiment of evil, Satan is frequently mentioned in the Bible and the Midrash, though rarely in halakhic literature. The Sages regarded Satan not as an autonomous power but as an agent that God used for a particular purpose, such as the temptation of Job (*BB* 47a). Satan's role in the world is threefold: he tempts man to sin, then accuses him of sinning and inflicts punishment. He devises all the evil in the world and has various names, including the Angel of Death (cf. *Wisdom of Ben Sira* 2:24 on Gen. 3).

Satan's function is associated with the basic Jewish concept of free will (*beḥirah*). Man is endowed with the capability of choice, but choice here does not mean his ability to choose the more effective or advantageous of any two possible actions.

He must freely choose between good and evil. In order for man to consciously exercise this power, two opposing forces were embedded in him – the good inclination (*yetzer ha-tov*) and the evil one (*yetzer ha-ra*). Both forces were creations of the Almighty.

The evil inclination is sometimes identified with "the adversary", namely Satan, but it can also figure as an "angel" (*mal'akh*), denoting "a messenger of God". Just as the Angel of Death[35] is none other than the emissary acting on God's orders, so the evil inclination is charged with the task of endeavouring to "turn man away" from his good inclination. In point of fact, 'Satan' is derived from the Hebrew root *satah*, "to turn away". The Talmud relates that two angels accompany a Jew home from the synagogue each Sabbath eve. One angel is good, the other bad, yet both are called "servants of the Almighty" (*Shab.* 119b).[36] Hence man is required to exercise his freedom of choice and to "choose good", which means to "choose life" (Deut. 30:15, 19).[37]

Resh Lakish encapsulated his colleagues' view of Satan in this aphorism: "The Adversary [*ha-satan*], the Evil Inclination [*yetzer ha-ra*] and the Angel of Death [*mal'akh ha-mavet*] are one and the same" (*BB* 16a).[38] Together with the *yetzer ha-tov*, they all fulfil their duties as messengers of God; both the yetzer ha-tov and the *yetzer ha-ra* are instruments through which man can serve Him. The Sages derived this teaching from the Biblical precept, "Thou shalt love the Lord thy God with all thy heart" (Deut. 6:5).[39] In Hebrew, *lev* is the normal spelling of "heart"; by doubling the letter *bet*, "thy heart" (*levavekha*) is extended to denote the heart's two attitudes – good and evil – which can both help to serve God (*Ber.* 54a). While this concept may be hard for man to grasp, it is only

---

35   מלאך המות
36   שני מלאכי השרת
37   ובחרת בחיים
38   אמר ריש לקיש הוא שטן הוא יצר הרע הוא מלאך המות
39   ואהבת את השם אל-היך בכל לבבך

in this way that he exercises his free will (Moshe Cordovero, *Shi'ur Komah* 25).

Judaism rejected the Manichaean belief in a cosmic struggle between the forces of good and evil, represented by light and darkness. "In the beginning" God Himself created these elements "and divided the light from the darkness" (Gen. 1:4).[40] The prophet Isaiah enunciated Jewish thought clearly: "I am the Lord, and there is none else; I form the light and create darkness; I make peace and create evil; I am the Lord that doeth all these things" (Isa. 45:6–7).[41] This teaching is repeated in the daily Morning Service shortly before the *Shema* declaration of faith: "He forms light and creates darkness; He makes peace and creates all things".[42] Nor would the Sages countenance the dualism of Gnostic philosophy, as in Zoroastrian cosmology, which taught that evil was the work of a separate power known as the Demiurge. Those upholding such views were proscribed as heretics – *minim* (TJ *Ber.* 9:1, 62b). Maimonides defined heresy as the belief that there are two or more powers of creation (Maim. *Yad, Teshuvah* 3:7).

When the Sages equated Satan with the *yetzer ha-ra*, they affirmed that man was both able and duty-bound to overcome Satan; otherwise, the evil impulse would bring about his death (*BB* 15a). The temptation of Eve in the Garden of Eden (Gen. 3) and the testing of Abraham and Isaac through the *Akedah* sacrifice were instigated by Satan (*Sanh.* 89b on Gen. 22; *Midrash Tanhuma, Va-yera* 22). He likewise misled the people of Israel into believing that Moses had died on Mount Sinai and urged them to make the Golden Calf. Here Satan was identified with the *yetzer ha-ra* (*Shab.* 89a, Rashi *ad loc.*; *Midrash Tanhuma* on Ex. 32:1).

Since "the adversary" induces man to do wrong, an extended petition is included in the daily Morning Service – *Vi-yehi*

---

40 ויבדל אל-הים בין האור ובין החושך
41 יוצר אור ובורא חושך עושה שלום ובורא רע אני ה' עשה כל אלה
42 יוצר אור ובורא חושך, עושה שלום ובורא את הכל

ratzon.[43] It reads in part: "Lead us not into the power of sin or temptation.[44] Let not the evil impulse[45] dominate us... and rescue me from the destructive Satan".[46] The *Hashkivenu* evening prayer ("Lay us down to sleep in peace") includes a plea to "remove the adversary" (Satan), who stands as an obstacle "before us" and an aggressor "behind us".[47] Satan was also believed to serve as prosecutor in the Heavenly court (Zech. 4; Lev. R. 38:7).

The Sages personified this abstract power of evil, identifying Satan as the motive force behind the *yetzer ha-ra* and all wrongdoing. One should therefore avoid mentioning a possible disaster and never say anything that might give Satan an excuse to cause mischief. "Don't open your mouth [i.e., never give an opening] to Satan", they advised (*Ber.* 19a, 60a).[48] Since "the adversary" was believed to take advantage of a man's predicament, it was also advisable to stay clear of risky situations (TJ *Shab.* 2; Gen. R. 91:9).[49]

"An arrow in your eye" was a phrase that expressed defiance of Satan (*Kid.* 30a).[50] The scholarly Pelimo often used this expression, but Satan once told him that it had no effect; he should use God's own words instead: "The Lord rebuke thee, O Satan" (Zech. 3:2; *Kid.* 81a–b).[51]

The Sages declared that Satan resented the fact that R. Matya ben Harash was in all respects a saintly individual. The Evil One employed every wile at his disposal to lure this man into sinning, but gave up when his plan failed (*Midrash Tanhuma, Hukkat*). The best way for any man to protect himself from Satan was through Torah study and performance of the

---

43	ויהי רצון
44	לא לידי חטא, ולא לידי עבירה ועון, ולא לידי נסיון
45	ואל תשלט בנו יצר הרע
46	משטן המשחית
47	והסר שטן מלפנינו ומאחורינו
48	אל תפתח פה לשטן
49	אין השטן מקטרג אלא בשעת סכנה
50	הוה אמינא לשטן גירא בעיניך
51	יגער ה' בך השטן

mitzvot which the Torah ordained.[52] Thus, on Yom Kippur, when one spends the whole day in fasting and prayer, Satan has no power over Israel (*RH* 17b; *Midrash Shoḥer Tov* 27).

Chapter 13

Contract – *Hozim*

13 Contract – <u>H</u>ozim

A. Introduction

Cases of monetary law[1] are distinct from religious, non-monetary matters.[2] The strict observance of religious prohibitions is considered more vital than judgments in monetary matters. In a debate between the schools of Hillel and Shammai the latter objected to a ruling by Hillel as follows: "You have been permissive in the matter of forbidden sexual relations,[3] where greater stringency is required; should you not therefore be permissive in a monetary matter that is not nearly so serious?"

The discussion involved a couple who travelled overseas,[4] the wife returning with a report that her husband had died there. The Sages discussed the circumstances in which the wife's evidence could be accepted so as to permit her remarriage. A statement by the wife lacking additional evidence would normally be regarded as inadequate and the court would not accept it, yet Bet Shammai ruled that she could remarry and also collect the payment owed to her according to the terms laid down in her ketubbah.[5] However, Bet Hillel declared that although the woman could remarry, her unsupported evidence did not entitle her to receive the money specified in her ketubbah.[6] Bet Shammai then objected to that decision, saying: "You have permitted her to remarry, which might involve a serious breach of the marriage prohibitions; should

---

ממון	1
איסור	2
עריות	3
האשה שהלכה היא ובעלה למדינת הים	4
תנשא ותטול כתובתה	5
תנשא ולא תטול כתובתה	6

we not therefore also grant her monetary claim, where a flawed request is of lesser importance?"[7] The Mishnah records that Bet Hillel assented to the other opinion and followed Shammai's ruling (*Yev.* 114b, 116b).[8]

In Hillel's view, the payment of her *ketubbah* was a financial claim and, according to the legal axiom, *hamotzi meihaveiro alav horaiah*, without irrefutable evidence the court had no right to extract money or property from the respondent who is presumed to be the rightful possessor (*hezkat mamon*) (*B.K.* 35a, 62a, *Tos.* "*Asu*"; *Ket.* 27b; *Shev.* 46a; *BB* 45b; *Git.* 14b, *Tos.* "*ve'hakhamim*"; Maim. *To'en ve'nit'an* 8:1; *Sh. Ar., Hoshen Mishpat* 133:1). This woman had to show that the money was in fact due to her: "The burden of proof rests upon the claimant" (*Sh. Ar., Hoshen Mishpat* 58:2, REMA).[9] Since Hillel had permitted her to remarry, he was obliged to accept the reasoning of Bet Shammai and to concur with them (M. Elon, *Jewish Law* [*Mishpat Ivri*], Vol. 1, p. 123).

A case of civil law may turn into an issue of religious law if, for example, the stipulation in a contract happens to clash with the Biblical laws of succession regarding a testator's estate. In normal circumstances, if a man stipulated that a given son or daughter of his was denied his or her share of the inheritance, that statement would be ineffective since it contravened Torah law and was therefore void (*BB* 115a, 122b).[10] The principle is that any condition defying a Biblical law is invalid (*Mak.* 3b). If someone declared, "I will sell you this article on condition that the law against overcharging[11] does not apply to it", that law would still retain its effect. Nevertheless, later Sages permitted greater freedom in contractual conditions, so that a stipulation that the purchaser would not accuse him of overcharging might be valid (*Mak.* 3b; Maim. *Shemittah ve-Yovel*, 9:10; *Sh. Ar., Hoshen Mishpat* 67:9). The same

---

7 התרתם ערוה חמורה ולא נתיר ממון הקל

8 חזרו בית הלל להורות כדברי בית שמאי

9 המוציא מחברו עליו הראיה

10 כל המתנה על מה שכתוב בתורה תנאו בטל

11 אונאה

ruling would apply to the prohibition of usury (*BM* 61a). Any condition requiring a breach of Torah law or criminal law is, of course, null and void (*BK* 93a; Elon, *op. cit.*, Vol. 1, p. 127).

Law Morals and Conscience

Torah law demands the observance of moral and ethical precepts just as it lays down the general code of established law. The prohibitive commandment, "Thou shalt not murder", and the precept, "Honour thy father and thy mother", are juxtaposed in the Decalogue (Ex. 20:12–13). The two are sometimes interrelated: when the court renders judgment in a trial and passes a death sentence, it is also obliged to fulfil the moral law, "Thou shalt love thy neighbour as thyself". Thus, even a criminal's execution should be performed with minimal disgrace, inflicting the least possible agony on the victim (*Sanh.* 45a).[12]

The civil law of contract is usually treated in a different manner from the religious or ritual laws. There are, however, many instances in which the court's decision will depend on the contractor's intention and attitude of mind when the contract was made. Although a normative legal judgment may involve penalties or sanctions, moral obligations may be invoked by the court, but they are not enforced. A moral imperative is declared to be the way a good and upright person conducts himself, the discharging of personal responsibility in which man's conscience is his guide.

Discussing the relationship between employer and employee, the Talmud records this morally based judgment that a prominent Sage handed down (see also Chapter 5 above).

Rabbah bar bar Ḥanan hired some porters to bring him a

barrel of wine. As they were carrying it, the barrel fell down and was broken. Since Rabbah felt that the damage had been caused by their negligence, he decided to recoup his loss by seizing their garments. The porters demanded that he return them and brought their complaint before Rav, the leading Babylonian scholar and head of the Sura Academy. "Give their clothes back to them", Rav ordered, whereupon Rabbah asked: "Is that the law? Surely the porters are liable for the damage they caused?" Rav replied: "Even so, in fulfilment of the teaching, 'That thou mayest walk in the way of good men'" (Prov. 2:20)." Rabbah accordingly returned their garments. The porters had a further complaint to make: "We are poor men; we have worked all day and need money. Are we to receive no pay?" Rav then ordered Rabbah to pay them their wages. "Is that the law?" Rabbah again asked, and Rav replied: "Even so, for the teaching further states, 'And keep the paths of the righteous'" (Prov. 2:20; BM 83a; Sh. Ar., Hoshen Mishpat 304:1, Arukh ha-Shulhan).[13]

The Quality of Conscience

If not enforced by law, the performance of one's moral duty is inspired and influenced by one's conscience. It can be assumed that man's conscience is a deep-seated mental faculty which gauges the moral quality of his motives and actions, impelling him to do what he judges to be right and inhibiting whatever he considers to be wrong. Thus, "obeying the dictates of one's conscience" usually means that one follows the path of virtue, even if there is no compulsion to do so. Ultimately, an individual's actions reflect the character or temperament that determines how he will behave. This final choice depends on the extent to which he accepts God's law or abides by ethical and religious teaching.

A further instance of "conscience correction" may be seen

when one party made an oral agreement to buy merchandise from another. Although no written contract had been drawn up, the purchaser was morally obliged to keep his word and complete the transaction, for otherwise the Sages would be displeased with him (Maim. *Yad, Mekhirah,* 7:8).[14] Anyone whose faulty conscience angered them was said to possess "a base soul".[15] Scrupulously ethical conduct was, however, applauded as "saintly behaviour" (*BM* 52b; Elon, *op. cit.,* Vol. 1, p. 148).[16]

The Sages recognized that the average person belongs to the middle rank of human nature. At times his evil impulse (*yetzer ha-ra*) is dominant, fostering passion, egoism, vanity, lasciviousness and greed; at other times his better impulse (*yetzer ha-tov*) gains the upper hand, determining his course of action. This points to the frailty and vacillation of man's conscience when he seeks to follow the right and proper way. As Jeremiah the prophet declared: "The heart is deceitful above all things and desperately sick". For man's conscience is unreliable – "Who can know it?" – and only God can "search the heart, rewarding man in accordance with his ways and the fruit of his actions" (Jer. 17:9–10).[17]

The man whose behaviour entitles him to be called a saint or a libertine is one who consistently harnesses his inclinations for the performance of good or evil. It is not a case of his mind or emotions being necessarily wicked or of his conscience misleading him. Should someone claim that the evil impulse leads him astray so that he is forced to behave wickedly, the Almighty replies: "You [man] have made him evil" (*Midrash Tanḥuma, Bereshit* 7).[18] The difference between the righteous and the wicked is that the latter plead that their conscience is at fault, to which the Sages reply: "The wicked are in the power of their heart (i.e, their sensual desires), whereas the

---

אין רוח חכמים נוחה הימנו	14
נפש רע	15
מדת חסידות	16
עקב הלב מכל ואנש הוא מי ידענו	17
אמר הקב״ה אתה עשית אותו רע	18

righteous have their heart in their power" (Gen. R. 34:10). The Rabbis urged man never to consider himself impotent in the face of an overwhelming evil desire; he should always drive his good impulse[19] into battle with his evil inclination[20] and endeavour to make the good one victorious (*Ber.* 5a).[21]

A Torah law primarily based on an act of the mind is the law of the "forgotten sheaf" (*shikhhah*): "When thou reapest thy harvest in thy field, and hast forgot a sheaf in the field[22], thou shalt not go back to fetch it; it shall be for the stranger, for the fatherless, and for the widow" (Deut. 24:19; Mish., *Pe'ah* 6:1; *BM* 11a; Maim. *Mattenot Aniyyim* 1:5). This law prohibits the husbandman from going back to collect a sheaf which, in his mind, he had forgotten to collect while the reaping was in progress.

Whether or not the reaper admits to having "forgotten", he will accept the mandate of the law; but if he is nevertheless intent on retaining his sheaf, he will prevaricate and try to justify his action by misrepresenting what actually occurred so as to evade liability. Such a course of action, revealing his true thoughts, is determined by the individual's conscience; and conscience reflects that man's nature, which he is ever capable of improving. Divine law judges the whole man and pays no regard to fanciful representations of his character. It is not a question of strength or weakness in his physical make-up, but of his firm resolve to do the right thing. "Who is mighty? He who subdues his passions", the Sages affirmed. "He who rules over his spirit is better then one who conquers a city" (*Avot* 4:1).

A man's conscience is subject to examination, less by himself (as he is naturally biased in its favor) than by the Almighty, who knows what that individual's mental choices really are. When the prophet Samuel chose Jesse's youngest

---

19   יצר הטוב

20   יצר הרע

21   לעולם ירגיז אדם יצר טוב על יצר הרע

22   ושכחת עומר בשדה

son to be king over Israel, rejecting his stalwart older brothers, God told him: "Man looketh on the outward appearance [only], but the Lord looketh on the heart" (1 Sam. 16:7).[23]

Some people resort to the excuse that they were born with a weak conscience while others may claim that their evil impulse was too strong for them to overcome, but no one can avoid censure by attributing his misdeeds to some genetic fault.

Liability in Heavenly Justice – Hayyav bi-yedei Shamayim

A court of law is able to judge known transgressions that incur varying punishments. The extent of some offences may, however, fall short of their legal definitions and thus escape the penalty ordained. Each individual knows if he chose to disregard the law and if his conscience did not prevent him from doing so. For such offences he is judged by the Heavenly tribunal (Mish. *Yevamot* 4:13; *Yev.* 49a)[24] and, if found guilty, incurs Divine punishment. In a number of cases the penalty is not visible. Where the liability of *karet* ("spiritual excision") has been incurred the death penalty is exacted by Divine punishment. R. Yohanan ben Beroka said: "One who has committed the sin of desecrating the Divine Name – *Hillul Hashem* – in secret will receive Divine punishment in the open (*Avot* 4:4).[25]

[References: Lev. 22:3; *Ker.* 2a; Soncino Talmud, *Kodashim* III, Introd. 1:1 – There are 36 transgressions punishable by *karet*; *Yev.* 49a[26]; *Avot* 2:12; *Avot* 1:3[27]; *Avot* 4:4, "Heavenly punishment", "Heavenly judgment";[28] *BK* 56a[29]]

The story of Balaam and Balak provides an example of

---

23 הקב״ה ליבא בעי דכתיב וה׳ יראה ללבב
24 חייב בידי שמים
25 כל המחלל שם שמים בסתר נפרעין ממנו בגלוי
26 לשם שמים – וכל מעשיך יהיו לשם שמים
27 ויהי מורא שמים עליכם
28 דיני שמים כגון כרת
29 השולח את הבערה ביד חרש שוטה וקטן פטור מדיני אדם, וחייב בדיני שמים

man's struggle against his own conscience. Balak, the heathen Moabite king, sought to curse and vanquish the people of Israel. Balak saw no moral problem in his design, although Israel had shown no hostility towards the Moabites. Balaam regarded himself as a prophet of the Almighty, however, and his conscience told him that it would be wrong for him to invoke curses on Israel. He realized that God did not wish him to curse the Israelites, a people whom the Lord had already blessed. Although Balak's offer of a rich reward was alluring, Balaam had to admit that his conscience would not allow him to do as Balak asked. Nevertheless, Balaam told the king to wait a while: perhaps a scheme could be devised that would fulfil his request.

Sorely tempted by the gold and silver that Balak had promised, Balaam struggled with his conscience and looked for a way to get around its demands. The Almighty still tried to dissuade him, even using Balaam's faithful ass to show that a Divine prohibition cannot be ignored. Yet Balaam insisted on following his own inclinations rather than the dictates of his conscience. God then not only permitted but ordered him to accompany Balak, warning him to speak only as the Lord commanded; otherwise, he would incur the penalty for disobedience (Num. 22:2–35; verse 3, Sforno, verse 35, Rashi *ad loc.*). Balaam's curses were turned into blessings for Israel, and he eventually perished with the Midianites (Num. 24; 31:8).

In a number of cases, where the misdeed is such that no court of law may punish the offender, spiritual "excision" (*karet*) is prescribed (Lev 18:29; *Yev.* 49a).[30] Thirty-six transgressions of this kind are listed in the Torah, ranging from unnatural vice and the defilement of Temple sacrifices to the consumption of leavened bread on Passover and violation of the Yom Kippur fast (Mish., *Ker.* 1:1).

This severe penalty, which entails the "cutting off" or

removal of a person's soul from Divine grace and protection, may also result in an untimely or sudden death. According to rabbinic tradition, "dying at the age of fifty is regarded as death by karet[31] and at sixty as death by Divine judgment;[32] whereas it is recorded that the prophet Samuel died at the age of fifty-two" (Ta'an. 5b). Rava, however, observed that "long life, the blessing of children and an adequate livelihood are not due to a person's worthiness; they are simply due to the astrological constellation at his birth" (MK 28a).[33]

There are many issues in life that must be resolved according to the dictates of a man's conscience: where his moral duty is not clearly defined, for example, or where it obliges him to divulge the thought that prompted his action, whether this be an honest intention or one making him liable to an adverse judgment in court. When negotiating a transaction or signing an agreement, if the nature of the contract depends on the intention of both parties, the honest or dishonest behaviour of either side will reflect the quality of his conscience. Any aberration is subject to Divine judgment.

The legal order per se cannot enforce compliance with moral obligations, since there is no objective criterion by which such compliance (or lack of it) may be judged according to the particular circumstances of the individual concerned. The intent or objective of the law would need to be measured with the intent or objective existing only in his mind and depending on the truth of his claim. A faulty conscience would allow him to distort the truth of his intention and rule out the possibility of any objective judgment.

Nevertheless, the rules of law and the ethical demand of "Thou shalt love thy neighbour as thyself" (Lev. 19:18) are fundamental to Judaism. Hillel the Elder taught: "Whatever is hateful to you, never do to someone else; this embraces the

---

31 מתת כרת
32 מיתה בידי שמים
33 אמר רבא חיי בני ומזוני לא בזכותא תליא מילתא אלא במזלא תליא מילתא

whole of Torah teaching" (*Shab.* 31a; Elon, *op cit.*, Vol. 1, pp. 141–144).[34]

There are instances in Jewish law where no liability may be incurred, yet redress is not left to the conscience of the perpetrator and liability is determined by a court judgment. This procedure was established in a wide range of injuries that may not suffice to require a penalty in the laws of torts, but which are held to make the perpetrator liable for redress by Divine law. Four instances were mentioned by the Sages (*BK* 55b). A Mishnaic ruling thus points to the law, "If a man... shall let his beast loose, and it feed in another man's field (Ex. 22:4).[35] Should a responsible adult have charge of an animal that grazes in another man's field, he (the agent) must pay for the loss incurred. However, the Sages ruled that if the person in charge of the animal inflicting the damage was incompetent (i.e., a deaf-mute, an imbecile or a minor), the owner – while not liable to pay compensation by human law – would be obligated to do so by Divine law (*BK* 6:4, 59b; Maim. *Yad, Nizkei Mammon*, 14:5; *Sh. Ar., Hoshen Mishpat* 32:2, 396:6, 418:7).[36]

Liability in Divine Justice – *Hayav Bedinei Shamayim*

Where a person is judged liable solely by Divine law, it is the court's duty to inform him that he is so liable. The matter is not left to the conscience of that individual, and the court must admonish him as follows: "We will not apply a sanction against you, but you must do your duty in the sight of Heaven, since Heaven will be your judge". Any subsequent failure by that man to appease his neighbor and make good the wrong is considered to be a grave transgression of Divine law that might well affect his standing in the eyes of the community. He is stigmatized as one "lacking in credibility and trustworthiness"

---

34   דעלך סני לחברך לא תעביד

35   כי יעבר איש שדה

36   פטור בדיני אדם וחייב בדיני שמים

(*BM* 49a; Maim. *Mekhirah* 7:8; Meiri, *Bet ha-Behirah*, *BK* 6:6; *Yam shel Shelomo*, *BK* 6:6).[37]

It may appear that the court has exceeded its authority by pressurizing the defendant, even threatening him with dire punishment,[38] to make him accept a liability far above the rules of law (*BM* 44a; Maim. *Mekhirah* 7:1–2; *BM* 37a–b; Maim. *Yad, Gezelah va-Avedah* 4:9–10). In Jewish law there is, however, a religio-moral sanction known as "fulfilment of one's duty in the sight of Heaven".[39] The Sages ruled here that while the *bet din* could not prescribe liability, the defendant must satisfy the claimant in the eyes of Heavenly justice, although they did not go so far as to invoke Divine punishment (*BM* 37a–b; Maim. *Yad, Gezelah va-Avedah*, 4:9–10; *Sh. Ar., Hoshen Mishpat* 365:2).

Generous Application of the Law – Lifnim mi-Shurat ha-Din

A court may give special consideration to a person's needs, instructing the defendant to act more generously than the strict law would require. The Sages called this a judgment *lifnim mi-shurat ha-din* – "inside the line of justice" (i.e., going beyond the strict letter of the law; see Chapter 5, "Ethics").[40] A man of principle should act in accordance with a higher moral standard than the law demands. He will have nothing to lose and everything to gain from such conduct, which amounts to *kiddush Hashem* – a sanctification of the Divine Name (*BK* 99b–100a; *BM* 30b; *Ber.* 7a; *BM* 83a, Rashi *ad loc.*).[41]

There are times when a judge is obligated to rule according to the principle of *lifnim mi-shurat ha-din*, especially if the circumstances or urgency of the case require that the law be applied in a flexible manner. Such a judgment may deviate

---

37	מחסור אמונא
38	מי שפרע
39	יצאת ידי שמים
40	לפנים משורת הדין
41	קידוש ה׳

from the strict letter of the law, but it is viewed as true justice guided by Divine inspiration.[42] If a judge fails to act in this way, he has not made a rightful decision (*Sanh.* 7a; Elon, *op. cit.*, Vol. 1, pp. 155–159).

Scripture calls upon man to do "that which is right and good in the sight of the Lord" (Deut. 6:18).[43] Morally, therefore, one should proceed *lifnim mi-shurat ha-din*, going beyond one's legal obligation (*ibid.*, Naḥmanides *ad loc.*).[44] The validity of a judgment where the facts of the case relate to acts of the mind by the parties concerned will thus depend on the reliability of a man's conscience. The Sages and the Bible repeatedly exhort man to speak the truth. Honesty alone merits the seal of God's approval (*Shab.* 55a).[45]

However often one gives way to temptation and backsliding, the essential virtue of admitting the truth about one's conduct is rewarded by Divine aid. The paradox of man's behaviour was expressly delineated in an aphorism: "Falsehood has no feet to stand on". The Sages fancifully explained that each letter of the Hebrew word *sheker* – "falsehood"[46] rests on one support; whereas each letter of the Hebrew word *emet* – "truth",[47] rests on two supports, signifying that while truth endures, falsehood falls away (*Shab.* 104a).

Scripture affirms that "the lip of truth shall be established forever; but a lying tongue is but for a moment" (Prov. 12:19). One should not be afraid to tell the truth, since God takes pleasure in honesty: "Lying lips are an abomination to the Lord; but they that deal truly are His delight" (Prov. 12:22).[48]

The civil law of contract and the ritual or religious laws are usually treated differently. There are, however, many

---

42   דין אמת לאמיתו

43   ועשית הישיר והטוב בעיני ה׳

44   לפנים משורת הדין

45   חותמו של הקדוש ברוך הוא אמת

46   שקר

47   אמת

48   תועבת ה׳ שפתי שקר ועשה אמונה רצונו

instances where the court's ruling will depend on the intention of the contractor and on his frame of mind when the contract was made.

B. Will and Consent

Pursuant to the will of the persons concerned, the law allows an individual to create, transfer or cancel rights, either unilaterally or bilaterally. A person may acquire or lose his rights by a declaration or manifestation of will and intent directed to that end.

A bilateral vestive act involves the consenting wills of two or more distinct parties, as in a contract, conveyance, mortgage or lease, and in each case the legal act is called an agreement. A unilateral act can take effect not only without the consent of the other party, but notwithstanding his dissent, as in his avoidance of a legally voidable contract. A will and testament involves only the intent of the testator, even though the beneficiaries are unaware of it. A person may relinquish or divest himself of his rights unilaterally, in accordance with his will, and his voluntary act becomes a legal one.

The essence of a contract between two parties is a meeting of wills between the parties in full and final agreement – consensus *ad idem*. Consensus is the basic requirement in creating an obligation and in a transaction. A contract, however, is a mental procedure and, in order to be satisfied that it truly obtains, the law requires what jurists term "the reality of consent", its being "true, full and free" and morally binding. Evidence that this condition exists may be obtained through various testifiable procedures.

A transaction of sale agreed upon verbally, but not in writing, is ineffective and voidable (Maim. *Mekhirah* 1:1; *BB* 49a).

[General references: W. R. Anson, *Principles of the English Law of Contract*, Oxford, 1876, 21st edition, ed.

Guest, p. 364*ff.*; F. Pollock, *Principles of Contract*, 13th edition, London, Weidenfeld, 1950, p. 364*ff.*; I. Herzog, *Main Institutions of Jewish Law*, London, Soncino Press, 1939, Vol. 1, p. 107; J. Salmond, *Jurisprudence*, 10th edition, ed. Glanville L. Williams, London, Sweet & Maxwell, 1947, par. 126, pp. 353, 374; A. Gulack, *Yesodei ha-Mishpat ha-Ivri*, Berlin, Devir, 1922]

C. Intention

Retroactive Determination – Bererah

The source of *bererah*[49] is widely discussed by the Sages of the Talmud, as well as later halakhic authorities (*posekim*),[50] in both ritual practice and commercial law. It is a manner of considering the fulfilment of a condition, the intention in the mind of a contractor or an object whose nature is in doubt. It is sometimes defined as the retroactive determination of an equivocal circumstance. Its application in the laws of contract requires some consideration.

We have seen above that the basic principle of every contract is a "meeting of wills" between two or more parties for which there must be (a) one party's full intention to confer legal ownership on another (*gemirat da'at*)[51] and (b) full confidence in the mind of the latter party that he will receive that for which he has contracted (*semikhat da'at*).[52]

To ensure that there will be consensus *ad idem*, each party must know to whom he is transferring his rights. Thus, in a matter of sale, he should first determine in his mind that he is transferring the object to the second party and that the second party relies on him to do so (Ḥazon Ish, *Sh. Ar., Ḥoshen Mishpat* 22, p. 51).

---

49 ברירה
50 פוסקים
51 גמירת דעת
52 סמיכת דעת

This contract requires a bilateral agreement. When a recognized person (A) sells to another recognized person (B), there can be a "meeting of wills". When A instructs B to sell the object to a designated person (C), we regard B as the messenger of A, since he is merely an extension of his principal (A) according to the law of agency (*Sh. Ar., Hoshen Mishpat, Shelihut*). The rule is that "a man's agent is like himself" (*Sh. Ar., Hoshen Mishpat* 182:1; *Kid.* 41a–b).[53]

In the case of a gift, the donor may instruct B to give it to whomsoever he wishes (C). We presume that C, having received a benefit to himself, is in agreement with A as regards acceptance of the gift which A has transferred to him. This contract may be of a unilateral nature. A problem would, however, arise about a "meeting of wills" in the following case. A instructs B to sell his field to either C or D, according to which of them agrees to buy it. Thus, at the time when his property was conveyed, the owner did not know to whom he intended to convey it (Herzog, *Main Institutions*, Vol. 2, p. 227).

The established law in *Halakhah,* allowing for the possibility of someone appointing an agent to sell his property to whoever will buy it, is derived from the undisputed Mishnaic ruling that a man may betroth his wife either in person or by an agent. This is the basis of the general principle that an act by a man's appointed agent is like one performed by himself.[54]

This rule drew its authority from the law of the paschal lamb, which every individual Israelite was commanded to sacrifice. Obviously, however, that sacrifice could be offered only once and by one person. It was therefore understood that a representative of every household should sacrifice a lamb for the entire family (Ex. 12:47; *Kid.* 41a–b).[55]

[References: *Yam shel Shlomo, BK* 5, for an extensive dissertation on the intricacies of "*bererah*" *Halakhah*; *Sedei Hemed,* vol. 7 (*Kelalim*), 43, *s.v.* "*Bererah*", for a discussion

---

53 שלוחו של אדם כמותו
54 שלוחו של אדם כמותו
55 כל עדת ישראל יעשו אותו

of the views of *posekim*; *Otzar Yisrael*, Vol. 3, *s.v.* "*Bererah*";
Talmudic Encyclopaedia, Vol. 4, *s.v.* "*Bererah*"]

The same principle was applied in the commercial law of
contract. Maimonides laid down the general rule that a man
can tell his agent to "go and sell real estate of mine or my
moveable goods" or else to "buy them for me," the agent's acts
then effecting such a sale or purchase on his behalf (Maim.
Sheluhin 1:1; *Sh. Ar., Hoshen Mishpat* 182:1).

Jurisprudentially, the procedure whereby an owner
conveyed his property to someone whose identity was
unknown to him raised the question of how the "meeting of
minds" required for every contract took place. Commercially,
the law recognized the validity of an offer made by a person
or his agent and its acceptance by the purchaser as a binding
transaction. If the owner stated that he left the property free
for anyone to take, this would be a different procedure – that
of "abandonment" (*hefker*). If he made it over as a gift to
either A or B, who desired it, even though he did not know
which one had accepted the gift, it might be presumed that the
recipient was the one to whom it was conveyed.

Acquisition without Intention

There can be a form of acquisition where the acquiring party
is totally unaware of the transaction. If the donor (A) wishes
to give an object or a sum of money to B, he may give it to
C with the stipulation that he is acquiring it for B. Once C
has taken hold of it as a mode of acquisition, the property
passes to B (*zekhiyyah*). Thus, the mode of *zekhiyyah* effects
the transaction even without the recipient's intention to
acquire. This procedure may be one of agency (*shelihut*), but
it may also imply that while there is no obvious intention to
acquire, that intention presumably exists *in potentia*, since the
payment is an obvious gain for the recipient. According to
the established rule, if someone conveys a gift to C for the
benefit of B, its receipt by C is an acquisition for B (*Git.* 14a;

Maim. *Zekhiyyah u-Mattanah* 4:2; *Sh. Ar., Hoshen Mishpat* 243:1).[56]

A typical Talmudic discussion of this sort occurs in one of the laws of divorce. It is an accepted principle that the bill of divorce (*get*) must be written with the sole aim of effecting the divorce of a specified man and a specified woman. The *get* must also be witnessed solely for the divorce of the specified man and woman (*Sh. Ar., Even ha-Ezer* 131:1; Maim. *Gerushin* 3:3–4).[57] This law follows the ruling of the Mishnah (*Git.* 24a).[58]

Thus, if a trainee *sofer* (scribe) chanced to copy the text of a *get* as a writing exercise and inserted the names of a particular man and wife living in the same town, such a *get* would be invalid for that couple's divorce. Furthermore, if it was written properly for a specified couple (but not used) and was then found by another couple with the identical names, it would not be valid for that second couple (see Chapter 10 above).

A Post-factum Choice – Bererah

If a man had two wives bearing exactly the same name[59] and ordered the scribe to write a *get* for the purpose of divorcing the one he would later choose,[60] the ruling of the early (Mishnaic) authority was as follows: Even though this *get* had been intended for the man and his wife, the divorce would be invalid as it was uncertain, at the time of writing, whether it was meant to divorce a particular wife, Torah law having stated: "He shall write her a bill of divorcement and give it into her hand" (Deut. 24:1).[61] The stipulation was "he shall

---

56 המזכה לחבירו מתנה על ידי אחר
57 צריך שתהיה כתיבת הגט וחתימתו לשם האיש המגרש ולשם האשה המתגרשת
58 כל גט שנכתב שלא לשום אשה פסול
59 היו לו נשים ושמותיהן שוות
60 ואיזו שארצה אגרש בו
61 וכתב לה ספר כריתות ונתן בידה

write her", in other words for a specific woman.[62]

Some Sages of the Gemara assumed that the Mishnaic teaching negated the idea that the man's ultimate choice was in fact what he had intended when the *get* was written (*Git.* 24b).[63] This ruling followed the principle that the authoritative law is always as stated in the Mishnah (*Sanh.* 86a).[64] Others argued, however, that although the law of divorce was restricted in accordance with the Torah's requirements, it might be claimed that in other cases (e.g., the division of an inheritance among brothers) the portion eventually received was the one bequeathed by the testator. Here, a different interpretation of *bererah* would determine whether a man received the property as a gift or purchased it from his brother (*Git.* 25a.; *Kid.* 42b.; *Betzah* 37a).

Similar problems in determining the law would arise in regard to establishing an *eruv* or "Sabbath boundary" (*Er.* 36b; 82a.). One example, mentioned elsewhere, involved someone who planned to meet his rabbi and did not know from which direction he would come. This man fixed his *eruv* on one side of town, but stipulated that he was acquiring a place on whichever side of town the rabbi appeared. The acquisition was thus dependent on *bererah* (*Er.* 36b).

There were those who maintained that if the eventual intention depended on the person himself, this would show that he had not made up his mind at the time, resulting in a negative effect. If, however, he exercised no choice and the result depended on an external event, he retained an open mind and such a possibility could not be excluded.

Another case of *bererah* may be found in the law of divorce, where it must be certain that the *get* was duly conveyed. Should a man who was seriously ill hand his wife a bill of divorce and tell her, "This will be your *get* in the event of my death," the conveyance of the *get* would depend on an

---

62   לה לשמה

63   לשמה קמ"ל דאין ברירה

64   הלכתה כסתם משנה כרבי מאיר

external eventuality. If the man passed away, the *get* executed before his death remained valid, although differing views were expressed by the Sages as to its effectiveness (*Git.* 73a).

In the law of marriage it was ruled that a man may appoint an agent to give *kiddushin* to a woman on his behalf. He may instruct his agent in general terms ("Betroth a woman for me") or name a specific woman. Since one of the prescribed methods of effecting *kiddush* is to give the bride a sum of money (*kesef*), the man hands this money to his agent but does not know to whom it will be given. This legal situation can only be explained by the validity of an eventual decision – *bererah* (*Kid.* 42a; *Sh. Ar., Even ha-Ezer* 27:1, 26:4, 35:1).

Some halakhic authorities explained this concept as one resembling a condition. When a landowner permits the needy to glean *leket* in his field (Lev. 23:22), he does not know how much produce will be taken or how much will be left. He therefore renounces ownership of what will be taken (making it *hefker*) and keeps whatever remains. Here the extent of his renunciation is not a matter of choice, nor is it known to him. In accordance with the principle of *bererah*, however, his cleaned crops are transferred to whichever person collects them (*BK* 69a).

Moreover, in regard to the Four Species taken on Sukkot, the Tabernacles festival, Torah law ordained that they must belong to that person: "Ye shall take for yourselves on the first day the fruit of goodly trees (*etrog*), branches of palm-trees (*lulav*), boughs of thick trees (*hadas*), and willows of the brook (*aravot*)." Torah law stipulated, "Ye shall take for yourselves" (*U-lekaḥtem lakhem*). Accordingly, if these items are stolen property, their use is invalid. The Sages ruled that they should be one's own property, not borrowed or stolen (Lev. 23:40; *Suk.* 27b, 29b, 41b; *Sh. Ar., Oraḥ Ḥayyim* 649:1).[65] A similar law would apply to the eating of unleavened bread (*matzah*) on the first night of Passover (Rosh, *Suk.* 35b).

In view of the fact that these Four Species were often in

short supply, it became standard practice for the owner to declare that whoever used them could regard them as his own.[66] A similar practice was followed when several people baked *matzah* in a communal oven and one person's dough could be taken by another, although the owner did not know to whom it was given. In these laws we utilize the principle of an undetermined choice – *yesh bererah* (R. Aryeh Leib ben Asher Gunzberg, Responsa *Sha'agat Aryeh*, no. 92).

Abandonment of Ownership – Yeush

There is also a mode of acquiring an object even though it had not been transferred by the owner to another individual. This can result where the owner's property has been lost or stolen, particularly when it was unidentifiable, and he despaired of it's recovery, losing all hope of regaining possession of it. His despair could be evidenced by his sorrowful behaviour or by his expression of his anguish that he had suffered this loss against his own will. This attitude of resignation to his loss is known as *yeush* (*BM* 23a).[67]

By the owner's abandoning his property removing from his mind all thoughts of repossessing it, his ownership ceases, and the object becomes 'ownerless' (*hefker*), so that whoever takes it with the intention of acquiring it acquires ownership of it. As a result of his *yeush* his ownership of the object ceases. By his simple act of the mind, without any active procedure he withdraws himself from any possibility of ownership, and his ownership of the object ceases.

However if the person who found it took it for himself where there has been no *yeush* on the part of the owner the obligation of restoring it to it's owner rests on him (Deut. 22:1).[68] Since the owner still hoped to recover his property he

---

66   כל מי שיגיע לולבו לידו הרי הוא לו במתנה

67   וי ליה לחסרון כיס, מיאש לה מינה

68   השב תשיבם לאחיך

thus retained his right of ownership of it, and it's unauthorized acquisition by another person would be considered as a crime of theft.

Among the Sages and the halakhic authorities (*poskim*), however, there were differences of opinion as to whether the incidence of *yeush* alone is sufficient to pass ownership to the finder or the thief.[69] Some asserted that ownership passed only if the object was now different from what it was when it was lost and it had now become an object with a different name or it could have been transferred to a third person.

Unclear Intention in Kiddushin

There are a number of situations in *kiddushin* where problems arise because the intention that the contractor has in mind is unknown or unclear. When performing *kiddushin*, a man may include a stipulation regarding his marriage. He may say, for example, "I give you this coin (*perutah*) and you will be married to me in 30 days", or he may declare: "Behold, you are betrothed to me by this *perutah* if I give you 200 *zuzim* within 30 days". If he gives her the money at some point within those 30 days, his marriage will then become legally established (Mish., *Kid.* 60a).[70] If he does not give her the sum agreed within that time, no betrothal has been effected (Maim. *Ishut* 7:11–12).[71]

In this case of a delayed marriage, if a second man offered to betroth the woman within those 30 days and the woman accepted, this second *kiddushin* would be fully effective, and she would be deemed fully and unquestionably betrothed to the second man, because the first betrothal had not yet taken effect when the second was made (Mish., *Kid.* 58b; Maim. *Ishut* 7:11).[72]

---

69 אם יאוש קונה או לא קונה
70 הרי זו מקודשת
71 אינה מקודשת
72 מקודשת לשני

If the man gave the woman his *perutah* and simply declared that she was now betrothed to him, the *kiddushin* was immediately effective. If, however, he used both formulas in his declaration, saying "You are betrothed to me now and after 30 days",[73] it would not be certain if "30 days" meant a condition of his present betrothal or a reconsideration (i.e., not immediately but only after 30 days).

Marital Rights and Duties

The rights of a wife in relation to her husband include the following:
1) *Nedunyah*, i.e., the wife's dowry (*Sh. Ar., Even ha-Ezer* 50:4, 51:1, 66:11; *Sh. Ar., Hoshen Mishpat* 43, 49, 118:9; *Sh. Ar., Even ha-Ezer* 90:13, 15, 17)
2) *Ketubbah*, the sum due to the wife as specified in her marriage document (*Sh. Ar., Even ha-Ezer* 55:1, 61:1, 62:9, 66:7, 13, 18).
3) *Tzon Barzel*, the property owned by the wife and held in trust by the husband who is responsible for its return in full (*Sh. Ar., Even ha-Ezer* 77:3, REMA; 85:2, 3; *Sh. Ar., Even ha-Ezer* 85:1, 3; 88:1*ff.*; *Bet Shmuel* 6; 90:14, 15, 17*ff.*, REMA; 96:1).
4) *Melug*, i.e., estate belonging to the wife before her marriage of which the husband may enjoy its usufruct, including gifts received by the wife designated as her personal property.
   The rights and duties of the husband in relation to his wife are also specified (*Sh. Ar., Even ha-Ezer* 69, 80, 83, 85, 90, for rights; 70, 73, 93, 94, 100 for duties; 66, 69, 70, 78, 79, 86, 89, 96 for the *ketubbah*).

Acceptability of a Claim Involving Observance of a Minhag

According to the law of betrothal, a bridegroom is obliged to give his bride *kesef kiddushin* – a sum amounting to 200 *zuzim* if she is a virgin or 100 *zuzim* if she is not (*Ket.* 10b; *Sh. Ar., Even ha-Ezer* 66:6; *Ta'anat betulim* – Etl. 68:1–2; Maim. *Ishut* 11:9–10; *Ket.* 11b, 12b, 46b).

What would happen if the husband declared before the *bet din* that he had married someone's daughter on the understanding that she was a virgin, and had accordingly paid the 200 *zuzim* stipulated in her *ketubbah*, but when they first had intercourse he found no "tokens of her virginity"?[74] If it transpired that she had engaged in sexual intercourse with another man after her betrothal to him, she would be liable to the death penalty; but if she had lost her virginity before her betrothal, the husband would be authorized to reduce her *ketubbah* payment to 100 *zuzim* on the basis that he had entered into a mistaken contract.[75] Should the bride's father then claim that the bridegroom had laid a false charge against his daughter,[76] the court's judgment would depend on the testimony of witnesses in support of either party (Deut. 22:13–21; *Ket.* 46a, 11b;[77] *Sh. Ar., Even ha-Ezer* 68:1–2; Maim. *Ishut* 11:9–10).

In view of the difficulties faced when obtaining evidence in this situation, a custom developed in Judea whereby, in preparation for the marriage, two attendants were assigned to the couple – one representing the bride's side and one representing the groom's. They accompanied the bride and bridegroom so as to ensure that neither practiced any deceit. If this custom had not been followed on his marriage, the groom forfeited the right to claim that his bride had not been a virgin

---

74 ולא מצאתי לה בתולים
75 מקח טעות
76 מוציא שם רע
77 טענת בתולים

and the father's denial of such a claim would be accepted as trustworthy (*Ket.* 2a; *Tosef., Ket.* 1:4; *Tur, Sh. Ar., Even ha-Ezer* 68:2; and cf. Elon, *op. cit.*, Vol. 1, "*Minhag*" [custom], p. 88).[78]

The acceptance of an established custom (*minhag*) as legally authoritative was based on the injunction: "Remove not the ancient landmark which thy fathers have set" (Prov. 22:28; Deut. 19:14). R. Mena*h*em Meiri (Perpignan, 13th cent.) also based this *minhag* on an extended interpretation of the verse: "Hearken unto thy father that begot thee, and despise not thy mother when she is old" (Prov. 23:22; Meiri, *Magen Avot*, Introd.; Elon, *op. cit.*, Vol. 1, p. 894).[79] The Sages likewise quoted the verse, "Hear the instruction of thy father, and forsake not the teaching of thy mother" (Prov. 1:8;[80] *Hul.* 93b; *Pes.* 50a–b, 51b[81]).

Traditionally, this dual expression referred to the validity of *minhag* as well as the prescribed *Halakhah*. Learning from the example of Moses, who ate no bread when angels accompanied him on Mount Sinai, R. Tan*h*um ben *H*anilai laid down a general rule that one should not depart from accepted custom (*BM* 86b).[82]

Civil Law Created by Custom

Every financial transaction may be made subject to a condition agreed to by the parties involved. When merchants follow a particular custom in their methods of acquisition and conveyance, such as a mark on the goods sold or a simple handshake, it is as if they have all agreed that a transaction so entered into shall be effective (*Hoshen Mishpat* 201:1–2),

---

78	הוי מעמידין שני שושבנים
79	ואל תבוז כי זקנה אמך
80	ואל תטוש תורת אמך
81	מקום שנהגו
82	לעולם אל ישנה אדם מן המנהג

even though the practice does not strictly accord with the requirements of *Halakhah*. The transaction is effective, since it was agreed upon with that understanding.

This effectiveness may relate to a civil law, even if its limitations are based on a religious one. Thus, religious law ordains the cancellation of all debts in a sabbatical year (*shemittah*): "This is the manner of the release: every creditor shall release that which he hath lent unto his neighbour" (Deut. 15:2; Maim. *Shemittah ve-Yovel* 9:1-3; *Git.* 36a).[83] It is, however, recorded that R. Asher ben Yeḥiel, the eminent codifier known as Asheri (Germany-Spain, 14th cent.), observed that the custom was prevalent in his time not to cancel debts in the sabbatical year. Since this had become standard practice, it was as though the creditor lent money on condition that the debt would not be cancelled, and this stipulation governed the contract.

Centuries earlier, with a view to lessening hardship in new social conditions, Hillel the Elder had authorized the collection of debts through a legal arrangement known as the *prozbul* (*Shev.* 10:3–4).[84] It thus became standard practice for debts to be collected in the *shemittah* year. Thanks to Hillel's institution of the *prozbul*, recognizing both the lender's concern to protect his money and the borrower's need to obtain a loan, his ingenious legal process had the effect of superseding a clear Biblical prohibition (Asheri, Responsa 64:4; Elon, *op. cit.*, Vol. 1, p. 904).

Marriage Gifts – Sivlonot

In the Talmudic era it was common practice for the bridegroom to send valuable gifts to his bride, as when Eliezer brought presents for Rebekah in anticipation of her marriage to Isaac (Gen. 24). However, this was usually done after the betrothal

---

83 וזה דבר השמיטה שמוט כל בעל משה ידו אשר ישה ברעיהו

84 פרוזבול

agreement[85] had been completed. Once a gift was received and accepted, the donor had no right to demand its return unless it was given on the understanding that certain conditions would be fulfilled (Maim. *Zekhiyyah u-Mattanah* 4:1 3:6; *Sh. Ar., Hoshen Mishpat* 241:9).

Should the marriage not take place, any gifts would revert to the donor. R. Yehudah ha-Nasi affirmed that while the law deemed such a gift non-returnable, the Sages held that if the marriage was cancelled because either the man or the woman had died, where it was customary to return the gift, it should be returned; where it was customary not to do so, it need not be returned. This ruling did not meet with general approval. R. Meir stated that a betrothal gift was not returnable. Others maintained that where presents were generally given back, as in Nehardea, they need to be returned, but tokens such as jewellery need not be given back, as was the practice elsewhere in Babylonia (*BB* 145a, Rashi).

If returning wedding gifts was accepted practice, they had to be returned on the basis of an understanding by both parties that this was part of their contractual agreement. That would apply even if no specific condition had been made, since local custom was regarded as automatically binding. If, however, the usual practice was not to return such gifts, even though the bridegroom had sent them to the bride in anticipation of their marriage and on condition that it took place (otherwise expecting their return), there was no need for her to give them back since accepted practice overruled even established *Halakhah*.

D. Conditions

Introduction

When a condition is attached to a contract, A conveys something to B if the condition is fulfilled; if it is not, the arrangement is cancelled. The contract thus has both a positive and a negative aspect.[86]

The problem that arises is whether a person's full intention,[87] deemed essential in every conveyance, was expressed by this contract, since it was uncertain whether the condition would be fulfilled or not. It may therefore be questionable whether a transfer of property took place, even if the condition was eventually fulfilled (Maim. *Mekhirah* 11:6). The applicable rules[88] laid down that every condition be made in both positive and negative forms, thus establishing the positive action without reference to any negative possibility, i.e., covering whichever action occurs. A valid condition in sale, gift or *kiddushin* must therefore be expressed in its double form.[89]

R. Meir derived this principle from the Biblical text relating how Moses agreed to bestow the land of Gilead on the children of Gad and Reuben, provided that they joined all the other tribes in occupying the land of Canaan. This undertaking was expressed in two forms: "If ye will do this... and every armed man of you will pass over the Jordan before the Lord... But if ye will not do so... "(Num. 32: 20–21, 23).[90] The positive statement was followed by a negative one, declaring that if Gad and Reuben did not participate in the general campaign, only a portion of Canaan would be allocated to them.

R. Ḥananyah ben Gamliel demurred, maintaining that this requirement applied in the case of marriage or divorce, but not

---

86	קיום המעשה ובטול המעשה
87	גמירות הדעת
88	משפטי תנאים
89	תנאי כפול
90	אם יעברו – ואם לא יעברו

in financial agreements. Some Geonic authorities accepted his view and the Sages quoted a number of other undertakings in which repetition was mandatory (*Kid.* 61a).

Maimonides ruled that every condition is valid only if it is expressed in both forms.[91] Moreover, the positive aspect of the agreement must be stipulated first.[92] Other requirements are (a) that the condition was made before the act of conveyance took place;[93] and (b) that its fulfilment is a real possibility (Maim. *Zekhiyyah u-Mattanah* 3:7).[94] R. Yosef Caro applied these rules to all commercial transactions (*Sh. Ar., Hoshen Mishpat* 241; *Tur, Even ha-Ezer* 38, *Bet Yosef ad loc.*; *Sh. Ar., Even ha-Ezer* 38:4).

E. Consideration

When brothers divide an estate which they have inherited into equal shares and the division is made by lot, each acquires possession of his share as soon as one brother's lot is drawn. When the Sages asked how exactly possession was acquired, R. Ashi explained that in return for the benefit of a mutual agreement on dividing the land, they resolved that possession be secured by lot alone. Each accordingly received a benefit from the other which sufficed for the acquisition (*BB* 106b; Maim. *Shekhenim* 2, 11; *Sh. Ar., Hoshen Mishpat* 173:2).[95]

A valid consideration usually means cash or an item that the transferee gives in order to satisfy the transferor that he receives something of value, thus inducing him to part with an object or right and give it to the other. That consideration need not always be something positive: it may also represent a virtual benefit affording psychological satisfaction. Thus, if

91   צריך שיהיה תנאי כפול
92   והן קודם ללאו
93   התנאי קודם למעשה
94   תנאי שאפשר לקיימו
95   בההוא הנאה דקא צייתי להדדי גמרי ומקנו להדדי

a paid bailee[96] responsible to the owner for the safety of his bailment also contracted with him as a borrower, this could be done without the need for an additional *kinyan*, since the borrower is now given an extra responsibility which is, in itself, of value to him. He acquires the reputation of being trustworthy, and this benefit is a consideration for which he readily obligates himself (*BM* 94a).[97]

A legally accepted payment of consideration to effect an agreement may be given without any actual money passing between the two sides. This may occur when a creditor discharges a debt by the law of waiver (*mehilah*). A debtor would have been willing to pay a certain amount to a third party so as to induce the creditor to cancel the debt. Since the creditor himself waives the debt, that waiver is worth whatever sum the debtor might have paid in return for his benefit. This consideration is a positive gain, resembling an actual cash payment. A further contract may thus be effected on receipt of the waiver, even if its value is not specified in a document but given by word of mouth. This procedure involves not a mutual contract but a release of the creditor's right to the debt, without the transfer of funds to another party, and it therefore does not require a legal form of *kinyan*. Such a benefit is termed *mehilah* (remission, renounciation) (*Sanh.* 6a; Maim. *Mekhirah* 5:11).[98]

Similarly, in regard to the payment of *kesef kiddushin*, if the woman had previously received a loan from her suitor and he now waives repayment, this favour is accepted as a worthwhile consideration (*Kid.* 6b; Maim. *Ishut* 5:14–15; Maim. *Mekhirah* 5:11).[99]

Another case in which receipt of a benefit (*hana'ah*) effects a contract is where A gives money to B, or is asked to lend him money, and C undertakes to stand surety (*arev*) for repayment

---

96 שומר שכר
97 בההוא הנאה דקא נפיק ליה קלא דאיניש מהיימנא הוא גמיר למשעבד נפשיה
98 יש דברים שאינו צריכים קנין- המוחל לחבירו חוב
99 המקדש בהנאת מלוה מקודשת

of the loan. C conveys his guarantee to A, for which he should receive a consideration. Here it is explained that C receives a benefit from the knowledge that he is trusted by A, who parts with his money on the strength of C's surety. That consideration is sufficient to bind C in his contract with A, and he is accordingly obligated to pay the sum due if the debtor fails to do so. This is particularly so if the *bet din* requires C to accept the liability of serving as A's surety, since he thus enjoys the reputation of being trustworthy (*BB* 176a–b; Maim. *Malveh* 25:2; *Sh. Ar., Hoshen Mishpat* 129:2).[100]

Symbolic Contractual Agreement – Kinyan Sudar

In the procedure known as *kinyan sudar*, a piece of cloth belonging to one party is grasped by the other party, thus constituting a type of fictional barter. However, in the *kinyan sudar*[101] procedure through which title is effected, can the cloth be deemed a consideration for a parcel of land? *Kinyan sudar* is a symbolic exchange or a symbolic form of delivery. Rav and Levi took opposing stands on the issue of *ba-meh kinyan?* – "by what means is a title effected?"[102]

In Rav's opinion, it was the cloth of the purchaser who thereby acquired the land. He gave it to the conveyancer in a symbolic act demonstrating his wish that the conveyancer should be satisfied to accept this from him and to convey his property in return.[103]

Levi apparently maintained that the cloth of the bestower[104] should be given to the recipient as a symbolic act of conveyance. The Sages explained that Levi's view could not indicate that the land was transferred as an adjunct to the cloth, since the law only provided for the opposite case, where a cloth was given as an adjunct of the land. Levi would therefore regard the

---

100   דבה הוא הנאה דמהמין ליה גמר ומשעבד ליה

101   קנין סודר

102   במה קונין

103   רב אמר בכליו של קונה

104   כליו של מקנה

kinyan sudar as a form of consideration. The bestower had the satisfaction of knowing that the recipient accepted his cloth as a gift and, in consideration of that pleasure, he wholeheartedly transferred the land to him. This was the consideration that he received (*BM* 47a).[105] Maimonides ruled, like Rav, that the purchaser gave his cloth as a symbol of his payment (Maim. *Mekhirah*, 5:5).[106]

The fictional barter and mode of *kinyan sudar* may resemble a consideration, but in reality *kinyan* is the ingredient of form. An estate worth a fortune may be transferred by *kinyan sudar*. The assignee hands over any article of use that may not even be worth a *perutah*, the smallest coin in circulation. This is not a case of barter, which normally means an exchange of equal value. In Jewish law, what answers to consideration is termed value[107] or exchange,[108] for which there are other modes of acquisition.

Kinyan sudar is essentially a legal form of transfer. Betrothal (*kiddushin*) is a special case based on a different concept. In betrothal, the gift that a bridegroom hands to his bride must be worth at least a *perutah*, which cannot be regarded as the actual price for a woman's betrothal to him, but as the bestowal of a gift conforming with one of the three modes needed to effect a betrothal, namely *kesef* – something of value (*Kid.* 2a; 3a, *Tos. s.v. "Ve-ishah"*).

A binding unilateral commitment (*ḥiyyuv*) to a transaction would require a formal, witnessed declaration ("Be ye witnesses that..."). Such a procedure would fulfil the need for form – *udita* (*Sanh.* 29b; Maim. *Mekhirah* 11:15; *Sh. Ar., Ḥoshen Mishpat* 40:1). Another example of a unilateral commitment is a note written by the obligator stating, "I owe so-and-so the sum of...", followed by his signature (IOU).

Another example of unsubstantial consideration is when

---

105 בה היא הנאה דקה מקבל מניה גמר ואקני ליה

106 בכליו של קונה

107 שווי

108 חליפין

the lender agrees to postpone the collection of his loan and to
change it from an old debt to a new one (*Kid.* 2a; 3a, *Tos.*, *s.v.*
"*Ve-ishah*").[109]

There may be cases where even if the requirements of
both consideration and form have been met, the transaction
is ineffective. This could be due to the absence of *semikhat
da'at* or *gemirat da'at*. Thus, a sale may have been concluded
in due form, but owing to prevailing circumstances there is
a lack of *gemirat da'at* on the part of the vendor because he
has doubts about the sale's completion until the full price has
been paid or a bill of sale (*shetar mekher*) has been delivered.
Jewish law fully recognized the validity of prevailing customs
among traders in support of the expected fulfilment (*semikhat
da'at*).

Past Consideration

In order for the vendor to be confident that the terms of the
transaction will be fulfilled (*gemirat da'at*), he must be aware
of having received an acceptable consideration when the
agreement was reached. That consideration must accompany
his agreement. Therefore, any consideration given to him in the
past will not be deemed operative in the current transaction.

This rule is also enunciated by the Sages in the laws of
betrothal, where it is obligatory for the man to give the woman
something worth at least a *perutah*. If he said to her, "I betroth
you with the value of my [past] service in helping you to ride
a donkey, or giving you a place on my wagon or my boat",
such value would not effect *kiddushin*. If, however, he said,
"With the value of my future service in helping you ride a
donkey", that would become a debt to which the man was now
committed and it would therefore be valid as a *kesef kiddushin*
payment (*Kid.* 63a).

---

109   בההוא הנאה דקה משתניא בין מלוה ישנה למלוה ליה חדשה גמר ומשעבד
נפשו

Another rule is *ha-mekaddesh ba-malveh einah mekuddeshet*, namely, when the man discharges a woman's earlier debt by *meḥilah*, but does not give her the required *kesef* at this time (*Kid.* 6b). If, however, the gift was *hana'at meḥilat malveh* (see above), this benefit has immediate value for her, since she would have paid someone else to obtain it – *mekuddeshet* (*Kid.* 6a).

F. Fraud and Misrepresentation

Introduction

Any misrepresentation raises the question as to whether one or both parties really agreed to the contract. Where true consent obviously did not exist, the misrepresentation casts doubt on the validity of the contract entered into and renders it voidable at the instance of the party deceived.

An act of misrepresentation giving a false impression of the article contracted for could simply be a mistake, one made quite innocently and with no intention to deceive. On the other hand, it could also be a fraudulent scheme aimed at inducing the other party to enter into the contract. The law held a fraudulent representation to void the contract and entitle the injured party to recover any goods or property transferred in pursuance thereof as a fraudulent action. Apart from the moral disgrace incurred (Lev. 25:17), any injurious effect produced knowingly could also be actionable in various situations as a breach of trust which could constitute a tort of fraud.

Where any loss incurred as a result of the fraud has been made good, the original agreement may subsequently be endorsed, provided that the requisite, genuine consent of both parties is obtained. The validity of the contract would then be restored.

[References: P. G. Osborn, *A Concise Law Dictionary*, 5th edition, London, Sweet and Maxwell, 1964, *s.v.* "Fraud, Misrepresentation"; D. M. Walker, *The Oxford Companion to Law*, Oxford, Clarendon Press, 1980]

Innocent Misrepresentation

The Sages discussed the following two cases:

1. A man contracted to lease from the owner a certain field, which (as he saw) was irrigated by a spring or planted with trees. Subsequently, the spring dried up or the trees were felled. He may not deduct the loss sustained thereby from the amount agreed as payment for the lease. The contract remains valid,[110] as there had been no fraudulent misrepresentation in the lease or sale.

2. If, however, the man added a stipulation when he made the contract, saying, "I particularly wish you to lease me this irrigated field" or "this plantation", and the spring later dried up or the trees were felled, he may reduce the rental payment in accordance with his loss.

In the first case, the lessor described the field as it was at the time, but that did not provide a warranty for the future. In the second case, the lessee declared that he especially wanted a field that was irrigated or planted with trees. If that condition was not fulfilled, he could justifiably reduce his rental. He had made it known to the lessor that there was a condition attached to his taking the lease, and that he would maintain the lease only so long as the field was properly irrigated and the trees remained in place (Maim. *Sekhirut* 8:4; *BM* 103b, *Tos., s.v.* "*Menakkeh*"; *Sh. Ar., Ḥoshen Mishpat* 321:1–2).

Criminal Falsehood

The Mishnah refers to a case in which two men appearing in court hold a garment.[111] One says "I found it" and the other says "I found it." One says "It's all mine" and the other says

---

110   אינו מנקה לו ממכירו
111   שנים אוחזין בטלית

"It's all mine", both maintaining their claim. One must swear that he owns at least half of the garment, the other must take the same oath and the value of the item found is then divided. The Sages ask: "But one man is telling a lie; if so, why should we require him to take a false oath?" Their answer is: "We do not say that one suspected of fraud in money matters should also be suspected of taking a false oath, since perjury is a greater crime than robbery (*Shab.* 33b). Fear of swearing a false oath would therefore induce a man to tell the truth. On the other hand, both may have picked up the garment simultaneously, in which case both are telling the truth" (*BM* 2a, 3b, 5b; *Shev.* 47a–b; Maim. *Malveh* 2:2, *Kesef Mishneh ad loc.*; *Sh. Ar., Hoshen Mishpat* 99:1, *Tur, Shulhan Arukh, s.v. "Ke-she-ra'u"*).

Furthermore, Torah law itself required that a claimant or defendant who was unable to produce evidence should take an oath.[112] Such a case was where a bailer claimed damages for his bailment and the bailee denied responsibility for any loss, since he had not misused the object or animal entrusted to him (Ex. 22:10).[113]

The power of an enforced oath lay in the fear and knowledge that swearing a false oath in court was a profanation of the Divine Name.[114] The Sages ruled, however, that one already suspected of taking a false oath would not be given such an opportunity to avoid his obligation (*Mekhilta* on Ex. 22:10).[115] They further ruled that if both parties were known to swear falsely, an oath should not be administered. Under the oath taken by Israel at Sinai prohibiting theft,[116] both parties would be held accountable.

---

112 שבועת הדיינים
113 שבועת ה' תהיה בין שניהם אם לא שלח ידו במלאכת רעהו
114 חילול ה'
115 חשוד על השבועה
116 לא תגזול

The Sages of Babylon declared that the oath prescribed in the Torah returned to its place of origin, Mount Sinai,[117] hence a person was denied the benefit of his own oath.[118] If a defendant admitted part of the amount claimed, he was required to swear accordingly. The Sages of the Land of Israel contended that if he was not allowed to take an oath, he would have to bear full responsibility for meeting the claim,[119] in which case the benefit of taking the oath was given to the claimant (*Shev.* 47a, Rashi *ad loc.*).

In Geonic times, fraudulent conduct became so widespread that potential creditors were unwilling to lend money, even to those in dire need. The Geonim therefore ruled that whenever a claim was denied, an oath of the most sacred and severe kind should be sworn over the holy Torah (Maim. *Malveh,* 2:2, *Kesef Mishneh ad loc.*).

Later authorities heightened the dread of a false oath by warning the persons concerned that they would become destitute if they swore falsely. A God-fearing man would rather pay a claimant than take an oath, even when he had no financial liability. Therefore, no oath was imposed on him (*Sh. Ar., Ḥoshen Mishpat* 99:1–2).

G. Duress – *Oness*

In Sale Agreements

In addition to an agreement about the price and object of the sale, there must be an identical understanding in the minds of both parties with regard to the substance of the transaction. There must be a meeting of wills or a confident meeting of minds (*semikhat da'at*). Signature before witnesses is usually

---

117   חזרה שבועה לסיני
118   מושבע ועומד
119   אינו יכול לישבע משלם

evidence of such a connecting of wills. The vendor's consent
is obviously in doubt if he sells under duress, even when he
expresses his agreement to the required elements of the sale.
Duress could have been exerted in various ways: through
actual or threatened physical violence or a subjective cause
(e.g., an urgent need of money for his own requirements or a
wish to avoid domestic conflict).

The Sages distinguished between these two kinds of *oness*.
They ruled that only duress exerted by an outside party could
invalidate a transaction, and assumed that no one would
willingly part with his land unless he had a compelling reason
to do so. If, however, a person's subjective state made him
agree to transfer possession,[120] the sale was valid. This did not
apply to the matter of purchase,[121] where free choice had to be
exercised, and any purchase made under duress was therefore
null and void (*Sh. Ar., Ḥoshen Mishpat* 205: 1, 12-14; Maim.
Mekhirah 10:1).

Even so, cases are mentioned where a sale made under
duress remained valid. A classic example was cited by R.
Huna. If people resorted to physical violence, compelling a
man to sell them his field ("they hung him on a tree until his
pain made him agree"),[122] the sale was valid. The reason given
is that whenever a man sells his possessions, he does so under
some form of external or internal compulsion. Although it was
not the owner's intention to sell,[123] the purchaser still acquired
full title to what he had bought.[124] The fact remains that the
former said, "I am willing to do so",[125] thereby transferring the
ownership for which he had, after all, received full payment.
The sale could have been invalidated and the transfer of title
avoided, had he earlier protested before witnesses that he was
only consenting under physical duress (*BB* 47b, Rashi *ad loc.*,

---

120   אגב אונסיה גמר ומקני
121   אנסוהו לקנות אינו קנין
122   תליהו וזבין זבינייה זביני
123   אפילו לא גמר ומקני
124   קונה לוקח
125   רוצה אני

48: Maim. *Mekhirah* 10:1; *Sh. Ar., Hoshen Mishpat* 151:3; *BB* 48b, RIF, RAN and Rashi *ad loc.*; *Sh. Ar., Hoshen Mishpat* 205:1).[126]

In the case of a gift or the remission of a debt (*mehilah*), evidence of *force majeure* renders them invalid. If someone, having previously indicated his unwillingness to bestow a gift, had received no consideration in return, it is assumed that he never consented to give it, since the governing factor here is the donor's wish to convey it to the donee. He clearly had no wish to do so and, even if no physical duress was involved, all matters concerning a gift are subject to the will of the donor (*Sh. Ar., Hoshen Mishpat* 205:6).[127]

When releasing anyone from a contract made under duress, the Sages needed to know that the witnesses were aware of the physical constraint prompting the sale (*BB* 47b). They further clarified the law by ruling that *ones* was not necessarily the result of physical violence: even the threat of financial loss would invalidate the sale.

The following case was referred to by the Sages. A mortgaged his orchard to a creditor (B), who was entitled to the usufruct provided that the orchard would revert to A after a maximum of ten years. However, A did not possess any deed or mortgage document. After B had enjoyed use of the orchard for three years, which normally gave continuous occupation the right of possession (*hazakah*), he demanded that A sell the orchard to him. If A failed to do so, B threatened to deny the existence of any mortgage agreement and to claim that the orchard was his own purchased property. Unable to furnish any evidence to the contrary, and despite his unwillingness to part with the orchard, A was thus compelled to sell it. Here the Sages ruled that the sale could be invalidated by a prior declaration before witnesses, who would then compose a deed of protest – *moda'ah* (*BB* 40b, RAN, Rashi and Rashbam; Maim. *Mekhirah* 10:1–2).

---

126   מודעא
127   אין הולכין במתנה אלא אחר גילוי דעת הנותן

A striking example of *oness* dates from the Talmudic era, when the Romans occupied Judea. A Roman official was then empowered to confiscate Jewish property under threat of death, if the owner (A) refused to transfer the land to him. This official was known as a *sikarikon* ("expropriator"). When the *sikarikon* later sold the field he had confiscated to B, the latter – wishing to substantiate his ownership under Jewish law, requested A to sell him the original title. A might not wish to do so, claiming that it was still his and had been stolen from him, but he feared the *sikarikon* and would reluctantly sell his title to B. The Sages declared the second sale invalid, as it was conducted under duress (*Git.* 55b, RAN; Maim. *Genevah* 5:1; *Sh. Ar., Hoshen Mishpat* 356:1; *Encyclopaedia Judaica,* 14:1529–1530).

Domestic Pressure

The act of marriage creates certain rights and duties binding a husband and wife. The husband has ten obligations towards his wife. These include providing her with due sustenance (*she'erah* or *mezonot*); clothes and lodging (*kesutah*); the amount stipulated in her marriage contract (*ketubbah*); her conjugal rights (*onatah*); any medical attention (*refu'atah*); ransom, if she is taken captive (*lif-dotah*); and burial (*kevuratah*).

In return for his fulfilment of these obligations the husband is entitled to the benefit of his wife's handiwork (*ma'asei yadeha*); her chance finds (*metzi'atah*); the usufruct of her property (*peroteha*); and the inheritance of her estate – *yerushatah* (*Ket.* 59a; Maim. *Ishut* 12:1–4; *Sh. Ar., Even ha-Ezer* 69:1–3).

Talmudic law states that the wife retains her personal possessions before marriage as well as gifts meant specifically for her personal use, and only she has the right to dispose of them. These assets include all property that she brings into the marriage, as stated in her *ketubbah*, and which she gives to her husband for his exclusive use. This constitutes her dowry (*nedunyah*).

Such assets fall under two categories (see Chapter 9). The first, if used by the husband, requires his surety (*aharayut*) for its eventual return to her or to her heirs at the full value which it possessed when he received it. This remains hers, in unbroken ownership, and it is figuratively called "property of iron sheep",[128] i.e., inalienably secure goods (mortmain). The second, known as "plucked property",[129] is any asset that she gives to her husband so that he may benefit from the usufruct (*perot*). The principal remains hers and it must be restored to her in the event of a divorce or her husband's death.

There is also a third category of possession, where the husband has no ownership and the property belongs only to the wife, unless she decides to convey part of it to him. This includes his financial obligation towards her, as required in their marriage agreement, for which he has a continuous responsibility (*shi'bud*). That obligation he must fulfil should the marriage be dissolved, although he may have been given the limited right of usufruct. All his own property is mortgaged in surety.

[References: Maim. *Nashim* 12–14; A. Gulak, *Yesodei ha-Mishpat ha-Ivri* Vol. 3, 3.14–16; *Encyclopaedia Judaica*, 8:1120 *ff.*, *s.v.* "Husband and Wife"; and 6:185, *s.v.* "Dowry"; *Sh. Ar.*, *Even ha-Ezer* 69, 80, 83, 85, 90 for the husband's rights; *Sh. Ar., Even ha-Ezer* 66, 69–70, 73, 78–79, 86, 89, 93–94, 96, 100 for the husband's duties; *Sh. Ar., Even ha-Ezer* 43, 49–51, 55, 61–62, 66, 77, 85, 88, 90, 96, 118 for the wife's rights; and *Sh. Ar., Even ha-Ezer* 66, 69–70, 73, 78–79 for the wife's duties; E. E. Scheftelowitz, *The Jewish Law of Family and Inheritance* 5–6, pp. 86–110]

Although the husband has the usufruct of his wife's property, he is not entitled to sell any of it.[130] The Sages declared that if the husband sold a field belonging to his wife's mortgaged

---

128   נכסי צאן ברזל
129   נכסי מלוג
130   גוף הקרן

property, the purchaser would still need the wife's consent; otherwise, the husband's transaction was invalid. If he sold either the principal or the usufruct without her consent, she then had the power to recover it from the purchaser (*BB* 50b). Even if she gave her consent, the Sages were divided as to whether such a sale was valid.

According to one opinion, she really did not wish to sell and her consent would have been given under duress, simply to avoid angering her husband if she refused. Because she agreed only in order to placate her husband,[131] the sale would be invalid.[132]

According to the other view, while having no ownership rights, the husband already enjoyed the use of his wife's property – to which she did not object. Therefore, she could not claim to have given her consent for fear of angering him. Had she refused, her husband would have admitted that only she had the right of disposal;[133] but if she agreed, her consent would be genuine, completing the sale, and that sale was valid.[134] Maimonides ruled according to the second view,[135] as did Caro in the *Shulḥan Arukh*.

[References: *BB* 49b, Rashi *s.v. "Tanya naḥat ru'aḥ"*; *Ket.* 80b; Maim. *Ishut* 22:5, 16, 35; *Sh. Ar., Even ha-Ezer* 90:16]

H. Mistakes

Flaws in Consent

In order to avoid any claim that the contents of a document had been misunderstood, the halakhic authorities expounded a ruling that the court must have the document read clearly

---

131 נחת רוח עשיתי לבעלי
132 מקח בטל
133 אין לה טענת נחת רוח
134 ממכרו ממכר
135 מכרן קיים

to the signatories before they endorsed it, to ensure that they grasped its meaning each in his own language (*Git.* 87b.; *Sh. Ar., Hoshen Mishpat* 45:2).

An agreement entered into before a non-Jewish court would be sustained by a *bet din* after the contents (written in a foreign language) had been read and explained to the signatories by reliable non-Jews (*Git.* 19b; *Sh. Ar., Hoshen Mishpat* 68:2). The *bet din* would not accept a claim that someone, being an ignoramus, had not understood what was written in the agreement before he signed it (*Git.* 19b; *Sh. Ar., Hoshen Mishpat* 61:13, 15).

It is a basic legal principle that the consent of each party must be "true, full and free". The achievement of consensus may thus depend on a subjective view of the contract, which could render it invalid on the grounds that misrepresentation by the plaintiff led the parties to draw up a contract on the basis of a wrong assumption. In these circumstances no real consensus existed. Nevertheless, it is impracticable to argue that a secret mental reservation by one or other of the parties could invalidate the obligation. The construction put on the terms of the contract is one that the two sides might reasonably entertain, not one that either of the parties claims to have had in mind (Anson, *English Law of Contract*, pp. 3–10).

In this respect the *Halakhah* laid down a general rule that intentions which are not expressed and which only exist in the mind are not legally binding (*devarim she'balev*) (*Kid.* 50a).[136] This law of contract is, of course, different from the ritual law of prayer, which depends entirely on the thought in a worshipper's mind. Where such activity was essentially a "service of the heart".[137] An exception to this rule would obtain if what a person had in mind, though unexpressed, was something normally understood. In that case we invoke the principle of *umdanah*, a generally accepted assessment (*BK* 41a).

---

136 דברים שבלב אינם דברים
137 עבודה שבלב

Nevertheless, an alleged mistake or misrepresentation could nullify the agreement. It might likewise be asserted that a person had expressed himself incorrectly, e.g., that he had undertaken to bring a sacrifice intended as a peace-offering (*shelamim*), but had mistakenly declared it to be an *olah*, a burnt-offering (Mish., *Ter.* 3:8; *Shev.* 26a).

Interpreting an Intention – Migo

The *bet din* would give favourable consideration to an exceptional claim in the following instance. A held a promissory note (*shetar amanah*) against B, who declared that the IOU had been signed in anticipation of a loan (*Sh. Ar., Hoshen Mishpat* 47b). If the loan was not advanced, a new principle would support his claim – on the grounds that if he had wanted to make a false declaration and the document could not be authenticated, he could have denied the document's authenticity or claimed that the debt had already been paid. This principle, known as *migo*, lays down that the claim is believed since he could have made a better one (*Ket.* 22a; *Git.* 51b, *Tos., s.v.* "*Ve-Rabbi Eliezer*"; *BM* 110a).

The weakness of a *migo* claim is evident from the rule that such a plea would not be entertained in the face of opposing witnesses (*BM* 81b; *Sh. Ar., Hoshen Mishpat* 126:13).[138] Nor would a *migo* claim be accepted if it ran counter to accepted practice (*BB* 5a; *Sh. Ar., Hoshen Mishpat* 126:13).[139] Even a valid claim in support of a defendant's plea would not serve to enforce a payment (*BB* 32b, *Tos., s.v.* "*amay*").[140]

---

138   מיגו במקום עדים
139   מיגו במקום מנהג, במקום חזקה
140   מיגו להוציא לא אמרינן

Mental Reservation – Mesirat Moda'ah

If a person claimed that he had entered into an agreement under duress, his mental dissent could render it null and void. Such a plea would be accepted, however, only if he declared before witnesses in advance that he had been subjected to coercion and that there was no *gemirat da'at*. In halakhic terms, this "mental reservation" formula was called *mesirat moda'ah*. The witnesses would have recorded his protest in a signed document before he entered into the agreement (*BB* 40a–42a; *Sh. Ar., Hoshen Mishpat* 205:1–2).

Mistakes in the Nature and Purpose of Sale

A mistake that was made regarding the conditions attached to an agreement could render it voidable. In the Babylonian city of Nehardea, for example, there was once a shortage of grain and panicky townsfolk even sold their villas to obtain a supply. Large cargoes of grain had actually arrived, however, and were then awaiting admission to the port. It was therefore ruled that the property sales be cancelled and the villas returned to their owners, since the deals were based on a wrong assumption (*mikkah ta'ut*). All things considered, these transactions had been a mistake – *zivinai be-ta'ut* (*Ket.* 97a).

Mistaken Identification of the Party with Whom a Contract Is Made

In contrast to English law (Anson, *op. cit.*, p. 251), the *Halakhah* attaches no importance to a mistake allegedly made in identifying the purchaser who signed a contract. The Talmud quotes an instance where A purchased land from B, telling him that he was buying it for C (the Exilarch, for example), although he really intended the purchase for himself. After the truth emerged, A requested B to draw up a new title deed in his own name. B then explained that he had used the name of the

Exilarch to protect himself, so that no one would discover that he had bought land. The Sages ruled that the sale must remain as it was contracted, and that A could not invalidate it because of a mistake in the purchaser's identity.[141] The vendor could tell the buyer: "It is for you to make arrangements with the person in whose name you bought the field" (*BK* 102b–103a, Rashi *ad loc.*; *Sh. Ar., Hoshen Mishpat* 184:3).

Mistakes in Content – Ta'ut Bemekah

Since there must be *consensus ad idem* in every contract, the minds of both the buyer and seller must be directed towards the same particular object, with no mistake as to the nature of the thing sold (Anson, *op. cit.*, pp. 3–10, 248–249).

The Talmud refers to a case in which A sold B all of the Bar Sissin estate.[142] A certain field in the possession of A was known as "Bar Sissin's field". The vendor, however, told the purchaser: "This is not really part of Bar Sissin's estate and I did not buy it from him. 'Bar Sissin's field' is only its traditional name, and it was not included in the sale". R. Nahman decided in favour of the purchaser, since it was on account of the field's name that his mind registered it as part of the contract, unless the seller could prove otherwise – in which case the sale would have been void on the grounds of a mistake *ad idem*. A was thinking of one piece of land while B was thinking of another (*BB* 30a; *Sh. Ar., Hoshen Mishpat* 218:25).

R. Nahman laid down the general rule that every *kinyan* made in error is voidable[143] and that any dispute is settled according to local practice (*Git.* 14a; Maim. *Mekhirah* 15:1, 26:7; *Sh. Ar., Hoshen Mishpat* 232:1).

---

141 הלוקח שדה בשם חבירו אין כופין את המוכר למכור זימנא אחריתי

142 כל נכסי דבר סיסין מזבנינא לך

143 כל קנין בטעות חוזר

If the mistake in a contract involved two completely different items, the sale was null and void. Thus, if someone contracted to purchase wine but was supplied with a different liquor or with vinegar, or if he agreed to purchase olive wood but was given sycamore, the sale was void. If, however, there was only a difference in the quality of the item supplied, the sale was voidable but could be maintained by an adjustment in the price (*BB* 83b; Maim. *Mekhirah* 17:2; *Sh. Ar., Hoshen Mishpat* 233:1; Salmond, *Jurisprudence*, par. 127, pp. 355–359).

Mistakes in Measure – Ta'ut ba-Middah

Rabbah affirmed that any sale based on measure, weight or number is voidable if a wrong measure is given. According to Rashi, this means that the sale is completely void – *batel ha-mikkah* (Maim. *Mekhirah* 15:1). Other commentators maintain, however, that the sale need not be void but only voidable, since mistaken measures can be rectified (*Nimmukei Yosef* on *BB* 103b; RAN on *Kid.* 42a).

Contracts Impossible to Fulfil

In a case where fulfilling the terms of a contract was impossible *ab initio*, as when an agreement was made for the sale of goods that had already perished at the time the contract was drawn up, without the seller's knowledge and without either party being at fault, the agreement was void. Such would also be the case where the contract applied to something no longer in existence or not yet in existence, or which existed but was not in the seller's possession or under his control. Likewise, if there was a legal or physical condition barring fulfilment of the contract.

[References: Hai Gaon, *Ha-Mikkah veha-Mimkar* 2; *Talmudic Encyclopaedia*, Vol. 7, p. 30, s.v. *"Davar she-lo ba la-olam"*; Osborn, *Concise Law Dictionary*, p. 160]

Non-Existent Objects

There are conflicting opinions among the Sages as to whether a person can transfer title to something that is not yet in existence. Those who rule in the negative maintain that the buyer cannot rely on the transaction[144] or that there is as yet nothing to which ownership can apply, hence it cannot be transferred. According to R. Meir, however, the object may not yet exist, but acquisition takes effect once it comes existence. This is a development on which the purchaser can surely rely if it means selling the next yield of his date-palm or other produce which, in the natural course of events, may be expected to grow.

We have seen that there is a difference of opinion as to the validity of a contract if the object does not yet exist but is expected to come into existence, such as fruit, produce, or an embryo. It is, however, perfectly obvious that if something no longer exists (having gone to the bottom of the sea, burnt or died), it cannot figure in a business transaction and any contract would be a nullity – *res corporales* (*Git.* 13b; *BM* 16a., 33b, Rashi; *Kid.* 63a; *Sh. Ar., Hoshen Mishpat* 209:4).[145]

[References: S. Albeck, in *Encyclopaedia Judaica*, 14:675–680, s.v. "Sale"; *Talmudic Encyclopaedia*, Vol. 7, *s.v.* "*Davar she-lo ba la-olam*", *s.v.* "*be-kinyanim*"; A. Gulak, *Yesodei ha-Mishpat ha-Ivri*, Vol. 1, Chap. 4, par. 28–29]

Mistakes in Price – Ta'ut baMekhir

Another kind of mistake in a transaction (*mikkah ta'ut*) is where the wrong price has been demanded, either by overcharging or by undercharging (*ona'at mikkah*).

As far as overcharging is concerned, there is a failure of consent in the mind of the purchaser, since the price

---

144 לא סמכה דעתיה
145 דבר שיש בו ממש צריך שיהא בעולם

ACTS OF THE MIND IN JEWISH RITUAL LAW

stipulated in the contract was more than he expected to pay.
That would invalidate the sale. Apart from this legal aspect,
if the overcharging was deliberate, swindling the purchaser,
it violated a prohibition of Torah law. The Sages viewed
the commandment in that light: "If thou sell aught unto thy
neighbour, or buy of thy neighbour's hand, ye shall not wrong
one another" (Lev. 25:14; *Tur, Hoshen Mishpat* 227; Maim.
Mekhirah, 12:1–2).[146]

In any case, whether deliberate or unintentional, the
difference must be returned and the contract is voidable. The
buyer may, however, uphold the validity of the contract if
he feels certain that the price will be adjusted. If, moreover,
the overcharge is not substantial, the buyer may be willing to
concede it (*mehilah*). Any fraud amounting to less than the
value of a *perutah*, the smallest coin, is not actionable (*BM*
55b).

According to the Sages of the Mishnah, the amount rendering
a sale voidable is "any increase or reduction that varies by
one-sixth from the correct price" (*shetut le-mikkah*), the exact
definition being "four out of twenty-four pieces of silver".[147]
Anything less than that is assumed to have been treated as a
write-off (*mehilah*) by the person wronged (*BM* 49a; Maim.
Mekhirah 12:1–2; *Sh. Ar., Hoshen Mishpat* 227:1–3).

Depending on the state of mind of the parties concerned,
certain types of possession are excluded from this law of *ona'ah*:
landed property (*karka'ot*), slaves (*avadim*), bonds (*shetarot*),
things consecrated and votive offerings (*hekdeshot*). In the
case of land, the buyer may consider a particular property of
special importance to him and thus agree to pay more than its
market value; or, vice versa, the seller may be in such need
of cash that he is ready to accept less than its market value.
Similar reasons may apply when the value of slaves, bonds or
votive offerings is assessed.

---

146   וכי תמכרו ממכר לעמיתך או קנה מיד עמיתך אל תונו איש את אחיו
147   האונאה ארבעה כסף מעשרים וארבעה כסף

In cases where there is no fixed market price, each party may negotiate the deal as he sees fit. However, an exorbitant overcharge (*laesio enormis*) of over 50 per cent may be declared void (*Kid.* 42b, *Tos. "hakhei nammei"*; ROSH, *BM* 56a; Maim. *Mekhirah* 13:8; *Sh. Ar., Hoshen Mishpat* 227:29).

Defect in Quality – Mum

The general principle is that a defect invalidates the sale. The vendor is always obliged to supply the promised article in good condition, and any defect must be inherent in the article itself, not extraneous. Thus, if A sold B a house which had a structural defect (e.g., a cracked wall), the sale would become void.[148] If, however, they were not aware that the house had been vandalized and that some walls, doors or windows had been damaged, the sale would not be void and the vendor could undertake to have the building restored to its original condition. Here, the defect was not intrinsic but the result of some extraneous event (*Sh. Ar., Hoshen Mishpat* 225:1, 232:5).[149]

In a case where eggs, cheese and similar items were clearly defective when purchased, nullification of the sale would depend on local business practice,[150] since the purchaser would have been aware of such a possibility (*Sh. Ar., Hoshen Mishpat* 232:6, 19).

The vendor is duty-bound to provide goods suitable for the purpose required. Seeds may thus be required either for planting or for consumption. If garden seeds failed to germinate, the vendor would be liable; but if edible seeds that someone had bought and planted failed to germinate, the vendor would not be liable (*BB* 92a–93b; *Sh. Ar., Hoshen Mishpat* 232:20–21).

The buyer assumes that goods supplied are reasonably fit

---

148 מום בגוף הבית
149 מום שאינו בגוף הבית
150 כל שהסכימו עליו בני המדינה

for the purpose intended. If a man bought an ox to plough land and did not mention this when purchasing it, while the vendor knew that it was the buyer's practice to buy oxen for ploughing, the vendor's sale of an ox fit only for slaughter would be voidable (*BB* 92a; *Sh. Ar., Hoshen Mishpat* 232:23).

If the goods sold were those ordered but not of the standard required, such as wheat of inferior quality, the buyer could cancel the sale or adjust the price, whichever he preferred. The same would apply in the opposite case, where the vendor sustained a loss (*BB* 83b; Maim. *Mekhirah* 17:1; *Sh. Ar., Hoshen Mishpat* 233:1).

There was a basic rule governing the sale of land, slaves, beasts or other property. If the buyer came across a defect (*mum*) in the amount or quality, of which he had been unaware when the purchase was made, he could return the property and void the contract whenever he noticed the defect, even if a number of years had elapsed, since the deal had been struck in error (*mikkah ta'ut*). If, however, it transpired that the purchaser, after coming across the defect, had nevertheless made use of the article without informing the seller of his claim, this demonstrated his acquiescence (*mehilah*) and he forfeited his right to void the contract. If his acquiescence was in dispute, the court would determine its validity (*Kid.* 42b; Maim. *Mekhirah* 15:1, 3; *Sh. Ar., Hoshen Mishpat* 232:3; *Arukh ha-Shulhan* 227:8).

Difference in Kind

If someone contracted to buy goods of a particular type but was supplied with items of a different kind (e.g., if he ordered whole wheat flour and received white flour, sycamore instead of olive wood, grape wine instead of grape vinegar, or vice versa), the sale was null and void. This applied even when the item received was more valuable than the one ordered, as it did not meet the purchaser's requirements (*BB* 83b–84a; Maim. *Mekhirah* 17:2; *Sh. Ar., Ḥoshen Mishpat* 233:1).

Non-fulfilment of a Known Intention

Some clear exceptions to the normal laws governing contract stipulations may be seen in the following instances. A man sold his house or other property, informing the buyer that he was doing so because he intended to emigrate and settle in the Land of Israel. For one reason or other, however, this man did not succeed in his quest: either conditions were adverse to settling there and he had to return or the journey proved too dangerous. In a case like this, he was entitled to nullify the sale. Likewise, if a prolonged drought forced a man to sell his property in order to buy wheat, whereupon rain started to fall and wheat became readily available, the sale could be cancelled. If the seller's aim in disposing of his property was not made known to the buyer (*gillui da'at*), and his intention was not fulfilled, the sale remained valid.

The Sages enunciated the principle that "thoughts in the mind which are not expressed verbally when the transaction is made cannot be determined and have no legal effect".[151] What the buyer is contracting for must be certain (*gemirat da'at*): he cannot say what is in the other party's mind unless it is expressed. If the buyer was told the purpose of the sale, however, the intended condition remained valid (*Kid.* 50a, Rashi *ad loc.*; *Sh. Ar., Ḥoshen Mishpat* 207:3, SMA).

The opposite situation would arise if someone disposed of a house or a field and, when the sale took place, told the buyer: "When I have enough money, I'll return your payment and then you will restore the house to me." Once the money was returned, the purchaser was obliged to restore the property. The sale was made on that condition and, once the proviso was fulfilled, the sale became void. Payment made by the buyer was considered as a loan and had to be returned. The buyer would likewise have to return any income from the produce of the field, since that represented a gain over and above the amount of his loan and it would constitute usury.

However, the buyer could avoid having to restore the net gain by volunteering to return the field on his own initiative, if the seller gave his unqualified consent (*gamar u-maskin*). In that case, a straightforward transaction (*ha-mikkah kayyam*) would take place and the arrangement would then constitute a voluntary undertaking made by the purchaser.[152] This would complete the deal and the buyer's offer would be seen as a gesture of goodwill that did not affect the nature of the sale (*BM* 65b; *Sh. Ar., Ḥoshen Mishpat* 207:6–7; *Sh. Ar., Yoreh De'ah* 174:1).

I. Gift – *Mattanah*

Introduction

A legal transaction for the conveyance of land or chattels may take place by means of an assignment made for a consideration, which is a sale. This agreement must be endorsed by both partners with *consensus ad idem*. An owner's right in land or other property may also be assigned to a beneficiary in a unilateral transfer of title, which is a gift.

Although a sale requires the consensual agreement of both parties, in the case of a gift an assignment may be made even without the knowledge of the beneficiary. Acceptance of the gift is, however, essential for the legal transfer of title. A gift may be rejected when the donee becomes aware of it, and such refusal nullifies the gift. Its acceptance by the donee is normally presumed, unless a refusal is indicated. A gift may be conditioned, but when duly executed it is final and irrevocable.

[Reference: Walker, *The Oxford Companion to Law*, p. 526]

Fraudulent Gifts

A gift made fraudulently is voidable. A person may fraudulently convey goods or landed estates, not as a *bona fide* gift but for some shady purpose: to delay or defraud creditors, or a future purchaser of the same property, or to avoid being identified as the owner.

A gift thus made may be rendered null and void at the instance of the future purchaser. In Jewish law it is a person's inward intention that governs the validity of the contract rather than his mere spoken or written word. Jewish law requires that there be no secret or "hidden" gift. The writ of assignment must be made openly, in public, except in the case of a dying man's last will and testament, where only witnesses are required (*Sh. Ar., Hoshen Mishpat* 242:3).[153]

If, however, the deed or instruction to witnesses included a stipulation that the donee should acquire the gift immediately (*me-akhshav*), this removes all doubt concerning the donor's wholehearted intention and the transfer bestows full and immediate possession (*Sh. Ar., Hoshen Mishpat* 242:3, REMA).

---

153   שתהא גלויה ומפורסמת

An Invalidated "Hidden Gift" – Mattanta Temirta

As stated, a "hidden gift" (*mattanta temirta*) has no validity. R. Yehudah laid down the general rule that "a deed of gift drawn up in secret is not enforceable" (*BB* 40b).[154] It is further explained that even when the donee already has such a gift in his possession, the *bet din* will order its retrieval from him.[155] Since the donor behaved deceitfully, the court resolves that the gift was not given *bona fide*, hence the donee does not acquire it (*ibid.*, ROSH 33).[156] Maimonides stated the law in explicit terms: "Whoever wishes to bestow a gift, in sickness or in health, must do so openly and in public. If he authorized the writing of a deed of gift for the donee to be given secretly, that act is worthless[157] because the intention is deceitful. Every valid gift of property must include a statement to the effect that it was made in public" (Maim. *Zekhiyyah u-Mattanah* 5:1–2).[158]

R. Papa quoted the following case, where this law would apply. A man wished to marry a woman who would only agree to the betrothal on condition that he assigned all his property to her, which he did. Before doing so, however, he secretly transferred all his property to his son. The Sages ruled that neither party acquired title. The man's real wish was for his son to acquire possession, not the woman, and the assignment to her was made under duress. The prior assignment to his son was, however, a gift made in secret and it was therefore not enforceable (*BB* 40b).

An analogous case was that of a widow contemplating marriage who sought to prevent her future husband from acquiring title to her estate, which the marriage would bring him. Accordingly, prior to the marriage, she transferred her estate to her daughter, declaring at the same time before

---

154   האי מתנתא טמירתא לא מגבינן בה

155   אם תפס מפקינן מיניה

156   אנו אומדין דעתו שלא גמר לתת לו בנפש חפצה

157   אינה כלום

158   מתנה גלוייה

witnesses that this assignment was only provisional and that her intention was for the estate to revert to herself in the event of divorce or her husband's death.

This woman and her husband were later divorced and she then claimed the return of her estate, but the daughter refused to surrender her gift. The Sages ruled that the deed of gift to the daughter was nothing more than a ruse and had no validity. Shemuel, the foremost halakhic authority, enunciated the principle that a spurious deed would not be recognized by the court. The mother's gift to her daughter had not been intended as a *bona fide* transfer of property, as it was assumed[159] that she would protect her own interests rather than hand over her estate to anyone else. Since this had never been a *bona fide* gift, it was null and void. Every gift must be accompanied by the donor's mental commitment and intention, and in this case the mother's gift was only a ruse to prevent her estate from falling into the hands of the husband or his heirs (*Ket.* 78b).[160]

If, before making the gift, she had voiced reservations, indicating that her daughter was not meant to acquire it, such a declaration before witnesses (*moda'ah*) would invalidate the transfer. Had she written two deeds, one secret and the other public, both the secret and the public deed would be considered invalid.

The Tur (R. Ya'akov ben Asher) disagreed with Maimonides' interpretation of the law. He ruled that the declaration of protest (*moda'ah*) invalidated the first gift but not the second, which was made in public. Having been duly assigned, the second gift remained valid and enabled the daughter to acquire it. The Sages thus meant to preclude the fraud of evasion. R. Yosef Caro ruled according to the view of the *Tur*.

[References: *Ket.* 78b, Rashi *ad loc.*; Maim. *Zekhiyyah u-Mattanah* 5:3–5, *Maggid Mishneh ad loc.*; Tur, *Hoshen Mishpat* 242:1–2]

---

159   אנו אומדין
160   שטר מברחתא לא קנה

The accepted rule is that any declaration of protest invalidating a transaction must be made in the presence of witnesses before the deed is executed. Such a protest is effective only if the transactor claims that he is acting under duress.[161] The witnessed declaration serves as evidence that the transaction is defective because one party's affirmed intention is lacking.[162] Such a protest must have an accompanying statement, which the witnesses may record in a separate document,[163] declaring that they are aware of the pressures exerted on someone to act as he did.

To ensure the reliability of a business transaction, it became standard practice, when a genuine deed of contract was written, for the witnesses to attach a statement confirming that the transactor was thereby waiving *ab initio* any such protest that might subsequently be lodged (*Sh. Ar., Hoshen Mishpat* 242:1, 2, 4, 5; A. Gulak, *Yesodei ha-Mishpat ha-Ivri* 3:17).[164]

Gift Made by a Dying Person

According to the *Halakhah*, if a person who is on the point of death or seriously ill[165] gives instructions in the presence of witnesses that certain property of his be handed over to a particular beneficiary, even if this was not entered in a deed of gift and regardless of whether the assignment was made on a weekday or a Sabbath, that property must be given to the beneficiary on the donor's decease. Such an assignment was valid, even without the formality of a symbolic transfer (*kinyan*) or a formal mandate to the witnesses.[166] The Sages explained that the formal laws were relaxed so that the dying man might have peace of mind, in the certain knowledge that

---

161   מחמת האונס
162   חוסר גמירת דעת
163   שטר מודעא
164   לבטל כל מודעא
165   שכיב מרע
166   אתם עדי

this wish would be fulfilled (*BB* 152a, 156a, *Tos. s.v. "konin"*; Maim. *Zekhiyyah u-Mattanah* 8:2, *Maggid Mishneh ad loc.*; *Sh. Ar., Hoshen Mishpat* 250:1).[167]

The Sages discussed a case in which a dying man had a deed written by witnesses, stating that he gave all his property to a certain beneficiary and that a *kinyan* had been made to that effect. Rav ruled that the gift had thus been duly assigned, since the dying man had made doubly sure that the gift would be so allocated after his decease. However, Shemuel, who was recognized as the highest authority in civil law cases,[168] ruled that the law in this case was problematical. The dying man could have assigned the gift merely by word of mouth. His superfluous instructions might therefore indicate that he had decided not to transfer possession to the beneficiary at once, but through the deed after his demise.

The accepted rule, however, was that no transfer of possession through a deed might be effected after the testator's death. No assignment could be made by a man once he was dead,[169] and no action could therefore be undertaken by the court. The gift was held to be revoked and the property would revert to the legal heirs. Furthermore, if the sick man recovered, the property remained his own and his gift could be withdrawn, as the court's assessment of his real intention (*umdanah*) led it to believe that he had made the gift only in anticipation of his death. RIF, Maimonides and Caro followed Shemuel's ruling (*BB* 152a, RIF and Rav *ad loc.*; Maim. *Zekhiyyah u-Mattanah* 8:10–11; 156a, *Tos. s.v. "konin"*; Maim. *Zekhiyyah u-Mattanah* 8:2, *Maggid Mishneh ad loc.*; *Sh Ar., Hoshen Mishpat* 250:1–2).

---

167 כדי שלא תטרף דעתיה עליו
168 דהלכתא כוותיה דשמואל בדיני
169 אין שטר לאחר מיתה

Assessment of Intention – Umdanah

The principle of *umdanah*, where the court assesses the real (albeit unexpressed) intention of the gift's donor, was elucidated by the Sages in the following case. A man's son left home for a distant land and the father, hearing that his son had died, assigned all his property to a stranger in a deed of gift. Subsequently, however, the man's son returned. The Sages debated as to whether his gift was valid and ruled according to the principle of *umdanah*. They assumed that if the father had known that his son was alive, he would not have given his property to a stranger, because he really meant his son to inherit it. Since the donor's intention was obviously flawed, the gift was declared invalid. By giving away all his property, the man had shown that he did not expect to survive; and as his son was reportedly dead and thus unable to inherit,[170] he had given his property to a stranger, whereas his real wish would have been for his son to acquire it (*BB* 146b, Rashi and *Haggahot ha-Rosh*; Maim. *Sh.Ar., Hoshen Mishpat* 250:2, 8).

Another case of a gift being deemed invalid was where a person had felt compelled by unusual circumstances to hand it over to someone else. In the court's estimate (*umdanah*), this was not his original intention and only a mistaken view of the circumstances had made him do so.

J. Inheritance – *Yerushah*

The concept of inheritance in Jewish law refers to a person's estate, which descends to his heirs in accordance with the established rules of precedence and their relationship with the deceased. The disposal of such legacies is predetermined by Torah law. The process of inheritance is governed by objective statutory laws that are not at the testator's discretion but apply automatically on his demise. This procedure is unlike the testamentary disposal of one's possessions, where the testator provides for the distribution of his property after his death, according to his own free will, though not to the exclusion of legitimate heirs (*BB* 133b; Maim. *Nahalot* 6:11; *Sh_Ar., Hoshen Mishpat* 276, 282:1; A. Gulak, *Yesodei ha-Mishpat ha-Ivri*, Vol. 2, 5:31–32).[171]

A testamentary will may also be revoked according to the testator's wish or replaced by another, later will. As a result, any such bequest is, strictly speaking, not an inheritance (*yerushah*) but a gift (*mattanah*).

Inheritance (*yerushah*) is a juridical relationship between an individual and his family consequent on his death, according to the priority of their relationship. No individual is empowered to establish a different manner of succession, nor can he deny the right of a statutory heir. He may, however, exercise his personal choice by bestowing "gifts" before his death according to his own inclination. After his demise, no other person is entitled to convey a gift (*Sh_Ar., Hoshen Mishpat* 276:1; 281:6, 7–10; Maim. *Nahalot* 1:1 *et seq.*, 6:1 *et seq.*).

Detailed regulations concerning the rights of inheritance binding a husband and wife, and extending their curtailment, were formulated by rabbinical decrees in various communities (*takkanot ha-kehillot*). Ordinances promulgated in the medieval German communities of Speyer, Worms and Mainz were accepted throughout Poland and Eastern Europe as "*Takkanot SHUM*".[172] In Spain, too, these inheritance laws were adapted to local needs and social conditions.[173]

---

171 אין רוח חכמים נוחה הימנו
172 תקנות שום
173 תקנות הקהילות טוליטולא ומולינא

Testamentary Bequests

The basis of a will is the declaration of a person's wishes regarding the procedures to be followed after his death, notably the disposal of his possessions (Gulak, Vol. 3, 6:52–72, pp. 113–145).

The bestowal of one's property, according to the rules of inheritance, is governed by ordained Biblical law. Any nonconforming bequest must be made in the form of a gift. The testator is free to dispose of his property in either form of bequest. The purpose of a will is to arrange the desired distribution of property within the laws of inheritance, and to distinguish between family obligations and the bestowal of external gifts. The Sages condemned any disposal of property in breach of the statutory laws of inheritance.

A will should be drawn up with great scrupulousness and legal nicety, so as to make the testator's wishes perfectly clear and avoid any future misunderstanding or distortion of his intent. However, since a person's last will and testament is often made when he is gravely ill and preoccupied with thoughts of his impending death, every effort must be made to ascertain, confirm and execute his intention. The Sages ruled that for the dying person to have peace of mind, he must be convinced that his wishes will be fulfilled. It is a *mitzvah* to implement the wishes of the deceased, whatever formula he has used (*Ket.* 70a; *Git.* 14b; *Sh. Ar., Hoshen Mishpat* 253:2).[174]

Should the testator recover from his illness, he is empowered to change the terms of his will. If he dies, the evidence of two people who witnessed it is accepted as clarification of his intent. A healthy person's testament[175] must be drawn up according to full contractual requirements, including a written deed and a formal act of *kinyan*,[176] after which its validity is binding.

---

174   מצוה לקיים דברי המת
175   צוואת אדם בריא
176   בשטר ובקנין

The testament of a very sick person confined to his bed is treated with considerable indulgence as far as the strict legal requirements are concerned (*Sh. Ar., Hoshen Mishpat* 250:5, 6).[177] Even the oral testament of a person who is critically ill[178] has the same validity as a will formally delivered (*BB* 156b; *Sh. Ar., Hoshen Mishpat* 250:1, 7).[179]

Whereas every testamentary gift must be made openly, in public, the will of a mortally ill person dividing his estate among his heirs may be written privately, with instructions that it should not be revealed until after his death, the testament itself becoming effective once he is dead (*Sh. Ar., Hoshen Mishpat* 243:3, 6).

Testator's Intention

Shemuel declared that if a dying man gave all his property in writing to strangers, although symbolic acquisition (by *kinyan*) took place, he may rescind the will if he recovers, as we know that he disposed of his estate only because he was expecting to die. Since the gift was made on his deathbed, there can be no doubt of his serious intention and the gift is valid in all cases. The codifiers further explain that even though he never referred to his imminent death when making this bequest, he was clearly aware of the situation and in these circumstances no formal acquisition (by *kinyan*) was required.

Rav and Shemuel differed as to what the testator had in mind when he wrote in his will that it was also being delivered by *kinyan*. The point at issue was whether the gift was final or if he could withdraw it in the event of his recovery. Rav held that by making his *kinyan* declaration the testator might well have implied that only the deed itself would complete the

---

177 צוואת שכיב מרע
178 שכיב מרע
179 ככתובים וכמסורים דמו

transfer of property after his death, and that no statement by word of mouth could do so.[180] The testator would certainly be in no position to make a *kinyan* or a conveyance after his death! The bequest therefore had no legal standing and could not be effected.[181]

Shemuel, however, ruled that the bequest was valid. He understood that the testator's aim was to reinforce the implementation of his bequest, although the law accepted that a dying man's bequest was valid even without a formal *kinyan*. This testator had included the term *kinyan*, not as a specific requirement but as a way of strengthening the donee's right to the bequest.[182] Shemuel believed that this was implicit in the donor's instruction: "Write and give".[183] Had he written that the *kinyan* was intended only as an empowerment (*yippui ko'ah*), it would certainly be valid. Shemuel nevertheless agreed that if the man recovered, his bequest could be withdrawn.

Maimonides adopted the view of Rav that there could be no *kinyan* after a man's death, so that the bequest was invalid. However, he also accepted Shemuel's view in one respect: if the donor had first made the bequest in his lifetime and then added, "Write and give" (*kitvu u-tenu*), this expression was intended as a reinforcement (*yippui ko'ah*) of the prior gift (*BB* 152a–b; Maim. *Zekhiyyah u-Mattanah* 8:12, RAVAD and *Maggid Mishneh ad loc.*, 8:13, 17; *Sh. Ar., Hoshen Mishpat* 250:1, 7–8).

Categories of a Testament

There are three different forms of will:
1. That made by a person who is critically ill (*tzava'at shekhiv me-ra*), which has the force of a document written and delivered. The condition of such a person is

---

180   לא גמר ומקני
181   בטל
182   יפוי כח
183   כתבו ותנו

defined by Maimonides as "a sick man whose entire body has grown feeble and whose strength has waned through illness, so that he is bedridden and cannot walk outside" (*BB* 149a; Maim. *Zekhiyyah u-Mattanah* 8:2, 27). Gifts made under such a will come into effect on the death of the legator, but may be withdrawn if he recovers (*Git.* 72b; *BB* 149a).

2. That made by a healthy person.[184] This gift is not bestowed as a *yerushah* according to the laws of inheritance.[185] The legator transfers his property to the legatee "from today and following my death" (*BB* 135b–136a, Rashbam *ad loc.*).[186] Scholars have differed as to whether the gift is transferred immediately or may later be revoked. It is therefore questionable whether the legator, on recovery, may withdraw the offer of his gift (*Sh. Ar., Hoshen Mishpat* 257:1, 6–7; Maim. *Zekhiyyah u-Mattanah* 12:13–14).

3. That made by a healthy person anticipating his possible demise.[187] Though not gravely ill, he fears that he may die suddenly and therefore wishes to bequeath his property as he chooses. Such a person is not confined to bed and is capable of walking outside the house with the aid of a stick (Ex. 21:18–19, *Mekhilta ad loc.*).[188] Such a will is mostly held to be like that of a person in sound health.[189]

Disputes may arise among the beneficiaries if there are opposing claims regarding the testator's state of health when the will was made. A legal heir is entitled to the property,[190] while other beneficiaries must furnish evidence to prove their claim (Maim. *Zekhiyyah u-Mattanah* 9:22; *Sh. Ar., Hoshen Mishpat* 251:2–3; 250:14, *Bet Yosef* 13).

---

184 מתנת בריא
185 דיני ירושה
186 מהיום ולאחר מיתה
187 מצווה מחמת מיתה
188 והתהלך בחוץ על משענתו
189 כמתנת בריא
190 מוחזק

A will of this type should be made by a person who is critically ill or in a dangerous, life-threatening situation. The Sages gave three examples (apart from ill health): anyone facing execution by the lawful authorities, leaving a caravan in the middle of a desert or embarking on a sea voyage (*Git.* 65b–66a, Rashi *ad loc.*). Whoever escaped any of these perils was duty bound to give special thanks to the Almighty (*Ber.* 54b).

For a disposition made by someone in mortal danger[191] no *kinyan* is necessary. This applies not only to wills but also (chiefly) to the instructions given for a divorce, where the strict formalities are dispensed with (Maim. *Gerushin* 2:12; *Sh. Ar., Ḥoshen Mishpat* 250, *Bet Yosef* 13).

Interpretation of Wills – Umdanah

When the claims of beneficiaries conflict, all issues are subject to the rules appertaining to documents. In the interpretation of wills, the guiding principle is one's duty to fulfil the wishes of the deceased (*Git.* 40a; *Sh. Ar., Ḥoshen Mishpat* 253:2, REMA).[192]

Every effort must therefore be made to fathom the testator's mind in order to gauge his true intention. A beneficiary presenting the deed in support of his claim against the legal heirs must always bear the burden of proof, since the heirs are deemed to be in automatic control of his property.[193] The legal principle is that anyone striving to appropriate an object in someone else's possession must prove his right to that object[194] or show that the testator had revoked any earlier disposition (*Ket.* 27b, 76b; *Tos.*, "*Kallah be-vet aviha*", *Ket.* 83b; *Bik.* 2:10).

---

191 מחמת מיתה
192 מצוה לקיים דברי המת
193 מוחזקים
194 המוציא מחברו עליו הראיה

The legator can prevent later disputes by giving added strength to his bequest, stating that it is clearly expressed and not open to some other interpretation (*Sh. Ar., Hoshen Mishpat* 42:9–10).[195] A dispute may, however, arise if the testator left contradictory instructions about the allocation of his property. The court's task would then be to ascertain what he really had in mind, according to either his first or his last instruction.

A case in point was that of a dying man who stated before witnesses that he bequeathed all his estate to A, but later declared that he gave part of it to B. Various questions had then to be answered. Did the second bequest nullify or diminish the first? Was the second bequest made in error, since he had already given all his estate to A? Or, alternatively, was he retaining part of the estate for himself while distributing the remainder? (Otherwise, the laws governing testamentary gifts would prevent all of the acquisitions.) The Sages ruled that the second legatee acquired ownership of his bequest while the first did not (*BB* 148b; *Sh. Ar., Hoshen Mishpat* 250:12). Similarly, if the man bequeathed his gift to A in a deed, but later bequeathed the same gift to B, the ruling was that B acquired the gift while A did not, on the grounds that the testator had changed his mind and revoked the first gift.

A comparable discussion, as to whether the first or second opinion should be followed, involves one of the ritual Sabbath laws.[196] Here, a person's intention is open to different interpretations according to the circumstances in which the problem arose.

Mishnaic law states, in regard to carrying on the Sabbath,[197] that the prohibition is only violated if one carries a specified minimum, depending on the use generally made of a particular object or commodity. The Sages prescribed different standards for a number of items. The standard measure for food was

---

195   דלא באסמכתא
196   על דעת ראשונה או על דעת אחרונה
197   איסור הוצאה

either the size of an olive (*ka-zayit*),[198] a dried fig[199] or a lentil.[200] If the commodity was less than the standard size, no transgression had occurred (*Shab.* 93b.; Maim. *Shabbat* 18:28).

The law accordingly states that if a man retains seeds for the purpose of sowing, for a sample or for use as medicine, and then carries them outside the Sabbath boundary, he is held liable whatever their size, even though less than the standard measure of all other commodities would not make him guilty of a violation. If, after carrying the seeds outside, he decides not to sow or use the seeds for his original purpose and then takes them back into the house, he is liable only according to the standard measure. In the first case, by carrying them outside for a specific purpose, he has attached a special value to the seeds – whatever their size may be.[201] However, by changing his mind, he cancels the designation.

According to these laws, culpability is a matter of intention. Abbaye described a case where someone put an object aside and forgot why he had done so. He then carried it outside for no specific purpose. The question that arose was whether the special purpose that he had in mind was retained by the object or whether, now that the original intention was forgotten, his change of mind cancelled the effect of that special purpose. From the Mishnah's general wording Abbaye derived the rule that if anyone undertakes a particular action, even nonspecifically (*setam*), that action's original importance is retained.[202] This ruling was accepted by the Sages (*Shab.* 90b, Rashi *ad loc.*; Maim. *Shabbat* 18:21).

---

198 כזית
199 כגרוגרת
200 כעדשה
201 אחשביה
202 כל העושה על דעת ראשונה הוא עושה

K. Warranty

A Collateral Undertaking – Asmakhta

An extended undertaking subsidiary to the contract is known halakhically as an *asmakhta*. This Aramaic term is akin to the Hebrew root *samakh* ("support"): in other words, such an undertaking was not intended as a material condition but as a subsidiary element adding assurance to the contract's guaranteed fulfilment. Any contract with such an undertaking (or surety) attached is regarded as an imperfect one; and the Sages had to decide whether, as a result of the warranty's being claimed, title was or was not transferred. The object referred to in the guarantee remained in the guarantor's possession and its transfer to the creditor depended on the implementation of his undertaking.

The person who obligated himself in this undertaking did so in the belief that such a conveyance would probably not materialize. That expectation weakened the decisiveness needed in the contract, showing that it was not entered into with the firm resolve (*gemirat da'at*) which every contract required. The introduction of subsidiary collateral diverted the contractor's mind from the essential purpose of the agreement, thereby diminishing the element of *gemirat da'at*.

A number of Sages reportedly expressed opposing views as to whether such a contract was binding or otherwise. Some maintained its validity, in that containing a particular stipulation which, if it were not fulfilled, would be a breach of contract (*asmakhta kanya*). Others ruled that a contract including such a collateral warranty was not binding but void (*asmakhta lo-kanya*). An agreement was flawed if it included a collateral warranty and thus nullified the entire contract.

In view of the many different interpretations given by Talmudic sources, there is no clear-cut definition of the law governing *asmakhta* and post-Talmudic jurists developed an extensive body of legal opinions, which resulted in a profusion of halakhic rulings.

An Impossible Condition

If, in drawing up a contract, one lays down an impossible condition, two questions arise: (a) Since that condition is farcical, could the entire transaction be meant seriously? (b) Is the condition itself of no effect, thus validating the contract? The Sages mentioned the following instance. On delivering her bill of divorce, a man tells his wife: "This is your divorce, provided that you rise up to heaven or cross the Great Sea on foot". As a rule, the divorce only becomes valid if the condition stipulated before the event is fulfilled. Should the condition negate a law of the Torah, it has no validity.[203]

Torah law thus ordains that in every marriage "her food, her raiment, and her conjugal rights shall he not diminish" (Ex. 21:10).[204] Hence, if a man stipulated that the marriage would take place on condition that such duties did not bind him, that condition would have no validity but the marriage itself would remain valid (*Sh. Ar., Even ha-Ezer* 38:5; Maim. *Ishut* 6:9–10). Similarly, in the case of a man who executed a legal function and attached a condition that was impossible to fulfil, such a condition would be disregarded but the operation itself would be deemed to have taken effect.

According to the principle set down by R. Yehudah ben Tema, whenever an impossible condition is made, it cannot be intended seriously; its purpose must surely be to irritate or make fun of someone. The legal act, however, remains binding (*Sh. Ar., Even ha-Ezer* 38:2).[205] Some authorities accepted this ruling in the vital matters of marriage and divorce, which had to be certain and unambiguous. In commercial matters, however, every condition was obligatory (Maim. *Ishut* 6:9–10).

---

203   המתנה על מה שכתוב בתורה תנאו בטל
204   שארה כסותה ועונתה לא יגרע
205   אינו אלא כמפליגה וכשר

This difference of opinion followed an earlier tannaitic dispute between R. Meir and R. Ḥanina ben Gamliel, where latter's view prevailed: although the condition was voided, the contract remained in effect. Hence R. Naḥman's authoritative ruling: *Halakhah ke-Rav Yehudah ben Tema* (*BM* 94a; Maimonides, Mishnah commentary *ad loc.*).

A classic passage in the Talmud illustrating the various approaches to *asmakhta* runs as follows. On entering into an agreement to participate in a joint venture, one person may transfer certain goods to another, who holds them as a security (*eravon*) for the former's discharge of some obligation. The transfer does not convey ownership, but represents the holding of a security that must be returned once the agreement is carried out or forfeited in the event of its noncompletion.

The following case was discussed by the Sages. When A gave a sum of money or chattels as a pledge to B, he made this stipulation: "If I fail to discharge my obligation, my pledge is forfeit to you". B in turn stipulated: "If I fail, I will double your pledge". This is an example of *asmakhta*, in regard to which R. Yose and R. Yehudah differed. R. Yose held that the conditions were binding, in accordance with the rule that an *asmakhta* agreement gives title (*asmakhta kanya*) and effects conveyance of the contract as a whole, together with the obligation of the warranty. R. Yehudah, however, maintained that the contracting of such an agreement was void and that the contract was valid only in the amount of the pledge. An auxiliary or extravagant promise simply indicated that a person meant to fulfil the agreement. This was an imperfect warranty, neither intended seriously nor legally binding, and its lack of determination (*gemirat da'at*) nullified the contract (*lo-kanya*).

In another case of *asmakhta*, A lent money to B, who gave him his field as security. A stipulated, "If you don't repay me within the next three years, the field is mine", and B agreed to this arrangement. The *tannaim* (Sages of the Mishnah) ruled that if B did not repay the loan within three years, the field would belong to the lender (*harei hu shello*).

The *amoraim* (Sages of the Gemara) debated at some length the presence of the *asmakhta* in this agreement. R. Naḥman ruled that according to halakhic law the contract was valid and the *asmakhta* conveyed title (*asmakhta kanya*). This decision was, however, overturned by R. Yehudah, and later R. Naḥman became convinced that R. Yehudah's view was correct. Having changed his mind, he adopted the majority ruling that an *asmakhta* did not convey title and voided the agreement – *asmakhta lo-kanya* (*BM* 65b). The fact that the lender had not acquired title gave rise to a problem if, in the meantime, A had enjoyed the usufruct of the field, which would be considered interest (*ribbit*).[206] Maimonides ruled accordingly (Maim. *Malveh* 6:4; *Sh. Ar., Yoreh De'ah* 164:4).[207]

The Sages discussed a further case where A paid some of the money he owed to B, then obtained a receipt for his part payment while B held the bond for the debt. It was agreed that the bond would be deposited with a third party (C) and A stipulated that if the balance was not paid by such-and-such a date, C would give the bond to the lender. B could thus recover the whole amount from A if the balance was not paid on time. R. Yose accepted the validity of this agreement and ruled that the entire bond should be given to the lender.[208]

R. Yehudah determined, however, that the agreement was flawed by reason of *asmakhta*. The agreement had not been meant seriously, as the borrower felt sure that there would be no grounds for putting it into effect. Rav followed R. Yose's ruling, whereas Shemuel followed that of R. Yehudah, which the Gemara finally accepted. In accordance with his opinion that an *asmakhta* arrangement did not give title, Maimonides also adopted the view of R. Yehudah – "For he [the borrower] did not resolve in his mind to convey" (Maim. *Mekhirah*, 11:2).[209] R. Yosef Caro ruled likewise (*BB* 168a; Maim. *Mekhirah* 11:5; *Sh. Ar., Ḥoshen Mishpat* 55:1).

---

206 ריבית
207 הרי זה לא קניא מפני שהיא אסמכתא
208 רבי יוסי אומר יתן
209 שהרי לא גמר בלבו להקנות

When someone takes part in a game of chance and places his bet, he agrees that (if he loses) the winner will take the money he has staked. The question facing the Sages here was as follows: When the winner took his money, did the loser (by agreeing to participate in the game) convey that sum to the winner, or did he hold on to his money all the time in the hope that he would win? In that case, the winner had taken money which the owner had not conveyed to him. The *tanna* of the Mishnah accordingly judged the winner to be guilty of misappropriation (i.e., theft). Such habitual contravention of the law discredited persistent gamblers and they would be disbarred from giving evidence in court.

This teacher therefore held that gambling was an agreement based on *asmakhta* and, as such, it did not convey title (*asmakhta lo-kanya*). Although the loser was resigned to forfeiting his money, the conveyance was an imperfect one.

Among those whom the Mishnah disqualifies as witnesses are people who risk their money in games of chance and lay bets on throwing dice or pigeon racing.[210] The Sages explained that such ventures had nothing to do with an individual's skill and only depended on sheer luck in the game, which he hoped to win. Although other Sages did not consider winning games of chance to be theft, the Rabbis censured the gambler for wasting time and money on such activities instead of engaging in work that was useful to society.[211] A punter might claim that the swiftness of pigeons winning a race was not just a matter of luck but the result of skilful training. The Rabbis declared, however, that the fault lay in the possibility of another man's pigeons joining his flock and being misappropriated (*Sanh.* 24b, *Tos. s.v. "Ve-elu hen"*; Maim. *Edut* 10:4; *Sh. Ar., Hoshen Mishpat* 34:16).

As many Sages ruled these to be valid conveyances (*kanya*) as held them to be invalid (*lo-kanya*). Those who adopted the *kanya* ruling took an objective view of the agreement,

---

210 ואלו הן הפסולין המשחק בקוביה ומפריחי יונים

211 לפי שאין עסוקין בישיבו של עולם

considering it like any other that made a stipulation which
would not usually invalidate the agreement. Those who
accepted the contrary ruling (*lo-kanya*) took the subjective
view that an individual making the agreement did not intend
to convey his property, which showed that the element of full
consent (*gemirat da'at*) was lacking (SMA on <u>H</u>oshen Mishpat
207).

Na<u>h</u>manides adopted a similar view, but made this
distinction. If someone had it in his power (*be-yado*) to
fulfil the undertaking, he relied on his firm belief that the
obligation to convey his property might be avoided, as in
the undertaking: "Should I not repay the debt within three
years, my field will become your property". He did not really
have it in mind to transfer his field: that would be a case of
asmakhta which vitiated the agreement. In this interpretation
Na<u>h</u>manides followed the ruling of R. Hai Gaon (Ramban
on Alfasi, *Ned.* 27a–b; cf. Rashi, *Sanh.* 26b; Rashba, quoting
Shittah Mekubetzet; *BM* 73b–74a).

There were circumstances in which some authorities
maintained that a defendant's claim of *asmakhta*, to avoid
responsibility in the contract, might be thwarted by simply
inserting a clause in the written agreement declaring: "It is
agreed that this contract does not make possible a claim of
asmakhta.[212] A typical instance would be that of a borrower
mortgaging his field as security for the payment of his debt; if
he failed to repay what he owed, the lender took this mortgaged
field, despite the contract's possible voidance by reason of
asmakhta (cf. *BM* 65b).

A clause was also inserted, "excluding any supportive
interpretation of the document's purpose" that might
be suggested in favour of the borrower's contention of
avoidance.[213] This remedy against the flaw of *asmakhta* was
approved by the Babylonian authority Saadiah Gaon (10th
cent.). However, though halakhically possible, this same

---

212 והוא שכתב לא דלא כאסמכתא

213 ודלא כטופסי דשטרי

device was later rejected by Caro "in accordance with everyday commercial practice" (*BB* 44b; *Tur, Hoshen Mishpat* 213:1; *Sh. Ar., Hoshen Mishpat* 113:3).

Conclusion

Maimonides accepted the view of R. Yehudah in the Mishnah (*BM* 48b) and followed the ruling given by his earlier halakhic authority and mentor, Hai Gaon, in a treatise dealing with commercial law (*Ha-Mikkah ve-ha-Mimkar*). French scholars quoted by the Tosafists evolved an interpretation that differed in some important aspects from that of the Spanish school represented by Maimonides. The Tosafist view was expounded by R. Yitzhak ben Shemuel (known as RI).

A summary of the opinions expressed by various schools is given by R. Ya'akov ben Asher in his code (*Tur, Hoshen Mishpat* 207). In his great Code of Law (*Shulhan Arukh, Hoshen Mishpat* 207) and in his *Bet Yosef* commentary on Maimonides (*Mekhirah* 11:2–7), R. Yosef Caro generally follows Rambam's interpretation.

The vast quantity of learning that has accumulated around this one topic of *asmakhta* illustrates the freedom of interpretation exercised by the great legal (halakhic) scholars of the Talmud and successive generations, leaving the whole subject open to discussion.

[References: Herzog, *Main Institutions*, Vol. 2, Chap. 6; A. Gulak, *Yesodei ha-Mishpat ha-Ivri*, Vol. 1, Book 1, 3:21; *Encyclopaedia Judaica* 5:923–933, *s.v.* "Contract"; Elon, *Mishpat Ivri*]

L. Suretyship – *Arevut*

An act of suretyship is a contractual engagement that establishes an obligation of right *in personam* between the contracting parties, whereby one undertakes to serve as a surety for the other who is legally obliged to perform an act for the benefit of a creditor. The surety is answerable for the other man's debt, in the event of his failing to repay a loan, by the guarantor's declaration that he will henceforth ensure that the loan is repaid and that the creditor has a legal right to demand it from him. When this assurance is consented to and acted upon by both parties, a contract is established by mutual agreement.

For the establishment of an effective contract between two parties, the law requires the existence of a consideration, which usually meets the purpose if it is worth having. Thus, something of value is given by one party in exchange for a promise given by the other. This contract is in the nature of a bargain: If I do something for you, you will do something for me, namely, a *quid pro quo*.

The consideration must offer some gain or benefit to the promisor in recompense for the burden of fulfilling his promise. It must also have some value of material interest to one or both parties; if such a consideration is lacking or insufficient, the contract is invalid. Jewish law regards any psychological satisfaction gained by the surety as a valid consideration.

[General reference: Salmond, *Jurisprudence*, Chap. 16, pars. 126–127]

The Guarantor – Arev

The normal application of suretyship is as follows. If, when the loan was transacted, C told A, "Lend money to B and I will stand surety",[214] C is obligated to repay the loan for which he is the surety. This basic ruling by R. Huna was accepted as the governing law. If, however, C told A, "Lend money to B and I will make every effort to ensure that he repays you", that does not make him a guarantor in the legal sense of *arev*. The pledge must be a full undertaking that he himself will pay. The *arevut* obligation applies when C assures A that B will repay him, that he will have the means to do so and that C himself undertakes to make the repayment if B defaults.

If, when making the loan, A relied on C's assurance, which proved to be untruthful, we conclude that A, by agreeing to lend on his security (i.e., determining his consent),[215] was misled by C, who therefore has an obligation to repay the loan (*BB* 104a; *Sh. Ar., Hoshen Mishpat* 129:2, REMA).[216]

A contract that imposes a legal obligation (*shi'bud*) is one in which a person assumes legal responsibility for having the contract fulfilled. He thereby undertakes to repay whatever is due should the borrower fail to do so. It might be maintained that such an agreement contains the flaw of *asmakhta* (as explained above), in that the guarantor's commitment depends on his assumption that the debtor will certainly repay. However, this flaw is remedied by the fact that the guarantor *does* receive a payment (consideration) in being deemed a man of means and integrity. That consideration will suffice to validate the contract.

A Court-appointed Guarantor – Arev Bet Din

An even stronger obligation is created when the guarantor's pledge is made incumbent on him by order of the court (*arev bet din*). Since every such undertaking requires the element of a consideration, the fact that the court is certain that a man will repay a debt gives him psychological satisfaction of value to him. This gain will suffice for his commitment.[217]

By accepting the obligation of a guarantor, the creditor secures the advantage of being not merely an *arev*, but an *arev bet din*. He may also acquire real estate that was, perhaps,

---

215 גמירת דעת
216 כי בטוח הוא ועשאו על פיו והיה שקר חייב לשלם
217 דבההוא הנאה דמהימן ליה גמר ומשעבד ליה

already mortgaged, but the creditor must first claim it from the debtor (*BB* 103b, 104b, 173b, 176b; *Sh. Ar., Hoshen Mishpat* 129:8).

A Guarantor Accepting Full Personal Responsibility – Arev Kablan

A further extension of the guarantor's degree of obligation may be seen when he takes direct and immediate responsibility for repayment of the loan, as if he himself were the borrower and, as guarantor, affirmed: "Lend him and I will repay you".[218]

The creditor may attach the guarantor's property, even if the debtor has enough of his own to repay the amount loaned. Such an obligation is created when the guarantor says, "Give him and I will be responsible" (i.e., the *kablan*).[219] This commitment is expressed in the Hebrew formula, *ve-ani kapchu* (an abbreviation of the letters *kuf, peh chet, vuv*) – *ve'ani kablan, pore'ah, chayav venoten*). The accepted rule is that the creditor may first call upon the guarantor, if he so wishes (*BB* 174a; *Sh. Ar., Hoshen Mishpat* 129:14–17).[220]

The terms of the surety's binding commitment, made in the presence of the *bet din*, are recorded in a bill giving details of the names and conditions involved. The complete text of such a document appears in an authoritative halakhic compilation, *Sefer ha-Ittur* (Part 2, s.v. "*arev ve-arev kablan*", end.). This excludes any ambiguity from the undertaking, in accordance with all the halakhic interpretations.

[General references: M. Elon, in *Encyclopaedia Judaica*, 15:524*ff.*, *s.v.* "Suretyship"; A. Gulak, *Yesodei ha-Mishpat ha-Ivri*, Vol. 2, pp. 88–95; I. Herzog, *Main Institutions*, Vol. 2, pp. 197–208; M. Elon, *Mafte'ah*, pp. 222–225]

---

218   תן לו ואני אפרע

219   תן לו ואני קבלן

220   קבלן לעולם יפרע ממנו תחילה אם ירצה

Chapter 14

The Rabbinic Concept
of Mind and Will

14 The Rabbinic Concept of Mind and Will

A. Agents of the Inner Person: Rabbinical Terminology

In Rabbinic literature, various terms meaning "will" or inner personality are used to describe faculties of the mind rather than "will" in its general sense.

(1) *Ratzon – Will*

Thus, in the Talmud, *ratzon* does not possess the general sense of "will" but denotes consent or approval. Performing an act with *ratzon* means that one does so willingly. Acting in a manner contrary to the *ratzon* of the Sages means that one does so without their approval; and acting in a manner opposed to their teaching means that one does so against their *ratzon*. To fulfil the *ratzon* of God is to act in accordance with His desire.

(2) *Nefesh – Soul*

In Rabbinic literature, *nefesh* generally possesses the sense of that term as used in the Bible. Simply, *nefesh* is an individual, a person, as used in the term *nefashot* (Gen 46:26; Ex. 12:4). This also includes a person's vitality or animal life, and thus by transference, denotes the person himself. *Nefesh* represents both the "blood soul" and the "breath soul" which leaves man when he dies. It is the life that may be endangered and, at times, even forfeited. Scripture ordains that the life of a murderer must be taken: "At the hand of man, even at the hand of every man's brother will I require the life of man" (Gen. 9:5).[1] The term *nefesh* is, however, also used in the Biblical sense of "will, wish or desire." A man of bad character may be said to possess an evil *nefesh*; and a person's wish or intention, good or bad, lies in his *nefesh* (*Arukh ha-Shalem*, ed. A. Kohut, Vienna, 1926, Vol. 5, fol. 368a et seq., s.v. "*Nefesh*").

In the Biblical conception, blood, *dam*, has a degree of sanctity as the carrier of life; hence, its consumption by man is prohibited "for the blood is the life" (Deut. 12:23; cf. Gen. 9:4).[2] When offering an animal sacrifice, the Israelite was forbidden to eat any of its blood, "for the life of the flesh is in the blood" (Lev. 17:11)[3] and "the life of all flesh is the blood thereof" (Lev. 17:14).[4]

The liver contains the largest conglomeration of blood in the body. Accordingly, the liver is sometimes used to designate man's soul, his entire being or personality. Such usage occurs in many ancient Semitic languages (Brown, Driver and Briggs, *Lexicon of the Old Testament*, s.v. "*Kaved*").

On this basis one may understand the translation of a verse in Psalms that has puzzled many commentators: "So that my glory may sing praise to Thee, and not be silent" (Ps. 30:13, RV, 30:12).[5] Here, the word *kavod* has been variously translated: as "the honoured people of the world" (Targum) or "praise to the Almighty without ceasing", as in Ps. 29:9;[6] "the soul" (Kimhi); or "the soul, which is the glory of the body" (*Metzudat Tziyyon*, ibid.).[7] In addition to its literal meaning (honour, glory), *kavod* may be associated with the word *kaved* (liver), which represents one's soul or entire life force. King

---

ומיד האדם מיד איש אחיו אדרש את נפש האדם	1
כי הדם הוא הנפש	2
כי נפש כל בשר דמו בנפשו	3
כי נפש כל בשר דמו היא	4
למען יזמרך כבוד ולא ידום	5
ובהיכלו כלו אומר כבוד	6
כבוד הוא הנשמה שהיא כבוד הגוף	7

David, the Psalmist, thus proclaims that his whole being "will sing Thy praises without remission".

Chapter 7 of Proverbs is devoted to cautioning an innocent young man against the harlot's wiles. She entices him with her perfume and blandishments; then, "as an ox that goeth to the slaughter", he falls into her trap. The text indicates that her arrow pierces his "liver": the infatuated youth hastens to her like a bird running into the fowler's net, little realizing that this will cost him his life (Prov. 7:23).[8]

The term *nefesh* is used in the Bible in connection with the law of the nazirite. According to Biblical law, a nazirite is required to bring a sin-offering at the secession of his naziriteship. Different reasons for the need for this atonement have been given by the Sages. The early exposition of the Targum states that the offering was a purification after defilement by contact with the dead (Num. 6:11).[9] In the Midrash *Sifri* it was further explained that R. Ishmael said, the duty of bringing an offering referred only to one who had been so defiled. This view was use in the translation of the Revised Version, "For he sinned by reason of the dead". R. Elazar Hakappar, however, said that an offering was brought by every nazirite because he had deprived himself of the benefit of wine in which the soul had delight. Such deprivation was an offence against the natural desire of his soul. This interpretation explained the literal Biblical reason for the offering, "for he hath sinned against the soul" (Num. 6:11).[10] Thus, the sin-offering had to be brought only if he had defiled himself by contact with the dead, in accordance with the interpretation given by the Targum (Num. ibid.).

In the above discussion we find two different uses of the term *nefesh*: a) the 'soul' of man, meaning the nature of his entire being; and b) a body, a deceased person (*Ned.* 9b; 10a; *Ta'anit* 11a; *Naz.* 4b).

עד יפלח חץ כבדו... ולא ידע כי בנפשו הוא   8

מדחב על מתא   9

כי חטא על הנפש   10

The classical commentators also gave varying interpretations. Rashi (ibid.) followed the view of Targum. Nachmanides (ibid.) explained that his sin was that he should have maintained the sanctity of being a nazirite for the rest of his life, and he sinned by discontinuing it. Maimonides (*De'ot* 3:1) wrote that a nazirite sinned by depriving himself of a physical pleasure which he was entitled to enjoy.

(3) *Lev – Heart*

Another expression for the seat of mind and thought is *lev* (heart). This term is especially applicable to workings of the mind that are not expressed, i.e., "secret thoughts" (*devarim she-ba-lev*). Although the fulfilment of most precepts requires a specific utterance, there are a number of precepts that can be effected by thought alone. These include belief in God, rejection of idolatry, avoidance of evil fancies and desires, sexual restraint, repentance and forgiveness. In some ritual matters also, a person's mental determination can suffice – in the removal of leaven before Passover (*bi'ur ḥametz*), for example, or designating the portions due to the priest, allocating tithes (*terumah* and *ma'aser*) and undertaking a self-imposed fast (*Ta'an.* 12a; Maim. *Ta'aniyyot* 1:100).[11] A mental decision can likewise effect a husband's confirmation or annulment of his wife's oath (Num. 30:7–13; *Ned.* 76b).[12]

[References: J. D. Eisenstein (ed.), *Otzar Yisra'el*, art. "*Devarim she-ba-lev*", Vol. 4, p.12; cf. M. Lazarus, *The Ethics of Judaism*, Part 1, Appendix 23, p. 291; J. H. Hertz, *Pentateuch*, pp. 32, 487, 803]

11   תענית שקיבל על עצמו
12   והחריש לה

(4) *Maḥashavah – Thoughtful Intention*

The concepts of thoughtful plan and intention are expressed in the Talmud by the terms *maḥashavah* and *kavvanah*. Work forbidden on the Sabbath is defined as anything that involves creative design or skilled labour – *melekhet maḥashevet* (*Ḥag.* 10b). An intention brought to a successful conclusion is a *maḥashavah* that bears fruit (*Kid.* 40a). When rewarding someone for his performance of a good deed, God adds the merit of a good intention – *maḥashavah tovah* (*Kid.* 40a). If, however, a man secretly plans an evil or deceitful act, he should know that God will inflict due punishment, since He is *Ba'al Maḥashavot*, the One who sees through all man's thoughts, actions and intentions (*San.* 19b). The Midrash teaches us that "he who steals men's confidence is chief among thieves" (*Mekhilta: Mishpatim*).

(5) *Kavvanah – Intention, Devotion*

The Rabbinic precept that *kavvanah* is needed to fulfil God's ordinances means that their performance must be accompanied by devotion or, at least, by one's intention to comply with the Law (*Ber.* 13a). Slaughtering an animal with the intention (*kavvanah*) of doing so in accordance with the laws of ritual slaughter (*sheḥitah*) is thus clearly distinguished from slaughtering the beast with no such ritual intent (*Hul.* 31a). The term *kavvanah* is also used in the sense of meditation, attention or devotion (cf. *Ber.* 13b; *Meg.* 20a). (A detailed dissertation on the subject of *kavvanah* is given above in chapter three.)

(6) *Hirhur – Inner Contemplation, Unspoken Words, Critical Thoughts*

Inner contemplation unaccompanied by speech or action is termed *hirhur*. This may equally refer to proper thoughts or improper fancies. In the latter case, it puts one in mind of the Biblical admonition, "That ye go not about after your own heart and your own eyes" (Num. 15:39), which alludes to the indulgence of one's physical desire or sinful imagination. To emphasize the danger of sinful thoughts, the Sages affirmed that a man who allows himself to indulge in such fancies, even without any actual wrongdoing, is excluded from the presence of God (*Nid.* 13a).

The fact that a person is not guilty of a palpable transgression does not necessarily mean that he is undefiled by sinful thoughts (*Shab.* 64a). Such thoughts are deemed even more injurious to one's spiritual health than the action itself. Why so? Because a transgression would be evident, thus inducing the offender to repent, whereas a sinful thought might easily be overlooked (*Yoma* 29a).[13] A person suffering from an unclean discharge may have been punished in this way for yielding to immoral thoughts (*Zav.* 2:2); when he avoids them by day, he is saved from impurity by night (*Av. Zar.* 20b; *Ket.* 46a).[14]

Legally speaking, idol worship involves the performance of an idolatrous act. Nevertheless, even observing idol worship (*hirhur avodah zarah*) is regarded as a contemplated transgression (*hirhur averah*), which is likewise forbidden (*Ber.* 12b; *Sanh.* 62b–63b, 90a). A righteous man who keeps his impulses in check is credited with the highest achievement (*Avot* 4:1;[15] *Sanh.* 104b[16]). When Torah instruction fills his heart, all evil thoughts are removed from him (*Avot de Rabbi Natan* 20).[17]

Meditating on words of holy Scripture in an unclean place is deemed unseemly (*Ber.* 24b). The Sages differed as to whether meditation (*hirhur*) was equivalent to speech. It is, however, stipulated that when anyone recites Grace after Meals, the *Shema,* the *Amidah* or blessings for other precepts,

---

13 הרהורי עבירה קשו מעבירה
14 ת״ר ונשמרת מכל דבר רע, שלא יהרהר אדם ביום ויבא לידי טומאה בלילה
15 איזהו גבור הכובש את יצרו
16 לא גבור בתורה אתה, מה תתהלל
17 כל הנותן דברי תורה על לבו מבטלין ממנו... הרהורי יצר הרע

the words should be articulated, unless ill health or defilement prevents him from doing so (*Ber.* 20b; cf. *Sh. Ar., Orah Hayyim* 62). Although speaking about one's regular weekday pursuits is forbidden on the Sabbath, merely thinking about them (*hirhur*) does not fall under the prohibition (*Shab.* 113b; cf. *Sh. Ar., Orah Hayyim* 16).

The word *hirhur* has two different senses. The first denotes the thought given to an action in a person's mind without the action itself being performed. Only the actual performance of a forbidden action constitutes a violation of the Sabbath; but whereas speaking about inappropriate matters is also forbidden on the Sabbath, thoughts about such matters are not prohibited (*Shab.* 103b).[18] Contemplating an immoral act is, however, forbidden and at times it is considered even worse than the act itself (*Yoma* 29a).[19]

The Sages taught that "the instant a person has it in mind to commit a sin, he is disloyal to God" (Lev. R. 8:5). Being "disloyal", however, still does not amount to an actual transgression. R. Nehemyah declared: "If a man intends to commit a sin, God does not hold him to account before he has done wrong; but if he intends to fulfil a precept, even when he has not yet managed to do so, God promptly credits it to him as if the *mitzvah* had already been performed" (*Midrash Tehillim* 30).

The performance of a *mitzvah* in obedience to God requires a state of physical cleanliness. One who is ritually unclean (*tamei*) is forbidden to recite a benediction (*Suk.* 26b; *Sh. Ar., Orah Hayyim* 40:7).[20] The statutory recital of the *Shema* is confined to particular hours of the morning and evening (*Sh. Ar., Orah Hayyim* 58:1, 5). If the due time has arrived and a man finds that he is "unclean", he may fulfil his obligation by simply pondering over the words of the *Shema* (*meharher be-libbo*). As mentioned earlier, the Sages disagreed about the

---

18   דבור אסור, הרהור מותר
19   הרהורי עבירה קשו מעבירה
20   בעל קרי אסור להניח תפלין

equivalence of *hirhur* to "speaking inwardly" (*Ber.* 20b.). So as not to exceed the time allowed for its recital, they eventually decided that meditating on the *Shema* was acceptable (*Sh. Ar., Oraḥ Ḥayyim* 62:3–4).

The alternative sense of *hirhur* is "finding fault with, suspecting" or even "thinking ill" of someone. Moses the lawgiver was once guilty of criticizing Divine justice. When Pharaoh ordered Israel to continue supplying the regular tally of bricks, although he refused to provide them with straw, Moses complained to the Almighty: After he spoke to the ruler of Egypt, demanding Israel's release from slavery at God's command, Pharaoh had intensified his oppression of the Israelites. Moses therefore asked God to explain why He had created so much trouble for Israel (Ex. 5:22–23).[21]

The Almighty then upbraided Moses for complaining that His promise to redeem the Israelites had not been fulfilled. "Abraham, Isaac and Jacob were promised the Land of Canaan as their inheritance, but that was not accomplished in their days. They never cast doubt on God's faithfulness, whereas you find fault with Him. What impels you to criticize His behaviour?"[22] As a result of this offence, Moses was only allowed a glimpse of the Promised Land; his people would enter it, but he would not (Ex. R. 6:4; Ex. 6:1, Rashi, *Ba'al ha-Turim*; MAHARAL, *Gur Aryeh,* ibid.; *Sanh.* 111a).

In Talmudic times, a man acknowledged by fellow scholars to be thoroughly proficient in Torah law and meticulously observant was honoured as a *talmid ḥakham* – one vested with religious and moral authority. Disparagement of such a learned man was considered an impertinence (*Sanh.* 104b).[23] While his opinions or interpretations might be questioned, vilifying his character or conduct was strictly forbidden (*Ber.* 19a).[24] One could be sure that if he acted wrongly one night, he would

---

21 למה הרעת לעם הזה

22 כמה פעמים נגליתי על אברהם יצחק ויעקב באל שדי ולא הודעתי להם כי שמי ה'
כשם שאמרתי לך ולא הרהרו אחר מדותי

23 לא גבור בתורה אתה, מה תתהלל

24 אל תהרהר עליו

repent and perform *teshuvah* the next morning (*Ber.* 19a).[25] A scholar was in a class above the general public (ibid.),[26] and the Sages declared that "he who welcomes a *talmid hakham* into his home is compared to one who associates with the *Shekhinah*, the Divine Presence (*Ket.* 111b; *Hul.* 9a; *Ber.* 43b; R. Yitzhak Aboab, *Menorat ha-Ma'or*, sect. 322).

B. *Da'at* – Mind, Knowledge, Intention

(1) *Knowledge and Consent*

The term most often employed in Talmudic literature to denote the inner person's mind and will is *da'at*, stemming from the verbal root *yada* (to know). In legal phraseology *da'at* is virtually equivalent to the English expression, "knowledge and consent". It sometimes indicates a sense of awareness, but can also signify actions performed "of one's own free will". Generally speaking, *da'at* refers to the mind as the faculty of intelligence and considered opinion.

(2) *The Basic Agent of Personality*

The term *da'at* has a particularly wide signification. It refers to "mind" as mental energy or the psychical source of intelligence and opinion (*Arukh ha-Shalem*, ed. A. Kohut, Vol. 3, p.105*ff.*, s.v. "*De'ah*").

Asher Gulak describes the vital importance of *da'at* in Jewish law. The creation or termination of every legal relationship between individuals requires both form and *da'at*. Jewish law bases the arrangement of every contract on

---

25 תלמיד חכם שעבר עבירה בלילה אל תהרהר אחריו ביום, ודאי עשה תשובה

26 אל תהרהר עליו

an accompanying identity of intention, the agreement of terms and purposes by the parties concerned and the expectation that such a contract's intent will be fulfilled (*gemirat da'at, semikhat da'at*). The external requirements of form ordained in Jewish law require that certain acts of conveyance (*kinyan*) take place, whereby evidence of the new legal relationship is publicly demonstrated. The legal formality undertaken by the individual is apparent; the subjective agent in the transaction, however, remains unseen and is called *da'at*.

[References: Gulak, *Yesodei ha-Mishpat ha-Ivri*, Vol. 2, 1922; *Toledot ha-Mishpat be-Yisra'el*, Vol. 1, 1939]

The essential element here is the fact that *da'at* was present at the establishment of the contract. *Da'at*, in this legal sense, means more than knowledge, wish or awareness. It is not always essential for the parties concerned to desire that the legal act take place, but it is always imperative that they intend, willingly or otherwise, that the particular act in which they are engaged be effected. This intention is not described as the individual's *ratzon* (will or wish), but as the product of his *da'at*. Jurisprudence makes this declaration: "Contract is that form of agreement which directly contemplates an obligation: the contractual obligation is that form of obligation which springs from agreement" (Anson, *Law of Contract*, 2).

C. Capacity

The fundamental importance of *da'at* can be gauged from the requirement that each party to an agreement or contract should, first of all, have legal capacity not only in personal status but also in *da'at* (i.e., intelligence).

The legal criterion of intelligence usually coincides with the age of puberty. Maimonides states that the power of agency is withheld from minors, "because they are not endowed with sufficient intelligence" (Maim. *Shelihut*, 2:2). The lowest degree of intelligence needed for some limited rights of acquisition is determined by the sense of discrimination that makes a person "throw away a pebble, but take a nut when it is handed to him". A deaf-mute (*heresh*) is considered to be mentally handicapped, on a level with a minor of minimum intelligence; an imbecile has no power of acquisition whatsoever (*BM* 71b;[27] *Git.* 64b; Maim. *Zekhiyyah* 4:6–7;[28] *Git.* 64b[29]).

The second requirement is an awareness of the nature of the act in which the two parties are engaged and of their intention to effect it in accordance with the terms and conditions known to both. Thirdly, both parties must be satisfied that the acts in which they are engaged are legally effective. *Da'at* thus embraces four essential elements: intelligence, awareness, intention and confidence (Henri Bergson, *Matter and Memory*, p. 231*f.*).[30]

In the case of a cerebral injury, it is not mind as an occult power that is damaged but the nervous system of the brain, the cerebral links which permit the memory to function. These may be obstructed by nervous disorders, not through some defect in the mind itself but through losing the brain's service to the mind (Jacques Chevalier, *Henri Bergson*, trans. L. A. Clare, New York, Macmillan & Co., 1928, pp. 166–170).

The brain is only one of many organs on which the manifestation of intellect depends. It is not just the brain that thinks but the man, the organism as a whole. All parts of the body have a sympathy with one another more acute than human intelligence can yet, or perhaps ever will, imagine (D. A. Gorton, *The Monism of Man*, 1893, pp. 54–56). Thought, memory, volition and desire are not simply functions of the brain or visible evidence of matter, although both these elements play an integral part in their manifestation. They all betoken the deeper and far more extensive power of conscious life, mind or soul. This conscious life is the principle of individuality, which may be called the will of the individual.

קטן אף על גב דלית ליה שליחות ... אית ליה זכיה מדרבנן   27

קטן שנותנין לו צרור וזורקו   28

קטנה היודעת לשמור את גיטה   29

גמירת דעת וסמיכת דעת   30

The will of the individual must be recognized as a principle and constituent having deeper roots than what is commonly taken to be the individual mind. Its energy, task and operation are assigned by the Divine Power of the universe.

[References: B. Bosanquet, *The Principle of Individuality and Value: The Gifford Lectures for 1911–12*, London, 1927, p. 354]

D. The Rabbinic System of Cosmogony

Astronomers and natural scientists investigating the mystery of creation have not managed to devise a process more telling than the simple and poetic one recounted in the Book of Genesis. It opens with the majestic hypothesis of a Divine Creator: "In the beginning God created the heaven and the earth". Science points to millions of changes that may have taken place in matter and energy, producing an infinite variety of forms (Smar, *The Origin of the Earth*, p. 8), but the Torah declares that God created the material nucleus from which later forms were capable of developing (Nahmanides on Gen. 1:1).

A philosopher once assured Rabban Gamliel that God found all the materials needed to create the world already in existence, namely, the "*tohu, bohu*, darkness, water, wind and deep" mentioned in Genesis. Rabban Gamliel, however, vehemently rejected the notion of primordial matter, asserting that the term "creation" itself supports the hypothesis that God was the first and sole Creator of all things (Gen. R. 1:12; Isa. 45:6–7).[31]

The philosophers attempted to explain the process of creation in various ways, but each theory was disproved by the next. Rabbinic teaching emphasizes the belief that everything depends on its creation and constant re-creation by the Master of the Universe. This principle is expressed in the Morning Service: "In His goodness He renews the process of creation every day" (*Ḥag.* 12b; Ps. 136:4; *Authorised Daily Prayer Book*, p. 39; Maim. *Guide*, 2:30, ed. M. Friedlaender, 1910).[32]

Maimonides endeavoured to present a system in which the philosophical and Rabbinic views were combined. He outlined the following sequence of events leading up to the creation of man and his soul.

(1) *Origin – Creation*

The earliest, and all subsequent, forms of life originated in the four elements (earth, water, air and fire), the making of which constituted an act of *creatio ex nihilo*. The Sages thus affirmed that all things were created together, but separated from each other consecutively (Maim. *Guide*, ibid., ed. M. Friedlaender, p. 213).

Through the motion of the spheres the elements mingled with one another and, through the further action of light and darkness, their constitution changed (Maim. *Guide*, ibid., p. 216). The first change was the formation of two kinds of mist, creating meteorological phenomena such as rain. This process also brought about the formation of minerals, plants, animals and, lastly, man.

The spirit of life vitalizing the animal kingdom was identical with that breathed into man. Hence the life force (*nefesh*) originating in the four elements, and known by the comprehensive term 'earth', is present in animal and man alike. This life force is held to reside in a creature's blood: "For as to the life of all flesh, the blood thereof is all one with the life thereof" (Lev. 17:14; Maim. *Guide*, *loc. cit.*).[33]

---

32   ובטובו מחדש בכל יום תמיד מעשה בראשית
33   כי נפש כל בשר דמו בנפשו הוא

When devising His supreme creation, God said, "Let us produce [lit. "make"] man" (Gen. 1:26). This refers to a union of God's creative forces with those of the earth, i.e., the four elements. While the earth contributed man's animal form of life, God endowed this creature with His own Divine spirit (Gen. 2:7). This combination of animal life and Divine spirit (*neshamah*) produced a new "living being" – *nefesh ḥayyah* (ibid.); and the added *neshamah* changed man from an animal into a human being endowed with intellect and speech (cf. *Targum Onkelos* on Gen. 2:7).[34]

Thus, man is described as having being created "in our image" (Gen. 1:26),[35] i.e., in the "image" of God and earth, signifying that he possesses the vital qualities of both. Man is later described as being created partly "in the likeness of God" (Gen. 5:1), because that aspect of his nature – his intellect and creative ability – is the special characteristic of man.

Although God breathed the "higher soul" into man after he already possessed the attributes of animal life, this Divine *nefesh* would not remain separate from the animal one. Both life forces combined to produce the new human being, distinct from the earlier *nefesh ḥayyah*, which now had (a) the elemental power of growth, as found in plants; (b) the power of movement, as in marine and terrestrial life; and (c) the human powers of active intellect and speech. All of these merged in one living soul, the *nefesh ḥayyah* that is man.

Each man's nature differs from the other's by reason of the varying constitution of the elements within him. Though not separate, these elements can bring different forces into play that may be opposed or assisted by forces originating from other parts of his constitution. The final result, however, in thought, speech and action, is man as a whole, not a part of him.

Man's urges derive from the earthly *nefesh*, i.e., the blind forces of animal life known as the *yetzer ha-ra* (evil

---

34   ויהי האדם לנפש חיה... תרגום: והות באדם לרוח ממללא

35   נעשה אדם בצלמנו כדמותנו

inclination). Those that derive from the God-given *nefesh*, i.e., the power of the Divine intellect, are called the *yetzer ha-tov* (good inclination). The desires of man's earthly *nefesh* are evil, however, only when the balance of the four elements has been upset. The Divine intellect instructs us as to what is proper in man; such would in fact even be the desire of the animal *nefesh*, if the elements were in true harmony.

Man has been compared to "Jacob's ladder", with its base on earth and its spiritual power descending from heaven. When Jacob lay down to rest at a place called Luz, on his journey northward from Beersheba, "he dreamed, and behold a ladder set up on the earth, and the top of it reached to heaven; and behold the angels of God ascending and descending on it" (Gen. 28:12).[36] The Sages explained that this ladder connecting heaven and earth represented Jacob himself: he, like every human being, possessed the earthly and heavenly qualities of which both men and angels can avail themselves. Moses succeeded in reaching heaven, as the Bible records that he "went up unto God" (Ex. 19:3),[37] and Jacob drew encouragement from the assurance that this power also existed within him (Gen. R. 68:16, 18).

Man in his basic elemental form is called *Adam*. As he ascends towards the Divine form he is called *Ish*. Only man is capable of self-improvement and of controlling his baser animal nature. Every creature is governed by a particular instinct and an unchangeable form of behaviour. All their traits, whether good or bad, can be found in man, but he alone possesses the unique ability to follow any inclination that he chooses and to change from one to another. When God said, "Let us make man in our image, after our likeness" (Gen. 1:26), He gave man the power to rule over all the creatures on earth and to master the qualities of each. Man is a microcosm, and his instinctive longing is for perfection (cf. *Sanh.* 38b).[38]

---

36   ויחלם והנה סלם מצב ארצה וראשו מגיע השמימה

37   ומשה עלה אל האל-הים

38   אדם הראשון מסוף העולם ועד סופו היה

[S. D. Luzzatto (Shadal), *Meḥkarei ha-Yahadut*, 1:2, s.v. *"tzelem Elohim"*]

Rabbi Elḥanan Wasserman, one of the six million Jews annihilated by the Nazis, endeavoured to explain how such wickedness could exist among men:

"It is taught in the *Zohar* that man, who was created last, possessed the characteristics of all the animals that preceded him. Some men behave like wolves, foxes or snakes, while others can behave like doves or sheep, lions or eagles. Each animal is bound by its own natural instinct, but man is endowed with freedom of choice... One may therefore be on a high cultural and intellectual level, yet act like a wolf or a snake. Man is, however, also capable of perfecting himself if he follows the teachings of Torah, through which he can bathe in the celestial light that the Creator reserved for the righteous.

"The task of man, in his striving for perfection, is to overcome those tendencies of his nature that lead to evil. In some men the evil urges are extremely powerful. Of Moses himself it is related that such evil impulses were naturally dominant. When his fame as Israel's deliverer from Egypt spread throughout the East, an Arab king who wished to discover the essential character of Moses commissioned an artist to bring him a portrait of the lawgiver. From the way the artist portrayed Moses' face, he was judged to be a man of the lowest character. The king rebuked the artist, stating that he could not have portrayed Moses correctly. To discover the truth for himself, the king journeyed to the Israelite encampment, compared the artist's portrait with what he saw in Moses and then discovered that the artist's portrayal was true to life.

"Recognizing that Moses was clearly 'a man of God', he asked him to explain this paradox. Moses admitted that he had from birth possessed all the evil traits of character visible in his portrait, but also affirmed that he had always kept these proclivities under strict control. Having managed to suppress them, he was now a man who naturally followed the ways of God. This story ends with a declaration that the greatness of Moses lay in the fact that, despite tremendous handicaps, he managed through his own constant effort to become a new person, and even to be called 'the man of God' – *ish ha-Elohim*" (*Tiferet Yisra'el,* Mishnah commentary by Yisra'el ben Gedalyah Lipschutz, Danzig, 19th cent., end of *Kiddushin* 4:4).

Although the Rabbis were aware of the danger posed by giving free reign to man's emotional impulses, they refused to consider these urges an inevitable source of evil and disaster. The emotions were an essential feature of human life, but they should not be let go in a completely subjective, brutish manner. When given conscious expression, with due regard for man's relationship with his fellow man and his place in God's creation, they could serve a vital purpose in helping to build a true civilization. Man's closest communion with God was expressed not in the form of intellectual adoration, but in the practice of *ahavah*: "Thou shalt love thy neighbour as thyself: I am the Lord" (Lev. 19:18).[39]

(2) *The Mind*

The mind is often considered the wellspring of all that is reasonable, good and Divine. In Biblical terminology and Rabbinic psychology, however, the mind (termed *lev*, heart) is also identified as the source of man's evil impulse: "Every imagination of the thoughts of his heart was only evil continually" (Gen. 6:5);[40] "for the imagination of man's heart is evil from his youth" (Gen. 8:21).[41] The mind generates the thoughts and devices, the promptings and purposes of evil, while the heart is thus often identified with the evil inclination (*yetzer ha-ra*).

---

39 ואהבת לרעך כמוך אני ה'
40 וכל יצר מחשבות לבו רק רע כל היום
41 כי יצר לב האדם רע מנעוריו

The Almighty thus commanded Israel to make "fringes" on the borders of their garments and, when looking at them, to recall His teaching, "that ye go not about after your own heart and your own eyes, after which ye use to go a-whoring" (Num. 15:39).[42] The Rabbis comment on this verse: "The heart [thought and imagination] and the eyes lead men into sin; but the eyes merely follow the heart, and there are blind men who stand condemned of every monstrous deed in the world" (*Sifrei*, Num. 5:115, cf. TJ *Ber.* 3c). Likewise, in the Apocrypha (2 Esdras 4:30), the "evil seed sown in the heart of Adam" is equivalent to the *yetzer ha-ra* in rabbinic literature.

The mind, which visualizes the delights of sin, is also responsible for planning the gratification of a man's desires and for making him carry that plan into effect. Temptation and the rationalizing of evil desires both originate in the mind. Though present in the mind and the emotions, the *yetzer ha-ra* is not identified with either of them. What we call the evil impulse is, in fact, a moral and theological concept. The "heart", as mind, embraces the faculties of reason, imagination, passion and purpose, all of which are at man's disposal. When these are wrongly utilized, whether in the scientific, religious or moral sense, the actions they inspire are viewed as workings of the *yetzer ha-ra*.

[References: Maim. *Guide* 1:31, ed. Friedlaender, p. 40; Solomon Schechter, *Aspects of Rabbinic Theology*, 1909, p. 267; George Foot Moore, *Judaism*, Vol. 1, 1927, p. 486]

(3) *The Person*

It is in the nature of man to be capable of experiencing numerous inclinations, moods and feelings, each of which may be linked with different, even conflicting motives. These inclinations are not, however, separate powers vying for control over the person. They are all creations of the person himself, who may sometimes hesitate before deciding which inclination to follow, but eventually chooses one in preference to the others.

The Torah not only instructs man to behave morally and rationally, but in the studying of it also inspires him with the ideal of Torah and its pursuit. By directing his thoughts to Torah wisdom, man gains a sense of responsibility and moral obligation that will henceforth constitute the natural basis of his conduct.

Man's sentiments can likewise be under effective Torah control. Regarding the injunction of the *Shema*, "Thou shalt love the Lord thy God" (Deut. 6:5), the *Sifrei* Midrash asks: "How can one be ordered to love, when love is purely a matter of sentiment? An action may be decreed, but how can this apply to a sentiment?" This law was expounded by Kant in the sense of "treat him as if we felt such affection" (Laird, *Moral Notions*, p. 63). The *Sifrei*, however, explains that the commandment applies to the following verse, "And these words... shall be upon thy heart", namely, the injunction to love means to study the Torah's words. Study, reflection and understanding of those words will also have an impact on man's feelings and create in him the actual disposition to love.

E. The Concept of the Will in Jewish Philosophy

(1) *Duties of the Heart* (Baḥya Ibn Pakuda)

According to Baḥya Ibn Pakuda (Spain, 11th cent.), if manifest actions are subject to the laws of God, so also, and even of greater necessity, are the non-manifest acts of the mind or will (*Hovot ha-Levavot*, Introd.). Since God ordered the performance of manifest acts, which cannot be complete without the participation of the will, He must also have ordered the performance of non-manifest acts, which can be described as motivations of the will in the performance of physical actions. It is possible, in philosophical analysis, to regard thought and action as two separate activities, but they are so closely connected that an instance of one may also be considered an instance of the other (Collingwood, *Philosophical Method*, p. 43).

The Torah lays down clear duties of the will, both positive and negative, which Baḥya calls "Duties of the Heart" (*Ḥovot ha-Levavot*). Man is required to obey them by directing his will to act in accordance with God's law. Among the positive duties Baḥya lists the following:

(i)   To believe in the existence of God as the Creator *ex nihilo*, that He is One and Incomparable;

(ii)   To serve Him in our heart and to contemplate the wonders of creation that are a reflection of Him;

(iii)   To trust in God, to humble ourselves before Him and to fear Him;

(iv)   To long to fulfil God's will and to devote our actions to His service;

(v)   To love Him and all those who love Him;

(vi)   To hate those who hate Him.

Among the negative duties Baḥya mentions the following: not to covet; not to bear vengeance or a grudge; not to desire or contemplate transgression; not to hate one's brother in one's heart, not to go astray after one's heart and one's eyes; and not to harden one's heart (*Ḥovot ha-Levavot*, Introd.).

The foundation of all Torah observance lies in the proper directing of man's will. The first step in fulfilling God's law is man's determination to act accordingly and, through his will, to "energize" that intention. Once man takes the initiative, God helps him to complete his action: "If he comes to purify himself, he receives heavenly assistance" (*Yoma* 38b).[43]

The Sages reiterated the importance of directing one's will to perform God's law with their use of the expression, "God requires the heart" – *Rahmana libba ba'i* (*Sanh.* 106b, Rashi ibid., s.v. "*Revuta*").[44] The fact that the *bet din* does not inflict the usual penalty for a transgression committed unawares (*bi-shegagah*) – e.g., for unintentional homicide, capital punishment is not laid down, and the unwitting transgression of a negative commandment does not incur the penalty of stripes (but only the bringing of a sin-offering) – demonstrates that the action is not considered complete if it is not motivated by the will. Likewise, the Sages declared that the fulfilment of a precept is only rewarded if the will to perform that *mitzvah* was its motivation. King David, however, was rewarded simply for wishing to build the Temple, although he never actually constructed it (1 Kings 5:17–19; 1 Chron. 22:7–10).[45]

Of primary importance in the fulfilment of all Torah laws is an understanding of what it means to serve God and, through the will, a coordination of that mental understanding with the physical action of the body. This requirement is summed up by Moses through the emphasis placed on one word in the text: "Thou shalt be whole-hearted (*tamim*) with the Lord thy God" (Deut. 18:13, American Jewish Version, JPSA, 1917).[46] This indicates that one's body and soul should both be directed in coordination with the will of God. The righteous man not only does righteousness but always wills the truth in his heart: "I will walk within my house with a perfect heart" (Ps. 101:2). A further exposition of "whole-hearted" teaches "do not seek the predictions of sooth-sayers, but be confident in the will of God" (ibid. Rashi).

Isaiah condemned solemn assemblies that people with sinful minds attended "I cannot away with iniquity and the solemn meeting" (Isa. 1:13).[47] In their regard for acts of the will, the Rabbis even declared that the motivation of an act

---

44 רחמנא ליבא בעי
45 ויאמר דוד לשלמה בנו אני היה עם-לבבי לבנות בית לשם ה' אל-הי
46 תמים תהיה עם ה' אל-היך
47 לא אוכל און ועצרה

determined its propriety. Thus, in the opinion of R. Nahman bar Yitzhak, a righteous act that unwittingly led to a transgression was more commendable than one that stemmed from an unrighteous intention (*Naz.* 23b Rashi ibid., s.v. *"gedolah"*; cf. *Pes.* 50b).[48]

(2) *Book of Beliefs and Opinions* (Sa'adyah Ga'on)

In his "Book of Beliefs and Opinions" (*Sefer Emunot ve-De'ot*), Sa'adyah ben Yosef (Babylonian Gaon, 10th cent.) writes as follows: "If someone contrives a wicked scheme, although he does not put it into effect, he is held guilty of the intent though not of the act, as Scripture affirms, 'The thoughts of wickedness are an abomination to the Lord' " (Prov. 15:26).[49] Moreover, no one is ever punished for his intentions or inner convictions (except for denying the existence of God, since that is a conclusion which is reached only by the mind). A whole burnt-offering is nevertheless required, by way of atonement for entertaining such evil thoughts (Lev. R. 7:3; *Tosef. Men.* 10:12).

A person will receive a considerable reward, however, if he rids his mind of unwholesome ideas, as it is written: "Let the wicked forsake his way, and the man of iniquity his thoughts" (Isa. 55:7).[50] We may not know how evil thoughts arise in the mind, but, however that may be, it is the duty of man not to harbour them.

An awareness of sin and the need for atonement pervade Jewish teaching. The confession of sins and prayers for forgiveness are an integral part of the Hebrew liturgy. The sense of having to depend on God for all one's needs is particularly marked when one struggles to overcome the temptations of

---

48 גדולה עבירה לשמה ממצווה שלא לשמה

49 תועבת ה' מחשבות רע

50 יעזוב רשע דרכיו ואיש און מחשבתיו וישב אל ה' וירחמהו

the *yetzer ha-ra,* since God had endowed man with the power of free choice (*behirah*), which the individual alone can direct. Man in this struggle recognizes his own insufficiency and prays to God for help.

F. The Universal Mind

Each individual has a primary nucleus that is unfolded in the course of his life history, sometimes termed "after its king". The primary nucleus of mind that one possesses and which naturally harmonizes with the universe is the soul. The soul that lies behind the mental "I" is "the inmost secret of each man's heart" (T. Mark, *The Unfolding of Personality*, London, 1910, p. 25). In the animist view, mind is fundamental in the universe of being, and all humanity shares in the common stock of universal mind; but each person does so in his own peculiar way, which constitutes his individuality (G. F. Stout, *Mind and Matter*, Cambridge, 1931, pp. 309, 311–315).

The special attributes that unite man with the Divine soul and separate him from the rest of creation are precisely the Divine attributes of rational and creative activity. Man's possession of will, intellect and freedom is what fashions him as a personality and moral being (I. Epstein, *The Faith of Judaism*, p. 216; cf. *Chambers English Dictionary*, s.v. "Mean = to have the mind, to intend, signify; Anglo-Saxon *maena*: German *meinen*, to think, from a root *man*, found also in Man and Mind").

Sa'adyah Ga'on describes the will as the basic "imperceptible air" of all creation which God implanted in nature for a special purpose and whose workings are eternally superintended and directed by Him (Commentary on *Sefer Yetzirah*, Chap. 4). He states, furthermore, that when the soul is united with the body, it possesses the three faculties of reasoning, appetite and anger that Biblical texts designate by the terms *neshamah, nefesh* and *ruah,* respectively (Sa'adyah, *Emunot ve-De'ot* 6:3).

Yehudah Halevi (Spain and Egypt, 12th cent.) believed that the faculties of man are his executive powers, which he trains to obey his orders (*Kuzari*, III, 2–5). Reason, being one of his faculties, is directed by him; the force of its direction may be called the power of will. According to Halevi's view of the insufficiency and fallibility of reason, man also possesses an inner vision that attains the height of prophecy and Divine influence. These powers, too, become faculties that man has at his disposal in the perfection of his being and personality (*Kuzari*, III, 7). In the process of moral judgment, man's hankering after evil is countered by his intuitive knowledge or consciousness that such base actions are prohibited by God, whose nature and authority far transcend the power of man (*Kuzari*, III, 19).

G.   The "Manikin" – The Soul as Encapsulation of Man

The notion that the soul is a miniature likeness of man's nature and personality, and that it dwells in the chambers of the heart, reflects the idea that the will is in fact the essential "manikin" in a person's totality. Thus, good willed by the heart is human virtue, just as evil willed by the heart is man's sin (*Ber.* 61a; Eccles. R. 1:38, s.v. "*dibarti ani im libi*"; *Midrash Tanḥuma*, ed. Buber, *Va-Yikra* 12; Moore, *Judaism*, Vol. 3, p. 149, note 205). This sheds further light on the Bible's association of the evil impulse with the heart (Gen. 6:5, 8:21; Moore, *Judaism*, Vol. 1, p. 486; Schechter, *Some Aspects of Rabbinic Theology,* pp. 255–261).

When man utilizes any of his faculties, the more will power he exerts in the action, the more effective that action will be. Thus, testing the smoothness of a knife depends for its effectiveness on the amount of sensory power behind the finger's touch. The concentration of this power of the will is not the business of reason or the senses but of man himself. His use of reason and intellect enables him to exercise all his faculties. Will is the power by which man directs all the appetitive, impulsive and cognitive faculties of the soul.

[References: Sa'adyah Gaon, *Emunot ve-De'ot* 10:2, ed. S. Rosenblatt, p. 361]

Describing the proper conduct of man, Yehudah Halevi affirms that when man truly exercises his personality, he governs all his mental and physical faculties as well as his senses. The nobility of such control is delineated in Scripture: "He that ruleth his spirit is better than he that taketh a city" (Prov. 16:32; *Kuzari*, III, 5); cf. William James's notion of "the will to believe", the "will to win" motivation in athletics, and Bishop South (*Sermons*): "Whosoever wills the doing of a thing, if the doing of it be in his power, he will certainly do it; and whosoever does not do that thing which he has in his power to do, does not properly will it".

In our daily prayers, we beg the Almighty to forgive our transgressions, quoting the following passage from Psalms: "For He knoweth our frame; He remembereth that we are dust" (Ps. 103:14).[51] This serves to remind God that He created our structure, from which the evil *yetzer* was energized. We are aware that the good *yetzer* derives from the soul's presence within us, but God knows that our physical being is part of man's creation from the earth – and this gives rise to our evil *yetzer*, which leads us to sin. God should accordingly pardon our wrongdoing, since He also bears responsibility for our conduct (ibid., Targum, Kimḥi).

H. Will – the Source of All Action

In his analysis of actions, both physical and mental, R. Yitzḥak Arama (Spain, 15th cent.) declared that three things are required for their successful performance: will, ability and skill. Ability and skill are the tools of the will (*Akedat Yitzḥak*, Deut., *Re'eh* Chap. 93).

Whereas Yehudah Halevi attributes the control of one's behaviour to the will, Maimonides apparently subordinates everything to reason, which in his view is the sole master of man. One should point out that Halevi was a Hebraist and empiricist, whereas Maimonides was a Hellenist and a rationalist (H. Wolfson, "Maimonides and Halevi", JQR, Vol. 2, no. 3, January 1912, p. 336). Maimonides, however, also considered reason to be an instrument of man. Through his perfection of this tool he becomes a truly intelligent being. The highest development of intelligence is the means whereby man performs his most effective activity.

When Maimonides discusses the attributes of God and denies any possible similarity between the attributes of God and those of man, he refers to these three: wisdom, power and will. Although the nature of these attributes in man are, Maimonides insists, not comparable to those of God, they may be comprehended through their relationship with His. Whereas in God these attributes are all perfect and complete, in man they are present to a lesser and different extent. Thus, even if man has enough power and understanding to perform a certain act, he may fail to do so through a lack of will. Whereas the pure will of God has supreme authority and driving force at its command, the will of man tends towards laxity and inertia due to the material constituents of his being (Maim. *Guide* 1: 56–58).

In the opinion of both Maimonides and Yehudah Halevi, man's duty is to realize through training the fullest capacity of his own intellect, power and will.

I. Volition

Volition has been described as the highest level of human mentality (Broad, *The Mind and Its Place in Nature*, Chap.14, pp. 634–637). The basis of all volition is the experience of various desires, impulses, emotions, resolves and intentions.

These may be divided into two types, namely, those that do or do not involve moral judgment. The latter type – whether, for example, to build a house of stone or wood, or whether to cross a river by swimming or building a bridge – may be decided by ratiocination. The former type, necessitating a choice between acts that generate good or evil, requires the exercise of moral judgment. In this case, volition or conation is no more than an idea that may result in good or evil. As such, the volition is neither creditable nor discreditable. It is translated into an action through the exercise of man's will. Neither an act of ratiocination nor one of volition can take effect without the application of man's will.

Ratzon, in the Talmud, refers to an individual's volition in the sense of personal wish or desire. This psychological element is deemed too subjective for acceptance as the criterion of any act performed under the law. Whereas some legal acts by an individual may be in accordance with his *ratzon* (wish or desire), far more may well be due to sheer necessity. If *ratzon* were to be the criterion of a legal agreement, the selling of one's home through pressure of circumstance would be voidable due to the absence of *ratzon*. The sale remains valid, however, since the vendor agreed (however reluctantly) to this transfer of ownership.

The main concern of the law is that performance of the act should be intended by the individual (*BB* 48a, Rashi and *Tos.*, s.v. "*ella*").[52] The psychical force of mind, which is the essence of the person considered in law, is termed *da'at*. If that element is present when the legal act takes place, the law is satisfied that the essence of the person has shared in it. The various considerations or external circumstances that have led – or even compelled – the individual to frame such an intention are regarded by the law as extraneous to the reality of his eventual intent and action. It is due to this conception of *da'at* that the Talmud also recognizes the validity of an act performed under physical pressure exerted by order of the court, as when it enforces a divorce or obliges a person to fulfil his sacrificial vow, which normally requires the person's own consent (*BB* 48a).[53] Maimonides held that failure to discharge an obligation was attributable to the evil spirit (*yetzer ha-ra*) in a man, which the pressure exerted by a court may vanquish, thus enabling the man to do his duty of his own free will (Maim. *Gerushin* 2:20).

In matters of alienation and acquisition, public policy requires that evidence be given of an objective act in law. The insistence on objective performance of an act is due, in particular, to the requirement that any surrender of his legal right be grounded on the subjective will of the assigner. Jewish law, in the final analysis, always requires the direction of will to achieve a legal result.

The essential part played by the will in the creation of a right is further visible in the distinction that Jewish law makes between original and derived acquisition. In derived acquisition, the new owner plays a more passive role than he does in original acquisition and therefore requires less capacity to effect the transaction, since there is a more active will alienating the property to him. In the case of original acquisition, *animus acquirendi* (i.e., the intention to acquire) is the essential coefficient. Here, therefore, the new owner's full capacity is essential, whereas in the case of derived acquisition one resorts to the legal maxim, *da'at aheret makneh*, which signifies that another active will is engaged in alienating the property (*BM* 11b).[54] In every instance it is clear that the underlying factor in the legal act is the activity of the will (*da'at*) in one part or other of the process.

[References: I. Herzog, *Main Institutions of Jewish Law*, Vol. 1, p. 275; cf. A. Gulak, *Yesodei ha-Mishpat ha-Ivri*, Vol. 1, Chap. 5, p. 103]

When he performs an action, a man exercises free will in two stages. Firstly, in reacting to the impulse of a volition,

---

he may decide how to act by using *behinah* (intellectual choice) in matters of ratiocination, or *behirah* (moral choice) in those involving moral judgment. If he exercises *behinah* or *behirah*, he will decide to act wisely and well. Secondly, having reached a decision on the proper course to follow, he is still at liberty to apply his will in translating his decision into action, to withhold it or to apply it in another direction. A man may know and wish to do what is right, yet fail to do so; he may therefore consider himself weak-willed. In fact, however, he is exercising complete freedom of will, since he has decided to reject the counsel of *behirah* in favour of some other prompting. Far from being denied the exercise of free will, he has voluntarily surrendered his power to choose what is right.

It is also possible that a man may not only decide in favour of some right action, but also apply his will in effecting it; however, due to some adverse circumstance, this fails to achieve what was intended. Apart from motivation by will and resolve, skill, strength and perseverance are indispensable in achieving the desired result. The volitions of a rational agent are determined not by any external cause, but only by himself and his own free will (H. J. Paton, *The Categorical Imperative*, p. 210).

Summation: The Will

In Jewish thought the will corresponds to man's entire self, ego or personality. The physical and psychical faculties that man possesses are faculties of the will; and every manifestation of reason, appetite or emotion results from some activity of the will. Various concrete terms are used to denote the many activities of the will and, as the source of all these activities, the will takes different personalized forms. These personifications, which typify Hebrew language and thinking, mirror the concept of *ratzon*, but not its true essence.

The total power of the will is more than just an individual's capacity: it is the power of that individual as a whole. When fully exercised by man, the will is a manifestation of his entire being. God seeks this integral man in all his complexity, and charges him with devoting himself to the service of the Almighty.[55]

The Book of Psalms, Israel's great manual of devotion, is a kaleidoscope of one people's entire experience, imbued with solace, strength and inspiration. The Psalms have also become the medium through which civilized humanity chooses to express itself, "a mirror reflecting the motions of each person's soul". They are "the prayer book and hymn book of the whole world... religion itself put into speech" (C. H. Cornill, *Culture of Ancient Israel*, 1914). The Book of Psalms – *Tehillim*, "contains the whole music of the heart of man, swept by the hand of his Maker. In it are gathered the lyrical burst of his tenderness, the moan of his penitence, the pathos of his sorrow, the triumph of his victory, the despair of his defeat, the firmness of his confidence, the rapture of his assured hope" (R. E. Prothero, *The Psalms in Human Life*, 1903).

The concluding verse of the last chapter ends with the words, "Let everything that hath breath praise the Lord. Hallelujah!" (Ps. 150:6).[56] The *Metzudat David* commentary expands their meaning in this way: "Whoever possesses a living soul and intellect (*kol ha-neshamah*), let him praise the Lord". Ibn Ezra associates these words with the call for man to praise God with every type of musical instrument, i.e., "With every breath used to play these instruments, praise the Lord". The Targum, for its part, renders the words as follows: "Let every *breath* praise the Lord". A further interpretation of the closing verse suggests that "praise emanating from the soul is the highest form of worship, as the soul is the heart of man", the wellspring of every thought and emotion. The different types of music spoken of by the Psalmist give expression, each in its

---

own way, to the entire range of mood and feeling that dwell in the heart of man. Just as music speaks to the heart, the heart speaks in music. Music can express all the intonations of the soul, by which man glorifies God. Accordingly, the Psalmist calls for the totality of man (*kol ha-neshamah*), every part of his soul and being, to "praise the Lord" (MALBIM; *Metzudat David*; Kimhi *ad loc.*).[57]

On the Torah's particularization of the sacrificial service, beginning with the words: "When any man of you bringeth an offering unto the Lord" (Lev. 1:2),[58] it is related that a woman once brought a handful of meal as an offering. The priest, who found fault with the meagerness of her offering, was told in a dream: "You should not despise her, but know that she has offered herself as a sacrifice" – *nafshah hikrivah* (Lev. R. 3:5).

When man is required by the Torah to strive for communion with God, he is exhorted to do so as a composite creation – "with all thy heart, and with all thy soul, and with all thy might" (Deut. 6:5).[59] The notion of the will here represents man's entire personality: "heart" (*lev*) thus refers to his natural instincts and urges (*yetzer*); "soul" (*nefesh*) to his intellect and power of choice; and "might" (*me'od*) to his vital energy. All these powers and faculties are the natural heritage of man, and together they constitute his will. They represent the whole of man and with that totality he is urged to serve his Maker, hence the *Shema* prayer's daily injunction to love God "with all one's heart, soul and might".[60]

Man possesses the ability, and is also required, to harmonize, perfect and purify the entire complex of his faculties. The perfection and purification that he achieves is the measure of his success in life. The effort that he makes in this process, be it strong or weak, good or bad, is his will.

---

57 רד״ק: ועל כל ההילולים הוא הילול הנשמה, והיא התבונן במעשה הא-ל יתברך
    ובידיעה כפי כח הנשמה

58 נפש כי תקריב קרבן לה'

59 בכל לבבך ובכל נפשך ובכל מאדך

60 ואהבת את ה' אל-היך

Yehudah Halevi, in his *Kuzari* (ed. Slutzki, p. 45), declared that all of man's faculties and emotions are enlisted in the service of God; but through the love of God and the precepts of His Torah, man is enabled to bring these various activities under control and to make proper use of their functions. The Sages affirmed that the *mitzvot* are intended to help man achieve his own perfection (Gen. R. 44).[61]

According to Rav A. Y. Kook, man is endowed with the Divine Spirit (*ru'ah ha-kodesh*), of which God is the focus. When we hear the beating of the heart, we can sense both its physical actuality and its spiritual significance. Commenting on the verse, "My beloved knocketh [saying]: 'Open to me, my sister, my love'..." (Song of Songs 5:2), Rav Kook declared that whenever an original thought or idea is formed in our mind, it is as if the angel of the Lord, beating at the door of our heart, calls upon us to open the heart and release the *ru'ah ha-kodesh* within, so that it may join that of God. Man thus experiences the Almighty calling to him, and only man has the power to respond (*Iggeret ha-Kodesh* 1:165; *Kuzari*, "*Kol dodi dofek*").

The Creator Himself does not alter man's nature. The outstanding feature of his creation is the God-given power to freely direct his will, so as to achieve his own improvement and perfection. For man's successful pursuit of virtue God bestows the reward of happiness. At all times, however, God preserves the exercise of man's free will and ability to choose (*behirah*), whereby he may consistently act in accordance with Torah and reason (*Shab.* 104a).[62] The intellect with which man is endowed can be supplemented and perfected through the teachings of Torah. The noblest conception of man's will is his effort to comprehend that of the Almighty and to obey his injunctions, hence David's call: "Thy face, Lord, will I seek" (Ps. 27:8).[63]

---

61   לא נתנו מצוות אלא לצרף בהן את ישראל
62   בא לטהר מסייעים אותו
63   את פניך ה' אבקש

When Adam disobeyed God's command by eating the
forbidden fruit, God called to him: "Where art thou?" (Gen.
3:9).[64] He obviously knew about the man's location; what He
asked him to realize was the position of his soul. "Until this
moment", God declared, "your soul has been perfectly aligned
with Mine. Now that you have fallen in with the serpent's
evil designs, you have turned into a different person". It is
this inner quality of man that the Almighty searches out and
wishes to uplift (Gen. R. 19:17, *Mattenot Kehunah, ad loc.*).

When Rabbinic moralists asserted that "God seeks man"
(*Ha-Elohim mevakkesh et ha-adam*),[65] they expressed the
Jewish view that He looks for the individual's all-embracing
persona, the totality of his being. Since man, in the process of
his creation, was endowed with freedom of choice, he is an
independent being with the power to choose good or evil. The
Almighty does not *order* him to choose good, but *implores*
him to do so. When He promised Abraham that the Land of
Israel would belong to his descendants, He said: "Lift up now
thine eyes, and look from the place where thou art... for all the
land which thou seest, to thee will I give it, and to thy seed for
ever" (Gen. 13:14–15).

In the Hebrew text of verse 14, *sa na einekha* ("Lift up now
thine eyes"), the word *na* actually means "Please" or "I pray
you". It does not express a command, but the hope and wish
that Abraham will accept God's promise and take possession
of the land. The text only then continues with an imperative
demand for action: *Kum hit'hallekh ba-aretz* – "Arise, walk
through the land in the length and breadth of it" (Gen. 13:17).
In all questions of moral choice, God turns to the complete
man and beseeches him (*bi-leshon tahanunim*) to choose that
which is right (R. Shelomo Efrayim ben Aharon, *Keli Yakar*
on Gen. 13:17, s.v. "*Kum*").

Job, in his distress, was told by Elihu that the Lord's
injunctions to serve Him are no more than a man can bear, so that

---

64 ויקרא ה' אל-הים אל האדם ויאמר לו איכה
65 האל-הים מבקש את האדם

he has the power to decide whether to obey. The commentary of Malbim (Romania, 19th cent.) states: "Everything God seeks from man in His service is what he is capable of doing" (R. Meir Leibush Malbim, *Ha-Torah ve-ha-Mitzvah*, on Job 33:12; *Metzudat David, ad loc.*).

Prior to his death, Moses admonished the people as follows: "And now, Israel, what doth the Lord thy God require of thee, but to fear the Lord thy God, to walk in all His ways, and to love Him, and to serve the Lord thy God with all thy heart and with all thy soul" (Deut. 10:12).[66] Yehudah Halevi declared that an awareness of the Divine Spirit within man endures in his consciousness. Man's response accords with his readiness as a free person to hear God's will (*Kuzari*, II, 24).[67]

Yalkut Shim'oni, a Midrashic work, quotes the Rabbinic interpretation of a verse, "The word of the Lord that came to Joel the son of Pethuel" (Joel 1:1). The Rabbis taught that Joel's father was named Pethuel because he won favour in the sight of God. To gain that favour, man need only humble his heart and confess, "I have sinned". When the Israelites were reprimanded by Samuel for worshipping the gods of the Philistines, they poured out their hearts in repentance before God and declared, "We have sinned against the Lord" (1 Sam. 7:6).[68] They were promptly forgiven and rescued from their enemies. Here, *Yalkut Shim'oni* quotes what R. Yirmiyahu said in the name of R. Shemuel bar Yitzhak: "You require nothing more from man than the confession: I have sinned".[69]

After their army removed the holy ark from Shiloh, the Philistines had reason to fear that it would bring them bad luck and Divine retribution; they then implored the Israelites to take it back. The ark was eventually moved to Kiriath-jearim near Jerusalem, but the Israelites also feared that some unwary act on their part might defile the ark's sanctity. When the prophet

---

ועתה ישראל מה ה' אל-היך שאל מעמך כי אם ליראה את ה' אל-היך   66

קול דודי דופק קריאת האל-הים לשוב נתן במצפון לבם   67

ויאמרו שם חטאנו לה'   68

כלום אתה מבקש מן האדם הזה אלא שיאמר חטאתי   69

Samuel was urged to seek God's help and deliverance from their enemies, the Bible relates: "Samuel cried unto the Lord for Israel; and... the Lord thundered with a great thunder on that day upon the Philistines, and confounded them... Then Samuel took a stone, and set it between Mizpah and Shen, and called the name of it *Even ha-Ezer* ['The stone of help']... So the Philistines were subdued, and came no more into Israelite territory" (1 Sam. 7:9–13).

The Sages taught that the Almighty requires man's heart – *Rahmana libba ba'i* (*Sanh.* 106b).[70] Doeg may have been one of the greatest Torah scholars in King David's time, but this proved of no avail to him before God's judgment seat. Doeg lacked sincerity and all the erudition on his lips was never in his heart (ibid.). When God told Samuel to choose David as king in preference to his older and handsomer brothers, He declared that while man pays regard to outward appearances, *Hashem yir'eh la-levav* – "the Lord looketh on the heart" (1 Sam. 16:7).[71] It is the inner man's perfection that God seeks, and He judges him by all his deeds: "Render unto every man according to all his ways, whose heart Thou knowest – for Thou, even Thou only, knowest the hearts of the children of men" (2 Chron. 6:30).

People notice a man's outward behaviour, but God sees into a man's heart and knows what he is really doing. The Almighty thus looks for his response as a true and complete individual. Even a murderer can sometimes pose as a respectable lawyer or physician. It is recognized that *jus naturale*, the law of reason, morality and justice, is taught by nature and implanted in mankind (Roman law, Justinian). Nevertheless, it is for each individual to decide whether he will follow this natural law or his own whim.

[References: *Yalkut Shimoni*, an anthology of the Bible, *Aggadah* and *Halakhah* (Oxford MS, 1308; Salonika MS, 14th cent.) compiled by R. Shim'on of Frankfurt (Shim'on

70   רחמנא ליבא בעי
71   ה׳ יראה ללבב

ha-Darshan, 13th cent.) and divided into paragraphs known as *remazim*]

The service of God is not a mechanical performance of certain religious rites, but the whole man's devotion to worshipping the Creator. Each individual must continually endeavour to perfect himself, and no one can be certain of his own virtue. R. Yudan taught: "Even a righteous person is not entitled to self-confidence as long as he remains on earth"; and Hillel said: "Do not believe in yourself until the day you die" (*Avot* 2:5). Each person's manner of worshipping God is unique, just as the Almighty Himself is unique in His world (*Sifra* 43d).

God may determine the life of man, but one decision is left entirely to him: whether he should follow the ways of God or be guided by his own appetites. The Sages declared that "everything is in the power of Heaven, except [man's] fear of heaven" (*Ber.* 33b).[72] At every moment in life it is man who chooses and directs his actions, and the Almighty then decides if the choice he made was right or wrong. The Sages accordingly taught that "man is judged every day and hour after hour" (*RH* 16a).[73] It is the complete man who makes the choices that God seeks, hence the appeal made in His Name to the Children of Israel: What does God ask of you? – To love and revere Him, to follow His ways, and to serve Him with all your heart and soul (Deut. 10:12, Rashi; *Ber.* 33b).[74]

In the Book of Ecclestiastes Solomon reflected on the aims and purpose of a man's life. He describes conflicting sources of human happiness, but finally concludes that by man's obedience to the word of God his life proves to be his real happiness. Man was created as a reflection of the image of God on the earth, and he possesses in his soul a spark of the Divine Presence (Gen. 1:27).[75] The purpose of man's life is to

---

72 הכל בידי שמים חוץ מיראת שמים

73 אדם נידון בכל יום בכל שעה

74 ועתה ישראל מה ה' אל-הים שואל מעמך כי אם ליראה את ה' אל-היך

75 ויברא אל-הים את האדם בצלמו בצלם אל-הים ברא אתו, זכר ונקבה ברא אתם

cherish that spark and keep himself ever close to the sanctity of his Creator. Thus Solomon concluded that the sum of all his strivings in life is "to fear God and keep his commandments, for this is the whole of man". God seeks such a soul in man, and this is the man that God seeks (Eccl. 12:13).[76]

APPENDIX

Appendix

Classical Hebrew Texts

Development of the Law

Jewish teaching records that Moses received the Torah by the Divine Revelation at Mt. Sinai (Ex. 24:12). Moses wrote the entire Torah himself placing a copy in the Ark of the Tabernacle as a witness of the true text (Deut. 31:26). Together with the Written Law Moses received also the interpretation of the Law which was not written down but was taught orally (*Git.* 60b). Moses taught the Oral Law to Joshua and the Seventy Elders, and Joshua passed it on to the prophets. Samuel received it from Eli and David received it from Samuel. In the post-prophetic era it was taught by the Men of the Great Assembly (*anshei kenesset ha-gedolah*), founded after the return from Babylonian exile (4th cent. BCE) by Ezra, who formulated much of what became normative Judaism. Their religious authority was passed on to the Sages of Torah and their schools learning and continued till the time of the High Priest, Shimon ha-Tzadik, about the year 200 BCE.

After some formulations by R. Akiva and R. Meir, it was realized that in the turbulent conditions of the time it was no longer possible to properly memorize and teach the Oral Law. The Sages wrote down the traditions that they had received from their teachers as they perceived them, and this new era of the Sages began with Shimon ha-Tzadik (*Avot* 1:1, 2). R. Judah Hanasi formulated a systematic account of the teachings received by his predecessors which became known as the Mishna, the Hebrew name implying, the texts that require studying and repeating (about the year 189 CE). This work became the handbook of all future study of the Oral Law.

Nature of the Texts

1. **The Bible**, Scripture – *Tanakh,* the Bible is composed of the 1) Torah, i.e, the Pentateuch, or *Humash*, comprising the Five Books of Moses (Gen., Ex., Lev., Num., Deut.); 2) *Nevi'im* – Prophets, the former prophets and later prophets; 3) *Ketuvim* – Writings, consisting of various books considered as sacred Writings (Psalms, Proverbs, etc.).

2. **The Talmud**, composed of the Mishna and Gemara.

   1) **Mishna**, embodying the earliest oral traditions of Jewish teaching as recorded by the early Sages, called the Tannaim; finally redacted by R. Judah the Prince (c.189 CE).
   The Mishna is divided into six parts (*shishah sedarim*):
   1. *Zera'im,* 'seeds' – religious, legal aspects of the land of Israel and its produce.
   2. *Mo'ed,* 'seasons' – the religious observance of the Sabbath and the Holy days of the year.
   3. *Nashim,* 'women' – mainly marriage and divorce.
   4. *Nezikin* 'injuries' – civil and criminal law.
   5. *Kodashim,* 'holy things' – sacrifices, vows to the sanctuary, consecrated objects.
   6. *Tohorot,* 'purifications' – levitical purity and impurity.

   2) **Gemara,** the legal and traditional elucidation of subjects of Mishnaic treatises as discussed in the academies of learning by Sages known as the Amoraim. The orderly editing of the Gemara and the determination of authorised *Halakhah* was the work of the Sages R. Ashi and Ravina in the 5-6th cents. In the 6th cent. the successors of the Amoraim were known as the Savoraim who concluded the final editing of the Talmud.

The leading scholars of the 6th and 10th cents. were known as the Geonim, particularly, the heads of the Babylonian Academies of Sura and Pumpedita. Codes of Talmudic law were written by the Geonim, Yehudai, Natronai, Amram, Saadya, Sherira, Hai Gaon.

The authority of halakhic scholars in determining the *Halakha* varied in different stages of Jewish history. It was, at first, considered that later scholars might not be as wise as their predecessors, who were closer to the original sources of the law. Thus, until the time of Abbaya and Rava in the middle of the 4th cent. the *Halakha* was decided according to the views of the earlier scholars rather than those of later dissenting scholars. From the time of Abbaya and Rava onward, however, it was accepted that the opinions of later scholars prevailed over the contrary opinions of an earlier generation – *kaima lan hilkheta kebatra'a* (*Naz.* 56b; Asher ben Yeḥiel, *Piskei ha-Rosh, Shab.* 23:1, *BM* 3:10, 4:21). It was considered that since the later scholars had wider knowledge of the statements of all earlier scholars and, after deliberating on them, they decided to differ from an earlier ruling, they took greater pains in presenting the *Halakha* (*Kid.* 45b, *Tos. s.v. "befeirush"*; Joseph Colon, *Responsa Maharik*, 84).

3. **The Zohar**, a Kabbalistic work embodying mystical motifs, reflections, teachings, and traditions. The name of the author is not stated but is generally associated with the name of R. Shimeon ben Yoḥai, Israel, 2nd cent.

4. **The Midrash**, the ethical and Aggadic interpretations of the Scriptures, known as the Midrashim, began in the tannaitic period. Their moral teachings were expounded during the synagogue services even

before the period of the Gemara (*Git.* 60a) and they continued their production till the 10th – 11th cents. The principal Aggadic Midrashim covered the five books of the Pentateuch and most of the remaining Scriptures.

Among the sources of Jewish law were also collections of halakhic Midrashim. The *Sifra*, a Midrash to the Book of Leviticus, contained a collection of tannaitic rulings (*beraitot*) expounding the Book of Leviticus verse by verse. The Book of Exodus was expounded in the *Mekhilta,* and Numbers and Deuteronomy in the *Sifrei* (*Sanh.* 85a, 86b).

Classical Talmud Commentators

Commentators

1. Rabbenu Gershom (10th cent.)
2. Rabbenu Hananel (11th cent.)
3. Rashi, R. Shelomo Yitzhaki, (11th cent.)
4. Tosafists (12th–13th cent.)

Codifiers

1. Alfasi, Isaac ben Jacob Ha-Kohen, (RIF), (Algeria, Fez, North Africa, Spain 1030-1103). At the close of the Gaonic period a more extensive codification, following the tractates of the Talmud, was written by the RIF. His work is often called "the small Talmud" (*Talmud Katan*). Much of the later Code of Maimonides followed the rulings of this code.
2. Moses Maimonides (Rambam), (Spain, Egypt 1135–1204). Author of the code *Yad Ha-hazakah*, a systematic presentation of the whole of Jewish law, consisting of

fourteen books covering authoritative rulings of all aspects of the *Halakha*: legal, ritual, doctrinal, and ethical. (The word YAD consists of the Hebrew letters bearing the number 14.) This code is also known as *Mishneh Torah*, i.e, a reconstruction, or a codification of all Torah Law, following the order of the six Orders of the Mishna.

3. Jacob ben Asher, (Germany, Spain 1270–1343), known as the TUR. His code consisted of four sections called the Four Rows, *Arba Turim*. The four parts are, *Orah Hayyim*, *Yoreh De'ah*, *Even Ha'Ezer*, *Hoshen Mishpat*.

4. Joseph Caro, (Spain, Turkey, Safed, 1488–1575), author of the authoritative systematic code of the *Shulhan Arukh* which was based on the system of the *Four Turim* of R. Jacob ben Asher, and was similarly divided. Caro's *Shulhan Arukh* embraced the differing opinions of all his predecessors, giving a decisive ruling which generally received the widest acceptance.

Early Halakhic Authorities

(chronologically arranged)

Rishonim (earlier authorities)

RIF (רי"ף): R. Yitzhak Alfasi, Spain, N. Africa, 11th cent. Compendium Laws of Talmud.

RASHI (רש"י): R. Shelomo Yitzhaki, France, 11th cent.

ARUKH (ערוך): R. Natan ben Yehiel, *Arukh Hashulhan*, Talmudic lexicon, Rome, 11th cent.

RASHBAM (רשב"ם): R. Shmuel ben Meir, France, 11th cent.

RAMBAM (רמב"ם): R. Moses ben Maimon (Maimonides), Spain, N. Africa, Egypt, 12th cent.

HA-ITTUR (העיטור): R. Yitzhak ben Alba Mari of Marseilles, France, 12th cent.

RAVAD (ראב"ד): R. Avraham ben David of Posquieres, France, 12th cent, (*Hassagot al Mishneh Torah shel ha-Rambam*; *Ba'alei ha-Nefesh*).

RABBENU TAM (רבינו תם): Tosafist, France, 12th cent.

RI HAZAKEN (ר"י הזקן): R. Yitzhak ben Shmuel, France, 12th cent.

RADAK (רד"ק): R. Dovid Kimhi, France 12th–13th cent.

RID (רי"ד): R. Yeshaiah ben Mali of Trani, Italy, 13th cent.

HA-MORDEKHAI (המרדכי): R. Mordekhai ben Hillel Ha-Cohen, Germany, 13th cent.

RAM MI-ROTENBURG (ר"ם מרוטנברג): R. Meir ben Baruch Ha-Cohen, Germany, 13th cent.

HAGAHOT MAIMONIYOT (הגהות מימוניות): R. Meir Ha-Cohen, France, 13th cent.

RAMBAN (רמב"ן): R. Moshe ben Nahman (Nahmanides), Spain, Israel, 13th cent.

RASHBA (רשב"א): R. Shelomo ben Avraham, Aderet, Spain, 13th cent.

ROSH (רא"ש): R. Asher ben Yehiel, Germany, Spain, 13th cent.

KOL BO (כל בו): a compendium of accepted Jewish practice, attributed to R. Aaron ben Yaakov Ha-Kohen, Germany, 13th cent.

RITVA (ריטב"א): R. Yom Tov ben Avraham, Spain 13th–14th cent.

HAMEIRI (המאירי): R. Menahem ben Shlomo Meiri, France, 13th cent.

MAGGID MISHNEH (מגיד משנה): R. Vidal Yom Tov of Tolosa, Annotations on Maim. *Yad Ha-hazakah*, Spain, 14th cent.

RAN (ר"ן): R. Nisim ben Reuven, Gerondi, Spain, 14th cent.

RASHBATZ (רשב"ץ): R. Shimeon ben Tzemaḥ Duron, Algiers, 14th–15th cent.

ABARBANEL (אברבנאל): Don Itzḥak Abarbanel, Spain, 15th cent.

MAHARIK (מהרי"ק): R. Yosef ben Shlomo Kolon, Italy, 15th cent.

R'AV (רע"ב): R. Ovadiah Mi-Bertinoro, Italy, Israel, 15th cent.

MINTZ (מינץ): R. Mosheh ben Itzḥak Segal, Mintz, Germany 15th cent.

MAHARIL (מהר"ל): an acronym for Morenu Ha-Rav Yaakov ben Mosheh Ha-Levi of Moellin, Germany, 15th cent., (*Sefer Minhagei Maharil*).

KESEF MISHNEH (כסף משנה): R. Yosef Caro, Spain, Turkey, Safed, 15th–16th cent.

Aharonim (later authorities)

DI-BUTON (די בוטן): R. Avraham ben Moshe Di-Buton, (*Leḥem Mishnah* on Maim., *Yad*) Salonica, 16th cent.

ASHKENAZI (אשכנזי): R. Bezalel ben Avraham Ashkenazi, (*Asifat Zekenim, Shitah Mekubetzet*) Germany, 16th cent.

RADBAZ (רדב"ז): R. David ben Shlomo ben Zimra, Israel, Egypt, 16th cent.

CARO (קארו): R. Yosef ben Efraim Caro, 16th cent. (*Shulḥan Arukh, Kesef Mishneh* on Maim., *Bet Yosef* on *Tur.*)

FALK (פלק): R. Yehoshua ben Alexander Katz, Poland 16th cent.

REMA (רמ"א): R. Mosheh Isserles, Poland 16th cent. (Annotations on *Shulḥan Arukh*, according to *Ashkenazi* halakhic practice)

YAFFA (יפה): R. Mordechai ben Avraham, Poland, 16th cent. (*Sefer Ha-Levush*)

MAHARSHAL (מהרש"ל): R. Shlomo ben Yeḥiel Luria, Poland, 16th cent.

MABIT (מבי"ט): (*Sefer Beit Elohim*), acronym for Mosheh ben Yosef Trani, Safed, 16th cent.

TASHBATZ (תשב"ץ): R. Shlomo ben Tzemaḥ Doron, Algiers, 16th cent.

BAḤ (ב"ח): R. Yoel ben Shmuel Segal Sirkes, Poland, 16th–17th cent. (*Bet Ḥadash* on the *Tur*)

MAHARIT (מהרי"ט): R. Yosef ben Moshe Mi-Trani, Safed, 17th cent.

TOS. YOM TOV (תוספות יום טוב): R. Yom Tov Lipman Heller, Prague, Poland, 16th–17th cents.

SHELAH (של"ה): R. Isaiah ben Avraham Ha-Levi Horowitz, Poland, Jerusalem, 16th–17th cent. (*Shenei Luḥot Haberit*)

MAHARSHA (מהרש"א): R. Shmuel Eliezer Edels, Poland, 16th–17th cent.

TAZ (ט"ז): R. David ben Shmuel Halevi, Poland, 17th cent.

SHACH (ש"ך): R. Shabetai ben Meir Ha-Cohen, Poland, 17th cent.

LIMA (לימא): R. Mosheh ben Yitzḥak Yehuda Lima (*Ḥelkat Meḥokek* on *Shulḥan Arukh*), Lithuania, 17th cent.

ROZANNES (רוזנס): R. Yehuda Rozannes, (*Mishneh Lemelech* on Maim., *Yad*) Turkey, 17th–18th cent.

NAVON (נבון): R. Efraim ben Aharom Navon (*Mahane Efraim*), Costa, 17th–18th cent.

FALK (פלק): R. Yaakov Yehoshua ben Zvi Hirsch Falk (*Penei Yehoshua*), Poland, Germany, 18th cent.

LAMPRONTI (למפרונטי): R. Yitzḥak Ḥizkiah Lampronti (Encyl. *Paḥad Yizḥak*) Italy, 17th–18th cents.

HA-GRA (הגר"א): R. Eliahu ben Shlomo Zalman, Vilna 18th cent.

ḤIDA (חיד"א): R. Ḥayim Yosef David Azulai, Italy, 18th cent.

ASHKENAZI (אשכנזי): R. Yehuda ben Shimeon, Germany, 18th cent.

EYBESCHITZ (איבשוץ): R. Yehonotan ben Natan Nata, Poland, Prague, 18th cent.

YA'VETZ (יעב"ץ): R. Yaakov Emden, Germany, 18th cent.

LANDAU (לנדא): R. Yeḥezkel ben Yehudah Halevi Landau (*Noda Biyehudah*), Prague, 18th cent.

KETZOT (קצות): R. Aryeh ben Yosef Ha-Cohen, Galicia, 18th – 19th cent. (*Ketzot Ha-ḥoshen*)

NETIVOT (נתיבות): R. Yaakov Mi-Lissa, Poland, 18th–19th cent. (*Netivot Hamishpat*)

ḤATAM SOFER (חתם סופר): R. Mosheh Sofer Schreiber, Pressburg, 18th–19th cent.

EGER (איגר): R. Akiva (Eger) ben Mosheh, Posen, 18th–19th cent.

MEDINI (מדיני): R. Hayim Hizkiah ben Rafael Eliah Medini, Russia, 19th cent. (*Sedei Ḥemed*)

EGER (איגר): R. Shlomo ben Akiva Eger, Lithuania, 19th cent.

HIRSCH (הרש): R. Shimshon Rafael Hirsch, Germany, 19th cent.

MALBIM (מלב"ם): R. Meir Loeb ben Yeḥiel Michael, Poland, Rumania, 19th cent.

ḤAFETZ ḤAYIM (חפץ חיים): R. Israel Meir Ha-Kohen, Poland, 19th–20th cent. (*Mishnah Berurah*)

ḤAZON ISH (חזון איש): R. Avraham Yeshayah Karelitz, Lithuania, Israel, 20th cent.

GLOSSARY

Glossary

A selected glossary of Hebrew and Aramaic terms

A

Adon-ai (**אד-ני**): The Lord. The sacred name of God describing the Almighty's sovereignty over all existence. The term *Adon-ai* is similar to the expression *Ribbono Shel Olam* – Master of the Universe. It is used in prayer as a substitute for the Tetragrammaton (YHVH) and replaced in everyday speech by *Ha-Shem* (or popularly *Adoshem*).

Aggadah (**אגדה**): A class of rabbinical literature which explains the Bible homiletically and frequently by allegory, as opposed to the legal interpretation. This interpretation in many of the books about the Bible is called *midrash* (*MK* 23a).

Agunah (**עגונה**): A deserted wife, yet "chained" in a state of marriage. A woman whose husband failed to execute the procedure of giving the *get* (bill of divorcement), or whose husband's death could not be established.

Ahavah (**אהבה**): Love. Love of man as a human being, as opposed to hate or indifference. Heterosexual affection of man and woman. Rabbinical tradition speaks of love as an expression of close and disinterested devotion, considered a basic principle of human and Divine relations.

Ahsheveih (**אחשביה**): He considered it (lit.). A rabbinic term taken from the laws of *hametz* on Pesach, whose more generalized sense is: In this particular case he attached increased importance to an act or an object.

Akkum (עכו"ם): Idolaters, heathens; acronym of *ovedei kokhavim u-mazzalot* – those who worship stars and planets.

Almanah (אלמנה): A widow. In Jewish tradition the well-being of a woman bereft of her husband entails the religious obligation of giving relief and protection according to the needs of the widow. This special protection is applied also to the *yetom* – the orphan bereft of a parent. A widower is termed *alman*.

Ammah (אמה): A cubit. A linear measure equalling the length of a person's forearm, from the elbow to the tip of the middle finger, usually varying between 18 and 23 inches (45–58 cm.).

Amen (אמן): The response on hearing a benediction that adds a prayer for its fulfilment.

Am Ha'aretz (עם הארץ): A person unlearned in Jewish law; ignorant of the details of Jewish observance; an untaught country workman.

Amidah (עמידה): The principal set of benedictions of the prayer service recited while standing in silent devotion, known also as the *Shemoneh Esrei* – (lit.) Eighteen Benedictions.

Amirah Lenokhri (מירה לנכרי): A request by a Jew for a non-Jew to do an act of "work" for him which is forbidden for a Jew himself to do on the Sabbath or a festival.

Amorah (אמורא): The name given to the rabbinic teachers in both Palestine and Babylon during the Talmudic period. They are distinguished from the earlier teachers of the Mishnah who are called by the title *tanna*.

Apikoros (אפיקורס): A heretic, sceptic. One determined not to uphold the observance of Torah law by reason of his philosophy or indifference to traditional religious authority.

Arev (**ערב**): A guarantor. A person who bears responsibility for the return or repayment of some property by a debtor as required by contract, and who undertakes to do so himself in the event of the debtor's nonfeasance.

Ashkenaz (**אשכנז**): Biblically, grandson of Japheth (Gen. 10:3). An early designation for Germany (Amram Gaon, Rashi); the term 'Ashkenazim', signifying Rhenish (German) Jews of the Middle Ages, is now also applied to their East European and other descendants throughout the world.

Asmakhta (**אסמכתא**): Reliance, support. The Sages used this term to describe a possible scriptural support for an Oral Law, or a rabbinical enactment in commercial law. *Asmakhta* may refer to an undertaking to forfeit one's property in certain cases without having received a sufficient surety, or a promise of exaggerated payment without due collateral security (*BB* 168a; *BM* 66a).

Asur (**אסור**): Prohibited. A thing or action that is forbidden according to religious law.

Aveida (**אבדה**): A lost thing. Also, the law governing the obligation of returning things that have been lost to their owner.

Aveirah (**עבירה**): A transgression violating any religious commandment whether ordained in a positive or negative form.

Av Melakha – Tolda (**אב מלאכה, תולדה**): Each of the 39 activities involved in the construction of the Holy Tabernacle and its services were enumerated by the Sages and entitled "a parent work" – *av melakhah*. Further derivative works from each category were called "offspring works" – *toldot*.

***Avodah* (עבודה)**: Work, labour; the use of farming or building implements; Divine service, worship, the Temple rite on the Day of Atonement; prayer, particularly the first of the concluding blessings of the *Amidah*.

***Avodah Zara* (עבודה זרה)**: Idolatry, the worship of a heathen deity.

***Ayin ha-Ra* (עין הרע)**: Evil eye (lit.). The jealous or envious disposition of a person, traditionally having the power to bring misfortune on those upon whom the "evil eye" is directed.

B

***Ba'al Hov* (בעל חוב)**: A debtor. One who is indebted to another, either financially or ethically. The same term is also used for one who has lent something to another, the *malveh* (*Ned.* 47b; HM 112:1, 113:1).

***Bar Da'at* (בר דעת)**: An intelligent person, an individual of understanding with the capacity for reasoning. The essential requirement for legal capacity (*BK* 54b; *BM* 80b).

***Bar Mitzvah* (בר מצוה)**: Son of the commandment (lit.). A boy at the age of thirteen and one day attains religious majority marking his conscious acceptance of Jewish religious responsibility to fulfil all the duties applicable to Jewish life.

***Barukh Ha'shem* (ברוך ה')**: "Blessed be His Name"; also equivalent to "thank God". An expression of gratitude to and recognition of God as the merciful source of all blessing.

***Batlan* (בטלן)**: An idler; a man without definite occupation. One unemployed in regular labour, therefore often available for this reason to be called on to give some community service.

Bat Mitzvah (בת מצוה): Daughter of the commandment (lit.). A girl of the age of twelve years and one day reaching her religious majority which marks her personal responsibility for the fulfilment of all Jewish practice.

Be-Emunah (באמונה): Faithfully; trust, honesty, and faithfulness.

Bekhor (בכור): The "firstborn" of the mother, both of man or animal.

Bemezid (במזיד): Intentionally; an act done with premeditation in full consciousness in doing a wrong.

Berakhah (ברכה): A blessing. An appropriate prayer or benediction on every occasion in recognition of gratitude to the Almighty.

Berakhah Levatalah (ברכה לבטלה): A benediction made in vain. Jewish ritual ordains an appropriate benediction for every occasion. Such a benediction may not be made incorrectly or in a manner not required, thus amounting to a superfluous use of the Holy Name.

Bereirah (ברירה): Choice (lit.); retroactive designation. A legal term describing a retrospective designation of an act whose purpose was previously undefined.

Bet Din (בית דין): Court of law. A duly constituted rabbinic court of law, usually consisting of three or more recognized scholars, pronouncing a judicial opinion on any matter of civil or religious law submitted to their judgement (*Sanh.* 2a; Maim. *Yad. Sanhedrin* 1:3, 2:1)

Bet Knesset (בית כנסת): Synagogue. The traditional Jewish house of assembly, a centre for communal worship, study and gathering.

Bet Midrash (בית מדרש): A house of study. A prayer house for communal Jewish study.

Betulah (בתולה): A virgin, a young girl. In a legal sense a girl between twelve and twelve and a half years old, after which age she reaches a state of maturity – *bagrut*.

Bezadon (בזדון): A wilful action. A sin knowingly and deliberately committed.

Bitahon (בטחון): Trust, faith, confidence, hope. The expression *bitahon* is usually used to refer to reliance upon God, who will assure protection and guidance and the ultimate triumph of that which is right.

Brit Milah (מילה ברית): The covenant of circumcision. Popularly abbreviated to *berit* or *brith*, the rite of circumcision marks the lasting bond of union between the newly born male child and God and the Jewish people.

D

Da'at (דעת): Knowledge, mind. Also used as describing understanding, consent and agreement.

Dan L'khaf Zehut (דן לכף זכות): To judge in the scale of merit (lit.). A sympathetic charitableness in one's judgement of the behaviour or opinion of other people.

Derash – Derashah (דרש, דרשה): Interpretation (lit.). A lecture, sermon. A rabbinical law derived from an interpretation of a Biblical verse.

Derekh Eretz (דרך ארץ): The way of the land (lit.). The observance of good manners in social conduct, thoughtful acts of consideration of the feelings of one's fellow man. Also used as a term of gainful and socially directed occupation.

Din (דין): Judgement. The authority of law in all issues of Jewish religion and society as finally enacted by Israel's saintly scholars. The administration of justice.

Dinar (דינר): A valuable coin of gold and a similar coin of silver of lesser value (1/24 of the gold *dinar*).

E

Eirusin (אירוסין): The ceremony of marriage betrothal preceding the full ceremony of marriage, which is known as *nisu'in*.

Eiruv (עירוב): Mixing. A symbolic act of "mixing" certain items, domains or food preparations to form one permitted item, thus permitting a person to do something which otherwise may not be done on the Sabbath or a festival.

Eiruv Tavshilin (עירוב תבשילין): Making (or joining) of foods. The symbolic combination of the food prepared for a festival with the food required for the Sabbath that follows immediately after the festival ends.

Eishet Ish (אשת איש): A duly married woman.

Eishet Hayil (אשת חיל): A woman of virtue (Prov. 31:10). One who conducts her life in accordance with the virtuous traditions of Jewish ways.

Emet (אמת): Truth (as opposed to falsehood). Righteous, trustworthy and faithful. Rabbinical teaching said the existence of the world depends on the pursuit of law, truth and peace.

Emunah (אמונה): Faith. Especially faith in the all-powerful Ruler of the Universe and His abundant mercy to man.

Ephah (איפה): A dry measure used for goods such as flour to signify a small measure or a large measure.

Erev Shabbat (ערב שבת): Sabbath eve. The eve of the Sabbath anticipating the Sabbath day which begins at sunset on Friday.

Erev Yom Tov (ערב יום-טוב): Festival eve. The eve of every Jewish festival beginning at sunset of the preceding day.

Etrog (אתרוג): Citron (a large lemon-like citrus fruit). One of the four plants used on the Festival of Tabernacles (Sukkoth) representing the harvest thanksgiving. The other three plants are the palm branch – *lulav*, myrtle – *hadas*, and the willow branch – *aravah*.

G

Gaon (גאון): Outstanding. The title of the heads of the two leading academies in Babylon in the 6th–11th centuries; *Sherira, Yehudai, Hai, Amram, Saadyah, Natronai.* Also a title of rare excellence applied to an exceptional rabbinical scholar of great renown.

Garush (m), ***Gerushah*** (f) (גרוש, גרושה): Divorcé, divorcée, divorced. A legally divorced man or woman as effected in accordance with Jewish law.

Gemarah (גמרא): Completion (Aramaic). The Six Orders of the Talmud (*Shas*) containing debates and decisions of the Sages (200–500 CE) that expand and elucidate earlier laws of the Mishnah; also a synonym for the whole Talmud.

Gemilut Hessed (גמילות חסד): An act of kindness. Particularly, a loan free of any interest. A simple loan, as an act of kindness such as a neighbourly loan to help another over a period of economic difficulty.

Gemirat Da'at (גמירת דעת): An identity of understanding. A coordination of understanding by both parties in an agreement; a conclusive agreement.

Genizah (גניזה): Put away (lit.). Sacred writings no longer useable are stored and hidden from public attention in a *genizah* (a loft, cave, etc.), because even unusable sacred writings had to be treated with respect.

Get (גט): A bill of divorcement. A religious document which legally effects a divorce dissolving the status of matrimony.

Gezelah (גזלה): Robbery, or the prohibition of stealing; also, the things which have been stolen.

Giluy Da'at (גילוי דעת): Making known one's thought (lit.). Defining the terms of an agreement or obligation as understood in the mind of the contractor.

Goy (גוי): Nation, gentile. One who does not belong to the Jewish nation and follows a different religion. The Jewish attitude towards other peoples is that of respect due to their being also God's children and human beings.

H

Ha'aramah (הערמה): Deceit. A deceitful evasion of a religious prohibition or duty.

Hafsakah (הפסקה): Interruption. An interval; the required time of ceasing from previous activity.

Hag (חג): Festival. The name given to every festival in the cycle of the Jewish calendar, particularly the three pilgrim festivals: Pesah (Passover), Shavuot (the Feast of Weeks) and Sukkoth (the Feast of Tabernacles).

Hakadosh Barukh Hu (הקב"ה): The Holy One Blessed Be He. The name of the Almighty most frequently used, and often abbreviated to HKB"H.

Hakhana (הכנה): Preparation. The preparation of something to a state of readiness for use or designated for use on the Sabbath or a festival.

Hakhehasha (הכחשה): Contradiction. Counter-evidence, the refutation of a testimony by means of further evidence contradicting the original claim.

Halakhah – Halakhot (הלכה, הלכות): Procedure. The term denoting the entire corpus of Jewish (rabbinic) law from the Mishnah to the *Shulhan Arukh*; authoritative rulings by the Sages that govern Jewish life (*Ker.* 12b; TJ *Betz.* 2:61b; TJ *Hor.* 3b end, 48c).

Halitzah (חליצה): Loosening. Torah law required the wife of her deceased husband, who had no children of his own, to marry the husband's brother; however, on his refusal to do so, they perform a ceremony of release, known as *halitzah* – "taking off his shoe", thus permitting the widow to marry whomever she wishes.

Hallel (הלל): Praise. Recitation of Psalms of praise and prayer expressing profound belief and exaltation of the Almighty; expressions of jubilation sung on happy occasions.

Halva'ah (הלואה): A loan. A prohibition of usury applies to all Israelites, although a loan in the form of a profit-sharing arrangement may obviate the technical prohibition of interest.

Hametz (חמץ): Leavened bread. The food forbidden to be eaten during the seven days of Pesah (Passover) when all leavened food is excluded from the Jewish home.

Hana'ah (הנאה): Pleasure, benefit or enjoyment which a person gains.

Hanukah (חנוכה): The Feast of Lights. Observed for eight days celebrating the rededication of the Temple by the Maccabees in the year 167 BCE.

Harata (חרטה): Regret, remorse for an act; sorrow for what has been done or has taken place.

Ha-Shem (השם): The Name (lit.). A respectful, abridged terminology for God, used instead of actually expressing the Holy Name of God.

Hatan Ve'Kallah (חתן וכלה): Bride and bridegroom.

Hatunah (חתונה): Marriage. The ceremony in the celebration of the union of man and woman as husband and wife.

Hatzer (חצר): A courtyard. An enclosed ground in the possession of its owner, or of a common ownership.

Havdalah (הבדלה): Division. The prayer dividing the six work days ahead from the concluded day of rest. The rubric of benedictions is recited at the conclusion of every Sabbath and festival. The ceremony is recited with appropriate benedictions over a cup of wine, spices and a flame or light.

Hayyav (חייב): Obliged, guilty. Legally bound to carry out a prescribed action; in Temple times obliged to bring a guilt offering.

Hazakah (חזקה): Holding. A legal term denoting presumptive title to landed property based on the occupier's undisturbed possession during a fixed period; usucaption. The term also refers to taking possession of landed property by openly performing an act of ownership, such fencing or digging.

Hazal (חז"ל): The Sages. An acronym describing 'the wise men of blessed memory' – *hakhamim zikhronam liverakhah.*

Hazama (הזמה): Counter evidence. In particular, a refutation of the testimony of a witness by the testimony of two further witnesses who state that the former witness was with them at another place where it was impossible for him to witness the event.

Hazmanah (הזמנה): Appointment. Refers to the preparation or designation of an object for a certain purpose.

Hefker (הפקר): Free, ownerless. That is, property which has no owner, or whose ownership has been renounced in favour of all and sundry.

Hekdesh (הקדש): Consecrated property. That which is dedicated to a sacred purpose, particularly as Temple property, or the dedication of the value of an object to Temple use. Something that had been consecrated to the Temple treasury or for the supply of altar sacrifices. Any consecrated property belonging to the Temple may not be made use of in any way for any other purpose which would incur the transgression of *me'ilah* (*Yev.* 66b; TJ *Ar.* 9:1; TJ *Ket.* 5:4; TJ *BM* 4:7; TJ *Ned.* 4:2).

Herem (חרם): Excommunication. A state of a person or thing excluded from general use or social company by reason of an act of religious sacrilege, or one disregarding an order of the religious authorities.

Heresh (חרש): Deaf. The legal status of a person who is a deaf-mute according to halakhic specifications.

Ḥesed (חסד): Kindness, compassion, benevolence.

Hesseḥ Da'at (היסח דעת): Diversion of attention. A loss of concentration, a distraction.

Heter (היתר): Permission. The relaxation of a prohibition by the authorized rabbinic authority; an action or thing on which there is no prohibition is termed *mutar* – permitted.

Ḥillul Ha-Shem (חילול ה'): The desecration of God's name. An ignoble or seriously unethical act of a Jew, bringing disrespect on the name of Israel and the law of God.

Hirhur (הרהור): Contemplation, thought. An unexpressed meditation or intention; considering an intention in one's mind, as opposed to expressing it.

Ḥol (חול): Ordinary. A day having no special religious sanctification, e.g., a weekday as opposed to a Sabbath or festival day.

Holy Day (חג, יום-טוב): A Jewish historical or religious festival.

Ḥumra (חומרא): Restriction. A ritual or legal restriction imposed in an especially strict interpretation of the law.

Ḥuppah (חופה): Canopy. A wedding canopy or chamber shared by the bride and bridegroom as an act of betrothal.

I

Im Yirtzeh Ha-Shem (אם ירצה ה'): If it please God (lit.). The plans of man or the fulfilment of his wishes are subject to the will of God. It is therefore customary to add a prayer, "Please

God". Man being conscious of his own limitations recognizes that all his hopes depend on the help of God. He therefore always adds the prayer "with God's help", *be'ezrat Ha-Shem* – בעזרת ה'.

***Issur* (איסור)**: A prohibition or forbidden thing. A Biblical prohibition or a rabbinical interdict; an extension of the law of the Torah by rabbinical enactment (TJ *Ber*. 1:3b).

K

***Kaddish* (קדיש)**: Sanctification. A hymn of praise, traditionally in an Aramaic form, recited in the rubric of a public prayer service by the reader leading the prayers, and also by a mourner, expressing confidence in Divine Providence.

***Kadosh* (קדוש)**: Holy, sacred; dedicated to the Temple.

***Kallah* (כלה)**: A betrothed woman or prospective bride.

***Karet* (כרת)**: Cutting off. A Divine punishment for certain transgressions removing the sinner from Divine grace; excision of the soul.

***Karka'ot* (קרקעות)**: Land, immovable property, real estate.

***Kasher* (כשר)**: Fit, proper. Ritually acceptable in accordance with Jewish practice, particularly referring to the type or preparation of foods, or indicating a person fit and accepted for some purpose.

***Katan* (קטן)**: Small (masculine). A boy under the age of thirteen years and one day (*bar mitzvah*), and thus below the age of ritual and observance obligation and legal competence.

Kavvanah (כונה): Concentration. Conscious deliberation before performing a religious precept; devotion in prayer; the aim and intention of an action.

Ke'adasha (כעדשה): A standard measure of the small size of a lentil, often understood as an Egyptian lentil.

Kepeidah (קפידה): Special, particular concern about the matter; punctilious.

Kesef (כסף): Silver, a silver coin, money or value in general.

Kesef Kiddushin (כסף קדושין): Money paid for marriage. Money or an article at least of the value of one *perutah* which a bridegroom is obliged to give to his bride at the marriage ceremony (*kiddushin*).

Ketanah (קטנה): Small (feminine). A girl under the age of twelve years and one day, below the age of ritual and observance obligation and legal competence.

Ketubah (כתובה): A written document, particularly the written marriage contract specifying the identification and mutual obligations of husband and wife, including the wife's marriage settlement which she is entitled to recover on her being divorced or on the death of her husband during her lifetime.

Kezayit (כזית): Olive size. A legally defined measure, the size of an olive, defining applicability to certain prohibitions or obligations.

Kiddush (קדוש): Sanctification. The traditional benediction over a cup of wine for the sanctification of every Sabbath and festival; the ceremony takes place usually at the beginning of the meal on the eve of the Sabbath or festival.

Kiddush Ha-Shem (קדוש ה'): Sanctification of the Divine Name. A courageous public act demonstrating complete loyalty and confidence in the law and righteousness of God.

Kiddushin (קדושין): The marriage ceremony sanctification completing the covenant of marriage.

Kigerogeret (כגרוגרת): Like a fig. A legally recognized standard size of a substance of the size of a dried fig.

Kinyan (קנין): Purchase. The legal acquisition of either landed or movable property.

Kinyan Sudar (קנין סודר): The acquisition of a scarf or cloth. A legal form of acquisition of objects or confirming agreements or obligations, executed by the symbolic act of the handing of a cloth by one contracting party to the other, representing the transfer of the object or the undertaking of the obligation.

Kohen (כהן): A priest of priestly status. A male descendant of the High Priest Aaron.

Korban (קרבן): Offering. A sacrifice offered on the Temple altar; a sacrifice generally.

L

Lifnim Mishurat Hadin (לפנים משורת הדין): Within the requirements of law. A judgement involving a liberal concession by a litigant over and above what he is obliged to do according to the law.

Likhevod Shabbat (לכבוד שבת): The honour of the Sabbath. An action done to enhance the Sabbath Day.

Lishemah (לשמה): For its own sake. An action performed entirely for its own religious sake and not for any private purpose.

Lug (לוֹג): A liquid measure, traditionally equivalent to the space occupied by six eggs.

Lulav (לוֹלב): A branch of the palm, used as one of the Four Species on the Feast of Tabernacles (Sukkoth).

M

Ma'amar (מאמר): An agreement of marriage by word of mouth expressed particularly in the marriage of the widow of a childless man by a brother of the deceased; a Levirate marriage.

Ma'aser (מעשר): The tithe. A "first tithe" due to the Levite, and a "second tithe" to be consumed by the owner in Jerusalem, or due to the poor every third year.

Mahshavah (מחשבה): A thought, plan or a mental intention.

Mamzer (ממזר): Illegitimate child. The offspring of an incestuous union and of any connection forbidden in the Torah.

Mar'it Ha'ayin (מראית העין): Sight of the eye. A semblance of wrongdoing which is forbidden for appearance's sake. A fear of the harm of "the evil eye".

Mashiah (משיח): The anointed Messiah of Israel. The promised future descendant of the House of David who will solve the problems of Jewry, ensure the protection of Israel and generate an era of universal peace.

Matanah (מתנה): A gift, present, donation. The term is also used to describe the sprinkling or smearing of the blood of a sacrifice on the Temple altar.

Matzah (מצה): The unleavened biscuit bread eaten throughout the Passover in place of leavened bread.

Mazal (מזל): Luck, good fortune. The term originally derived, according to tradition, from the Hebrew word for 'constellation' or 'planet', governing the destiny of one born under the planet's influence.

Mazal Tov (מזל טוב): "Good luck", congratulations; a greeting of good wishes extended on happy occasions and for noteworthy achievements.

Megillah (מגילה): Scroll. Any one of the five scrolls – Song of Songs, Ruth, Lamentations, Ecclesiastes, and Esther – which form part of the Biblical Writings; the term is chiefly applied to *Megillat Esther*, the handwritten parchment scroll read in synagogue on the Festival of Purim.

Mehilah (מחילה): Forgiveness, pardon. Also, remission of a debt; forgoing a due credit.

Me'ilah (מעילה): An offensive act, particularly the unlawful use of sacred property, or a sanctified object; wrongful conduct.

Mekah (מקח): A purchase, purchasing or buying, as in 'buying and selling' – *mekah umemkar*; financial transaction.

Melakhah (מלאכה): Work, trade or task, particularly one of the 39 forbidden forms of work on the Sabbath.

Melehet Mahshevet (מלאכת מחשבת): A thoughtful activity. Productive work, purposely done is prohibited on the Sabbath or a festival.

Menorah (מנורה): Candlestick, candelabrum, lamp. The seven branched candelabrum placed in the Temple sanctuary.

Mepharshim (מפרשים): Commentators. Erudite rabbinical scholars who have written recognized commentaries on the Torah, Talmud, and the codes, such as *Rashi* (*R. Shlomo Yitzhaki)* and *Tosafot.* Recognized rabbinical authorities determining *Halakhah* (law).

Mesirah (מסירה): Handing over. A form of legal acquisition executed by the seller in his delivering the object of sale and the receiving of delivery by the purchaser.

Mesorah, Massorah (מסורה): Tradition. The traditional scriptural text copied exactly but without the pointing indicating vowel pronunciation. The traditional vocalization is known as *Mikra*, the reading version of the text. The term *mesorah* also refers to the traditions of law and wisdom handed down from Moses to the elders of Israel.

Metaltelin (מטלטלים): Goods that can be handled. A technical term used for movable goods, movables and chattels.

Mezonot (מזונות): Food. The support due to be given by a husband to his wife to supply her food and various needs; alimony.

Mezuzah (מזוזה): Door post. A piece of parchment inscribed with the first two paragraphs of the *Shema*, rolled in a casing affixed to the right door post of every entrance.

Middat Ha-din (מדת הדין): The measure of law. The divine application of the strict law of justice in His universal rule. In contrast to *middat ha-rahamim*, a merciful judgement.

Middat Ha-Rahamim (מדת הרחמים): The measure of mercy. The quality of mercy, leniency and sympathy tempering the strict application of justice by mercy. The combined guidance of both relationships of *din* (law) and *rahamim* (mercy) is indispensable to true justice.

Mide'orayta (מדאוריתא): From the Torah (Aramaic). Jewish law of Biblical origin. Fundamental Jewish law expressing the highest Jewish legal authority of the Torah.

Miderabbanan (מדרבנן): From the Rabbis (Aramaic). Jewish law of rabbinic authority; laws ordained by the Sages derived from the legal authority of the Torah.

Midrash (מדרש): Interpretation. A rabbinic compilation of homiletic commentaries on a scriptural text.

Mikkah Ta'ut (מיקח טעות): A business mistake. A sale or agreement transacted in error by one of the parties, enabling the loser to correct the agreement (*BB* 97b).

Mikveh (מקוה): The ritual bath used for purification after ritual defilement.

Milah (מילה): The religious covenant of circumcision of a male child, normally on the eighth day of his birth.

Minyan (מנין): Number, a quorum. A gathering of ten men above the age of thirteen forming a quorum for worship.

Mishnah (משנה): The collection of rulings, discussions and Biblical interpretations by the early Sages (*tannaim*), as edited by R. Judah Hanasi around the year 200 CE.

Mishpat (משפט): Justice, judgement; the strict law.

Mit'asek (מתעסק): Engaging one's attention to do one thing while intending to do something else; to do a forbidden act by mistake on the Sabbath or a festival; to do a thing without intending it to have its practical purpose but merely to practice or experiment.

Mitzvah (מצוה): A religious commandment or duty. These include the 613 religious observances with the addition of doing any good deed or meritorious act.

Miun (מיאון): Refusal. A woman's protest against a marriage contracted during her minority with the intention of annulling the marriage by divorce.

Moda'ah (מודעה): A declaration of protest. A notification by a party in the formation of a contract that the action he is about to make is not really intended by him but is done under duress.

Muktzeh (מוקצה): Set apart. The prohibition of using or handling items which before the Sabbath or the festival had not been expected to be used and therefore are 'set apart', 'cut off', 'set aside', excluded from normal use on that day.

Mutar (מותר): Permitted, or released from an obligation.

Musaf (מוסף): The additional *Amidah* prayer included in services on the Sabbath, the New Moon, and festivals.

N

Nasi (נשיא): A prince; chief. The head of the Great Sanhedrin in Jerusalem and of the successor courts of lesser Sanhedrin.

Nedunia (נדוניא): Dowry (Aramaic). Originally, a bridegroom gave the dowry and a gift to the bride's father in return for the privilege of taking his daughter away from her parental home. Later on, in the time of the Mishnah, the husband promised his bride additional gifts which were prescribed in the written document of marriage – *ketubah*. A further practice became the provision by the father of the bride of her ceremonial garb and the wedding equipment.

Nefesh (נפש): The soul, life or a person; the will, desire, disposition; the essential element of the life-blood.

Ne'ilah (נעילה): The concluding prayer on Yom Kippur, the Day of Atonement.

Ner Tamid (נר תמיד): The perpetual lamp. The lamp whose light burned unceasingly in the Temple and subsequently in every synagogue.

Neshamah (נשמה): Soul. The principle of life as a distinct entity separate from the body; the spiritual part of man as distinct from the physical part; the emotional part of a man's nature expressing his feelings, thought and sentiments.

Niddah (נדה): A menstrual woman, or the state and period of menstruation.

Nisuin (נישואין): Marriage. The actual performance of the halakhic procedure of the complete state of marriage.

O

Olah (עולה): A sacrificial offering. A sacrifice totally burned on the altar, voluntary or ordained, or ritually prescribed.

Omer (עומר): The first sheaf of barley harvested on the night following the first night of Passover and offered as a sacrifice in the Temple (Lev. 23:10), thereafter, counting the preceding 49 days, the Festival of Shavuot, marking the wheat harvest, is celebrated.

Ona'ah (אונאה): Overreaching and the imposition of its redress; fraudulent representation; a feeling of being imposed upon.

Oneg Shabbat (עונג שבת): Sabbath joy. In addition to the halakhic observance of the Sabbath as a day of rest, a sense of joy fills the Jewish home and the day is enjoyed as a spiritual happening.

Oness (אונס): Force. A wrong act committed under compulsion.

P

Parnas (פרנס): The leader of a Jewish community and administrator of communal practice.

Parnasah (פרנסה): Livelihood. Regular gainful employment; earnings providing self-support.

Patur (פטור): Released, exempt, free from obligation or liability.

Peirot (פירות): Fruit (lit.). The right of usufruct of goods, the products of trees or soil of limited ownership.

Perutah (פרוטה): The smallest copper coin of small value mentioned in rabbinic literature.

Pesaḥ (פסח): Passover. The Feast of Passover marks Israel's deliverance from Egyptian bondage. The festival is observed for seven days beginning with the 15th day of the month of Nissan. Passover is also known as the Festival of Unleavened Bread – *Ḥag Ha-matzot*. Matza, known as the Bread of Affliction, symbolizes Israel's journey from slavery to freedom.

Pesik Reishei (פסיק רישיה): To cut off its head, but not intending it to die (lit.). The unavoidable result of an act for which the doer must take responsibility.

Pharisees (פרושים): "Separatists". A sect of Judaism maintaining "separation" from ritually impure people and things, noted for their adherence to the Oral Law.

***Piku'ah Nefesh* (פיקוח נפש):** A danger to life. A condition endangering a person's life or threatening to endanger it, which requires immediate action to save life thus, in principle, putting the saving of life above *Halakhah* except in cases involving idolatry, murder and forbidden sexual relations.

***Piyyut–Piyyutim* (פיוט, פיוטים):** Liturgical poems included in the statutory prayers.

***Posek–Posekim* (פוסק, פוסקים):** Decider(s) of an issue. Recognized rabbinical legal authorities who pronounce rulings on debated issues of *Halakhah*, and/or codifiers who arrange systematic compilations of Talmudic law, such as Maimonides (*Yad Hahazakah*); Alfasi (*Sepher Halakhot*) and Joseph Caro (*Shulhan Arukh*).

***Prozbul* (פרוזבול):** Before the assembly of councillors (lit., Greek). Specifically, a legal declaration on transacting a loan with the effect of preventing the law of limitation applying at the onset of the Sabbatical Year.

***Purim* (פורים):** Lots (lit.). The festival which commemorates the frustration of Haman's plot, based on the casting of lots to decide the date on which to destroy the Jews of Persia in the reign of Ahasuerus/Xerxes (5th cent. BCE).

R

***Rabbi, Rav* (רב):** Master. A Jewish scholar whose religious authority is derived from ordination conferred on him by a senior learned rabbi of great repute.

Rahmanut (רחמנות): Mercifulness, compassion; the eschewing of callousness and the domination of compassion.

Rambam (רמב״ם): Acronym of Maimonides, Moses ben Maimon (Spain, North Africa, Egypt, Israel, 12th cent.), jurisprudent, philosopher and codifier.

Ramban (רמב״ן): Acronym of Nahmanides, Moses ben Nahman (Spain, 13th cent.), Talmud and Bible commentator, exponent of religious tradition.

Rasha (רשע): A wicked person. A purposeful transgressor of divine law, given to unscrupulous conduct in his relationships with God and man (1Kings 8:47). A wrongful claimant judged as false and strongly censured (*Sanh.* 27a).

Rashi (רש״י): Acronym of Rabbi Shlomo Yitzhaki (R. Solomon ben Isaac, 1040–1105). Known as the "Prince of Commentators" on the Bible and Talmud, he lived in north-western France.

Ratzon (רצון): Will, desire, willing, wish, intentional, acceptable.

Rema (רמ״א): Acronym of Moses Isserles. Authoritative halakhic codifier whose rulings are followed particularly in Ashkenazi communities (Poland, 16th cent.).

Reshut (רשות): A domain; permission; power of control.

Responsa (שאלות ותשובות): Questions and answers. A branch of rabbinic literature recording answers to halakhic questions addressed to recognized scholars.

Ribit (רבית): Usury, interest on a loan.

Rif (רי״ף): Acronym of Isaac Alfasi (Spain, 11th cent.). The Rif was an early Talmudic authority of prime importance, following the Babylonian *geonim*.

Rosh Hashanah (ראש השנה): The New Year. The first day of the month of Tishrei, designated as the religious New Year.

Roshei Teivot (ראשי תיבות): Heading of words (lit.). A form of abbreviation, specifically an acronym. A combination of the first letters of a few words of a name, title or subject joined together to form an acronym, e.g., RAMBAM (*R*abbi *M*oses *b*en *M*aimon), GEMACH (*gem*ilut *h*asadim).

Rosh Hodesh (ראש חדש): The first day of the new month calculated according to the monthly reappearance of the new moon.

Ruah (רוח): Wind, air, spirit, direction, disposition.

S

Safek (ספק): A doubt. An uncertainty of the appropriate decision of law. A doubt whether the action committed involved a transgression or not. Uncertainty regarding the facts of a case (TJ *Ker.* 4:1; *BM* 2a; *Yev.* 37b).

Sages (חז"ל): Acronym for the Scholars of Blessed Memory – *Hakhamim Zikhronam Liverakhah* in Hebrew. The rabbinic Talmud teachers, *tannaim* and *amoraim*.

Sanhedrin (סנהדרין): The Supreme Court. The highest council of the Sages consisting of 71 members, or a lesser court of 23 members. The Sanhedrin, located in Jerusalem, was empowered to originate or dispense all types of religious law.

Saris (סריס): A tenant farmer who gives half his produce or an agreed part as rent for the field he works on; a metayer.

Satan (שטן): Adversary (lit.), accuser. Symbolically a person's withdrawal from the presence of the Lord makes room for the hostility of the Satan, thus inviting misfortune and confusion.

Se'ah (סאה): A measure of volume, usually of produce or land.

Seder (סדר): Order. The ritual home celebration on the first (and second, outside of Israel) night(s) of Passover.

Sefaradim (ספרדים): Jews whose families originated in Spain and some countries in Eastern Europe and in the Middle East.

Sefer Torah (ספר תורה): The Book of the Law. The holy book containing the Pentateuch written by a scribe on parchment in the form of a scroll.

Sekhakh (סכך): Covering. The layer of boughs placed as a cover of the booth dwelt in during the Festival of Tabernacles (Sukkoth).

Semikhah (סמיכה): Laying on of hands (lit.). The official ordination, authorizing a scholar to judge matters of ritual or civil law. The *semikhah* was originally performed by the laying of hands by the recognized authority upon the scholar being ordained. The term is also used for the certificate of authorization.

Semikhat Da'at (סמיכת דעת): The assured reliance on the ability and the intention of both parties in carrying out the terms of an agreement.

Setam (סתם): Something undefined. A transaction without particular terms. An opinion recorded without specification of the author.

***Seyag La-Torah* (סייג לתורה):** A fence around the law. The rabbis, at times, ordained a further restriction beyond the strict law in order to protect the law itself and prevent its transgression (*Avot* 1:1).

***Sha'atnez* (שעטנז):** A cloth made of a mixture of wool and linen together (Lev. 19:19; Deut. 22:11).

***Shabbat* (שבת):** The weekly day of rest on the seventh day of the week as ordained in the Scriptural account of the creation (Gen. 2:3).

***Shaḥarit* (שחרית):** Morning prayer. The liturgical group of prayers recited at the beginning of the day.

***Shaliaḥ* (שליח):** A messenger, an agent; *sheliḥut* – agency.

***Shalom* (שלום):** Peace, absence of strife, completeness, well-being.

***Shalosh Regalim* (שלש רגלים):** The three pilgrimages. The three festivals which were celebrated as days of pilgrimage to the Temple in Jerusalem, namely, the Passover, Feast of Weeks and Feast of the Tabernacles.

***Shas* (ש"ס):** The six Orders of the Mishnah, a title extended to the rabbinical literature of the Talmud. The word is an acronym of the Hebrew *Shishah Sedarim.*

***Shavuot* (שבועות):** The Feast of Weeks. This harvest festival is celebrated seven weeks from the second day of Passover, on the sixth day of the month of Sivan. In its spiritual aspect, the festival commemorates the Revelation of the Torah on Mt. Sinai.

***Shevu'ah* (שבועה):** An oath. A testimony by oath having in Jewish law a character of legal evidence; substantiating a claim by swearing a solemn oath.

Shegagah (שגגה): Error. An inadvertent act, an unintended transgression.

She'heheyanu (שהחיינו): A special benediction of thanksgiving to the Almighty on enjoying some new experience or an act performed for the first time during the current calendar year.

Shehita (שחיטה): The slaughtering of an animal or fowl according to Jewish ritual requirements.

Shekel (שקל): A technical currency coin or weight of the value of ten small coins called *ma'ah*; the Biblical sacred shekel was worth twice the value of the common *shekel*.

Shekhinah (שכינה): The Divine Presence. Another name for the Almighty. The sacred presence of God as it reveals itself in the life of pious souls.

Shema (שמע): Hear (lit.). The name taken from the opening word of the Biblical passage, "*Hear*, O Israel", which is recited daily in the Hebrew liturgy.

Shemittah (שמיטה): The year of release. The seventh year of each cycle of the Jewish calendar.

Shetar (שטר): Legal document, promissory note. A deed of sale or gift used in a conveyance containing the date, place, and names of the parties, stipulations and conditions; the signatures of witnesses are appended to the document.

Shevut (שבות): Rest. An occupation forbidden by the Rabbis – although not by the Bible – because it does not harmonize with the nature of the Sabbath, or where one may forget and do something rabbinically forbidden.

Shiddukh (שידוך): The arrangement for a forthcoming marriage negotiated by the parents of the bride and bridegroom.

Shinnuy Ha-Shem (שינוי השם): Change of name. The name of a person in some adversity is changed or a new name is added to the original name. The custom implies the creation of a new person with a new character and having an additional lease of life.

Shi'ur (שיעור): A halakhically defined measure of quantity or size.

Shoḥet (שוחט): Slaughterer. A religious professional qualified to perform the slaughter of animals or fowls according to Jewish ritual.

Shuttafut (שותפות): Partnership. A term denoting joint ownership or commercial partnership.

Shofar (שופר): A ram's horn. Used as an instrument sounded in the synagogue on the New Year and at the conclusion of the Day of Atonement.

Shulḥan Arukh (שולחן ערוך): Code of Laws. The collected code of laws that defined all virtual and legal questions, compiled by Joseph Caro (Spain, Israel, 16th cent.).

Siddur (סדור): Arrangement (lit.). Prayer book containing the order and literary arrangement of the rubric of Jewish worship.

Sifri (ספרי): An ethical interpretation of the Scriptures and the practical law as part of early Midrashic literature.

Simḥat Torah (שמחת תורה): Rejoicing in the Law (lit.). The festival celebrated in honour of the conclusion of the public reading of the Pentateuch at the conclusion of the Festival of Tabernacles.

Sodom (סדום): A Biblical city infamous for its wicked conduct.

Sotah (סוטה): A wife who is suspected of adultery and undergoes the Biblical ordeal of "the bitter waters".

Sukkah - Sukkoth (סוכה, סוכות): A booth; the Feast of Tabernacles. The festival of thanksgiving for the ingathering of the harvest in the land of Israel. The festival occurs after the High Holy Days in the autumn on the fifteenth day of the month of Tishrei and continues for eight days.

T

Takkanah (תקנה): An enactment of the authorized Sages and legislators of Israel, usually constituting a new supplementary law.

Tallit (טלית): A woollen prayer shawl with fringes attached to the four corners, worn during certain prayer services.

Talmud (תלמוד): Teaching (lit.). A codex of legislation derived from both the Written and Oral Law. A composite collection of legal and moral teachings discussed and sanctioned by the early and later Sages, which includes the Mishnah, Gemara and Aggadah. The collection compiled by the Babylonian Sages is called *Talmud Bavli*, and that collected by the scholars residing in the Holy Land is called *Talmud Yerushalmi*.

Tanna – Tanna'im (תנא, תנאים): The early Sages quoted in the Mishnah or Boraita.

Targum (תרגום): Aramaic translation. The Aramaic translation and interpretation of the Scriptures. Among traditional versions are *Targum Onkelos*, *Targum Yerushalmi*, and *Targum Yehonatan*.

Ta'ut (תעות): Mistake, error. A mistake in a matter of fact or law; a misunderstanding or wrong evaluation; an error in the performance of a required action.

Tefillah (תפילה): Prayer. The central prayer of the *Amidah* in the daily worship.

Tefillin (תפילין): Phylacteries. Two black leather boxes containing appropriate scriptural passages, bound on the left arm and hand and worn on the head as ordained in scriptural law.

Teḥum Shabbat (תחום שבת): Sabbath limit. The distance of two thousand cubits in any direction from the outskirts of the town in which one resides, beyond which limit walking is prohibited.

Teshuvah (תשובה): Repentance. The abandonment of wrong or evil ways of conduct and a reaffirmation of one's return to Divinely inspired regulations.

Terumah (תרומה): The portion of a sacrifice or of the produce which was set aside as due to the Priest (*Kohen*).

Tevel (טבל): Produce set aside to fulfil the obligation of the giving of sacred and priestly gifts. A declaration of such intent renders the produce forbidden for eating until the act is performed.

Toke'a (תוקע): One who sounds the *shofar* (ram's horn) by blowing through it; the sound emitted is termed *teki'ah*.

Torah (תורה): The Law. Strictly, the teaching of the Pentateuch as distinct from the Prophets. Also, the entire body of Jewish teaching based on the written Scriptures and the oral traditions connected with them.

Torah Sheba'al Peh (תורה שבעל פה): The Oral Law. An outgrowth and development of the Written Law, containing legal decisions handed down by tradition and recorded by the Sages.

Torah Shebikehetav (תורה שבכתב): The Written Law. The written Hebrew text of Scripture as traditionally received down through the ages.

Tosefot (תוספות): A collection of legal notes and decisions supplementary to the commentary of Rashi on the Babylonian Talmud, the scholars being frequently the grandsons of Rashi.

Tovat Hana'ah (טובת הנאה): The benefit of a pleasure. The satisfaction which one feels in obliging someone; the satisfaction gained in doing a service for which the other person will feel obliged.

Trefah (טריפה): Torn (lit.). Meat unfit for consumption according to Jewish ritual law; an animal found after slaughter to be suffering from a physical or fatal organic defect or disease rendering the meat forbidden as specified in Jewish ritual law.

Tzaddik (צדיק): A righteous person. A pious, virtuous and just person, one who is honest and upright, God-fearing and zealous in the performance of his religious duties. *Zekher tzaddik liverakhak* – "the memory of the righteous shall be for a blessing" is a phrase traditionally quoted (Prov.10:7) when mentioning a deceased person's name (Gen.18:23; Hab. 2:4; *Avot* 6:1).

Tzedakah (צדקה): Charity, philanthropy. The performance of benevolent actions for the needy with no expectation for material reward. A charitable fund used for the alleviation of the needs of humanity.

Tzedek (צדק): Justice or righteousness.

Tzvi (צבי): A deer, gazelle. Something beautiful desired by all.

Tzitzit (ציצית): Fringes attached to the corners of a garment or prayer shawl – *tallit.*

Tzi'un (ציון): A land mark, such as a pillar of stone, indicating the neighbourhood of an impurity such as a burial place.

Tzorkhei Tzibur (צרכי ציבור): Community needs. The maintenance of Jewish communal life supporting social needs, philanthropic and educational institutions, and synagogues for worship and learning. Whoever occupies themselves in the needs of the community is expected to do so in faithfulness.

U

Udita (אודיתא): Confession; admission of indebtedness.

Umdana (אומדנא): Estimate, assessment, opinion.

V

Vidduy (וידוי): Confession. The traditional form of confession of sin being an established ritual form of repentance.

Y

Yayin Nesekh (יין נסך): Libational wine. A prohibition against the partaking of wine prepared by gentiles because of possible extra doctrinal intent.

Yedi'ot Meḥalkot (ידיעות מחלקות): Intermittent awareness. A succession of transgressions done unwittingly, but the realization in the interval between the acts that they were prohibited.

Yetzer Ha'ra (יצר הרע): The evil inclination. The inclination towards evil conduct, as opposed the *yetzer tov* – the good inclination.

Yerushah (ירושה): Inheritance. The disposition of one's material possessions and the acquisition of such possessions by the inheritors after the death of the testator.

Yeshivah (ישיבה): Academy of advanced Jewish learning, often in junior and senior categories, the head being called the *rosh yeshivah*.

Yeshuah (ישועה): Salvation, help, redemption. Trust in the salvation of God is a basic ethic in man's conduct.

Ye'ush (יאוש): Abandonment. A property whose owner has abandoned all hope of its recovery from loss or theft. The owner resigns himself to his loss and gives up his right of possession. Despair in the hour of need and the tragic denial of God's compassion.

Yevamah (יבמה): The widow of a husband who has died without issue, and who is due to be married to the deceased husband's brother (Deut. 25:5–10).

Yibum (יבום): The act of a Levirate marriage.

Yirat Shamayim (יראת שמים): Fear of Heaven (lit.). Fear of the Lord; a God-fearing man reveres God and conducts himself in complete faith in the Almighty's justice and mercy.

Yi'ud (יעוד): Designation of a Hebrew handmaid in betrothal to her master or his son, having the effect of a marriage (*Kid.* 18b–19a).

Yom Kippur (יום כפור): The Day of Atonement. The tenth day of the month of Tishrei, which is observed throughout by complete abstention from food and drink, being a solemn occasion dedicated to devoted prayer and the conduct of divine service.

Yom Tov (חג, יום-טוב): A good day (lit.). Every religious Holy Day, synonymous with *hag*; a Biblical festival, particularly the three pilgrim festivals of Passover, Pentecost and Tabernacles.

Yovel (יובל): Jubilee. The fiftieth year at the end of seven successive seven-year cycles.

Z

Zekhiyah (זכייה): Acquisition. The process of one person acquiring property from the owner, or lost or ownerless property from the previous owner.

Zekhuth (זכות): A worthy action, favourable judgement. Justification in the juridical or theological sense; documentary evidence confirming an advantage of legal right; merit or virtue.

Zimmun (זימון): Appointment. Designated for some particular purpose; participation in the recital of Grace after a common meal, requiring a minimum of three persons, hence, an invitation to join as a guest in a meal. Also, a summons to appear before a court.

Zommem (זומם): A witness whose testimony is refuted by two other witnesses testifying that the former witness was in another place where he could not have seen the event which he claims to have witnessed.

Zug (זוג): A pair, a marital couple.

Zuz (זוז): A silver coin equal to a *dinar*, being a quarter of a *shekel*.

BIBLIOGRAPHY

List of Hebrew Books Consulted
(Many Editions)

Bibliography

List of Hebrew Books Consulted (Many Editions)

Aboab, Isaac. *Menorat ha-Maor.*

Abudraham. *Perushim al ha-Tefillot.* R. David ben Yosef Toledano.

Akedat Yitzhak. Yitzhak ben Moshe Arama.

Albo, R. Joseph. *Ikkarim.*

Alshekh. Bible Commentaries. Mosheh Alshekh. Salonika, Safed.

Arukh ha-Shulhan, Shulhan Arukh. Codes. Yehiel Mikhal ben Aharon ha-Levi Epstein.

Avodat Yisrael. Siddur. Behr, Seligman, Israel.

Ba'alei haNefesh. RAVAD.

BAH, Yoel Sirkes. *Bayit Hadash, Peirush al ha-Turim.*

Bahya ben Asher. *Kad ha-Kemah.*

Bachya. *Hovot Halevavot, passim.*

Bayit Hadash, Peirush al Ha-Turim. BAH, Yo'el Sirkes.

Be'er Hagolah. *Hagahot.* Moshe ben Naftali Hirsch. Rawkesh, Vilna.

Behr, I. *Siddur Avodat Yisrael.*

Bet Elohim. *Faith and Religion.* MABIT – Mosheh ben Yosef mi-Trani.

Bet Shmuel. Commentary on Even ha-Ezer. Shmuel ben Uri Shraga Feivish.

Berlin, R. Chayim. *Nefesh Hayyim.*

Bertinoro (RA'V). Mishnah Commentary. R. Ovadia Mi-Bertinorah.

Binat Adam al Hokhmat Adam, Yoreh De'ah. Avraham ben Yehiel Mikhel Danziger.

Birkat Kohen. Novellae on Even ha-Ezer. R. Kopel Kahana.

Birkei Yosef, Hagahot. Azulay, Hayyim Yosef David ben Refael Yitzhak Zerahya.

Caro, Joseph. *Shulhan Arukh – Orah Hayyim, Yoreh De'ah, Even Ha-Ezer, Hoshen Hamishpat; Bet Yosef.*

Darkhei Mosheh, Hagahot al ha-Shulhan Arukh. R. Moshe ben Yisrael Isserles (REMA).

Derekh Eretz Zuta. Minor Tractate. Rabbah.

Derekh Ha-Hayyim. Siddur. YA'VETZ (R. Yaakov Emden).

Derekh Ha-Hayyim. Siddur. Ashkenaz rite. R. Yaakov mi-Lissa.

Dinei Mishpahah. Schereschewsky. Jerusalem: Mass, 1967.

Emunot ve-De'ot. Saadiah Gaon.

Eshel Avraham. Avraham David ben Asher Anschel Wahrmann. Ukraine, 19th cent.

Eshel Avraham. Avraham Hayyim ben Menahem Mendel Na'eh.

Etz Hayyim. R. Hayyim Vital. 1573. Many editions.

Even Ha'Ezer

FALK. *Hagahot.* Yehoshua ben Alexander ha-Kohen.

Gemirat Da'at Bekinyanim. Study on Commercial Law. Deutsch, Sinai. Tel Aviv University, 1973.

Gerondi, Rabbenu Yona. *Sha'arei Teshuva.*

Gombiner, Avraham ben Hayyim Halevi. *Magen Avraham.*

Gulak, A. *Yesodei ha-Mishpat ha-Ivri.*

Gunsberg, R. Aryeh Leib ben Asher. Responsa. *Sha'agat Aryeh.*

Ha'amek Davar. Commentary on Pentateuch. Naftali Tzvi Yehuda Berlin mi-Volozhin.

Hadat Ve'arkhei Ha'adam. Roth, H.Y. Jerusalem: Magnes Press, Hebrew University, 1973.

Ḥafetz Ḥayyim, Yisrael Meir ha-Kohen mi-Radin. *Mishnah Berurah.*

Hafla'ah, *Sefer Hafla'ah.* Novellae in Halakha. R. Pinchas ben Tzvi Hirsch Halevi Horowitz.

Hai Gaon. *Halakhot Pessukot, She'iltot.* Talmud Codes.

Hai Gaon. *Ha-Mekaḥ veha-Memkar.*

Ha-Ittur. Compendium of Halakha. R. Meir Yonah ben Shmuel, ed.

Halakhot Pessukot, She'iltot. Talmud Codes. Hai Gaon.

Halevi, R. Judah. *Kuzari.*

Ha-ma'amad Ha-ishi Be-Yisrael. Silberg, M. Jerusalem: Hebrew University, 1961.

Ha-mekaḥ Veha-memkar. Commercial Law. Hai Gaon.

Ha-Mikneh. Compendium of Halakah, Commercial Law. R. Zussman Eliezer ben Mordekhai Efraim Sofer. New York: Grossman, 1872.

Ha-Mordekhai. Halakhic Compendium on Talmud. R. Mordekhai ben Hillel Ashkenazi.

Ha-Nefesh ha- Ḥokhmaah, Kabbala. Moses de Leon.

Ha'Otiot. SHELAH (R. Isaiah ben Avraham Ha-Levi Horowitz).

Ha-philosophia shel Yahadut. Guttman, Y.J. Jerusalem: Mosad Bialik, 1953.

Hareidim, Sefer. Precepts of R. Luria (ARI). Eliezer Azikri.

Hasidim, Sefer. Ethics. Judah ben Samuel ha-Hasid.

Hayyei Adam. Reconstruction of Orah Hayyim. Avraham ben Yehiel Mikhel Danziger.

Hazon Yehezkel, Tosefta. R. Yehezkel Abramski.

Heikhal Yitzhak, Even ha-Ezer. Responsa. R. Isaac Herzog ha-Levi.

Herzog, Rabbi I. Responsa. *Heikhal Yitzhak, Even ha-Ezer.*

Hokhmat Adam, *Yoreh Dei'ah.* Avraham ben Yehiel Mikhel Danziger.

Horowitz, R. Isaiah. *Shenei Luhot ha-Berit.*

Horowitz, R. Pinhas Halevi. *Sefer ha-Hafla'ah.*

Hovot Halevavot, passim. Bachya.

Hut ha-Meshulash. R. Haim ben Yitzhak mi-Volozhin (R. Haim Volozhiner).

Isserles, Moshe ben Yisrael (REMA). *Darkhei Moshe, Hagahot al ha-Shulhan Arukh.*

Ikkarim. R. Joseph Albo.

Jakobson, Issachar. *Netiv Binah, Iyyunim al Seder ha-Tefillot.* Tel Aviv: Sinai, 1968.

Kad ha-Kemah. Bahya ben Asher.

Kesef Mishneh. Commentary on *Mishneh Torah.* R. Joseph Caro.

Ketzot ha-Shulhan. Commentary on *Hoshen Mishpat.* Aryeh Leib Heller.

Kitevei Maharal mi-Prag. Maharal (Judah Loew ben Bezalel). Ed. Avraham Kariv.

Kitzur Shulḥan Arukh. Shlomo Gantzfried. Ed. David Feldman. Manchester, UK: 1951. Eng. trans. Gerald Friedlander. London: Shapiro, Vallentine, 1949.

Kli Yakar. Commentary on Pentateuch. R. Ephraim Shlomo ben Aaron mi-Luntshits.

Kook, A.I. *Olat Ra'ayah; Seder ha-Tefillah; Iggeret Teshuvah.*

Kovetz Shi'urim. Novellae. R. Elḥanan Wasserman.

Kuzari. R. Judah Halevi.

Landau, R. Ezekiel. *Tziun le-Nefesh Ḥayyah.*

Leḥem Mishneh. Commentary on *Mishneh Torah*. R. Avraham di Buton.

Luzzato. *Mesilat Yesharim.* Chap. 1.

MABIT. Responsa. *Kiryat Sefer al ha-Rambam.* R. Moshe bar Yosef mi-Trani.

Magen Avraham. Commentary on *Shulḥan Arukh, Oraḥ Ḥayyim.* R. Avraham Abele ben Ḥayyim ha-Levi Gombiner.

Magen David. Commentary on *Shulḥan Arukh.* R. David ben Shemuel ha-Levi.

Maggid Mishneh. Commentary on *Mishneh Torah.* R. YomTov Vidal mi-Tolosa.

MAHARAL. R. Yehuda Loev ben Bezalel. *Kitvei Maharal Miprag.* Novellae on Talmud. Ed. A. Kariv. Vol. 1, p. 206. Jerusalem: Mosad Harav Kook, 1982.

Maḥzor Vitri, Prayer Book. Simḥa ben Shmuel mi-Vitri, pupil of Rashi.

Maimonides. *Sefer ha-Mitzvot;* Code, *Yad ha-Ḥazakah, passim.*

Mekhilta. Tannaitic Midrash on Book of Exodus. Rabbi Ishma'el.

Menasseh ben Israel. *Nishmat Hayyim.*

Menorat ha-Maor. Isaac Aboab.

Mesillat Yesharim. Ethics. R. Mosheh Hayyim Luzzatto.

Metzudat David. Commentary on Bible. R. David Alamshuler.

Midrash Halakha, Torat Kohanim, Behukotai.

Midrash Rabba. Aggadic Midrash on Pentateuch and Scriptures.

Minhagei Israel. Sperber, D. Jerusalem: Mosad Harav Kook, 1993.

Mishnah Berurah. Hafetz Hayyim. R. Yisrael Meir Ha-Kohen mi-Radin.

Mishneh le-Melekh. Commentary on *Mishneh Torah.* R. Yom Tov Vidal mi-Tolosa.

Nefesh ha-Hayyim. R. Hayyim Soloveitchik mi-Volozhin, R. Hayyim Brisker. Vilna: 1824.

Netiv Binah, Iyyunim al Seder ha-Tefillot. Jakobson, Issachar. Tel Aviv: Sinai, 1968.

Nishmat Adam al Hayyei Adam, Orah Hayyim. Avraham ben Yehiel Mikhel Danziger.

Nishmat Hayyim. Moral Philosophy. Manasseh ben Israel.

Noda bi-Yehudah. Responsa. R. Yehezkel ben Yehudah Halevi Landau.

Olat R'ayah; Seder ha-Tefillah; Iggeret Teshuvah. Rabbi A.I. Kook.

Or ha-Hayyim. Commentary on Pentateuch. R. Hayyim ben Mosheh Ibn Atar.

Otzar ha-Tefillot. Siddur. Edited collection of prayers. Author not stated.

Otzar Yisrael. Encyclopaedia. Ed. J. D. Eisenstein.

Pahad Yitzhak. Talmudic Enyclopaedia. R. Yitzhak ben Shemuel Lampronti. Talmudic Encyclopaedia, 13 vols.

Peri Hadash. Responsa. R. Hizkiah ben David de Silva.

Peri Megadim. *Hagahot*. Yosef ben Meir Te'umim.

Pirkei de R. Eliezer. Amoraic Aggadic Midrash. R. Eliezer ben Hyrcanus.

RA'V, **Bertinoro**. R. Ovadiah ben Avraham Yare mi-Bertinoro. Commentary on Mishna.

RADBAZ. R. David ben Shlomo ben Zimra. Responsa.

RAN. Nissim ben Reuven Gerondi. Commentary on ha-Rif.

RASHBA. R. Shelomo ben Avraham. Novellae on Talmud.

RAVAD. Abraham ben David. *Hassagot al Mishneh Torah shel ha-Rambam; Ba'alei ha-Nefesh; Sefer Halakhot.*

RAVEN. R. Eliezer ben Natan. Responsa on *Even ha-Ezer*.

REMA. R. Moshe ben Yisrael Isserles. *Hagahot al ha-Shulhan ha-Arukh.*

Reshit Hokhmah. Kabbalah. R. Eliyahu de Vidas.

RIF. Yitzhak ben Yaakov Alfasi. Compendium of Talmud Law – *Gufei Halakhot*.

Rinat Yisrael. Siddur. Ed. Tal, Shlomo. Jerusalem: 1984.

RITVA. R. Yom Tov ben Avraham Ashvili. Novellae on Talmud.

RIVAL. R. Yosef ben Lev. Responsa. No. 11.

ROSH. Rabbeinu Asher ben R. Yehiel. Halakhic Compendium on Talmud.

Sa'adia Gaon. *Emunot ve-Deot 5.*

Sedei Hemed, Talmudic Compendium. Hayyim Hizkiyah Midini. 10 vols.

Sefer ha-Mitzvot. Compendium of Torah Laws. Maimonides.

Sefer ha-Hinukh. Commentary on *Mitzvot ha-Torah.* Anonymous, perhaps Aaron ben Yosef Halevi mi-Barcelona.

Sefer Kavvanot. Meditations on Prayer. Venice, 1620.

Sforno. Commentary on Pentateuch. R. Ovadia ben Yaakov Seforno.

Sh'agat Aryeh. Responsa. R. Aryeh Leib ben Asher Gunsberg.

Sha'ar Efrayim. Responsa. Aryeh Yehuda Leib ben Efrayim ha-Kohen.

Sha'ar Efraim. RITVA – R. Yom Tov ben Avraham Ashvili.

Sha'arei Talmud Torah. Levy, Leo. Jerusalem: Olam Hasefer Hatorani, 1981.

Sha'arei Teshuva. Rabbenu Yona Gerondi.

Sha'arei Teshuvah. *Hagahot.* Margolioth, Hayyim Mordekhai.

SHAKH. *Hagahot.* Shabetai Ha-Kohen ben Meir Katz.

Shemirat Shabbat Kehilkhatah. R. Yehoshua Shaiah Neuwirt.

Shenei Luhot Habrit. R. Isaiah ben Avraham Halevi Horowitz (SHELAH).

Shitah Mekubetzet. Responsa, Novellae. R. Bezalel Ashkenazi.

Shoher Tov. *Midrash.*

Shulhan Arukh – *Orah Hayyim, Yoreh De'ah, Even ha-Ezer, Hoshen ha-Mishpat; Bet Yosef.* Joseph Caro.

Shulhan Arukh. R. Shneur Zalman me-Lubavitch. Biozefaff: 1875.

Siddur. Amram Gaon.

Siddur Bet El. YA'VETZ. R. Yaakov Emden.

Siddur ha-Gera, Orhot Hayyim. Vilna Gaon.

Siddur Sefardi. Ritual Siddur of R. Ovadia Yosef.

Siddur Tzeluta, de-Avraham. Rav Avraham Landau of Czechenov. Ed. R. Yaakov Verdiger. Tel Aviv Institute of Jewish Liturgy, 1963.

Ta'amei Yisrael. Heinemann, I. 1959.

Ta'amei Minhagim. R. Avraham Yitzhak Shohet. Compilation. Lemberg, 1911.

Tamhuma. Amoraic Aggadic Midrash. R. Tanhum bar Abba.

TAZ. Hagahot. David ha-Levi.

TAZ. Turei Zahav. Commentary on *Shulhan Arukh.* R. David ben ben Shemuel Ha-levi.

Tiferet Yisrael. Commentary on Mishna. R. Israel Lipschitz, Danzig.

Tikkun Mitzvot ha-Nefesh. Ibn Gabirol.

Tokef Tzava'ah be-Archa'ot ba-Mishpat ha-Ivri – Dinei Israel. Deutsch, Sinai. Tel-Aviv University.

Toledot ha-Mishpat be-Yisrael. Gulak, A. Jerusalem: Hebrew University, 1939.

Torah Temimah. Commentary on Pentateuch. Barukh ben Yehiel Mikhal ha-Levi Epstein.

Torah Umussar. Reines, H.Z. Jerusalem: Mosad Harav Kook, 1954.

Torat ha-Bayit. Novellae on *Talmud Midrash Halakhah.* RASHBA, R. Shlomo ben Avraham Aderet.

Tosefta, Hazon Yehezkel. Abramski.

Tosphot Yom Tov. Commentary on Mishnah. R. Yom Tov Lipman ben Natan Halevi Heller.

TUR, Arba'ah Turim. Codes. Ya'akov ben Asher.

Tzitz Eliezer. Responsa. R. Eliezer Yehudah Waldenberg.

Tziun Lenefesh Hayyah. R. Ezekiel Landau.

Volozhiner, Haim (R. Haim ben Ytizhak mi-Volozhin). *Nefesh Hayyim.*

Wassserman, R. Elhanan. *Kovetz Shiurim.* Novellae.

Yad ha-Hazakah. Code. Maimonides.

Yad Ahavah, Seder Tefillot. Maimonides.

Yalkut Shim'oni. Midrash Anthology. Rabbeinu Shimon mi-Frankfort.

Yam Shel Shlomo. Novellae on Talmud. R. Shlomo Luria.

Yesodei ha-Mishpat ha-Ivri. Gulak, A.

Zohar. RAM. Vilna, 1911.

BIBLIOGRAPHY

Selected List of English Books

Biliography

Selected List of English Books

Aḥad Ha'am. *Essays, Letters, Memoirs.* Ed. Simon, L. The Sabbath and Zionist Dream. 1944.

Albo, Josef. *Ha-Ikkarim.* Ed. and trans. Husik, I. 1930.

Anson, W.R. *Principles of the English Law of Contract.* 21st ed. Guest, ed.

Babylonian Talmud. English translation. Ed. Epstein, I. London: Soncino Press, 1935–1953.

Baeck, Leo. *The Essence of Judaism.* New York: Shocken, 1967.

Bain, Alexander. *The Senses and the Intellect,* 1855; *The Emotions and the Will,* 1859; *Mind* (journal, from 1876).

Berlin, Meir and Zevin, Shlomo, ed. *Encyclopaedia Talmudica.* Eng. trans. of Hebrew. Jerusalem: Yad Harav Herzog, 1956, etc.

Bible. *The Holy Scriptures.* Philadelphia: Jewish Publication Society of America, 1947. Cambridge University Press, 1958.

Bible. *Soncino Books of the Bible.* Ed. Cohen, A. London: Soncino, 1949, etc.

Buechler, A. *Types of Jewish Palestinian Piety.* Oxford University Press, 1926; *Studies in Sin and Atonement in Rabbinic Literature.* London: Jews' College Publications, Oxford University Press, 1928.

Bunim, I.M. *Ethics from Sinai.* New York: Feldheim, 1964.

Cannon, W.B. *Bodily Changes in Pain, Hunger, Fear and Rage.* 2nd ed., revised. Harvard, 1942.

Cohen, A. *Everyman's Talmud.* London: Dent, 1932.

Cohen, Boaz. *Jewish and Roman Law.* 2 vols. New York: Jewish Theological Seminary of America, 1966.

Danby, H. *The Mishnah.* Eng. trans. Oxford University Press, 1933.

Dunbar, F. *Emotions and Bodily Changes,* 1954; *Psychosomatic Diagnosis,* 1943.

Elon, M. *Jewish Law.* Eng. trans. from Heb. B. Auerbach and M.J. Sykes. 4 vols. Philadelphia: JPS, 1994.

Epstein, I. *Judaism.* London: Epworth Press, 1939; Harmondsworth Middlesex UK: Penguin Books, 1959. *The Faith of Judaism.* London: Soncino, 1954. *Judaism of Tradition.* London: Goldston, 1931.

Finkelstein, L. *The Jews: Their History* (Vol. 1), *Their Religion and Culture* (Vol. 2), *Their Role in Civilisation* (Vol. 3). New York: Schocken, 1971; *The Pharisees.* Philadelphia: JPS, 1938.

Freud, S. *New Introductory Lectures on Psychoanalysis.*

Friedlander, M. *The Jewish Religion.* London: Shapiro, Vallentine, 1937.

Grunfeld, I. *Eternal Judaism* London: Soncino, 1957; *Judaism Eternal.* 2 vols. Ed. I. Grunfeld. London: Soncino, 1956.

Herford, R.T., ed. *The Ethics of the Talmud.* New York: Shocken, 1966.

Herford, Travers R. *The Pharisees.* London: Allen and Unwin, 1924.

Hertz J.H. *The Authorised Daily Prayer Book.* London: Soncino, 1947, etc.; *The Pentateuch.* London: Soncino, 1938; *A Book of Jewish Thoughts.* New York: Oxford University Press; *Affirmations of Judaism.* Oxford University Press, 1929.

Herzog, I. *Main Institutions of Jewish Law.* 2 vols. London: Soncino, 1936.

Hirsch, S.R. *Horeb: Essays on Jewish Life and Thought.* 2 vols. Ed. Grunfeld, I. London: Soncino Press, 1962.

Husik, I. *A History of Medieval Jewish Philosophy.* Philadelphia: JPS, 1930.

Idelsohn, A.Z. *Jewish Liturgy and Its Development.* New York: Henry Holt, 1932.

Jacobs, Joseph. *Jewish Ideals.* London: David Nutt, 1896.

James, W. *The Religious Experience: A study in human nature* (Gifford Lectures), Edinburgh, 1902.

Jewish Encyclopaedia. New York: Funk & Wagnalls, 1925.

Josephus, Flavius. *Antiquities of the Jews*, *The Jewish War.* Eng. trans. from Greek. *Complete Works.* Ed. Whiston, W. Loeb Classical Library. Thackeray, ed. St. John, 1926–65.

Kadushin, M. *Worship and Ethics: A Study in Rabbinic Judaism.* Evanston: Northwestern U. Press, 1964.

Kagan, K. Kahana. *Three Great Systems of Jurisprudence.* London: Stevens, 1955.

Katz, S.T. *Jewish Ideas and Concepts.* New York: Schocken, 1977.

Kaufmann, Yehezkel. *The Religion of Israel.* Trans. and abridged by Moshe Greenberg. London: Allen and Unwin, 1960.

Lazarus, M. *Ethics of Judaism.* Trans. from German *Die Ethik des Judentums.* Philadelphia: JPS, 1901.

Lehrman, S.M. *The Jewish Festivals.* London: Shapiro, Vallentine, 1953.

Maimonides. *The Guide for the Perplexed.* Trans. from Hebrew *Moreh Nevuchim* by M. Friedländer. London: Routledge, 1910.

Maimonides. *Shemonah Perakim, Yad: De'ot,* Intro. to *Pirkei Avot,* s. *The Ideal of the Middle Way.* English translation. London.

Marmorstein, A. *The Doctrine of Merits in Old Rabbinical Literature.* London: Jews' College Publications, Oxford University Press, 1925; *The Old Rabbinic Doctrine of God.* London: Jews' College Publications, Oxford University Press, 1926.

Melamed, S.M. *Psychologie des judischen Geistes.* Berlin, 1921.

Mielziner, M. *Introduction to the Talmud.* New York: Bloch, 1925.

Montefiore, C.G. and H.J Lowe. *A Rabbinic Anthology.* London: Macmillan, 1938.

Moore, G. F. *Judaism.* 3 Vols. Cambridge: Harvard University Press, 1927–1932.

Osborn, P.G. *A Concise Law Dictionary.* 5th ed. London: Sweet and Maxwell, 1964.

Oxford Dictionary of the Jewish Religion. R.J. Werblowsky and Geoffrey Wigoder, editors-in-chief. New York: Oxford University Press, 1997.

Pentateuch. Ed. Hertz, J.H. London: Soncino, 1947.

Pollock, F. *Principles of Contract.* 13th ed. London: Weidenfeld.

Prayer Books (**Eng. Trans.**). *Singer's Authorized Daily Prayer Book*. J.H. Hertz, *Daily Prayer Book*; *Artscroll Prayer Book*.

Quint, E. *A Restatement of Rabbinical Law*. New Jersey: Aronson, 1996.

Rabinowitz, H. *A Guide to Hassidism*. New York: Yoseloff, 1960.

Rankin, O.S. *Israel's Wisdom Literature*. Edinburgh: T. and T. Clark, 1936.

Roth, Cecil, editor-in-chief. *Encyclopaedia Judaica*. 16 vols. Jerusalem: Keter, 1972.

Salmond, J. *Jurisprudence*. 10th ed., Ed. Glanville, L. Williams. London: Sweet and Maxwell, 1947.

Schechter, Solomon. *Aspects of Rabbinic Theology*. New York: Schocken, 1961; *Studies in Judaism*. 3rd series. Philadelphia: JPS, 1924.

Scheftelowitz, E.E. *The Jewish Law of Family and Inheritance in Palestine*. Tel Aviv: Feuchtwanger, 1945.

Silver, D.J. ed. *Judaism and Ethics*. New York: KTAV, 1970.

Singer, S. *Authorised Daily Prayer Book*. London.

Soloveitchik, Joseph B. *The Halakhic Mind*. New York: Seth Press, 1986; *The Halakhic Man*. Philadelphia: JPS, 1983. Based on the Hebrew *Ish ha-Halakha,*1979.

Spero, M.H. *Judaism and Psychology: Halakhic Perspectives*. New York: KTAV, 1980.

Strack, H.L. *Introduction to the Talmud and Midrash*. Philadelphia: JPS, 1931.

Walker, D.M. *The Oxford Companion to Law*. Oxford: Clarendon Press, 1980.

Waxman, M. *Judaism, Religion and Ethics.* New York: Yoseloff, 1958.

Wechsler, D. *The Measurement of Emotional Reactions.* New York, 1925.

Weisman, Yehoshua. *The Law of Property and Concurrent Ownership.* Hebrew. 1997.

Werblowsky, Z. and Wigoder G., ed. *The Encyclopedia of Jewish Religion.* Jerusalem: Massada-PEC Press, 1932.

Wolff, H.G., Wolf George. "Studies on the Nature of Certain Symptoms" in *Psychosomatic Medicine,* vol. 8, pp. 293-319 (1946).

Yust, Walter. Editor-in-chief, *Encyclopaedia Britannica.* London: 1955.

Zimmels, H.J. *Ashkenazim and Sephardim.* Oxford University Press, 1958.

Zohar, trans. to Eng. Sperling, H. and F. Simon. 5 vols. London: Soncino Press, 1931, 1949.

ABBREVIATIONS

Abbreviations

Ar.	Arakhin
Avot	Avot de-Rabbi Natan
AZ	Avodah Zarah
BB	Bava Batra
BCE	Before Common Era (BC)
Bekh.	Bekhorot
Ber.	Berakhot
Betz.	Betzah
Bik.	Bikkurim
BK	Bava Kamma
BM	Bava Metzia
CE	Common Era (AD)
cent.	Century
Chr.	Chroniciles
Dan.	Daniel
Dem.	Demai
Deut.	Deuteronomy
Eccl.	Ecclesiastes
Eccl. R.	Ecclesiastes Rabbah
Ed.	Eduyyot
EH	Even ha-Ezer
Er.	Eruvin
Est.	Esther
Est. R.	Esther Rabbah
Ex.	Exodus
Ex. R.	Exodus Rabbah
Ezek.	Ezekiel
ff.	Following
Gen.	Genesis
Gen. R.	Genesis Rabbah
Git.	Gittin
Hag.	Hagigah

Hal.	Hallah
HM	Hoshen Mishpat
Hor.	Horayot
Hos.	Hosea
Hul.	Hullin
Isa.	Isaiah
Jer.	Jeremiah
Josh.	Joshua
JPSA	Jewish Publication Society of America Bible translation
Judg.	Judges
Kel.	Kelim
Ker.	Keritot
Ket.	Ketubbot
Kid.	Kiddushin
Kil.	Kilayim
Kin.	Kinnim
Lam.	Lamentations
Lam. R.	Lamentations Rabbah
Lev.	Leviticus
Lev. R.	Leviticus Rabbah
Ma'as.	Ma'aserot
Ma'as Sh.	Ma'aser Sheni
Maim.	Maimonides
Mak.	Makkot
Makh.	Makhshirim
Mal.	Malachi
Meg.	Megillah
Mekh.	Mekhilta
Men.	Menaḥot
Mic.	Micah
Mid.	Middot
Midr.	Midrash
Mik.	Mikva'ot
Mish.	Mishnah
MK	Mo'ed Katan
Nah.	Nahum

Ned.	Nedarim
Neg.	Nega'im
Neh.	Nehemiah
Nid.	Niddah
Num.	Numbers
Num. R.	Numbers Rabbah
Ob.	Obadiah
OH	Orah Hayyim
Ohol.	Oholot
Orl.	Orlah
Pes.	Pesahim
Prov.	Proverbs
Ps.	Psalms
R.	Rabbi (title)
RH	Rosh ha-Shanah
RV	Revised Version (English Bible)
Sam.	Samuel
Sanh.	Sanhedrin
sect.	Section
Shab.	Shabbat
Sh. Ar.	Shulkhan Arukh
Shek.	Shekalim
Shevu.	Shevu'ot
Sof.	Soferim
Song	Song of Songs (Canticles)
Song R.	Song of Songs Rabbah
Sot.	Sotah
Suk.	Sukkah
Ta'an.	Ta'anit
Tam.	Tamid
Tanh.	Tanhuma
TB	Babylonian Talmud
Tem.	Temurah
Ter.	Terumot
TJ	Jerusalem Talmud
Toh.	Tohorot

Tos.	Tosafot
Tosef.	Tosefta
Uk.	Uktsin
Yad.	Yadayim (Maim. Yad = Mishneh Torah)
Yal.	Yalkut
YD	Yoreh De'ah
Yev.	Yevamot
Yoma	Yoma
Zav.	Zavim
Zech.	Zechariah
Zeph.	Zephania
Zev.	Zevaḥim

INDEX

Index

capacity: mental illness with lucid intervals; temporary insanity; consent by a deaf-mute; child marriage. L. The *get* written on a tablet. M. Precautions when marrying after death of husband. N. Mental surrender of *ketubbah*. O. Annulment of marriage. P. Conditions in divorce – *hamegaresh al tenai*. Q. Cancellation of *kiddushin* by the *bet din*.

E

Emunah – Belief: chap. 1

Eruv: chap. 3, 7. *Eruv*: eruv te<u>h</u>umim; eruv hatzerot; eruv tavshillin.

Ethics: chap. 5. A. Introduction. B. Creating a different person: *gerut*; holiness of mind and thought. C. Deceit – *sheker*. D. Envy – *kina'ah*. E. Generosity and gratitude. F. Forgiveness. G. Vengefulness. H. Consideration for others: *mipenei darkhei shalom*; *mishum derekh eretz*; *li-fenim mi-shurat ha-din*; *mipnei tikkun ha-olam*; *dan le-khaf zekhut*; *derekh eretz*. I. Inconsiderate behaviour. J. Acts known only to the heart. K. Wrongful speech: hurting another's feelings – *ona'at devarim*; misleading advice – *eitzah sh'einah hogenet*. L. Humility – *anavah*. M. The Biblical prohibition of usury – *ribit*.

Etrog: chap. 8

Evil Eye – *Ayin ha-Ra*: chap. 12. A. Introduction: psychological considerations. B. Subjective aspects. C. Objective aspects. D. Protection from the evil eye: prayer; amulets. E. Satan.

F

Faith: chap. 1

Fasts: chap. 8. The Day of Atonement; Ta'anit Esther; Tisha'ah be-Av; Tenth of Tevet; Third of Tishrei; Seventeenth of Tammuz.

Festivals: chap. 8. Major Festivals: New Year, Day of Atonement; Three Pilgrim Festivals: Passover, Pentecost, Tabernacles, Sim_hat Torah; Historical Festivals: Hanukah, Purim. Work on Festival; preparation of food; *muktzeh* – preparation and designation; the firstborn animal; the problem of *muktzeh*; designation for use – *hakhanah*; avoidance of the appearance of a transgression; work on intervening days of the Festival – *_hol hamoed*.

Forbidden Relations: chap. 9

G

Gittin: chap. 10

Gud A_hid: chap. 3

Gud Asik: chap. 3

H

Ha'aramah: chap. 7

Hakhanah: chap. 8

_Halitzah: chap. 10

Hallel: chap. 3

_Hametz: chap. 8

I

K

N

O

S

Sabbath: chap. 7. A. Introduction; concept of the Sabbath; Sabbath lights; prohibition of work; special strictness. B. *Muktzeh*. C. Medications on Sabbath; extenuating circumstances; sickness and women in labour. D. Work by a non-Jew. E. *Eruv*: effect of intention, consent in participation; *Eruv*: *eruv tehumim, eruv hatzerot, eruv tavshillin*. F. Intention, intended and unintended – *tzerikhah legufah*; inevitable transgression; constructive and destructive results; error; evasion; fastidiousness; divorce; witchcraft; irascibility; intervening awareness; intention and culpability; work for constructive purposes; the place of thought in action; the joy of the Sabbath – *Oneg Shabbat*.

Sacrifices: chap. 11

Satan: chap. 12

Sekakkh: chap. 3, 8

Shavu'ot: chap. 8

Shegagah: chap. 3

Shehita: chap. 3

Sheker: chap. 5

Shelihut – Agency: chap. 10

Shema: chap. 3

Shemittah: chap. 3, 5, 13

Shevut: chap. 7

Shofar: chap.3, 8

Sickness: chap. 7; labour pains: chap. 7

Simhat Torah: chap. 8

Sivlonot: chap. 13

Soul: chap. 14

W

Y

ABOUT THE AUTHOR

Rabbi Dr. Isaac Cohen is the former Chief Rabbi of Ireland, where he distinguished himself in his outstanding leadership of the Jewish community. He previously occupied the position of Rabbi of Edinburgh. During the period of World War II, he ministered to the Jewish community in Leeds and served as Officiating Chaplain to H.M. Forces. His first ministerial appointment was to the new London communities of Harrow, Kenton and district. He has been a prominent member of the Executive of the Conference of European Rabbis. After attending The Portsmouth Grammar School and Aria College, he was educated in the Rabbinical Seminary of Jews' College and University College, London, took a Ph.D. from Edinburgh University. He was born in Wales in 1914. He was married and lived in Jerusalem until his death on November 30, 2007.